D0467606

WITHDRAWN

The Great Admirals

THE GREAT ADMIRALS

Command at Sea, 1587–1945

General Editor
JACK SWEETMAN

NAVAL INSTITUTE PRESS
Annapolis, Maryland

Library of Congress Cataloging-in-Publication Data

The great admirals : command at sea, 1587–1945 / general editor, Jack Sweetman.
p. cm.
Includes bibliographical references (p. –) and index.
ISBN 0-87021-229-X (alk. paper)
1. Admirals—Biography. I. Sweetman, Jack, 1940– .
V61.G74 1997
359′.0092′2—dc21
[B] 97-8503

Printed in the United States of America on acid-free paper ∞

04 03 02 01 99 98 97 9 8 7 6 5 4 3 2

First printing

To the Memory
of
My Father

JACK SWEETMAN
(1896–1988)

Quartermaster Third Class
USS *New Hampshire*
Atlantic Fleet
1912–14

Corporal
Company A, 26th Engineers
American Expeditionary Forces
France
1917–19

Contents

Illustrations

Prints and Photographs

Maps and Charts

Acknowledgments

First of all, I must express my thanks to the nineteen distinguished historians whose essays illumine the following pages. No editor could have asked for a more knowledgable or a more cooperative team of contributors. To work with them was a delight.

At the Naval Institute Press, Dr. Paul Wilderson provided a sympathetic ear and sage advice throughout the book's gestation. Mr. J. Randall Baldini, Ms. Linda W. O'Doughda, and Ms. Sandra W. Adams skillfully supervised its transition from manuscript to published work. Mr. Charles Mussi helped obtain the illustrations, and Ms. Karen White and Mr. Jeffrey S. Klavon shared their insights into the matter of photo reproduction.

Others to whom I am indebted include Ms. Lynn Gemmel, copy editor par excellence; Petty Officer Jenny Buikhuisen of the Royal Netherlands Navy Audiovisual Service, who drew maps 5 and 6; the book's designer, Mr. Dennis Anderson; and Professor Emeritus E. B. Potter, U.S. Naval Academy, whose comments were greatly appreciated.

As always, however, my greatest debt is to my wife, Gisela *geborene* Tetzel, tireless helpmate and true companion.

INTRODUCTION

A book entitled *The Great Admirals* owes its readers an explanation of the criteria that guided the selection of its subjects. The most fundamental is suggested by its subtitle, *Command at Sea, 1587–1945*, which is meant to be taken literally. The common denominator of the admirals treated in these pages is that all held command in fleet actions, the climactic event of war at sea, during the four centuries since the advent of standoff tactics gave naval combat a recognizably modern form. The subjects of *The Great Admirals* were fighting admirals.

Compared to the several thousand general engagements that armies fought during those same centuries, fleet actions have been relatively few. The total will vary according to the measures applied, but by a generous reckoning it would not exceed 135: no more than three or four on the average in each of the thirtysome conflicts in which they occurred. This disparity reflects one of the major historical differences between land and sea warfare. However unpalatable the prospect, sooner or later an army could always be obliged to offer battle. A fleet, in contrast, could refuse action as long as it liked simply by staying in port, shielded by fortifications that prior to the invention of aircraft would usually safeguard it from unwanted attentions. An enemy could hardly compel it to put itself in harm's way. Even when hostile formations came into contact on the high seas, the mechanics of naval warfare made it difficult for a fleet to force a decisive battle on another that did not share its agenda. Most fleet actions took place by mutual consent. Either both sides were seeking battle or the one that would have preferred to avoid it was committed to a mission that justified its acceptance. Neither of these situations obtained very often.

The number of admirals who held command in fleet actions is therefore far fewer than that of the generals who commanded comparable engagements ashore. The nineteen admirals featured in this volume flew their flags in more than forty such actions—approximately a third of all those fought in modern times. Still, they are a minority of the admirals who led fleets into battle. What considerations governed the choice of these nineteen?

First of all, I should emphasize that, eagerly as the counsel of fellow historians was solicited and gratefully as it was received, the final responsibility for the selections is mine alone. In an effort to counterbalance the element of subjectivity that must enter any such exercise, two criteria reasonably susceptible to objective evaluation were applied: personal ability and historical importance. Some subjects qualified in both respects; others, in only one. It would, for example, be hard to argue that Tegetthoff, fated to devote his life to a dying empire, can be characterized as a great admiral in terms of historical importance: even his brilliant victory at Lissa could do no more than palliate the humiliation of a war lost on land. But I believe readers will agree that in personal ability he was indeed a great admiral. Conversely, the egregiously baroque plan that Yamamoto approved for the Midway campaign must raise grave doubts as to his ability, but his sponsorship of the attack on Pearl Harbor admits no doubt of his importance.

The consideration of potential subjects proceeded on a strictly individual basis. No attempt was made to achieve any particular national or chronological division. On the other hand, I did try to look beyond the two navies that predictably dominate Anglo-American naval historiography. As it worked out, the admirals chosen came from nine navies, as follows:

Great Britain	Drake, Blake, Hawke, Nelson, Jellicoe, Cunningham
United States	Farragut, Dewey, Spruance, Halsey
Japan	Togo, Yamamoto
The Netherlands	Tromp, de Ruyter
Austria	Tegetthoff
Denmark	Juel
France	Suffren
Germany	Scheer
Greece	Miaoulis

Chronologically, the breakdown appears below, with men whose careers spanned two centuries assigned to that in which they attained greatest renown:

16th century	Drake
17th century	Tromp, Blake, de Ruyter, Juel
18th century	Hawke, Suffren
19th century	Nelson, Miaoulis, Farragut, Tegetthoff, Dewey
20th century	Togo, Jellicoe, Scheer, Cunningham, Yamamoto, Spruance, Halsey

Many readers will no doubt question the inclusion of certain admirals and the exclusion of others. Probably no two students of naval history, asked to compile a list of great admirals according to this collection's definition, would produce identical rosters. Nevertheless, I believe that the majority of these admirals would appear on every roster. The stipulation that all must have commanded fleets in battle accounts for the absence of a number of figures—King and Nimitz among them—who might be expected to be found in any gallery of great admirals, but who exercised command from headquarters ashore.

Some readers may also question the decision to limit this particular gallery to admirals who held command in battle. In the first place, it may be argued, battles are not important in themselves. They are merely a means to an end, the condition that a century ago Captain Alfred Thayer Mahan, the evangelist of sea power, christened "command of the sea"—that is, the ability to use the world ocean as a highway for one's own military and commercial purposes, while preventing the enemy from doing the same. In the second place, battles are determined by tactics, the employment of forces in combat, an activity often dismissed by other than its practitioners as mundane and trivial in comparison to strategy, the deployment of forces in a campaign or a conflict as a whole.

The answer to these objections and the rationale of this book is that battle, in the form of fleet actions, is the crowning act of naval warfare and the supreme test of the naval profession. In conflicts between sea powers and enemies whose fleets are negligible to nonexistent, the former will enjoy all the rewards of victory in battle without having to fight for them: the happy situation in which the U.S. and allied navies found themselves in the Korean, Vietnam, and Gulf wars. If, however, the enemy possesses a substantial navy, command of the sea cannot be attained until that navy has been either neutralized by blockade or destroyed in battle, and since no blockade can be absolute, battle has always been preferred. Over the centuries weaker navies have consistently sought to achieve success through a means other than battle by attacking the enemy's merchant marine—or, to use the terms coined by seventeenth-century French theorists, by *guerre de course* (commerce raiding) rather than *guerre d'escadre* (fleet operations). This policy was pursued by the French navy in six wars with England between 1702 and 1814, the Continental Navy in the American Revolution, the U.S. Navy in the War of 1812, the Confederate navy in the Civil War, and the German navy in the latter part of World War I and throughout World War II. In every instance, the raiders wreaked havoc. In none did their depredations prove decisive.*

So, while battles are indeed only a means to an end, they are a means

*The U.S. Navy's submarine offensive, which destroyed more than half of Japan's merchant fleet in World War II, might appear to have been a successful *guerre de course*, but the reality was more complex. The Pacific conflict was unique in that the attack on Japanese trade proceeded in tandem with a colossal *guerre d'escadre* that absorbed attention and resources which could otherwise have been devoted to countering the war on commerce.

without which, if it is contested, that end cannot be attained. The relationship between strategy and tactics shows a similar dynamic. Good tactics will rarely redeem a bad strategy, but bad tactics will usually ruin a good one. The lesson of the past four centuries is that fleets that cannot win battles do not win wars at sea.

In keeping with this rationale the essays that follow focus on the exercise of command in battle. To develop this theme, each contributor was asked to assess the combination of personal attributes and professional experience that shaped his admiral's leadership, and to analyze a battle in which that leadership could be observed in action—in both senses of the word. Within these terms of reference, the contributors approached their subjects from whatever perspective they deemed most productive and pursued the logic of their presentations to their own conclusions. As will become evident, several authors found serious fault with some aspect of the performance of the admirals they treated. All gave fair warning, the answer to which was that the object of the book was biography, not hagiography. For the benefit of readers who would like to learn more about one or another admiral, each essay concludes with a note on sources. A number of these notes contain information that, so far as I am aware, has not previously been available in the English language.

One point that becomes clear from reading these essays is the tremendous influence these great admirals exerted on the outcome of the actions fought under their command. The matériel school of naval strategy that flourished around the turn of the century and is not yet altogether extinct holds that battles are won by technology; the fleet with the best and most ships and weapons is to all intents and purposes assured of victory. The battles detailed in this volume reveal that unless the imbalance was overwhelming, historically that has not been the case. In only four actions—Mobile Bay, Manila Bay, Tsushima, and Leyte Gulf—was the outcome effectively foreordained by the matériel inequality of the opposing forces, and two of them required command decisions far more daring than they may appear to posterity, which knows, as the men who made them could not, that they would lead to triumph rather than disaster. In the other fifteen engagements, victory was gained against a roughly equivalent or, as at Gerontas Bay, Lissa, and Midway, a significantly superior force. The moral seems clear: good hardware is a servant of, not a substitute for, good leadership.

All the same, it is undeniable that the options available to an admiral have at all times been broadly defined by the state of what might be called the tools of his trade: naval and weapons technology, obviously, but also command relationships, communications, doctrine, intelligence, and logistics. All of these tools have undergone great change over the centuries, and to appreciate the actions taken by an admiral in any given era it is necessary to have some understanding of the characteristics and capabilities of those at his disposal. For this reason, the essays are complemented by six surveys outlining the evolution of the instruments of naval warfare from ancient times to the near present. The content of these surveys is entirely my responsibility, and does not necessarily represent the interpretations and opinions of the contributors.

Leadership, or the art of command, is among the most studied and at the same time most elusive aspects of the military profession. The identity of great commanders is perfectly apparent after the fact, but no means has ever been devised to identify them beforehand, when such information would be of maximum utility. These essays illustrate the difficulty. The admirals they portray differed widely in personality, style, and values. Some, like Blake, Jellicoe, and Spruance, were cool, reserved men; others, like Nelson, Miaoulis, and Halsey, were passionate, outgoing ones. Most lived their lives within the social and professional conventions of their day, but there were spectacular exceptions: Drake viewed himself as the cutting edge of God's will; Nelson conducted his affair with Lady Hamilton indelicately enough to shock the sensibilities of contemporary English society, no easy task; Miaoulis spent his young manhood outside the law and, later, as a national hero, rebelled against the government he had helped create; and Suffren was outrageously sui generis. Drake, Suffren, Nelson, Tegetthoff, Dewey, Jellicoe, and Yamamoto were highly ambitious; the remainder seem basically to have been content to do what they conceived to be their duty. Perhaps none were intellectuals, but nearly all were thinkers as well as doers in regard to naval matters, and several possessed far above average intelligence. The majority were good bosses; a few could be real pains. Only Tromp, de Ruyter, Nelson, Halsey, and perhaps Cunningham seem to have had the X factor—call it charisma—that makes a leader loved as well as respected.

Despite their differences as individuals, as commanders these men for the most part had four key characteristics in common. First, all except Blake were professional seamen, well versed in the ways of naval warfare, even those who began their careers in the merchant marine; and Blake, a general, was able to apply his experience of war on land to fighting at sea. Second, all possessed the mental toughness to act on their own responsibility and accept great albeit closely calculated risks. Third, all were imbued with the spirit of the offensive, although Jellicoe's awareness that he was, as Churchill put it, the only man who could lose the war in an afternoon caused him to act with what many have adjudged undue caution. Fourth, all exhibited personal bravery in the face of dangers demonstrated by the fact that four of them lost their lives as a result of enemy action. In sum, they shared the attributes of technical competence, initiative, boldness of conception, and courage, both moral and physical.

Of course, the value of these qualities is not restricted to the naval profession.

About the Contributors

Edward L. Beach, Captain, U.S. Navy (Ret.) (*Farragut*), was commander of the Regiment of Midshipmen at the U.S. Naval Academy, from which he graduated in 1939. During World War II he took part in twelve Pacific submarine patrols, progressing from assistant engineer to captain of his own boat and winning ten decorations for gallantry, including the Navy Cross. From 1953 to 1957 he was Naval Aide to President Eisenhower. In 1960 Captain Beach commanded the nuclear submarine *Triton* in the first submerged circumnavigation of the globe, a 41,000-mile voyage that still holds the record for submerged speed and endurance. His first book, the nonfiction *Submarine!,* appeared in 1952, and was immediately listed in the New York *Times* best-seller list. It was followed in 1955 by the novel *Run Silent, Run Deep,* which has been recognized as the classic account of the American undersea war against Japan. Since then he has written two more novels, also best-sellers, and four nonfiction works, including *The United States Navy: 200 Years,* and has coauthored four other books. Captain Beach's contributions to naval literature have been honored by the Alfred Thayer Mahan Award for Literary Achievement of the Navy League of the United States and by numerous other awards.

Hans Christian Bjerg (*Juel*) is Head of the Military Archives of the Danish National Archives, Historical Adviser to the Danish Naval Staff, and Lecturer in Naval History at the Royal Naval Academy. He holds a degree from the University of Copenhagen. The founder and first editor of *Marinehistorik Tidsskrift* (Review of Naval History), and a member of the boards of the Marinehistorik Selskab (Naval History Society) and the Danish Naval Museum, he is the author of ten books on Danish naval history. The most recent, a study of the navy's technical services from 1739 to present, was published in 1989.

William B. Cogar (*Blake*) is Museum Director and Associate Professor of History at the U.S. Naval Academy. He was awarded his D.Phil. by St. Edmund Hall, Oxford University. A specialist in the history of the Commonwealth Navy, he has research interests on both sides of the Atlantic. At present he is compiling a biographical dictionary of the flag officers of the

American sea services. Two volumes, *Dictionary of Admirals of the U.S. Navy, 1862–1900* and *1900–1918,* have appeared to date. Dr. Cogar also edited the proceedings of the seventh, eighth, and twelfth Naval History Symposia, *Naval History* (1988) and *New Interpretations in Naval History* (1989 and 1997).

JAMES GOLDRICK, Commander, Royal Australian Navy (*Jellicoe*), graduated from the R.A.N. College in 1978. He holds a B.A. and M.Litt. Besides much sea duty, his career has included tours as Aide de Camp to the Governor-General of Australia, Research Officer to the R.A.N.'s Chief of Naval Staff, and International Research Fellow at the U.S. Naval War College. Currently he is captain of HMAS *Sydney.* His study of the opening months of World War I in the North Sea, *The King's Ships Were at Sea,* appeared in 1984, and *No Easy Answers,* a history of the navies of the Indian subcontinent, will soon be published. He has edited or co-edited several other works on naval history and contributed to a number of periodicals and publications, including *The Oxford Illustrated History of the Royal Navy.*

ERIC J. GROVE (*Cunningham*) has been a Lecturer in International Politics and Deputy Director of the Center for Security Studies at the University of Hull since 1993. From 1971 to 1984 he taught at the Royal Naval College Britannia at Dartmouth, during which time he spent a year as exchange professor at the U.S. Naval Academy. Leaving Dartmouth as Deputy Head of Strategic Studies, he became a freelance defense analyst and historian, also teaching at the Royal Naval College Greenwich and Cambridge University. Professor Grove has authored, coauthored, or edited ten books on naval subjects, among them *Vanguard to Trident,* a study of postwar British naval policy, and the revised, two-volume edition of the well-known *Sea Battles in Close-Up* series.

GERALD JORDAN (*Nelson*) is an Associate Professor of History at York University in Ontario, Canada. A veteran of eight years' service in the British merchant navy, he received his doctorate from the University of California, Irvine, in 1974 for a dissertation supervised by Professor Arthur Marder. His publications include *Naval Warfare in the Twentieth Century: Essays in Honour of Arthur Marder* and *British Military History: A Guide to the Literature since 1970,* both as contributing editor, and a number of articles on British naval and political history. He is now at work on a book on the East India Company and the port of Singapore, 1819–1867.

EDWARD STUART KIRBY (*Togo*) is Professor Emeritus of Aston University, Birmingham, England, and Senior Associate of St. Antony's College, Oxford University. He was born of British parents in Japan in 1909 and remembers witnessing the funeral procession of the Emperor Meiji in 1912. Educated in Japan, Switzerland, and England, he received a doctorate in economics from

London University and taught at Tohoku University, Sendai, Japan, in the 1930s. During World War II he served to the rank of Lieutenant Colonel in the British Indian Army as Assistant Military Attaché in Teheran, as Official Interpreter in Japanese to the Government of India, and in the British Military Mission to China, finally taking part in the surrender of Japanese forces in Hong Kong. Following his return to academe, he held professorships in England, Canada, Hong Kong, and Thailand. He has published widely on the Far East and Russia.

JOHN B. LUNDSTROM (*Spruance*) holds degrees from the University of Wisconsin, Milwaukee. Curator of American and Military History at the Milwaukee Public Museum, he is now writing a biography of Admiral Frank Jack Fletcher. Among his previous publications are *The First South Pacific Campaign: Pacific Fleet Strategy, December 1941–June 1942; The First Team: Pacific Naval Air Combat from Pearl Harbor to Midway; The First Team and the Guadalcanal Campaign: Naval Fighter Combat from August to November 1942;* and, coauthored with Steve Ewing, *Fateful Rendezvous: The Life of Butch O'Hare.* He also contributed the introduction to the Classics of Naval Literature edition of Thomas B. Buell's *The Quiet Warrior: A Biography of Admiral Raymond A. Spruance.*

RUDDOCK F. MACKAY (*Hawke*) is the author of *Admiral Hawke, Fisher of Kilverstone,* and *Balfour: Intellectual Statesman.* During World War II he served as a rating in the Royal New Zealand Navy. From 1949 to 1965 he taught at schools in England and New Zealand and at the Royal Naval College, Dartmouth. In 1965 he joined the faculty of the University of St. Andrews, Scotland, from which he retired as Reader in Modern History in 1983. He was awarded the degree of D.Litt. by St. Andrews in 1975. His edition of *The Hawke Papers* was published by the Navy Records Society in 1990.

PHILIPPE MASSON (*Suffren*) has been Chief of the Historical Section of the French Service Historique de la Marine since 1965. In addition, he is Professor of Maritime History at the Higher School of Naval Warfare and a member of the faculty of the Catholic Institute. Dr. Masson's many works on naval and military subjects include *Napoléon et la Marine; Histoire de la Marine* (two volumes); *Histoire des batailles navales; Misère et grandeur des gens de mer; De La Mer et de sa stratégie; L'Homme au Combat au XXe Siècle; Histoire de l'armée allemande, 1931–1945; Une guerre mondiale, 1939–1945,* and, as contributing editor, *Dictionnaire de la Seconde Guerre mondiale* (two volumes).

ABRAHAM VAN DER MOER, Vice Admiral, Royal Netherlands Navy (Ret.) (*de Ruyter*), is a member of the Commission for Maritime History of the Royal Netherlands Academy of Science and was president of the commission assisting in the preparation of the official history of the R.N.N. in World War II. He entered the navy as a midshipman in 1936. In 1940 he was ordered to the Netherlands East Indies, where he later took part in the Battle of the Java Sea. Subsequently he served with patrol forces in Dutch Guyana (Surinam), returning home in 1946. A 1958 graduate of the Naval Command Course at the U.S. Naval War College, Admiral van der Moer performed three tours of duty in Netherlands New Guinea during the confrontation with Indonesia. He retired from the post of Admiral Netherlands Fleet, commanding Dutch naval forces in European waters, in 1972. Always keenly interested in naval history, he has since devoted much of his time to studies in this field and has authored several works on sixteenth- and seventeenth-century Dutch naval operations and explorations, numerous articles on maritime affairs, and three historical novels.

HELMUT PEMSEL (*Tegetthoff*) was born in Lower Austria. During World War II he left high school at the age of sixteen to join the home defense antiaircraft artillery and later served in a Panzer division on the Western Front. He attended the University of Vienna after the war and has been active as an independent businessman since 1960. In 1974 he organized the Study Group for Austrian Naval History, and for most of the fourteen years of its existence served as editor of its quarterly journal, *Marine—Gestern, Heute*. He has published five books on naval and maritime history, including *Von Salamis bis Okinawa*, which appeared in English as *A History of War at Sea*, and *Seeherrschaft: Eine maritime Weltgeschichte von den Anfängen der Seefahrt bis zur Gegenwart* (Command of the Sea: A Maritime World History from the Origins of Seafaring to the Present) (two volumes).

CLARK G. REYNOLDS (*Halsey*) received his doctorate from Duke University. He is the author of *The Fast Carriers: The Forging of an Air Navy; Command of the Sea: The History and Strategy of Maritime Empires; Famous American Admirals; The Fighting Lady: The New* Yorktown *in the Pacific War; History and the Sea: Essays on Maritime Strategies;* and *Admiral John H. Towers: The Struggle for Naval Air Supremacy*, and co-author with Admiral Joseph J. Clark of *Carrier Admiral*. Dr. Reynolds has taught at the U.S. Naval Academy, the University of Maine, the U.S. Merchant Marine Academy, and the University of Charleston, South Carolina. Long active in the International Commission for Maritime History, he was a co-founder of the North American Society of Oceanic History.

ANTHONY N. RYAN (*Drake*) retired as Reader in History at the University of Liverpool in 1991. A Julian Corbett Prizeman and Fellow of the Royal Historical Society, he was Honorary General Editor of the Navy Records Society from 1973 to 1991. Editor of *The Saumarez Papers: The Baltic, 1808–1812*, and coauthor, with David B. Quinn, of *England's Sea Empire, 1550–1642,* Professor Ryan has contributed to a number of other works, including *The New Cambridge Modern History,* as well as learned journals, on subjects ranging from the defeat of the Spanish Armada to the Royal Navy and the Continental System. He is a member of the editorial board of the Society for Nautical Research and a vice president of the Navy Records Society.

JACK SWEETMAN (*Surveys*) graduated from Stetson University and served as a company commander in the U.S. Army before becoming a Ford Fellow at Emory University. He received his doctorate in 1973. He is the author or editor of a number of Naval Institute Press titles, including *The Landing at Veracruz: 1914. The U.S. Naval Academy: An Illustrated History*, and *American Naval History: An Illustrated Chronology*. Retired from the history faculty of the U.S. Naval Academy, he serves as series editor for the press's Classics of Naval Literature collection, forty volumes of which have appeared to date, and as consulting editor of the U.S. Naval Institute's bimonthly periodical, *Naval History*. In 1988 he received the Alfred Thayer Mahan Award for Literary Achievement.

KONSTANTINOS VARFIS, Commodore, Hellenic Navy (Ret.) (*Miaoulis*), was a professor at the Naval Cadets School in Piraeus and President of the Greek Commission on Maritime History. He graduated from the Naval Cadets School in 1956. His sea duty, mainly in destroyers, included command of several vessels and a tour as Commander, Light Forces. He also served on the Naval General Staff and at NATO Headquarters. In 1972 he resigned from the navy in protest of the rule of the military junta, rejoining upon the restoration of democracy in 1974. Following his retirement in 1980, Commodore Varfis was appointed Vice President of the War Museum, a position he held until 1989. That same year he received his doctoral degree from the Department of Political Science and International Studies, Panteios University, Athens. The author of four books and numerous articles, from 1984 until his death in 1994 he directed the preparation of the official history of the early Hellenic Navy.

GARY E. WEIR (*Scheer*) received his doctorate from the University of Tennessee, Knoxville, in 1982. He is currently both head of the Contemporary History Branch of the Naval Historical Center, Washington, D.C., and an Associate Professor of History for the University of Maryland University College. Dr. Weir is the author of *Building the Kaiser's Navy: The Imperial Naval Office and German Industry in the Tirpitz Era, 1890–1918; Building American Submarines, 1914–1940;* and *Forged in War: The Naval Industrial Complex and American Submarine Construction, 1940–1961.* For the latter he was awarded the Theodore and Franklin D. Roosevelt Naval History Prize. He also contributed the introduction and notes to the Classics of Naval Literature edition of Lowell Thomas's *Raiders of the Deep.*

JOHANNES JACOBUS ANTONIUS WIJN (*Tromp*) has served as Historical Adviser to the Jan Blanken Drydock Foundation at Hellevoetsluis, the Netherlands, Deputy Head of the Historical Department of the Netherlands Naval Staff, and Curator of the museum ship *Amsterdam.* He received his doctorate from the State University of Leiden in 1982. His principal interest is the history of the material aspects of Dutch sea power. Mainly in this field, he has written a number of articles and edited *Tussen Vloot en Politiek: Een eeuw Marinestaf, 1886–1986* (Between Navy and Politics: The Naval Staff Centenary, 1886–1986). With Rear Admiral K. H. L. Gerretse, R.N.N. (Ret.), he coauthored *Drie-cylinders duiken dieper: De onderzeebooten van de Dolfijn-klasse van de Koninklijke Marine, 1942–1992* (Three-Cylinder Boats Dive Deeper: Dolphin-Class Submarines in the Royal Netherlands Navy, 1942–1992). He is a member of the board of the Lindschoben-Vereeniging, a scholarly society that edits rare journals of travels on both land and sea.

H. P. WILLMOTT (*Yamamoto*) holds an M.S. from the National Defense University, Washington, D.C., and Ph.D. from King's College, University of London. From 1972 to 1979 he was a member of the British airborne reserve forces. A Fellow of the Royal Historical Society and research fellow with the Institute for the Study of War and Society, De Montfort University, he has taught at the U.S. National War College and several American universities. Dr. Willmott is the author of thirteen books on modern naval and military subjects, including *Empires in the Balance* and *The Barrier and the Javelin,* the first two volumes of a general reexamination of the Pacific War; *Sea Warfare: Weapons, Tactics and Strategy; The Great Crusade: A History of the Second World War;* and the forthcoming *When Men Lost Faith in Reason: Reflections on Warfare in the Twentieth Century.*

JOHN F. WUKOVITS (*Dewey*), who received a bachelor's degree in history from the University of Notre Dame in 1967, earned his master's degree in American history the following year from Michigan State University. Since then he has taught history and writing to junior high school students, most recently at Monguagon Middle School in Trenton, Michigan. Over the past ten years he has written extensively on naval matters, including his 1996 biography of World War II Admiral Clifton A. F. Sprague, *Devotion to Duty.* He has also written biographical essays on Admirals Raymond Spruance and William Halsey, as well as more than one hundred articles for various national publications, such as *Naval History, World War II, Journal of Military History,* and *Naval War College Review.*

The Great Admirals

Survey I

The Ship and the Gun

(1500–1688)

The naval history of the Western World spans approximately four thousand years. Although the ancient record is dim and intermittent, its beginnings can be traced to circa 2000 B.C., when Egypt and, presumably, Minoan Crete established naval forces to protect their maritime commerce and coasts against pirates and invaders. The earliest known depiction of a sea battle, a wall carving in the tomb of Ramses III at Medinet Habu, near Luxor, commemorates an Egyptian defeat of the rampaging Sea Peoples about 1190 B.C. The oldest written report of a specific engagement, the Ugarit Tablet, describes a clash between the Hittites and the Sea Peoples off Cyprus around the same date. Assyrian and Egyptian memorials identify several subsequent battles during the centuries that intervened before ships of Corinth and Corcyra (modern Corfu) met in 664 B.C. to fight the first fleet action recorded by Greek civilization. From that date onward, Western history is replete with accounts of naval battles and campaigns, gradually increasing in detail and reliability as they approach the present.

The countless engagements that fill this long history notwithstanding, fundamental changes in the forms of combat have been few. In tactical terms, the four millennia since navies came into being can be divided into three periods:

> The Age of Shock Action, from earliest times to the Battle of the Spanish Armada,
> The Age of the Gun, from the Armada battle to World War II, and
> The Age of Air-Sea Warfare, from World War II to the present.

Like most exercises in historical compartmentation, the preceding division is to an extent arbitrary and subject to many exceptions. The Battle of Lissa, for example, was decided by shock action in 1866, nearly three hundred years after the Armada battle introduced the Age of the Gun, and charging destroyers eliminated a number of surfaced submarines by the same method in both world wars. No form of combat has ever quite disappeared; it has simply become an anachronism.

Tactics are dictated by technology. The Age of the Gun and the Age of Air-Sea Warfare were precipitated by technological innovation. The Age of Shock Action was prolonged by technological limitation: the lack of a reliable means through which ships could do one another serious harm from a distance. Two weapons with pretensions to that function did, in fact, appear. These were the catapult, first used in sea warfare around 400 B.C., and Greek fire, a flaming jet—probably a mixture of naptha, sulphur, and quicklime—that the Byzantine navy began spraying from primitive flamethrowers in the seventh century A.D. Neither proved decisive. Catapults, the largest mounted on Lazy Susan–like platforms that could be rotated to bear on the enemy, hurled oversize arrows, containers of burning charcoal or pitch, and stones weighing up to fifty-eight pounds, but an effective range of less than two hundred yards confined them to an auxiliary role. Greek fire achieved some striking initial successes, contributing greatly to the frustration of Muslim attempts to blockade Constantinople during the great sieges of 677 and 718. Subsequently, however, its effectiveness dwindled with the discovery of means by which it could be deflected (supposedly, sheets of felt or cowhides soaked in vinegar) and extinguished (sand), and the closely guarded secret of its delivery system disappeared with the Byzantine navy in the thirteenth century.

Absent an instrument to inflict damage on an enemy beyond arm's length, the only way of doing so was to come into physical contact with him—in other words, by shock action. The galleys that monopolized naval warfare throughout ancient times and most of the Middle Ages existed to deliver this shock. Their aim was either to disable the enemy by ramming or to capture him by boarding, with ramming or grappling as a preliminary. The odds against an attacker backing water quickly enough to avoid being boarded by the ship he had struck were so steep that few fleets attempted to use pure ramming tactics, and none practiced them successfully for long. As a rule, both parties set out with the intention of boarding, an action conducted by the marines who constituted a galley's main armament. For all the menace implicit in the sturdy ram protruding from its bows, the oared warship was little more than a vehicle for transporting infantry into battle on a floating field. Typically, fleets advanced in line-abreast formations, like armies ashore, to seek victory by such quintessentially military maneuvers as turning the enemy's flank or breaking his front. Once battle was joined, order disappeared as fleets dissolved into islands of ships won and lost through the hand-to-hand combat that swept over their decks.

In northern European waters, never hospitable to oared vessels, the galley began to give way to sailing warships around 1200 A.D., but the change scarcely affected the age-old format of war at sea. While battles between fleets under sail might be prefaced by a competition to gain the weather gage—that is, to get upwind, the position favoring an attacker—the paramount objective remained to overwhelm the enemy by boarding. The ships themselves were the standard northern merchantmen of the late Middle Ages, beamy, single-masted, high-riding craft called cogs, modified for martial activities by the addition of "castles"—raised fighting platforms for men-at-arms—fore and aft. A characteristic action would open with an exchange of antipersonnel fire in the form of arrows, crossbow bolts, spears, stones, and other handy objects, perhaps with a few pots of incendiary materials literally thrown in, meant to soften up the enemy for the close combat to follow. When ships coalesced into a cluster, boarding parties might throw planks across their decks to facilitate movement from one to another, and friendly ships awaiting attack sometimes lashed themselves together for mutual support. The chronicler Froissart left a vivid picture of a medieval naval battle in his account of "L'Espagnols sur mer," an engagement off the Channel coast between an English fleet commanded by King Edward III and a convoy of forty Spanish armed merchantmen in August 1350:

> The Spanish . . . might easily have refused the battle, . . . for they . . . had the wind in their favour . . . but their pride and presumption made them act otherwise. . . .
>
> When the king of England saw . . . their order of battle, he ordered the person who managed his vessel, saying, "Lay me alongside the Spaniard who is bearing down on us; for I will have a tilt with him." . . . The king's ship was large and stiff; otherwise she would have been sunk, for that of the enemy was a great one, and the shock of their meeting was more like the crash of a torrent or tempest; the rebound caused the castle in the king's ship to encounter that of the Spaniard: so that the mast of the latter was broken, and all in the castle fell with it into the sea, when they were drowned. The English vessel, however, suffered, and let in water, which the knights cleared, and stopped the leak, without telling the king anything of the matter. Upon examining the vessel he had engaged lying before him, he said: "Grapple my ship with that; for I will have possession of her." His knights replied: "Let her go her way: you shall have better than her." That vessel sailed on, and another large ship bore down, and grappled with chains and hooks to that of the king. The fight now began in earnest, and the archers and cross-bows on each side were eager to shoot and defend themselves. . . . The English had not any advantage; and the Spanish ships were much larger and higher than their opponents, which gave them a great superiority in shooting and casting stones and iron bars on board their enemy, which annoyed them exceedingly. The knights on board the king's ship were in danger of sinking, for the leak still admitted water: this made them more eager to conquer the vessel they were grappled to . . . and at last they gained the ship, and flung all they found in it overboard, having quitted their own ship.[1]

When Edward fought the Spanish at sea, the Age of Shock Action was nearing an end. In the course of the following century, two initially unrelated innovations, the ship and the gun, would be combined to create a weapon system destined to revolutionize the pattern of naval combat. The gun came first. Europeans learned the formula for gunpowder about 1260. Hand-held firearms appeared around the turn of the following century, and cannon were being used in sieges by 1331, if not before. Gunpowder weapons began to be taken afloat at least as early as 1338, when the French captured an English vessel with a handgun and three cannons aboard, and to be used in action no later than the Battle of Helsingfors in 1362, a contemporary account of which reports that a Danish prince was killed by a ball from a German *Donnerbüchse* (Thunder-box). Soon the addition of gunfire to the usual missile-exchange became commonplace. By the middle of the fifteenth century, galleys were mounting cannons in their bows, and well-armed cogs carried cannon and smaller guns in their castles, now permanent structures, and a few more cannons on deck.

Initially, these weapons were employed in support of the customary boarding action. Their full potential would not be realized until the appearance of the ship, using that word in its technical sense to denote a square-rigged vessel having three or more masts. The first vessel to approximate that description, the carrack, came into being in the first half of the fifteenth century. Most carracks were not true ships, retaining a lateen (triangular) sail on their mizzenmast, like Columbus's *Santa María,* but they possessed most of their advantages. Clearly intended to synthesize the best features of the cog and the lateen-rigged Mediterranean cargo carrier, the carrack combined the former's high castles, stern rudder (introduced about 1300), and square sail with the latter's multiple masts and hull construction. The result was an ocean-sailing vessel of unprecedented efficiency, which by 1500 had replaced her predecessors in the dual role of Western Europe's premier merchant and fighting ship. Hinged gunports, believed to have been devised by a French shipwright in 1501, provided the finishing touch by making it possible to mount cannons below deck. The installation of broadside batteries in such ships set the stage for a new era in naval tactics.

The instruments and practice of shock action gave way slowly. The galley and the galleass—oared warships' last gasp, a big, decked-over galley carrying a broadside of her own—remained reasonably effective in the constricted waters of the Mediterranean, the Black Sea, and the Baltic for another three centuries, sometimes massing to overwhelm becalmed sailing ships, while within decades the carrack was supplanted by the slimmer-waisted, more maneuverable, less toplofty galleon; yet all that is beside the point. The first broadside fired from a carrack signaled the approach of the Age of the Gun.

The consequences extended far beyond the realm of naval tactics. In the sixteenth century, gun-armed sailing ships served as the vehicle of the amazing overseas expansion that made so critical a contribution to the rise of Europe's literal and figurative fortunes. Not only did these vessels carry European expeditions to the four corners of the earth, they assured the outcome of clashes with indigenous sea forces. Home with them to still semifeudal societies they brought an apparently inexhaustible stream of riches from beyond the seas. Portugal and Spain, first out the gate on voyages of discovery, were first to reap the rewards, but the effects and allure of their maritime bonanza soon became felt beyond the Pyrenees. The Netherlands, which revolted against Spain in 1568, began to encroach upon the Iberian monopolies, an example England was not slow to follow, while Spain dispersed her colossal share of the New World's treasures throughout Western Europe to support her campaigns against the two Protestant powers. Together with assorted other stimuli, the deluge of seaborne wealth triggered a dramatic upsurge in the European economy. Medieval monarchies had been too poor to afford standing military establishments. Land and sea forces were raised according to need and disbanded once the need passed. The increase in their revenues accompanying the economic growth that occurred after 1500 lifted governments out of penury. They began to be able to meet the costs of maintaining permanent, professional armies and navies and, no less important, the administrative infrastructures necessary to support them.

Of course, professional navies did not come into existence overnight. Practices and standards had to be established, and the old freebooting ways of thought replaced by a sense of corporate discipline. The transition took generations. Sir Francis Drake, the earliest of the great admirals to whom this book is devoted, was a superb commander, but his mindset was hardly that of a member of a military hierarchy. Not until the mid-seventeenth century did navies begin to acquire the institutional attributes that would qualify them as professional forces by modern standards—or, indeed, by progressive contemporary standards. Even then, the transformation remained incomplete. Governments continued to count on merchant ships commanded by skittish merchant skippers to flesh out fleets in time of war, high birth to ensure preferential consideration for high command, and subordinate commanders, high-born or not, to display considerable selectivity in obedience of orders. The development of the bureaucracies that administered and, if all went well, paid and provisioned navies proceeded at a similar pace. Although great strides were made between 1650 and 1700, the emergence of thoroughly professional navies and support services had to await the new century.

The evolution of naval tactics was also gradual. For decades after the appearance of the broadside-firing ship, boarding remained the prevalent form of combat. Fleets advanced in the traditional line-abreast formation, bows-on to the enemy, unable to use their broadside guns until they entered the melee, where their fire was delivered as a prelude to boarding. The reason for this ostensible underutilization of firepower may have been that firepower was still not very great. Sixteenth-century crew lists show that ships carried too few gunners to have approached the round-per-minute rate of fire achieved later, and the evidence indicates that until around 1625 guns were secured against recoil and reloaded by men climbing outboard on temporary scaffolding. This awkward procedure probably would have made it impossible to get off more than one shot every five minutes. In any event, only two standoff gun battles—engagements in which one side refused to close—are known to have been fought between 1500 and 1550. The first occurred in 1502, when a Portuguese squadron that entered action in line-ahead formation annihilated a fleet of Indian dhows off the Malabar coast, but as the next combat of the kind did not take place for forty-five years, it obviously failed to inspire imitation. Standard tactical practice at mid-century was reflected in two sets of fighting instructions issued by Lord Lisle, High Admiral of England, in 1545. Both called for the fleet to gain the weather gage, come down on its foe in line abreast, and "to lay aboard the principal ships of the enemy, every man choosing his mate as they may. . . ."[2]

The English were soon to devise new tactics. Beginning in 1572, maritime guerrillas like Drake waged a semiprivate, colonial sea war against Spain for more than a decade before the decision to support the Dutch revolt brought England formally into the conflict. In the course of their depredations the Elizabethan sea rovers learned to fight standoff gunnery actions, exploiting the superior sailing qualities of their sleeker, lower, "race-built" galleons to avoid being boarded by the superb infantry with which Spain's clumsy galleons were usually stuffed. These tactics dominated the Battle of the Spanish Armada, the great action—altogether, the opposing forces numbered nearly three hundred ships—that demonstrated the ascendancy of the gun.

La felicissima armada, as Spanish officialdom styled it, sailed for the English Channel early in May 1588. The most fortunate fleet knew very well the form of opposition it would find there. In his instructions to its commander, the Duke of Medina-Sidonia, King Philip II wrote, "You are especially to take notice that the enemy's object will be to engage at a distance, on account of the advantage which they have from their artillery . . . and . . . the object of our side should be to close and grapple and engage hand to hand."[3]

This was excellent advice. Unhappily for its author's aspirations, the Armada proved unable to profit by it. Despite its best efforts, Philip's fleet did not succeed in boarding a single English ship. Conversely, the damage inflicted on it by English gunfire was less than catastrophic. Between 31 July, when the battle opened at the western mouth of the English Channel, and 10 August, when the Spanish shaped a long course for home north around the British Isles, the Armada lost at most seven ships. Its ruin occurred off the coast of Ireland, where a great storm claimed at least forty.

Yet by the time the Armada began its disastrous return voyage, it was already beaten. During the running fight up the Channel, the Spanish had nearly exhausted the ammunition for many of their ships' guns—mostly short-range pieces intended for preboarding bombardment—and the fireships launched against the Armada at anchor off Calais on the night of 7–8 August showed that the English had no intention of leaving them in peace to take on more. (The English also ran short of powder and shot, but resupplies reached them from home.) Furthermore, and most important, by then both sides realized that the Armada was ensnared in a form of combat it could neither imitate nor counter. As its commanders had become oppressively aware, all the ammunition in Christendom would not have enabled the Spanish fleet to come to grips with its nimble tormentors. It was true that, as the Spanish lamented, a Protestant wind destroyed the Armada, but Protestant ships and guns had defeated it.

The Armada campaign marked the beginning of the end of Spain's Golden Century of imperial grandeur. Some historians believe that the Armada's failure was a blow from which Spanish self-confidence never recovered. Philip II fitted out new fleets in 1596 and 1597, but both were shattered by storms before reaching English waters. Other defeats on land and sea followed, and little by little Spain slipped from the ranks of great powers.

The decline of Spain coincided with the rise of the rebellious territories she tried so persistently to bring back under her control, the United Provinces of the Netherlands. The Dutch republic drew its fortunes from the sea: from the rich harvest of its fisheries and the products of spice islands wrested from the Portuguese, but, above all, from its ubiquitous merchant marine, which virtually monopolized the carrying trade between the Atlantic, northern Europe, and the Baltic. All of these activities were supported by sophisticated business practices developed to facilitate international commerce. By 1650, the Netherlands had become the wealthiest country in Europe.

Unfortunately for the republic, its prosperity aroused the envy of its erstwhile ally across the English Channel. In 1651 Oliver Cromwell's Parliament passed the first of several Navigation Acts designed to curtail Dutch trade. Good businessmen that they were, the Dutch sought to achieve a compromise by negotiation, but the only thing the English were interested in negotiating was an end to Dutch maritime supremacy. Three wars resulted. These conflicts, waged between 1652 and 1674, witnessed the emergence of the tactical patterns and problems that characterized naval combat throughout the Age of Sail.

The evolution of the ships themselves was gradual, as would remain the case until the coming of steam and iron. In design, the combatants of the Anglo-Dutch Wars were descendants of the race-built galleons of the Elizabethan era, now almost wholly square-rigged, with their forecastles flattened nearly out of existence and their aftercastles reduced to an upswept quarterdeck. They had also grown larger, and improvements in their rig, such as the introduction of fore-and-aft sails on stays between their masts, enhanced their maneuverability.

The respect in which warships built after mid-century differed most from their predecessors, however, was in the extent and size of their armament. More than a century passed after the appearance of gunports before a ship was built with more than one complete, internal gun deck. The breakthrough came in 1610, when the English shipwright Phineas Pett launched the *Prince Royal,* the first warship to have two full gun decks, which, together with a partial battery on her upper deck, mounted a total of 55 guns. Almost three decades later, Pett and his son Peter collaborated on the first true three-decker, the *Sovereign of the Seas,* which carried 102 guns—nearly two-and-a-half times as many as the most heavily armed English ship in the Armada battle. Though these leviathans, maritime status symbols with which the early Stuarts aimed to magnify their majesty, had no immediate issue, they heralded a trend toward bigger ships mounting more guns that prevailed throughout the last half of the century. In 1652, only 3 of the 97 fighting ships in the English navy carried 60 or more guns; in 1685, 63 of 143 did so.

The growth of naval gun power was accompanied by the debut of distinctly naval tactics. Force of circumstance had obliged the English to fight standoff battles during the war with Spain (1585–1604), but once the threat of being inundated by Spanish infantry had passed they went back to the old ways. The Commonwealth navy entered the first Dutch war (1652–54) with a tactical repertoire that, other than calling on captains to exercise common sense in such matters as supporting friendly ships, did not extend beyond seizing the weather gage in preparation for the time-honored melee. Yet by that time three developments had taken place that would contribute to the new format of war at sea, in which fleet engagements took the form of broadside gunnery duels between columns of ships locked in the follow-my-leader formation known as the line of battle.

The earliest of these developments was the division of major combatants into "rates," a practice initiated in England in 1618 and subsequently adopted by the other naval powers. The original four rates were soon subdivided into six, a total retained throughout the Age of Sail. The basis of classification underwent repeated change—from tons' burthen to crew strength in 1653, to number of gun crew in 1677, and, in 1714, to number of guns—but all of these measurements were means to the same end, categorizing vessels according to size, and all would have yielded much the same result.

No matter the standard, first and second rates were always three-deckers. Their high cost ensured that first rates remained a rare type, usually employed as flagships. Including the *Sovereign,* only eleven had been built in England by the century's end. Those in service on the eve of the third Dutch war (1672–74) mounted between 90 and 100 guns, measured up to 131 feet in length at the keel (and perhaps another 30 feet overall), and depending on their size and station, required crews numbering from 520 to 815 men. Second rates, also very expensive ships, were almost as large, but carried fewer guns, from 64 to 80, and only two-thirds as many men. Third rates were two-deckers that, like the upper two rates, mounted an incomplete battery on their upper deck. The biggest boasted up to 72 guns and 420 men. Ships of the fourth through sixth rates were called frigates, after the small, fast, single-deckers (*frégats*) developed by the Dunkirk corsairs. The earliest English frigates, dating from the 1640s, had been faithful copies of these craft, but in a few years the design had been inflated beyond recognition, so that by 1672 the word had become a generic term for the lower three rates. Fourth rates were small two-deckers, no more than 108 feet at the keel, carrying from 42 to 58 guns and between 180 and 280 men. Much inferior to third rates, they were greatly superior to fifth and sixth rates, little one-and-a-half and single-deckers well under 100 feet at the waterline, with batteries counting at most 32 guns and crews of fewer than 150.[4] Furthermore, the number of guns they mounted was only one element in the enormous difference in firepower between upper and lower rates; the other and more important was the size of those guns, especially in their main batteries. These ranged from 42-pounders in a first rate to 8-pounders in a sixth. The consequent inequalities in the weight of their broadsides were immense.

Strictly speaking, the rating system had no tactical significance. Its purpose was to determine the number of officers authorized a given vessel and the scale of their pay: the bigger the rate, the better the money. Still, by its very existence the system provided a means of rationalizing fleet configuration and tactical tasking. The role it played in these respects was reinforced in 1677, when, in a pioneering essay at standardization, the English

Admiralty laid down the first of a succession of repeatedly revised "Establishments" specifying the armament, manning levels, and dimensions of each rate.

The shift in tactical paradigms was also facilitated by the regularization of fleet organization. In the closing centuries of the Age of Shock Action, sailing fleets had deployed in the line-abreast order used by their oared predecessors—left wing, center, and right wing, often plus a reserve—but such formations were ad hoc. By the onset of the Dutch wars, however, English admirals routinely divided their fleets into three squadrons, which soon came to be designated the red, the white, and the blue. These colors, flown by the "flagships" of the squadron commanders, were an index of seniority. Admirals of the red squadron, in which the fleet commander sailed, took precedence over their counterparts in both other squadrons, and admirals of the white squadron over theirs in the blue. In linear formations, the white squadron customarily formed the van, the red squadron the center, and the blue squadron the rear. In large fleets, squadrons were subdivided into the same three elements. Nothing intrinsic to these arrangements favored the rise of the new tactics, but they supplied a mechanism through which an admiral might retain a degree of control over his forces in a standoff action, although the waywardness of squadron commanders made that degree problematic. Consistently effective control would only be achieved in the more disciplined fleets of the succeeding century.

The third development that fostered the emergence of the line of battle was technological in nature and, in comparison to those outlined above, more immediate in impact. This was the appearance of inboard loading, a procedure made possible by the introduction of "tackle"—a cat's cradle of pulleys (in nautical parlance, blocks) on rope slings stretched between eyebolts sunk into a ship's sides and decks and rings on a gun's barrel and carriage—by means of which its crew could "run" a piece in to load and out to fire, recoil alone sufficing to return it to the loading position after the first shot. Exactly when and where this apparatus came into use is unknown. There was nothing of the sort in Sweden's mighty 64-gun ship *Vasa* in 1628, when she capsized within minutes of launching to spend the next 333 years on the bottom of Stockholm's teredo-free harbor before being raised to become the only and almost perfectly preserved seventeenth-century warship in the world today, but the standoff battle Tromp fought at the Downs in 1639 indicates that Dutch ships were equipped with it by then. In any event, the English as well as the Dutch fleet had effectively completed the conversion by 1652. The result was to increase rates of fire by 250 to 500 percent, from a shot every five minutes to a shot a minute for bursts of peak activity and one every two or three minutes for an indefinite period. With inboard loading, a ship could maintain a practically continuous broadside fire while sailing a steady course, and what a single ship could do, a column of ships could do also.

Tromp's tactics at the Downs notwithstanding, at the opening of the First Anglo-Dutch War both fleets sought melees. Then, on 29 March 1653, the Commonwealth's three "Generals at Sea," Robert Blake, Richard Deane, and George Monck (the future Duke of Albemarle), issued instructions "for the better ordering of the Fleet in Fighting" that through their requirement, thrice reiterated in slightly different words, for "every ship . . . to keep in a line with the admiral,"[5] are generally regarded as the first official prescription for the formation of a line of battle.

That this was their intent is borne out by contemporary accounts of the first engagement following their dissemination—the Battle of Gabbard Bank, in June—which, if deficient in detail, make clear that the English did, in fact, employ line-ahead tactics throughout most of the action to win a handsome victory. What prompted the issue of these particular instructions at this particular time can only be conjectured. Certainly, the confusion that enveloped a fleet in a melee must have been appalling to the Generals at Sea, veteran military men (all had served with distinction in the English Civil War) accustomed to the much greater control a general could at least aspire to exercise in engagements ashore, and even though the English fleet had done well in the war's opening battles, they may have reasoned that with more cohesive tactics it would have done better still. It may also be that the fresh perspective these soldiers brought to sea helped them to recognize that, unlike other weapon systems, sailing ships could not bring their full firepower to bear on a target toward which they were advancing, but only against one to which they presented their side. Whatever moved the generals to frame the new instructions, the results must have been satisfactory, for a year and two major battles (Gabbard Bank and Scheveningen) later, they reissued them essentially unchanged.

The maintenance of the line of battle received increasing emphasis in the fighting instructions issued to the Royal Navy (as Charles II entitled it following the Stuart restoration) during the next two Dutch wars. On 22 November 1664, with the second conflict unofficially under way, the fleet commander, Charles's brother, James, Duke of York, released a revised version of the fighting instructions of 1653. Among the few changes were two that told captains to "put themselves into the place and order which shall have been directed them in the order of battle" and "to engage with the enemy according to the order prescribed,"[6] which make it evident that each ship had now been assigned a definite position in the line.

James repeated the identical instructions on 10 April 1665, but only eight days later he set out ten additional instructions clearly intended to concentrate tactical control of the fleet in his hands. This document also included the first official stipulation of the interval to be maintained between ships in the line of battle: half a cable's length (100 yards), a distance the Royal Navy would observe for almost two hundred years. By the end of May, on the eve of the Battle of Lowestoft, the duke had distributed two more sets of additional instructions reinforcing their predecessors' provisions. At Lowestoft, James won a very one-sided victory over a not very inferior Dutch fleet; nevertheless, complaints that he failed to press the pursuit caused him to be sent ashore. Appointed co-commanders in his stead were Prince Rupert and the Duke of Albemarle. Their first fighting instructions, dated 1 May 1666, were a repetition of those Albemarle had cosigned as General Monck in 1653.

The sanctity that the line of battle had attained on paper was not necessarily respected at sea. All of James's injunctions to the contrary, at Lowestoft there were times when his line shivered into four or five little lines, and after Rupert and Albemarle's defeat by de Ruyter in the Four Days Battle in June 1666, Admiralty official Samuel Pepys confided to his celebrated diary that Admiral Sir William Penn (who was not present at the action) had told him it proved "We must fight in a line, whereas we fight promiscuously, to our utter and demonstrable ruine: the Dutch fighting otherwise—and we, whenever we beat them."[7] But these observations by an officer who had no love for either of the co-commanders were, perhaps deliberately, misleading. As Pepys's full text reveals Penn was well aware, the cause of the defeat was as much strategic as tactical, Rupert and Albemarle having unwisely divided their fleet before the battle, with the result that the former could not reach the scene of action until late on the third day; and granted that as tacticians both were too venturesome for Penn's taste, he must also have known that they had not simply indulged in a free-for-all. Despite the abyss that often opened between doctrine and performance, the Royal Navy was firmly committed to the line of battle as its primary fighting formation.

The onset of the Third Anglo-Dutch War found the Duke of York back in command at sea. In the spring of 1672, he distributed fighting instructions that in their essentials recapitulated those issued during the preceding conflict, and in late 1672 or early 1673 he released the first printed book containing both sailing and fighting instructions, the latter consisting of twenty-six articles combining the most useful of all those promulgated since 1653. These *Instructions for the better Ordering His Majesties Fleet in Sayling* and ditto *in Fighting,* several times reprinted, remained in general use until 1688, when the Glorious Revolution that drove James from the throne prompted its replacement by the first such manual issued by the English government, the economically entitled *Sailing & Fighting Instructions* published in 1689. By then, the line had been adopted as the basic order of battle by every European sailing fleet.

Before the new order's potential could be fully realized, a degree of homogeneity had to be imposed on its components. Previously, little fifth and sixth rates had been able to sail merrily into melees, trusting that they could either find someone their own size to pick on or gang up against big ships. These options vanished when they were laced into a line and obliged to engage their opposite numbers in the enemy formation, by which they might be dwarfed. That extreme mismatches could jeopardize the integrity of an entire formation became evident during the Anglo-Dutch Wars, and in 1677 the English Parliament authorized the construction of thirty major combatants that were perhaps the first vessels deliberately planned to be "ships of the line," although the term did not gain currency until the turn of the century. There was nothing dramatically different about the ships themselves; the major change was tactical rather than technological. In the future, places in the line of battle would be restricted to members of the first four rates. Fifth and sixth rates retained the responsibility of reconnaissance, patrolling, convoy escort, commerce raiding, and carrying dispatches. Those present at fleet actions took station on the unengaged side of their line, ready to repeat a flagship's signals, to defend the line from fireships, and take charge of surrendered enemy vessels. Fourth rates, 50- or 60-gun vessels handy enough to double as cruisers, originally comprised the largest contingent of ships of the line. This held true until midway the following century, when advances in the third and fifth rates outmoded them as both line of battle ships and cruisers.

With these developments the warship's metamorphosis from assault ferry to gun platform, the principal impetus to the rise of the line of battle, was conceptually complete. The line did more than maximize a fleet's firepower, however. It also provided a means through which its commander could attempt, not always successfully, to exercise what modern military analysts abbreviate as C_2—command and control. This attribute was made all the more important by the absence of anything resembling an adequate signals system. Flags had been used for signaling ever since the fourteenth century, but they had yet to acquire intrinsic meanings; that is, different colors and designs did not represent specific letters or numerals. They designated articles in the sailing or fighting instructions, the particular article being indicated by the flag itself, the position in which it was hoisted, and whether the hoist was accompanied by the display of other flags or the firing of a given number of guns.

The limitations this system imposed on fleet communications were severe. The pivotal instructions of 1653, for example, comprised a mere fourteen articles, four of which were standing orders (e.g., not to fire at an enemy ship at the risk of hitting a friendly one) and two prescribed signals to be made by ships retiring to repair damage or in distress. Only eight established discretionary commands for issue according to tactical circumstances. At times, frigates and small craft were used to carry extemporaneous orders from a fleet flagship to squadron commanders, but this expedient left much to be desired, as did the increase in the store of standard commands contained in the more fulsome fighting instructions issued later in the century. An admiral was practically tongue-tied when it came to addressing his fleet.

Historians often describe the evolution of fleet tactics under sail in terms of a contest between two "schools," the formalist and the meleeist. These are defined as having differed in that while both held the line of battle to be the proper formation for a fleet entering action, formalists insisted that it should be retained until the enemy had been put to rout, whereas meleeists believed that under some circumstances it could be discarded in order to force a decision.

Insofar as it is understood to indicate schools of thought, this is a convenient characterization, allowing ready distinction to be made between the outlooks of individual admirals such as Penn and Albemarle. On the other hand, it should not be taken to imply that adherents of these schools arrayed themselves in parties to promote the view they espoused—an activity of which there is no record. The triumph of linear tactics was not brought about by the efforts of a formalist lobby. It resulted from a combination of causes: the appeal of the line itself, which not only maximized a formation's firepower but protected the most vulnerable portions of a ship's anatomy, the bow and stern, of all except its first and last members; the need to curb the independence to which captains and squadron commanders wished to remain accustomed; the rudimentary state of signals communications; even, it has been suggested, the intellectual mood-music of the Age of Reason, an age that placed the highest premium on the qualities of order, regularity, and control.[8]

Whatever a commander's tactical inclinations, battle was slow-moving, close, and deadly. At sea, ships quickly lost speed owing to the accumulation of barnacles and marine growth on their hulls. The most that upper rates, not built as greyhounds, could make in hot pursuit ("general chase") of an enemy in a moderate breeze was probably seven to eight knots, and the requirement for its members to keep station must have restricted a line of battle to two to four knots. In clear weather, lookouts' field of vision extended approximately twenty miles, while the maximum effective range of ships' guns was only about two-thirds of a mile (1,000 yards). Fleets steering straight for one another at a speed of three knots would therefore be in visual contact for upwards of three hours before they actually engaged, and fleets did not necessarily steer straight for one another. Jockeying for the weather gage or other advantage might keep them in sight but out of range for many more than three hours; indeed, in some instances, for days on end.

Though fire could be delivered more or less effectively up to 1,000 yards, fleets intent on action usually sought to close to the roughly 350 yards that was considered point-blank—that is, the maximum range at which a shot fired at zero elevation would strike its target before beginning to fall. From there, they might press on to "a pistol shot"—15 to 30 yards—or even closer. The detailed accounts available of late eighteenth- and early nineteenth-century battles reveal that at times ships were actually touching. Boarding then became possible, but seldom occurred in fleet engagements, although not uncommon in duels between cruising vessels.

The fire fleets exchanged included a variety of missiles. By far the most common were roundshot, solid iron cannonballs that would smash a ship's hull and upper works as well as throwing up showers of man-killing wooden splinters. Special-purpose projectiles called chain-shot and bar-shot, the former consisting of two roundshot connected by a chain and the latter of the halves of a single shot joined by a bar, might be used against masts and rigging; clusters of slightly different types of small shot—grape-shot, case-shot, and langridge—could be sprayed at rigging and exposed personnel; and, commencing at about one hundred yards, musket balls fired by ships' marine complements would pepper an enemy's decks. Good gunnery was a matter of rate of fire, for the limitations of naval ordnance and the dense, black-powder smoke that soon blanketed the battle area precluded very effective aiming. This was why offensive fleets strove to get at such close quarters. As range decreased, hits increased.

Despite the punishment to which they might be subjected, wooden ships were rarely sunk in the course of a day's battle. They might be dismasted or crippled by the loss of rigging; their guns might be silenced; they might sustain such grievous damage that they would slowly founder; but their inherent buoyancy and the efforts of damage-control parties usually kept even the most badly battered afloat for hours. Almost the only way a ship could be destroyed in an immediate sense was if fire or accident set off her magazine.

Ships' companies were less durable. The effects of the varieties of shot described above on human flesh are all too easily imagined. Thus it is perhaps not so surprising as it first seems to learn that, though statistics from the period should be treated with discretion, they leave no doubt that proportionately (and often absolutely) the great battles of the seventeenth, eighteenth, and early nineteenth centuries were quite as bloody as their later nineteenth- and twentieth-century counterparts. Ranked in terms of casualties suffered by one side, the most sanguinary naval battle in history is Leyte Gulf (1944), in which the Japanese lost 10,500 dead and several thousand wounded, but it is followed by Chesme (1770), in which at least 8,000 Turks are conservatively estimated to have perished when Russian fireships ignited their embayed fleet. Of the eighteen next-deadliest battles, twelve took place under sail, with casualties in killed and wounded running from 7,000 Spanish at the Downs (1639) to 2,700 Anglo-Dutch at Malaga (1704)—the latter being approximately the same number the U.S. Navy sustained at Pearl Harbor (1941).

The reader of the following essays will observe that these totals include a goodly number of admirals, whose position on their quarter-decks left them as much exposed to enemy fire as the most recently joined landsman. In the three fleet engagements of the Second Anglo-Dutch War (1665–67), for example, eleven admirals—seven Dutch and four English—were killed in action. Five of them fell at Lowestoft, where the Duke of York was much admired for his composure upon being drenched with blood and slightly wounded by a flying skull fragment when a Dutch chain-shot dismembered three of his retinue.

As the heir to his childless brother's throne, the Duke of York had staff to spare. The average admiral was not so well served. A flag-captain relieved him of the responsibility of commanding his flagship and could, of course, be consulted on operational matters. Otherwise, the only assistants of whom he could be assured were a secretary, who managed the considerable correspondence a fleet engendered, and a clerk. The commander of a large fleet might be assigned a chief of staff, in the Royal Navy called a "first captain" or "captain of the fleet," to act as his adviser and take charge of administration and logistics, but the position was not always filled. Admirals of the Age of Sail not only exercised command under potentially very dangerous circumstances, they did so almost singlehandedly.

NOTES

1. Sir John Froissart, trans. Thomas Johnes, *Chronicles of England, France, Spain, and the Adjoining Countries* (London: Henry G. Bohn, 1852), I: 198.

2. Julian S. Corbett, *Fighting Instructions, 1530–1816* (N.p.: Navy Records Society, 1905), pp. 22–24.

3. Major General J. F. C. Fuller, *A Military History of the Western World* (New York: Funk & Wagnalls, 1954–56), II: 14–15.

4. Smaller combatants remained outside the system, as did fireships, which constituted an ingredient of an admiral's arsenal as long as warships were made of wood.

5. Corbett, op. cit., p. 100.

6. Brian Tunstall, ed. Dr. Nicholas Tracy, *Naval Warfare in the Age of Sail: The*

Evolution of Fighting Tactics, 1650–1815 (Annapolis, Md.: Naval Institute Press, 1990), p. 22.

7. Robert Latham and William Mathews, eds., *The Diary of Samuel Pepys* (Berkeley: University of California Press, 1972), VII: 194.

8. William Maltby, "Politics, Professionalism, and the Evolution of Sailing-Ship Tactics, 1650–1714," in John A. Lynn, ed., *Tools of War: Instruments, Ideas, and Institutions of Warfare, 1445–1871* (Urbana: University of Illinois Press, 1990), pp. 67–69.

I

Francis Drake

God's Corsair

(1543?–1596)

Anthony N. Ryan

"WITH REASON," WROTE THE SPANISH HISTORIAN CESAREO Fernández Duro of the operations commanded by Sir Francis Drake in Iberian waters in 1587, "do historians maintain that there is not in the annals of England an expedition comparable to it."[1] Drake's expedition must also be unique in the annals of England in its immunity from both criticism by contemporaries and debunking by historians. Richard Hakluyt,[2] Robert Leng, author of the only extant narrative by a participant,[3] and Sir William Monson, an Elizabethan seaman and writer of naval tracts, speak to us in its praise with an almost united voice. Monson, never a complacent compiler, described the voyage as having "proceeded prosperously and without exception; for there was both honour and wealth gained, the enemy greatly endamaged, the merchants fully satisfied, and our country sufficiently secured for that year."[4]

Partly because of their dependence upon the testimony of contemporary witnesses, the assessments of historians have tended to chime in with it. For Sir Julian Corbett there was in all the wars of Elizabethan England no campaign to match that of 1587. Writing three centuries later, he declared that "To this day it may serve as the finest example of how a small well-handled fleet, acting on a nicely timed offensive, may paralyse the mobilisation of an overwhelming force."[5] Garrett Mattingly concluded that Drake so disrupted Spanish plans that no Armada could sail for England in 1587.[6] Kenneth Andrews attributes the success of the expedition to Drake's brilliant opportunism in "combining a lightning intuitive grasp of the possible with the technical capacity, verve and sheer personal force to translate possibilities into near-certainties."[7]

The 1587 expedition was the outstanding success, both strategic and financial, of Drake's career. The history of English maritime offensives against Spain, including others in which Drake held or shared command, provide numerous instances of incomplete success and almost total failure. When sixteenth-century English fleets operated in distant waters, the odds were stacked against them. Logistical strains, disease, conflicts of interest between the state and private entrepreneurs, upon whom the government was always in part dependent for ships and money, and social and disciplinary tensions within an inchoate hierarchy of command often added up to failure. Present on all great naval occasions, they make it easier to understand Drake's failures at Lisbon in 1589 and in the Caribbean in 1595–96 than to understand his success in 1587.

Francis Drake was born into a family of tenant farmers near Tavistock, Devonshire, in the early 1540s. Before he was ten years of age, the family was forced to uproot itself. His father, Edmund Drake, was an ardent and radical Protestant, publicly identified with the dissemination of the faith. Devonshire was no place for such a man during the West Country uprising against the Reformation in 1549. Having fled its home, the family settled in an area of Protestant sympathy, Gillingham on the River Medway, which was beginning a new era in its history as the main anchorage of the royal warships built by Henry VIII. Here the Drakes lived in straitened circumstances and, during the reign of Mary Tudor (1553–58), under the threat of persecution. There is no reason to doubt that Francis Drake absorbed from his father the dedication to Protestantism and detestation of Catholicism that, in an age of religious strife, were to give a cutting edge to his secular ambitions.

Drake was certainly literate and in manhood may well have acquired a working knowledge of French. His formal education, however, was largely vocational. Apprenticed to the master of a coastal bark, he learned the business of seamanship in a great nursery of seamen, the testing waters of the Thames Estuary and the Narrow Seas. He emerged from this apprenticeship a master of his craft. He was also endowed with a natural gift, perhaps inherited from his lay-preaching father, for the exploitation of the spoken word and with the self-confidence that so often goes with it. By 1568 he was commanding a ship, the *Judith* of fifty tons, in the service of John Hawkins.

Drake owed this advancement to ability and to a blood relationship with the Hawkinses, the Plymouth family that pioneered English efforts to subvert, by force if necessary, the Spanish and Portuguese claims to commercial monopoly within their respective empires. Fate decreed that this employment should bring him into violent confrontation with the Spaniards in the Mexican harbor of San Juan de Ulloa on a voyage led by John Hawkins in 1567–69 to sell slaves obtained in West Africa to Spanish colonists in the Caribbean. Drake regarded the Spanish attack as a treacherous onslaught that cried out for revenge. On returning home, he entered into the first of two childless marriages and planned his future.

Out of the wreckage of San Juan de Ulloa, Drake carved a career as leader of unofficial hostilities against Spain. His first enterprise of note was an expedition in 1572–73 to the Isthmus of Panama where, in collaboration with a French pirate, he succeeded in seizing a consignment of silver during its passage across the isthmus from Panama to Nombre de Dios. Thereafter Drake was firmly identified with the anti-Spanish movement in England, so much so that during the Anglo-Spanish *rapprochement* of the mid-1570s it was deemed politically opportune that he should serve in Ireland. He reemerged to lead the famous circumnavigation of 1577–80, a privately financed enterprise of reconnaissance and plunder that was undertaken with the probable connivance of Queen Elizabeth but without her public commitment. Had Drake failed, he would have been disavowed. The reward of success was a knighthood. He achieved two firsts. He became the first Englishman to circumnavigate the globe and the first to break into the Pacific Ocean, then widely regarded as a Spanish lake. He returned to Plymouth in September 1580 with booty beyond men's wildest dreams.

Between 1580 and 1585, during which period he purchased Buckland Abbey near Plymouth and married for a second time, Drake was involved in promoting a variety of ventures without, as far as is known, going to sea. In 1585, however, this prince of maritime guerrillas graduated from guerrilla warfare to command of a force backed and in part financed by the government to carry out reprisals in response to the Spanish imposition of an embargo upon English ships in Iberian ports. The objective was the West Indies and Drake led the raid with élan. Handicapped by sickness that enfeebled both seamen and soldiers and put the greatest prize of all, Panama, out of reach, he nonetheless swept through the Caribbean, leaving a trail of pillage and destruction. Although the profits were less than expected, Drake created a state of chronic insecurity in the colonial world and shook the nerves of European bankers upon whom King Philip II depended for advances to finance the great-power status of Spain. A Spanish official with whom he negotiated a ransom for Santo Domingo recorded an impression of Drake in his prime:

> Drake is a man of medium stature, blond, rather heavy than slender, merry, careful. He commands and governs imperiously. He is feared and obeyed by his men. He punishes resolutely. Sharp, restless, well-spoken, inclined to liberality and to ambition, vainglorious, boastful, not very cruel.[8]

In 1587, with Anglo-Spanish differences apparently irreconcilable, Drake was a natural leader of the forces mobilized to strike at Spain before Spain could strike at England. He had a successful record as commander of arduous and audacious enterprises. He enjoyed the backing of the two most influential advocates of war in the queen's entourage, Robert Dudley, Earl of Leicester, and Sir Francis Walsingham, principal royal secretary. In an age when many people believed in the God of battles, Drake believed he was fighting God's battles. In the context of war against Spain he had no sense of conflict between godliness and gain. In 1587 a note of religious exaltation pervaded much of his correspondence:

> But whereas it is most certain that the King doth not only make speedy preparation in Spain, but likewise expecteth a very great fleet from

> the Straits and divers other places to join with his forces to invade England, we propose to set apart all fear of danger and by God's furtherance to proceed by all good means that we can devise to prevent their coming. Wherefore I shall desire you to continue a faithful remembrance of us in your prayers that our present service may take that good effect as God may be glorified, His Church, our Queen and country preserved, and the enemy of the truth utterly vanquished that we may have continual peace in Israel.[9]

In writing thus, Drake was in tune with much of the music of his time. Yet he was hardly an unblemished hero. Across him lay the shadow of the execution of Thomas Doughty, one of the "gentlemen adventurers" embarked on the circumnavigation, at Port St. Julian on the coast of South America in 1578. The execution of Doughty, found guilty of treachery after a trial of doubtful legality, may be explained as the response of the leader of a hazardous undertaking to the emergence of a challenge to his authority. It may also have gone deeper. In his magisterial *Drake and the Tudor Navy,* Sir Julian Corbett tentatively identified Doughty as a possible representative within the squadron of a "peace party" at court, whose function was to divert the expedition from the acts of depredation that Drake and his collaborators planned against Spain.[10] The evidence, such as it is, points to Doughty having been an unscrupulous individual of piratical inclinations who resented the increasingly subordinate role in which Drake cast him.[11] But Drake appears to have had no reservations about exterminating Doughty as a threat to his self-appointed mission as leader of a personal war against Spain. This sense of mission was a source of strength. In an age of anti-Spanish and anti-Catholic sentiment, it enabled Drake to build up a following in the seafaring community and to bind it to him with the cement of shared plunder. Plunder brought him through the social barriers of the Elizabethan Age to a position of power as the embodiment of aspirations widely diffused in English society.

Drake led his squadron out of Plymouth Sound on a fair wind for Spain on 2 April 1587* "to stand for our gracious queen and country against Antichrist and his members."[12] The force numbered twenty-three ships, of which four fighting galleons—the flagship *Elizabeth Bonaventure* (550 tons), *Golden Lion* (550 tons), *Rainbow* (500 tons), and *Dreadnought* (400 tons)—and two pinnaces—*Spy* (50 tons) and *Cygnet* (15 tons)—were described as "her Majesty's ships and pinnaces." Other vessels were the property of the Lord

* Dating throughout this chapter is in accordance with the Julian calendar. To determine the equivalent date in the modern calendar, ten days must be added.

Admiral of England, Charles, Lord Howard of Effingham, who would command against the Armada in 1588, and of Drake himself. But the most powerful contingent of privately owned ships consisted of eleven vessels, some barely distinguishable from those of the queen, belonging to entrepreneurs of the city of London. This so-called London fleet was commanded by veterans of the guerrilla war against Spain, and its principal promoters were involved in a range of privateering activities throughout the world.

In short, Drake's force consisted of two fleets, separately organized, financed, manned and victualed, temporarily allied as competitive collaborators in an enterprise calculated to achieve public benefit through the encouragement of private gain. Drake himself was an arch-exponent of the idea of maritime war as an activity in which the participants' strategic responsibilities should be harmonized with their financial aspirations. Commissioned by the queen as General of the Expedition, he also headed a list drawn up later of the London promoters who were described as "parteners and interessed in the prise."[13]

Collaboration between crown and subjects in fitting out fleets was rooted in tradition, dating back to times immemorial, that the navy of England was the multitude of the shipping of the realm; which had meant, in reality, the employment of the most sturdy merchantmen, seized or hired by the crown and converted for war service. Technical advances in shipbuilding and in the use of artillery at sea, which would produce the professional navy of the later seventeenth century, were already influencing the character of the national sea forces in the Tudor age. Their outward sign in the 1580s was the queen's ships, a force when fully mobilized in 1588 of thirty-four warships ranging in size from the tiny *Cygnet* to the *Triumph* of 760 tons.[14] These vessels were royal property, funded by the royal exchequer, supported by royal dockyards and managed, within the administrative limitations of the age, by royal officials. They were, however, only one component of the navy of England. Because of the restrictions imposed upon naval expenditure by inadequate public revenue, the crown was still dependent on the contribution of private shipowners. Elizabeth I commanded neither a state navy nor the funds to support one.

There being no professional navy, there was no professional officer corps. Command was vested in the hand of irregulars. Ad hoc appointments to specific commissions were the order of the day. They might go to noblemen, courtiers, and landowning gentry, selected primarily because their social prestige was held to qualify them for posts of honor and profit in the service of the crown. Fighting seamen were also candidates for appointment. Connected with civilian shipping and trade, they had made their re-

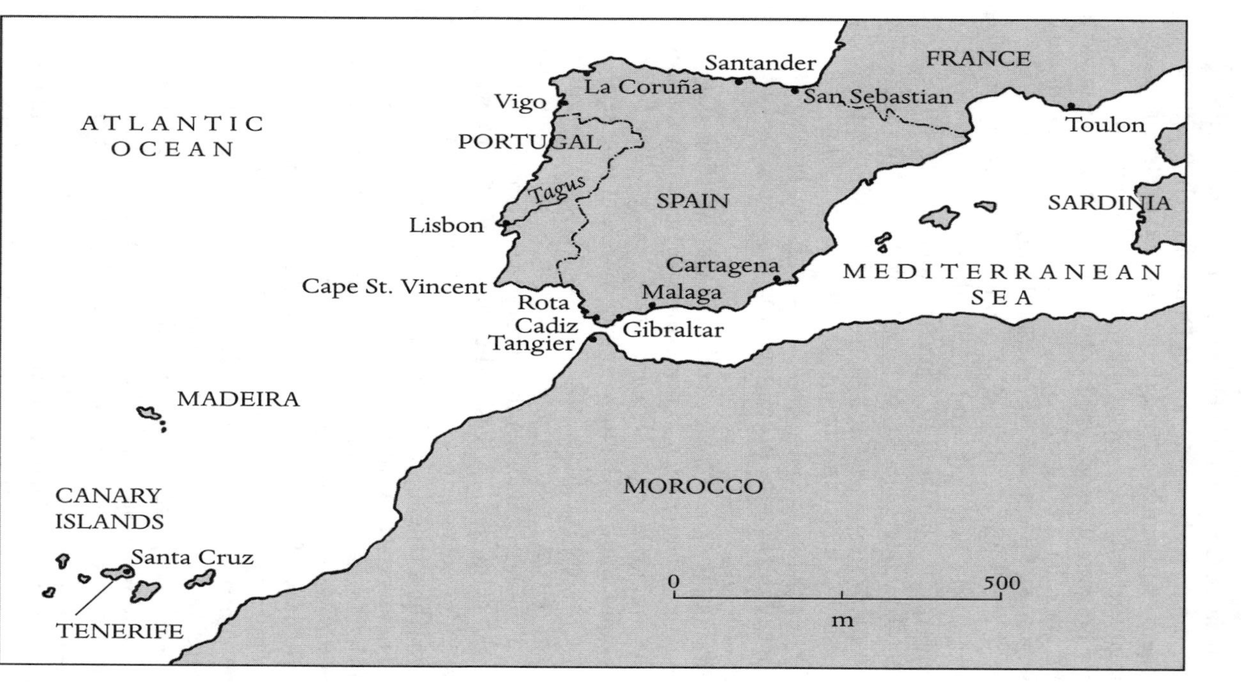

1. English Campaigns in Iberian Waters, 1587 and 1656–57.

putations and, in some cases, their fortunes in armed assaults upon Iberian colonial monopolies and in an unremitting war of plunder against Spanish shipping. They were maritime guerrillas whose aptitudes and skills made them indispensable to the government in time of war. The names of the most prominent individuals and families crop up again in the fleet lists of the 1580s and 1590s. Their highly developed predatory instincts seemed to guarantee that the maritime war could be made to pay for itself at the expense of the enemy.

The primary objective in 1587 was to impede the massing at Lisbon of a combined naval and military force whose ultimate destination was England. However, the queen and her advisers did not share Drake's apocalyptic vision of Anglo-Spanish relations as the setting for war to the death between good and evil or, as he might have put it, between the Lord of Hosts and Antichrist. They attempted to preserve a distinction between unlimited war and operations designed to achieve limited objectives that might enhance England's security and even help to achieve a truce of sorts between the two states. The suspicions that Drake focused upon Doughty and his supposed backers at court in 1578 surfaced again in 1587. That spring he attributed the desertion of mariners at Plymouth, hardly an uncommon experience, to "some practice of some adversaries to the action."[15] On the lookout for symptoms of treachery, he was to discover more during the course of the campaign.

The original orders under which Drake sailed are no longer extant. Shortly after his departure, however, the government amended them, supposedly in consequence of reports that the Spaniards had ceased preparations for an invasion of England. These amended orders, which survive, directed Drake to take "a milder course."[16]

The milder course was to forbear from assaulting Spanish ports, offering violence to any Spanish town or shipping within harbor, or committing any act of hostility upon land. Drake remained authorized to attack Spanish shipping at sea, specifically that coming from or going to the Indies. The amended orders, dated 9 April, seven days after he sailed from Plymouth, never reached him. While not excluding a serious intent on the part of the queen not "to exasperate matters further than they are,"[17] the timing hardly suggests a serious intent to restrict Drake's freedom of action. The government was thus provided with a means of disclaiming responsibility for his conduct should it be deemed politic to so do, without depriving itself of any advantages that he might win.[18] Drake therefore lay under the threat of disavowal, especially if he should fail.

In the interchangeable roles of queen's admiral and queen's corsair, Drake rapidly seized the initiative and never lost it. Acting in accordance with the idea which he was to express in 1588, that "the advantage of time and place in all martial actions is half a victory,"[19] he lost no time in descending upon Cadiz. This action, seemingly unpremeditated, was inspired by intelligence obtained at sea that a fleet of storeships had been assembled there preparatory to sailing for Lisbon. Most of these ships lay in the outer harbor, which was easily accessible on the fair wind Drake enjoyed in the afternoon of 19 April. The defenders were caught unawares by the sudden entry of the English force and also by the inability of the Mediterranean war galleys to drive off the heavily gunned sailing ships of the North. Drake knew that time was not on his side. It was certain that enemy reinforcements with artillery would arrive; it was possible that the wind would fail, immobilizing his ships and putting them at a potential disadvantage if combat with the oar-propelled galleys were renewed. During twenty-four hours of intense activity, some thirty merchantmen were destroyed or taken and Drake himself led a daring sortie into the inner harbor to burn an unarmed galleon belonging to the Marquis of Santa Cruz, the commander-designate of the "Enterprise of England."

Having shaken the Spaniards and acquired a useful quantity of provisions and wine, Drake extricated the squadron with remarkably few casualties. Rated in the English hall of fame as a major victory, the "singeing of the King of Spain's beard" at Cadiz was perceived by Drake as an introduction to the main business of the campaign. "Now being well furnished with necessary provision," he wrote to John Wolley, a government secretary, on 27 April, "our intent is (God willing) to impeach the fleet which is to come out of the Straits and divers other places before it joined in with the King's forces, in the accomplishment whereof neither willing minds or industry shall be wanting."[20]

At Cadiz Drake obtained information of the whereabouts of the Spanish squadrons destined to rendezvous at Lisbon with the Marquis of Santa Cruz. The most interesting news was that the Biscayan squadron under Juan Martínez de Recalde was cruising off Cape St. Vincent. This intelligence proved outdated, however, as Recalde had been recalled to Lisbon as part of the Spanish reaction to the English presence. Thwarted of his prey, Drake decided to occupy the cruising ground off Cape St. Vincent, where he would dominate the shipping lanes between the Mediterranean and the Atlantic. He had in mind an extended stay, for which he needed a secure and well-situated anchorage where his ships could be watered and kept clean. Having selected the bay overlooked by the castle of Sagres, just east of the cape, his next move was to lead a landing party to disarm the castle and nearby fortifications, thus making the anchorage secure. Although this act gave rise to controversy, in view of Drake's aims and responsibilities the arguments in its favor were unassailable. No sixteenth-century fleet had any chance of remaining healthy unless it had access to supplies of fresh water and facilities for cleaning the ships and refreshing the crews. The attack on Sagres involved enormous risks, especially as the landing party was without artillery. But the very fact that the risks were high endowed Drake with the advantage of surprise. Drake's instinct for the unexpected, though it might disconcert his followers, was one of his outstanding qualities.

Having reduced the number of Spanish vessels and stockpile of supplies through the raid on Cadiz, Drake proceeded to scour the waters off Cape St. Vincent. Here he captured many ships, including some bound for Lisbon with barrel staves for the manufacture of casks and water butts, to deficiencies in which are attributed some of the problems suffered by the Spanish Armada in 1588.* He also harassed the enemy's fishing fleets.

This effective campaign of attrition did not satisfy Drake. As champion of England and of the Protestant cause, he wished to put things to the test of combat. He therefore made an appearance off the mouth of the Tagus, challenging Santa Cruz to come out and give battle. With Santa Cruz unable to sail and Drake unable to force his way up the river to Lisbon, the affair ended as a demonstration, an unnerving one for the Spaniards, of Drake's mobility and freedom of enterprise.

Off Cape St. Vincent, Drake expressed himself freely on the long-term advantage of possessing so admirable a cruising ground. After describing the Spaniards in a letter to Walsingham of 17 May as enemies to the truth and upholders of Baal or Dagon's Image, he forecast a prolonged campaign:

> As long as it shall please God to give us provisions to eat and drink, and that our ships and wind and weather will permit us, you shall surely hear of us near this Cape of St. Vincent, where we do and will expect daily what her Majesty and your honours will further command. God make us thankful that her Majesty sent out these few ships in time.[21]

Nevertheless, on 22 May Drake led the fleet away from Cape St. Vincent and headed out into the Atlantic for the Azores.

If Drake set down his reasons for this sudden change of mind, the record has not survived. The only contemporary explanation emanates from Monson, who claimed that Drake's London associates were becoming restive because they saw no prospect of rich prizes and prevailed upon him to sail for the Azores in search of a Portuguese carrack homeward bound from the Indian Ocean.[22] Since a swoop upon enemy shipping in the Atlantic was already on the agenda, this rings true. In an age of entrepreneurial warfare

* It is generally agreed that defective water butts and casks, hastily made from unseasoned timber, exacerbated the Armada's victualing problems.

Drake was under pressure, not only from his associates but from his responsibility to a penurious government, to crown the cruise with profit. This was, of course, entirely in accord with his own instincts.

Drake was also under pressure arising out of dissension with his second-in-command, William Borough, captain of the *Golden Lion*. Not only was Borough an experienced seaman, he was also an officer of the Tudor naval administration, Clerk of the Ships. As such, he represented the regular forces of the monarchy. He believed that his status gave him the right to tender advice and to have a say in the conduct of the campaign. Drake, who owed his rise to individual endeavor, believed that he had a right to invite advice and, if he saw fit, to disregard it.

The quarrel, though it included differences over the conduct of affairs, was primarily over the nature of command. This is evident in Borough's protest of 30 April that he "could never perceive any matter of council or advice touching the action and service for her Majesty with the fleet now under your charge to be effectually propounded or debated."[23] Drake's reaction to the protest was a diagnosis of treachery. This prompted him to strip Borough of command. Then, following the desertion of the *Golden Lion*, he convened a court-martial that sentenced Borough in absentia to death.[24] Drake had no doubt that right was on his side. After the expedition's return to England, he made publicly clear his determination to see the sentence carried out.

On route to the Azores in blustery weather, the London ships parted company with Drake. He may have had no further service for them; in any case, he laid no charge of desertion against them, remained on good terms with his London associates, and participated in the distribution of prize money on the terms already agreed. With the remainder of his force, Drake continued in pursuit of a financial bonanza. His nose for a prize did not fail him. The climax of the cruise and of the campaign was the capture of the carrack *San Felipe*, homeward bound from the East Indies. Her cargo was valued at £114,000, a vast sum by the standards of the age. Having, in the words of Hakluyt, "assured themselves every man to have a sufficient reward for his travel," Drake's men set sail for England and "arrived in Plimouth the same sommer with their whole Fleete and this rich booty, to their owne profite and due commendation, and to the great admiration of the whole kingdom."[25]

While Drake himself and all concerned, including the queen and her council, were congratulating themselves on the happy financial outcome of the campaign, they seem to have been much less alive to its strategic significance. This was partly because they were obsessed with making the war a paying proposition and partly because they did not have the knowledge to comprehend the illogicality of events. When Drake surrendered the strategic initiative off Cape St. Vincent, he did what Philip II feared most. Late in April the Spanish council of war worried that Drake's appearance might be the prelude either to a combined attack upon the forces being assembled at Lisbon or to a joint onslaught upon Spanish shipping by English and Algerine sea forces, with possible backing from the Ottoman Empire. But as they got things into perspective, the councillors felt less concern over the Cadiz raid and the English presence off Cape St. Vincent than over the prospect of another round in the battle of the Atlantic, with Drake bent on the destruction of the Indies fleets. They duly recommended a major offensive in the Atlantic against the marauders by a force dispatched from Lisbon, even at the risk of delaying preparations for the invasion of England. This recommendation echoed the conviction the king had held from the outset that priority should be given to the defense of Spain's communications.[26] The "departure of Drake and the security of the fleets" had the effect, quite unforeseen by Drake, of forcing Santa Cruz to sea with a strong fleet at the end of June on a cruise of almost three months.[27] This constituted a serious setback for Philip II, who had been planning an invasion of England in the autumn of 1587. He continued to press for action, even arguing in favor of launching the operation at the close of year, but the condition of ships and crews on their return from the Atlantic made that impossible.

With the advantage of hindsight, it is possible to detect in Drake's conduct anticipations of the strategic doctrine defined three hundred years later by Alfred Thayer Mahan and his disciples: for example, that England's first and last line of defense was dominion in enemy waters. But hindsight can be a disadvantage in a search for understanding of Drake's conduct in 1587. It may encourage the use of inappropriate strategic models as an aid to judgment and it may foster belief in an unreal distinction between Drake the admiral and Drake the corsair. As long as the state, because of its inability to fund a professional navy, was in considerable measure dependent upon private adventurers, maritime war had to be conducted at the enemy's expense. In other words, there could be no service without profit, despite the potential for conflict between them. Unsupported by any sort of naval staff, Drake owed his strategic and financial success in 1587 to intuitive opportunism and an instinctive flair for confusing the enemy.

Drake's vendetta against William Borough, however, ended in failure. His implacable resolve to achieve the death or, failing that, the ruin of a man whom he regarded as a coward, a deserter, and an instrument of his adversaries was frustrated by those who viewed the same man as a loyal servant of the crown. Borough retained both his life and his office.[28] In the circumstances of the time Drake's services may have been indispensable, but the queen's council had no intention of allowing him to behave as if they were. Despite his operational success, therefore, Drake had reason to be dissatisfied with the government. Given his financial success, he may not have cared very much about a disavowal that went no further than words. But he had cause to feel that his authority had been undermined and that the opponents of war with Spain were still influential.

The government, for its part, had reason to be dissatisfied with Drake, not so much because he had technically exceeded his orders, but because he had turned the relatively minor business of Borough's protest into an occasion for a capital charge. His exaggerated response was viewed by his political masters as the sort of conduct that could precipitate the disintegration of a sixteenth-century fleet. They still needed his services, but they clearly considered it preferable that he should serve under command rather than in command during the national mobilization of sea forces for the trial of strength with Spain in 1588.

Drake's reputation was now such, however, that he was popularly regarded both at home and abroad in 1588 as the embodiment of English sea power. Whether it be fact or fiction, the story of Drake calmly finishing his game of bowls on Plymouth Hoe with the Armada already in sight of the English coast, tells us something of the aura that shone about him. His actual role was that of an influential second in command to the Lord Admiral of England, Howard of Effingham, who was by no means merely a figurehead. Drake took a prominent part in debate, though his was not the only voice to which Howard listened, and as a squadron leader he was in the thick of the fighting in the Channel skirmishes and the battle off Gravelines. Of his tactical ideas, nothing is known. He remained a controversial figure, taking the Andalusian squadron's damaged flagship, *Nuestra Señora del Rosario,* in circumstances which prompted accusations that he sought to monopolize the prize money.[29] Even in the hour of victory, his reputation as a corsair overshadowed that as an admiral of the queen.

In 1589 Drake was back at the helm in joint command with General Sir John Norris of a combined expedition to the Iberian peninsula.[30] The enterprise was stricken by conflicts of interest between the crown and private adventurers. During the winter of 1588–89 queen and council became convinced that the primary object should be the extirpation of Spanish sea power through the destruction of the surviving warships of the Armada campaign, which had fetched up in the northern ports of Santander and San Sebastian. This sober assessment of strategic priorities by no means coincided with that of Drake and his associates. Eight years earlier, Spain had occupied Portugal. Fortified by a promise from the Portuguese pretender, Dom Antonio, that if they helped him gain the throne he would open the Portuguese empire to English merchants, they aimed to expel the Spanish administration. Indigenous assistance, it was hoped, would be forthcoming. This hope was misplaced. The English army failed to rouse the population on its march to Lisbon. Weakened by sickness, it was forced to withdraw to the ships. In their zeal to win Portugal, the expedition's leaders had disregarded the queen's point of view. In an attempt to compromise, they made a futile attack on La Coruña, the main consequence of which was the spread of infection. Conduct so at variance with official interests brought royal disfavor. Drake remained on the beach until 1595.

His return to active service was ill-fated. Sharing command with Sir John Hawkins, Drake sailed from Plymouth for the Caribbean for the last time in August 1595. The expedition was to make for San Juan de Puerto Rico where, according to reports, a disabled treasure ship might be found. From there it would continue on to strike at the Isthmus of Panama and return home by mid-May 1596. Largely at the insistence of Drake, who was short of victuals, the fleet detoured to the Canary Islands in search of supplies. The time thereby lost in crossing the Atlantic was never regained. The delay enabled the Spaniards to obtain information about English intentions, which, by putting their defenses in order, they were able to thwart. John Hawkins died off Puerto Rico. After being repulsed at Panama, Drake was stricken with a malignant dysentery. He died off Porto Bello on 28 January 1596 and his body was consigned to the deep.[31]

The modern study of Francis Drake dates from the late nineteenth century, when didactic historians were attempting to educate the Royal Navy and the reading public in the eternal principles of maritime strategy as revealed by the past. They emphasized the evidence that seemed to bring out the lessons bequeathed by Drake to the great strategic traditions of the British navy. Nowadays historians are more concerned with understanding the realities of sixteenth-century maritime warfare as practiced by Drake and his contemporaries. And they recognize that, compared with the professional naval officers of the eighteenth century onward, Francis Drake was a man from another world.

Notes

1. C. Fernández Duro, *Armada Española desde La Union de Castilla y de Aragón*, 9 vols. (Madrid: Sucesores de Rivadeneyra, 1895–1903), III: 15.

2. Richard Hakluyt, *The Principal Navigations, Voyages, Traffiques and Discoveries of the English Nation,* 8 vols. (London and Toronto: J. M. Dent, 1927), IV: 281.

3. Clarence Hopper, ed., "Sir Francis Drake's Memorable Service done against the Spaniards in 1587. Written by Robert Leng, Gentleman, One of his Co-adventurers and Fellow Soldiers," *The Camden Miscellany* (London: The Camden Society, 1844), V: 13.

4. M. Oppenheim, ed., *The Naval Tracts of Sir William Monson,* 5 vols. (London: Navy Records Society, 1902–14), I: 138 (hereafter, *Monson's Tracts*).

5. Julian S. Corbett, *Drake and the Tudor Navy: With a History of the Rise of England as a Maritime Power,* 2 vols. (London: Longmans, Green, 1898), II: 108 (hereafter, Corbett, *Drake*).

6. Garrett Mattingly, *The Defeat of the Spanish Armada* (London: Jonathan Cape, 1959), p. 122.

7. Kenneth R. Andrews, *Drake's Voyages: A Re-assessment of their Place in Elizabethan Maritime Expansion* (2nd ed., London: Panther Books, 1970), p. 146.

8. García Fernández de Torrequemada to Philip II, 2 February [N.S.], 1587, Irene A. Wright, ed., *Further English Voyages to Spanish America, 1583–1594* (London: Hakluyt Society, 2nd ser., vol. 99, 1951), p. 225.

9. Drake to John Foxe, 27 April 1587, Julian S. Corbett, ed., *Papers Relating to the Navy during the Spanish War, 1585–1587* (London: Navy Records Society, vol. 11, 1898), p. 111 (hereafter, Corbett, *Spanish War*). It is interesting to find Drake corresponding with the famous Protestant martyrologist.

10. Corbett, *Drake,* I: 254ff.

11. Andrews, op. cit., pp. 77ff; David B. Quinn, *Drake's Circumnavigation of the Globe: A Review* (Exeter: University Press, 1981), p. 3.

12. Drake to Walsingham, 2 April 1587, Corbett, *Spanish War,* pp. 102ff.

13. "The Names of the Suertyes to be bounde to her Majesty for £50,000 endorsed 31 October 1587," Hopper, op. cit., p. 27.

14. Mia J. Rodríguez-Salgado and the Staff of the National Maritime Museum, *Armada, 1588–1988: An International Exhibition to Commemorate the Spanish Armada: The Official Catalogue* (Harmondsworth: Penguin Books in association with the National Maritime Museum, 1988), pp. 156ff.

15. Drake to Walsingham, 2 April 1587, Corbett, *Spanish War,* pp. 102ff.

16. Walsingham to Stafford, Corbett, *Spanish War,* p. 106; see also Conyers Read, *Mr. Secretary Walsingham and the Policy of Queen Elizabeth,* 3 vols. (Oxford: Clarendon Press, 1925), III: 231ff.

17. Council to Drake, Corbett, *Spanish War,* pp. 100ff. This letter is dated 9 April 1587 by Hopper, op. cit., pp. 28ff.

18. Burghley to Andreas De Looe, 28 July 1587, Corbett, *Spanish War,* pp. 146ff. De Looe, an agent of the Duke of Parma, Philip II's governor in the Netherlands, was assured by Burghley that "so unwitting, yea unwilling, to her Majesty those actions were committed by Sir Fras. Drake, for the which her Majesty is as yet greatly offended with him." For comments on this act of disavowal, from which the capture of the *San Felipe* was carefully excluded, see Corbett, *Drake,* II: 75ff and 122ff.

The disavowal, insincere though it probably was, lends some credence to Drake's view that in the prevailing political murk adversaries to the action were not wanting.

19. Drake to Queen Elizabeth I, 13 April 1588, J. K. Laughton, ed., *State Papers Relating to the Defeat of the Spanish Armada, Anno 1588*, 2 vols. (London: Navy Records Society, 1894) I: 147ff.

20. Drake to John Wolley, 27 April 1587, Corbett, *Spanish War*, pp. 109ff.

21. Drake to Walsingham, 17 May 1587, ibid., p. 133.

22. *Monson's Tracts*, I: 137. For Monson's views on the inadequacy of private forces as a basis of naval strength, see David B. Quinn and A. N. Ryan, *England's Sea Empire, 1550–1642* (London: George Allen and Unwin, 1983), pp. 211ff.

23. Borough to Drake, 30 April 1587, Corbett, *Spanish War*, pp. 123ff.

24. "A general courte holden for the service of Her Majestie abourde the *Elizabeth Bonaventure* the xxxth day of Maye before Sir Ffrauncis Drake, knighte, generall of Her Majestie's fleete; Thomas Fennard, Vice-Admirall; Anthony Platte, Lieutenant-generall; John Marchant, serjant-major, and the reste of the captaines and masters of the fleete as followeth," M. Oppenheim, *A History of the Administration of the Royal Navy and of Merchant Shipping in Relation to the Navy: From MDIX to MDCLX with an Introduction Treating of the Preceding Period* (London: The Bodley Head, 1896), Appendix B, pp. 382ff.

25. Hakluyt, op. cit., p. 285.

26. Rodríguez-Salgado, op. cit., pp. 22ff.

27. Philip II to Cardinal Archduke Albert, September 1587, George P. B. Naish, ed., "Documents illustrating the History of the Spanish Armada," C. C. Lloyd, ed., *The Naval Miscellany, Volume IV* (London: Navy Records Society, vol. 92, 1952), p. 7.

28. Corbett, *Drake*, pp. 111ff and 122ff. See also Borough to Burghley, 21 February 1588, Laughton, op. cit., I: 74ff.

29. "Mathew Starke's Deposition, 11 August 1588," Laughton, op. cit., II: 101ff.

30. There is a lucid account of this expedition in R. B. Wernham, *After the Armada: England and the Struggle for Western Europe, 1588–1595* (Oxford: Clarendon Press, 1984), pp. 48ff. The documents are printed by Wernham, ed., *The Expedition of Sir John Norris and Sir Francis Drake to Spain and Portugal, 1589* (London: Navy Records Society, vol. 127, 1988).

31. For a contemporary account of Drake's illness and death, see "Thomas Maynarde's Narrative," K. R. Andrews, ed., *The Last Voyage of Drake and Hawkins* (London: Hakluyt Society, 2nd ser., vol. 142, 1972), pp. 100ff.

Note on Sources

Thanks to the Hakluyt Society, founded in 1846, and the Navy Records Society, founded in 1893, there is in print an abundance of contemporary evidence about the career of Francis Drake. The voyage of 1577–80 is documented by W. S. W. Vaux, ed., *The World Encompassed by Sir Francis Drake* (London: Hakluyt Society [H.S.],

1st ser., vol. 16, 1855) and by Zelia Nuttall, ed., *New Light on Drake* (London: H.S., 2nd ser., vol. 34, 1914), which includes material from Spanish archives. Mary Frear Keeler, ed., *Sir Francis Drake's West Indian Voyage, 1585–86* (London: H.S., 2nd ser., vol. 148, 1981) documents the "great West Indies raid." Spanish documents relating to this episode are printed by Irene A. Wright, ed., *Further English Voyages to Spanish America, 1583–1594* (London: H.S., 2nd ser., vol. 99, 1951). The last voyage and death are documented by K. R. Andrews, ed., *The Last Voyage of Drake and Hawkins* (London: H.S., 2nd ser., vol. 142, 1972).

The first volumes published by the Navy Records Society (N.R.S.) are the indispensable J. K. Laughton, ed., *State Papers Relating to the Defeat of the Spanish Armada, Anno 1588*, 2 vols. (London: N.R.S., vols. 1 and 2, 1894). Petruccio Ubaldino's "Drake-centered" narrative of 1588 is printed by George P. B. Naish, ed., "Documents illustrating the History of the Spanish Armada," C. C. Lloyd, ed., *The Naval Miscellany, Volume IV* (London: N.R.S., vol. 92, 1952). Julian S. Corbett, ed., *Papers Relating to the Navy during the Spanish War, 1585–1587* (London: N.R.S., vol. 11, 1898) is a major source for the study of Drake's conduct in 1587. References to Drake are scattered through M. Oppenheim, ed., *The Naval Tracts of Sir William Monson*, 5 vols. (London: N.R.S., vols. 22, 23, 43, 45, 47, 1902–14). Correspondence and narratives of 1589 are printed by R. B. Wernham, ed., *The Expedition of Sir John Norris and Sir Francis Drake to Spain and Portugal, 1589* (London: N.R.S., vol. 127, 1988).

The only extant narrative by a participant in the 1587 operation is Clarence Hopper, ed., "Sir Francis Drake's Memorable Service done against the Spaniards in 1587. Written by Robert Leng, Gentleman, One of his Co-adventurers and Fellow Soldiers," *The Camden Miscellany*, vol. V (London: The Camden Society, 1844). There is a brief account in Richard Hakluyt, *The Principal Navigations, Voyages, Traffiques and Discoveries of the English Nation*, 8 vols. (London and Toronto: J. M. Dent, vol. 4, 1927).

The most recent syntheses of the era are K. R. Andrews, *Trade, Plunder and Settlement: Maritime Enterprise and the Genesis of the British Empire, 1480–1630* (Cambridge: Cambridge University Press, 1984), and David B. Quinn and A. N. Ryan, *England's Sea Empire, 1550–1642* (London: George Allen and Unwin, 1983). J. A. Williamson, *The Age of Drake* (2nd ed., London: A. & C. Black, 1946) remains a useful study. The British Library's "Drake Exhibition" in 1977 was accompanied by the publication of *Sir Francis Drake: An Exhibition to Commemorate Francis Drake's Voyage around the World, 1577–1580* (London: The British Library, 1977), an illustrated introductory survey of Drake's career. Julian S. Corbett, *Drake and the Tudor Navy: With a History of the Rise of England as a Maritime Power*, 2 vols. (London: Longmans, Green, 1898) is indispensable; but see Kenneth R. Andrews, *Drake's Voyages: A Reassessment of their Place in Elizabethan Maritime Expansion* (1st ed., London: Weidenfeld and Nicholson, 1967; 2nd ed., London: Panther Books, 1970) for criticism of Corbett's assessment of Drake as a naval strategist. Andrews's fundamental contribution to our understanding of the war of plunder and, hence, of Elizabethan sea warfare in general may be studied, inter alia, in *Elizabethan Privateering: English Privateering during the Spanish War, 1585–1603* (Cambridge: Cambridge University Press,

1964) and *The Caribbean: Trade and Plunder, 1530–1630* (London: Yale University Press, 1978). David B. Quinn, *Drake's Circumnavigation of the Globe: A Review* (Exeter: University of Exeter Press, 1981) is a succinct interpretation. In a compelling study of the Armada campaign, Garrett Mattingly, *The Defeat of the Spanish Armada* (London: Jonathan Cape, 1959), does justice to Drake's contribution, as do Colin Martin and Geoffrey Parker, *The Spanish Armada* (London: Hamish Hamilton, 1988). Many of the modern works cited above have extensive bibliographies.

David B. Quinn, *Sir Francis Drake As Seen By His Contemporaries* (Providence: The John Carter Brown Library, 1996), was received too late to be used in the writing of this chapter. It includes a bibliographical supplement by Burton Van Name Edwards.

2

Maarten Harpertszoon Tromp
Father of Naval Tactics
(1598–1653)

J. J. A. Wijn

MAARTEN HARPERTSZOON TROMP WAS BORN ON 23 APRIL 1598 in Brielle, the same small city where twenty-six years earlier the "Seabeggars" gained their first victory in the Dutch revolt against Spain. The first flag of the Dutch republic had flown from the tower of St. Catherine's Church, in which Maarten was baptized on 3 May.

He belonged to a seafaring family. His grandfather, Maarten Lambertszoon van der Wel, was a fairly successful coastal trader and his father, Harpert Maartenszoon, also made his living at sea. Harpert ran away from home to join the young Dutch navy and became known as a fine seaman. To join the fleet, he had to drop his family name van der Wel and for unknown reasons adopted that of Tromp.[1] The van der Wels lived in Delft but when Harpert married the widow Jannetgen Barents in 1597, the young couple settled in Brielle.

Maarten was raised by his mother while Harpert served alternately with the cruising fleet at sea or the blockading squadron off Dunkirk. Cruising and escorting were necessary to protect Dutch merchantmen and the numerous herring boats from Spanish ships, Dunkirk privateers, and English men-of-war. A constant blockade of Dunkirk was considered a necessity, for this port was not only the home of the dreaded raiders, but had fallen into Spanish hands. The Duke of Parma, the Spanish commander in chief, encouraged and even paid the Dunkirk corsairs to attack Dutch shipping.

Maarten's father gradually rose in rank and in April 1606, when Maarten was eight years old, the family moved to Rotterdam, where the Tromps could afford a large house of their own. A month later, Harpert was appointed captain of a small man-of-war by the Rotterdam Admiralty.[2] He thereupon resolved to take charge of his son's upbringing and prepare him for a career as a seaman like himself. Convinced that life aboard ship would produce better results than religious-tinged training at home, he took Maarten with him as his cabin boy. Firsthand experience was considered much more worthwhile than theory, although by then Maarten was already able to read, write, and do arithmetic.

In February 1607 Harpert and Maarten sailed in the Rotterdam squadron under Commodore Moy Lambert as part of the Dutch fleet of Lieutenant-Admiral Jacob van Heemskerck to blockade the Spanish coast. The objective of Heemskerck's expedition was to intercept an enemy fleet being sent to expel the Dutch from the East Indies. On 25 April, a sharp action was fought off Gibraltar, resulting in a great Dutch victory. After this impressive start

Maarten stayed on board his father's ship, cruising and blockading in the stormy and fitful waters of the North Sea and the English Channel, constantly on watch against Spanish men-of-war and Dunkirk privateers. This schooling proved to be very important for the attentive cabin boy, for these waters would soon become important battlegrounds for the Dutch navy and Maarten Tromp would take advantage of the knowledge he had begun to acquire at such an early age. By visiting ports in France and England he also picked up a fair knowledge of both languages, enough to be able to communicate with fellow seamen, navy contractors, tradesmen and, still later, with foreign captains and admirals.[3]

In 1609 a truce was signed between Spain and the Dutch republic that lasted for twelve years. The Dutch army and navy were cut back sharply following the ceasefire, as would be the case during interludes of peace throughout the century. Harpert remained on duty for another year, because the truce did not affect the Dunkirk corsairs and the navy had to continue its cruising activities against them.

After leaving the navy, Harpert chose to stay at sea. With his own money he bought a merchant ship and joined the Guinea trade to the west coast of Africa, which was very profitable during these years. Naturally, he took Maarten with him. An English pirate attacked Harpert's ship near Cape Verde on the Tromps' first voyage south. The Dutch vessel carried a few guns, but the pirate proved too strong for her. Soon she was boarded and her crew overwhelmed. Harpert was killed in the struggle and his corpse thrown into the sea. Twelve-year-old Maarten, who had fought very bravely, was forced to serve as the pirates' cabin boy for the next two years. Little is known of this period of his life, but contemporary accounts by other captives make clear that it was no sinecure. Maarten led a miserable existence, but at the same time he became a hardened seaman. He learned how it felt to be humiliated and mistreated and what it meant to serve as a common sailor. During these years, his character was forged into a model of sobriety, will power, persistence, and consideration for his fellow men. It is said that his trust in God, in those days of endless religious wars more manifest than at present, prevented him from having feelings of hatred or revenge.[4]

In 1612, Maarten managed to escape from his captors in an Italian harbor and returned to Rotterdam. Back home he undertook to support his mother and three younger sisters, who first learned of the death of their husband and father from him. He went to work on the Rotterdam wharfs, but he was not happy there, for he had lost his heart to the sea. Occasional short voyages in merchantmen eventually led to his return to the navy, and on 23 June 1617 he was delighted to be appointed leading seaman in *De Leeuwinne* (The Lioness), commanded by Moy Lambert, his father's former comrade-in-arms. In this vessel Tromp participated in successful operations against Mediterranean pirates in 1618 and 1619. He earned promotion to first mate during these seasonal campaigns, but on 15 May 1619 he resigned.

Dutch overseas trade had grown explosively during the relatively calm years of the truce and Tromp, still responsible for his mother and sisters, decided to try his luck in the very lucrative *straatvaart,* the trade through the Straits of Gibraltar into the Mediterranean, a region he knew fairly well by now. His fortunes definitely did not lie with the merchant fleet, however. He mustered on *Het Tuchthuis*—House of Correction, an odd name for a ship, but indicative of the state of affairs in vessels of that day!—and sailed the pirate-infested southern waters for some time. But in 1621 *Het Tuchthuis* was captured by Tunisian pirates and for the second time Tromp was held as a slave. He was released within a year, either as part of an exchange of prisoners or by the payment of ransom by the Admiralty. In June 1622 he returned home safe and sound, never again to reenter either the Mediterranean or the merchant marine.[5]

Now that the Twelve Years Truce had expired and hostilities with Spain resumed, Maarten Tromp rejoined the navy and became lieutenant of the *Bruinvisch,* spending two years cruising the coast of Europe from Flanders to Gibraltar, convoying homeward-bound *straatvaarders* and attacking enemy shipping. That he did not spend all his time at sea is proven by his marriage on 7 May 1624 to Dina de Haas, daughter of Master Cornelis de Haas.[6] The following month he was appointed to the captaincy of the "yacht."* *Sint Antonius.* In this, his first command, Tromp's duties consisted of convoying the huge herring fleets and escorting merchantmen. After six months he was transferred to the blockading fleet off Dunkirk and received a larger command, the ship of the line *Gelderland,* of which he remained captain for four years.

Another aspect of Tromp's character was formed during this period. The land war was not going well, which caused the republic to devote most of its resources to the army. The navy was starved of ships, crews, and money, and Tromp had to struggle constantly to persuade the Admiralty to furnish the material, provisions, and funds needed to keep his ship in fighting condition. In the process, he developed an absolute tenacity of purpose.

To a considerable extent, the problem that would plague the navy and its leaders throughout the seventeenth century (and later) stemmed from the extraordinarily decentralized nature of the federation of the seven provinces that formed the Dutch republic or, more formally, the United Provinces. In many respects, they were doggedly disunited provinces. Each

* In Dutch naval terminology, a small sailing vessel with a crew of a few dozen men.

retained its own parliament (*States*), which sent delegates to the national States-General. Executive power belonged to the *Stadtholder,* a sort of hereditary presidency vested in the princely House of Orange. This power was, however, severely constrained by provincial particularism. To complicate matters still further, the navy was itself a collection of provincial components. In the course of the struggle against Spain, no less than five separate admiralties had been established—three in the Province of Holland (including the Rotterdam admiralty that Tromp served), one in Zealand, and another in Friesland—each with its own fleet, officers, yards, and revenues. There were, of course, arrangements to coordinate their activities. Half of each admiralty board was composed of representatives from the other six provinces; a council of delegates from all the admiralties met periodically at The Hague under the chairmanship of the Stadtholder, who was also head—Admiral-General—of the navy; and the States-General determined strategy and, in consultation with the Stadtholder, appointed flag officers. Inevitably, however, so complex a system was difficult to manage efficiently, especially as different authorities often aimed at conflicting goals, but every attempt to replace it with a more centralized organization was defeated by the opposition of the provinces.

Although Tromp engaged in no major actions during his command of the *Gelderland* except for a fight against five large Dunkirkers in the spring of 1627, he attracted the attention of his Admiralty. Early in 1629 the newly appointed Lieutenant-Admiral of Holland, Piet Heyn, asked Tromp to be captain of his flagship, *De Groene Draeck* (The Green Dragon). Heyn wrote that while he had other brave captains, in Tromp he recognized all the qualities of a great leader. Unfortunately, the collaboration between these two outstanding men did not last long. During their first action, with ten corsairs off Dungeness on 17 June 1629, Heyn was mortally wounded. Tromp continued flying his admiral's flag throughout the battle, which the Dutch won after a day's severe fighting. Afterward, he carried Heyn's corpse to Rotterdam and was awarded by the States of Holland with a gold chain.

In the following years Tromp continued to operate against the Dunkirk corsairs, achieving consistent success. On one occasion he captured the governor of Dunkirk and delivered him to Rotterdam as a prisoner. For this exploit, he received another gold chain and other rewards, this time from the Admiralty.[7]

When his new commander in chief, Vice-Admiral Liefhebber, went ashore to supervise the building of a flagship, Tromp temporarily became chief of the cruising squadron. On 16 March 1630, Stadtholder Frederick Henry appointed him to the rank of post captain. This meant that Tromp held the permanent rank of captain, apart from the actual command of a ship. In addition, he received the title captain-commodore and a gold medal from the States-General. He now belonged to the group of sixty captains who held permanent appointments, and his portion of the prize money for captured vessels increased considerably.

Characteristic of Tromp's stature was the fact that he shared his successes with his subordinates. More than once he requested and obtained rewards for members of his crew. For his friendly manner of speaking, his even temper, and his superb leadership, he received the nickname *Bestevaer,* literally meaning "Granddad" or "Old Fellow," but which in his case came to signify "the best man to sail with." After him, only de Ruyter was accorded this sobriquet.

Late in 1631, an accident occurred that caused Tromp much sorrow. His famous *De Groene Draeck* was lost two miles west of Flushing through a pilot's negligence. Six months later, he assumed command of the *Prins Hendrik,* the newest ship in the fleet.[8]

The next years proved disappointing for Tromp for a number of reasons. A shortage of ships caused a quarrel between the Admiralties and the States-General over the employment of the single squadron remaining in home waters. The members of the Rotterdam Admiralty wished to please their fellow tradesmen by giving convoy to the merchant fleets. In contrast, the States-General emphasized the importance of protection against corsairs and the interception of troop transports, monies, and munitions being sent from Spain to the enemy army in Flanders. To achieve both objectives, the fleet was kept almost constantly at sea, without adequate rest for its crews or maintenance for its ships. On top of these problems came the choice of a new commander in chief. Tradition dictated that a member of the nobility should hold the highest post, regardless of his abilities. In the case of Piet Heyn, Frederick Henry had been able to override this ridiculous rule, but after Heyn's unexpected death tradition regained the upper hand and the Honorable Philips van Dorp, with whom Tromp was not on speaking terms, was appointed commander in chief.

When Tromp's wife died in November 1633, leaving him with three young sons, he made up his mind. On 30 May 1634, he resigned from the navy. It was a sign of van Dorp's incompetence and a reflection of the deplorable state of affairs within the navy and the country that no effort was made to persuade Tromp to remain.[9]

Maarten Harpertszoon found a quiet job as deacon and devoted himself to raising his sons. He found new happiness in a second marriage to Aeltgen van Arckenbout on 12 September 1634. No more than fifteen months later, however, the States of Holland begged him to rejoin the navy as nothing less than its vice-admiral. The previous summer the feared Dunkirk corsair Jacques Colaert had been able to run the Dutch blockade with a fleet of fourteen fine ships and six frigates and was wreaking havoc on the fishing fleets, their feeble escorts, and the navy's cruising squadrons. Now it looked as if the States admitted the fleet's need of a professional leader. Nevertheless, Tromp declined the offer, recalling all too well his frustrating quarrels with van Dorp, the reluctance of the Rotterdam Admiralty to refund the sums he personally had spent in the upkeep of his ship, and the troubles he had experienced in mustering enough men for his crew. Even the intercession of Frederick Henry failed to sway him. With exquisite courtesy, Tromp explained his refusal by saying that he did not wish to affront the commander in chief by sailing with the fleet while leaving "the gentlemen"—van Dorp and Liefhebber—ashore! Neither of the two admirals showed any appreciation for his absolutely correct course of action.[10]

In the meantime, the care and maintenance of the fleet deteriorated. The complicated organization of the five admiralties and the rivalries between them, the States, the States-General, and the Stadtholder, combined with a reluctance to spend money on the fleet, led to disaster. In 1636 there was no blockading force off the Flemish coast and the enemy raided the North Sea at will. The States-General tried to improve conditions through the installation of boards of directors, separate from the admiralties, to take charge of fitting out the navy's ships; Tromp became head of the Rotterdam Directory. But even this emergency measure was doomed to failure as a result of the devastating Dutch particularism. Only in the face of an immediate threat was the republic able to act, although then, as history shows, it acted with great vigor.

On 27 October 1637, Lieutenant-Admiral van Dorp resigned his position. This was a great day for the young nation, for it cleared the way for the States of Holland to ask Tromp for a second time to accept the leadership of the navy.[11] This time he agreed, but in doing so he laid down conditions that guaranteed him greater authority than had been held by the navy's previous commanders. Because he knew from bitter experience how badly the fleet had been neglected by the same body that now begged him to take command of it, he demanded an adequate number of ships, well equipped and well manned. The States solemnly promised to act in accordance with his wishes. The terms of Tromp's official appointment from the Stadtholder further strengthened his position versus the admiralties and the States. Two days later, his townsman Witte Corneliszoon de With, a year younger, very brave but brutal and bad-tempered, was appointed his vice-admiral.

Tromp began by restoring the neglected blockade of Dunkirk, the root of all evil in the North Sea. At the same time, he strove to improve conditions throughout the navy. Personally taking command of the blockading squadron, he went cruising in the English Channel, attacking enemy shipping, tracing the many shifting shoals and sandbanks, and exercising his ships and crews, not only during the sailing season but throughout the long winters as well. Within a short time he was able to restore discipline, motivation, skills, and cooperation among his subordinates. A spirit of strength and self-confidence emerged. This spirit was backed by better logistics from the shore. The improvement in the latter was also due to Tromp, who used his rare interludes at home to convince the authorities to give him the necessary support. Despite the opposition of the city of Amsterdam, which sought only its own interest, and the lukewarm cooperation of de With, a jealous and independent character, he gradually managed to get a firm grip on the navy. A cordial relationship with Stadtholder Frederick Henry proved advantageous in solving difficult problems. Together they preserved the custom of holding the *generaal rendez-vous,* an assembly of all the fleets off Hellevoetsluis at the start of a campaign, and they also managed to change Tromp's one-year appointment into an indefinite one. They did not succeed, however, in discouraging the Amsterdam merchants' lucrative—and to modern sensibilities, shameless—practice of selling warships to Spain.[12]

To understand the importance of Tromp's actions up to this moment and in the battles to come requires a brief look at the situation in which the republic found itself during this hectic period. The Eighty Years War had begun in 1568 as a revolt against the despotic rule of King Philip II of Spain. The Dutch national government had been organized by the Union of Utrecht in 1579 and by the time of Philip's death in 1598 the United Provinces had convincingly asserted their independence, but the refusal of his successors to recognize the loss of the northern Netherlands meant that the conflict would continue for another half-century.

As the United Provinces grew in importance, strength, and wealth, they gradually became the pivot of European politics. Thus, after the Twelve Years Truce expired in 1621, the Dutch found themselves at the storm-center of the Thirty Years War (1618–48), the struggle between the hereditary enemies Bourbon France and Habsburg Spain, through which was interwoven the fanatic religious conflict between Catholics and Protestants. The French minister Cardinal Richelieu sought to break the Habsburg encirclement of France. Possessing large territories in the north and south of Europe, the Spanish had been able to move their troops overland throughout the European theater. The French armies and the Swedes under Gustavus Adolphus successfully disconnected Spain and northern Italy from the Low Countries, thus gaining an enormous strategic advantage. In order to retain the southern Netherlands—basically, modern-day Belgium—as a stronghold and fleet base in northern Europe, the Spanish were obliged to transport their troops through the Atlantic and the English Channel to Dunkirk. This passage had been blocked in 1588, when the "invincible Armada" was destroyed by the English and Dutch fleets and, the Spanish said, a Protestant wind. After a long war with the Dutch rebels, the Spanish managed to reconquer most of the Flemish ports. In 1605 they tried to reinforce the army in Flanders by sea but were checked by a Dutch fleet off Dover, and two years later Heemskerck was able to scotch the Spanish threat off Gibraltar, on the enemy's doorstep—the occasion on which young Maarten Tromp received his baptism of fire.

But from 1631 onward, the Spanish succeeded in sending annual reinforcements through the Channel. For reasons explained above, the Dutch navy was not always fit to react, while the English government of King Charles I played a curious double game, fearful of Dutch and French naval expansion and jealous of Dutch commercial supremacy, but at the same time anxious to check the spread of the militant Counter-Reformation supported by Spain.

Tromp's task was to stop further transport of enemy troops to Flanders, not only to support the United Provinces' struggle for independence, but also to assist their allies, France and the German Protestant states. Intelligence reports had convinced Tromp and the States-General that a powerful Armada was being assembled in Spanish harbors and might sail for the Low Countries at any time from 1637 onward. Tromp was fully aware of the strategic importance of his mission, as well as of the tactical implications of encountering the enemy fleet with his small squadron.

This is why both Tromp and de With kept cruising throughout the years 1637 and 1638, not only in summer but also in the harsh winters. De With was luckier in his engagements and took more enemy shipping than Tromp, but the latter improved his already enormous knowledge of the Channel and his crews grew accustomed to the views and methods of their new admiral. Once more, he became their *Bestevaer*.

In view of the rumors of bustling activity in the northern Spanish harbors and Dunkirk, Tromp decided to put to sea early in 1639. The enemy needed not only to transport fresh troops to the Netherlands, but also to bring a sizable force of veterans home from that theater to meet an imminent French attack on northern Spain. So Tromp was at his post with twelve ships when on 18 February the Biscayan corsair Miguel de Orna left Dunkirk with a strong fleet via the southwestern outlet called Het Scheurtje (The Little Fissure). A fierce action resulted. During the next four hours the Dutch took three vessels and chased the remainder back to port. Tromp had to return to his base at Hellevoetsluis to repair his damage. The States-General, delighted to learn of this victory after a long series of abortive attempts to check the Dunkirk raiders, bestowed chains and medals on Tromp and his captains.

The admiral himself took the opportunity to urge the States of Holland to outfit more ships, for he knew that this victory was not the final one. But his plea was to no avail. The States did not press the repair of his vessels and were not at all disposed to increase the number of men-of-war under his command. In the meantime, the Dunkirkers worked feverishly to make good their damages and were able to sail unopposed on 12 March. On 6 April, Tromp took an outraged stand in the States of Holland. At last he was able to convince the representatives of the seriousness of the situation. A few days later, on 13 April, Tromp lost his second wife, leaving him with another three motherless children. He nevertheless put to sea at the end of the month, bound for the Straits of Dover with twenty sail to await Spain's new Armada.

This Armada was the largest fleet Spain had assembled since the 1588 disaster. In La Coruña ten thousand troops were waiting to sail north. More than forty-five men-of-war and about thirty transports crowded with soldiers left harbor at the end of August. The admiral, Don Antonio de Oquendo, was a skilled seaman.[13] He had strict orders to attack any French or Dutch ships encountered, even if he had to violate English neutrality. His departure was delayed by a brief French blockade, the late arrival of an escort fleet from the Mediterranean and the West Indies, and last but not least, because of the fact that Spanish absolutism was no better a guarantee of naval efficiency than Dutch particularism.

In the meantime, Tromp spent a very busy summer cruising the Narrows and inspecting every merchantman that passed to collect information about the enemy. This caused a new problem for the Dutch, because the English, aroused by complaints provoked by these inspections, sent a squadron under Admiral Sir John Pennington to the Downs to keep an eye on Tromp.

Finally, on 15 September 1639, Dutch patience was rewarded: Oquendo's fleet was sighted. Tromp dispatched one of his thirteen ships to warn de With (five ships) and Joost Banckert (twelve ships). The next morning, after de With joined Tromp, they had seventeen ships at their disposal against Oquendo's sixty-seven.

Determined to prevent the Spanish from passing through the Channel, Tromp held a last meeting with his captains on board his flagship *Aemilia,* and outlined his tactical plan. Much to the surprise of Oquendo, who sailed ahead in his flagship *Santiago* to show his captains how to attack a Dutchman, Tromp maintained a straight, uninterrupted line with his ships stem to stern. Working up against a northwesterly wind, he chose the lee-side and, declining to close, commenced firing broadsides that cut up the Spanish rigging. In this manner Tromp continued his attacks for hours with his faster, more maneuverable ships, denying the Spanish an opportunity to engage in a melee, which was the usual tactic of the time and would have been disastrous for the small number of Dutch vessels. Tromp's only loss occurred when one of his ships' powder magazine exploded.

At four o'clock in the afternoon the Spanish broke off the action and tried to sail eastward to Dunkirk. Coming in sight of the English coast near Folkestone, they dropped anchor during a lull in the wind. Tromp followed. At midnight he lost contact with the enemy fleet and also anchored. The next morning a reconnaissance located the Spanish force, but a calm held the fleets a mile apart off the English coast all day. As the wind freshened that evening, Tromp decided to attack at night, another highly unusual decision whose wisdom was soon proved. To enable his ships to recognize each other, he ordered two lights to be placed in the stern and one on the mast and a piece of canvas to be wrapped around the poop. By then, the arrival of two ships from Hellevoetsluis had raised the number of vessels under Tromp's command to eighteen. Sailing again in a close line-ahead formation with a southeasterly wind, they surprised the unsuspecting Spanish fleet in the act of weighing anchor for Dunkirk. The ensuing gunnery action lasted until morning, damaging the large Spanish galleons and exhausting Tromp's ammunition. At this moment Banckert's squadron of twelve sail reported to the admiral and enthusiastically resumed the battering of the Spanish ships. The fighting continued into the afternoon, when Tromp was forced to disengage because of an acute shortage of powder and shot.

Having demonstrated his tactical ability, Tromp now displayed his strategic understanding. His night attack had revealed Oquendo's intentions, which Tromp proceeded to frustrate. Knowing these waters by heart from his cruising during 1637 and 1638, he sailed to Calais Roads. By this movement he blocked the southwestern entrance of Dunkirk, Het Scheurtje, while he could resupply the ships from Calais with the warm support of Richelieu. Oquendo did not dare risk another engagement, not even in view of Tromp's evident shortage of ammunition, and fled to the Downs, where he hoped to gain time to repair his extensive damage. Here his fleet was temporarily halted by Pennington, who had instructions from his king to be friendly to Oquendo, but nevertheless asked him to haul down his colors upon entering the roads. This was too much for the proud Spaniard and a long quarrel broke out between the two men.[14] It lasted until dawn, when Tromp arrived at the Downs with twenty-four fully provisioned ships. The sight of his small fleet caused a sort of a panic among the Spanish captains, who cut their cables and fled behind the shoals and banks to the north of Pennington's squadron. Tromp followed and took up a position to the south, where he could keep a keen eye on the enemy.

In the meantime, the States-General, aware of these events, showed a remarkable activity in supplying the Dutch admiral with provisions and men. A constant stream of ships was equipped in Dutch harbors and sent to the Downs. But the States-General's most important initiative was a strict and secret order to Tromp, dated 21 September 1639, to attack and destroy the Spanish fleet, in the vicinity of whatever nation, and notwithstanding the presence of whatever fleet.[15] For weeks the three fleets in the Downs held the attention of western Europe. Crowds of Englishmen came to see the spectacle of hundreds of ships so close together. Several notables presented themselves on board the flagships of Pennington, Tromp, and even Oquendo. Everyone wondered if Tromp would dare to violate English neutrality by attacking the Armada.

And that was precisely what Tromp had in mind. He was only awaiting an opportunity to avoid giving Pennington too much offense and persuading Oquendo to come out. His conduct during these weeks revealed Tromp's diplomatic skills and his sense of humor in dealing with delicate problems. Pennington, who in his heart sympathized with Tromp and, like most Englishmen, detested the Spanish, repeatedly informed his government of the correctness of Tromp's actions. Pennington's flag-captain, Peter White, daily visited the *Aemilia, Bestevaer*'s famous flagship, and left a vivid logbook that describes a number of humorous scenes staged by Tromp to appease his English opponent. White's account also provides an insight into what was going on in Tromp's mind. Through his friendly relationship with the Englishman, *Bestevaer* was able to control shipping in the areas simply by listening to White's reports and making suggestive comments in reply.

At the Downs, both Tromp and Oquendo had to contend with the unreliable King Charles I. Although English policy supposedly tilted toward Spain, Charles played no favorites. He approached the situation with an evenhanded intention of obtaining the greatest possible political and financial profit from both parties, demanding payment from France in exchange for giving the Dutch fleet a free hand and overcharging Oquendo for assistance of often dubious quality. The discovery of a thousand Spanish soldiers who had been concealed aboard three English vessels in August gave Tromp a means of gaining the diplomatic advantage. By removing the soldiers but leaving the ships' rich cargoes untouched, he exposed the king's duplicity while avoiding a clash with Pennington.

Oquendo was less fortunate. He was obliged to pay exorbitant prices for poor-quality English powder and the passage of Spanish troops to Dunkirk in English ships. New masts, spars, and rigging that he ordered in Dover failed to appear. Informed of this, Tromp ordered one of his captains, Dorreveld of the rowing-yacht *Amsterdam,* to pick up the spare parts and deliver them to the Spanish fleet. This took place on 7 October. Tromp even offered his adversary a fair share of his own Calais powder free of charge, so eager was he to lure Oquendo into open waters.[16]

The last had not been heard of Captain Dorreveld, however. As he refused to accept payment for his deliveries—behavior that nowadays would be considered extremely unDutch—the Spanish rewarded him with a quantity of wine. He took such pleasure in their gift that in an excess of high spirits he attacked an English coastal vessel. Tromp apologized for this action to Pennington with his quick-witted style, saying that his captain must have been drunk on the Spanish wine and that he would have gladly replaced him, if there were no Spaniards present. Pennington swallowed this excuse with mild skepticism.

On the morning of 21 October Tromp had at his disposal a total of ninety-five ships and eleven fireships, which he had organized into six squadrons, each with its own task. He had informed Pennington of his intention to attack the Armada by a letter in which he again enumerated all of Oquendo's violations of English neutrality. He concluded, "I trust that His Majesty of England will be very pleased with what I am doing."[17] The *Aemilia* fired a cannon as a signal and the fleet weighed anchor. Tromp had positioned his fireships in front of the men-of-war. When the Spanish captains saw the fireships coming their way, they opened fire. The Dutch answered with heavy and sustained salvos. Pennington, who had instructions to take action against the Dutch, half-heartedly engaged de With's squadron. De With, for his part, simply ignored the English and fell upon a Portuguese squadron in the Spanish fleet, leaving Pennington undisturbed to direct his broadsides into the waters of the Downs.

In the following hours, a fierce battle developed. The Dutch again declined to close and bombarded the Spanish ships from a distance with fairly accurate broadsides. In banks of billowing mist that deprived Oquendo of any view of his enemy, twenty Spanish galleons were driven ashore and

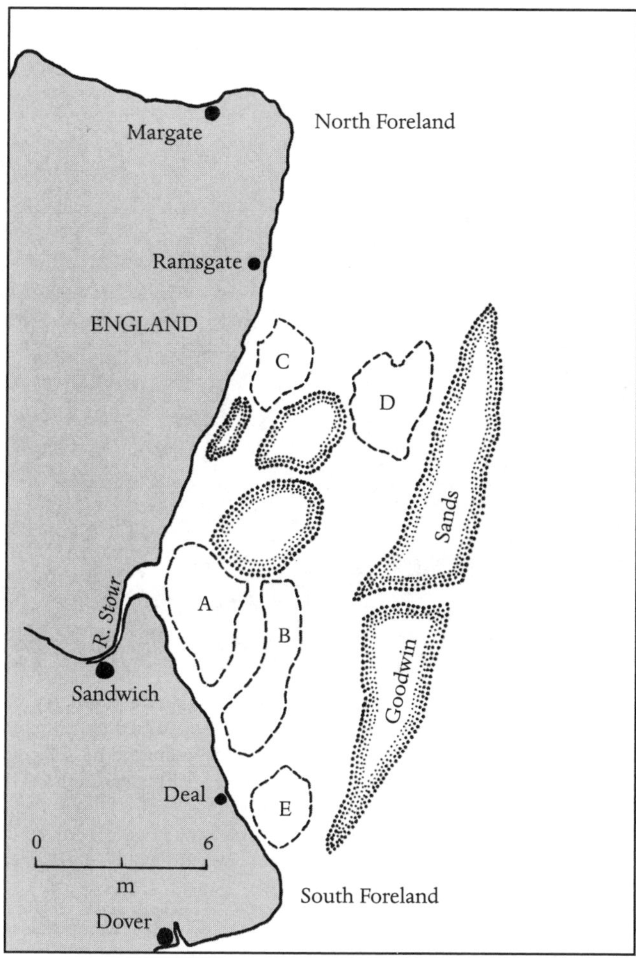

2. The Battle of the Downs, 21 October 1639. (A) The Spanish fleet. (B) First position of the English fleet, subsequently occupied by Tromp. (C) De With's squadron. (D) Banckert's squadron. (E) Second position of the English fleet. Based on a map published in Amsterdam about 1643.

wrecked. The remnants of his fleet were forced out of the Downs, attacked by fireships, and battered by Tromp's guns until nightfall. By then, all but twelve of Oquendo's men-of-war had been destroyed, captured, or driven aground. The proud *Santa Teresa,* at 2,400 tons the largest of his ships, was a burned-out wreck. More than seven thousand of the soldiers on board the

1. The Battle of the Downs, 21 October 1639. A section of a contemporary German print shows Tromp's flagship, the *Aemilia* (at the right center, identified by an A on her stern), closely engaged with an enemy galleon (B), which is also menaced by a burning ship (C). Though the key to the print has been detached, (B) probably represents the Portuguese squadron's flagship *Santa Teresa,* which burned after the crew of a Dutch ship that had become entangled with her set fire to their own vessel, and the large galleon crossing directly ahead of the *Aemilia* would be Oquendo's *Santiago.* (The Beverley R. Robinson Collection, U.S. Naval Academy Museum.)

Spanish vessels were killed or drowned, as well as the majority of their unlucky crews.

Tromp lost a single vessel, which became entangled with the *Santa Teresa* and was set on fire by her own crew. Most of her company was rescued. Only one hundred Dutch sailors died in the entire engagement. Oquendo himself escaped in the night and made it to Dunkirk with a riddled *Santiago.* The next morning Tromp made a sweep south to Beachy Head, where he spotted a few lost Spanish galleons, which immediately surrendered or were burned. Besides the *Santiago,* only eight Spanish ships reached Dunkirk, all in a more or less disabled condition.

On 23 October, Tromp returned to the Downs to see if there were any Spaniards left afloat; none were. His salutes were not answered by the English vessels, nor by the English shore batteries, but Pennington, who was left alone in the Downs, boarded the *Aemilia* and asked Tromp what he was looking for, after having offended the king in his own backyard. Cordially, Tromp replied that he had not the least intention of affronting His Majesty, but was merely obeying the orders of the States-General; he only came to see if all the Spaniards had been disposed of, and if not, he would love to dispose of them now. Finding his work finished, Tromp left twenty vessels to blockade Dunkirk and sailed for home. On 29 October, he personally presented his report to the States-General. He was rewarded with a huge grant of money, and a commemorative medal was struck in his honor.[18]

With this victory the Dutch republic established its reputation as a sea power. Confidence in the navy as a defense for the fishing and merchant fleets was restored. The enemy naval vessels and privateers operating from Dunkirk would not receive significant support from Spain for some time to come. Without too much exaggeration, it might have been said that the English Channel had become Dutch home waters. The battle's effect on the land war was equally positive, for it meant that the severed land routes between the Spanish possessions would not be replaced by an ocean highway. In this sense, the Downs was a victory for France, Sweden, and the German Protestant states as well as for the republic.

Commander in chief for only two years, Tromp had managed to forge the neglected fleets into an effective and well-trained body that was not only prepared to perform endless and monotonous cruising duties, but would enthusiastically follow its leader in determined attacks against an apparently overwhelming enemy. In retrospect, we can identify the qualities and decisions that led to Tromp's triumph at the Downs: the weeks of waiting in the Channel, the blockade of Dunkirk, his tactful diplomacy toward the English, his audacity in giving battle on 16 and 18 September and his use of the fleet in a single line of battle, without allowing his aggressive, glory-hunting captains to fight their own little wars; his unconventional but decisive night attack of 18 September; his subsequent caution before 21 October, when the issue was certain and there was no sense in running needless risks; his phenomenal knowledge of the sea and the sandbanks; his sympathetic handling of both superiors and subordinates, and his cordiality and humor. All these things made him beloved as a man as well as renowned as a shrewd tactician and wise strategist. When he returned to Brielle the bells of St. Catharine's, where he had been baptized, pealed in his honor.

Tromp saw the small signs of his time, but also had a keen eye for the long run, as he proved again later when constantly fighting for a strong navy, prepared for the unexpected. He did not, however, succeed in this object.

Soon after hostilities came to an end late in 1639, the States-General, the Provincial States, and the admiralties immediately neglected the fleet, despite Tromp's proposals. Not until the approach of war with England thirteen years later did the authorities acknowledge the wisdom of his arguments for maintaining a substantial, permanent sea force. Nevertheless, Tromp himself was honored by the States-General, who granted him a huge award and another gold chain. He was also knighted by the French King Louis XIII. The erstwhile cabin boy had reached the highest circles of society; yet aboard ship he remained the same hardy, unpretentious seaman that he had always been.

Being twice a widower, with six children to care for, Tromp now married for a third time. On 1 February 1640, a radiant Maarten Harpertszoon wed Cornelia Teding van Berckhout, the daughter of a wealthy and distinguished old family in the Province of Holland. Sadly, his success made him the focus of envy as well as warmhearted congratulations. Anonymous pamphlets appeared in which he and his family were mocked and ridiculed. Even his courage was called into question. Tromp responded to these slanders with a dignified silence.

In the meanwhile, Tromp resumed his naval activities, blockading the Dunkirk pirates, who were still a menace to Dutch trade albeit that they lacked the support of the Spanish navy. He and Witte de With incessantly urged the admiralties to keep up the fleet, but to no avail. At the Peace of Westphalia in 1648 Spain gave the long-awaited formal recognition of the independence of the Republic of the Seven United Provinces, which provided the States and the admiralties with still another excuse to neglect the navy. These authorities failed to see that the republic's outstanding position in world trade and at the center of European politics was based on hegemony at sea. After the defeat of Spain new empires would arise, across the Channel and below the Scheldt, eager to challenge the preeminence of the small but powerful republic. It would seem that the signs should have been obvious. In October 1651 England proclaimed the First Navigation Act, discriminating against Dutch seaborne trade and setting the stage for the first of the three exceptionally hard-fought confrontations known as the Anglo-Dutch Wars. Farsighted as always, on 15 March 1652 Tromp presented a highly important memorandum to his superiors, "Consideratien, ingesteld op de jegenswoordige occasie ter zee" (Considerations on the Present Situation at Sea), in which he further developed his ideas on tactics, based upon the principle of attacking before the enemy had the opportunity to act.[19]

The First Anglo-Dutch War (1652–54) unofficially opened on 29 May, when forty men-of-war under Tromp encountered twenty-five English vessels under General at Sea Robert Blake off Dover. Tromp's refusal to dip his colors to the English squadron, as prescribed by the Navigation Act, prompted Blake to fire two shots across his bow. Tromp responded to a third shot with a broadside and the fight was on. Despite his numerical advantage, Tromp did not press the action. His principal concern was the safety of a merchant convoy and he withdrew after losing two ships. Declarations of war were exchanged in July (see map 3).

For the republic, the conflict revolved around the protection of its fishing fleets and critically important merchant shipping to the Baltic, the Mediterranean, and the Far East. Initially, the navy attempted to defend these interests with the remnants of the long-neglected fleet, augmented by a collection of chartered vessels; later, it was reinforced by a number of fine new ships built according to Tromp's program of March 1652. In the end, the Dutch were unsuccessful in the North Sea and at the signing of peace the republic agreed to respect the provisions of the Navigation Act, reverses that were partly offset by victories in the East Indies and the Mediterranean; but Tromp would not live to see the outcome of the struggle.

In the weeks following the Battle of Dover, Tromp reentered the Channel to collect homecoming convoys of Dutch merchantmen. At the Downs he encountered and started to attack Sir John Ayscue's small English squadron, when a sudden calm frustrated his intention. He then proceeded to the North Sea to shepherd the Baltic convoys into friendly waters. An English fleet under Blake was present in the North Sea at the same time, despoiling the Dutch herring fishery, but the two forces did not come into contact and Tromp returned home to a storm of criticism for not having safeguarded the catch.

Politics also came into play. On 16 November 1650, Stadtholder William II had died, aged twenty-four. A week later, his widow gave birth to his son. Instead of designating a mature member of the House of Orange to act on behalf of the child, the Dutch merchant oligarchy, ever jealous of the family, seized the opportunity to vest executive power in a board of "Regents." Tromp's reputation as a loyal Orangist therefore represented a mark in his disfavor in the eyes of the patricians who controlled the States-General and the highly influential municipal government of Amsterdam.

The shameful result was that in August 1652 the States-General asked Tromp to relinquish command of the fleet, while retaining his rank and titles. Disgusted as he must have been by this treatment, he continued to give the government the benefit of his advice on the conduct of the war. His abilities were too valuable to be overlooked for long, however, and in October he was restored to command.

Tromp returned to sea with the mission of escorting outgoing and incoming merchant convoys through the Channel. On 10 December, he defeated an inferior English fleet under Blake at the Battle of Dungeness. Legend holds that afterward Tromp wore a broom to his masthead, signifying that he had swept the Channel of the enemy, but there is no contemporary evidence of this action, which would have been out of character, in any event.

The English soon reassembled a substantial force, and in February Blake attacked Tromp while the latter was escorting a homeward-bound convoy up the Channel. The odds were nearly even, with approximately seventy warships on each side, but the English vessels were more powerfully built. In the Three Days Battle (also called the Battle of Portland, 28 February to 2 March 1653, the enemy eventually broke through the Dutch screen, taking eleven naval vessels and thirty merchantmen. Nevertheless, Tromp succeeded in saving most of the convoy.

The damages both fleets had sustained led to a pause in the war at sea, but before the end of May Tromp sailed to escort a merchant convoy of two hundred ships home from the Baltic. Afterward, he made a raid into the Channel, where on 12–13 June he was defeated by a numerically superior English fleet under General at Sea George Monck at the Battle of Gabbard Bank. The English capitalized upon their victory by imposing a blockade on the Dutch coast.

The States-General's initial reaction was to seek peace, but the severity of the terms England offered steeled the Dutch to make another attempt to gain command of the sea. Accordingly, two squadrons were fitted out, one under Tromp at Flushing and the other in the Texel under de With. Getting to sea early in August, the Dutch succeeded by skillful maneuvering in uniting their forces in the presence of Monck's fleet, to which they gave battle on 10 August. Each fleet counted more than one hundred sail. The greater number and, more importantly, the greater strength of the English vessels proved decisive in the ensuing Battle of Scheveningen, and Tromp's fleet was driven back into port with the loss of fifteen ships. Both sides suffered heavy casualties. The Dutch effort had not been altogether in vain, however. Monck's battered fleet had to return home for repairs, making possible the revival of Dutch trade, and the English government lowered the price of peace.

Tromp himself was killed toward the close of the action on the quarterdeck of his flagship, the *Brederode,* by a musket ball through the chest. His last words were "Ik heb gedaan, houdt goeden moed"—I'm finished, but keep up your courage. On 5 September 1653, the country he had served so well gave him the final honor of a state funeral in the Old Church at Delft.

NOTES

1. Johanna K. Oudendijk, *Maerten Harpertszoon Tromp* (The Hague: H. P. Leopolds Uitgevers Maatschappij N.V., 1942), p. 4.

2. F. Graefe, *De kapiteinsjaren van Maerten Harpertszoon Tromp,* Werken uitgegeven door de Commissie voor Zeegeschiedenis V (Amsterdam: N.V. Noord-Hollandsche Uitg. Mij., 1938), p. 4.

3. Ibid., p. 5.

4. Ibid., p. 11.

5. Ibid., pp. 15–16; Afdeling Maritime Historie van de Marinestaf (AMH) (Historical Department of the Naval Staff), Archief Milo, Nr. 81.

6. Central Bureau of Genealogy, The Hague (CBvG), *Genealogy Tromp.*

7. Journaal van commandeur Maerten Harpertszoon Tromp, van 23 november 1629 tot 14 maart 1630, in Rijksarchief Utrecht, Archief Staten van Utrecht, Nr. 665.

8. Algemeen Rijksarchief Den Haag (ARA) (National Archives), Admiralty of Rotterdam: Commissieboeken 86, Nr. 125–126.

9. CBvG, *Tromp;* AMH, Milo, Nr. 81.

10. Graefe, op. cit., pp. 88–91.

11. ARA, Staten Generaal 1626–1639, Inv. Nr. 12271, Folio 256, V.

12. W. P. C. Knuttel, *Catalogus van de pamflettenverzameling berustende in de Koninklijke Bibliotheek,* 9 vols. (The Hague: Koninklijke Bibliothek, 1889–1920), Nr. 462a.

13. M. G. de Boer, *De Armada van 1639* (Groningen: P. Noordhoff, 1911), pp. 20–21.

14. Ibid., p. 43.

15. ARA, Staten Generaal, Secreete Resolutien 21–september 1639.

16. De Boer, *Armada,* pp. 57–58.

17. M. G. de Boer, *Tromp en de Armada van 1639,* Werken uitgegeven door de Commissie voor Zeegeschiedenis VI (Amsterdam: N.V. Noord-Hollandsche Uitg. Mij., 1941), p. 123.

18. S. P. l'Honoré Naber, "Het Journaal van den luitenant-admiral Maarten Harpertszoon Tromp, gehouden aan boord van 's Lands schip Amelia in den jare 1639," in *Bijdragen en Mededelingen van het Historisch Genootschap* (1931), LII, 319; de Boer, *Tromp en de Armada,* p. 128.

19. ARA, Staten-Generaal, Inv. Nr. 7164; J. E. Elias, *De vlootbouw in Nederland in de eerste helft den 17e eeuw, 1596–1655,* Werken uitgegeven door de Commissie voor Zeegeschiedenis I (Amsterdam: N.V. Noord-Hollandsche Uitg. Mij., 1933), pp. 84–88.

Note on Sources

While there is no full-scale biography of Tromp in the English language, his role in the First Anglo-Dutch War is treated in more or less detail in many naval histories. For the background to the conflict, see C. R. Boxer, *The Dutch Seaborne Empire, 1600–1800* (London: Harmondsworth, 1965; 2nd ed., 1973), a broad and accurate overview of seventeenth- and eighteenth-century Dutch maritime history. More recent are the works of J. I. Israel, *The Dutch Republic and the Hispanic World, 1606–1661* (Oxford: Oxford University Press, 1982) and *Dutch Primacy in World Trade, 1585–1640* (Oxford: Oxford University Press, 1989), more or less rewritten in a magnificent volume, *The*

Dutch Republic: Its Rise, Greatness and Fall (Oxford: Oxford University Press, 1995). An illuminating combination of naval and social history is presented by J. R. Bruijn in *The Dutch Navy of the Seventeenth and Eighteenth Centuries* (Columbia: University of South Carolina Press, 1993), which sheds new light on the influence of the Dutch republic and its navy on modern history. C. R. Boxer published a profile of Admiral Tromp entitled "M. H. Tromp, 1598–1653," in *Mariners' Mirror*, 1954, pp. 33–53. English translations of documents from the closing years of Tromp's life appear in S. R. Gardiner and C. T. Atkinson, eds., *Letters and Papers Relating to the First Dutch War, 1652–1654*, 6 vols. (London: Navy Records Society, 1899–1930). Some of the translations are rather curious, however, and a useful addition was made by A. C. Dewar, *Corrigenda to the Letters and Papers* (London: Navy Records Society, 1932). Tromp's unceasing struggle to build an adequate fleet is described in J. J. A. Wijn, "Shipbuilding and Strategy, an Ever-changing Interaction," *Revue International d'Histoire Militaire* 58 (1984), pp. 187–221. A German publication by C. Ballhausen, *Der Erste Englisch-Holländische Seekrieg, 1652–1654, sowie der Schwedisch-Holländische Seekrieg, 1658–59* (The Hague: Martinus Nijhoff, 1923), includes everything that the author could find about Tromp, whether fact or fiction, true or false.

Of course, the majority of the studies on Tromp are in Dutch. A full bibliography is given in Johanna K. Oudendijk, *Maerten Harpertszoon Tromp* (The Hague: H. P. Leopolds Uitg. Mij. N.V., 1942), whereas J. C. M. Warnsinck offers a brief but vivid account of Tromp's life in *Twaalf doorluchtige zeehelden* (Amsterdam: P. N. van Kampen & Zoon N.V., 1941). Most of the six volumes of the important work by J. E. Elias, *Schetsen uit de geschiedenis van ons zeewezen, 1568–1654* ('s-Gravenhage: Martinus Nijhoff, 1916–1930), deal extensively with Tromp. They describe not only his skills as a maritime strategist and tactician, but also his day-to-day cares and complaints, his motives and objectives, and his joys and sorrows. F. Graefe, *De kapiteinsjaren van Maarten Harpertszoon Tromp* (Amsterdam: N.V. Noord-Hollandsche Uitg. Mij., 1938) traces his career as a ship's captain, and M. G. de Boer, *Tromp en de Duinkerkers* (Amsterdam: N.V. Noord-Hollandsche Uitg. Mif., 1949) discusses the ceaseless battle with the Dunkirk privateers who constituted a standing nuisance to Dutch trade. A notable new work by Anne Doedens and Liek Mulder, *Tromp, het verhaal van een zeeheld* (Baarn: Hollandia, 1989), resulted from its authors' discovery of a number of Tromp's long-lost letters and journals from the period 1629–30 in the archives of the University of Utrecht. Transcribing these materials into modern Dutch, the authors assembled a virtually autobiographical narrative of Tromp's command of *de Groene Draeck*. Many of Tromp's other letters and the major part of the resolutions of the States-General, the Provincial States, and the Boards of Admiralty are preserved in the National Archives (Algemeen Rijksarchief) in The Hague.

A number of works deal specifically with the campaign of 1639. C. R. Boxer, *The Journal of Maarten Harpertszoon Tromp Anno 1639* (Cambridge: Cambridge University Press, 1930) is a comprehensible English translation of the seventeenth-century Old Dutch text. Two complementary logbooks of 1639 are described by S. P. l'Honoré Naber in *Bijdragen en Mededelingen van het Historisch Genootschap* (*BMHG*). "Het journaal van M. H. Tromp in den jare 1639" (*BMHG*, 1931) presents Tromp's view of the situation, while "Het journaal gehouden door Peter White in den jare 1639" (*BMHG,* 1932) relates the impression that Tromp made on the English naval officer Peter White, Sir John Pennington's flag captain, with whom he spoke almost daily during the dramatic weeks at the Downs. A contemporary Portuguese account of the battle, Dom Francisco Manuel de Melo, *Conflito do Canal de Inglaterra entre as armes Espanholes e Olandesas* (Lisbon, 1660), was translated into Dutch by M. de Jong as *De strijd en het Engelse Kanaal tussen de Spaansche en Hollandsche wapenen anno 1639* (Den Helder: C. de Boer jr., 1939). M. G. de Boer devoted three works to the events culminating in the decision at the Downs: *De Armada van 1639* (Groningen: P. Noordhoff, 1911); *Tromp en de Armada van 1639* (Amsterdam: N.V. Noord-Hollandsche Uitg. Mij., 1941); and *Het proefjaar van Maarten Harpertszoon Tromp* (Amsterdam: N.V. Noord-Hollandsche Uitg. Mij., 1946).

3

Robert Blake
The State's Admiral
(1599–1657)

William B. Cogar

IN THE LATE SUMMER OF 1657, THREE ENGLISH WARSHIPS SAILED up the Western Approaches of the Channel toward Plymouth. The *George, Newbury,* and *Colchester* were part of the squadron returning from a resounding victory over a large and rich Spanish fleet at Santa Cruz de Tenerife in the Canary Islands. On board the *George* was that squadron's dying commander, Robert Blake, and the victory was the crowning achievement of his naval service to England. In great pain yet clear in mind, Blake hoped to live to reach shore. Upon entering Plymouth Sound on 17 August, the captain of the *George* wrote to the government that "it pleased the Lord to order. . . . Death seized on him and he departed this life about 10 o'clock in the morning," noting how difficult it was to write "this sad account of so great a loss to the State and nation."[1]

In the midst of the celebrations of the long-awaited victory over a Spanish fleet, England changed its mood upon hearing of the death of its most famous naval commander. The government of the English Commonwealth promptly ordered that Blake receive a funeral befitting his rank and achievements. Taken by ship to Greenwich where it lay in state in the Queen's House, Blake's corpse was removed on 14 September by barge up the Thames and interred in Henry VII's Chapel in Westminster Abbey.[2]

Much as the English public mourned Blake's death, perhaps no one lamented it more than the Lord Protector himself. Oliver Cromwell recognized the loss of a commander renowned throughout Europe. The Venetian ambassador to England was only partially correct when he wrote that the government regretted "the loss of so worthy a man, who on every occasion had proven his . . . loyalty and an unswerving devotion to the present regime."[3] It was neither to Cromwell's nor to any other regime that Blake swore his initial and lasting fidelity. Blake was unswerving in his loyalty to England. In religion, "he was one of the party with whom puritanism was a matter of morals and conduct, rather than of dogma."[4] Because of his qualities and characteristics, Blake's reputation, some say his legend, has transcended the controversy surrounding his country's experiment with puritan republicanism, and he remains one of England's foremost naval heroes.

From the time he received a command afloat at nearly fifty years of age until his death, Blake became synonymous with the success at sea that England enjoyed during the Interregnum. It was Blake who pursued those ships loyal to the exiled Stuarts as far as the Mediterranean. It was Blake who emerged the hero of what would be the first, and most successful, of three very bloody and fiercely contested wars against the Dutch. It was Blake who to a considerable extent repressed the North African pirates and showed the flag in the Mediterranean for the two years following the Dutch war. Finally, it was Blake who defeated a Spanish fleet at Santa Cruz, a victory that served as practically the only good news for England in what was otherwise a frustrating war. Equally, Blake contributed significantly to the increasingly disciplined and professional quality of the English navy. During a time when political and religious controversy dominated England's domestic scene, Blake "left a character without a stain; he rendered great services to England; he set an example . . . well imitated and followed."[5] Who was this man who so impressed both his contemporaries and posterity?

Robert Blake came from England's West Country, the traditional "nursery of seamen." Very little is known of his early life. He was born in September 1599 at Bridgwater in Somerset, the eldest son of Humphrey Blake, a wealthy and important member of the local gentry who, besides owning land around Bridgwater, traded in wines and other commodities to France and elsewhere.[6] After an early education at the King James's Grammar School in Bridgwater, Blake matriculated in early 1615 at Oxford University. Whether he went up to Oxford on his own volition to pursue an academic career or to follow the wishes of his father is unknown. In all likelihood, Blake sought the education that his rank in society dictated for him, the heir to a modest but not inconsiderable estate.[7]

Blake's academic career was undistinguished. He tried without success to win a scholarship and later a fellowship at two Oxford colleges. Sometime in 1617, doubtless finding more comfort "amongst his own," he became a Commoner of Wadham College, founded especially for West Country men. He received the B.A. degree in February 1618, returning shortly thereafter to Somerset, where he entered his father's business.[8]

Blake was not necessarily the dour Puritan characterized by future Royalists, but he was far from a cavalier. Serious and generally quiet, though not without humor, while at Oxford he was probably viewed as a rather provincial figure. He stood about five feet, six inches tall, and had a broad face and sturdy, thickset frame. His temperament, in the words of one biographer, "seems to have been almost irritatingly serene and well balanced."[9]

Between coming down from Oxford and the outbreak of civil war in 1642, Blake practically disappears. These "missing years" have been a source of frustration to historians, but it seems safe to conclude that he simply got on with his life. When his father died in 1625, he inherited the Blake estate and trading interests. This naturally included traveling around the kingdom as well as overseas. There can be little doubt that one reason for Blake's appointment as General at Sea in 1649 was his nautical experience. Other than as a youth before going up to Oxford, when would he have gained that experience, had it not been in managing the family business?

As head of the family, Blake was also occupied with raising his numerous brothers and sisters. Either on this account or because, as some insinuated, he was of a "monkish" nature, Blake never married, and there is no hint of a romantic episode at any stage of his life.[10]

In accordance with the law, Blake was baptized in the Church of England. But like so many others throughout England in the 1630s, he objected to the failure of King Charles I to reform the Established Church along puritan lines. According to one historian, himself a clergyman, Blake's clear-cut, uncomplicated puritanism grew stronger as he grew older. In almost every one of his surviving letters there is a consistent religious, and especially puritan, theme. In all likelihood, when Blake was given a command, "he conceived of himself as a man selected of God for great purposes, which he was therefore bound to carry out."[11] It cannot have been surprising that Blake, a man of local prominence possessing a natural interest in the state of the realm, was returned from Bridgwater to the Parliament that convened in April 1640. However, his first parliamentary experience was brief. The Short Parliament was dissolved by the king after sitting for only a month. In November 1640 Blake was not returned to what would become the Long Parliament. Given the paucity of his political statements and his subsequent career as a man more inclined to action than to debate, he may have been happy not to be returned to Westminster.[12]

As the possibility of civil war loomed larger, Blake does not seem to have hesitated to take up arms for the Parliament. While some of his biographers suspect that he held republican sympathies while at Oxford, the evidence is flimsy. What probably persuaded Blake to fight against Charles was the general belief that the king was wrong, religiously, politically, and constitutionally, and that England's happy and balanced world needed restoring. Perhaps the naval historian John Knox Laughton was right when he wrote that Blake "was ruled by his judgment of passing events, which, as he interpreted them, gave him but the choice between submission to arbitrary tyranny and a manly resistance."[13]

What prior military experience Blake had is unknown. It is probable that he had none, other than perhaps as a militia officer. Nevertheless, he was a well-respected member of the Somerset gentry and, by early 1641, one in whom the Parliament clearly had confidence. Having cast his lot with the Parliament, Blake gravitated to the Pophams, a more influential Somerset family who had chosen the same side, and obtained a commission in the regiment they raised.[14]

While Blake did not fight in any of the famous Civil War battles such as

Marston Moor or Naseby, he participated in three memorable actions in the West Country, demonstrating resolute courage and outstanding leadership. All were in defense of besieged places. The first occurred at Bristol in July 1643, when the small fort that he commanded fought on for a day after the governor had surrendered the city. Having been relieved of its arms and equipment, the garrison was released—not uncommon practice in the war—and Blake rejoined his regiment to find that his conduct had won him the commendation of the Parliament and promotion to lieutenant colonel.

The next action in which Blake took part was the defense of Lyme. In the year following the fall of Bristol, this small town on the Dorsetshire coast became one of the few places in the west to hold out for Parliament. Used to launch raiding parties against Royalist forces and supplies, its capture was deemed vital by the Royalists in controlling the country between the River Severn and the Channel as well as giving the king access to the Channel. Officially, Blake held the position of third in command, but by the end of the siege his initiative and readiness to assume responsibility had made him the real leader of the defense.

The third and most important episode in Blake's army career was the defense of Taunton, a city of strategic importance of which he became governor in July 1644. This was his first independent command. Despite numerous casualties and tremendous damage to the city, Blake's obstinate defense ensured victory for the parliamentary cause during a low period in its fortunes. It was only in July 1645, after the Parliament's victory at Naseby, that a force was sent to raise the siege. Widely celebrated, the defense of Taunton made Blake known and admired in important military and political circles.[15]

By the summer of 1646, the war in the west was all but over. During the previous autumn Blake had been elected to Parliament for Bridgwater, although he was prevented from taking his seat until May 1646 because of assorted military obligations.[16] According to one biographer, the future General at Sea objected to the increasingly radical developments at Westminster "and under the influence of his humane convictions, declared openly that he would as freely venture his life to save the King as ever he had done to serve the Parliament." The same biographer believed that Cromwell and others were jealous and suspicious of Blake.[17] Letters by and about Blake, however, offer no confirmation of this interpretation. He was certainly not ignorant of or uninterested in political and religious developments during these tumultuous years. But for whatever reason or reasons, and unfortunately for modern scholars he made few comments of a political or personal nature, he did not participate in the trial and execution of Charles I.

Although he survived the purge of the Long Parliament by Colonel Thomas Pride, Blake demonstrated a characteristic reluctance to engage in political activity. Given his essentially conservative nature, he probably was disturbed by the events in London. If so, those who held power during the tumultuous winter of 1648–49 remained sufficiently confident of Blake's reliability to appoint him one of the three men who would command the fleet. Having passed through one civil war, apparently he had resolved that henceforth he would simply remain loyal to England, and that meant whichever regime was in power. He remained aloof from political developments throughout the remainder of his life, concentrating on keeping England safe from invasion and asserting the increasingly important role of her navy in international affairs.

In February 1649, only a few days after the execution of Charles I and the establishment of a unicameral republican commonwealth, the Rump Parliament turned its attention to the vital issue of setting out a fleet to secure control of the waters around England. Appointed Generals at Sea in joint command of the fleet were Colonels Edward Popham, Robert Blake, and Richard Deane, with seniority in that order. They were responsible for protecting England's coasts and trade, reducing those vessels sailing under Royalist commissions, and upholding "the sovereignty of the commonwealth in the seas."[18]

Blake's connection with the Pophams certainly played a part in his appointment as a General at Sea. But he and his two colleagues were appointed for practical as well as political reasons. Each had distinguished himself in command of parliamentary forces during the Civil War, yet each had experience at sea. On 28 April 1649 and at the age of nearly fifty, Robert Blake first went aboard a warship as the commanding officer, and thus embarked upon a naval career that would cause him to be remembered as one of England's great admirals.[19]

The navy's first duty in 1649 was to suppress the remnants of Royalism at sea. Vessels sailing under the formidable Prince Rupert had profited from the political turmoil and the weakened state of the English fleet to play havoc with English shipping. With Popham remaining in London and Deane helping transport Cromwell's army to Ireland, the task of clearing the English and Irish Seas of Royalists fell to Blake. Throughout the late spring and summer, Blake and his squadron of about ten vessels blockaded Rupert in Kinsale, Ireland.

Although he had become a naval commander rather late in life, Blake found his new career to his liking. In the summer of 1649, Cromwell invited Blake to return to the army, offering him the command of a regiment and the rank of major-general. Learning of Cromwell's invitation, Deane wrote to Popham saying that if Blake left, "I wish we may have as honest a man in his room. . . ." Fortunately for England, the Parliament left the decision to Blake, who declared his willingness to serve in any capacity, but made known his preference to retain a naval command. This decision to forego a military command and remain in the navy would endear Blake to his sailors for the rest of his life.[20]

In October bad weather forced Blake to seek shelter in southern Wales, and Rupert took advantage of his absence to escape. Although Blake's blockade failed to snare Rupert's small fleet, it contributed materially to the Commonwealth's efforts to subdue Ireland by controlling the sea and prompting revolts in favor of the Parliament in Cork and Youghal. For the next several weeks, the whereabouts of the wily prince were unknown. A squadron under Blake and Deane were posted off Land's End, assuming that Rupert would make for the Scillies, still under Royalist control. Word finally arrived that Rupert was off Portugal, and the Parliament sent Blake in pursuit in early 1650.[21]

Blake sailed to Portugal in early March with a squadron of about a dozen ships and some smaller vessels, joyfully discovering Rupert and his squadron in the Tagus. Believing that the "King [of Portugal] would raise no objection to the extermination of the pirate," Blake began preparations to do just that. Very soon, however, he learned that his assumption was in error; the king had taken the Royalist squadron under his protection. After a prolonged standoff, the Parliament authorized the blockading force to exert more than diplomatic pressure by seizing Portuguese merchantmen. Blake and Popham, who had brought reinforcements from home, did a splendid job of this, netting fourteen of twenty-three vessels in a convoy homeward-bound from Brazil. Their success brought England and Portugal to the brink of war, but in the end King John reconsidered and urged the Royalist ships to depart. In the early autumn, with the blockaders temporarily off station, Rupert's squadron slipped out of the Tagus and made its way into the Mediterranean.

Blake quickly took up the pursuit, chasing some of Rupert's ships into Cartagena harbor and setting them afire, and hounding the three remaining vessels as far as Toulon. The need for supplies then forced him back to Cartagena, where he received orders to return home. Reaching England on 20 February 1651, Blake was welcomed as a hero, voted the thanks of the Parliament, and awarded £1,000 for his great services to the state. Not only was Blake winning fame at home, but his actions off Iberia were gaining him a reputation abroad.[22]

The only home territories still held by the Royalists were the Isles of Scilly and Jersey. The responsibility for reducing them was given to Blake. In the spring of 1651, he commenced operations against the Scillies, whose capital surrendered on 13 June. The conquest of Jersey had to await the defeat of an invasion by the young Charles II at Worcester in September, but it, too, fell by the end of the year. The elimination of the last Royalist forces in and around England marked an important chapter in Blake's naval career.[23]

When Deane returned to the army in May 1651 and Popham died in August, the Parliament made no immediate move to appoint successors. It probably believed that three Generals at Sea were no longer necessary. The various squadrons designed to meet any Royalist threats and to police the British waters had been satisfactorily commanded by vice and rear admirals. Subsequently, Robert Blake became the sole General and supreme commander at sea. He remained the latter until his death.[24]

Blake's stature and reputation were now great, both in and out of England. He was elected for the first time to the Council of State, the Parliament's executive, although he chose to be a rather inactive member, typical of his attitude toward politics. As it turned out, an increase in the longstanding tensions between England and the United Provinces made his absence from sea duty brief. In March 1652, the government directed Blake to attend the business of fitting out ships for the forthcoming summer guard, for which "there is extraordinary occasion."[25]

After ridding the British Isles of Royalist forces, the Parliament wasted little time in trying to wrest the lucrative European carrying trade from the Dutch republic. In 1651 it passed the first Navigation Act aimed specifically at Dutch commercial preeminence, prohibiting the importation of goods in foreign vessels other than those of the vendor nation. In addition, the Parliament resurrected the old and somewhat presumptuous claim of sovereignty over the Narrow Seas, ordering naval commanders to insist that foreign ships acknowledge the same upon meeting English vessels by rendering a salute. This demand produced the spark igniting the two Protestant republics into the First Anglo-Dutch War.[26]

While not completely ready for war, the English navy by early 1652 was better equipped, administered, and commanded than it had been since the end of the previous century. England also enjoyed the geographical advantage of her position astride the Dutch trade routes. The Dutch, in contrast, were severely handicapped by the necessity of constantly having to convoy their many merchantmen in and out of the Narrow Seas. Combined with the political rivalry within the Netherlands between the republican and Orangist factions and the jealousies of the republic's provincial admiralties, these factors put the English at a distinct advantage.[27] That the contest was so stubborn testifies to the hardihood of the Dutch sailors and the skill of their commanders, Maarten Tromp and Michiel de Ruyter.

In May Blake sailed from the Downs with a fleet of about twenty-five ships westward along the English coast to Rye. On 28 May, a Dutch fleet of about forty ships under Tromp appeared and anchored off Dover. Tensions were already high owing to a brief scrap between English and Dutch forces

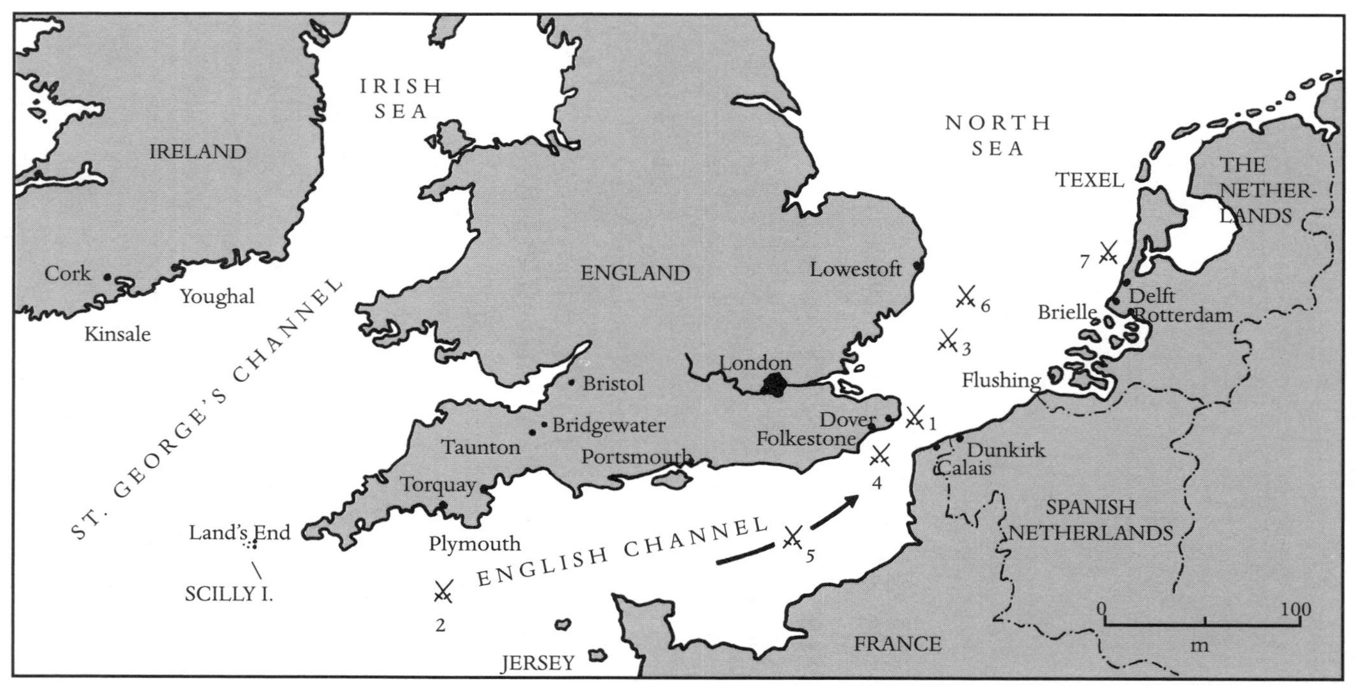

3. The First Anglo-Dutch War. (1) The Battle of Dover, May 1652. (2) The Battle off Plymouth, August 1652. (3) The Battle of Kentish Knock, October 1652. (4) The Battle of Dungeness, December 1652. (5) The Three Days Battle, February–March 1653. (6) The Battle of Gabbard Bank, June 1653. (7) The Battle of Scheveningen, August 1653.

elsewhere in the English Channel a few days earlier. About five o'clock in the afternoon of 29 May, Tromp ran his fleet down toward the English without abiding by the English demand that foreign ships strike their flag or lower their topsails. To encourage the Dutchman to recognize England's suzerainty, Blake twice fired a shot across Tromp's bow. The third time he did so, he was met with a broadside, and battle commenced.

Tromp's ships, entering action without any real formation, quickly clustered around Blake's flagship, the *James,* which had outsailed the rest of his fleet. Blake began to receive the worst of the fight. Although more solidly built than the Dutch vessels, the *James* sustained considerable damage and suffered more than forty casualties before the remainder of Blake's force came up and engaged the enemy. At the same time, the English squadron in the Downs quickly weighed anchor and fell upon the rear of the Dutch fleet. The action lasted about four hours until darkness and the loss of two of his ships forced Tromp to withdraw. With the morning light, the Dutch decided to forgo further battle and bore away to the east.[28]

With war a certainty, Blake began to initiate a significant change in the method of commanding vessels and one that helped to make for a more professional sea force in the future. Up to this time fleets were composed of ships belonging to the monarch or state, supplemented according to need by merchantmen hired or conscripted for service. Most of these vessels remained under command of their merchant captains, who normally had a financial interest in their ships and sensibly hesitated from placing them in harm's way. Blake perceived the tactical problem this posed and, due largely to his urging, the government began to install its own officers in private as well as state vessels.[29]

Indicative of the war's commercial purpose, the Parliament directed Blake to capture as many Dutch merchantmen as he could, realizing that those returning home were mostly ignorant of the hostilities and would be easy prey. Early in July 1652, Blake sailed north to intercept the Dutch East India convoys homeward-bound by the northern route around Scotland, as well as to attack the Dutch fishing fleets in the North Sea. He enjoyed much success, capturing fifteen vessels in a Dutch convoy and ridding the Dutch busses of their herring before sending them to Holland empty-handed. Tromp had been sent out to escort the returning merchantmen and to drive off Blake. Severe weather prevented the two fleets from meeting, however, and Tromp sailed home to face severe criticism by political opponents in a nation under increasing economic strain. He was relieved of command as a result.[30]

During the late summer and fall of 1652, Blake cruised off the Dutch coast in hopes of intercepting the other Dutch fleet, then returning up the Channel under the command of Admiral de Ruyter. He did not succeed, and de Ruyter slipped into the safety of his harbors under cover of foul weather. Refitted and strengthened, the Dutch fleet soon emerged in search of battle under the command of Admiral Witte Corneliszoon de With, who was quickly joined by de Ruyter.

Each fleet consisted of about sixty-five ships when they met on 8 October. The Battle of the Kentish Knock, named for the shallow in the northern part of the Thames estuary, commenced in late afternoon and lasted until dark. Neither side formed a true line of battle. Instead, individual ships or, at best, small groups of them fought independent actions. The larger, more powerful, and aggressively handled English vessels dominated the encounter. The "Butterboxes," so called derogatorily by the English, displayed an unwillingness to press the engagement because of divisions within their command structure, reflecting the political disunity within the Netherlands. At dawn, learning that they had lost three ships and suffered considerable damage to others, the Dutch chose not to renew the action.

Blake wrote a letter to the Parliament relating the events of the battle. In it, he demonstrated an appreciation of the military predicament by emphasizing the fleet's urgent need of repairs and provisions to follow up the victory and defeat the Dutch navy completely. The government failed to heed his recommendations, mistaking the victorious battle for a decisive one. On its orders, Blake's fleet was dispersed and he was left to guard the Channel with some forty ships in need of supplies.[31]

Following de With's defeat, the United Provinces restored Tromp to his position as fleet commander. Throughout the autumn of 1652, the Dutch busied themselves fitting out a fleet of some eighty ships to convoy several hundred merchantmen to La Rochelle and there pick up an incoming fleet of merchantmen. In order to succeed, Tromp knew that he had to dislodge Blake, then in the Downs with a vastly inferior force. In December, Tromp put to sea with a fleet estimated at 450 warships and merchantmen. Upon learning that the Dutch had sailed, Blake called a council of war at which his officers supported their commander's wish to engage the enemy. It may be that Blake did not realize just how superior a force he faced until the two fleets were in contact. But the odds did not deter him, and on 10 December, the Battle of Dungeness, some thirty miles down the coast from Dover, proved to be the war's most heatedly contested action.

In two roughly parallel lines, the opposing fleets sailed into battle. By nightfall, the English had lost six ships, and a number of others, including Blake's flagship, had suffered severe damage. Reluctantly, Blake broke off the action, anchoring off Dover under cover of darkness. Unable to pursue Blake because of contrary winds, Tromp stood off toward the French coast. For the next few weeks, Tromp watched as Dutch merchant ships proceeded through the Straits of Dover unmolested.

The ships that followed Blake into battle fought gallantly against heavy odds, but several vessels purposely, it seemed, held back, and Blake's report to the government pointed to this fact. He wrote that "there was much baseness of spirit, not among the merchant-men only, but many of the State's ships. . . ." He continued to say that one major problem was the large number of merchantmen used as men-of-war. While clearing his chest of this, Blake accepted complete responsibility for the defeat, and asked the government "to think of giving me, your unworthy servant, a discharge from the employment, so far too great for me. . . ." He added that he had full confidence that the two recent additions as Generals at Sea were worthy men.[32]

Since the outset of war, Robert Blake had been the sole General at Sea. Most likely, the Parliament believed that the war would be decided quickly by one great battle. That had not been the case, though, and by the autumn of 1652, the navy had become too large and the squadrons too far separated to be effectively commanded by one man. When considering renewing Blake's commission four days before Dungeness, the Parliament appointed Richard Deane (for the second time) and George Monck to be Generals at Sea.

Dungeness was a serious setback for England, but the Parliament had full confidence in Blake. His resignation was not accepted, and expressions of confidence were sent to him. During the following weeks, the three Generals at Sea busily oversaw the fleet's refitting, and early in February 1653 the Parliament congratulated them on their work in putting the fleet back into a seaworthy condition in so little time.[33]

During this period, Blake proved that he was as able an administrator as he was a commander. Many of the reforms that the navy underwent had Blake's hand in them, and his subsequent successes at sea ensured that these changes became permanent. Blake was especially concerned with the welfare of the sailors. In December 1652, informing the government of the needs of the fleet, he mentioned "errors and defects, especially the discouragements and want of seamen." A week later, he wrote to the House

> imploring all speedy and possible means for the reinforcing of his fleet; for his loss of seamen is extraordinary, and unless there be speedy care taken in paying them off their money, and furnishing out new assistance, we shall be but in a sad condition. For indeed they cry out extremely for money, and refuse to engage again. . . .

Blake stated that the Dutch seamen were better paid and rewarded than his own, which "sticks in their stomachs and quells their valour, which otherwise might prove happily instrumental in the good of this nation."[34]

The improvements in the size and quality of the English fleet were quickly made evident. By the middle of February 1653, some seventy-five ships were readied with the intention of seeking out Tromp's fleet, expected up the Channel from La Rochelle with a large convoy. The ensuing engagement, known as the Battle of Portland, was waged over three days from 28 February to 2 March. The first day's action, bravely fought by both sides, was on the whole indecisive. Tromp ordered his convoy to proceed to Holland while his fleet covered its passage. The second day saw a running battle up the Channel with the English trying to break through the Dutch warships and overhaul the merchantmen. By the time Blake attacked Tromp on the morning of the third and final day, the Dutch commander had only about thirty ships of his original seventy in fighting order. Even these ran out of ammunition, and when the English, with their speedier frigates, caught up to the rear of the Dutch convoy, Tromp could do little to defend it. With darkness, the action ended and England could celebrate a great victory.

Overall, the Dutch lost eleven warships, thirty merchantmen, and nearly two thousand dead; the English, one warship and about a thousand dead. One of the casualties was Blake himself, wounded in the thigh. Put ashore at Portsmouth, he became seriously ill, and command of the fleet passed to Monck. There was speculation that the state of Blake's health would prevent him from ever returning to sea.[35]

Recovering enough to travel, Blake was moved to Westminster, arriving there on 20 April 1653, the very day that Oliver Cromwell dissolved the Rump Parliament. Blake's auspicious arrival led to rumors that he opposed Cromwell's action. Some historians believe that this was true, but his most recent biographer reasons that Blake actually welcomed the new regime in the hope of a stronger civil authority. As far as the evidence, or lack of evidence, shows, if Blake opposed the dissolution of the Rump, he refrained from commenting on it, accepted the situation as a fait accompli, and chose to serve under it. Although there is no evidence to substantiate it, tradition has it that Blake declared, "It is not for seamen to mind State affairs but to keep foreigners from fooling us."[36]

By late spring, the Dutch had refitted their fleet and made a quick sortie to escort some merchantmen home and attack English shipping. More than one hundred vessels under the command of Richard Deane and George Monck were stationed off the North Foreland to meet the enemy. Throughout May, Blake slowly mended, trying as best he could in his weakened state to put the full fleet back to sea as quickly as possible and in a strength that would ensure victory. Learning that the Dutch were at sea, he joined his new flagship, the *Essex,* in the Thames.

Before Blake could reach the scene with his squadron of eighteen ships, the Battle of Gabbard Bank had already begun on 12 June. His arrival late in the afternoon decided the battle, and the following day the Dutch retired into the Flemish shallows after losing about twenty ships and nearly 1,400 men. The English lost one vessel and about four hundred men, including General at Sea Richard Deane.

Monck and Blake immediately blockaded the Dutch coast. Soon it became clear that Blake was far from recovered, and he went ashore again in early July. One official wrote that he found the General

> in a very weak condicion, full of paine, both in his head & left side, wch had put him into a feaver, besides the anguish he endures by the Gravell in his kidneys, insomuch as he takes no rest night nor day but continues groaning verie sadly.

Rumors circulated that Blake would not be able to resume his command if he survived, and possible successors were discussed.[37]

Blake remained too ill to participate in the last major action of the war, the Battle of Scheveningen, in early August 1653. The victory belonged to Monck and resulted in the death of Blake's old nemesis, Tromp. Blake did manage to return to the fleet in September, but the war was all but over. Peace was signed on 15 April 1654.[38]

The First Anglo-Dutch War, and the role Blake played in it, was a watershed in English naval history. Taking nearly four times the number of prizes lost during the conflict, England began her rise to maritime supremacy. The war also stimulated the professional development of the English navy, most notably, perhaps, by the appearance of the *Instructions for the better ordering of the Fleet in Fighting* in 1653. This directive, the first attempt to establish a tactical doctrine, advocated the use of line formations and attacks from the weather gage.[39]

The conclusion of the war left England with a naval force of more than 150 ships. Cromwell, now holding supreme power as Lord Protector, decided to use that force principally against England's chief rival, Spain. By attacking the rich West India trade, he hoped to divert to England the vast mineral wealth coming from the New World and thus alleviate his increasingly precarious financial situation, not to mention restoring England's reputation as the Protestant champion against Catholic Spain.

Barely two months after the end of the Dutch War, Cromwell assembled a large fleet in the Downs, one part of which would proceed to the West Indies, and the other to the Mediterranean. He decided that the force directed to attack the West Indies, the "Western Design," would be under the naval command of William Penn. Blake would command the fleet sent to revive English prestige in the Mediterranean, where the Spanish, French, and Barbary corsairs had exploited the republic's preoccupation with the

Dutch to interfere with English shipping. Both fleets sailed without a formal declaration of war in hopes of snapping up riches before adversaries could react.[40]

After the usual delays in the delivery of supplies, Blake left the Downs with a force of twenty-seven warships in mid-October 1654. He steered for Sardinia, intent on intercepting a French squadron reported near Sicily, but on 14 December he learned that his quarry had returned to port. Blake then sailed to Leghorn, where he received instructions to attempt to prevail upon the dey of Tunis to release the English captives he held and make restitution for the seizure of an English merchant ship. Like the other Barbary States nominally under the suzerainty of the Sultan of Turkey, Tunis was for practical purposes an independent principality. For centuries it had raised revenues by demanding tribute from maritime nations to refrain from attacking their trade. English vessels were supposedly protected by a treaty in 1646, but its provisions had lost their potency.[41]

Informed that ships were being assembled at Tunis for the Sultan's service, Blake hurried there from Leghorn, arriving on 18 February 1655. The anticipated force proved to be merely a rumor, but while off Tunis, he tried unsuccessfully to open negotiations with the dey. Withdrawing to resupply, Blake proceeded to Porto Farina, where he discovered nine of the dey's war galleys, lying unrigged but under the guns of the castle and several shore batteries. Concluding that it would be too costly to attack the galleys in this position, he continued to Cagliari to take on provisions, leaving seven vessels to blockade the Gulf of Tunis. By the latter part of March, Blake was back off Tunis, resolved "to put an end to the business there." A second attempt to negotiate with the dey met as haughty a rebuff as the first. Clearly exasperated by this "insolence and contumely," Blake called a council of war, at the end of which he decided to attack the galleys at Porto Farina.

Arriving off the harbor on the afternoon of 13 April, Blake found the vessels "still lying under the batteries, a pistol shot from the shore, [and] the coast lined with musketeers, while some sixty guns peered from the castle and works." Having beseeched the Lord's help, Blake attacked on the next morning. Entering the harbor behind a light westerly breeze, he managed to anchor his entire force of sixteen ships within musket shot of the castle, upon which they directed their broadsides.

The elements smiled on the English. "The Lord being pleased," as Blake wrote, "to favour us with a gentle gale off the sea, which cast all the smoke upon them and made our work the more easy." The castle's guns were silenced after an action of five hours. With smoke continuing to blanket the shore batteries, boat parties from the frigates rowed over to burn the nine galleys, whose crews fled ashore. By eleven o'clock in the evening the English ships were warping their way out of the harbor. Blake's squadron suffered twenty-five men killed and forty wounded. The general's account of the action is characteristic of his deference to the providential hand. "It is also remarkable by us," Blake reported,

> that shortly after our getting forth, the wind and weather changed and continued very stormy for many days, so that we could not have effected the business, had not the Lord afforded that nick of time, in which it was done.[42]

In the wake of this triumph, Blake attempted to intercept the rich Spanish Plate fleet from America believed to be headed toward Cadiz. Anchoring off Rota about 1 June, he also received orders to prevent the fleet then in Cadiz from sailing for the West Indies (see map 1). Although some provisions had reached him from home, by early July 1655 his squadron was running desperately low in almost all commodities and his ships were in need of repairs. Obtaining no news of the Plate fleet, Blake proceeded to Lisbon, despatching an urgent plea to London for supplies, without which he would be forced to return to England. In mid-September, none having arrived, he sailed for home.

Both Blake's fleet and the one under William Penn returned to England in the autumn of 1655. To Cromwell, neither had been successful in their missions. The "Western Design" had not taken Cartagena, and Blake had failed to intercept the Plate fleet, although this had not been one of his original objectives. It appeared that the Protector's policy of war against Spain came to nothing. Cromwell was so angry at the disastrous voyage to Cartagena that he sent Penn to the Tower of London.[43]

By the close of 1655, Robert Blake was the only General at Sea in command at sea. After a short stint in the Tower, Penn was retired in disgrace. George Monck became commander in Scotland, and John Desborough, who had been appointed General at Sea with Penn in December 1653, remained ashore attending to affairs there.[44] Subsequently, Cromwell turned to a loyal follower, Edward Montagu, who had commanded a regiment in the New Model Army. Although Montagu lacked any naval experience, he was appointed a General at Sea in early 1656.[45]

Meanwhile, preparations went ahead to prosecute the war against Spain. For the navy, this meant another turn at trying to capture the Plate fleet, expected to return to Spain in the summer of 1656. Success would not only expand English influence in European politics, but ease what was becoming a disastrous financial situation at home. With credit stretched to the limit, and much difficulty in procuring ships, supplies, and seamen, a fleet of about fifty vessels under Blake and Montagu sailed for the Mediterranean in March 1656.[46]

Arriving off Cadiz in mid-April, Blake learned that he had missed the arrival of some Plate ships. Just what he should do next was unclear. The instructions from Cromwell have not survived, but it can be assumed that Blake and Montagu were given considerable latitude. After holding his customary council of war, Blake rejected the possibility of an attack on the Spanish West Indies. He also ruled out an attack on Cadiz itself, whose defenses were reportedly being strengthened in anticipation of just such an eventuality. The only thing left to do was to establish a blockade in hopes of intercepting a Plate fleet. Blake must have dreaded another long period on blockade, which in the mid-seventeenth century was not only a new function for a fleet but one made doubly difficult by the absence of an advanced base and inadequate logistical support from home.[47]

Blake kept his fleet divided throughout the summer of 1656. One squadron, under the command of Captain Richard Stayner, remained off Cadiz to watch for the Plate fleet. The other squadrons, under Blake and Montagu, either sailed on forays against Spanish shipping from as far north as Vigo through the Straits of Gibraltar to Malaga Roads, or visited friendly ports such as Tangier or Lisbon in search of supplies. While Blake and Montagu were at the latter in mid-September, English fortunes changed for the better. Stayner's squadron met a small Spanish fleet of seven ships returning from the West Indies, capturing two and sinking two others before the remainder escaped into Cadiz. Although most of the treasure went to the bottom in the sunken vessels, the loss was a serious one for Spain.[48]

In the meantime, Blake and Montagu had written Cromwell, asking permission to send their larger ships home for the winter. Replying in late August, Cromwell approved their request, convinced that the Spanish would not send any ships to sea over the winter season. Typically, Blake chose to remain off the enemy coast, keeping about twenty vessels with him, while Montagu sailed for home with twelve ships. The latter reached England in early October, bearing letters from Blake with strong pleas for more and better supplies for his fleet.[49]

From prisoners taken by Stayner, Blake learned that a considerable amount of specie in Mexico was awaiting shipment and that a larger and richer Plate fleet was expected sometime early in the new year. The general realized that this time the Spanish would not sail directly to Cadiz without first making sure that the way was clear of English ships. He believed that instead they would put in at a convenient port from which they could gather information as to the disposition of their English enemies. Blake concluded that the most likely port was Santa Cruz de Tenerife in the Canary Islands.[50] In the meantime, he settled down to the depressing prospect of another winter on blockade, made worse by the lack of a regular supply of fresh victuals from England. Throughout the following months, Blake's fleet cruised between Cape St. Vincent and the Straits, while maintaining a small squadron close to Cadiz. The general's health continued to deteriorate. His old leg wound plagued him; he had kidney stones and he was likely suffering from edema.[51]

Early in 1657, Blake received intelligence of the awaited Plate fleet that supported his belief. An English merchant ship reported that a Plate fleet was west of the Canary Islands, and in mid-April, another report confirmed Blake's conjecture. The Spanish fleet had indeed put into Santa Cruz and was there awaiting news of the whereabouts of the English fleet before making the final leg of its journey.[52]

Blake sailed for Tenerife on 24 April, arriving there four days later. Santa Cruz presented him with a formidable challenge. The harbor faced east, with a crescent-shaped shoreline running roughly a mile and a half in a north-south direction. A stone jetty provided a breakwater behind which ships could load and unload their cargoes. The town and harbor were protected by two large forts connected along the sea front by redoubts and breastworks for artillery and musketeers. Accounts differ as to the exact number of Spanish vessels at anchor, but agree that the smaller vessels, numbering around seven, were closest to the shore. Six or seven larger galleons were anchored to seaward, but still under cover of the fortifications, in line-ahead formation with their broadsides bearing on the harbor mouth. All of the Spanish ships had sent their cargoes of gold and silver ashore for safekeeping.

After consulting with his ships' captains "how to order the attempt" and "earnest seeking to the Lord for his presence," Blake resolved to attack, using the same tactics that he had employed at Porto Farina. Ill health is generally the bane of boldness in naval and military commanders. For a man in Blake's pitiable condition to have made the—virtually unprecedented—decision to attack a European fleet in a fortified harbor is a testimonial to both his determination to serve England and his faith in himself as an instrument of the Lord. He awaited only the coming of a sea breeze, which would allow him to sail into the harbor and carry the smoke from his guns toward shore, blinding his adversaries, after whose ruin he would warp back out to sea. On 30 April his patience was rewarded.

Upon the unanimous recommendation of his commanders, Blake divided his fleet into two squadrons. The first, twelve frigates led by Richard Stayner, maneuvered between the two groups of enemy ships, concentrating on the shore batteries and forts. After about an hour, Stayner's ships anchored some three cables' length—approximately six hundred yards—from the shore, within pistol range of the enemy ships yet far enough to be able to swing around safely after the fight. In this position, they were effectively masked from the fire of the fortifications, whose "overs" threatened the galleons and whose "unders" imperiled the smaller vessels. Here they brought their superior and disciplined gunnery into deadly effect on the smaller vessels. Within three hours after the English had entered the harbor, all of the smaller Spanish vessels either had struck their colors or were in flames.

The other English squadron, another twelve frigates under Blake, divided its broadsides between the galleons and the principal fort. By early afternoon, the shore batteries had all but been silenced and the galleons were afire, the two Spanish flagships blowing up in rapid succession. Around 4:00 P.M., Blake's fleet began the difficult maneuver of warping out of the harbor. The operation was complicated by the efforts made by several captains to tow out prizes. Blake was forced to send his reluctant subordinates three successive orders to burn the Spanish ships instead, seeing that the attempt to take prizes would jeopardize the fleet's withdrawal.

While their inability to take the Spanish treasure must have been a great disappointment, the action was an overwhelming success for Blake and the English fleet. Every Spanish ship was destroyed, whereas the English did not lose a single vessel, although several sustained extensive damage. From the English accounts, 60 men were killed or died of their wounds, and 120 were wounded.[53]

News quickly spread of the victory. The Parliament promptly appointed 16 June as a day of Thanksgiving and voted Blake a jewel valued at £500. A week later, Cromwell wrote to Blake saying that England could not "but take notice also how eminently it hath pleased God to make use of you in this service, assisting you with wisdom in the conduct and courage in the execution. . . ."[54] Even exiled royalists were very impressed by this English victory. Clarendon wrote that the entire

> action was so miraculous that all men who knew the place concluded that no sober men, with what courage soever endued, would have done; whilst the spaniards comforted themselves with the belief that they were devils, and not men, which had destroyed them in such a manner.[55]

Upon returning to the Spanish coast, Blake received instructions from Cromwell to send part of his fleet home and distribute the remainder to maintain the blockade of Cadiz and protect English commerce off the entrance to the Straits. From the pessimistic references to his health in letters written shortly before the attack on Tenerife, Blake must have sensed that he was close to death. Now that he had achieved an overwhelming victory, he decided that the time had come to return to England. His hope was that he would survive long enough to die on shore. After selecting the ships and officers to remain on station, Blake departed in the *George* for

England on 17 July. Four weeks later he died within sight of land on Plymouth Sound.[56]

NOTES

1. Robert Blake, *The Letters of Robert Blake,* ed. J. R. Powell (London: Navy Records Society, vol. 76, 1937), pp. 462–63 (hereafter, *Letters*).

2. Michael Baumber, *General-at-Sea: Robert Blake and the Seventeenth-Century Revolution in Naval Warfare* (London: John Murray, 1989), p. 237; J. R. Powell, *Robert Blake: General-at-Sea* (London: Collins, 1972), pp. 308–9; *Letters,* p. 335; *Calendar of State Papers, Venetian,* 1657–59 (hereafter, *Cal.S.P.Ven.*), pp. 102, 105, 110–11; John Clarke, *The Clarke Papers,* ed. C. H. Firth, 4 vols. (London: Camden Society, 1891–1901), III: 115; Edmund Ludlow, *Memoirs of Edmund Ludlow,* ed. C. H. Firth, 2 vols. (Oxford: Clarendon Press, 1894), II: 37; Bulstrode Whitelocke, *Memorials of the English Affairs,* 4 vols. (Oxford: Oxford University Press, 1853), IV: 311. Baumber is justified in wondering how Blake, a confirmed republican and puritan, would have reacted to being buried amidst pomp, circumstance, and monarchs (Baumber, op. cit., p. 237).

3. *Cal.S.P.Ven.,* 1657–59, pp. 101–2.

4. David Hannay, *Admiral Blake* (London: Longmans, Green, 1886), p. 183.

5. Ibid., p. 190.

6. Tradition has it that Blake was born on 17 August 1599. What is certain is that his baptism was recorded on 27 September in Bridgwater's St. Mary's Church. Humphrey Blake married the widow Sarah (Williams) Smither. Besides the future admiral, they had fourteen children, of whom twelve were sons. Roger Beadon, *Robert Blake: Sometime Commanding all the Fleets and Naval Forces of England* (London: Edward Arnold, 1935), pp. 14–16; William Hepworth Dixon, *Robert Blake: Admiral and General at Sea* (London: Bickers & Son, 1889), p. 5; Baumber, op. cit., pp. 3–14.

7. Hannay, op. cit., pp. 5–6; Edward Hyde, Earl of Clarendon, *The History of the Rebellion and Civil Wars in England,* ed. W. D. Macray, 6 vols. (Oxford: Clarendon Press, 1888; reprint, 1958), VI: 37; C. D. Curtis, *Blake: General-at-Sea* (Taunton: Barnicott and Pearce, The Wessex Press, 1934), pp. 5–9.

8. Ibid., pp. 5–6; Beadon, op. cit., pp. 16–20; Baumber, op. cit., pp. 4–7.

9. Ibid.; Hannay, op. cit., p. 184.

10. Powell, op. cit., pp. 15–20; Baumber, op. cit., p. 6; Sir Charles H. Firth, "Sailors of the Civil War, the Commonwealth and the Protectorate," *The Mariner's Mirror,* XII (July 1926), p. 245; Beadon, op. cit., pp. 19–23; Clarendon, op. cit., VI: 37; Hannay, op. cit., p. 6.

11. Powell, op. cit., p. 17.

12. Beadon, op. cit., pp. 18, 25; Hannay, op. cit., p. 7; Baumber, op. cit., pp. 18–23.

13. J. K. Laughton, "Blake," *Dictionary of National Biography* (hereafter, *DNB*).

14. Hannay, op. cit., pp. 10–12; Curtis, op. cit., pp. 17–21; Dixon, op. cit., p. 37; Powell, op. cit., p. 21.

15. Curtis, op. cit., pp. 22–57; Hannay, op. cit., pp. 15–34; Baumber, op. cit., pp. 26–64; Powell, op. cit., pp. 21–30, 32–64; Beadon, op. cit., pp. 27–58; Dixon, op. cit., pp. 44–87; Laughton, "Blake," *DNB.*

16. Powell, op. cit., pp. 47–64; Hannay, op. cit., p. 34.

17. Dixon, op. cit., pp. 87–89.

18. *Journal of the House of Commons* (hereafter, *C.J.*), VI: 136, 138, 149, 150, 340, 342, 537–38, 543; *Acts and Ordinances of the Interregnum,* eds. C. H. Firth and R. S. Rait, 3 vols. (London: 1911) (hereafter, *Acts and Ordinances*), II: 13–14, 17; *Calendar of State Papers, Domestic,* 1649–50 (hereafter, *Cal.S.P.Dom.*), pp. 20, 23.

19. *Letters,* pp. 8–9; Baumber, op. cit., pp. 67–73; Dixon, op. cit., p. 101.

20. *Cal.S.P.Dom.,* 1649–50, pp. 326, 328; *C.J.,* VI: 301; *Royal Commission on Historical Manuscripts, Reports,* Leyborne-Popham, pp. 34–35, 38; Baumber, op. cit., pp. 77–78.

21. Powell, op. cit., p. 89; John Thurloe, *A Collection of State Papers of John Thurloe,* ed. T. Birch, 7 vols. (London: F. Gyles, 1742), I: 134–36, 137; *Letters,* pp. 10–11.

22. Laughton, "Blake," *DNB; Letters,* pp. 11–19; Baumber, op. cit., pp. 81–93; Hannay, op. cit., pp. 55–61; R. C. Anderson, "The Royalists at Sea in 1650," *The Mariner's Mirror,* XVII (Apr. 1931), pp. 135–68.

23. Powell, op. cit., pp. 108–20, 121–33; J. R. Powell, "Blake's Reduction of Jersey in 1651," *The Mariner's Mirror,* XVIII (Jan. 1932), pp. 64–80; *Letters,* p. 96.

24. W. N. Hammond, "The Administration of the English Navy, 1649–1660" (Ph.D. diss., University of British Columbia, 1974), p. 50; W. B. Cogar, "The Politics of Naval Administration, 1649–1660" (D.Phil. thesis, Oxford University, 1983), pp. 58, 62, 115, 162, 173, 196; *C.J.,* VII: 97; London, Public Record Office, State Papers, Domestic (hereafter, S.P.), 25/66/412, 413.

25. *Letters and Papers Relating to the First Dutch War, 1652–1654,* eds. S. R. Gardiner and C. T. Atkinson, 6 vols. plus corrigenda (London: Navy Records Society, 1899–1931) (hereafter, *Letters and Papers*), I: 110.

26. Hannay, op. cit., p. 77; Charles Wilson, *Profit and Power: A Study of England and the Dutch Wars* (London: Longmans, Green, 1957), p. 40; *Letters and Papers,* I: 48–53.

27. Ibid., I: 53–58; Cogar, op. cit., pp. 100–108; Baumber, op. cit., pp. 109–20.

28. *Letters and Papers,* I: 170–298; Hannay, op. cit., pp. 80–81; Oxford, Bodleian Library (hereafter, Bodl. Lib.), Tanner MSS. 53, f.35; Powell, op. cit., pp. 139–50.

29. This situation would become a very important cause for Blake's defeat a year later at Dungeness. Hannay, op. cit., p. 84.

30. Ibid., pp. 85–88; *Letters,* pp. 164–71.

31. Bodl. Lib., Tanner MSS. 53, f.128; Powell, op. cit., pp. 169–80; Beadon, op. cit., pp. 152–61; Baumber, op. cit., pp. 151–63; *Letters and Papers,* II: 217–388.

32. Powell, op. cit., pp. 181–90; *Letters,* pp. 182–86; *Letters and Papers,* III; 1–129; Laughton, "Blake," *DNB.*

33. *Cal.S.P.Dom.,* 1651–52, pp. 89, 150, 506, 509; *C.J.,* VII: 222, 256; S.P., 25/68/27, 30, 37.

34. *Letters and Papers,* III: 96–452, IV: 1–64; *Letters,* pp. 185, 188; Granville Penn, *Memorials of the Professional Life and Times of Sir William Penn,* 2 vols. (London: 1833), I: 458.

35. Powell, op. cit., pp. 207–23; *Letters and Papers,* IV: 65–197; Bodl. Lib., Tanner MSS. 53, ff.210, 215; S.P., 18/34/29, 36, 46; Bodl. Lib., Rawlinson MSS. A.227, f.48.

36. *Declaration of the Generals at Sea,* 22 Apr. 1653; *Perfect Diurnal,* 25 Apr.–2 May 1653, pp. 2669–70; Bodl. Lib., Clarendon MSS. 45, ff.335, 336; S. R. Gardiner, *History of the Commonwealth and Protectorate, 1649–1660,* 2 vols. (London: Longmans, Green, 1897), II: 270–71, III: 33; Clarendon, op. cit., V: 288; Powell, op. cit., p. 231; Beadon, op. cit., p. 191.

37. *Letters and Papers,* IV: 199–396; V: 1–146.

38. Ibid., pp. 147–429.

39. Helmut Pemsel, *A History of War at Sea* (Annapolis: Naval Institute Press, 1977), p. 48.

40. Clarke, op. cit., III: 203–8; British Library, Stowe MSS. 185, ff.83–84; *DNB,* "William Penn"; Powell, op. cit., pp. 252–53.

41. *Letters,* pp. 266–88; Powell, op. cit., pp. 252–58; Sir Julian S. Corbett, *England in the Mediterranean: A Study of the Rise and Influence of British Power Within the Straits, 1603–1713,* 2 vols. (2nd ed., London: Longmans, Green, 1917), I: 271–93; John Weale, "The Journal of John Weale, 1654–1656," ed. J. R. Powell, *The Naval Miscellany,* vol. IV (London: Navy Records Society, vol. 92, 1952), pp. 88–100.

42. *Letters,* pp. 272–75; Bodl. Lib., Rawlinson MSS. 24, ff.235, 503; Baumber, op. cit., pp. 195–210; Powell, op. cit., pp. 259–64; Corbett, op. cit., I; 294–311; Beadon, op. cit., pp. 223–26; Weale, loc. cit., pp. 100–113.

43. *Letters,* pp. 275–79; Powell, op. cit., pp. 269–72; Weale, loc. cit., pp. 113–26; Corbett, op. cit., I: 314–17.

44. Ludlow, op. cit., II: 37; *C.J.,* VII: 361–62; Bodl. Lib., Clarendon MSS. 46, f.327.

45. S.P., 25/76/344, 449; British Library, Additional MSS. 9305, f.220; F. R. Harris, *Edward Montagu, K.G., First Earl of Sandwich,* 2 vols. (London: John Murray, 1912) I: 1–87.

46. Clarendon, op. cit., VI: 17, 187; Harris, op. cit., I: 90n; *Letters,* p. 322; Cogar, op. cit., pp. 196–99; Powell, op. cit., pp. 273–78; Weale, loc. cit., pp. 126–31.

47. *Letters,* pp. 324–26; Thurloe, op. cit., V: 399–400, 432; Hannay, op. cit., pp. 141–43; Weale, loc. cit., pp. 131–37.

48. Powell, op. cit., pp. 278–90; *Letters,* pp. 373–74; Hannay, op. cit., pp. 159–64; Cogar, op. cit., pp. 208–10.

49. *Letters,* pp. 329–30.

50. Ibid., pp. 330–31, 423–26, 440, 453–54; Weale, loc. cit., p. 144.

51. *Letters,* pp. 381–82; Hannay, op. cit., p. 175; Sir Richard Stayner, "Narrative of the Battle of Santa Cruz," ed. C. H. Firth, *The Naval Miscellany,* vol. II (London: Navy Records Society, vol. 40, 1910), pp. 127–35.

52. "A Short Narrative of Engagement Before Santa Cruz," in *Letters,* pp. 458–60; Weale, loc. cit., pp. 144–46; *Letters,* pp. 453–54, 383–85.

53. Stayner, loc. cit., pp. 131–36; *Letters,* pp. 385–92; Baumber, op. cit., pp. 225–35; Powell, op. cit., pp. 293–311; Curtis, op. cit., pp. 148–60; Weale, loc. cit., pp. 146–47.

54. Thurloe, op. cit., VI: 342.

55. Clarendon, op. cit., VI: 36.

56. *Letters,* pp. 381, 383–84, 462–63. Although buried with honors in Westminster Abbey, Blake's body was exhumed after the Restoration along with other Interregnum notables and thrown ignominiously into a common grave on the north side of the Abbey. Ibid., p. 335.

NOTE ON SOURCES

There is an abundance of primary source material on Robert Blake. This includes many letters written by him as well as documents on events connected with him or facets of his life. Most of these sources are located in the major collections on mid-seventeenth-century English history. Among them are the Domestic Series of the State Papers and the Admiralty Records, both for the Interregnum period, located in London's Public Record Office. Furthermore, many letters are included in the Additional Manuscript collection in the British Library, London, and in the Tanner and Rawlinson Manuscript collections in Oxford University's Bodleian Library.

A considerable number of these records have been published. *The Letters of Robert Blake, Together with Supplementary Documents,* edited by J. R. Powell (London: Navy Records Society, vol. 76, 1937), contains over three hundred entries by, on, or associated with Blake. *Letters and Papers Relating to the First Dutch War, 1652–1654,* edited by S. R. Gardiner and C. T. Atkinson (London: Navy Records Society, 6 vols. plus corrigenda, 1899–1931), is extremely important for Blake's activities during that conflict. The *State Papers of John Thurloe,* edited by T. Birch, 7 vols. (London: 1742), is no less important for Blake's activities between the Dutch War and his death. In addition, G. E. Manwaring edited "Two Letters from Blake and Montagu, 1656–1657," in *The Naval Miscellany,* vol. III (London: Navy Records Society, vol. 63, 1927), pp. 333–38. For this same period of Blake's career, John Weale's "The Journal of John Weale, 1654–1656," edited by J. R. Powell, *The Naval Miscellany,* vol. IV (London: Navy Records Society, vol. 92, 1952), pp. 85–162, is very helpful.

On the battle for Santa Cruz, see Sir Richard Stayner, "A Narrative of the Battle of Santa Cruz," edited by C. H. Firth, in *The Naval Miscellany,* vol. II (London: Navy Records Society, vol. 40, 1910), pp. 127–36. Firth also wrote "Blake and the Battle of Santa Cruz," in *English Historical Review,* vol. 20, 1905. Much work needs to be done on this battle, especially with regard to Spanish primary sources.

Although numerous letters by Blake exist and are easily accessible, Blake continues to frustrate the scholar who seeks to discover the person behind the commander. In all his letters, Blake chose to relate facts rather than to express opinions about political events, personalities, or religion. While this in itself says much about him, for biographers the attraction of a considerable amount of letters is dashed by the lack of "personality" in them. Perhaps for this reason, no biography of Blake has yet been entirely satisfactory, although the most recent effort comes closest by far. The first biography, if that is not too flattering a term, of the admiral appeared in 1704 in a collection entitled *Lives English and Foreign,* whose unnamed author claimed to have known some members of Blake's family. In 1740, *A History and Life of Robert Blake, Esquire, General and Admiral of the Fleets and Naval Forces of England* was written by John Oldmixon. However, the noted naval historian J. K. Laughton, in his sketch of Blake in the *Dictionary of National Biography,* rightfully styled Oldmixon's work "an impudent and mendacious chap-book."

William Hepworth Dixon's *Robert Blake, Admiral and General at Sea* (London: Chapman and Hall, 1852) falls far short. Again to quote Laughton, Dixon's "account of Blake's public life is grossly inaccurate, and much of it is entirely false; he betrays throughout the most astonishing ignorance of naval matters, and a very curious incapability of appreciating or interpreting historical evidence." Blake became the subject of a reputable historian for the first time when David Hannay wrote *Admiral Blake* (London: Longmans, Green, 1886) as part of the *English Worthies* series edited by Andrew Lang. This short and very well-written biography catches the essence and spirit of Blake better than any other biography to date, and while more recent studies have used more primary material, Hannay's fine work is not seriously undermined and remains essential.

Two biographies on Blake appeared in the years before World War II. Roger Beadon's *Robert Blake: Sometime Commanding all the Fleets and Naval Forces of England* (London: Edward Arnold, 1935) is rather long-winded yet includes much of the very fine research undertaken by naval historians during the late nineteenth and early twentieth centuries. It thus fills in many of the gaps in Blake's life and activities found in earlier biographies. The same holds true for C. D. Curtis, *Robert Blake, General-at-Sea* (Taunton: Barnicott and Pearce, The Wessex Press, 1934). The latter also includes several valuable appendixes about Blake or on closely related topics.

Until very recently, the only other biography of Blake was J. R. Powell's *Robert Blake: General-at-Sea* (London: Collins, 1972). As editor of the Blake Papers and other mid-seventeenth-century naval documents, Powell drew material from a wide variety of valuable sources, but his biography lacks sufficient analysis and is simply too much a narrative. Michael Baumber's *General-at-Sea: Robert Blake and the Seventeenth-Century Revolution in Naval Warfare* (London: John Murray, 1989) is the best full-length biography of this elusive naval commander as well as a solid study of seventeenth-century naval warfare. Like its predecessors, however, it rests largely on English materials. To really round out an understanding of Robert Blake and his place in history, an examination of non-English sources, particularly Dutch, Spanish, and French, would be most helpful.

4

Michiel Adriaenszoon de Ruyter

Ornament of His Age

(1607–1676)

A. van der Moer

MICHIEL ADRIAENSZOON WAS BORN OF HUMBLE PARENTS IN Flushing, Zealand, on 24 March 1607. His father, a beer carrier, had once been a seafaring man. The fourth of eleven children, Michiel was high-spirited, enterprising, and ambitious. In later years, he said that in his youth he "was good for nothing but the sea."[1] He answered its call early, joining his first ship as a boatswain's boy at the age of eleven in 1618. In this modest manner began a career in which, to quote the magnificent biography of de Ruyter by the Reverend Gerard Brandt, published barely a decade after its subject's death, the boatswain's boy was destined to "climb along the steps of all ship's duties and every danger of the sea and from enemies to the highest naval functions."[2]

The future admiral spent most of the next thirty-two years in the merchant marine. In 1622, he volunteered as a gunner in the army, but after a few months he returned to sea. By application, good conduct, and courage, he rose to gunner, boatswain's mate, first mate, *schipper* (skipper) of a merchant vessel, and eventually, captain of his own ship. His nautical experiences also included service in whalers (1633–35), and, briefly, as captain of a privateer (1637). He used the name "Ruyter" for the first time in 1633, later adding the "de." This was a sobriquet taken from his maternal grandfather, who had served as a *ruiter* (cavalryman) in the army.

During this period sailing often meant fighting, and *schipper* de Ruyter saw his share of action. As a young sailor, he was wounded in the head and made prisoner by Spanish privateers in the Bay of Biscay. After being taken ashore, he escaped in company with two other sailors and made his way home overland, tramping and begging through France. Later, as a ship's captain, he proved himself to be a bold but at the same time a prudent commander. Summing up this phase of de Ruyter's career, Brandt wrote, "His cautiousness, gallantry, and good fortune or, to speak more Christian-like, divine assistance, always seemed to conspire in order to give him good results and to save him from the greatest dangers."[3]

In December 1640, after an occupation of sixty years, Portugal rebelled against the rule of the Netherlands' archenemy, Spain. The States-General decided to send twenty ships to support the insurgents; *schipper* de Ruyter's *De Haze* (The Hare) was chartered by the Zealand Admiralty to take part in this expedition. De Ruyter himself was chosen to act as rear admiral of the little fleet, an appointment that testifies to the excellent reputation he had acquired. The expedition accomplished little. An attempt to intercept a Plate fleet led to an inconclusive action off Cape St. Vincent with a superior Spanish force, not long after which colonial frictions caused the Netherlands to withdraw its support of Portugal. De Ruyter felt no regrets. Although he had conducted himself very well, he was not at all impressed with the general performance of the fleet, and upon its return home in 1642 he happily resumed his merchant career.

De Ruyter was not only a good seaman; he was also a good manager. By 1652, he had amassed a modest fortune. In January of that year he married his third wife (having been twice a widower) and decided that the time had come for him to retire from the sea. Fate willed otherwise.

A year earlier, Anglo-Dutch commercial rivalry had led the English Parliament to pass the First Navigation Act, discriminating against the Dutch carrying trade. War broke out in the summer of 1652. The Dutch republic realized full well that its future was at stake. Accordingly, it began to build up the navy and to recruit capable mariners. Men with de Ruyter's wealth of experience were needed on the quarterdeck and the States of Zealand took the initiative of asking him to join the fleet.

At first, the *schipper* flatly refused; he had plans of his own. But the authorities kept urging him to reconsider, appealing to his patriotism in flattering terms. De Ruyter was not susceptible to flattery, but the appeal to his patriotism moved him. Sailing as a captain in the navy for the first time in 1641, he had written, "I shall act sincerely as an honest captain, in the hope that God will bless the work we are sent out to do in honor of our dear Fatherland."[4] His devotion to his "dear Fatherland" remained unchanged, and although he knew that, due largely to Maarten Harpertszoon Tromp, the navy had improved since he had served in it, he saw "trouble ahead, external and internal."[5] External, because the ships of the English fleet were larger, more numerous, and stronger than those of the Dutch, and the English sailors were better trained and more skilled in battle. Internal, because of the discord that plagued the country, brought about mainly by the differences between the patrician *Regenten* (Regents) headed by the brothers Johan and Cornelis de Witt and the common people, who favored the rule of the House of Orange. The last Stadtholder, William II, had died at an early age in 1650, leaving a posthumous son, Prince William III. The Regents who then assumed power saw to it that no new Stadtholder was appointed and rejected the Orangists' proposal to name the young prince captain general and admiral general, with an able member of the Orange family to act on his behalf until he attained his majority. This dissention also delayed the outfitting of the navy, which was predominantly Orangist in sentiment.

Finally, de Ruyter was persuaded to engage himself for the duration of a single cruise, albeit, as he wrote, "with much reluctance and worry."[6] So on 29 July 1652, the States appointed "our dear loyal Captain Michiel de

2. The Action off Plymouth, 26 August 1652. The first action in which de Ruyter held command was fought when an English squadron under Sir John Ayscue attempted to intercept a westbound merchant convoy that he was escorting through the English Channel. This contemporary Dutch print shows de Ruyter's force engaging the English, while the convoy (upper right) goes safely on its way. (The Beverly R. Robinson Collection, U.S. Naval Academy Museum.)

Ruyter, because of his good qualities and his proven loyalty, bravery and experience in naval warfare" vice commodore. This was not a fixed rank and only implied that he was to be the main assistant to Vice Admiral Witte de With in his squadron of the fleet commanded by Maarten Tromp.

For de Ruyter, the ensuing campaign was the commencement of a succession that would extend over more than two tumultuous decades. In Brandt's words:

> His unblemished valor, which he demonstrated in the face of critical dangers and most difficult embarassments, and his shrewd caution (those two greatest warlike virtues) would become apparent to friends and enemies in seven wars, more than forty engagements and fifteen great sea battles, seven of them under his own command.[7]

The first of the battles occurred off Plymouth on 26 August 1652, when de Ruyter repulsed an English attempt to intercept a westbound convoy under his escort. In 1653 he commanded the rear of the Dutch fleet in all three of the year's major actions—the Three Days Battle (28 February to 2 March); Gabbard Bank (12–13 June); and Scheveningen (8–10 August), in which Tromp met his death. The Battle of Scheveningen was the last fleet engagement to occur before the war ended with the signing of the Peace of Westminster in April 1654.

De Ruyter had been commissioned vice admiral by the Amsterdam Admiralty on 11 November 1653. This time he elected to remain in the navy after the conclusion of peace and during the following decade he sailed in expeditions to the Baltic, the North Atlantic, and the Mediterranean to support Dutch interests in wars with Sweden, Portugal, and the Barbary powers. In 1660 he was granted Danish nobility in reward for his part in the allied capture of the island of Fünen from the Swedes the preceding year.

As the geographical range of de Ruyter's activities would suggest, the Dutch maritime empire had rapidly recovered from the setback of the First Anglo-Dutch War. Amsterdam remained the financial capital of Europe and ships flying the tricolor of the United Provinces still dominated the world's carrying trade. This situation did not, of course, escape the attention of England. The Commonwealth had been replaced by the restoration of the Stuart monarchy in 1660, but Charles II showed himself as eager as Cromwell had been to overthrow Dutch commercial supremacy. In 1663 and 1664 expeditions were dispatched, without benefit of a declaration of war, to attack Dutch colonial possessions. Hostilities soon spread to European waters and in January 1665 the Netherlands declared war on England.

The first major engagement of the Second Anglo-Dutch War, the Battle of Lowestoft, took place on 13 June, when the Dutch commander in chief, van Wassenaar van Obdam, attacked a slightly superior English fleet under the Duke of York. The outcome was disastrous. After an action lasting almost twelve hours, the Dutch were put to flight, losing seventeen ships and upward of four thousand men against the English loss of a single vessel and eight hundred men. The dead included the commander in chief, killed with almost everyone else aboard when his flagship's magazine exploded, and the second in command, Lieutenant Admiral Egbert Meussen Cortenaer. The news of this defeat, by far the worst the Dutch navy had ever suffered, spread a pall of gloom throughout the Netherlands.

De Ruyter was absent on a long cruise to the Mediterranean, west Africa, and the Americas at the beginning of the war. He returned home *achterom*—"the back way about," that is, north around the British Isles—shortly after the Battle of Lowestoft and anchored in the northern Dutch port of Delfzijl on 6 August. The Dutch people had been anxiously awaiting his return and a wave of hope swept over the country. Thousands came flocking to welcome him, paying him greater homage than any other admiral had ever received. His enormous popularity was probably enhanced

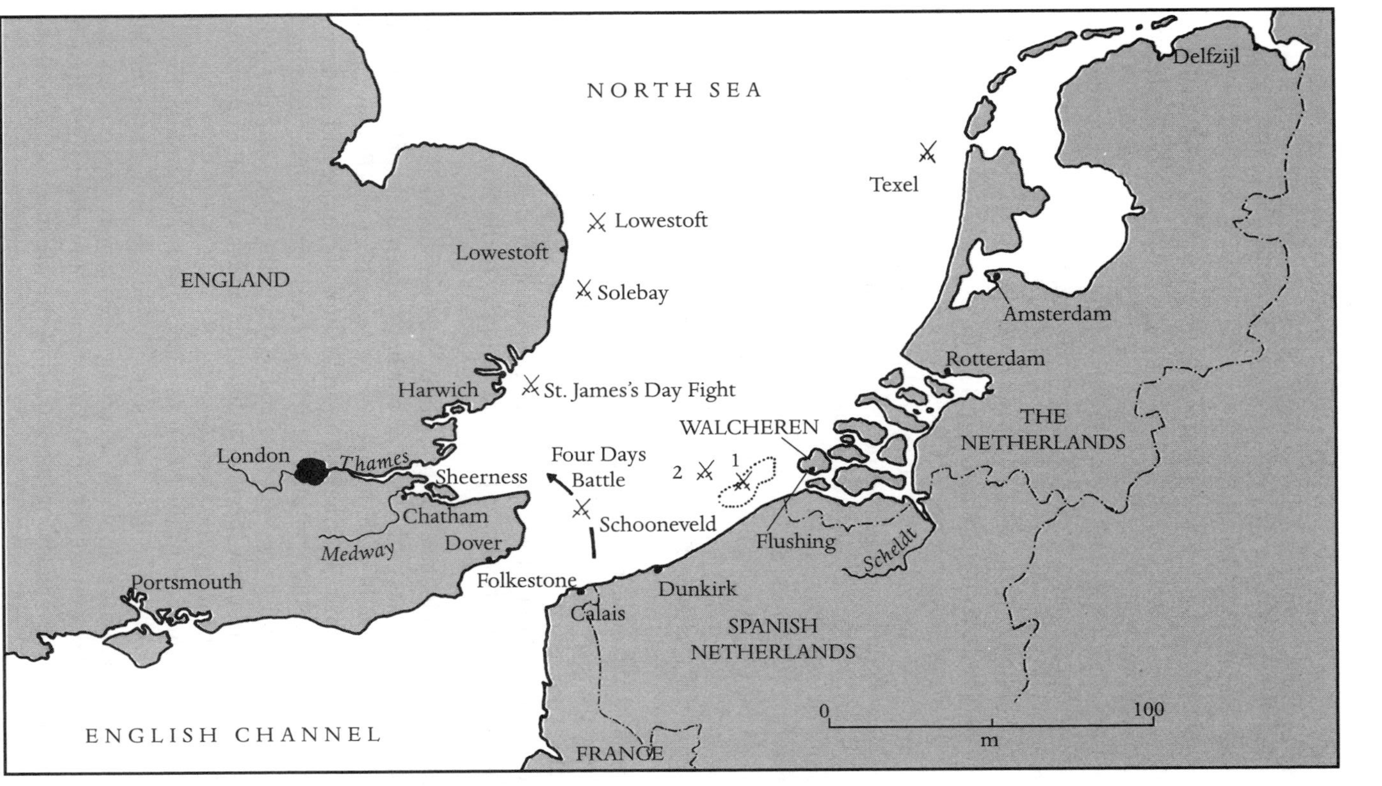

4. The Second and Third Anglo-Dutch Wars.

because there was no Stadtholder, for in the hour of danger the Dutch needed a national figure to rally around. This need could be fulfilled only by a member of the House of Orange. Johan de Witt could not serve as a substitute, but de Ruyter could.

Being considered "without controversy the most able"[8] of the country's admirals, on 11 August 1665 de Ruyter was appointed lieutenant admiral of Holland and commander in chief of the Dutch navy. The events of the ensuing years confirmed that the choice was a wise one. In what remained of the campaigning season of 1665, he escorted a big East India Company convoy home from Bergen, where it had been bottled up by the British, and then took station off the mouth of the Thames estuary to safeguard the passage of other Dutch merchantmen. The following year de Ruyter fought two of the most severe actions of the Age of Sail. In the Four Days Battle (11–14 June 1666) he defeated an English fleet commanded by George Monck (now Duke of Albemarle) and Prince Rupert, taking or destroying seventeen ships and inflicting eight thousand casualties on the enemy at a cost of six ships and two thousand men of his own. The English quickly outfitted another fleet, and Monck and Rupert met de Ruyter again at the St. James's Day Fight on 4–5 August. Both forces numbered approximately ninety men-of-war and twenty fireships. Due mainly to the misconduct of the commander of the Dutch rear, Maarten Tromp's son Cornelis, who left formation to fight a little battle of his own, de Ruyter was defeated. The masterful manner in which he extricated his force limited his losses to only two ships. On 8 August, however, a daring English raid burned 150 Dutch merchantmen at anchor in the Texel. De Ruyter returned to sea before the end of the month with the hope of achieving a success to offset these reverses, but a combination of circumstances prevented another battle from being fought before winter came.

In the meanwhile, peace negotiations had been opened at Breda in the Netherlands. The costs of the war had pinched the resources of both governments, especially the English. In an effort to economize and despite the protests of Monck, Charles II ordered England's ships of the line laid up, leaving squadrons of frigates to continue attacking Dutch trade. Upon learning of this development Johan de Witt resolved to strengthen the Dutch negotiating position by striking a spectacular blow: an attack on the English main fleet base at Chatham, on the Medway.

De Ruyter sailed from the Texel to carry out this bold project with a fleet of twenty-four of the line, twenty smaller vessels, and fifteen fireships early in June 1667. Cornelis de Witt accompanied him as a special representative of the States-General. Their audacity was amply rewarded. Capturing the fort at Sheerness guarding the mouth of the Medway on 20 June, the

Dutch pushed resolutely upstream, breaking through the defended river obstructions at Upnor, to burn eight English warships and, perhaps most gratifying of all, to capture the *Royal Charles,* the English fleet flagship. When they dropped downstream on 23 June, they had, in the words of a modern English historian, delivered "one of the most brilliant strokes with the most immediate and obvious effects in the history of naval warfare."[9] In London there was panic and fear of invasion; and throughout England, an outcry for peace.

During the following weeks, Dutch forces maintained a menacing presence off the Thames estuary. After an unsuccessful attack on Fort Landguard, near Harwich, on 10–13 July, de Ruyter divided his fleet in two. One part, under Lieutenant Admiral Aert van Nes, was detailed to blockade the Thames while de Ruyter took the other into the English Channel, exciting great anxiety among the coastal population. It was during this period that diarist Samuel Pepys heard a member of the Admiralty exclaim, "By God, I think the devil shits Dutchmen!"[10]

De Ruyter remained in the Channel until the end of August, when he received news of the ratification of the Treaty of Breda. The impact and aftermath of the Medway expedition ensured that the terms of peace would favor the Netherlands. The provisions of the English Navigation Acts affecting Dutch trade were relaxed and each side was allowed to keep the colonies that it had taken from the other in the course of the struggle. Their conquests on the west coast of Africa and in the East Indies made the Dutch the net gainers in this exchange, although their losses included the North American settlement of New Amsterdam, which the English renamed New York.

De Ruyter's life has inspired many authors. He is one of the few prominent figures of the Dutch Golden Age about whom we possess some information from his youth and years in obscurity. Brandt, although primarily interested in the admiral, occasionally mentions particulars that give us an insight into the man and a glimpse of the husband and father. Hence our picture of de Ruyter is clearer than those of most other men of his era. That picture has never changed. In our time it has become customary to tarnish the memory of great historical figures by showing that, notwithstanding their merits, they were only human. As far as is known, no one has ever tried to tarnish de Ruyter's reputation. No one would succeed if he did. The greatest seaman ever to sail under the Dutch flag was not just an outstanding admiral, but an excellent human being. Any attempt to diminish his reputation would founder on the facts. Upon becoming acquainted with the life of Michiel Adriaenszoon de Ruyter, one has to pass through a period of mild disbelief. The picture that emerges is almost too perfect. Yet the facts are incontestable, and they fill the student with veneration, not only for the admiral, "the Right Hand of the States-General," but for the man in whom the Dutch people, regarding him as one of their greatest sons, recognized all the virtues they used to admire.

In the stained-glass window that since 1966, the tricentennial of the Four Days Battle, has adorned the Great Church in Flushing, where de Ruyter was baptized, one finds the motto *Soli Deo Gloria*—The Glory Belongs to God Alone. Nothing could better characterize him. His entire life was a testimonial to his deep and sincere piety. To quote Brandt, "Amongst all things miraculous and praiseworthy in this life the most wonderful . . . is that he, esteemed so highly by others, thought so little of himself: considering that he did not deserve any honor for the victories gained under his flag, but attributing all his works and successes to God."[11] This was actually the case. After his great victory at the Battle of the Texel in 1673, de Ruyter's words were: "What shall I say? Mouths and tongues fail us to announce and proclaim God's goodness to us. The blessing is great. We must only hope to be so fortunate as to be able to show the right amount of thankfulness."[12] Today one is inclined to suspect that such sayings are merely conventional and do not express true conviction. But throughout his life de Ruyter never said or wrote anything that he did not believe. The quotation is entirely characteristic. Like many others by which it could be supplemented, it sprang from the depths of his pious heart and evidenced a faith with which few were blessed, even in that more reverent age.

It was not only in piety and patriotism that de Ruyter excelled. Contemporary sources also attest to his bravery, humility, honesty, simplicity, selflessness, and superb leadership. We cannot avoid the conclusion that these noble qualities of character contributed to the great part he played in the Dutch Golden Age. Yet a noble man does not necessarily make a good admiral; nor is nobility of character a prerequisite to be one. So we must look for other reasons to explain the greatness of Admiral de Ruyter.

There is, of course, his broad experience. Having begun his career before the mast and made many voyages as a member of ships' companies, he was familiar with all aspects of a sailor's life. Later, as a *schipper* and businessman, he often had to use his innate tact in dealing with authorities abroad. In this manner he developed diplomatic skills that stood him in good stead when, as an admiral, he was sent on delicate, more or less diplomatic missions. During his years in the merchant marine and as a privateer, he had seen considerable combat, from the hand-to-hand fighting of boarding actions to the battle of ship against ship. When he went to sea as a boy, there was no real difference between merchant and naval vessels and the way they were handled. In his lifetime, however, distinctively naval tactics came into being, especially in the Dutch navy under the innovative leadership of Admirals Piet Heyn and Maarten Tromp. Among the new tactical procedures introduced were the line ahead, the battle on parallel or opposing courses, breaking the enemy line, and convoy formations. De Ruyter thus began his career as a flag officer in a period of transition, during which old tactics were used beside the new and the orderly battle often ended in an old-fashioned melee.

As a commander de Ruyter was, in accordance with his character, cautious and prudent. Strategically, he always did his utmost to keep the fleet concentrated and in good order. He was willing to run great risks, but never rashly to hazard the survival of the fleet, upon which he realized that the very existence of the republic depended. In reaching decisions, he took account of the strategic situation as well as the tactical circumstances. A master in distinguishing between matters of major and minor importance, he never lost sight of the ultimate aim and always put the most important things first. He appreciated the value of timely intelligence, continuously sending out scouts to gather as much information as possible and adapting his plans to changing conditions. The study of de Ruyter's operations also makes clear that he paid much attention to mobility, logistics, surprise, morale, and discipline. In this list the reader may recognize the principles of warfare, which the admiral applied without theorizing about them.

In matters of strategy Dutch naval commanders were bound by the instructions of the States-General or its delegates, who sometimes joined the fleet. De Ruyter often sailed with such delegates in company. Naturally, he influenced the shaping of naval strategy, but he always bowed to his "masters." As commander in chief in March 1666, he wrote a letter to Johan de Witt in which, with characteristic modesty, he asked the regent to give him guidance from time to time, because, having just been appointed to this high position, he judged himself "in such great matters still very ignorant."[13] When de Witt sent him a plan for a naval campaign against the English, however, he commented soberly: "Not bad, provided it could be put into practice in the way one can put it in writing, but so many accidents may intervene, that it is impossible to put them all on paper."[14]

During the great naval wars, when operations took place near the Dutch coast the States-General usually furnished strict guidance. On expeditions to distant waters, the admiral would not be in touch with the government for months on end, so he had to decide for himself. Yet he was not entirely on his own, for tradition and often instructions dictated that all important matters were to be discussed in a council of war consisting of the flag officers and captains. From his earliest years in command, it was de Ruyter's custom to consult his subordinates frequently and to inform them continually about the situation and his intentions. This practice undoubtedly contributed to the lack of written evidence about his deliberations. Almost everything was dealt with verbally. During some expeditions the *pitsjaersein*—talk signal, from the Malay word *bitjara:* talk about—was hoisted almost daily. In this way de Ruyter succeeded in introducing unity of doctrine into the navy. From a historical standpoint, however, it is regrettable that he seldom wrote about the considerations that influenced his decisions and, if at all, very sparingly. Later in this chapter, an attempt will be made to analyze the tactical and strategic factors that caused him to act as he did during the First Battle of Schooneveld in 1673.

As a tactician, de Ruyter was unsurpassed. We are able to deduce this not only from his successes, but also from the testimony of his contemporaries. In his operations he skillfully took every possible advantage to be gained from wind and weather, sun and moon, tides, shallows, and banks. His prudent reconnaissances, unexpected attacks, the strict maintenance of formation upon which he insisted, the employment of fireships, the use of signals, and frequent fleet maneuvers were a tactical school for everyone who sailed under his command. How much importance de Ruyter attached to maintaining an orderly formation is apparent from a circular letter dated 10 August 1671, which he wrote during a peacetime training period:

> We daily observe with great regret the disorder, which some flag officers and captains cause in the fleet, by not following the orders to sail and anchor in good order at all times and such manner as if we were continuously in contact with or near the enemy. Considering that this is highly detrimental to the country and against the intentions of Their High Mightinesses the Gentlemen of the States-General we, attending to this matter ex-officio, hereby again most seriously order and command all officers and captains of the fleet to follow all given orders for sailing and anchoring strictly and punctually.[15]

De Ruyter was also an inspiring leader. While we do not know whether it proceeded from a conscious aspiration, throughout his life he set a shining example. The men who served under him felt not simply admiration but, above all, trust and confidence in their commander. His mere presence gave hope and courage to the Dutch, alarm and fright to their adversaries. Very significantly, he was the only admiral after Maarten Tromp whom Dutch seamen honored by the sobriquet *Bestevaer*—literally "grandfather" or "dear father," but in this context "the best man to sail with."

In everything he undertook, de Ruyter had only one interest at heart: that of his country. He did not allow himself to be influenced by personal considerations such as thirst for glory or applause. He never attempted to court public opinion or attract publicity. Whenever possible, he chose for harmony and concord and avoided pushing matters to extremes. The admiral preferred the whole to the parts, the future to the present, and discipline, moderation, and sound preparation to recklessness, impetuousness, and rash improvisation. He abstained from politics. A loyal member of the Reformed Church, he enjoyed the company of clergymen but objected to their intervention in worldly affairs, a point of view he shared with most of the Regents. Many others, especially the common people, felt otherwise; in his case, however, this difference did not give rise to conflicts.

Notwithstanding his modesty, de Ruyter became a person not only of national but of European importance. He was granted Danish and Spanish nobility—the latter in 1676—and only his refusal to visit the court of Charles II prevented him from being honored in the same way by the English. The king had let it be known that, next to the Prince of Orange, no one would be as welcome as the admiral. King Louis XIV invested him with the Order of St. Michael (1666). Colbert, the French minister of marine, called him *"le plus grand capitaine qui ayt jamais été en mer"*—the greatest commander who has ever been to sea.[16] Several foreign countries, receiving naval support from the States-General, specifically asked that de Ruyter be appointed to command the fleet, and many foreign officers requested permission to sail in Dutch ships in order to observe the admiral at work and to learn from his example. In 1677 an English biography of de Ruyter was published in London. Although written by a former enemy—who never even mentioned the Medway expedition!—it was full of praise: "In fine, so good a man, so devout and pious a Christian, so stout a Soldier, so wise, expert and successful a General; and so faithful, trusty and honest a Lover of his Country, that he deserves justly to be recommended to Posterity as an ornament of his age, the darling of the Seas and the delight and honour of his Country."[17]

Most of de Ruyter's career coincided with the so-called Stadtholder-less period, 1650–72, a time of internal discord when the chief executive authority in the republic was held by Johan de Witt. De Ruyter himself was not a partisan; to him, the national interest alone mattered. Although he remained a good Zealander, his province came second. Because it was only in the Province of Holland that he would be able to rise to the highest naval positions, in 1653 it had been considered necessary for him to leave the Zealand Admiralty for that of Amsterdam. At first he was unwilling, but de Witt persuaded him. Subsequently de Ruyter, a Zealander living in Amsterdam, Lieutenant Admiral of Holland and commander in chief of the Dutch navy, would fly his flag in the Rotterdam ship *De Zeven Provinciën* (The Seven Provinces). As the "Right Hand of the States," he was one of the most important pillars supporting the foreign policy of Johan de Witt and, later, Prince William III—a policy that made the Netherlands, at that time the world's foremost sea power, play an international role that was beyond the country's capabilities and therefore could not endure for very long.

De Ruyter got along very well with both the brothers de Witt, but also with the Orangist sailors. During these years the "Child of State," young Prince William III, though without public functions, gained increasing influence as the focus of Orangist loyalties. In 1672 alarm over the series of defeats sustained by Dutch land forces following the outbreak of war with France led the States to call the prince to the post of his father. His accession posed no problem for the admiral. De Ruyter wrote to the prince, assuring him that he and the navy rejoiced in the elevation of His Highness. He wished the new Stadtholder God's blessing and promised him his loyalty.[18]

Though the gray admiral and the young prince were on excellent terms, the change in government did not induce de Ruyter to disavow his friends Johan and Cornelis de Witt in their tragic downfall, as self-interest led many others to do. When Cornelis, who had accompanied him on the Medway expedition, was arrested and falsely charged with plotting against the prince, de Ruyter wrote a letter to the States-General to defend him. Afterward, a "distinguished gentleman" asked the admiral where he had left his judgment and his prudence to write such a letter. De Ruyter replied, "If it is the case, here in our country, that one may not speak the truth, things are very bad indeed, but I shall speak the truth as long as my eyes are open."[19] Sadly, his intercession was in vain; in August a furious mob broke into the jail where Johan de Witt was visiting Cornelis and beat the brothers to death.

The course of the war that brought disaster to the de Witts lay in the ambition of Louis XIV to add the Dutch republic to his realm. To support this design, in 1670 he secretly concluded a treaty with England's unscrupulous King Charles II, according to which the latter pledged, in return for an annual allowance of £200,000, to join in an assault on the republic (and to reimpose the Catholic faith on his country). Louis also made offensive alliances with the German principalities of Cologne and Münster. Thus in March 1672 the Dutch found themselves under attack by the French and Germans on land and the British at sea. Their little army was pushed steadily back. Only by the drastic expedient of opening the dikes did they succeed in halting the enemy advance.

At sea, de Ruyter awaited the opportunity to strike at the numerically superior force created by the junction of the English fleet under the Duke of York and a sizable French squadron under Comte Jean d'Estrées. His chance came when the enemy, returning from an uneventful cruise in the North Sea, anchored at Solebay off the Suffolk coast. The allied fleet consisted of approximately 150 vessels, including 71 ships of the line. De Ruyter took it by surprise on the morning of 7 June, attacking from the windward with 130 ships, including 62 of the line. At dusk he withdrew, having inflicted more damage than he had sustained and temporarily paralyzed allied operations.

Shortly thereafter, the strength of the Dutch fleet was reduced by one-third through the detachment of crewmen to serve in the hard-pressed land forces and de Ruyter was obliged to remain on the defensive for the rest of the campaigning season. The allies put to sea at the end of June in an unsuccessful attempt to intercept homecoming Dutch merchant convoys, but no actions occurred. In September, the French squadron sailed for home. That winter de Ruyter commanded the maritime defenses of Amsterdam while the city withstood a siege by a French army under the Prince de Condé. With the coming of spring, the admiral prepared to return to sea.

In May 1673 de Ruyter sailed for the Thames with the objective of blocking the river and bottling up the English fleet before it could unite with the French.[20] The republic's military situation still was precarious. Half of the country was in enemy hands. Because of the danger on land, Friesland's contribution to the fleet was negligible and the Zealand ships were not ready to sail. Only those of the three Holland admiralties followed de Ruyter's flag. Altogether, his force consisted of thirty-one ships of the line, twelve frigates, eighteen fireships, and a number of small craft. Accompanying them were eight heavily ballasted merchant vessels destined to be sunk in the most important channels of the Thames estuary. The admiral and his council of war had planned the operation in the minutest detail. To their disgust, however, a reconnaissance revealed that most of the English warships were already at sea or near the locations chosen for the blockships. The operation had to be called off.

Under these circumstances, de Ruyter decided to assemble his fleet in Schooneveld (Clean Field), a stretch of sea some fifteen nautical miles west of Flushing between the Flemish and Zealand banks and shoals. With depths of more than five fathoms it offered a good anchorage and gave easy access to the Scheldt and Meuse estuaries. From there it was also possible to keep an eye on the entrances to the Thames and the Narrows. Moreover, the prevailing southwesterly winds made it a good starting point in case the fleet had to move north along the Dutch coast. Schooneveld had been used as a fleet rendezvous in all of the republic's European wars. In England and France it was known as "de Ruyter's hole" or his "fort between the banks." In August 1666 the admiral had saved the Dutch fleet after the St. James's Day Fight by retreating to Schooneveld and in June 1667 he had used it as the starting point for his expedition to the Medway.

One of the attractive features of Schooneveld was its inconstancy. Banks and shoals tended to shift. Contemporary charts were far from accurate, but for the Dutch Schooneveld belonged to home waters. Their enemies regarded it as very tricky and probably overestimated the dangers, which made de Ruyter's hole all the more appealing to the States admirals.

The strength of the Dutch fleet that anchored at Schooneveld on 16 May 1673 was less than half that of the English. It could have met the French fleet, believed to be bound for Dutch waters, on an equal footing, but the Dutch deemed it inadvisable to leave the North Sea, because intelligence indicated that the English were preparing an invasion.

A number of vessels joined de Ruyter in the latter half of May. Cornelis Tromp arrived with seven Amsterdam vessels. He and de Ruyter, who had been at odds since the St. James's Day Fight, were reconciled under strong pressure from Prince William III. On 30 May, delegates from the prince and the States-General came on board de Ruyter's flagship, *De Zeven Provinciën*. During a High Council of War with all the flag officers present, the admiral's plan was unanimously adopted. The fleet would wait at Schooneveld until the enemy either attacked or attempted a landing, in both cases counterattacking with utmost vigor. The delegates dined on board and then went ashore.

On 1 June, the entire fleet raised sail and spent the day practicing. Upon completion of the maneuvers the commander in chief and his flag officers were guests on Tromp's flagship, the *Gouden Leeuw* (Golden Lion). During this meal, a pleasant occasion, the first reports were received of the approach of the Anglo-French fleet.

The English fleet was commanded by Prince Rupert, who flew his flag in the squadron of the red in the allied van. The French squadron of Comte d'Estrées formed the allied center squadron of the white and Sir Edward Spragge's English squadron of the blue brought up the rear. Rupert had instructions to land troops and, if necessary, defeat the Dutch fleet. In England ten thousand men had been assembled to reinforce the invasion force embarked in the fleet.

On the evening of 1 June, more than one hundred enemy vessels, seventy-six of them ships of the line, anchored off the Flemish banks, ready to attack the following day. De Ruyter remained at anchor with his fifty ships of the line—as some called them, our *Kleen hoopken* (Old Dutch for little bunch). Early the next morning Prince Rupert raised sail and the Dutch did the same. In a few hours the fleets had closed to a distance of ten nautical miles. Then the wind died and both forces anchored to await more favorable conditions. Their approximate positions are shown in map 5. (Because we are insufficiently informed about the banks and shoals of 1673, the chart is based on twentieth-century conditions.) That night a heavy gale came up and blew for four days. All during that time the two fleets lay ten miles apart,

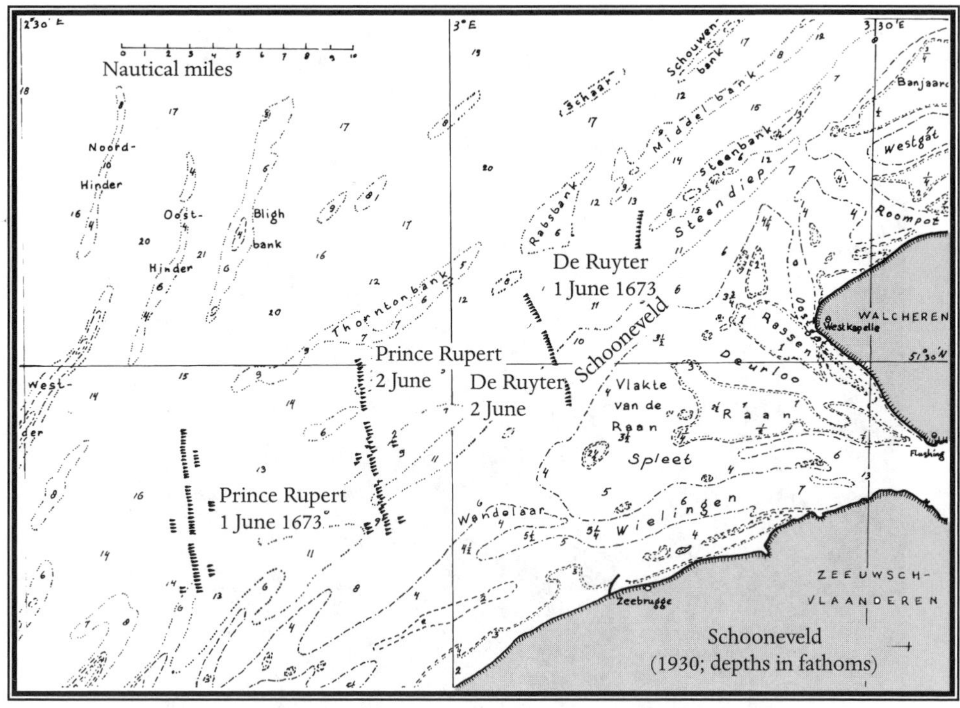

5. The Schooneveld.

grynsend (grinning) at each other. On 4 June, a Sunday, on de Ruyter's initiative, the men of the Dutch fleet partook of the Lord's Supper.

Prince Rupert anticipated that upon seeing the superior allied fleet approaching, de Ruyter would attempt to avoid battle by seeking shelter in the mouth of the Scheldt. To prevent him from doing so, Rupert planned to send thirty small, swift vessels forward to occupy the Dutch until his heavy ships could come to grips with them. Most of these small vessels were taken from the allied center and rear. They were not given a single, overall commander, but sailed under their own senior captains. When the weather changed for the better on 7 June, the prince put this plan into effect. About nine o'clock that morning, the tide being favorable, the allied fleet weighed anchor and set course for the Dutch. The vanguard of small ships was some miles ahead, followed by Rupert in the van, d'Estrées in the center, and Spragge in the rear. De Ruyter's flag flew over the Dutch center, while Tromp commanded the van and Vice Admiral Adriaen Banckert the rear.

3. The First Battle of Schooneveld, 7 June 1673. The ferocity of the melees that characterized the Anglo-Dutch Wars is evident in this spirited print published in Amsterdam later in 1673, although, in fact, the encounter was less sanguinary and more controlled than it indicates. In the center foreground Cornelis Tromp's flagship, the *Gouden Leeuw* (1), is wedged between two enemy vessels; note the boarding action in progress in the waist of the ship at right. De Ruyter's *Zeven Provinciën* is the fourth from left (2) in the knot of vessels at upper left. The Dutch vessles (4, 5, and 6) in the melee under way at upper right belong to Banckert's squadron. (The Beverley R. Robinson Collection, U.S. Naval Academy Museum.)

De Ruyter's reaction was not what Rupert had expected. Instead of attempting to retire, he formed a line of battle (map 6, fig. 1). This meant that there was no longer any point in sending the special vanguard forward, but no signal was available to recall it and confusion ensued. Tromp's squadron threatened to gain the weather gage, so the allied vanguard and Rupert's squadron had to change course. Against Tromp's well-ordered line the allied fleet had to fight with a mix of ships haphazardly thrown together and unaccustomed to acting in concert. Many of them were unable to fire because others got in their way.

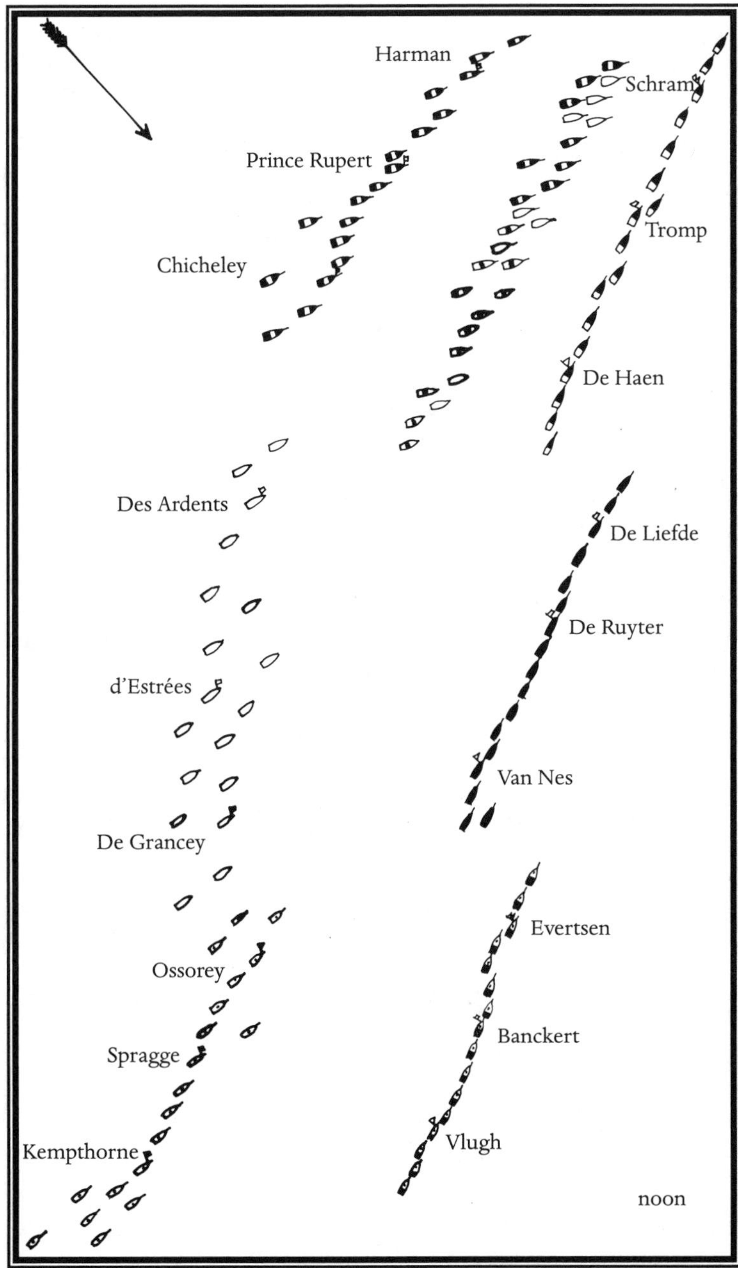

6. (Fig. 1) The First Battle of Schooneveld, 7 June 1673.

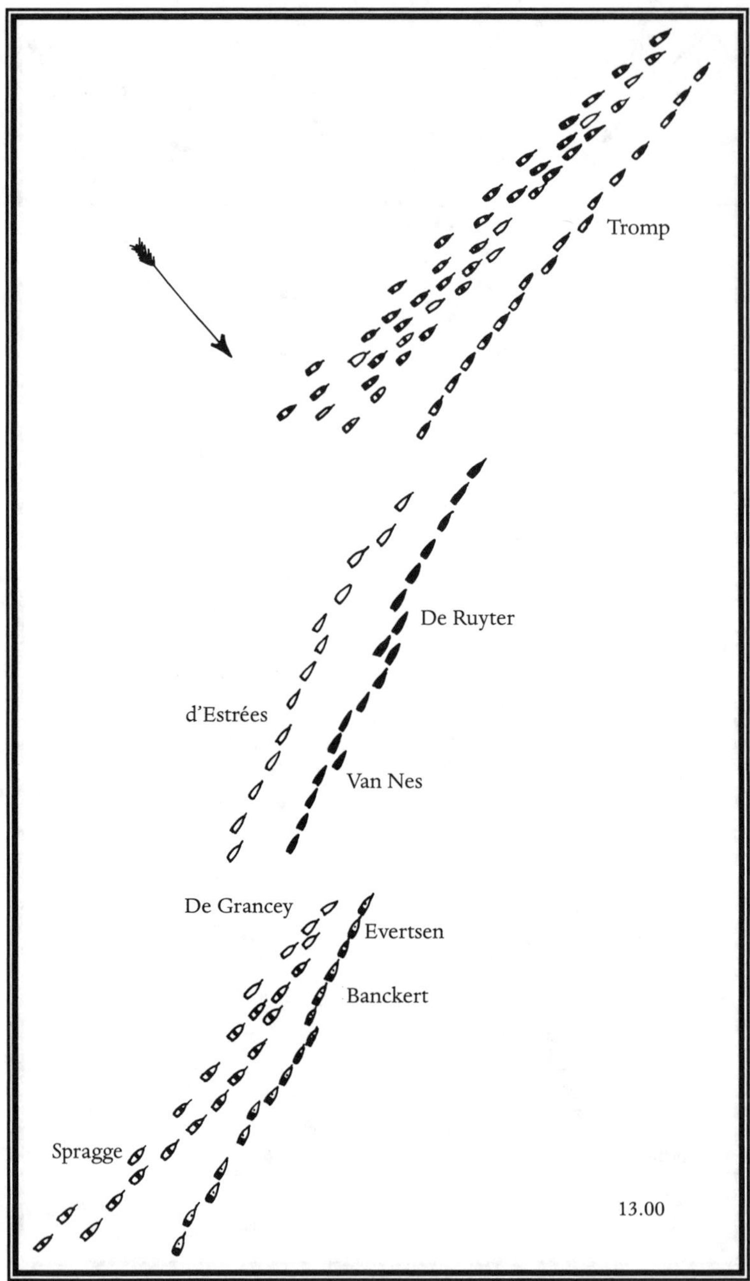
Tromp
De Ruyter
d'Estrées
Van Nes
De Grancey
Evertsen
Banckert
Spragge
13.00

Fig. 2

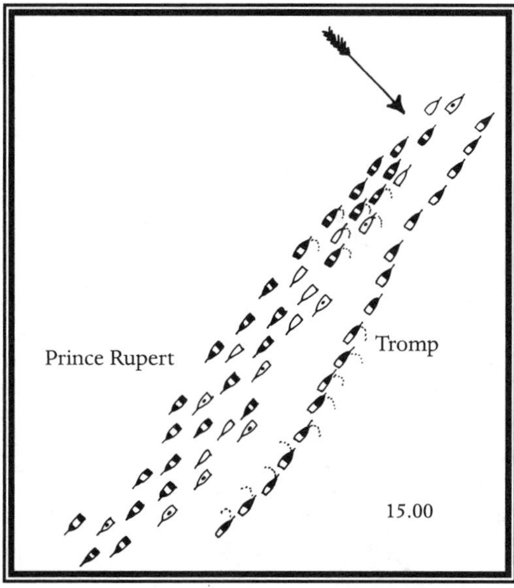

Fig. 3

D'Estrées set course toward de Ruyter's squadron. The latter steered north-northeast. The French lagged slightly behind, with the result that de Grancey, bringing up their rear, missed the last division of de Ruyter's squadron and sailed toward Vice Admiral Cornelis Evertsen's division, heading the Dutch rear. Thus Banckert found himself under attack by part of d'Estrées's squadron as well as all of Spragge's (fig. 2).

By then, Tromp had given up trying to win the weather gage from Rupert and was engaged in a running battle to the northeast with the prince's squadron and the special vanguard. For two hours his fifteen Dutch ships fought against almost forty allied vessels as the opposing forces gradually neared the shoals northwest of Walcheren. Fortunately, the allied ships continued to mask one another's fire and the freshening wind prevented them from using their lower gunports, so the Dutch were able to hold their own. At three o'clock in the afternoon Prince Rupert, becoming anxious about the diminishing depths, decided to put his ships about and stand to the southwest (fig. 3). He might have attempted an all-out attack from windward, but he feared the shoals. Tromp chose to accompany his adversaries in hopes of rejoining his commander, so the battle continued on the opposite course.

In the meanwhile, de Ruyter's own squadron had been in action with the reduced allied center. He rightly concluded that of his subordinate ad-

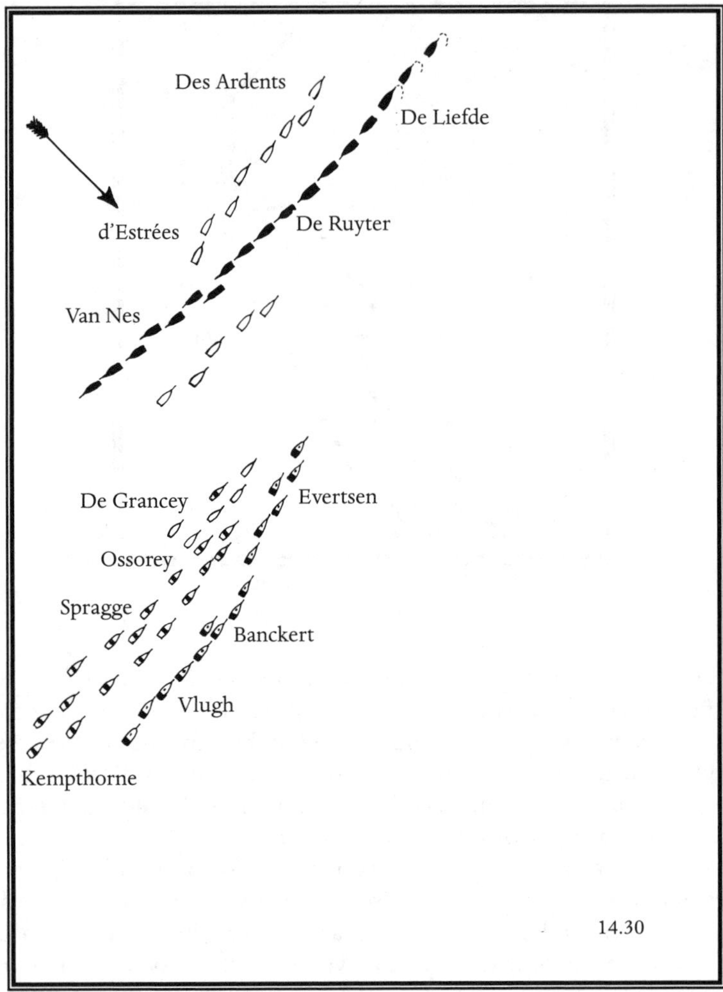

Fig. 4

mirals, Tromp and Banckert, the latter found himself in the greatest danger. The most effective way to aid him would be to come down on his adversaries from the windward. To do so, de Ruyter would have to put about and cross the French line. Seeing Tromp moving farther north, he sent a message by aviso (dispatch boat) ordering Tromp to change course and follow him. De Ruyter's turn to a southwesterly course (fig. 4) greatly surprised the French admirals. In their reports they expressed admiration for this decision and the precision with which the maneuver was executed.

De Ruyter's description of the evolution in his journal was very brief: "At three o'clock we tacked southwest to Prince Rupert and the blue flag. . . ." Apparently he did not know that at that moment his opposite number was actually fighting Tromp. In his report to the Prince of Orange, de Ruyter wrote, "We kept going northeast until about two o'clock in the afternoon; judging the time and opportunity were there to turn about to the southwest I made a signal to that effect and informed Admiral Tromp by aviso." It is only in the French after-action reports that the importance of this move is explained to posterity. When d'Estrées saw the Dutch squadron approaching, he tried to keep to windward and succeeded in passing just above *De Zeven Provinciën*. The two flagships exchanged broadsides as they passed. Some other French ships also managed to keep to windward, but a number did not and suffered in consequence as the Dutch line forged past. After persisting to his northeasterly course for a while, d'Estrées turned and followed his enemy (fig. 5).

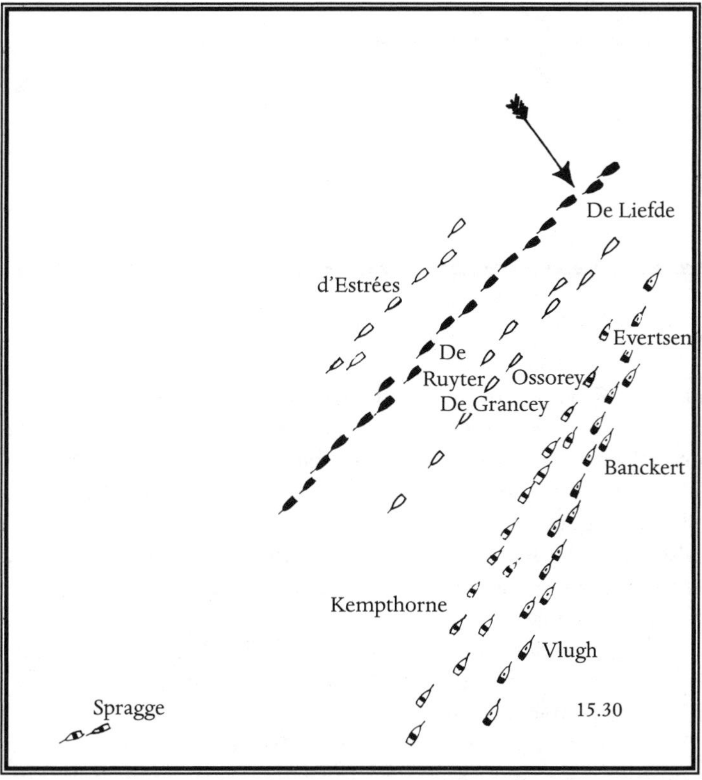

Fig. 5

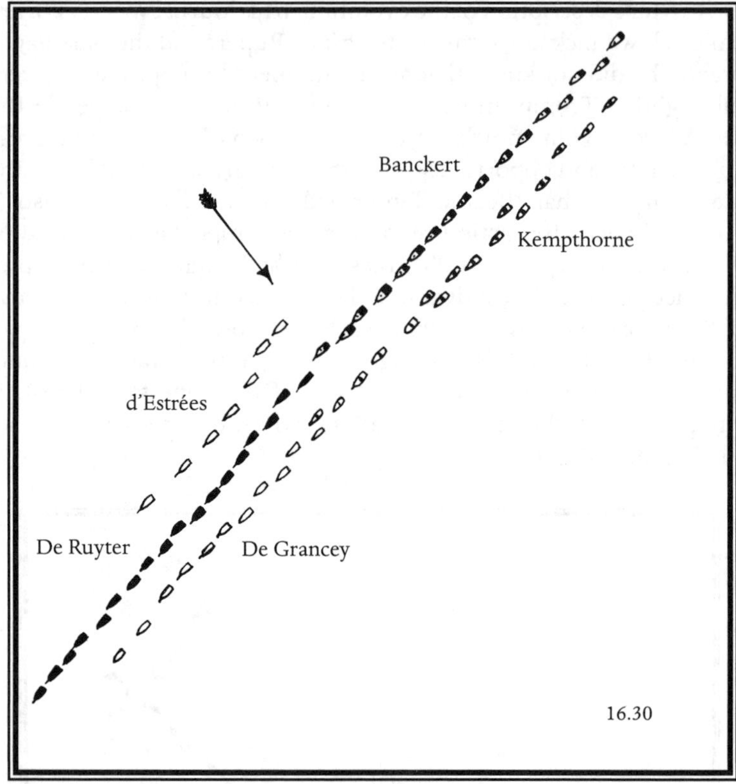

Fig. 6

When de Ruyter observed that many French ships avoided his flagship, he remarked, "The enemies still have respect for *De Zeven Provinciën.*" He was certainly referring to the ship, but he could also have meant his country, the seven united provinces that formed the Netherlands. Gradually the admiral's squadron neared de Grancey's division, which joined the other French ships in the lee of the Dutch and then changed course. Banckert's squadron did the same and followed the commander in chief. The situation was now as shown in fig. 6.

While these events were in progress, de Ruyter observed that Tromp had not followed his movements. Either the aviso had not reached him or he had so many enemy vessels to contend with that he was unable to conform. The anxiety de Ruyter felt about Tromp's squadron prompted his third command decision since the onset of the action. With the words

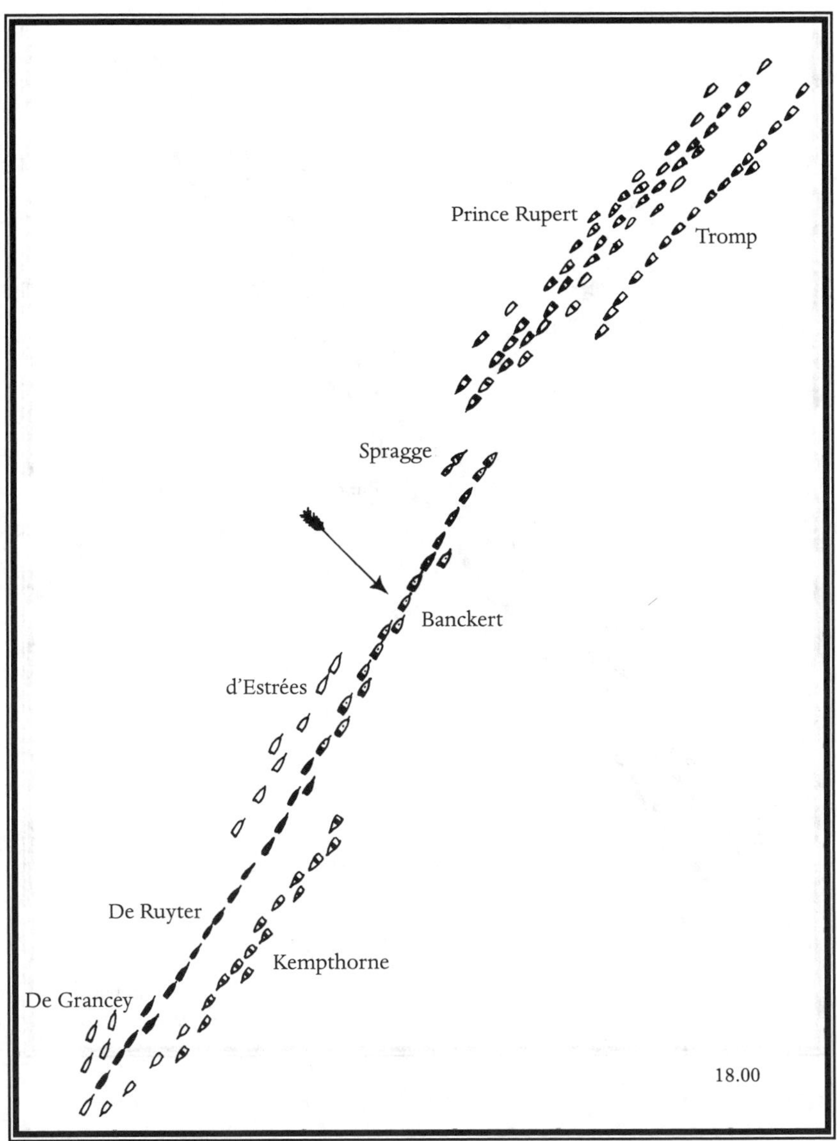
Prince Rupert
Tromp
Spragge
Banckert
d'Estrées
De Ruyter
Kempthorne
De Grancey
18.00

Fig. 7

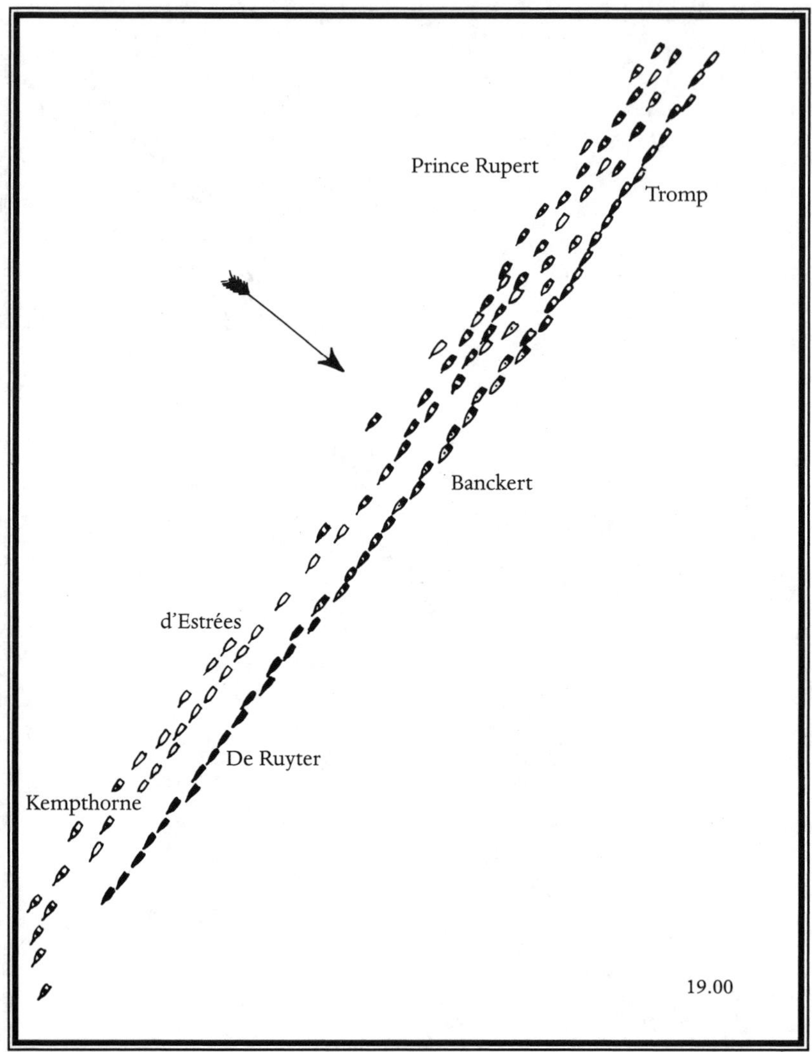

Fig. 8

"What matters most must come first. It is better to help friends than to hurt enemies," he ordered his and Banckert's squadrons to change course in order to join Tromp (fig. 7).

At about six o'clock de Ruyter's ships observed the missing squadron approaching from the northwest, still fighting. During the afternoon Tromp had lost sight of the rest of the fleet. By now he was flying his flag from his fourth successive flagship, the first three having been damaged. Upon seeing de Ruyter's force, he exclaimed, "Men, there is *Bestevaer!* He is coming to help us, and I shall not leave him as long as I can breathe!" According to one report, he had this encouraging word spread to lift his men's spirits before he actually saw anything.

At the appropriate moment, de Ruyter ordered his squadron and Banckert's to resume a southwesterly course. The entire Dutch fleet now formed one long uninterrupted line of battle. The allies followed this example and the result was a running battle as shown in fig. 8. Many of the French and English ships were not in position to take part in the action, so the allied superiority of numbers no longer had much significance. De Ruyter sought to profit from the comparative disorder in the enemy line by ordering several breakthroughs by division. These increased the confusion.

Dusk prevented de Ruyter from reaping the full fruits of the day's work. While the allies bore off to seaward, he reassembled his fleet and anchored in formation. The allies remained under sail until five o'clock in the morning, when they anchored approximately twelve nautical miles from the Dutch. One of Rupert's captains recorded what seems to have been the general opinion: "That hole is too little and the sands too dangerous for us to venture among them again."

As seventeenth-century naval engagements go, the First Battle of Schooneveld was not a costly affair. Several fireships and smaller craft were lost on both sides but no ships of the line by either, and only one Dutch and two English vessels had been so badly damaged that they had to be sent home. Personnel casualties were also comparatively light.

Tactically the battle was not a Dutch victory and strategically it was not decisive. Nevertheless, the allies' attack had been repulsed and their plans for a landing frustrated. Moreover, de Ruyter's position after the battle was better than it had been before. It would be relatively easy for his fleet, operating in home waters, to replace losses and obtain supplies. The allied fleets, in contrast, were a considerable distance from their bases, and the wind, which now turned to the east, added to their difficulties.

During the night the Dutch repaired the damage to their ships. De Ruyter was ready to attack the next morning, but a change in the weather prevented the resumption of the action. Unfavorable conditions continued until 14 June, when the Dutch fleet seized the initiative and, at the Second Battle of Schooneveld, succeeded in driving the enemy back to the English coast. For the time being, the danger that threatened the Netherlands from the sea had been warded off.

In August, after several small intervening engagements, the allies tried again. An invasion force of twenty thousand men was assembled in England, almost half of which embarked in an allied fleet of ninety frigates and ships of the line under Prince Rupert. De Ruyter, with seventy-five comparable vessels, met the enemy at the Battle of the Texel on 21 August 1673, and, once again, repelled the invasion.

This was the last major action of the third and final Anglo-Dutch war. Disgusted by the performance of the French fleet and outraged by the discovery that Charles II had been in French pay, Parliament compelled the king to conclude the Second Peace of Westminster with the Netherlands in February 1674. The terms of the treaty basically provided for a restoration of the prewar status quo.

Despite the peace with England, the war with France continued. Early in 1675, the latter undertook to wrest control of Sicily from Spain, thereby creating the conditions for naval collaboration between the Dutch republic and its traditional foe. When the republic decided to send a small fleet to the Mediterranean to aid in the defense of Sicily, the Spanish requested that de Ruyter go in command.

De Ruyter himself did not approve of the project. In planning sessions he pointed out that, in his opinion, the French naval forces in the Mediterranean were far more formidable than the Spanish and his fleet would be insufficient to redress the balance. During the deliberations "a certain gentleman of the Admiralty" told the sixty-eight-year-old admiral, "I do not think, sir, that in your old age you are beginning to be afraid and to lose courage!" To this taunt, de Ruyter quietly replied, "No, I am not losing courage. I am prepared to sacrifice my life for the state; but I am surprised and grieved that the gentlemen are prepared to risk and sacrifice the flag of the state." Pressed to accept the command, his objections notwithstanding, he declared, "The gentlemen do not have to beg me. They must command me, and if I were ordered to fly the flag of our country on one single ship, I should put to sea with it. Where the gentlemen of the States trust their flag, I will risk my life."[21]

In December 1675, de Ruyter sailed for the Mediterranean with fifteen frigates and ships of the line. His doubts about the adequacy of this expedition would soon be justified, but first he was to achieve a final triumph. It occurred near Stromboli, a small island north of Sicily, on 8 January 1676, when an allied Dutch and Spanish force of nineteen ships of the line and frigates under his command encountered a superior French fleet of twenty of the line under Admiral Abraham Duquesne. Attacking from windward, the French were beaten off by de Ruyter's close-hauled line in a defensive action that became celebrated as a model of its kind.

The next engagement, fought off eastern Sicily on 22 April, found the enemy at an even greater material advantage. The French fleet numbered twenty-nine ships of the line mounting 2,200 guns. Duquesne was again in command. The allied fleet consisted of seventeen of the line and nine frigates mounting 1,300 guns, but, unfortunately, de Ruyter was not again in command. That responsibility had been entrusted to the Spanish Admiral Don Francisco de la Cerda, who also led the allied center. De Ruyter commanded the van; the Dutch Vice Admiral Jan de Haen, the rear. Despite the odds, de Ruyter exploited the weather gage to close to point-blank range of the French van. De la Cerda failed to support his attack, which left the French center free to envelop de Ruyter's squadron, placing it between two fires. Disaster was averted by the initiative of de Haen, who led his squadron forward to de Ruyter's relief. The battle then sputtered to an inconclusive end. In its course, de Ruyter had been wounded in the legs. He died aboard his flagship, the *Eendragt* (Unity), in harbor at Syracuse on 29 April.

The curtain fell on the republic's Mediterranean misadventure a little more than a month later, at the Battle of Palermo (2 June), in which the allied fleet was destroyed by an overwhelming French force. Later, in conversation with de Ruyter's son, himself an admiral, Charles II declared, "I was amazed that the gentlemen of the States-General risked your father, so great an admiral, by sending him to Sicily with such a small force."[22] It is indeed a black page in Dutch history. Brandt's verdict is unsparing: "That inestimable blood was shed all too lightly."[23]

De Ruyter's body was carried back to the Netherlands for interment. Although France and the republic remained at war, Louis XIV ordered that salutes should be fired in the admiral's honor when the ship bearing his remains passed French ports. All that was mortal of Michiel Adriaenszoon de Ruyter reached Helevoetsluis on 30 January 1677 and was given a state funeral in the *Nieuwe Kerk* (New Church) in Amsterdam on 18 March. His tomb bears the inscription *Intaminus Fulget Honoribus*. Brandt translates this as: He shines in unblemished honor.

Notes

1. Gerard Brandt, *Het leven en bedrijf van den Heere Michiel de Ruiter* (Amsterdam: Wolfgang, Waasberge, Boom, Van Someren en Goethals, 1687), p. 6.
2. Ibid., p. 5.
3. Ibid., p. 16.
4. P. J. Blok, *Michiel Adriaansz. de Ruyter* (The Hague: Martinus Nijhoff, 1928), p. 36.
5. Brandt, op. cit., p. 23.
6. Ibid.
7. Ibid., p. 986.
8. Blok, op. cit., p. 221.

9. Peter Padfield, *Tide of Empires: Decisive Naval Campaigns in the Rise of the West* (London: Routledge & Kegan Paul, 1982), II: 63.

10. Henry B. Wheatley, ed., *The Diary of Samuel Pepys,* 2 vols. (New York: Random House, n.d.), II: 600.

11. Brandt, op. cit., p. 2.

12. Ibid., p. 862.

13. Blok, op. cit., p. 243.

14. Ibid., p. 245.

15. J. C. M. Warnsinck, *Admiraal de Ruyter. De zeeslag op Schooneveld* (The Hague: Martinus Nijhoff, 1930), p. 132.

16. Blok, op. cit., p. 323.

17. Quoted, ibid., p. 414.

18. Brandt, op. cit., p. 694.

19. Ibid., p. 758.

20. The account of the First Battle of Schooneveld and the accompanying figures are based on Professor Warnsinck's *Admiraal de Ruyter.*

21. Brandt, op. cit., p. 712.

22. Ibid., p. 1003.

23. Ibid., p. 1010.

NOTE ON SOURCES

In the year of his death, a brief biography of Admiral de Ruyter was included in a Dutch book about illustrious seafarers by Lambertus van den Bos. This work was used by the anonymous author of an English biography published by Dorman Newman (London, 1677): *The Life of M. A. De Ruyter, Admiral of Holland,* from which the subtitle of this chapter is taken.

In de Ruyter's own country, the writing of his biography was undertaken by the Reverend Gerard Brandt, who began his monumental work shortly after the admiral's death. Brandt himself died before its completion but his sons finished the work. Entitled *Het leven en bedrijf van den Heere Michiel de Ruiter* (The Life and Deeds of Michiel de Ruyter, Gentleman), it was published by Wolfgang, Waasberge, Boom, Van Someren en Goethals in Amsterdam in 1687. All subsequent publications about de Ruyter are based on this magnificent biography. It has often been reprinted, most recently in 1988, and has served as the main source for all de Ruyter studies. In 1996 Dr. Prud'homme van Reine published a new biography, *Rechterhand van Nederland* (Right Hand of the Netherlands). This brilliant study contains quite a number of new facts, based on sources not available to Brandt, but the general picture of the admiral is in accordance with that of Brandt. Other works among those listed below which are based on a wide study of other—mostly foreign—sources are those of Warnsinck, which was used for the analysis of the First Battle of Schooneveld, and van Foreest and Weber.

Blok, P. J. *Michiel Adriaansz. de Ruyter.* The Hague: Martinus Nijhoff, 1928. This work also appeared in an English edition translated by G. J. Renier, *The Life of Admiral de Ruyter.* London: Ernest Benn, 1933.

Boxer, C. R. *The Anglo-Dutch Wars of the 17th Century.* London: Her Majesty's Stationary Office, 1974.
Foreest, H. A. van, and R. E. J. Weber. *De Vierdaagse Zeeslag, 11–14 juni 1666.* Amsterdam: N.V. Noord-Hollandsche Uitg. Mij., 1984.
Jonge, J. C. de. *Het Nederlandsche Zeewezen.* 'S-Gravenhage: Van Cleef, 1833–1848.
Lunshof, H. A. *De stuurman van de Groene Leeuw.* Amsterdam: Elsevier, 1941.
Moer, A. van der. "Aenschouw Den Helt." *Marineblad,* April 1976.
Mollema, J. C. *Geschiedenis van Nederland ter Zee.* Amsterdam: Joost van den Vondel, 1939–42.
Prud'homme van Reine, R. B. *Rechterhand van Nederland.* Amsterdam-Antwerp: De Arbeiderspers, 1996.
Romein, J. M., and A. Romein-Verschoor. *Erflaters von onze beschaving.* Amsterdam: Querido, 1938–40.
Warnsinck, J. C. M. *Admiral de Ruyter. De zeeslag op Schooneveld.* The Hague: Martinus Nijhoff, 1930.

5

Niels Juel
The Good Old Knight
(1629–1697)

Hans Christian Bjerg

THE THIRTY YEARS WAR REACHED THE TWIN MONARCHY OF Denmark-Norway in 1626. Danish King Christian IV entered the conflict expecting to improve his country's position in northern Germany. For various reasons he was unsuccessful and hostile forces invaded the Jutland peninsula. The remainder of the country was saved by the fact that the navy maintained command of the Baltic approaches and prevented the enemy from reaching the Danish islands and Norway.[1]

The influential nobleman Erik Juel, whose estate was located at Thy, in northernmost Jutland, sent his wife, Sophie Sehested, and a little son to safety in Norway in 1627. He later joined them there, and on 8 May 1629,* Sophie gave birth in Christiania (now Oslo) to a boy christened Niels.[2] In that same month, the war ceased in Denmark, and the Juels returned to their estate, where another son, Jens, was born in 1631.

Up to the age of thirteen Niels Juel was reared in part by his parents and in part by his aunt, Karen Sehested, on her estate of Stenalt near Randers in Jutland. This well-educated noblewoman had been tutor to the children of the king. During his years with her Niels became familiar with books and manuscripts.[3]

In April 1643 the young Niels Juel was sent to serve as a page to Duke Frederik, later King Frederik III. The duke was then administrator of the diocese of Bremen-Verden in northern Germany. A short time after the boy's arrival Swedish troops invaded the Danish territory from the south, and Frederik was forced to flee.

As part of his education, in 1647–48 Niels Juel was enrolled in the Chivalric Academy for Young Nobles at Soroe on Zealand. An essential element in the upbringing of the sons of noblemen at this time was the so-called Grand Tour of Europe, through which they were expected to acquire a first-hand knowledge of foreign countries and to establish useful connections abroad. Niels's Grand Tour started in March 1650 with a journey through Germany to France, where he seems to have remained until 1652. During this period he must have become interested in naval affairs, for in that year he proceeded to the Netherlands in order to join the Dutch navy.

The young Dane's decision was well timed. The commercial rivalry be-

* In conformity with Danish historical custom, all dates are given according to the Julian calendar in use at the time. To reconcile them with the modern calendar (introduced in Denmark on 1 January 1700), ten days must be added.

tween the Netherlands and England had just led to the outbreak of the First Anglo-Dutch War (1652–54). This conflict was the first to take place after the full-rigged, broadside-armed sailing ship had evolved into the weapon system, combining gunfire with maneuver, that was to dominate war at sea until the mid-nineteenth century. The new type of warship demanded the development of new, distinctly naval tactics.[4] These tactics in turn required a new type of education for the officers serving on board the ships. From now on, a sea officer had to be both a skilled tactician and a skilled seaman. This combination created the naval officer of the seventeenth century. The Dutch navy was aware of the new demands and had instituted a program for training officer-aspirants at sea. (Naval academies as such were founded later, in the eighteenth century.)

Niels Juel enrolled in the Dutch navy as an *adelbors* (officer trainee) and participated in the war with England. The sources relating to this period of his life are not rich, but it appears that he fought in most of the big battles. He had the opportunity to follow and observe such leaders as Maarten Tromp and Michiel de Ruyter. Just after the conclusion of peace he became the captain of a ship in a fleet that sailed to the Mediterranean under the command of de Ruyter in 1654.[5]

When Niels Juel came home to Denmark in 1656 he possessed a comprehensive and up-to-date knowledge and experience of the naval warfare of his day. King Frederik, who had ascended the throne in 1648, welcomed his former page, and Niels Juel at once became an officer in the Danish navy.* A year earlier trouble had arisen between Sweden and Poland. The Swedes tried to blockade Danzig (now Gdansk), one of the support points of the Dutch Baltic trade. The Netherlands therefore despatched a fleet to the Baltic. As King Frederik supported the Dutch interest in the area, this force was followed by a Danish fleet in 1656. Niels Juel sailed with it as captain of the first-rate ship *Sorte Rytter* (The Black Rider). Sweden and the Netherlands reached a peaceable understanding, however, and the fleet returned home without having seen action.[6]

In the following year, 1657, relations between Denmark and Sweden became very tense, and in May, on the king's orders, a squadron commanded by Niels Juel began to seize Swedish merchantmen in the Sound. The expected war with Sweden came in June. That same month Niels Juel was appointed admiral and commander in chief of Holmen, the main base of the Danish navy in Copenhagen. He was then only twenty-eight years old, and despite the preferment customarily accorded to noblemen, this was a re-

* Actually, the Danish-Norwegian navy, but as a matter of convenience, in this and subsequent references to the twin monarchy and its institutions only the Danish element is named. The union between the two countries continued until 1814.

markable promotion. The command of the base was an important and influential one. Niels Juel's experience and his calm character were already proving useful to the Danish navy.

Soon the war at sea made the young admiral needed in the fleet. In September the Swedes attempted to invade Zealand, but were intercepted by a Danish fleet off Falsterbo on 12–14 September. The Danish commander was Admiral Henrik Bjelke, with Niels Juel as one of his vice admirals. Neither side could call the battle a victory, but the Swedes were forced to abandon the invasion—a classic example of the influence of sea power.

In Scandinavia the winter of 1657–58 became the most severe in recorded history. The sea was paved with a dense sheet of ice. In consequence the Danish navy, the only force the country could rely on, was put out of action, and Swedish King Karl X Gustav led his army across the frozen-over Danish Straits and suddenly appeared outside Copenhagen. King Frederik was forced to surrender at Roskilde near the capital on 26 February 1658.

Later that year the Swedes resumed the war and besieged Copenhagen. During the siege Niels Juel was often in action as commander in chief of the crews of the ice-bound vessels and the workers of the Holmen naval base. The naval personnel fought on the fortifications side-by-side with the inhabitants of the capital. In October a Dutch fleet under Admiral van Wassenaer van Obdam approached the city with badly needed supplies. The Danish fleet sortied from Copenhagen to support it, and the Swedish naval blockade was broken in an engagement called the Battle of the Sound.[7]

The war ended with the death of the Swedish king in 1660. It left the finances of the Danish monarchy in a deplorable state. The crisis was complicated by the refusal of the nobility, the wealthiest element of the population, to surrender its traditional exemption from taxation. At Holmen Niels Juel had a hard time. The navy had sustained heavy losses during the struggle with Sweden and resources were insufficient to rebuild it to its former strength.[8] Nevertheless, Niels Juel found the leisure to marry Margrethe Ulfeldt in 1661. She was twenty years old, twelve years junior to her husband.

The financial crisis forged an alliance between the king and wealthy commoners to establish an absolute monarchy, by which the nobility was subjected to taxation and its influence curtailed. The introduction of the absolute monarchy also resulted in major reforms of the state administration. Each sphere of activity was allotted a governing council, which bore a collective responsibility to the king. For naval affairs an admiralty was instituted, consisting of all of the admirals in the navy. Admiral of the Fleet Henrik Bjelke became its chairman, but as he belonged to the old school of officers, an operational commander was also needed. Niels Juel would have been a good choice, but he was passed over. The king called instead on Cort Adeler, a Norwegian-born officer living in the Netherlands. Born in 1622,

Adeler had joined the Dutch navy as an *adelbors* in 1647, just as Niels Juel did a few years later. In the following decade he entered the navy of the Republic of Venice and distinguished himself in the wars against the Turks. When he returned to the Netherlands, he had acquired a European reputation. It is therefore understandable that the king offered such a figure the post of admiral of the Danish navy. Adeler arrived in Copenhagen at the beginning of the 1660s, and was in charge of the navy from 1665, when he was appointed general-admiral.[9]

Cort Adeler proved to be a capable administrator. As general-admiral he began rebuilding the Danish navy, a task in which the evidence shows that he received the full cooperation of Niels Juel. After 1670 support for the reconstruction of the navy increased because of the interests of the new king, Christian V (1670–99).

Upon the death of his father Niels Juel succeeded to his family's estates, but he does not seem to have been interested in their management and sold them early in the 1660s. In 1666, however, he purchased and began to improve the estate of Sæbygaard in northern Jutland. He also had interests as a shipowner, a normal practice among naval officers of his day. As his wife inherited some estates, too, he must have been very busy attending to both naval and private affairs.

Soon after his accession to the throne Christian V asked for information about the condition of the navy. As a result of his initiative, a number of new regulations were issued, provisions similar to those in force in the Dutch navy were made for training officers, and the strength of the navy was increased. In 1673 the king set up a special commission to investigate the navy as an institution and all matters connected with it. The commission worked very rapidly but was extremely thorough.[10] Its recommendation produced several radical changes in the navy. Niels Juel, for instance, had to relinquish some of his administrative responsibilities to others. Still, he remained third in command after Henrik Bjelke and Cort Adeler, and in 1674 he was admitted to the recently established Order of Dannebrog.

The struggle for hegemony in Europe spread to Scandinavia that same year. In view of their rivalry, it was natural that Denmark and Sweden aligned with the opposing sides in the great contest. Sweden allied with France, while Denmark joined a coalition consisting of the Netherlands, Spain, the Duchy of Brandenburg, and the Holy Roman Empire. Denmark's treaty obligations were defensive in nature, in that the country was to take an active role only if Sweden entered the war on the side of France. This eventuality came to pass when Swedish troops invaded Brandenburg late in 1674. Christian V welcomed the approach of hostilities, in which he hoped to recover the formerly Danish territories in southwestern Sweden. The ensuing conflict officially began in the summer of 1675. It is known as the

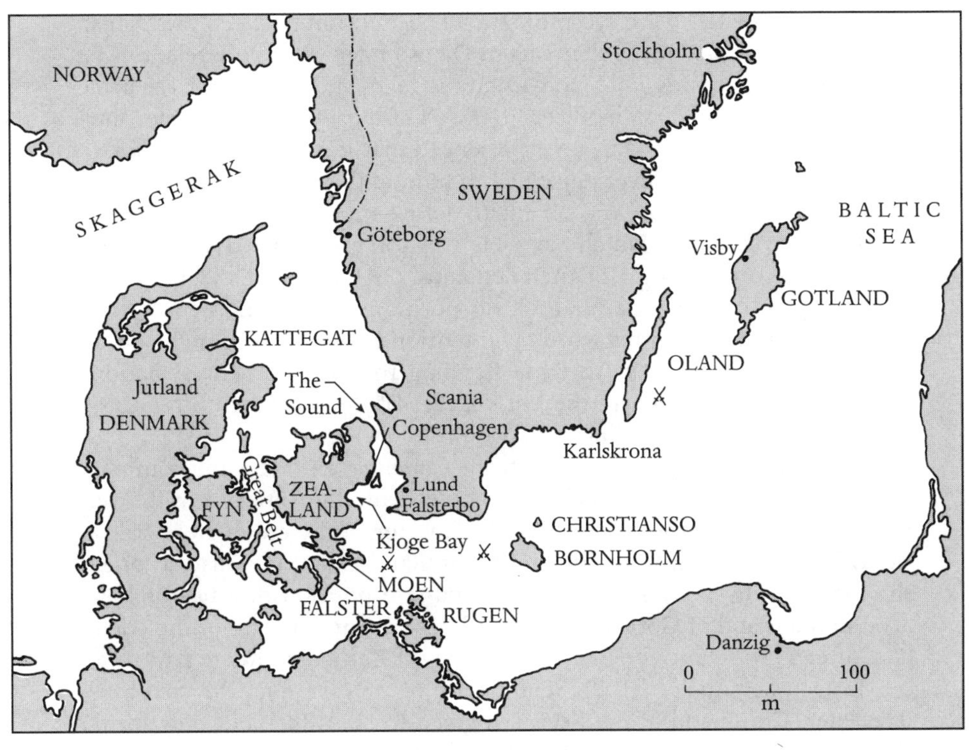

7. The Scanian War, 1675–79.

Scanian War, after the Swedish province in which land operations took place.

The Danish fleet had been ready for sea since May 1675. In accordance with the treaty of alliance, the Netherlands sent a squadron of eight ships to Copenhagen. Its commanding officer was Captain Binckes, who showed himself to be a troublemaker from the start. The Danish admiralty decided to send a fleet of twelve ships, together with the Dutch squadron, to the Baltic. The main task of this force was to intercept the transport of troops from Sweden to the theater of war in northern Germany. But first the admiralty had to decide what to do about Captain Binckes's demands regarding his rank in the combined fleet. Although he was willing to serve under Cort Adeler, he insisted that as an independent squadron commander he should be second-in-command. The captain was finally allowed to have his way by the obviously unsatisfactory expedient of keeping a Danish admiral and squadron at home.

Such difficulties were symptomatic of the tension between the Danish-Norwegian and the Dutch elements in Danish navy. The close relations between the Netherlands and Denmark in the 1660s and 1670s led to the placement of a number of Dutch officers in the Danish navy. Generally, the Dutch were better educated and more experienced than their Danish and Norwegian colleagues—and never neglected to remind them of that fact.[11]

Apparently Niels Juel was unable to defuse the clash of interests despite his prior service in the Dutch navy. He was too great a patriot to be influenced by the often arrogant Dutch demands. On the other hand, he refused to participate in intrigues. He took his positions openly and people knew that they could rely on his word. The tension between the Dutch and the Danish is one of the keys to understanding the development of national naval power in Denmark in the last decades of the seventeenth century, a process in which Niels Juel played a vital role.

The Danish-Dutch fleet sailed from Copenhagen under the command of Cort Adeler in August 1675 but was beset with difficulties from the very beginning. The weather was bad and a quarter of the crews were sick. In the Baltic the Swedish fleet confronted similar conditions. This was one of the reasons why it chose to adopt the passive position of a fleet-in-being around the island of Gotland. The allied fleet did not encounter the enemy and, after a cruise into the Baltic, anchored off Zealand in Kjöge Bay.

In October Adeler fell ill. Sent ashore on 2 November, he died a few days later. Command of the fleet was given to Niels Juel, but only for the time being. For all his experience, he was still not considered qualified to hold that post permanently. The king believed that it was necessary to have a foreign expert as commander in chief of the navy, a viewpoint that leading circles in the Netherlands strove to encourage. During the winter the Danish government opened negotiations with the Dutch Admiral Cornelis Tromp, a son of Maarten Tromp. In the outcome, he accepted its invitation to take command of the Danish navy and arrived in Copenhagen in May 1676. Although Niels Juel had been passed over again, he loyally accepted the king's decision.

Before Tromp's arrival, Niels Juel led a Danish fleet on a cruise to the Isle of Rügen off the German coast. Following a secret plan, he then steered for the Swedish island of Gotland, put two thousand soldiers ashore, and attacked Visby, the island's capital from both land and sea. The city surrendered on 1 May. With the whole island under his control, Niels Juel began to reorganize its administration and appoint new, pro-Danish officials. The successful execution of this mission was a personal triumph for the admiral. It appears as though he had taken advantage of the absence of the navy's Dutch commander to demonstrate his own ability.

Later in May, Niels Juel sailed to Bornholm, where he joined a Dutch fleet under the command of Admiral Philipp van Almonde. On the twenty-fifth of that month the allied forces met a numerically superior Swedish fleet. Although Niels Juel had orders not to accept battle against unfavorable odds, there was no way for him to avoid the enemy force. Fortunately, the Swedes were not inclined to press the issue, and after a brief engagement both sides withdrew.

Several letters written by Niels Juel during this period throw light on his attitude toward the Dutch influence in the Danish navy. In a letter to Admiral Bjelke, he declared that he could place as much courage and devotion in the service of the king as anyone, and continued: "I hope that God and Fortune sometime will give me the opportunity, so His Royal Majesty can see that he can get the same service from his own subjects as from any foreigner."[12]

After the Battle of Bornholm the Dutch Admiral Almonde accused the Danish captains of cowardice, but they were cleared by a court-martial. In a letter to Niels Juel the king expressed his satisfaction with the admiral's outstanding conduct during the battle.

On 27 May 1676 Admiral Tromp assumed command of the allied fleet, which was anchored just off Falsterbo on the southwestern coast of Sweden. Niels Juel was given command on the van and Almonde of the rear. The force then sailed in search of the Swedish fleet, which was located near the Isle of Oland on 1 June. The allied fleet of twenty-five ships of the line (ten of which were Dutch) and ten frigates was slightly inferior to the Swedes' twenty-seven ships of the line and eleven frigates.

The weather was foul, with strong winds and showers. The Swedish Admiral Lorentz Creutz, who was not a trained seaman, ordered his flagship, the *Kronan* (Crown), to go about while carrying a great press of sail and with most of her gun-ports open. During the turn the ship capsized and a fire broke out. When it reached her powder magazine, the *Kronan* exploded. Very few of her crew survived, and Admiral Creutz was not among them.

After the loss of the *Kronan,* Tromp and Niels Juel attacked the *Svardet* (Sword), flagship of the Swedish second in command, which surrendered but was blown up by a Dutch fireship before she could be boarded. The battle rapidly developed into a melee. The Swedish ship of the line *Neptunus* also hauled down her colors, and eventually the enemy resistance ceased. Most of the Swedish ships succeeded in reaching Stockholm, although the *Applet* (Orb) struck a rock and sank.

For the Swedish, the Battle of Oland was disastrous. It had cost them four ships of the line, three small frigates, and about four thousand dead. The allied fleet's losses were insignificant. In his report Niels Juel associated the symbolic meaning of the names of the lost Swedish ships with the actual meaning of the Swedish defeat. The Crown, Sword, and Orb were symbols of the realm—and Neptune the symbol of sovereignty over the sea. The allied fleet had in fact obtained command of the sea in the Sound and off southern Sweden, and retained it for the rest of the year.

King Christian took advantage of this fact and transported an army to invade the former Danish territories in western Sweden. Later in the year this army ran into trouble, and the king ordered crews from the laid-up fleet to reinforce it. As Tromp was ill, a detachment of approximately thirteen hundred seamen was placed under the command of Niels Juel, who suddenly found himself an army officer. The use of such troops proved a complete failure. They were very poorly armed and most of them were cut down by Swedish cavalry in the Battle of Lund on 4 December 1676.[13]

The Danish position at the opening of 1677 was not very good. The future of the Danish troops in Sweden appeared uncertain. Only through the retention of command of the sea could the lines of supply and communication to the army be secured. Furthermore, in accordance with the treaty of alliance, Denmark had been forced to declare war on France, and this mighty nation was expected to send a fleet into the Baltic.

In the face of this threat—which, fortunately, failed to materialize—the Danish government decided to send Admiral Tromp to the Netherlands to assemble a second Dutch fleet to support the Danish navy. In February 1677, Tromp set out on his mission, leaving Niels Juel in temporary command of the fleet.

The strategic objective of Swedish sea power in this situation was to try to cut the maritime lines of communication to the Danish army in Sweden. The Swedish navy was divided into two elements: a main fleet in the Baltic and a squadron based at Göteborg in the Skagerrak. The logical way to use these forces was either to have them launch concerted attacks on the Sound from the north and south or to have the Göteborg squadron combine with the Baltic fleet and attack the Sound together from the south.

Despite the anticipated arrival for a support fleet from the Netherlands, Niels Juel hastened to outfit the Danish navy for the coming campaign. When at the end of May the Swedish Göteborg squadron put to sea, the Danes were ready to react. Tromp was still in the Netherlands, so Niels Juel commanded the Danish fleet that sailed from Copenhagen on 23 May. He had two missions: to protect the transport of troops from northern Germany to Copenhagen, and at the same time to prevent the Göteborg squadron from joining the Swedish fleet in the Baltic.

Emerging from the Great Belt, the Göteborg squadron found Niels Juel awaiting it south of Gedser on the Isle of Falster. With nine ships of the line and two frigates, his fleet was significantly superior to its seven ships of the line. The two forces came into contact on the night of 31 May–1 June. The following day the battle continued along the Isle of Falster and off the Isle of Moen.

The first part of the engagement was fought during a dead calm, and the ships had to lower boats to tow them into action. During this phase, a Swedish ship of the line was captured by boarding. In the morning the wind came up and the Danish fleet found itself holding the advantage of the weather gage. Niels Juel could therefore force the Swedes northward, away from the mouth of the Baltic. In the course of the day, four more Swedish ships of the line were taken by boarding and fifteen hundred men, including the Swedish Admiral Sjöblad, made prisoner.

Niels Juel's victory in the Battle of Moen had great strategic importance. The Danish fleet maintained command of the sea and had reduced the potential main body of the enemy. The victory also eased the pressure on Denmark and reduced the great anxiety felt in Copenhagen over the delay in the arrival of the fleet that Tromp was bringing from the Netherlands. The battle itself showed Niels Juel to be a skilled tactician. For a second time, he had demonstrated that he was capable of commanding a fleet. The outcome of the battle therefore strengthened his position vis-à-vis the Dutch officers serving in the Danish navy.

After the battle Niels Juel withdrew to a position between Stevns on Zealand and Falsterbo on the Swedish coast. It is indicative of his strategic insight that he chose not to enter Kjöge Bay, where he could be surprised by the enemy. Niels Juel tried hard to use the available time to prepare for the inevitable battle with the Swedish Baltic fleet. On 13 June, he notified the naval base in Copenhagen: "I have several times written about the shortage of ammunition, cordage, timber, and beer, but I have only got a few hammocks, which can be of little help to the fleet in fighting the enemy."[14] Conditions in the fleet were in fact very bad, but the government authorities in Copenhagen showed no interest in providing for its needs. None of the king's councilors wanted Niels Juel to enter action alone and the supplies were reserved for Tromp's fleet.

On 21 June, Niels Juel received intelligence that the Swedish Baltic fleet was at sea and had been sighted off Bornholm. This news placed the Danish king and admiralty in a dilemma. The approach of Tromp's fleet indicated that the best course for the Danish navy would be to avoid a battle until its arrival. On the other hand, a purely defensive posture would deprive the Danish forces of any opportunity to seize the initiative in the event of a Swedish attack. Without the Dutch fleet, Niels Juel was in the same position that Admiral John R. Jellicoe occupied more than two centuries later—that

Strength of the Danish and Swedish Fleets at the Battle of Kjöge Bay

type	nationality	numbers	guns	crews
1st rate ships	Danish	16	970	5,286
50+ guns	Swedish	18	1,164	6,380
2nd rate ships	Danish	10	360	1,496
30–49 guns	Swedish	9	337	1,450
3rd rate ships	Danish	1	18	50
18–29 guns	Swedish	3	54	330
4th rate ships	Danish	11	64	160
4–12 guns	Swedish	18	96	476
Total	Danish	38	1,412	6,992
	Swedish	48	1,651	8,636

of a man who could "lose the war in an afternoon." If the Swedes succeeded in preventing the Danish fleet from continuing its support of the army in Sweden, Denmark was in serious trouble.

It is beyond question that Niels Juel perceived this strategic dilemma, but he also faced a human dilemma, because personally he wished to give battle to the Swedes prior to the appearance of the Dutch. At the same time, he recognized the danger that an attempt to fulfill his ambition might lead to the loss of the fleet and bring his country to the brink of disaster. The instructions he received from Copenhagen were mutually contradictory. His brother, Jens, was one of the advisers to the king. He was sent to join Niels in the fleet as a kind of political counselor. The circumstances virtually compelled the monarch to give Niels Juel a free hand to act as he thought best if he was attacked and could not avoid a fight.[15]

In the meanwhile, the Swedish fleet under the command of General-Admiral Henrik Horn steered northward out of the Baltic toward the Danish fleet positioned between Stevns and Falsterbo. The Swedish force consisted of forty-eight ships of the line and frigates, plus six fireships. Its strategic objective was obviously to isolate the Danish fleet from its base and from southern Sweden, so that it could no longer protect the supply lines to the Danish troops there.

Niels Juel awaited the enemy with a fleet of thirty-eight ships and three fireships. For a closer examination of the opposing forces, see the table.

The two fleets sighted each other around 4:00 A.M. on 1 July 1677. At that instant all considerations and speculations about the advantages of an action before or after the arrival of the Dutch disappeared, for their relative positions forced Niels Juel to accept battle. Today the engagement is usually referred to as "The Battle of Kjöge Bay," but contemporaries called it "The Battle between Stevns and Falsterbo," which is more accurate, because it took place just outside the bay.[16]

At the moment visual contact was made, the Swedish fleet found itself to the south and west of the Danish. General-Admiral Horn, who must have been well pleased by this discovery, shaped a course—toward Stevns on the Danish coast—that would interpose his fleet between Niels Juel's and its

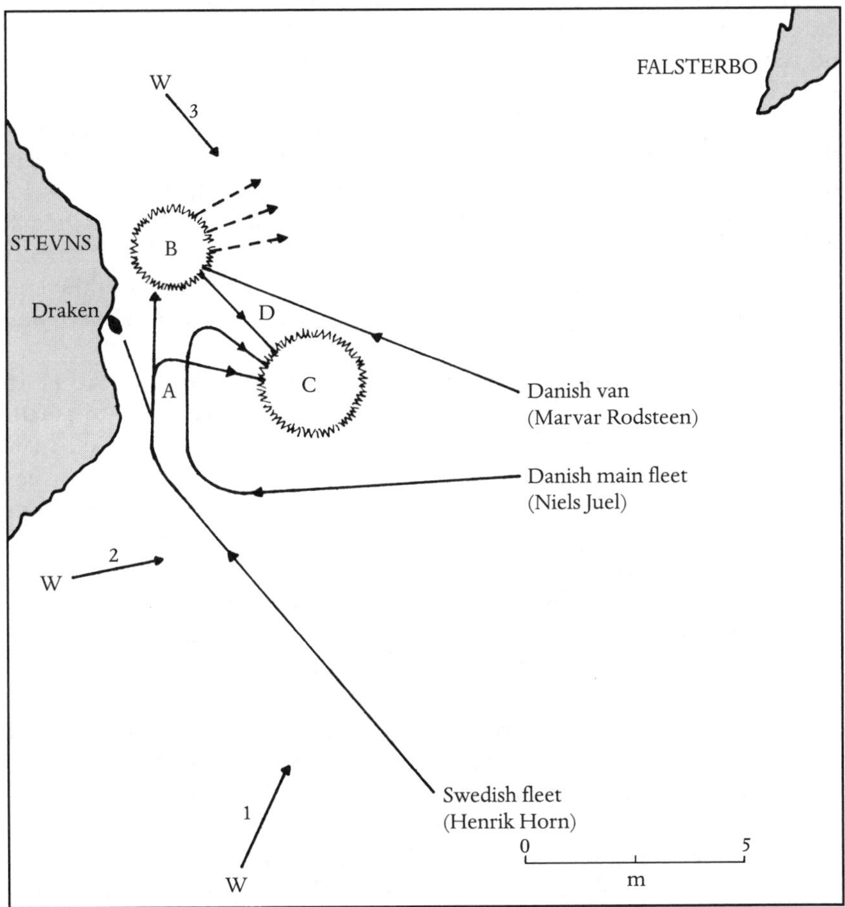

8. The Battle of Kjöge Bay, 1 July 1677. (A) The van of the Swedish fleet continues north while the center and rear turn east in an attempt to gain sea room. (B) The Danish van engages the Swedish van. (C) A melee develops between the main bodies of the Danish and Swedish fleets. (D) After dispersing the Swedish van, the Danish van joins the melee. The wind direction (W) changed three times during the battle.

base. The wind was southerly, giving the Swedes the weather gage, but in the course of the day it veered from westerly to northwesterly, in favor of the Danes.

Niels Juel responded to the Swedes' approach with a maneuver that put him in control of the battle. After the custom of the time, the opposing fleets were divided into three squadrons: the van, main body, and rear. Niels Juel set his main body and rear on a collision course with the Swedish fleet, presenting the enemy admiral with the alternatives of accepting a melee or sailing closer than he had intended to the Danish coast. Horn chose the latter. The Danish van, under Admiral Marvar Rodsteen, was steering too northerly a course to be able to participate in this phase of the battle.

To keep from running aground, Horn turned northward along Stevns. He sought to gain sea room for his fleet by sending some fireships against the Danish line. The attack was unsuccessful and Niels Juel turned and went on a parallel course with Horn. The two lines were slightly staggered, with the Swedish ahead. During the fight between the Danish flagship *Christianus Quintus* (Christian V) and the enemy van, the Swedish *Draken* (Dragon), 64 guns, was so badly damaged that she was forced to drop out of the line. The Danish rear continued to engage her, however, and the *Draken* was forced to run aground on Stevns.

The whole battle area was gradually blanketed by powder smoke. Horn let his van continue northward, deliberately tempting Niels Juel to pursue it. When the Danish line had passed, Horn would turn east with his main body in order to regain the open sea. The Danish van, which had not been able to enter action until now, succeeded in closing with the enemy van, and a melee developed north of Stevns.

As planned, Horn turned on an easterly course through the smoke to win maneuvering room and evade the Danish attempts to close. Niels Juel discovered the maneuver, followed Horn in the turn, and overtook the Swedish main body. The battle then changed into a melee with individual duels between ships. The ferocity of the struggle is indicated by the fact that Niels Juel was compelled to shift his flag to the *Fredericus Tertius* (Frederik III) and then to the *Charlotte Amalia*. In the meantime, the Danish van had destroyed or dispersed the enemy van. The Danish van then joined the melee between the main bodies. After its arrival, the Danish succeeded in cutting off sixteen Swedish vessels, including seven ships of the line. The cohesion of the Swedish fleet then disintegrated. The ships that remained able began to withdraw from the scene and Niels Juel ordered a general chase.

The Danish victory was as crushing as it was complete. The Swedes lost ten ships of the line and frigates (including seven captured), three fireships, and nine smaller vessels, while not a single Danish ship was lost and only

4. The Battle of Kjöge Bay, 1 July 1677. The melee with which the battle climaxed is captured in this tapestry woven by the Dutch artist Bernt von der Eichen between 1684 and 1692 and now hanging in Christiansborg Castle, the seat of the Danish Parliament. The view is to the south, with the coast of Zealand at right. The boarding action at lower right represents the capture of the Swedish ship *Mars* by the Danish *Tre Lover* (Three Lions). Danish vessels may be distinguished by the twin-tailed pennants bearing a white cross on a dark (red) field. (The Royal Collections, Rosenborg Castle, Denmark.)

four seriously damaged. Swedish casualties amounted to two admirals and approximately 3,000 men made prisoner and 1,500 killed and wounded; the Danish, to 350 killed and wounded.

The very same day that the battle took place Tromp arrived at Copenhagen with the Dutch support fleet. He could actually hear the thunder of Niels Juel's cannons in the distance. A change in the command of the Danish fleet had been very close.

The consequences of the victory were obvious. The supply lines to the Danish army in Sweden were secured, the Danish fleet had retained command of the sea, and the strength of the enemy navy had been significantly reduced. An important long-term result of the battle was the elimination of the Dutch influence on the naval affairs of Denmark-Norway.

Christian V watched the battle from the top of the church steeple in Falsterbo. He was delighted by what he saw. The next day he received a report of the action from Jens Juel, who had observed the fighting from a small vessel belonging to the fleet. The king promoted Niels Juel to lieutenant general-admiral and appointed him a knight of the Order of the Elephant, Denmark's highest distinction. A medal was struck in honor of the admiral and his victory. The inscription reads: "In this way will disturbances in the Baltic be curbed."

Niels Juel's victory attracted attention throughout Europe. Interest was especially evident in London because of the ongoing debate between adherents of the formalist and the meleeist schools of tactics.[17] Which school did the outcome of the battle favor? Many modern historians have viewed the battle as a purely formalist one in which Niels Juel, leading a line ahead, made a classic breakthrough of the Swedish line. A closer reading of the scanty sources to the tactical maneuvers seems to indicate that the breakthrough was rather a "cut off" of some elements of the Swedish formation, which were then destroyed in a melee. Apparently it would be more correct to characterize the battle as a combination of formalist and meleeist tactics. In any case, Niels Juel showed himself to be a great tactician, who lived up to his motto,

NEC TEMERE NEC TIMIDE

which means "Neither rash nor timid." The battle was his masterpiece as a naval commander. He had demonstrated that he was a skilled leader in both peace and war.

The formalities were still respected, and after the battle Tromp resumed command of the Danish navy. However, his position had been made uncertain by Niels Juel's great victory. The allied fleet held control of the sea for the rest of the year, but no major operation occurred.

In the following year, Tromp relinquished his command. The prerequisites of his employment in Denmark had disappeared. The Netherlands was on its way out of the war, and the Battle of Kjöge Bay had convinced King Christian that the Dutch could be eliminated from the naval affairs of his country. In May 1678 Tromp left Copenhagen for good, and on the thirtieth of that month Niels Juel hoisted his flag over a fleet that consisted solely of Danish warships. Their crews welcomed his assumption of command, for the naval knight's even temper and quiet nature had made him popular on the lower deck.

No longer considering the Swedish navy a strategic threat, in the last phase of the war Niels Juel used the fleet to harass the enemy's coast and maritime supply lines. The war began to die down at the beginning of the summer of 1679, and the treaty of peace was signed on 26 September. King Christian expressed his thanks to the navy, whose retention of command of the sea had saved his realm from a number of disasters. Unfortunately for his ambitions, Denmark's successes at sea had been balanced by defeats on land, and the terms of peace simply restored the prewar status quo.

Admiral Henrik Bjelke was relieved of duty as chairman of the admiralty that same year, and from then on Niels Juel was the real leader of the Danish navy. He had been given a seat on the king's council in 1678. When Bjelke died in 1683 Niels Juel formally became chairman of the Board of Admiralty. His path to that post had been difficult and long.

Niels Juel continued to develop the navy and its installations on behalf of the king. A major base was established at Christiansö to observe the new Swedish naval base in Karlskrona on the southern coast of Sweden. The conditions of the crews were improved, and new regulations issued. The enlarged fleet required additional facilities, and in the late 1680s Niels Juel started to fill in an area outside Copenhagen called Nyholm, where a new base was established for the navy. Today the main base of the Danish navy is still located there.

In addition to the honors it brought him, the Battle of Kjöge Bay had made Niels Juel a very rich man. His share of the prize money for the captured Swedish ships was about 25,000 rix-dollars, which corresponded to five times his annual salary as a lieutenant general-admiral. He purchased several estates, most notably Valdemar Castle on the island of Taasinge, south of Fünen. In Copenhagen he bought one of the best plots in the city at the king's New Square. There he built a stately mansion, completed in 1686, which he used primarily as a winter residence. He became as popular with the people of Copenhagen as he had been with his crews, and as he aged they began to refer to him as "The Good Old Knight."

As far as is known, Niels Juel enjoyed a happy family life. One of his sons became a high-ranking government official and maintained the estate of Valdemar Castle. A daughter was married in 1687 to one of his closest colleagues, Admiral Christian Bjelke.

The first reports that Niels Juel's health was weakening date from 1690. That year he worked very hard. The king had ordered him to assess the fitness of all the officers in the navy. In itself this list of evaluations is a remarkable testimonial to the old admiral's good judgment and his knowledge of and care for his officers.[18]

After 1693 Niels Juel underwent a severe physical decline, but he still performed his daily work at the admiralty. The old hero died at 11:00 A.M. on 8 April 1697. His funeral took place on 17 June, with full honors. He is interred in Holmens Kirke, the church of the Danish navy in Copenhagen. Under a relief associated with his sarcophagus there is a long poem, the ninth verse of which is considered one of the masterpieces of Danish literature.[19] It reads as follows:

> Stand, traveller, and contemplate a sea hero of stone,
> And if you are not made of stone yourself,
> pay homage to his dead bones.
> Because you look at Knight Niels Juel,
> whose marrow, bones and blood,
> With ardent heart for his king's honor stood.
> Whose manhood's urges in so many sea battles stand,
> And go honored through sea, air and land.
> A man of older virtues and a sincere and frank Dane,
> Of yes, and no, and what is honest and plain.
> His soul is with God, and his bones in this grave,
> As long as there is water in the seas,
> the remembrances his name will save.

NOTES

1. For a general view of these conflicts, see R. C. Anderson, *Naval Wars in the Baltic during the Sailing-Ship Epoch, 1522–1850* (London: C. Gilbert-Wood, 1910).

2. The most modern and comprehensive treatment of Niels Juel appears in Jørgen H. Barfod, *Niels Juel: Liv og gerning i den danske søetat* (Aarhus: Universitetsforlaget i Aarhus, 1977); see also Hans Christian Bjerg, "Niels Juel," *Dansk Biografisk Leksikon* (Copenhagen: Gyldendal, 1981), VII: 471ff.

3. For Niels Juel's childhood, see Jørgen Lundbye, "Nogle Oplysninger om Søhelten Niels Juels Barndom i Thy," *Historiske Aarbøger for Thisted Amt,* 1909, p. 15.

4. For the development of naval tactics, see Giuseppe Fioravanzo, trans. Arthur W. Holst, *A History of Naval Tactical Thought* (Annapolis: Naval Institute Press, 1979), and Hans Christian Bjerg, "Søtaktikkens Udvikling 1650–1805," *Tidsskrift for Søvæsen,* 1979, p. 209.

5. Barfod, op. cit., pp. 22ff.

6. Finn Askgaard, *Kampen om Østersøen, 1654–1660* (Copenhagen: Nyt Nordisk Forlag, 1974).

7. Ibid., pp. 235ff.

8. H. D. Lind, *Frederik den Tredjes Sømagt: Den dansk-norske Sømagts Historie, 1648–70* (Odense: Milo'ske Boghandel, 1896).

9. Preben Holck, *Cort Adeler* (Copenhagen: Gyldendal, 1934).

10. H. D. Lind, "Marinecommissionen, 1673," *Tidsskrift for Søvæsen,* 1895, pp. 281, 341.

11. About this subject, see Christian Brunn, *Niels Juel og Hollænderne* (Copenhagen: Gyldendal, 1871).

12. Letter of 2 May 1676, Niels Juels korrespondancebog, Søetatens arkiv, Rigsarkivet. See also Barfod, op. cit., p. 144.

13. Th. Bjerre, "Niels Juel og bådfolkets skæbne i slaget ved Lund den 4. december 1676," *Tidsskrift for Søvæsen,* 1957, p. 569.

14. Letter of 13 June 1677 to Admiral of the Fleet Henrik Bjelke; see Barfod, op. cit., p. 180.

15. H. D. Lind, "Da Tromp var i vente, 1677: En historisk Oversigt," *Tidsskrift for Søvæsen,* 1918, pp. 466, 513.

16. For more details on the battle, see Hans Christian Bjerg, ed., *Slaget i Køge Bugt 1. Juli 1677: Forudsætninger, forløb og følger* (Copenhagen: Søe-lieutenant-Selskabet, 1977).

17. The tactical debate is discussed in S. S. Robison and Mary L. Robison, *A History of Naval Tactics from 1530 to 1930* (Annapolis: U.S. Naval Institute, 1942).

18. C. F. von der Recke, "Niels Juells Conduiteliste over Marinens Officerspersonale Anno 1690," *Tidsskrift for Søvæsen,* 1861, pp. 168, 241.

19. The poem was the work of the famous Danish poet Thomas Kingo (1634–1703).

NOTE ON SOURCES

Regrettably, no general history of the Danish navy has yet appeared in English.

The documentary sources to the life and activities of Niels Juel are located primarily in the Danish National Archives (Rigsarkivet) in Copenhagen. Two memorial addresses delivered during the admiral's obsequies and subsequently published also contain a great deal of valuable contemporary information, albeit in a predictably hagiographic style. These are Peter Jespersen, *Ligtale over Niels Juel* (Copenhagen: n.p., 1699) and Marcus Giøe, *Sørgetale over Niels Juel* (Copenhagen: n.p., 1753). For modern biographies, see Jørgen H. Barfod, *Niels Juel: Liv og gerning i den danske søetat* (Aarhus: Universitetsforlaget i Aarhus, 1977); the same author's short English-language survey, *Niels Juel: A Danish Admiral of the 17th Century* (Copenhagen: Marinehistorik Selskab, 1977); and the present author's article, "Niels Juel," in *Dansk Biografisk Leksikon,* vol. VII (Copenhagen: Gyldendal, 1981).

The friction between the Dutch and Danish elements in the Danish navy in the latter half of the seventeenth century is treated in Christian Bruun, *Niels Juel og Hollænderne* (Copenhagen: Glydendal, 1871).

The Battle of Kjöge Bay is examined in detail in Jørgen H. Barfod, *Slaget i Køge Bugt den 1. Juli 1677* (Copenhagen: Marinehistorik Selskab, 1952) and Hans Christian Bjerg, ed., *Slaget i Køge Bugt 1. Juli 1677: Forudsætninger, forløb og følger* (Copenhagen: Søe-lieutenant Selskabet, 1977).

Survey II
The Line of Battle
(1688–1830)

The great sea wars of the classic age of fighting sail were waged between Britain and France. There were seven of them altogether; in effect, three sets of two, punctuated by a grudge-match between the second and third. The first set, the War of the League of Augsburg (1689–97) and the War of Spanish Succession (1702–13), were primarily Continental struggles provoked by the ambitions of Louis XIV.[1] They were followed after more than twenty years of détente by the War of Austrian Succession (1740–48) and the Seven Years War (1756–63). While these, too, were general European conflicts, their Anglo-French aspect included a grand competition for colonial empire. The stinging defeat France suffered in this rivalry prompted her to intervene in the War of the American Revolution in 1778 with the aim not so much of advancing her interests as of injuring Britain's. The success of that expensive undertaking aggravated the chronic fiscal problems that shortly thereafter triggered the overthrow of the Bourbon monarchy. This event in turn led to the last set of Anglo-French wars, those of the French Revolution (1793–1802) and the French Empire (1803–14, 1815), which were actually a single, predominantly Continental contest interrupted by a truce masquerading as a peace.

Among the circumstances that enabled Britain to emerge victorious from all except one of these struggles, none was more important than geography. The critical difference between the antagonists was that an unfriendly army could not reach Britain by marching. Immunity to overland invasion allowed the British to devote the principal portion of their defense expenditures to the navy, whereas the vulnerability of their northern frontier obliged the French to accord the army priority. The level of expenditure made possible by Britain's expanding economy compounded the disparity. Recognizing the advantage to be gained by forcing France to divide her resources, Britain consistently sought and subsidized Continental allies to take the field against her. The one war *perfide Albion* did not bring to a successful conclusion was the one she fought alone—the War of the American Revolution.

Another geographical disadvantage France confronted in her wars with Britain was the possession of two sea coasts separated by the Iberian peninsula. She was therefore compelled to divide her fleet into Atlantic and Mediterranean squadrons, the former based at Brest and the latter at Toulon, and the naval force necessary to screen the great cross-Channel invasion that represented the ideal solution to the problem of defeating Britain could not be assembled unless these squadrons combined—an eventuality against which the Royal Navy was on guard. The failure to carry out or coordinate this combination aborted invasion projects in 1692, 1759, and 1805, and attempts to substitute the Spanish and Dutch fleets for the Toulon squadron were crushed in 1797. Only once did it appear as though the conditions for an invasion had been met. Late in the summer of 1779, with 40,000 troops and their transports waiting in French ports, the junction of the Brest squadron and the Spanish fleet gave the French command of the Channel, but an outbreak of smallpox and scurvy aboard ship forced them to quit the sea before anything could be accomplished.

The instruments of naval warfare and the nature of naval combat proved almost as constant as the coastlines of France. Ships of the line gradually grew larger, finally attaining the maximum length wooden frames could support under existing methods of construction without "hogging" (drooping at the ends). For third rates, this was about 170 feet at the gundeck; for first and second rates, which gained strength from their third deck, approximately 210 feet. Their beam also increased, so that by the end of the eighteenth century first and second rates displaced about a third more than they had at the beginning and third rates almost twice as much. Refinements in their rigging and sail systems enhanced all big ships' maneuverability, and beginning in 1770 the use of copper sheathing and bolts below their waterline prevented accumulations of marine growth from slowing their speed during long deployments. Meanwhile, around mid-century, the 74-gun third rate became the mainstay of the line of battle, from which ships mounting fewer than 60 guns were dropped, and the frigate reappeared as the quintessential cruiser, a 30- to 44-gun fifth rate able to outrun whatever it could not outfight. None of these developments affected a fleet's optimal capabilities to any great extent. It was much the same story with naval ordnance. Although after 1780 several simple innovations, such as flintlock firing mechanisms, facilitated the practice of shipboard gunnery, guns continued to throw the usual types of projectiles the usual short distances. Naval technology held no surprises.

The course of the first Anglo-French war at sea established a strategic pattern that remained essentially unchanged through all the rest. This pat-

9. The Anglo-French Wars.

tern was quite different from that which had prevailed in the Anglo-Dutch Wars. During those conflicts, geography and the Dutch dependence on trade caused both navies to identify battle as their raison d'être: only by fighting could the English close the Narrow Seas to Dutch commerce, and only by fighting could the Dutch keep them open. In subsequent struggles, the Royal Navy continued to pursue a combat strategy aimed at the elimination of the enemy fleet. Initially, the French navy did the same. Its fleets aggressively sought action in the Mediterranean campaigns of the mid-1670s, and at Beachy Head in July 1690 a skillful attack by seventy ships of the line under Vice Admiral Count Anne-Hilarion de Tourville gained the greatest tactical victory a French fleet would ever win, destroying sixteen of fifty-seven Anglo-Dutch ships of the line. That victory was also potentially of utmost strategic importance, for with it came command of the English Channel, but as no preparations had been made for an invasion, the opportunity could not be exploited.

Not quite two years later, in May 1692, the tables were turned. This time the French had laid plans to invade England, but they were bad plans that obliged Tourville to put to sea before the concentration upon which they were predicated could be achieved, under strict orders, personally postscripted by the king, to engage any enemies he encountered, whatever their number. Accordingly, when Tourville with forty-four of the line found himself to the windward of what was obviously a vastly superior Anglo-Dutch fleet—it included ninety-eight of the line—under Admiral Edward Russell off Cape Barfleur, he promptly attacked. The French did remarkably well in the battle itself, sinking two ships without loss to themselves and breaking contact after the allies began to hem them in. But their battered fleet disintegrated during its retreat, and in the following days allied fireships and boat parties destroyed fifteen French ships that had taken refuge at Cherbourg and in the Bay of la Hogue.

Under the circumstances, the defeat did not redound to the navy's discredit. Louis XIV, who was partly responsible for it, took the news well. "I feel more joy," he said, "in knowing that forty-four of my ships fought ninety of my enemies' throughout a day than I do sorrow over the loss I have suffered."[2] Nevertheless, the glorious defeat at Barfleur was the earliest in a succession of events that led to a fundamental and lasting reorientation of French naval strategy: the renunciation of *guerre d'escadre* (literally, squadronal warfare, meaning fleet operations) and the adoption of *guerre de course* (literally, cruiser warfare, meaning commerce raiding). The other events were the financial crisis precipitated by the disastrous crop failure of 1693–94 and the unrewarding outcome of the campaign of 1694, in which the

Brest and Toulon squadrons united to support a French army's offensive on the Mediterranean coast of Spain. Fleet operations had already been suspended when late in 1695 Marshal Sébastian de Vauban proposed the strategy the French navy would follow for more than a century in his *Mémoire sur la course.*

France's foremost soldier, Vauban had become interested in naval affairs two decades earlier while rebuilding the fortifications of Dunkirk. In his *Mémoire* he posited that "up to now people have had an exaggerated idea of the value of a battle fleet, which has completely failed to live up to the hopes that the king placed on it," and seemed unlikely ever to fulfill them against the Anglo-Dutch coalition.[3] What France should do was mount a great *guerre de course:* first, by making every effort to encourage the traditional practice of privateering—the capture of enemy shipping by privately owned vessels licensed to combine patriotism and profit-seeking; and second, by detailing naval vessels and even small squadrons to join the assault on trade. Vauban did not regard this program as a matter of making a virtue of necessity. He believed that besides enabling the war at sea to become self-supporting, it would force England and Holland to their knees in three years. But Vauban did not advocate laying up the main fleet. Merely by remaining in being it would tie down enemy forces that could otherwise be deployed against the *course.* It could also be assigned to perform specific tasks in support of the war effort.

Although he provided their classic exposition, these views were not unique to Vauban. Together with the disappointing experiences that provoked them, they resulted in the rise of a doctrine which held that fighting battles was extraneous to the pursuit of higher strategic goals. After 1695, French admirals did not set out to destroy enemy fleets in order to win command of the sea. They set out to perform some particular mission: to escort a convoy, screen an invasion, aid forces ashore, and so forth. If that mission required them to initiate or accept battle, they would do so most gallantly, but always with a view of getting on with what they regarded as serious business. Suffren was the great exception, and perhaps because of the wreck of the French officer corps in the Reign of Terror, he had no successors.

The results of the *guerre de course* were intrinsically impressive. Though existing documentation does not permit a precise accounting, estimates are that in the War of the League of Augsburg French raiders, public and private, took approximately 4,000 prizes; in the War of Spanish Succession, 4,500; in the War of Austrian Succession, 3,300; in the Seven Years War, 4,000; and in the wars of the French Revolution and Empire, about 11,000. Obviously, the *course* was effective; but it was not decisive. Great as the numbers of prizes appear, and great as the distress they caused, statistically they were almost insignificant. In the wars of the French Revolution and Empire, for example, captures comprised a mere 2.5 percent of the tonnage of the British merchant marine. When in 1807 the success of French arms and the acquiescence of Russia finally gave France hegemony over western Europe, it was Napoleon's inability to exert perceptible economic pressure on Britain at sea that led him to attempt to do so on land, sealing European ports to British trade by the imposition of the Continental System. This measure was probably more than any other single factor responsible for bringing about the collapse of the Franco-Russian entente and setting the Grande Armée on the fatal road to Moscow.

The change in French strategy was reflected in a change in French tactics. In contrast to the British and Dutch, who fired low, into an enemy's hulls, to overwhelm his fighting power, the French fired high, into an enemy's sail system, to cripple his motive power, and unless their mission obliged them to attack, they preferred to fight from the leeward, the position favoring an attempt to disengage. Napoleon supposedly said the trouble with the French navy was that its admirals did not like to be killed, but that was a calumny. Numerous examples could be cited to show that French admirals were quite as brave as their British counterparts. They were simply imbued with a different doctrine.

The development of British doctrine down to the government *Sailing & Fighting Instructions* issued in 1689 was reviewed in the preceding survey. These instructions were reprinted with slight changes by Admiral Edward Russell in 1691 and remained in effect at the time of his victory at Barfleur. In 1702 they were reissued, again with minor alterations, by Admiral Sir George Rooke, who commanded the Anglo-Dutch fleet at Malaga (24 August 1704), the only major sea battle in the War of Spanish Succession. The action occurred when a French fleet hastened to challenge the seizure of Gibraltar by troops Rooke had landed earlier that month. The opposing forces were evenly matched, each including about fifty of the line, but Rooke's ships had expended much of their ammunition bombarding Gibraltar before the landing. In the course of a day's hard fighting, his line foiled French attempts to "double" (envelop) its van and break through its center. Although neither fleet lost a ship, together they suffered nearly 4,500 casualties. That evening a French council of war decided that it would be rash to renew the action with only 126,000 of the fleet's 229,000 cannon shot remaining, unaware that the Anglo-Dutch supply had been reduced to 3,500.

Strategically, Malaga was a major victory for the English, who retained possession of Gibraltar. Tactically, the battle was inconclusive, despite which both parties were well pleased with its outcome at that level: the English for obvious reasons, the French because they inflicted more harm than they sustained and at day's end retained possession of the "field of battle." In consequence, both navies grew more than ever convinced of the wisdom of maintaining a line of battle until the enemy had been put to flight. Once that was accomplished, or if the enemy fled before he had been engaged, formation could be broken to conduct a "general chase."

Malaga was the last stand-up battle—meaning an action between two lines with at least five ships in each—that the Royal Navy was to fight for forty years. In the meanwhile, the instructions Rooke used there had been perpetuated in the Admiralty's printed *Sailing & Fighting Instructions for His Majesty's Fleet,* stocks of which were kept on hand to send admirals readying fleets for sea. Early in the twentieth century naval historians, assuming this document represented official Admiralty doctrine, began to refer to its last half as the Permanent Fighting Instructions. That label is misleading. The "General Printed Instructions," as contemporaries often called them, were not standing orders; they were an administrative convenience, available to spare a newly appointed commander in chief the trouble of producing a set of his own. Not until he issued signed copies to his ship and squadron commanders did they enter into force. Nor was he obliged to adopt the Printed Instructions in exactly the form in which they reached him; he could amend their contents and postscript additional signals and instructions.[4] Indeed, their susceptibility to modification was perhaps as important as the weight of convention in excusing them from thorough-going revision. Be that as it may, the Printed Fighting Instructions, and in particular the seemingly sacrosanct articles relating to actions with enemy fleets arrayed in line of battle, formed the core of British tactical doctrine for more than three-quarters of a century.

Between the wars of Spanish and Austrian succession, the Royal Navy fought only a single sea battle of any sort: Cape Passaro (1718), an exemplary general chase action in which twenty-one of the line under Admiral Sir George Byng virtually annihilated a somewhat inferior Spanish fleet.[5] This interlude was ended by the Battle of Toulon (1744), and by the time of the Battle of the Saints (1782), the Royal Navy had fought no fewer than nineteen major engagements: six general chase actions and thirteen stand-up battles. All six general chase actions were victories.[6] All thirteen stand-up battles were indecisive.[7] Then, beginning with the Saints, where thirty-six of the line under Admiral Sir George Rodney broke a French fleet's line and captured five of the thirty-one ships in it, there was a drumroll of victories in stand-up battles unblemished by the loss of a single British ship: the Glorious First of June (1794), where twenty-five of the line under Admiral Lord

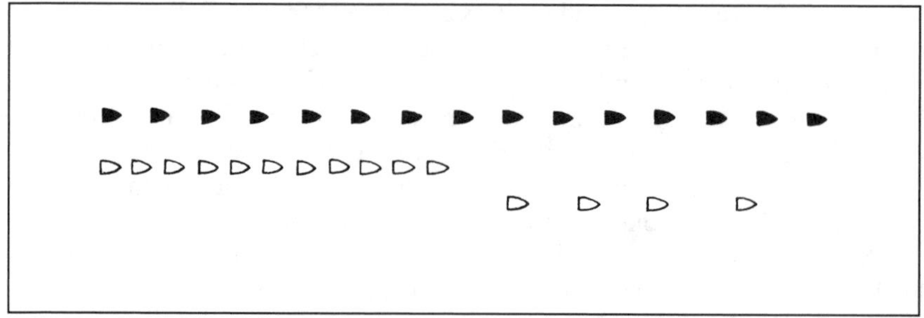

Fig. 1. Massing, in this example against the enemy rear.

Richard Howe broke a French line of twenty-six and sank or captured seven; Cape St. Vincent (1797), where fifteen of the line under Admiral Sir John Jervis (subsequently Earl St. Vincent) broke into a disorderly Spanish formation numbering twenty of the line and captured four of them; Camperdown (1797), where sixteen of the line under Admiral Adam Duncan broke a line of sixteen Dutch ships and took nine; the Nile (1798), where thirteen of the line and a 50-gun ship under Rear Admiral Horatio Nelson doubled an anchored French fleet and captured or destroyed eleven of its thirteen ships of the line; and, finally, the climax at Trafalgar (1805), the apotheois of British sea power, where with twenty-seven of the line Nelson accounted for eighteen of the thirty-three ships in a Franco-Spanish fleet after breaking its line in two places.

A question that has occupied naval historians ever since is why this revolution should have occurred. What had taken place to stimulate the tactical creativity the Royal Navy began to display in the century's closing decades? There had been no inspirational advance in naval weaponry, and everything known about the means of defeating a line of battle in 1797 had been known in 1697, the year Père Paul Hoste, a Jesuit who had served as Tourville's chaplain, published the first great study of naval tactics under sail, *L'Art des armées navales*. There were three possibilities:

- *Massing,* in which the attacker concentrated the principal portion of his line against a segment of the enemy's, reducing the interval between his ships in order to achieve a decisive superiority at that point, while his other ships stretched ahead or trailed astern to contain the remainder of the enemy line (fig. 1).
- *Doubling,* in which the attacker passed a portion of his fleet around one end of the enemy's line in order to take the ships there under a cross fire. Tour-

ville had doubled the allied van at Beachy Head. Hoste favored this tactic, as did the author of the next major tactical treatise, Admiral Viscount Bigot de Morogues, whose *Tactique Navale* appeared in 1763, but both cautioned that it could be practiced only by a numerically superior fleet (fig. 2).

- *Breaking,* in which the attacker penetrated the enemy's line. This maneuver could be carried out by an entire fleet or a portion thereof either to precipitate a melee or to accomplish one or both of the above. It was the method endorsed by the first British work to compare with those of Hoste and Morogues, *An Essay on Naval Tactics,* published in installments between 1782 and 1797 by John Clerk, laird of Eldin, a wealthy Scots merchant who had made a lifelong study of the subject (fig. 3).

Of course, countermeasures could be taken against all of these maneuvers; but for most of the century there was no need for them. After Malaga, no commander on either side attempted to mass against or double or break an enemy line until the War of the American Revolution. Previously, and in

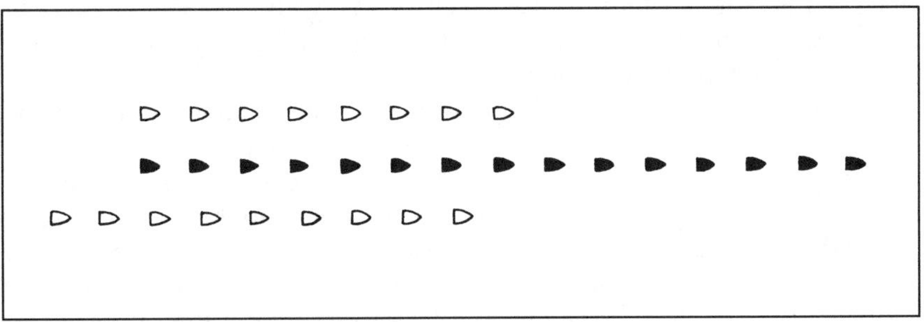

Fig. 2. Doubling, also against the enemy rear.

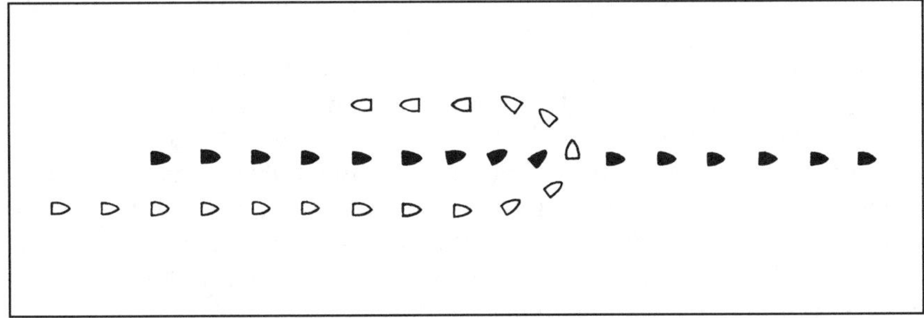

Fig. 3. Breaking, in this example in order to double the enemy rear.

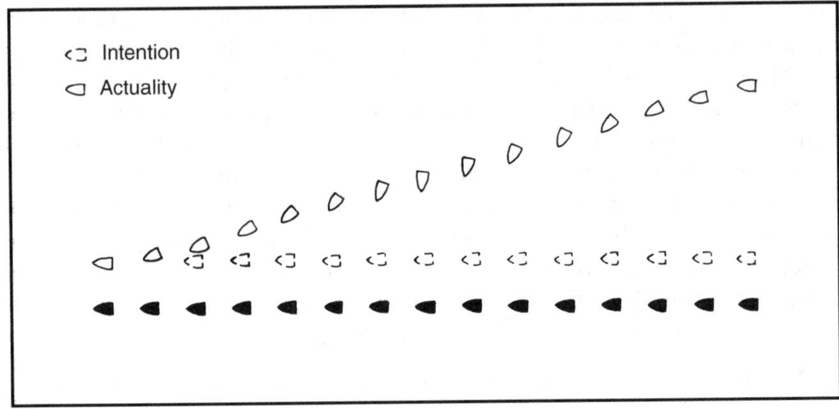

Fig. 4. The difficulty of bringing a line of battle into battle.

some cases thereafter, they sought to engage the enemy in a conterminous line—van-to-van, center-to-center, rear-to-rear, with each ship aligning on its opposite—and even in this, they often failed. Diagrammed on paper, it looks as though nothing could have been simpler. That was not the case at sea. In order to maintain a line's integrity, its leading ship had to be the first to begin to turn toward the enemy. The helmsman of the second ship would wait to put his helm over until he saw her start to come around, the helmsman of the third would wait until he saw the second do the same, and so on down the line. The result was that, instead of keeping parallel to the enemy, the attacker's line would angle toward him in such a way that from a bird's-eye view the two fleets would form a V, with its apex at their vans (fig. 4). Hours might pass before their rears came into action—at times, they never did—and then there was a possibility that the defensive fleet could compel the attacker to repeat the entire procedure by falling away and forming a new line. These were the circumstances that caused St. Vincent to assert, "Two fleets of equal strength can never produce decisive events, unless they are equally determined to fight it out or the Commander-in-Chief of one of them so bitches it as to misconduct his line."[8]

For the Royal Navy's persistence in this unrewarding tactic, the Printed Fighting Instructions were partly to blame. Although most of their thirty-two articles either established discretionary commands or dealt with relatively routine matters, three laid down rules that seriously limited an admiral's options in the conduct of battle.

Article 17 specified that when a British fleet holding the weather gage met an enemy fleet approaching from the opposite direction, it was to make sail until its van drew abreast the enemy rear and its rear abreast his van, at which point it would tack so as to retain its relative position beside the enemy line and continue the engagement on the opposing course. The intent was to prevent contact from being lost after a passing action, but since British fleets normally strove to win the weather gage and enemies inclined to accept battle normally turned toward them, the effect was to ordain the opening move of virtually every engagement.

Article 19, a single pregnant sentence, stipulated that "If the admiral and his fleet have the wind of the enemy, and they have stretched themselves in a line of battle, the van of the admiral's fleet is to steer with the enemy's and there to engage them."[9] This was the prescription for the conterminous line, the disadvantages of which have been noted.

Article 21 prohibited any British ship from leaving the line "till the [enemy's] main body be disabled or run."[10] This made it impossible for any element of a line to exploit a moment of tactical opportunity.

Conspicuous by its absence was an article, last seen in the Duke of York's instructions of 1672–73, for breaking an enemy's line. Although theoretically other articles could have been orchestrated to carry out the maneuver, there was no longer a place for it in the Royal Navy's tactical repertoire.

It has also been argued that the stultifying effect of the Printed Fighting Instructions was increased by the Battle of Toulon or, rather, the courts-martial that followed. In early February 1744 the British Mediterranean Fleet, twenty-eight of the line under Vice Admiral Thomas Mathews, was blockading a Spanish squadron of twelve of the line that had taken refuge in the port of Toulon. Britain and Spain had been at war since 1739. France, though still officially neutral, was expected to intervene at any moment, and Mathews had orders to attack the French as well as the Spanish should they put to sea together. On the morning of 8 February, they began to come out, headed by sixteen French ships of the line. In overall command was the French Admiral la Bruyère de Court. His instructions were to break the blockade but to place the onus for initiating hostilities on the British by having the French ships hold fire until fired upon.

At the time de Court left port, Mathews was anchored in Hyères Bay, east of Toulon. For the next three days, uncooperative winds frustrated both commanders, ruining de Court's plan to trap the British in the bay and thwarting Mathews's efforts to get his fleet into a proper line of battle. Mathews's difficulties were increased by a lack of cooperation from Vice Admiral Richard Lestock, who had apparently resolved that his squadron, bringing up the British rear, would remain several miles astern of the center. According to one account, after the fleet had come to anchor on 9 February, Lestock, a mid-sixtyish man nearly crippled by gout, made what was for him an arduous visit to the flagship to inquire if Mathews had any instructions. In response, the fleet commander observed that it was a cold night and bade him good evening. If this really happened, it would do much to explain the mulishness Lestock demonstrated throughout the ensuing operations.

By the morning of 11 February, Mathews was growing desperate. De Court had succeeded in forming a line of battle the preceding day, while his own van had still not aligned on his center and Lestock continued to lag; and now, with the speed advantage conferred by its ships' clean hulls, the combined fleet was beginning to leave him behind. Around midday, after several vain attempts to shepherd his squadrons into a line, Mathews concluded that it was imperative to bring the enemy to battle without further delay, "tho' in never so irregular a manner."[11] Thereupon, in hopes that the van and rear would conform to his movements, he made the signal to engage and, with the line-ahead signal raised hours earlier still flying, turned his flagship toward the enemy fleet and led the center down on it in a ragged line abreast.

Rear Admiral William Rowley, commanding the British van, took the cue and brought his squadron into action in similar fashion. Since it had fallen too far back to reach the head of the French van, the result was the formation of a distinctly nonconterminous British line opposing a little more than the last half of de Court's fleet. The weight of the attack thus fell mainly on the Spanish squadron. Soon this force found itself hard pressed, its flagship, the *Real Felipe,* heavily engaged by Mathews's flagship and another British vessel, the two ships assigned to support her driven out of the line, and a third captured by an enterprising young captain named Hawke. Lestock inched forward enough for his leading ships to open a long-range fire at the end of the Spanish column, but otherwise took no part in the action. Seeing the trouble at the rear of his line, de Court turned back with the French squadron, recaptured Hawke's prize, and relieved the *Real Felipe.* The numerical disadvantage at which this placed the British van and center, the damage they had suffered, and their disarray left Mathews no choice but to withdraw.

This debacle eventuated in courts-martial of Mathews, Lestock, and eleven captains from the squadrons actually engaged. Although Mathews was found not guilty of some of the fifteen charges against him, he was convicted of enough to be cashiered. His principal offenses, in the judgment of the court, were to have come down on the enemy without first forming a line of battle; to have violated Article 19 of the Printed Fighting Instructions by initiating the engagement at a time when his van was not abreast of the enemy van; and to have endangered his fleet by bringing his flagship into action with the *Real Felipe* while leaving his van to contend with a superior force. He was also censured for failing to maintain contact with the enemy after the battle.

Lestock, charged with seven counts of failing to do his utmost to defeat the enemy, was acquitted of them all. His defense rested on the assertion that Mathews's two signals were mutually exclusive: he could engage the enemy or he could maintain a line ahead, but he could not do both. Under those circumstances, he had decided that his correct course was to maintain the line. Even though informed opinion ascribed the favor this argument found with the court more to Lestock's political influence than the merits of his case, the fact remained: an admiral who had acted on the premise that fighting the enemy was more important than following the rules had been condemned, while an admiral who ostensibly had acted on its opposite had been exonerated.

Of the captains, one died, one disappeared, two were acquitted, and seven were cashiered. Four of those cashiered were found to have evinced insufficient initiative by not bearing down on the enemy, notwithstanding that this would have required them to leave their places in the line—following the rules was not as good a defense for a captain as for an admiral; three to have exhibited an excess of that same quality by stretching ahead of Rowley's line to keep the French from doubling it. Happily, four were later reinstated and two others placed on half-pay.

How these verdicts influenced British tactics in the following decades can be debated. The traditional interpretation is that their effect was wholly negative, leading the Royal Navy's officers to conclude that the safe thing was to adhere to the letter of the Printed Fighting Instructions without regard to the outcome. One respected student of British naval history summed up this view by describing the Toulon courts-martial as the point at which doctrine petrified into dogma.[12] Conversely, an authoritative recent work on the evolution of tactics under sail holds that Toulon and its unpleasant aftermath stimulated the tactical developments that bore fruit later in the century.[13]

Whether or not this is so, they certainly did not stimulate Admiral John Byng at the Battle of Minorca. A son of the victor of the Battle of Cape Passaro, Byng had been among the members of Mathews's court-martial. In April 1756, reports that France was planning to seize Minorca (won by Britain in the War of Spanish Succession) moved the British cabinet to send Byng into the Mediterranean with a small fleet carrying reinforcements for the island. By the time he reached the scene on 19 May, the French had already landed and were besieging Port Mahon. The French fleet screening the invasion appeared almost simultaneously, but night fell before a battle could be arranged.

The next morning, having gained the weather gage, Byng shaped a course that caused the fleets to pass one another on more or less parallel tracks. Both numbered twelve ships of the line, but the French vessels carried a somewhat heavier armament. Byng's force was divided into two divisions rather than the usual three squadrons: a van and rear, the former composed of seven ships under his personal command and the latter of the remaining five under Rear Admiral Temple West.

Byng's maneuver placed him in one of the situations in which the Printed Fighting Instructions specified a commander's next step. In conformity with Article 17, he must wait until his fleet had come fully abreast of the enemy, whereupon he would signal for it to come about to continue the engagement in a conterminous line on the opposite tack. West's division would thus become the British van.

A disadvantage of this maneuver was that it exposed ships making it to a dangerous raking (head-on) fire as they turned toward the enemy. Byng decided to execute a subtle variant. Instead of signaling his fleet to tack the moment its van was even with the enemy rear, he waited until its leaders sailed past it. This would allow his ships to escape being raked by coming up with the enemy from slightly astern.

Unfortunately, Byng had never discussed this maneuver with his subordinates, there were no signals to explain it, and no one in West's division understood what was intended. While the ships under Byng's immediate command angled toward the French line, West's five pressed ahead to overtake and approach it in the customary fashion, with the result that a gap soon opened between the British divisions. This gap increased after characteristically high French fire damaged the sail systems of two of Byng's ships, disordering and delaying the others' advance. In these distressing circumstances, Byng asked his flag captain, Arthur Gardiner, what he thought should be done. Gardiner recommended putting on more sail to get the flagship out of the confusion and into the action. Byng rejected this advice. Pointing out that the signal for the line ahead was flying, he declared, "You would not have me, as the admiral of the fleet, run down as if I were going to engage a single ship. It was Mr. Mathews's misfortune to be prejudiced by not carrying his force down together, which I shall endeavour to avoid."[14]

In the outcome, Byng's division never really reached the battle. West's division suffered considerable damage aloft, and the French continued on their way. Byng lingered off Minorca for four days and then, with the concurrence of a council of war including Admiral West, their ships' captains, and the senior army officers embarked, he withdrew to Gibraltar. Port Mahon fell in June.

The care Byng took to refrain from what had been ruled to be Mathews's mistakes did not avert his court-martial. The charges were that he had not done his utmost to defeat the French fleet and relieve Minorca. He was convicted of both counts, which carried the death penalty. Despite the court's unanimous recommendation that he be granted clemency, none was forthcoming. On 14 March 1757, the admiral was executed by firing squad on the quarterdeck of his own flagship—in Voltaire's famous phrase, "pour encourager les autres." If any moral could be drawn from this lamentable affair, it seemed to be that too much prudence was as unacceptable as too little.

In the meanwhile, however, the Royal Navy had achieved unequivocal victories in three general chase actions: the First Battle of Cape Finisterre (5 May 1747), in which a fleet including seventeen of the line and twelve smaller ships commanded by Rear Admiral George Anson gobbled up an entire French convoy escort—two of the line, four smaller warships, and three armed East Indiamen; Second Finisterre (14 October 1747), in which fourteen of the line under Rear Admiral Edward Hawke took six of eight ships of the line and an armed East Indiaman escorting another French convoy; and Havana (1 October 1748), in which seven of the line under Rear Admiral Charles Knowles captured one of a Spanish squadron of six of the line and hounded another into a bay where her crew burned her.

The experience gained at First Finisterre was reflected in a highly important set of additional instructions issued by Hawke in August 1747, shortly after assuming command of the Channel Fleet. Historians suspect that their fifteen articles actually emanated from Anson, but they were fully consistent with Hawke's outlook, and, in any case, it was their content, not their authorship, that mattered. The three key articles dramatically increased a fleet's offensive potential by providing that in action with a numerically inferior fleet, the ships that overlapped the enemy line were to leave station without waiting for orders (contrary to Article 21 of the Printed Fighting Instructions) and rake its exposed end; that in a general chase, the ships that outstripped the main body were to form a line ahead in order of sailing that would not only engage the enemy rear but endeavor to overtake and delay the van until the slower ships could come up; and that as those ships did so, they would join this ad hoc line without regard to the established order of battle. These articles were added to the printed instructions in 1756. Still, they applied only to enemies who were outnumbered or in flight. The problem of dealing with one who was neither remained unresolved.

Yet the dynamics of combat under sail and the influence of the Printed Fighting Instructions were not solely to blame for the indecisiveness of stand-up battles. The difficulties to which they gave rise continued to be exacerbated by the lack of signals that could do more than indicate articles in sailing and fighting instructions. Failures in communications occurred in five of the thirteen inconclusive actions fought between 1744 and 1782 (Toulon, Minorca, Ushant, Martinique 1780, and the Virginia Capes) and marred two of the six chase victories (Havana and Lagos Bay).

For most of the century, French signals, though equally devoid of intrinsic meanings, were superior to British signals in the wealth of instructions their elaborate tables enabled a commander to convey. Then the French made a wrong turn. In the 1740s a senior officer in the French East India Company's service, Count Mahé de La Bourdonnais, devised a numerical code using ten pennants with which literally thousands of signals could be sent. Bourdé de Villehuet, another East India Company officer, publicized this system in *Le manoeuvrier,* a treatise appearing in 1765. The French navy's leaders were thus presented with the opportunity to introduce truly modern signals. Instead, they preferred an extremely comprehensive but equally complicated model of the traditional system developed by a regular naval officer, the Chevalier du Pavillon. French fleets continued to use Pavillon's or similar signals for years after the Royal Navy had adopted an infinitely more capable numerical system.

Like the period of stasis that preceded it, the tactical breakthrough that took place near century's end was the product of a combination of circumstances. Perhaps the most fundamental was a growing consensus that although maintaining the line was a good way not to lose a battle, it was not a good way to win one; indeed, that sometimes the delay involved in forming a line might make it impossible to bring the enemy to battle at all; and, finally, that, as Lord Howe put it, "Some occasions in our profession . . . will justify, if not require, more hazard than than can be systematically defended."[15] That such sentiments had become current by the War of the American Revolution was evidenced by the century's third great naval court-martial, that of Admiral Augustus Keppel for his conduct of the Channel Fleet at the Battle of Ushant (27 July 1778).

The tactical scenario bore a marked similarity to that of the Battle of Toulon. For four days Keppel, with thirty of the line, had been sparring for a position from which to attack a French fleet of approximately the same strength, which had left Brest on what was meant to be a training cruise. Eventually, on the morning of the twenty-seventh Keppel saw his chance. By then his fleet had become somewhat disorganized, with ships and squadrons out of alignment and at irregular intervals, while the French retained a relatively orderly line of battle, but he did not hesitate to engage. Opening as a straightforward passing action, the battle sputtered to an end after some complicated maneuvers in which the British rear became separated from the rest of the fleet. Though Keppel repeatedly signaled for it to rejoin so that he could renew the action, hours passed before it complied, and by then contact had been broken.

The charges brought against Keppel combined those for which Mathews and Byng had been condemned: one specifying that, like Mathews, he had attacked without having formed an orderly line of battle, which was quite true; and four detailing ways in which, like Byng, he had not done his utmost to defeat the enemy. The court dismissed all five. Its verdict was welcomed by the Royal Navy's officers, who took it to signify that a commander would no longer jeopardize his career by exercising his initiative.

An even greater encouragement to innovation was the electrifying example of the Battle of the Saints (12 April 1782), in which Admiral Sir George Rodney broke a French line in three places. That this achievement was unpremeditated and in part involuntary did not diminish its impact in naval circles. The opposing fleets were fighting a close passing action off Dominica, south of the islets called the Saints, when a sudden shift in the wind forced the French ships to turn toward the British to maintain steerage way. Inevitably, gaps opened between them. Rodney's first captain, Sir Charles Douglas, urged him to seize the opportunity to break the enemy line. After some hesitation the admiral assented, and the flagship and the five ships immediately astern of her passed through the French formation. In the smoke of battle, her next ahead duplicated their maneuver without realizing it until enemy vessels were sighted on both sides. All twelve members of the British rear did the same. A melee did not occur. The ships involved simply sailed through the French line, but the damage they inflicted and the confusion they created made it possible to capture five vessels during the ensuing pursuit. The Royal Navy's first tactical success in a stand-up battle since Barfleur, the Saints showed what could be accomplished by a fleet not bound to the convention of the conterminous line. No more was heard of the old Printed Fighting Instructions after 1783.

The preconditions for the tactical revolution were completed by the introduction of a numerical signal code and dynamic new fighting instructions. Both were provided by Lord Richard Howe. One of the navy's most senior officers, Howe had begun working with signals as a young captain during the Seven Years War. By the time he took charge of the North American Station in 1776 he was ready to reverse the traditional subordination of signals to instructions, issuing the navy's first official *Signal Book for the Ships of War,* with a separate book of instructions as a sort of annex expanding upon the concise "significations" it contained. In 1790, on assuming command of the Channel Fleet, Howe crowned his reforms by the institution of a numerical system based on ten flags numbered 0 to 9. As many as four could be displayed in a single hoist, making it possible to indicate 9,999 instructions, although only a few hundred were actually established.

Howe's initiative was not exactly a bolt from the blue. Villehuet's *Manoeuvrier* had become known in the Royal Navy and several officers besides Howe had devised more or less numerical codes, but he was the first to employ one at sea. Its advantages were immediately apparent, and within a few years his system had been adopted in toto or with minor modifications by every British fleet commander. In February 1797, Jervis used a variant developed in the Mediterranean Fleet at Cape St. Vincent; Duncan used the original at Camperdown later that year; Nelson used the Mediterranean version at the Nile in 1798; and when in 1799 the Admiralty distributed the first signal books for use throughout the navy, it employed Howe's signals and did little more than embroider upon his instructions.

These instructions were also innovative. Placed in command of the Channel Fleet for the first time shortly after the Battle of the Saints, Howe proceeded to issue fighting instructions that included provisions for breaking the line. Other commanders in chief had done the same, but with a difference. They envisioned intersecting the enemy line, with each ship making the penetration at the same point and retaining its position in the line of battle, which would emerge intact on the opposite side—the maneuver projected in the Duke of York's instructions of 1673 and executed in fragmentary fashion by the last half of Rodney's line at the Saints. Howe, in contrast, intended that once his line was ranged beside the enemy's, each ship would turn to pass under her opposite's stern and come about on that vessel's previously unengaged side in order, as the 1799 signal book phrased it, "to break through the enemy's line in all parts. . . ."[16] Not only would this action instigate a melee in which the British rate of fire could be relied upon to prove decisive, when executed from the weather gage it would frustrate the usual French tactic of falling away to the leeward. Howe did not expect that all his ships would get through, but he believed that an enemy vessel would be lost for every one that succeeded.

Innovators are often fated to see others put their ideas into practice. Howe had the opportunity to do so himself. At the outbreak of war with the French Republic in 1793 he was, at age sixty-six, again appointed to command the Channel Fleet, and a year later, at the Glorious First of June, he broke the line of a well-ordered French fleet to the leeward. Of the twenty-five British ships engaged, only Howe's flagship, the 110-gun *Queen Charlotte*, and six others actually forced their way through, but the remainder pushed forward into extremely close quarters. By the end of the melee that followed, six French ships had been captured and a seventh sunk in a victory even greater than the Saints.

For all its capacity, however, Howe's code could not convey a message that had not been, so to speak, prerecorded in his instructions. The breakthrough to extemporaneous communication came with the invention by Captain (later Rear Admiral Sir) Home Popham of the "telegraphic signals" to which he drew attention by a manual of that title (. . . *or Marine Vocabulary*) published in 1803. His system employed the same ten numerical flags already in use. Its first twenty-five numbers designated the letters of the alphabet, one serving for both I and J, which had not quite divorced. The succeeding numbers up to 2000 stood for words especially relevant to naval operations and a final 1000 for sentences and place names—for example, 2529 signified "She sailed in the night."[17] Words not included in the vocabulary could be spelled.

In 1816, a more sophisticated version of Popham's system replaced Howe's as the Royal Navy's signals code. Until then they coexisted, the latter being used to transmit tactical and navigational instructions, and the former for everything else. Without it, Nelson could not have reminded his fleet that "England expects that every man will do his duty" at Trafalgar. Each of the first eight words was indicated by a three-flag hoist; ironically, only "duty" had to be spelled. Nelson's final signal, to "Engage the enemy more closely," was Howe's number 16 and required only a single, two-flag hoist.

In 1731, when Richard Howe was five years old, the British Admiralty issued its first set of *Regulations and Instructions*. The expression of an assertive officialdom's determination to standardize administrative practices throughout the fleet, this publication might serve to symbolize the rationality and expanding sway of eighteenth-century naval bureaucracies. The performance of Europe's admiralties and ministries was far from flawless. Britain's well-financed Admiralty, for example, sometimes let seamen's pay to fall years past due, a leading cause of the disturbances that temporarily paralyzed the Home Fleet in 1797, and in Parliament members often attacked its shortcomings and abuses. Yet to have maintained and managed as successfully as it did what in wartime became the largest and costliest department of state—in June 1812, the Royal Navy had 1,048 ships in commission or under repair—testifies to an underlying efficiency. During Cromwell's Spanish war, inadequate logistical support had made it terribly difficult for the Commonwealth navy to blockade the Atlantic coast of Spain. By the last of the French wars, the level of such support had so improved that, though it grumbled about its victuals, the Royal Navy had little difficulty blockading the European continent.

During the same period, naval officer corps assumed a modern form, with permanent ranks, uniforms, rules (sometimes circumvented) for entry and promotion, standards of conduct, and perhaps most important of all, a sense of corporate identity. Of course, as in the case of administrative hierarchies, much remained to be done before they became truly modern. In Britain political influence could play a critical role in an officer's career, and in pre-revolutionary France a patent of nobility was almost essential; moreover, no mechanism existed to thin out seniority lists by mandatory retirement of the superannuated and the inept. Through no fault of his own, an officer might spend his active life as a lieutenant. Still, the mold had been established. Never again would middle-aged soldiers find themselves commanding fleets. Naval service had become a profession.

NOTES

1. These included the annexation of the Netherlands, which had allied with England at the end of the Anglo-Dutch wars. The Republic preserved its independence, but the strain of fighting France on land and sea overtaxed its resources and its navy fell from the first rank.

2. Ch. de la Roncière and G. Clerc-Rampal, *Histoire de la Marine Française* (Paris: Librairie Larousse, 1934), p. 115.

3. Geoffrey Symcox, *The Crisis of French Sea Power, 1688–1697: From the* Guerre d'Escadre *to the* Guerre de Course (The Hague: Martinus Nijhoff, 1974), p. 183.

4. John Creswell, *British Admirals of the Eighteenth Century: Tactics in Battle* (Hamden, Conn.: Archon, 1972), pp. 28–29; Ruddock F. Mackay, *Admiral Hawke* (Oxford: Clarendon Press, 1965), pp. 57–58, 182–83.

5. The clash resulted from Spain's attempt to recover Italian territories she had lost in the War of Spanish Succession, an enterprise defeated by Austria, Britain, France, and the Netherlands in the War of the Quadruple Alliance (1718–20).

6. First Finisterre (1747), Second Finisterre (1747), Havana (1748), Lagos Bay (1759), Quiberon Bay (1759), and the Moonlight Battle (1779).

7. Toulon (1744), Negapatam (1746), Minorca (1756), Cuddalore (1758), Negapatam (1758), Pondicherry (1759), Ushant (1778), Grenada (1779), Martinique (1780), Cape Henry (1781), Martinique (1781), the Virginia Capes, also called the Chesapeake (1781), and Sadras (1782).

8. Brian Tunstall, ed. Dr. Nicholas Tracy, *Naval Warfare in the Age of Sail: The Evolution of Fighting Tactics, 1650–1815* (Annapolis: Naval Institute Press, 1990), pp. 6–7.

9. Julian S. Corbett, *Fighting Instructions, 1530–1816* (N.p.: Navy Records Society, 1905), p. 192.

10. Ibid.

11. Tunstall and Tracy, op. cit., p. 86.

12. Michael Lewis, *The Navy of Britian: A Historical Portrait* (London: George Allen and Unwin, 1949), pp. 532–33.

13. Tunstall and Tracy, op. cit., p. 91.

14. Alfred T. Mahan, *The Influence of Sea Power upon History, 1660–1783* (Boston: Little, Brown, 1890), p. 187.

15. Rear Admiral S. S. Robison, USN (Ret.), and Mary L. Robison, *A History of Naval Tactics from 1530 to 1930: The Evolution of Tactical Maxims* (Annapolis: U.S. Naval Institute, 1942), p. 412.

16. Corbett, op. cit., p. 255.

17. Brian Lavery, *Nelson's Navy: The Ships, Men and Organisation, 1793–1815* (Annapolis: Naval Institute Press, 1989), p. 261.

6

Edward Hawke

Risk-Taker Preeminent

(1705–1781)

Ruddock F. Mackay

EDWARD HAWKE'S RANKING AMONG THE GREAT NAVAL commanders is securely based. For Britain he won victories over the French in two major conflicts—the War of Austrian Succession (1740–48) and the Seven Years War (1756–63)—which on each occasion proved conclusive. In 1747, as a very junior admiral, he unexpectedly found himself entrusted with command of the Western Squadron, the main British fighting force, at a time when a heavily escorted French convoy was about to sail from Rochefort and Rochelle to the West Indies. By dint of aggressive tactics, Hawke inflicted so sharp a reverse on the enemy that the war at sea was not seriously resumed. After the peace of 1748, continuing Anglo-French colonial rivalry led to the decisive Seven Years War, wherein Hawke played a leading role. If in 1747 a French squadron had fallen rather easily into his clutches, this was far from the case in 1759, when he achieved an overwhelming victory at Quiberon Bay. To that year of British victories Hawke's long blockade of Brest had already made a basic contribution before the onset of autumnal gales allowed the French fleet at Brest finally to escape. With a huge lead, it made for Quiberon Bay, where an army corps was waiting to be conveyed to Scotland. How Hawke managed to catch the French squadron in the nick of time and the breathtaking risks he took to destroy it are examined in the following pages. First, however, it will be useful to sketch Hawke's career and his development as a leader.

Born in 1705, Edward Hawke was the only son of a barrister of Lincoln's Inn who was likewise named Edward Hawke and came of Cornish stock. His mother, Elizabeth, stemmed from the Yorkshire gentry. From 1720, when he began his naval service as a volunteer on board the frigate *Seahorse,* he counted on the patronage of his mother's brother, Lieutenant Colonel Martin Bladen. After seeing active service in the Low Countries, Bladen held a seat in Parliament from 1715 until his death in 1746. Without some connection of this kind, a young naval officer's chances of advancement were slight.

Until 1746, then, the political and social support for Hawke's naval career was fairly adequate. If he proved himself in his profession, he could rise. By 1725 he had been commissioned a lieutenant and by 1733 he was in command of a sloop. Serving mostly in the then-pestilential West Indies, by surviving he had demonstrated the strength of his physical constitution. In 1734 he was posted captain of the frigate *Flamborough* of 20 guns. The following year he returned to England and went on half-pay.

In 1737, at the age of thirty-two, Hawke married Catharine Brooke, who was then seventeen. Four of their children survived infancy. In his family, Hawke was affectionate and well loved. Of gentlemanly but modest bearing, he was a life-long Christian. As an officer, he was forthright but humane. At sea he achieved high levels of fighting efficiency without habitual reliance on punishment.

When war with Spain began in 1739, Hawke was again sent out to the West Indies, this time in command of an aging fourth rate, the *Portland,* 50 guns. He was exclusively involved in protecting trade, especially between Barbados and North America. This entailed refits at Boston during the hurricane season but no encounters with the enemy. By late 1742 he was back in England.

Six months later, Hawke received command of a real ship of the line, the *Berwick.* His orders were to man this new ship of 70 guns and take her out to reinforce the Mediterranean Fleet, then commanded by Admiral Thomas Mathews. When, in January 1744, Hawke joined Mathews in Hyères Road, near Toulon, he was well versed in seamanship, not least in foul weather, and he was practiced in the crucial, though still bewildering, art of maintaining good health aboard ship during extended cruises. Now, at the age of thirty-nine, he awaited his first experience of battle.

At that moment, France seemed about to join Spain against Britain, and a large Franco-Spanish fleet was preparing to sail from Toulon. Mathews had a somewhat smaller but still very considerable fleet of thirty of the line with which he intended to attack the allies if they came out.

On 9 February, the allied fleet emerged. Having spent the tenth getting out of Hyères Bay, on the eleventh Mathews fought the inconclusive and rather discreditable action known as the Battle of Toulon.

While the allies, with a light northeasterly breeze, continued to steer south, Mathews tried to get his fleet into action. The long Franco-Spanish line was forging steadily ahead to starboard of the British, who were badly strung out. Owing in part to the sluggishness of Vice Admiral Richard Lestock, commanding his rear division, Mathews could not match the advance of the allies. Therefore, in breach of the formal rules, he left his line and bore down on the enemy, flying signals for the line and a close engagement in the hope that his captains would do their best to bear down with him. By the time he and some of his disconcerted center division came within gunshot, the French van and center had gone ahead. In this situation, Mathews steered toward the flagship of the Spanish rear. Rear Admiral William Rowley in the van, with Hawke close behind him, tried to bear down on the French center, but the enemy proved evasive. It was only by breaking conspicuously away from the disorderly and hesitant British line that any captain could effectively get to grips.

Hawke alone took the risk. Now that the whole of the French center had sailed out of reach, he bore down on the leaders of the Spanish rear. The *Poder,* 64 guns, predictably edged away to leeward. Hawke not only pursued her but, according to an observer, "he went close under her stern and went up again on [her] lee side, and hauled his wind upon her lee bow and there engaged her till her mainmast fell."[1] An hour later, the Spaniard surrendered. The fact that she suffered very disproportionate casualties says much about Hawke's attention to gunnery in his new ship (which had been difficult to man).

This was the only definite success achieved by either side that day. Long remembered in the British service, it was the product of individual initiative, fighting spirit, good tactical judgment, and outstanding moral courage. Hawke showed himself proof against both the dead hand of formalism and the prevailing uncertainty.

Hawke was now near the top of the captains' list. It was mainly for this reason that Mathews and his successor appointed him to command various squadrons detached from the Mediterranean Fleet during 1744–45. The experience stood him in good stead when, a year or so later, prime responsibility was suddenly thrust upon him.

Meanwhile, evidence about Hawke's conduct off Toulon was a bright feature in the courts-martial of Mathews and a number of others for their ineffectiveness in that action. Yet when in 1747 Hawke fell due for promotion to rear admiral, he was nearly passed over. The reason was that his uncle and only patron, Colonel Bladen, had died the year before. Had it not been for the personal intervention of King George II, who refused to have *his* captain "yellowed"—that is, placed among the superannuated rear admirals—Hawke's active career would have terminated when he was only forty-two! Under the conventions of the time, Hawke's outstanding, if unorthodox, performance off Toulon did not enlist enough Admiralty support to ensure his promotion.

On his promotion in July 1747 Hawke took up the potentially unexciting command at Plymouth. Since 1744, however, the strategic picture had radically changed. The French government, preoccupied with the continental aspects of the war, concentrated its available money on the army and, by 1747, France's beleaguered colonies were withering for lack of replenishment by sea. In May, Vice Admiral George Anson demolished the sizable escort of a French convoy. By July the Admiralty knew that another convoy for the relief of the French West Indies was preparing in the Biscay ports.

Since 1745 the Western Squadron, on the moderate scale now sufficient to control the Channel and the Bay of Biscay, had been reestablished as the main British naval force. After his victory Anson was succeeded in the command by Vice Admiral Sir Peter Warren. Early in August, however, Warren put into Plymouth, incapacitated by scurvy. The Admiralty found that only the junior rear admiral at Plymouth was instantly available to act in his place. Loaded with instructions from Warren and the Admiralty, Hawke duly went out and took command of the squadron, consisting of a dozen or so ships of modest power.

After cruising for sixty-four days, Hawke intercepted the French fleet west of Ushant in the meridian of Cape Finisterre. The ensuing battle, fought on 14 October, is usually known as the Second Battle of Cape Finisterre (Anson's victory in May being the First). Here Hawke's characteristics as a battle-winner were unmistakably demonstrated. While the French convoy's escort amounted only to eight of the line against Hawke's fourteen, those eight were of superior power, with five of them carrying a heavier armament and a larger crew than the most powerful British ship.

As Hawke approached from the leeward, the French sailed close-hauled in a line ahead, hoping that he would conform and exchange broadsides at some distance while the convoy escaped. To their consternation, Hawke proceeded to handle his squadron in the aggressive spirit he had shown off Toulon. Although he was commanding only as Warren's deputy, in daily expectation of being superseded, he made the boldest possible use of the articles in the Fighting Instructions relating to the "chase." These freed individual captains from the rules for a formal battle. The result was a progressive envelopment of the French line, from rear to van, with Hawke himself setting a fine example. Six French ships were taken. British domination of the seas was now complete and irreversible for the duration of the War of Austrian Succession.

By the coming of peace in 1748, Hawke had been made a Knight of the Bath and promoted to vice admiral. At the unofficial start of the Seven Years War in 1755, he supervised the mobilization of the fleet at Portsmouth and put to sea in command of the Western Squadron. With intermissions, he continued in this post till 1762. Anson, First Lord of the Admiralty since 1751, saw the squadron as the strategic key to success in the war as a whole. As long as it covered the approaches to the Biscay ports, a French invasion of the British Isles was impracticable and the French colonies could be taken one by one.

The year 1759 proved decisive. From May to November, Hawke maintained a close blockade of Brest, where a squadron was getting ready to cover an invasion of Britain. Beyond this blockade, which was extended by posting light squadrons farther down the Bay of Biscay, Quebec lay at the mercy of British forces. At the same time, French seaborne trade was greatly constricted while Britain's flourished.

During these months on blockade, with his main force near Ushant constantly ready to act on intelligence supplied by the inshore squadron off

Brest, Hawke amply confirmed that he possessed qualities adequate to his task—patience, tenacity, and administrative grasp. He soon assured the Admiralty that he would enforce a blockade that would be not only continuous but close—except, of course, when the main squadron was blown off station by hard westerly gales. If the wind veered easterly, the enemy might be able to emerge before Hawke's return. When in June Hawke was forced to bear away to Torbay, the French were not ready to sail. He then settled down to the task of keeping twenty or more ships of the line, together with detached cruisers and frigates, continuously at sea off the notoriously dangerous Biscay coast and in a high state of fighting efficiency. While under Anson's capable direction the Admiralty and supply services made unprecedented efforts to sustain a policy that was hard on both ships and men, out in the Bay of Biscay Hawke saw to it that the policy worked. He kept a grip on the movement of reliefs and supplies. Scurvy and other familiar ills did inevitably make themselves felt, but on the day of battle in November the general level of health and morale remained exceptional.

At length, on 11 October, a hard gale blew from the west-southwest and forced Hawke to bear up a second time, on this occasion for Plymouth. He assured the Admiralty that he would be back off Brest before the French could make their intended move to Quiberon Bay, where General d'Aiguillon was waiting with his expeditionary corps. Indeed, on 20 October he found them still in port.

Hawke was now an Admiral of the Blue, aged fifty-two. His French opponent, Count Hubert de Conflans, who had done well in the previous war and had just been promoted to the top French rank of marshal, was some twelve years older. By October the enthusiasm that Conflans had felt for his mission—in part his own brainchild—had finally evaporated. An attempt to reinforce him with twelve ships of the line from the Toulon squadron had been defeated by Admiral Edward Boscawen at the Battle of Lagos Bay in August. Moreover, the Brest squadron was manned largely with sailors devoid of naval experience. Hawke's persistent attentions had checked any attempt to exercise the French squadron as a unit and, if the British for the moment had been driven away, the swift reappearance of the inshore squadron implied that Hawke would soon be back a few miles out to the northwest. In sum, Conflans no longer believed in his mission: that he could slip out of Brest, penetrate the northerly recesses of Quiberon Bay, collect the transports, escort them as far as the northern coast of Ireland, detach a division to see them into the Firth of Clyde, and return with his other two divisions to Brest. By 20 October Hawke had duly returned, despite the prospect of autumnal gales, and 5 November found Conflans writing to the navy minister, Berryer, that his basic intention was to avoid a fleet action.[2]

On 6 November a great gale began to blow at northwest. Hawke's squadron struggled against it but by the tenth was forced to put into Torbay. In a dispatch to the Admiralty Hawke admitted the possibility that the enemy might get out and push for Quiberon "with their whole squadron."[3] He did not need to say that, in that event, he would do likewise. All the intelligence pointed to the Morbihan, an almost landlocked harbor on the northern shore of Quiberon Bay, as Conflans's objective.

By 12 November Hawke was able to get his squadron out of Torbay, but that night a hard gale at southwest blew him back in. The damage was considerable and on the fourteenth he had to shift his flag from the *Ramillies* to the *Royal George*. During that period, links between admirals and their flagships (like those between captains and their ships' companies) were close and Hawke had worn his flag in the *Ramillies* since 1757. Nevertheless, his transition to the *Royal George* was accomplished without discernible upset. She was quite a new ship of 100 guns, designed as a flagship. Her commander was John Campbell, a Scot without a patron who had caught Anson's eye and, since then, had deservedly advanced in the service. When Hawke came on board, it meant a sharp step down for Campbell from the private command of a first-rate ship to be the admiral's flag captain, but such was Hawke's directness of manner and professional stature that no personal difficulties arose. The problems Admiral George Rodney experienced in 1762, when he wished to shift his flag aboard a ship commanded by the same Robert Duff who served prominently under Hawke in 1759, vividly illustrate the tensions so easily generated on such an occasion.[4]

On 14 November Hawke (like Conflans) found the wind favorable, but that same afternoon he had to send Rear Admiral Francis Geary and his scurvy-ridden flagship into Plymouth. To act as commodore commanding the rear division, Hawke appointed a senior captain, James Young of the *Mars*, 74 guns. In this case, too, the British performance on the day of battle suggests that neither morale nor efficiency suffered from the unavoidable last-minute change. In terms of spirit and cohesion, a more complete contrast with the half-heartedness of Mathews's fleet off Toulon in 1744 could scarcely be imagined.

On the same day (the fourteenth), Conflans sailed from Brest with twenty-one of the line and four frigates. In his race against Hawke to reach Quiberon Bay, he had a start of 200 miles with only 120 miles to go. What both admirals wanted was a favorable westerly wind. The fact that it was slow to come improved Hawke's chances. During the next six days, the seamanship of the two squadrons was put to the test.

For the first five days Conflans was annoyed by contrary winds, but he did not, on the evidence of his later dispatch,[5] seriously envisage the possibility that Hawke could catch up with him before he found safety in Quiberon Bay. His recent accession of some experienced seamen may have made him feel that his lead was unassailable. On 15 November he reached a position only some thirty miles short of the west end of Belle Isle.[6]

The next day, however, an easterly gale arose, and without appreciating the possible consequences, the French bore up and ran before it to the west. By 18 November, with the wind lighter but still easterly, they were again working up toward Belle Isle. Throughout the day some of them could be seen to leeward by the British frigate *Vengeance,* which was off the northwesterly tip of Belle Isle.[7] On the nineteenth, at 11:00 P.M., Conflans noted that the wind was at last beginning to blow from a westerly quarter and shortened sail in order to avoid nearing Belle Isle before daylight. He intended to carry his squadron into Quiberon Bay and make for the Morbihan the following day.

However, at about 7:00 A.M. on 20 November, Conflans discovered some British ships ahead of him, not far south of Belle Isle. He correctly identified them as belonging to the light inshore squadron commanded by Commodore Robert Duff. Since late summer, they had been watching the entrance to the Morbihan, wherein General d'Aiguillon's transports lay. Duff's eleven ships—mostly frigates and sloops—had contrived to escape from Quiberon Bay through the Teignouze Passage (which was apparently unknown to the French).[8] It was not reassuring to meet Conflans in full force, but Duff had at least found room in which to run.

With fresh gales blowing from west-southwest and Duff's ships starting to run north and south, Conflans saw no reason why he should not signal a chase. But no sooner had he begun the pursuit than sails began to appear behind him, crowding down before the wind. How had Hawke achieved this critical surprise? And with what tactical intentions did he come?

On 14 and 15 November, with the wind at northeast, Hawke had made good progress toward Ushant. On the sixteenth he sent the 18-gun sloop *Fortune* to warn Duff against being surprised and trapped by the Brest squadron, directing him to station some ships to watch the approaches to Belle Isle. However, these orders did not get through. The *Fortune* soon encountered the *Hébé,* a French frigate of 40 guns that had been damaged in the gale on the sixteenth and had lost touch with Conflans's fleet. In a hard-fought action the *Fortune* was heavily damaged and her acting captain killed.

That evening Hawke was about forty-five miles west-northwest of Ushant when he met a victualler returning home from Quiberon Bay. The master reported that the French fleet had been seen on the fifteenth some sixty-five miles west of Belle Isle with the wind easterly; also, that the captain of the frigate *Juno,* having been chased by the French earlier that day, had detached the sloop *Swallow* from the victuallers and sent her to warn Duff.

It was during the night of the sixteenth, while Conflans was running before an easterly gale, that Hawke began to catch up with him. In Hawke's vicinity the wind, having been at southeast, freshened to a hard gale at south-southeast. Despite this unfavorable development, whereby he was inevitably driven westward, he was able to report to the Admiralty on the seventeenth that he had "carried a pressure of sail all night" and that he made "no doubt of coming up" with Conflans "either at sea or in Quiberon Bay." On the strength of the victualler's information, he added that Conflans had eighteen of the line and three frigates, while he had twenty-three of the line and one frigate.[9]

From Hawke's point of view, this piece of intelligence was rather convenient. It exaggerated the disparity between the two fleets, insofar as Conflans actually had twenty-one of the line, and it therefore encouraged the idea of using the chase. In any case, Hawke's conduct as a captain off Toulon in 1744 and as an admiral on 14 October 1747 suggests that he was bent on fighting the closest possible action and argues that he hoped, once again, to make the fullest use of the chase allowed by the Fighting Instructions. From his experience in 1747 he knew that a general chase tended to produce superiority of force against the rear of a retreating enemy line. If, on the other hand, the French doubled back and outnumbered his leading ships for a time, he relied on superior seamanship and a quicker rate of fire to meet the contingency. So much may be readily inferred from his own past record and from his conduct, so free from any sign of hesitation, during the battle to come.

On 17 November, while Hawke was being driven to the west of Ushant, the sloop *Swallow* encountered Captain John Reynolds of the *Firm,* 60 guns, who, with two frigates, was watching Port Louis. Reynolds had recently been with Duff in Quiberon Bay and forthwith dispatched the *Vengeance,* 28 guns, as more likely than the *Swallow* to carry the warning to him in good time.[10]

By noon on the eighteenth Hawke reckoned that he was about forty miles southwest of Ushant.[11] The wind had veered right round to northeast and he could stand almost directly toward Belle Isle, which lay not much more than one hundred miles to the west-southwest. However, at noon on the nineteenth he was still some seventy miles west of Belle Isle. Like Conflans, he was now contending with variable easterly winds.

Meanwhile, the *Vengeance,* which had watched the French fleet working up toward Belle Isle on the eighteenth, was negotiating the north coast of the island. By 10:00 A.M. on the nineteenth she sighted Duff's squadron at anchor in Quiberon Bay. Her captain, Gamaliel Nightingale, thereupon "made the signal of seeing an enemy of superior force and fired minute guns." At 3:00 P.M., with the wind at southeast, he could see Duff's ships making sail for the difficult Teignouze Passage but he persisted with his warning guns for a further hour. During the night, the wind veered round to west and freshened to a gale, but by daybreak Duff and all his ships had rounded the west end of Belle Isle. Soon after 7:00 A.M. they sighted the enemy fleet to the southwest and scattered with the French in pursuit. But Conflans was about to suffer his first surprise.

On 17 November Hawke still had only a single frigate in company but had since, to his satisfaction, been joined by the *Maidstone* and *Coventry*, both of 28 guns. These frigates he had posted ahead of the squadron. When, during the night of the nineteenth, the wind veered to the west, he rode before it for a few hours. From 3:00 to 7:00 A.M. on Tuesday, 20 November, he and his squadron lay to. Estimating that Belle Isle lay not many miles to leeward, he waited for daylight before making his final—and decisive—dash for Quiberon Bay.

Soon after 7:00 A.M. the British were again crowding sail before the fresh gales and hard squalls that continued to blow from west-northwest throughout the morning. At 8:30 the *Maidstone* let fly her topgallant sheets to signal a fleet ahead. Her report was repeated by Captain Richard Howe in the *Magnanime*, 74 guns, in the van of the main body, and Hawke at once signaled for a line abreast. This had the effect of getting the squadron together in the interest of cohesion and control, but it did not appreciably retard its advance, according to the masters* of the *Royal George* and *Magnanime*.[12] Toward 9:45 the *Magnanime* confirmed that the ships ahead comprised an *enemy* fleet. Soon afterward, Hawke hoisted the crucial signal to which he steadfastly adhered throughout the day. In the words of his subsequent dispatch: "Observing, on my discovering them, that they [the French] made off, I threw out the signal for the seven ships nearest to them to chase and draw into a line of battle ahead of me and endeavor to stop them till the rest of the squadron should come up, who were also to form as they chased, that no time should be lost in the pursuit."[13]

This statement closely follows the wording of the Additional Fighting Instructions of that date. These provided for a white flag with a red cross to be hoisted at the admiral's main topmast head when he wanted the whole squadron to chase. If he also fired three guns, his first seven ships would, regardless of order, form a line ahead while doing so. Upon reaching the enemy's rear, they were to engage it until more ships came up. Then they would sail ahead up the enemy's line. Insofar as Anson, as First Lord of the Admiralty, had been very active in revising the Fighting Instructions, Hawke took some trouble to show how he had used the rules relating to the chase.

In 1758, after an unfortunate brush between Hawke and the Admiralty, Anson had taken command of the Western Squadron for some months and given high priority to tactical training. For some of that time Hawke had served as second-in-command. While Hawke himself always emphasized the

* The master was a specialist officer responsible for sailing and navigating his ship.

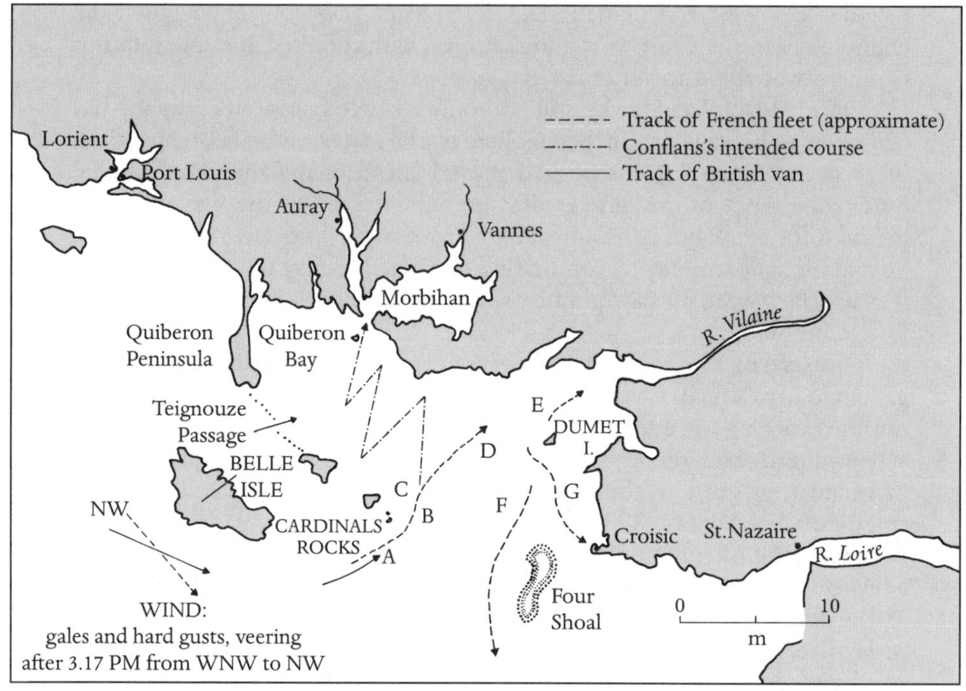

10. The Battle of Quiberon Bay, 20 November 1759. (A) At about 2:45 P.M., Hawke's van engages the French rear. (B) At 3:17, the French line is thrown into disorder by a hard northerly gust, after which the wind is at northwest. (C) From 4:00 to 5:00, a pell-mell action is fought between here and Dumet Island. (D) At 5:30, Hawke anchors here. One group of French ships (E) stands toward the Vilaine, while another steers for Rochefort (F) and after dawn the *Soleil Royal* runs for Croisic (G).

simple virtues of a very close engagement, brought on as swiftly as possible, Anson can doubtless be credited with some of the doctrine underlying his signals on 20 November. In the days of sail such intimate dependence on the freaks and fluctuations of the wind enhanced the merits of an aggressive yet flexible tactical philosophy that did not rely on complex instructions or an elaboration of doubtfully visible signals. Hawke assumed high standards of seamanship, morale, and gunnery in each individual ship, and within the bounds set by his simple orders, his fighting spirit, and his personal example, once battle was joined he set each captain free to do his utmost.

When at about 10:00 A.M. Conflans learned of the appearance of Hawke's squadron, he promptly called off his pursuit of Duff. Most of Duff's ships soon joined Hawke and became, in effect, privileged observers of the ensuing events. Just as Hawke had decided well before the battle on his likely course of action, so had Conflans decided on his. Louis XV had impressed on him that the first priority was the safety of the transports awaiting him in the mazelike anchorages in the Morbihan below Vannes and Auray. On reaching Quiberon Bay, Conflans was expected to destroy Duff's squadron but not to do battle with Hawke.

Despite these instructions, Conflans proceeded to invest time in trying to form a line ahead. While his objective was the Gulf of Morbihan, he assumed that he would be able without interruption to lead his line round the Cardinals Rocks into Quiberon Bay. Believing that Hawke had as many as thirty of the line and knowing that he faced unfamiliar dangers in such confined waters, it seemed obvious to Conflans that Hawke, too, would pause to form his line before following the French into Quiberon Bay. What with the gales and intermittent hard gusts, the possibility that Hawke would chase in after him pell-mell simply did not occur to him. Having got his squadron safely into the bay, Conflans intended to execute a series of tacks to the northwest. If Hawke followed, he would be able to fight a defensive action from windward not far south of the Morbihan.

All this helps to explain why Conflans did not see a fleet action in the open sea south of Belle Isle as a serious option. As he remarked in his dispatch of 24 November, he stood no chance of getting to windward of Hawke. Had Conflans stood in a line of battle toward the south or southwest, Hawke would probably have kept the chase signal flying and have progressively swallowed up the French line, from rear to van, as in 1747. Moreover, Hawke would have been given more time for fighting before night fell—perhaps as early as 5:00 P.M. In sum, Conflans would doubtless have lost more ships, and Hawke fewer, had the battle been fought in the open sea south of Belle Isle.

While Conflans bore away for the Cardinals, Hawke, impelled by very fresh gales at west-northwest, set every sail he could. Topsail reefs were shaken out and even topgallant sails were set. According to Thomas Conway, master of the *Royal George,* a speed of nine knots was achieved between 11:00 A.M. and noon. The flagship was heading due east. At noon, she was still some fifteen miles southwest of Belle Isle.[14] Up ahead was Augustus Keppel in the *Torbay,* 74 guns, one of the seven leading ships. By his reckoning, at noon the northwestern tip of Belle Isle lay north by east at nine miles distance and the French fleet, at east by south, was some nine miles ahead of him.[15] So Hawke was probably a good dozen miles behind the French rear at this stage, but as the gap between the fleets steadily diminished, most of the imperfectly formed French line could be discerned from his quarterdeck.

By 2:00 P.M. it was observed that Conflans's flagship, the *Soleil Royal,* 80 guns, had rounded the Cardinals. The gales continued at west-northwest at speeds of more than forty miles an hour. The waves were high, densely streaked with foam, and with their crests rolling over. (The paintings done some years later by Serres and Paton understate the sea that was running.) Ships suffered damage to canvas, yards, and rigging as they pressed ahead under a crowd of sail. The master of the *Royal George* put her speed between noon and 2:00 P.M. at a constant eight knots. She had set topgallant sails soon after the chase began and her example was enthusiastically followed by the fleet. The *Magnanime*—well up among the leaders—carried away her main topgallant yard. While repairs were being effected Howe, in tune with the spirit prevailing in the fleet, exhorted his men to hold their fire till they could touch the muzzles of the enemy's guns.[16] Despite the delay, the *Magnanime* was one of the first ships to get into action with the French rear.

Knowing by 2:00 P.M. that Conflans was leading his van into the bay beyond the Cardinals, Hawke did not shift from his resolve to persist with the chase. He was about to hazard the main British battle fleet among the countless hidden rocks and shoals in Quiberon Bay. The French would serve as pilots. The time when, to quote a contemporary seaman's verse, "Hawke did bang/Mounseer Conflang" had now come. Seldom in history has an admiral acted with such audacity.

At 2:45, Hawke could see that his leading ships had come up with three ships of the French rear division and were opening fire. He thereupon hoisted the red flag for a general engagement and kept it flying just below the chase signal till the end of the day. Conflans had so seriously misjudged the relative speeds of the two squadrons that his last three ships had been cut off outside the Cardinals. As Midshipman Edward Pakenham of the *Dunkirk,* 60 guns, noted in his journal, the French "were under an easy sail all day, yet we were carrying all the sail we could crowd from 7 in the morning to near 3 in the afternoon before we got up with them."[17]

Not long after 3:00 P.M., when Hawke was still a few miles from the Cardinals, the wind suddenly changed. By that time Conflans and his first two divisions had advanced, as he afterward reported, a considerable distance into Quiberon Bay, close-hauled on the larboard tack. Then there was a hard northerly gust, after which, according to Conflans, the continuing fresh gales came from north-northwest instead of west-northwest. The French line, never perfectly formed, was thrown into great disorder. Among the British, too, there were repercussions. Nightingale of the *Vengeance,* one of the frigate captains standing clear of the action, was well placed to observe developments. He had noted "the French fleet ahead under an easy sail." Then, at "17 minutes past 3 a very heavy squall came on at North." This caused the *Chichester,* 70 guns, to lose a topsail yard and three other ships to run afoul of each other, incurring damage and loss of way.[18]

According to Hawke, for the rest of the day the wind blew from the northwest, though Conway, the flagship's master, agreed with Conflans in putting it at north-northwest. Even without the gales and heavy sea, a ship of the line could hardly be made to sail within 70 degrees of the wind. Conflans was therefore constrained to steer approximately northeast and contemplate a revised series of tacks. But this alone need not have made him abandon his basic plan. What was now bothering him a great deal was the amount of sail that the British continued to carry, despite the circumstances. They kept coming up to leeward, often in superior numbers. Conflans, sharing the French predilection for formalism, was also much upset by the disorder into which his line had fallen on the abrupt change of wind. But, above all, he finally accepted that Hawke, far from forming a line of battle, was determined to persist with his barely credible chase.

Conflans thereupon jettisoned his own plan and hoisted the countermarch signal. He was then probably about six miles west-northwest of Dumet Island. His flagship managed to go about by tacking, but a number of ships in the van division failed to duplicate this evolution and lost much ground by having to wear. Consequently, for the rest of the battle there was no single French line, though Conflans was followed by about a dozen ships. Still, it is difficult to see, as has often been alleged, that his reversal of course was a tactical error. Swarming into the bay, the British no longer found it a simple matter to cluster in superior numbers to leeward of the French as they slowly advanced in their rather irregular line.

Meanwhile, by 3:55 Hawke in the *Royal George* had got around the Cardinals. Seeing the *Formidable,* 80 guns, flagship of Saint-André du Verger, *chef d'escadre* of the French rear, surrounded by British ships, Hawke pressed on into Quiberon Bay. To his great satisfaction, the *Soleil Royal* could be clearly seen heading back toward him. Hawke at once ordered Thomas Conway to place the *Royal George* alongside the French admiral. According to tradition, it was then that the master represented the dangers involved and Hawke replied: "You have now done your duty in apprising me of the danger, let us next see how well you can comply with my orders. I say, lay me alongside the French admiral."

Whatever was said, Hawke had already taken the really big decision to persevere with the chase, despite the dangers to his whole fleet, some hours earlier. By 1:00 P.M. it was clear that Conflans was leading his extended line toward the Cardinals and Quiberon Bay. During the next two hours, the perils of the pursuit were squarely faced by Hawke, and it would be surprising if there was no conversation on the subject between him, flag captain Campbell, and Conway. Before 3:00 P.M. they could see the French rear being fiercely attacked. To confirm and reinforce the chase signal, Hawke added the red flag for a general engagement. Nonetheless, as the rival flagships converged, Conway may well have made some remark to Hawke about the danger, in that Dumet Island lay not far to the northeast.[19] Certainly

Hawke's response, as quoted above, was characteristic. As at Second Finisterre, there was nothing he wanted more than a direct confrontation with the French admiral.

Soon after 4:00 P.M. Hawke knew that the *Formidable* ("pierced like a cullender," according to one observer[20]) had struck to the *Resolution*, which came up after the *Magnanime*, *Torbay*, and several others had left her shattered. He was also aware that another French ship of the line had sunk—an event quite exceptional in battles fought under sail. In the melee that developed northeast of the Cardinals, the *Thésée*, 74 guns, had been hotly engaged with Keppel's *Torbay*. Firing her main battery while to windward, the *Thésée* was caught by one of the recurrent gusts and rolled onto her beam ends. The sea poured into her lower gun-ports and she rapidly foundered. Though Keppel apparently had his leeward ports closed, he also shipped much water. "I immediately hoisted out the boats," Keppel noted, "and sent them to the wreck to endeavour to save as many people as they could."[21] In the tempestuous conditions, his boats, with those from other ships, did well to save twenty-nine men.

Meanwhile, Conflans, heading back toward the entrance of the bay, opened fire on some British ships that were handing out severe punishment to the *Juste*, 70 guns. In the flagship's wake came the Chevalier de Bauffremont, flying his *chef d'escadre*'s flag in the *Tonnant*, 80 guns, and a dozen other ships. Hawke entered action by 4:35. At his approach, Conflans and the ships following him wore and fired broadsides at the *Royal George*. Hawke closely engaged the *Superbe*, 70 guns, a mile or two west of Dumet Island. On receiving his second broadside at 4:41, the *Superbe* abruptly sank.[22] Hawke pressed ahead and tried to rake the *Soleil Royal* but was frustrated by the *Intrépide*, 70 guns. Conflans hoped to lead his ships out into the open sea but, as he maneuvered, two of them fell aboard him and he was carried some way to leeward of Dumet Island in the direction of the little port of Croisic. The light was fading and, realizing that he could not weather the Four Shoal, he anchored not far from Croisic.[23] The *Héros*, 74 guns, anchored nearby. Belonging to the French rear division, she had earlier been hammered into submission, but the weather was so bad that a boat could not be sent to take possession of her.

Bauffremont, with the rest of the ships following Conflans, had hauled his wind at about 5:00 P.M. and avoided being embayed. During the night he led several ships out of the bay and made for Rochefort. Altogether, eight French ships of the line reached that port.[24] Another group consisting of seven of the line and two frigates steered in the opposite direction. Having weathered Dumet Island, they anchored off the mouth of the Vilaine. The river was difficult of access but offered a possible refuge if the ships could be sufficiently lightened.

5. The Battle of Quiberon Bay, 20 November 1759. This view of the action was painted in 1779 by Dominic Serres, who took great care to ensure the technical accuracy of his compositions. In the center, Hawke's flagship, the *Royal George,* enters action flying his plain blue flag (of an admiral of the blue) on her main topmast head and the chase signal above that for action on her fore topmast head. The French *Intrépide,* immediately to the flagship's right, may be seen thwarting her attempt to rake the *Soleil Royal,* next right, which flies Conflans's white French admiral's flag at her topmast head. (The National Maritime Museum, Greenwich, England.)

At 5:00 P.M. or a little later, as night was falling, Hawke made the signal for the fleet to anchor. The *Royal George* was then rather more than two miles west by south of Dumet Island. The British were, as Hawke wrote, on a coast of which they were "totally ignorant, without a pilot, as was the greatest part of the squadron," and it was "blowing hard upon a lee shore."

Despite the shortness of the day, much had been achieved. A flagship of 80 guns had been captured and two other ships of the line had been sunk. The French fleet, on which widespread damage had been inflicted, was irrevocably split and could expect to suffer further losses. So successfully had Hawke's ships used the French as pilots that not one had been lost during the hours of daylight.

At daybreak the wind was still blowing hard from the north-northwest. Hawke saw the *Soleil Royal* and the *Héros* trapped near Croisic. His own fleet and the Four Shoal stood between the two ships and the open sea. Nearer at hand, the *Resolution,* 74 guns, could be seen aground on the western side of the Four. She had struck hard while trying to rejoin Hawke during the night. Observing the *Soleil Royal* cut and run toward Croisic, Hawke signaled the *Essex,* 64 guns, to slip and pursue her. In attempting to get into Croisic, the *Soleil Royal* and *Héros* ran ashore just south of the entrance and were burned—the former by the French, the latter by the British. Meanwhile, however, the *Essex* had struck on the Four Shoal where she, like the *Resolution,* became a wreck.

Elsewhere that day (21 November), the *Juste* was wrecked on the Grand Charpentier rock while trying to enter the Loire.[25] Six French ships of the line and two frigates managed to get into the Vilaine, but the *Inflexible,* 64 guns, grounded in the attempt. On 23 November Commodore Young reported to Hawke that a ship "on the starboard entrance on her beam ends" was thought to be a frigate. Hawke therefore never claimed the *Inflexible* as one of the French ships of the line lost in the sequel to the battle, but she disappears from the French accounts after 20 November and there is direct British evidence specifying her loss.[26]

Altogether, then, the French lost seven ships of the line, including two flagships; the British lost two of the line. For the remainder of the war, British command of the sea was nowhere seriously contested. A French invasion of the British Isles—the one potentially conclusive move on offer—was entirely ruled out. The future of Canada and India would rest with Britain rather than France. French seaborne trade had been brought virtually to a standstill.

Having in 1747 seized the unexpected chance of winning a crushing victory, Hawke had, on a grander scale and under uniquely daunting circumstances, met the challenge of Quiberon Bay in a similarly decisive manner. Confident of the professional quality of his officers and men, and embodying in his person and record an aggressive but flexible tactical doctrine, he fulfilled his promise to catch up with Conflans either outside or within Quiberon Bay. On 20 November, his key decisions were to hoist the chase and to adhere to it throughout the daylight hours. After months of close watching and of constant attention to his own ships and personnel, he was prepared, as he wrote in his dispatch of 24 November, to run "all risks to break this strong force of the enemy." Looking back over the events of the twentieth, he was surely justified in observing: "Had we had but two hours more daylight, the whole had been totally destroyed or taken."

What ultimate conclusions can be drawn about Hawke's qualities as a leader? He cannot be seen as the product of a school or the disciple of any particular precursor. While he derived his basic professional competence from considerable service in the West Indies, this service was not out of the ordinary. As a leader, he was born rather than made. When, as a captain in 1744, he was first tested in battle, he showed himself to be confident, resolute, bold, and formidable, possessing great moral strength and sound tactical judgment. As an admiral he displayed similar characteristics. He was not a complicated man. Gentlemanly in bearing and straightforward in manner, he inspired confidence in those under his command. A sincere Christian, he maintained high standards of decency on board ship, was a firm but humane disciplinarian, and consistently promoted the health and welfare of his ships' companies as far as the established system allowed. In wartime, he was persistent in seeking offensive opportunities. Appropriately, he chose the motto STRIKE when granted his coat of arms. The corresponding tactic, used by him on two contrasting occasions to such conclusive effect, was the general chase. He did not take risks lightly, but in 1759 above all, he showed that he could embrace them when the time was right.

Hawke continued to command fleets off the French coast until 1762. From late 1766 to early 1771, he was First Lord of the Admiralty. Raised to the peerage as a baron in 1776, he died in 1781.

Notes

1. Public Record Office Admiralty (hereafter ADM.) 1/5282, court-martial of Captain R. Pett, 1st day, 19 November 1745 (evidence of Captain Philip Tom).

2. G. Lacour-Gayet, *La marine militaire de la France sous le règne de Louis XV* (2nd ed., Paris: H. Champion, 1910), pp. 348–52, 522.

3. ADM. 1/92, Hawke to Clevland, 10 November 1759.

4. On Rodney and Duff, see David Spinney, *Rodney* (London: Allen & Unwin, 1969), pp. 202–5.

5. From here onward, the account of Conflans's role derives mainly from his dispatch of 24 November 1759, printed in O. Troude, *Batailles navales de la France,*

4 vols. (Paris: Challamel ainé, 1867–68), I:385–95. For tracing his movements from 14 to 20 November, certain British logs are useful, e.g., those cited in Notes 6 and 7.

6. ADM. 51/3834, captain's log of the *Firm*. This reports the *Swallow's* account of sighting the French on 15 November.

7. ADM. 51/1029, captain's log of the *Vengeance*.

8. Geoffrey Marcus, *Quiberon Bay* (London: Hollis & Carter, [1960]), p. 108 and note.

9. ADM. 1/92, Hawke to Clevland, 17 November 1759. This covers Hawke's proceedings from the 12th onward.

10. See Notes 6 and 7 above.

11. ADM. 51/811, captain's log of the *Royal George*.

12. ADM. 52/862 and 52/935, masters' logs of the *Royal George* and *Magnanime*. These give the speeds, estimated hourly.

13. ADM. 1/92, Hawke to Clevland, 24 November 1759. This is the prime source for Hawke's role on 20 and 21 November.

14. ADM. 51/811.

15. ADM. 51/1001, captain's log of the *Torbay*.

16. Marcus, op. cit., pp. 146–47.

17. The journal kept by Pakenham (subsequently Captain Lord Longford) is in the Longford Papers at the National Maritime Museum, Greenwich, England. It includes general comment on the battle, together with some timed observations of French maneuvers, thus usefully supplementing the content of the *Dublin*'s captain's log (ADM. 51/287).

18. ADM. 51/1029. See also Marcus, op. cit., pp. 150–51.

19. Ruddock F. Mackay, *Admiral Hawke* (Oxford: Clarendon Press, 1965), p. 247, has further comment on the verbal exchange.

20. Quoted in Marcus, op. cit., p. 152.

21. ADM. 51/1001.

22. ADM. 51/811.

23. Troude, op. cit., I:391–92.

24. Lacour-Gayet, op. cit., pp. 360–61.

25. ADM. 1/92, Hawke to Clevland, 2 December 1759.

26. National Maritime Museum, HWK/11, Young to Hawke with enclosure, 23 November 1759. See also Mackay, op. cit., pp. 244 and 253, for a copy of Pakenham's chart, which marks the location of the various wrecks, including the *Inflexible*, and for reference to other relevant sources (but Lacour-Gayet's list of the French navy is on his p. 542, not p. 522). Pakenham also claims the *Inflexible* in his journal (Note 17, above)—the *Dunkirk* having been one of the ships sent by Hawke to investigate the Vilaine.

Note on Sources

The best general account of Hawke's tempestuous victory is *Quiberon Bay*, by Geoffrey Marcus (London: Hollis & Carter, [1960]). It is based on thorough research and an impressive range of sources. On Hawke's career and development as a commander, *Admiral Hawke,* by Ruddock F. Mackay (Oxford: Clarendon Press, 1965), may be consulted. Some corrections of detail in that biography are embodied in the foregoing essay. This applies also to the volume of *Hawke Papers* edited by me for the Navy Records Society. Duly furnished with introductions and notes, it was published in 1990. It includes a run of documents for 1759 that can be read as a narrative; also much detail, from court-martial evidence, of Hawke's victory in 1747.

The original biography is the *Life of Edward, Lord Hawke,* by Montagu Burrows, published in London by W. H. Allen in 1883. It should be noted that its second and third editions (1896 and 1904) are abridged and exclude much of the documentary material given in the first edition.

For Hawke's role at Quiberon Bay, the basic primary sources are his own dispatches to the Admiralty dated 17 and 24 November 1759 (for which see Notes 9 and 13 above), while the lengthy dispatch written by Conflans on 24 November (see Note 5) provides a detailed account of his own actions. Various British captains' and masters' logs are also helpful, although, understandably, they vary a good deal over the timing of events on the afternoon of 20 November. (In the logs, the entries run from noon to noon. Thus, the events of the afternoon of the 20th are entered in the logs under the 21st, where, as usual, P.M. entries precede A.M. ones.) All the Admiralty documents mentioned are kept at the Public Record Office, Kew, London.

French naval policy in 1759 is authoritatively treated by G. Lacour-Gayet, *La marine militaire de la France sous le règne de Louis XV* (Paris: H. Champion, 1902, and revised ed., 1910), which contains useful information about Conflans and other French participants.

7

Pierre-André de Suffren de Saint-Tropez

Admiral Satan

(1729–1788)

Philippe Masson

Translated by Jack Sweetman

FOR MORE THAN TWO CENTURIES, PIERRE-ANDRÉ DE SUFFREN de Saint-Tropez has been the object of profound veneration. Admiral Raoul Castex (1878–1968), generally considered the foremost French naval thinker, placed him in the front rank in the pantheon of great naval commanders, beside de Ruyter and Nelson. During the celebration of the bicentennial of the American War of Independence, the French navy designated 1983 as Suffren Commemoration Year. From 1789 to 1962, nine French warships were named in honor of this great seaman.

Suffren's extraordinary fame stems from his campaigns in the Indian Ocean. The adventure began in 1781, when Ministre de la Marine de Castries decided to give a new impetus to the war with Britain, which had been dragging on for three years without decisive results. Two fleets sailed from Brest on 22 March 1781. The first, thirty ships of the line strong under Admiral Count de Grasse, was to conquer certain of the British Antilles. The second, under Suffren's command, consisted of five of the line, a corvette, and eight transports. The minister intended this little fleet to play a diversionary role, defending the Dutch colony at the Cape of Good Hope against a fleet that was just leaving England under Commodore George Johnstone and, insofar as possible, reanimating the war in the Indian Ocean.

The two formations separated on 29 March. De Grasse headed west, while Suffren turned south. The latter was far from unknown in the navy. Born into the petty nobility of Provence on 17 July 1729, Pierre-André de Suffren de Saint-Tropez was admitted into the Order of Malta as a "knight of minority" in 1737. At that time the order still maintained a sovereign existence on its island stronghold and its galleys, in incessant conflict with Muslim corsairs, provided training for many young Frenchmen embarking on naval careers. In 1743 Suffren entered the *Ecole des gardes de la Marine*—Naval Cadets School—at Toulon. He made his first cruise at the age of fifteen and fought in his first engagement, the Battle of Cape Sicié, on 24 February 1744.

During the War of Austrian Succession (1740–48), Suffren served in a squadron in the West Indies and in an unsuccessful expedition to Canada in 1746. The following year he was captured at the Second Battle of Finisterre and remained a prisoner until the conclusion of peace.

From 1748 until 1754 Suffren performed duty in the "Galleys of the Faith" at Malta, where he took the vows of the order and held several commands. Returning to France upon the outbreak of the Seven Years War (1756–63), he took part in campaigns in Canada and the Mediterranean before being made prisoner for a second time when the French Mediterranean squadron was defeated by a British fleet under Admiral Edward Boscawen at the Battle of Lagos Bay (18–19 August 1759).

Following the restoration of peace, Suffren participated in a bungled attack on the corsair base of Larache, Morocco, under the orders of Rear Admiral Duchaffault. His abilities brought him exceptionally rapid advancement: commander at the age of thirty-seven in 1767, captain at the age of forty-two in 1772. After a period of training in Duchaffault's practice squadron, he received command of the ship of the line *Fantasque* in 1777. In February 1778 France intervened on the side of the American colonies in their war against Great Britain and Suffren took part in the operations of Admiral Count d'Estaing's squadron at Newport, Grenada, and Savannah in 1778 and 1779.

Despite a difficult character and an already impressive embonpoint, during this period Suffren became known as an officer overflowing with activity—audacious, aggressive, and professionally expert. Notwithstanding his membership in the Order of Malta, he did not trouble himself over its rules of poverty and obedience. If he observed the vow to remain unmarried, he proved very liberal in the matter of chastity. Despite his taste for action, Suffren was also a reflective man. He read and meditated much on the great naval campaigns of the past, especially those of de Ruyter. Before sailing for India, he carefully studied the operations of his predecessors in that theater, Bourdonnais, d'Aché, and d'Orves.

Suffren also took an interest in the technical aspects of the navy. He argued in favor of improving ordnance by the adoption of firing locks, caronnades, and explosive shells, in imitation of the Royal Navy, and advocated the installation of additional ship's boats and lightning-conductors aboard ships. Unlike too many officers of the era, he by no means neglected the health of his crews. On 23 February 1773, upon "returning to the king" the frigate *Mignonne,* he noted: "The precautions that I have taken to conserve the salubrity of the air on board and to preserve my crew have happily succeeded and I have had only a few serious illnesses."[1]

On numerous occasions, Suffren applied himself to investigating particular military problems. In 1762 he wrote a note to the minister of marine on the defenses of Gibraltar and ways to attack them. This was followed in 1765 by a memoir on the protection of French interests in Morocco and in 1770 by study on "the means of curbing the corsairs of Algeria." While emphasizing, as had de Ruyter, the futility of bombarding cities, he called for the organization of convoys and patrols of exposed areas such as Sardinia and the coast of Provence.

Suffren enjoyed the advantage of powerful protectors, including Duchaffault, d'Estaing, and Chief Clerk Blouin, the head of the officers' bureau. He also benefited from the support of Sartine, who had preceded de Castries as minister of marine; Vergennes, foreign minister from 1774; and de Castries himself, who on 4 March 1781 expressed the intention "to give him the occasion to distinguish himself."[2]

The occasion was not long in coming. After separating from de Grasse, Suffren proceeded toward the Cape Verde Islands to take on fresh water. Arriving off Porto Praya on 16 April he was surprised to discover Johnstone's ships and transports riding at anchor. With extraordinary decisiveness and at the risk of imperiling his entire mission, he immediately went over to the attack—a decision that planted the seeds of trouble in his captains' minds.

On board his flagship, the *Héros,* Suffren entered the roadstead followed by only two ships and raked the British vessels. Dumbfounded at first, the English quickly recovered and returned a heavy fire. The French vessels, seriously damaged, were driven from the roads.

This tactical reverse proved to be a strategic victory. Grappling with severe damage, Johnstone had to postpone his departure for fifteen days. The delay permitted Suffren to reach the Cape of Good Hope and see to its defenses, thus obliging the English to cancel the attack and limit themselves to the capture of a few merchant ships. Immediately upon becoming known in Europe the affair at Porto Praya provoked a sensation. Suffren was acclaimed a hero. The cabinet at Versailles granted him the rank of rear admiral, and the Order of Malta the title of *bailli,* the highest grade of the order.

After that first spectacular success, Suffren reached Ile de France (now Mauritius) after a difficult voyage, during which he captured the English 50-gun ship *Hannibal.* There he found himself, in principle, under the orders of the governor, Monsieur de Souillac, and the command of Count d'Orves, an old seaman, ill and exhausted, who soon expired. His death gave Suffren almost complete freedom of action. With eleven ships of the line, three frigates, three corvettes, and some transports at his disposition, Suffren decided to get under way for India and carry the war to the coast of the Carnatic, where the situation was not at all brilliant.

In the theater that until then Versailles had considered quite secondary, the English had been able to proceed with the occupation of all the French and Dutch "factories"—trading posts—including Trincomalee on the east coast of Ceylon. At the same time, they were endeavoring to break the resistance of France's Indian ally, Hyder Ali, the nabob of Mysore. The English counted on controlling the sea with the fleet of Admiral Sir Edward Hughes, a dozen ships of the line supported by well-equipped bases at Madras and Bombay.

After declining an engagement off Madras, Suffren attacked Hughes's

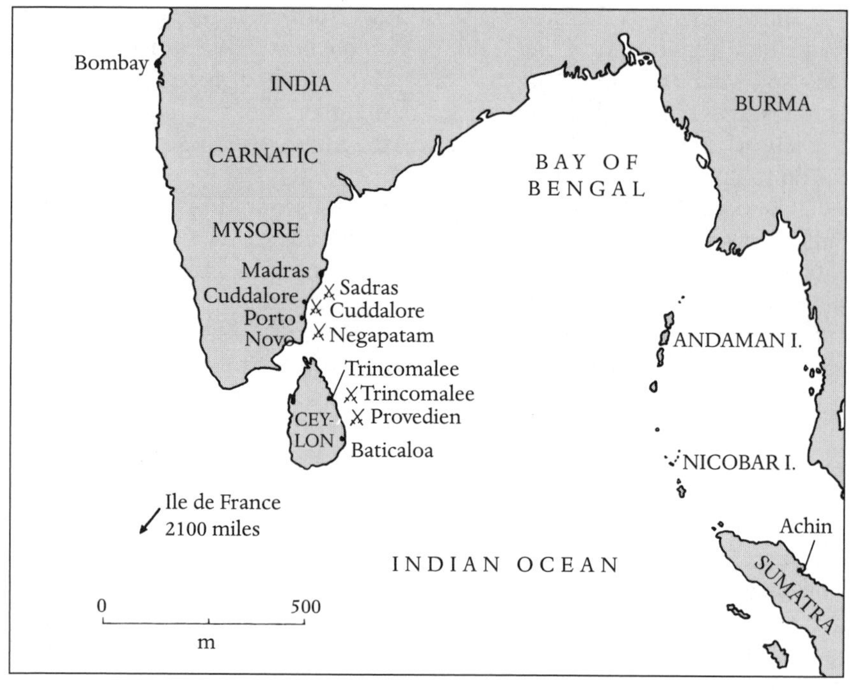

11. Suffren's Campaigns in the Indian Ocean, 1782–83.

squadron off Sadras on 17 February 1782 and forced the enemy to withdraw. The disembarkation of a small body of troops led to reoccupation of the Indian port of Cuddalore and opened direct contact with Hyder Ali. Two months later, on 12 April, Suffren failed to obtain a decisive success over Hughes at Provedien, off the east coast of Ceylon. This check frustrated his intention of seizing Trincomalee and he had to enter port at Baticaloa on the southeastern coast of the island.

On 6 July, Suffren resumed the offensive and fought a third engagement off Negapatam, India. It, too, proved a disappointment. The battle was indecisive and the English remained in control of the Dutch factories. Suffren retired to Cuddalore. Early in September, however, he succeeded in capturing Trincomalee by an audacious combined operation and repulsing a counterattack by Hughes.

Suffren wintered his well-tested fleet at Achin on the coast of Sumatra. He returned to the attack in January 1783. After scouring the Bay of Bengal, at Trincomalee he at last made his junction with a small expeditionary corps, escorted by three ships of the line, sent from France under the command of the Marquis de Bussy. This force, whose arrival had been repeatedly delayed, reinforced the troops at Cuddalore. On 20 June 1783 Suffren fought his fifth and last battle against Hughes's fleet, which was blockading the city, and compelled his adversary to withdraw. A few weeks later the proclamation of the Peace of Versailles put an end to a campaign that had already been accepted as a masterpiece of the art of war and had brought its author remarkable renown.

Several circumstances contributed to this phenomenon. Without being the scientific type of officer, trained in astronomical calculations, Suffren nevertheless appeared to be a great sailor, possessing an extraordinary sense of the sea. To his most ardent admirers, he also proved himself a superb tactician, filled with the spirit of the offensive, rejecting the conformity of his day characterized by the fetish of the line of battle, scientific maneuvers, and inconclusive engagements. Suffren attacked from the windward and closed to within pistol range. He sought the decisive battle, the battle of annihilation. Time and again he attempted to double his adversary's rear, taking it between two fires in order to bring about its destruction.

Nevertheless, a question suggests itself. Was Suffren really an innovator? He would not seem to be so, without overlooking de Ruyter or Tourville, the outstanding French admiral who succeeded in enveloping the Anglo-Dutch van at the Battle of Beachy Head (Bévéziers) in 1690. On several subsequent occasions, men such as Boscawen and Hawke had also succeeded in doubling their opponent's rear.

Doubling the enemy's line appeared so little revolutionary that it figures prominently in Bigot de Morogue's treatise, *Tactique Navale,* which was published in 1763 and, in a sense, constituted the bible of French naval officers. An entire paragraph is devoted to methods of doubling the enemy's van or rear, as well as ways to oppose it.

Suffren's originality lay elsewhere. It combined an aggressive temperament with a capacity to seize "the moment" on the field of battle and to shake off accepted rules. Without ever possessing a marked superiority, Suffren practiced or, rather, tried to practice doubling the line, despite Bigot de Morogue's admonition that this maneuver must be reserved to the more numerous fleet.

In a sense, Suffren conducted his campaign in the manner of a corsair or the commander of a light squadron. His offensive spirit assured him the ascendancy over his opponent. The man whom the English started calling "Admiral Satan" almost always took the initiative in the attack. He repeatedly returned to the charge, despite severe losses and significant material damage.

That style, that élan, impressed contemporaries. Following the American war, several treatises such as Grenier's *Art de la guerre sur mer,* appearing in 1787, and d'Amblimont's *Tactique navale,* published a year later, drew upon the lessons of the campaign in India and argued in favor of more flexible, more offensive doctrine, free from the rigors of formalism. In his *Essay on Naval Tactics* (1797), John Clerk emphasized the audacity of the actions of Sadras and Provedien and did not conceal his enthusiasm for Suffren, "an officer of genius and great enterprise."[3]

Still, the fact remains that none of the battles Suffren fought were decisive. Despite repeated attempts, he never succeeded in destroying all or part of the opposing fleet. It is true that in Admiral Hughes he confronted a skillful antagonist thoroughly familiar with the theater, where he had served from 1773 to 1777. "Mother Hughes," as the French dubbed him, avoided risks and parried Suffren's blows with rare aplomb.

The reverses Suffren experienced have been the subject of many studies. Some authors have evoked the imprint of the Order of Malta as favoring single combat to the detriment of combined action of the squadron battle. Others have emphasized Suffren's impulsive temperament and the absence of precise instructions to his captains, confused by his improvisations ever since the Battle of Porto Praya.

These explanations can scarcely be sustained. Under the orders of Duchaffault, l'Etenduère, and even more of d'Estaing, Suffren learned the rules of squadron action. In the Indian Ocean he repeatedly specified his intentions with maximum clarity. His letter of 6 February 1782 clearly explained to his division commander Tromelin his intention to double the enemy line and the role that he meant to reserve for him. His memorandum of 2 June of the same year constituted, in the opinion of Admiral Castex, "a model of clearness, concision and vigor."[4]

Likewise, many authors have rushed to blame Suffren's subordinates. To Castex, Suffren's disappointments were explained solely by the passivity of his officers, prisoners of formalism and the fetish of the line of battle, and totally disoriented by the liberties their commander took with customary concepts. While much more might be said about the sclerosis of tactical ideas in this era, the problem would have been particularly acute among officers who had spent long years in the Indian Ocean, were strangers to combined maneuvers, and had never had an opportunity to serve in the practice squadrons.

The question may be asked, however, if there was not something else, if the passivity of some officers at Sadras, Negapatam, and Trincomalee was not akin to conspiracy, to a refusal to obey, to deliberate sabotage by certain headstrong individuals determined to frustrate the plans of a commander for whom they felt no affection.

This touches on one of the dominant traits of the French navy of the

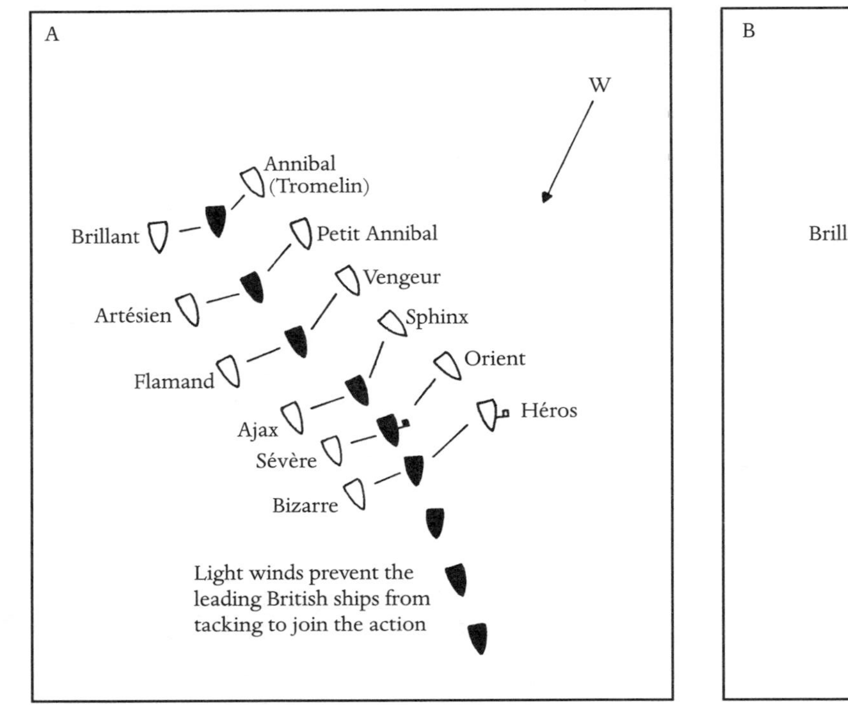

12. The Battle of Sadras, 17 February 1782. (A) The action as Suffren intended it to be fought, with Tromelin's division doubling the British rear. (B) The action as actually fought; only the *Brilliant* and *Flamand* double Hughes's line.

eighteenth century, which was characterized more by a spirit of insubordination, disparagement, and jealousy than by the absence of initiative or combativeness. The phenomenon was by no means particular to Suffren's squadron. D'Estaing and de Grasse experienced the same problem, if not to the same degree, during their operations in American waters. Nor did this spirit of disputation spare the Royal Navy, as is evidenced by the lively altercation that broke out between Admirals Hood and Graves after the Battle of the Chesapeake (5 September 1781), in which de Grasse repulsed their attempt to rescue the British army trapped at Yorktown. Suffren himself was an old hand in the matter. In March 1779 he described one of the navy's senior officers as "fallen from imbecility into infancy" and two years later, upon the announcement of the promotions of two officers whose abilities he despised, he remarked that "It remains rather amusing that one gets ahead better by being good for nothing than by being good for something."[5]

In sum, certain historians have not hesitated to denounce a cabal, a plot against Suffren's authority. Two men could have been at the origin of a spirit of subordination, two Indian Ocean officers, Tromelin and Bidé de Maurville, whom d'Orves appointed to command the *Annibal* and the *Artésien* following Suffren's arrival at the Ile de France owing to their seniority, not to their ability. Because of their interests in the colony, these two appear to have joined a difficult and interminable campaign on the coast of India with the worst possible grace. They did not forgive their removal from female companionship and the profitable activities that Suffren had denounced ever since his arrival.

On 15 November 1781 he wrote de Castries:

> I have been even more affected to see that the long and great remoteness from authority, the riches acquired and the hope that time and distance will erase everything, have given birth to ideas scarcely analogous to the military spirit of which subordination is the basis. The king can be well served in distant lands only when commanders have great powers and the strength to make use of them.[6]

Be that as it may, in the wake of the Battle of Negapatam Suffren resolved on drastic action. Before a shift in the wind threw both fleets into confusion, the ships of the French center and rear had taken an extremely feeble part in the battle. In consequence, four officers were relieved of command: Cillart, for having panicked and temporarily hauled down the flag of his ship, the *Sévère;* Bidé de Maurville (*Artésien*), for having added to the faults already evident at Sadras and Provedien; Forbin (*Vengeur*), for not having made amends for his bad conduct on 12 April; and Bouvet (*Ajax*), for medical reasons. Suffren recognized that Bouvet was "very ill." "All the mistakes that he had made, and they are great in number, can be attributed solely to senility."[7] These decisions, exceptional for the era, were approved by de Castries.

Another crisis erupted in September, after the Battle of Trincomalee, which was again marked by great confusion, a disorderly engagement, and an almost universal lack of combativeness, as well as the tardy arrival on the scene of action of the rear led by Tromelin. Suffren experienced a fit of despair, as was evidenced by the letter he wrote to de Castries three weeks after the battle:

> Monseigneur, I have had my heart broken by the most general disloyalty. I have just lost the opportunity to destroy the English squadron. I had fourteen of the line and the *Consolante,* which I had put into the line. Admiral Hughes turned about without fleeing; rather, he fled in order, conforming to speed of his worst sailer. . . . It was not until three o'clock in the afternoon that I could overtake him. My line almost formed, I attacked and signalled the *Vengeur* and the *Consolante* to attack the rear. No one came up. Only the *Héros,* the *Illustre* and the *Ajax* fought at close range and in line. The others, without regard to their post, without making any maneuver, fired from long range or, rather, almost, outside range.
>
> Everyone, yes, everyone could have come up, since we were to windward and ahead and no one did. Several of them have acted bravely in other engagements. I can attribute this horror only to the desire to terminate the campaign, to ill-will [and] to ignorance, for I dare suspect nothing worse. . . .[8]

What was most serious in this affair was that the very day after the engagement four officers asked to be relieved of command and given leave to return to Ile de France. Contrary to every expectation, Suffren granted the officers' request "with pleasure." Among the four captains was Tromelin, which cannot have come as a surprise. But the others were men whose previous conduct had been wholly praiseworthy and had entertained cordial relations with Suffren in the opening months of the campaign.

Moreover, the Trincomalee crisis was not the first. Another serious incident had occurred several weeks earlier, after Provedien, as was recorded by Huet de Froberville, an army officer embarked in the squadron:

> For some time an extraordinary laxity has manifested itself in the performance of duty. The commander-in-chief's activity displeases many individual members of the naval officer corps scarcely accustomed to bend and who do not find in their chief that insufferable corps spirit, so harmful to the public interest, on which its cadets are suckled and which prerogatives, honors and age reinforce in those who grow old in the service. We

> had the proof of it in the cabal that brought forth the resignations of thirty or forty of these officers.[9]

On this occasion, however, Suffren had proven intractable and rejected the request for leave en masse.

In wake of these incidents it is tempting to examine Suffren's own leadership methods. Time and again he was violent, abrasive, and harsh in his relations with his ships' captains. This conduct did not keep him from exercising his charm on young officers and demonstrating the most extreme demagoguery toward the seamen, even in cases of flagrant breaches of discipline.

After Provedien, it was in the most brutal manner that Suffren informed his captains of his intention to pursue the campaign to the shores of India. This decision was justified by his strategic plan but ran counter to the customary practice of brief incursions to the Coromandel coast and long periods of rest at Ile de France. He communicated it to his captains, none of whom he had consulted, in a voice like thunder:

> Very well, gentlemen, I have only a few words to you. I have decided to stay in India. Why, you know as well as me. But you may be ignorant of the tenor of the general instructions which Monsieur d'Orves received from the king: "His Majesty's wisdom does not permit him to dictate any particular operations. He knows that it would be imprudent to determine practicalities from a distance of four thousand leagues and, in consequence, he is content to inform the Sieur d'Orves that what he chiefly forbids is the inactivity of his squadron."
>
> Better to burn the squadron below the walls of Madras than to withdraw before Admiral Hughes! Until we are masters of Trincomalee, the unfamiliar roadsteads of Coromandel must suffice for us!
>
> Please communicate my orders to your officers and your crews.[10]

That was all.

Suffren tried to ignore the exertions and sacrifices exacted by the repeated and terribly costly actions fought by ships in poor condition and with improvised and incomplete crews. Five captains had already been killed and several others seriously wounded. On occasion the admiral's criticism bordered on injustice, even bad faith. Could the *Consolante* and the *Vengeur* honestly be blamed for not having been able to double the British rear off Trincomalee, when the first ship was disabled by enemy fire and the second, commanded by a first-rate captain, Cuverville, was on fire and had exhausted her ammunition? Contradictions of this kind occur in connection with the majority of the squadron's engagements. It was not uncommon, for Suffren himself, once he had recovered from his disappointments, to request awards for officers who had been harshly treated in the beginning. Even if it was not the sole reason, such conduct can only have contributed to the spread of disaffection and the birth of cabals.

What was the explanation for Suffren's animosity, not toward all of the officers, but at least toward all of the captains placed under his orders? Was it a form of revenge for the contempt that members of the *grand corps** nourished for the knights of Malta and even officers from the petty nobility of Provence, who were adjudged less honorable than the offshoots of Normandy and Brittany? Or should it rather be blamed on certain paranoiac aspects of Suffren's character, aggravated by a long and trying campaign? There is no doubt that the man was steeped in arrogance and ambition and thirsty for fame. His correspondence provides proof of that.

Did not he affirm, hardly having left Brest, that the campaign in India would allow him to acquire "glory, that phantom for which one does so many things"? Unfortunately, as his missives to his dear friend Madame d'Alès attest, his partial success deprived him of "glory," of "that immorality" to which he believed he had a right. His disappointments were resented not as frustrations of his duties to the king or the navy, but as personal injuries.

Following the Battle of Trincomalee these disappointments, which cannot be attributed solely to the shortcoming of his subordinates, aroused a veritable genius for persecution. Trublet, a young officer heaped with favors by Suffren, which makes his testimony all the more interesting, confirms this:

> Monsieur Suffren remains convinced that the majority of his ships meant to abandon him or at least neglected to come to his aid as promptly as they should have. His dissatisfaction was extreme, he made his resentment felt by several captains who had neglected nothing to share the dangers and to save him from the peril in which he found himself.[11]

It never occurred to Suffren to wonder whether it was really possible, without possessing a marked numerical superiority, to win a complete victory with a tired, mismatched fleet manned by overworked crews riddled by disease. A single explanation for his disappointments recurs like a leitmotif: the shortcomings and soon the treason of his captains. He considered himself above all criticism. At the conclusion of his report to de Castries, he

* Line officers, principally stemming from aristocratic families of the northern coastal provinces, who held commands at sea, as opposed to the middle-class *petit corps* of shore-based administrators.

wrote, "I have made mistakes in the war. Who has not? But none of those which lost engagements can be imputed to me." A single regret and a reproach. If he had been given Albert de Rioms as second-in-command, as he had requested before leaving Brest, "we would be masters of India."[12]

Still, it may be asked if Suffren's bearing toward his officers did not proceed as much from a spirit of deliberate provocation as from a commander's intention to singularize himself, to make himself legendary, as Napoleon would do fifteen years later. Already obese on sailing for India, Suffren became enormous, elephantine, unfurling an impressive paunch, although he did not lose his agility. Afflicted by bulemia, he ate voraciously, disgustingly, ignoring his knife and sometimes his fork.

Before his ships' captains, immaculate in full-dress uniform, Suffren customarily appeared dirty, slovenly, with eight days' growth of beard, and exuding an almost unbearable odor. A Briton's portrait has become classic:

> Of bizarre dress and figure, . . . he looked more like an English butcher than a Frenchman. About five feet, six inches in height, very corpulent, with little hair on the top of his head but more on the sides and back. Although quite fat he used neither powder nor pommade, wore no curls and had a short queue three or four inches long tied with an old bit of twine. . . . He was wearing a pair of old shoes from which the straps had been cut, and unbuttoned trousers. . . . Stockings of cotton or yarn and not of the cleanest hung over his legs . . . a linen shirt completely soaked with sweat.[13]

The admiral also affected a vulgar, chaffing, and provocative language.

Following the September engagement Suffren, convinced that he was surrounded by enemies, fell into a deep depression; "each step that we have taken since the conquest of Trincomalee was marked by a disaster." Two ships, the *Orient* and the *Bizarre,* disappeared, victims of the sea. Hughes received important reinforcements with the arrival of the five ships of the line. The winter harbor at Achin proved a disappointment. The local ruler was "an atrocious despot, somber and withdrawn, who counts victims rather than subjects."[14] The news that de Grasse had been defeated at the Battle of the Saints, which became known on 25 October 1782, plunged Suffren into despair. To add to his worries, the reinforcements under Bussy were late in arriving.

In January 1783, however, Suffren roused himself and regained his energy. He ravaged British shipping in the Bay of Bengal, finally made his junction with Bussy at Trincomalee and landed troops at Porto Novo to support Tippoo Sahib, Hyder Ali's successor. At last, on 20 June, at Cuddalore he

6. The Battle of Cuddalore, 20 June 1783. The Ministry of the Marine had recently issued an order requiring admirals to exercise command from a frigate outside their line of battle. At Cuddalore, Suffren flew his flag in the frigate *Cléopâtre,* here shown to the left of the French line. He did not consider this experiment a success. (Musée de la Marine, Paris.)

fought the battle that obliged Hughes to retire. Upon this success Suffren became himself again. Glory had made the rendezvous.

Whatever his defects, Suffren had accomplished the feat of conducting a frenetic campaign, almost two years in duration, whose diabolical tempo seems to foreshadow that of Bonaparte in Italy in 1796–97. Again like Bonaparte, Suffren exceeded the bounds of a mere tactician. He had the enormous merit of conducting for the first time an important geostrategic operation at a great distance, more than two months' voyage, from his nearest base. Suffren was one of those rare French admirals who understood that command of the sea does not constitute an end in itself. It must serve to support strategy and permit the association of naval and military operations. On the whole, Suffren's battles occurred within the framework of a maritime strategy oriented toward the land.

At the same time, he by no means ignored the effects of naval demonstrations. The arrival of his squadron before Cuddalore on two occasions, in July 1782 and June 1783, impressed the inhabitants and the garrison and constituted a favorable prelude to his meetings with Hyder Ali and Tippoo Sahib.

Throughout the campaign, Suffren interpreted his instructions in the most offensive possible manner. There was even an instance of flagrant disobedience. Entrenching himself behind the old directives received by d'Orves, Suffren refused to return to Ile de France to await Bussy's ships and transports, as de Castries suggested. On 1 May 1782 he wrote Governor Souillac:

> I choose to remain; with regret, because although the only thing to do, it will not be to anyone's taste, I will be criticized by everyone. Besides, if I leave the coast shortly after the action, Monsieur Hughes, whom I beat on 17 February and 12 April, will not hesitate to say that I have been beaten.[15]

An account of the campaign in India would be incomplete without mentioning Suffren's extraordinary talent for improvisation. Upon arriving at the Cape following the Battle of Porto Praya, he found material sufficient to allow only a partial repair of the damage that his squadron had sustained. The work could not be completed until he reached Ile de France, and at the cost of exhausting the colony's resources.

Entirely dependent on his own devices on the coast of India, Suffren gradually perfected a logistical triangle based on Coromandel, Ceylon, and Sumatra, the sides of which did not exceed twenty days' sail. From these bases, the fleet drew water, provisions, and wood. With the aid of the Dutch, it was possible to proceed with repairs and copper sheathing, to land the sick, and open hospitals. The thorniest problem concerned masts and yards; after every action, there were permutations from one frigate to another or from a frigate to a ship of the line. Suffren nevertheless succeeded, if the phrase is applicable, in living off the land. Large-scale commerce raiding, especially in the Bay of Bengal, enabled the squadron's needs to be answered.

The same improvisation occurred in regard to the crews, decimated by battle and disease. Of the 430 men who sailed in the *Ajax,* in 52 months of campaigning 43 were killed in action or by accident and 185 died of disease. It was regularly necessary to fill the crews by recruiting local manpower: blacks from Mozambique, Sepoys, Malays, soldiers. At the conclusion of the campaign, the shortages were on the order of 30 percent of a mismatched, patchwork fleet, half of whose ships lacked copper sheathing, two of which were kept afloat only by the constant action of their pumps.

It was fortunate that peace intervened in July 1783. Suffren probably would not have been able to hold out very long against Hughes's far better supported and recently reinforced fleet. The situation ashore was no more promising.

Thus, despite its tempo, the balance sheet on the campaign was hardly positive. Suffren's diversion did not lead the British to commit important forces to the Indian Ocean. The reinforcements sent to Hughes were limited to five ships of the line. Moreover, Suffren's success became known too late to affect the preliminaries of the peace. By the Treaty of Versailles, France recovered the five defenseless factories that had been accorded to it by the Treaty of Paris in 1763—a return to the status quo ante.

Some authorities contend that the dispatch of more sizable forces would have had profound repercussions, greatly improving France's political position in India. This is doubtful. There is nothing to indicate that the capture or destruction of a few English vessels would have led to a revolt by the Hindu princes and shaken British predominance.

In any event, the French navy could not fit out more than sixty or seventy ships of the line. It lacked the means to conduct offensive operations in two distinct theaters. Strategic priority was rightly accorded to the Atlantic and the cabinet at Versailles could not commit more than 15 to 20 percent of its forces to the Indian Ocean.

How then to explain the fabulous echo, in France as well as England, of an entirely marginal campaign? To begin with, the public relations aspect must not be overlooked. Suffren knew how, by his reports and his letters, to exalt his successes, to give his operations an epic appeal. He succeeded in making government offices and public opinion tremble with delight. Immediately after his reverse at Trincomalee, Suffren wrote Versailles:

> Here are nevertheless the results since I have been in India. I have been master of the sea. I have taken five vessels belonging to the king of England, three to the [Honourable East India] Company and more than sixty private ships. I have supported our army; I have furnished it with provisions and money. . . .[16]

There was more. Suffren's exploits occurred in the midst of a terribly costly and disappointing war. Despite two serious attempts, the French and their Spanish allies were never able to make a "descent" on England. They were equally unable to capture Gibraltar. In the Atlantic the campaigns of d'Estaing and de Guichen ended in lackluster and indecisive actions. Certainly, de Grasse's fleet and Rochambeau's expeditionary corps had played vital roles in the grand strategic combination that led to the capitulation of Cornwallis's army at Yorktown and thereby to American independence. But to a fickle public that success had been overshadowed by the humiliating defeat of the Saints.

In Suffren the French found a commander after their heart, capable of improvisation, of audacity, of panache, along the line of the great admirals of the seventeenth century—Tourville, Duquesne, Jean Bart, Duguay-Trouin. They had a sense of having regained ascendancy over the Royal Navy. In the phrase Louis XIV had used to honor Tourville after the Battle of la Hogue in 1692, Suffren knew how to shed glory on the navy, the kingdom, and the king. His exploits appeared to avenge the disappointments of the War of Austrian Succession, the Seven Years War, and, of course, the unhappy day of the Saints.

This sentiment explains Suffren's triumphal return. He was received as a conqueror at Ile de France. At the Cape, his reception was sumptuous. In reward for having saved the colony, the Dutch presented him with a magnificent sword, its blade enlaid with gold and its hilt encrusted with diamonds. Better yet, British officers who called at the Cape did not disguise their admiration and asked to be presented to the admiral in the *Héros* who had become a hero himself.

At Toulon, Suffren's arrival was triumphal, and even more so a few weeks later at Paris and Versailles. For a month, he was the toast of the court and the city. Louis XVI heaped him with favors. Promoted to the grade of lieutenant general* after Cuddalore, Suffren was made a knight of the Ordre du Saint-Esprit, the kingdom's highest award. By special decree, a fourth position of vice admiral was created for him. Provence was delirious. Poets celebrated his merits. Besides the pool at Berre an admirer had a replica of his flagship, 30 meters long, carved into a monolith, with the inscription:

BIG MOTIONLESS SHIP
WHICH COST ME A LOT OF MONEY. . . .

The stern of this enormous offering exists today.

Suffren was only partly satisfied. He felt that he was receiving only what was due him. He even showed some disappointment. He wanted to be made a marshal of France, as Tourville had been in 1693. De Castries turned him down. The minister's report to the king could not have been more flattering, however:

> Your Majesty knows that opinion in Europe, in England and in his kingdom places this officer on the same plane as the greatest seamen. . . . It is principally to him that is due the tone of superiority that the navy of France has regained in the opinion of all Europe. . . .

The reason for the refusal was simple. By virtue of his seniority, it would also have been necessary to accord the dignity of marshal to d'Estaing, but he did not deserve it. The minister executed a pirouette to bolster his refusal: "The principles of an enlightened administration impose

* This military-sounding rank was the French equivalent of the British vice admiral. The French *vice-amiral* was an appointment rather than a rank.

the obligation always to leave something to be desired by a man whom it is important to call upon for new services."[17]

Suffren ended his life in pomp and a sort of isolation. He was not consulted in the drafting of the Ordinance of 1786, which reorganized the navy, and he did not take part in the king's visit to inaugurate the construction of the great mole at Cherbourg. At the time of the Anglo-French crisis of 1787, however, he was given command of the Brest squadron.

Suffren died in Paris on 8 December 1788. For many years the conviction reigned that he had been killed in a duel. Some believed that he had been the victim of a sordid quarrel upon leaving a house of pleasure that the great fancier of women was accustomed to visit. Others held that the duel was a settling of scores and Suffren the victim of the former captain of the *Sévère,* Cillart, whom he had sacked after Provedien. In reality, things were much more prosaic. Suffren simply died of disease, the combination of a cold, the gout, and a "putrid abcess," treated by repeated bloodlettings in the approved practice of the day.

That Suffren figures in the front rank of French admirals cannot be contested. That he occupies the first place can be disputed. Certainly, no one could deny his enormous talents: his energy, his tenacity, his flair for improvisation, his strategic genius. He ranks high above d'Estaing and de Guichen. He reached the level of Tourville, Duquesne, and de Grasse, and he demonstrated greater strategic insight than Tourville, who proved incapable of exploiting the command of the sea he had won at Beachy Head. Yet he never held command in a decisive theater, which left him great ease of mind, and he never had more than fifteen of the line under his orders.

Still more important, Suffren lacked a certain dimension necessary to enter into the society of very great seamen. He knew how to make himself obeyed and respected. He never learned how to make himself loved, nor how to create a team spirit among his lieutenants. In this regard, he ranks far below de Ruyter, Nelson, and Halsey. As Las Cases, a former seaman himself, would write in the *Mémorial de Sainte-Hélène:* "Monsieur de Suffren had genius, originality, great ardor, strong ambition, a will of iron. . . . Very tough, very strange, extremely egotistical, hard to get along with, a bad comrade, he was loved by none but admired and appreciated by all."[18]

Notes

1. A. Carré, "Aspects médicaux de la campagne de l'Inde," *Revue Historique des Armées,* No. 4, 1983, p. 51. (Extract from Suffren's report to the king, 23 June 1773.)

2. De Castries to Comte d'Hector; Etienne Taillemite, *L'histoire ignorée de la marine française* (Paris: Perrin, 1988), p. 215.

3. Ibid., p. 232.

4. Raoul Castex, *Les idées militaires de la marine au XVIIIe siècle* (Paris: Fournier, 1911), p. 317.

5. Léon de la Varende, *Suffren et ses ennemis* (Paris: Flammarion, 1968), p. 61.

6. Taillemite, op. cit., p. 219.

7. Archives Nationales, Marine C7 314, dossier Suffren, p. 28.

8. La Varende, op. cit., p. 251.

9. Huet de Froberville, *Mémoires pour servir à l'histoire de la guerre de 1781 des Français avec les Anglais dans l'Inde* (Blois: Chailles, 1986), p. 75.

10. La Varende, op. cit., p. 207.

11. Trublet, *Histoire de la campagne de l'Inde* (Rennes: Brutet, 1788), p. 156.

12. Archives Nationales, Marine C7 314, dossier Suffren.

13. La Varende, op. cit., p. 42.

14. Trublet, op. cit., p. 160.

15. Castex, op. cit., p. 310.

16. Suffren to de Castries, Archives Nationales, Marine B4 207.

17. Archives Nationales, Marine C7 314, dossier Suffren, p. 43.

18. Count Emmanuel Las Cases. *Mémorial de Sainte-Hélène* (Paris: Editions Garnier Frères, 1961), vol. II: 524.

Note on Sources

Suffren still awaits an English-language biography. His Indian campaigns are, however, the subject of a long and laudatory chapter in Alfred Thayer Mahan's *The Influence of Sea Power upon History, 1660–1783* (Boston: Little, Brown, 1890). A more recent, brief account appears in E. H. Jenkins, *A History of the French Navy: From Its Beginnings to the Present Day* (Annapolis: Naval Institute Press, 1973).

The French literature is extensive. Trublet's early, eye-witness *Histoire de la campagne d'Inde* was published in 1788 (Rennes: Brutet). Other primary sources are the *Mémoires* of the Chevalier de Mautort (Paris: Plon, 1895) and Huet de Froberville's *Mémoires pour servir à l'histoire de la guerre de 1781 des Français avec les Anglais dans l'Inde* (Blois: Chailles, 1986). Biographical studies include Charles Cunat, *Histoire de bailli de Suffren* (Rennes: A. Marteville et Lefas, 1852); Léon de la Varende, *Suffren et ses ennemis* (Paris: Flammarion, 1968); and Roger Glachant, *Suffren et le temps de Vergennes* (Paris: France-Empire, 1976). A collection of Suffren's correspondence has been published as *La campagne des Indes: Lettres inédites du bailli de Suffren* (Nantes: L'école de guerre navale en liaison avec Petit Mantais, 1941).

The Service Historique de la Marine has produced several valuable monographs on Suffren's operations, beginning with Paul Cusset, *La deuxième partie de la campagne de Suffren* (1933). Others are Lieutenant Auguste Faure, *L'océan Indien dans la guerre d'indépendance américaine jusqu'à l'arrivée de Suffren* (1938); Lieutenant André Marloy, *La campagne de Suffren dans l'Inde (Sadras et Provedien)* (1921); and Lieutenant Charles Vedrines, *La campagne de Suffren dans l'Inde (Negapatam et Trinquemale)* (1921). Another capital work, reexamining Suffren's tactics, is Rear Admiral François Caron, *Le mythe de Suffren: La campagne en Inde, 1781–83* (Vincennes: Service Historique de la Marine, 1996). Also noteworthy is the issue "La Marine au temps de

Suffren" of the *Revue Historique des Armées* (No. 4, 1983), containing J. Meyer, "La campagne de Suffren"; J. P. Busson, "Suffren et ses amis d'après sa correspondance"; A. Carré, "Aspects médicaux de la campagne de l'Inde"; and M. Acerra, "Les arsenaux au temps de Suffren."

Of course, Suffren figures in every history of the French navy. The most specialized treatment remains G. Lacour-Gayet, *La marine militaire de la France sous le règne de Louis XVI* (Paris: Librairie spéciale pour l'histoire de la France, 1905). Two useful later works are Philippe Masson, *Histoire de la Marine,* vol. 1: *L'ère de la voile* (Paris: Lavauzelle, 1981), and Etienne Taillemite, *L'histoire ignorée de la marine française* (Paris: Perrin, 1988). Admiral Castex presented his interpretations in *Les idées militaires de la marine au XVIIIe siècle* (Paris: Fournier, 1911).

Original materials are contained in the Archives des Colonies, Série C2, Nos. 161–66, and the Archives Nationales (Série marine), Série B2, Nos. 417–25; Série B4, Nos. 196–98, 207, 216, 268, and 312; and Série C7, No. 314.

8

Horatio Nelson
A Man to Be Loved
(1758–1805)

Gerald Jordan

JUST BEFORE SUNSET ON 1 AUGUST 1798, IN A T'GALLANT NNW breeze, fourteen British ships of the line under Rear Admiral Sir Horatio Nelson sailed into Aboukir Bay, a few miles northeast of Alexandria, where in a fierce three-and-a-half hour action, they annihilated a French fleet of thirteen ships of the line, including the 120-gun *Orient,* and four frigates, under Vice Admiral François-Paul Brueys. Only two French line-of-battle ships and two frigates escaped. No British vessels were lost. The Battle of the Nile crowned a campaign during which, for the first time, all the elements of Nelson's genius came together to achieve victory on the grand scale. Its results were far-reaching. First and foremost, it forcibly reestablished British naval presence in the Mediterranean. A French army under Bonaparte was bottled up in Egypt where, without sea supply lines and communications, it could do little to threaten the British presence in the area or their route to India. At home, news of the victory gave a much needed boost to a government struggling with military and naval unrest, quieted republican sentiments, and even spurred some radical groups to rally around the flag in the fight against France. Overnight, Nelson became the personification of British patriotism and sea power.

For the almost two hundred years that have elapsed, Horatio Nelson has been a household name in Britain. Tales of his derring-do and his humanity have become part of the national mythology, to the point that fact is often difficult to distinguish from fiction. More biographies have been written about him than any other naval figure and continue to appear with great regularity. Britain's National Maritime Museum is virtually a shrine to his fame. Ever since his death at the Battle of Trafalgar on 21 October 1805, the search for a Nelson reincarnate has been for the Royal Navy an elusive venture akin to a quest for the Holy Grail.

Why all this should be so is not difficult to understand. The last of a long line of illustrious leaders of the days of sail, Nelson became a legend in his own lifetime. Vernon, Anson, Hawke, Rodney, Hood, and Howe had developed a tradition of naval supremacy to which Nelson was the heir. But their victories were limited in scope. Decisive naval victories were rare in the Age of Sail. Nelson won three: at the Nile in 1798, at Copenhagen in 1801, and at Trafalgar in 1805.[1] At a time when genuinely popular heroes were equally rare, Nelson's popularity with his captains and men, as with the crowd ashore, could never be doubted. "Nelson was a man to be loved," declared Sir Pulteney Malcolm, who as captain of the 74-gun *Donegal* sailed with Nelson during the pursuit of Villeneuve's fleet to the West Indies before Trafalgar. Nelson had that rare capacity to inspire to great heights those who served under him. An impulsive generosity of spirit and a colorful personality with a vibrant sense of theater, joined with rigorous sea training, an intuitive, commonsense grasp of tactics, and great physical bravery, matched the circumstances of the wars to produce a leader unique in the annals of naval warfare.

Horatio Nelson was born at Burnham Thorpe in Norfolk on 29 September 1758, the third surviving son of the Reverend Edmund Nelson, rector of the village. At the age of twelve he joined as midshipman the 64-gun HMS *Raisonnable,* commanded by his uncle, Captain Maurice Suckling. The next year, 1771, he voyaged to the Caribbean in a merchantman, from which he returned "a practical Seaman, with a horror of the Royal Navy, and with a saying, then constant with the Seamen, 'Aft the most honour, forward the better man.'"[2] From his early experience of the merchant service, Nelson acquired great respect for the seamen, which stood him in good stead in the future. By 1777, when he passed the examination for lieutenant and was appointed to the frigate *Lowestoffe,* he had gained considerable sea experience and was fast learning what each kind of ship was capable of doing in all weathers and climates. In 1773 he served on a polar expedition, followed by two years on the East Indies Station and, during the terrible winter of 1776–77, as acting-lieutenant on the 64-gun *Worcester* escorting the Gibraltar convoys. While serving under Rear Admiral Sir Peter Parker on the West Indies Station during the War of American Independence, Nelson received his first command, the schooner *Little Lucy,* early in 1778, but was soon transferred as first lieutenant to the flagship, the 50-gun *Bristol.* He received command of the brig *Badger* in December. In June 1779, a few months short of his twenty-first birthday, he was appointed post-captain in command of the 20-gun frigate *Hinchinbroke.*

From then on, Nelson's naval career was secure. Captains were promoted by seniority, and eventual flag rank was assured if they survived the rigors of naval life. After several years in the Caribbean, Nelson returned to England in July 1787 as captain of the 28-gun frigate *Boreas,* accompanied by his bride of four months, Fanny, whom he married on the island of Nevis. The ship paid off on 1 December.

For the next five years, Nelson was on half-pay, living mainly in Norfolk and constantly badgering the Admiralty for another ship. At last, in 1793, he was appointed to the *Agamemnon,* 64 guns, and served in the Mediterranean under Lord Hood, Admiral Hotham, and Sir John Jervis. On 1 June 1796, he hoisted his broad pennant as commodore in the 74-gun *Captain.* Under Jervis, he played an important part in the victory over Cordova's superior Spanish fleet at the Battle of Cape St. Vincent on St. Valentine's Day 1797, for which he was created a Knight of the Bath and promoted to rear admiral. In June 1798 he was given command of the powerful squadron that hunted and destroyed Brueys's fleet at the Battle of the Nile. Honors were showered upon him, including the title Baron Nelson of the Nile and Burnham Thorpe. For the next year and a half, he remained in the Mediterranean, where he became embroiled in a torrid and very public love affair with Emma Hamilton, wife of the British minister to the Kingdom of Naples. In July 1800, Nelson and the Hamiltons left Leghorn overland for England.

Despite the fears of his mentor, Lord St. Vincent, and the opprobrium of the priggish King George III, the affair seems not to have affected Nelson's career. The following year he was promoted vice admiral and, under Sir Hyde Parker, attacked the Danish fleet at Copenhagen. For this action, he was created a viscount. On the breakdown of the Peace of Amiens in 1803, Nelson was appointed commander in chief, Mediterranean, and for the next two years blockaded the south coast of France. In January 1805, Villeneuve's fleet broke out and was chased by Nelson to the West Indies and back. After a brief interlude with Emma and their daughter, Horatia, at Merton in Surrey, Nelson was recalled to command the fleet blockading the combined French and Spanish fleets at Cadiz. The enemy sallied out of port and were engaged off Cape Trafalgar on 21 October 1805. Nelson died of a wound as decisive victory was assured.

Nelson's autobiographical sketch, written in 1799 and from which much of the above information is taken, is remarkably modest and straightforward, giving the lie to the common charge of vanity. It only hints at the qualities of leadership that Nelson perfected during those years. There is no mention that, well before the Nile, he had acquired a reputation as a ferocious warrior, untamed by physical injury (he had lost an eye in Corsica in 1794 and an arm at Tenerife in 1797), who had led the boarding of the *San Josef* and *San Nicolas* at the Battle of the Cape St. Vincent in February 1797, or that the efficiency of his commands was maintained by strict discipline combined with a genuine concern for the well-being of his men. His physical courage, unswerving sense of duty, and almost childish craving for battle and glory are not considered worthy of discussion. On the other hand, the sketch pays generous tribute to those from whom Nelson learned his trade or to whom he owed preferment, particularly Viscount Hood, Sir John Jervis (Earl of St. Vincent), and HRH Prince William, Duke of Clarence (the future King William IV), with whom he served in the West Indies.

Such support was important. As a young captain on the Leewards Station, Nelson was rebuked twice by the Admiralty for his lack of "attention to the rules and practice of the service," and probably only his friendship with Prince William saved him from the full force of its wrath.[3] In 1783 Lord Hood presented Nelson to King George III, who "was exceedingly attentive" and honored the young captain with an invitation to Windsor to visit Prince William.[4] More importantly, when the need arose, the Admiralty recognized Nelson's talents and did not fail to make use of them. Early in 1798, when French activity was reported in Toulon, Earl Spencer, the First Lord of the Admiralty, gave Nelson the *Vanguard* and sent him to join St. Vincent's fleet. In 1802, Spencer's successor, Lord Barham, placed Nelson in command of the fleet that was eventually to destroy Franco-Spanish naval power at Trafalgar. As commander in chief on the former occasion, St. Vincent anticipated Lord Spencer's recommendation to advance Nelson over more senior officers to command the squadron reentering the Mediterranean and thus initiated the campaign that led to the Nile. St. Vincent also appointed some of his most experienced captains to serve under Nelson: Edward Berry had been Nelson's lieutenant in the *Agamemnon* and the *Captain;* Alexander Ball had served under Rodney at the Battle of the Saints in 1782; Thomas Louis had been a captain since 1783; R. W. Miller had commanded Nelson's flagship *Captain* at the Battle of Cape St. Vincent; Samuel Hood had seen action during the War of American Independence and had been at the occupation of Toulon in 1793; Benjamin Hallowell had been with Nelson in Corsica at the sieges of Bastia and Calvi and had been supernumerary on Jervis's flagship at Cape St. Vincent; Thomas Troubridge had led the fleet into action at Cape St. Vincent and was with Nelson in the attack on Tenerife; Thomas Hardy, who was to be remembered as Nelson's flag-captain at Trafalgar, Thomas Foley, and James Saumarez had fought at Cape St. Vincent. All became part of the "band of brothers" who won fame at the Nile.

For his part, Nelson strove to build a positive relationship with his captains. Frequent conferences transmitted to them his enthusiasm and forged cohesion, tactical understanding, and the recognition that in the uncertainty of battle individual commanders were expected to seize any initiative that arose. On the latter point, Nelson himself had set the precedent when he veered out of the line to interrupt the Spanish withdrawal at Cape St. Vincent. His battle skills were not simply intuitive but developed over the years of learning. A longtime student of tactics, he had been well schooled by Admiral Hood, who in 1783 promised Prince William Henry that the young captain "could give him as much information [about naval tactics] as any officer in the fleet."[5] Nelson's flag-captain, Berry, wrote in a memoir published after the Battle of the Nile that during the search for Brueys's fleet the *Vanguard*'s quarterdeck became a

> school of captains . . . [where] he would fully develop to them his own ideas of the different and best modes of attacks, and such plans as he proposed to execute upon falling in with the enemy, whatever their position or situation might be by night or day. . . . There was no possible position

> in which they could be found that he did not take into his calculations, and for the most advantageous attack of which he had not digested and arranged the best possible plans. With the masterly ideas of their admiral, therefore, on the subject of naval tactics, every one of his captains was most thoroughly acquainted; and upon surveying the situations of the Enemy they could ascertain with precision what were the ideas and intentions of their Commander, without the aid of any further instructions.[6]

Such thorough briefing of Nelson's officers brought greater efficiency to fleet operations at a time when flag signaling was still by ideograms. The first vocabulary signal books reached the British fleet off Cadiz in September 1805.[7] Not surprisingly, when the moment for action came at the Nile and at Trafalgar, signals were hardly needed. Indeed, at Trafalgar, Nelson's famous "England expects that every man will do his duty" elicited from his second-in-command, Collingwood, an annoyed "I wish Nelson would stop signalling, as we all know well enough what we have to do."[8] There lay the key to the "Nelson Touch." Nelson had brought his captains to the point where they reacted instinctively as he would want them to when unexpected situations arose in the heat of battle. And so the ships and their captains became, in effect, extensions of their admiral's will.

The battle tactics that Nelson and his captains executed at the Nile and Trafalgar were not entirely new and they were not reckless, but they were daring and did break the rules. The Fighting Instructions, dating back to the seventeenth century, laid down formalized maneuvers for sea battles that were in their essentials the same as those prescribed for armies fighting on land. In both cases, the objective was not annihilation of the enemy but to achieve strategical advantage and to maintain the fleet or the army-in-being. Adherence to the line of battle clearly put aggressive admirals at a disadvantage and allowed a defensive-minded enemy to escape all too easily. By the time that Graves's timid holding to the line of battle at Chesapeake Bay in 1781 cost him the chance to destroy de Grasse's fleet, more venturesome British admirals were breaking the enemy's line in an effort to prevent his escape. Nelson brought this tactic to its logical conclusion by using it to concentrate his forces, "doubling" to attack the enemy from both sides, and so bring about the annihilation of the opposing fleet. Here Nelson was an innovator. At the Glorious First of June, 1794, Howe with twenty-five ships had made partial penetration of the French line to capture six of twenty-six enemy sail of the line; at the Battle of Cape St. Vincent in 1797, Jervis's fleet of fifteen had taken four of twenty-seven Spanish ships, two of them by Nelson as a consequence of his veering out of the line; at Camperdown in October 1797, Duncan with sixteen sail had broken the enemy line in two places and taken eight of fifteen Dutch ships. At the Nile, Nelson took or destroyed eleven of thirteen enemy ships of the line; at Trafalgar, where Nelson commanded twenty-seven ships of the line, twenty of the enemy's combined fleet of thirty-three (eighteen French and fifteen Spanish) were taken or struck their colors.

No doctrine of annihilation, no imaginative tactics or captains' daring could succeed unless the sailors obeyed orders, worked as a team, and fought well. Although their conditions of service were often more harsh, British crews generally were better than those of French and Spanish warships. As well as often more daring commanders, they had more sea time, more gunnery practice, and greater battle experience. Nelson never forgot that the fleet and the individual ships were held together by personal bonds and that his successes were largely dependent on the men he commanded. His reputation attracted officers and seamen alike. During the great fleet mutinies of June 1797, when the commander in chief, St. Vincent, was hanging mutineers from the yardarm, a letter signed simply "Ship's Company" assured Nelson and his flag-captain, Miller, that "We are happy and comfortable and will shed every drop of blood in our veins to support them, and the name of the *Theseus* shall be immortalized as high as the *Captain*."[9]

The basis of Nelson's popularity lay in the practical concern he showed for the well-being of his sailors. The record is voluminous; a few examples will illustrate the point. As a junior captain in 1783, when he left the frigate *Albemarle* and the whole crew had volunteered "if I could get a ship, to enter for her immediately," he spent three weeks pestering the Admiralty, "attempting to get the wages due to my good fellows, for various Ships they have served in the war."[10] Victory and fame did not change him. After the Battle of the Nile he ordered read to the ships' companies a letter offering them his

> most sincere and cordial Thanks for their very gallant behaviour in this glorious Battle. It must strike forcibly every British Seaman, how superior their conduct is, when in discipline and good order, to the riotous behaviour of the lawless Frenchmen. The Squadron may be assured the Admiral will not fail . . . to represent their truly meritorious conduct in the strongest terms to the Commander-in-Chief.[11]

Nor did he fail. Indeed, he made himself quite unpopular with Earl Spencer by billing the Admiralty for an additional £60,000 prize money for French ships set on fire after the action. "An admiral may be amply rewarded by his feelings and the approbation of his superiors," he wrote to the First Lord, "but what reward have the inferior officers and men but the value of the Prize?"[12]

Hope of wages and prize money alone did not attract sailors to Nelson or turn a man-of-war into an efficient fighting machine. Health and efficiency, Nelson believed, went hand-in-hand. "It is easier for an officer to keep men healthy than for a Surgeon to save them," he wrote to a friend in 1804.[13] The idea was not unique to Nelson. Forward-looking commanders like St. Vincent insisted so far as possible on decent food, particularly limes and onions, to keep their crews in fighting health. Lord Howe had brought officers and men into a closer relationship with the introduction of divisions, led by lieutenants, subdivided into squadrons under midshipmen, who were responsible for the supervision of the sailors. Nevertheless, Nelson does seem to have been exceptional in the lengths to which he went to ensure the well-being of his crews. Dr. Gillespie, physician to Nelson's fleet during the two years' campaign in the Mediterranean and West Indies that culminated at Trafalgar, reported that of about seven thousand seamen and marines, the total number of deaths on board were one hundred. Gillespie believed the high state of health to be "unexampled perhaps in any squadron heretofore employed on a foreign station." This he attributed "to the attention paid by his lordship to the victualling and purveying for the fleet," to the use of stoves and ventilators below decks, and "the constant activity and motion in which the fleet was preserved." Nelson differed from most commanders by adding other and, at a time when discipline was normally maintained by the lash, more unusual methods of morale boosting. "Intemperance and skulking," Gillespie wrote,

> were never so little practiced in any fleet as in this. . . . Cheerfulness amongst the men was promoted by music and dancing and theatrical amusements: the example of which was given by the commander in chief in the *Victory,* and may with reason be reckoned amongst the causes of the preservation of the health of the men.[14]

So well known and remarkable was this that the political cartoonist Gillray once depicted quite inaccurately Nelson carousing on the quarterdeck with his sailors.

Brought up in the Anglican faith, Nelson did not neglect the spiritual health of his crews. Upon joining the *Vanguard* at Spithead in March 1798, one of his first acts was to request Bibles and prayer books from the Society for Promoting Christian Knowledge.[15] After the victory at the Nile, Nelson had services of thanksgiving held on board the ships of his fleet. And as the fleets closed for battle at Trafalgar on 21 October 1805, Nelson composed the prayer that highlights the conjunction of Christianity, patriotism, and duty:

> May the Great God, whom I worship, grant to my country, and for the benefit of Europe in general, a great and glorious Victory; and may no misconduct in anyone tarnish it; and may humanity after Victory be the predominant feature in the British fleet. For myself, individually, I commit my life to Him who made me, and may His blessing light upon my en-

> deavours for serving my Country faithfully. To him I resign myself, and the just cause which is entrusted to me to defend. Amen. Amen. Amen.

His Anglican upbringing helps to explain the nature of Nelson's patriotism and the intensity with which it was directed against antireligious, republican France. Although there is no doubt that a few of Nelson's seamen were inspired by the conviction that they were doing the work of the Lord, there is no indication that religion played a vital role in the lives of very many of them. There was, however, a conflation of Nelson and divinity in the minds of many sailors. George Charles Smith, captain of the foretop in the *Agamemnon* at the Battle of Copenhagen, wrote many years later that "Nelson was considered our Saviour and our God. . . . We gloried . . . that we followed in the wake of Nelson, as the only Jesus Christ or Saviour we acknowledge in the fleet."[16]

The care that Nelson took to ensure the well-being of the crews did much to mitigate the harshness of sea life and to maintain efficiency and discipline on the vessels under his command. He was not a lax disciplinarian. Although never plagued by mutiny himself, he applauded St. Vincent's severity in hanging in *St. George*'s leading mutineers. "Now your discipline is safe" was his crisp reaction.[17] As an admiral, Nelson left the day-by-day enforcement of discipline to the ship's captain. Edward Berry, flag-captain at the Nile, took his cue from Nelson and resorted to flogging only in the most exceptional circumstances. Nelson does not seem to have been disturbed, however, by Hardy's much more frequent use of the lash to maintain discipline when he was flag-captain in the *Victory* during the Trafalgar campaign. As a captain, Nelson seldom ordered a flogging. His personal touch, the respect with which he treated seamen as well as officers, was sufficient to maintain discipline on the ships he commanded. Although mutual trust and regard were more difficult to gain as commander of a fleet, Nelson's reputation preceded him, so that his ships had noticeably less trouble obtaining and keeping crews than was usual in the Royal Navy.

The test of every aspect of Nelson's leadership came in finding the enemy and then annihilating him in battle. In 1798, Nelson made the educated guess that Napoleon Buonaparte was making for Egypt. When, after the long search, he found the enemy in Aboukir Bay, he took the calculated risk of putting the fleet ashore in shoal waters to attack the French line on two sides. Given the training, aggressiveness, and high morale of the British crews, the maneuver practically guaranteed the enemy's destruction.

The 1798 Mediterranean campaign of which the Battle of the Nile was the culmination regained for Britain the initiative in the naval war. In 1796 Bonaparte's armies had crushed Austria and overrun much of the Italian peninsula. The Franco-Austrian settlement at Campo Formio the following year put the seal on the French hegemony of most of western Europe. Spain changed sides and allied herself with France. Prussia remained neutral and a Franco-Russian alliance appeared possible. A French invasion army was encamped across the English Channel. For the first time during the war, Britain stood alone.

A constant concern for the Admiralty was to prevent the Toulon fleet from breaking out into the Atlantic. Royal Naval squadrons at Gibraltar and Lisbon could possibly prevent that happening. But control of the Mediterranean itself was of great strategical importance to Britain. Protection of the route to the East, particularly India, made imperative the continued independence of the Kingdom of Naples and the Ottoman Empire, including Egypt. As a bonus, a British battle-fleet in the Mediterranean forced France and Spain to divide their naval forces, thus preventing their concentration in the Atlantic.

Bonaparte's victories relieved the British government of any immediate strategic reason to maintain a fleet east of Gibraltar. Without Continental allies, British ships of the line could do little either to impede French armies or to persuade threatened states like Naples to stay within the British orbit. The overcautious British commander, Vice Admiral Sir William Hotham, on two occasions in 1795 had declined to engage the Toulon fleet and so failed to secure maritime control of the Mediterranean.[18] The number of frigates and smaller vessels with which to harass French merchant shipping and coastal troop convoys was totally inadequate. Victualing of British warships in Mediterranean ports had always been precarious and in these circumstances became almost impossible. For as long as the main French fleet in Toulon remained inactive, a temporary withdrawal of the British navy from the Mediterranean made good sense.

In March and April 1798, however, reports reaching the Admiralty indicated a massive buildup of French shipping and estimates of up to 80,000 troops in Toulon. Spencer, First Lord of the Admiralty, and Dundas, Secretary of War, feared that the French might attempt to break out through the Straits of Gibraltar into the Atlantic and sail to Brest in preparation for another invasion of Ireland. To confuse matters, some reports suggested that Bonaparte's target might be Naples, Egypt, or the Levant. Whichever the case, the French fleet could not be allowed to put to sea unchallenged. Prime Minister William Pitt the Younger was trying desperately to form a second coalition against France. Prospective allies might be swayed by a reassertion of British naval power in the Mediterranean. They would certainly be dissuaded by a French fleet sailing freely about the Mediterranean and the consequent threat to the Ottoman Empire and the important communication lanes of the Adriatic. To the British government, as Spencer with pardonable exaggeration told St. Vincent, it seemed that "the appearance of a British squadron in the Mediterranean is a condition on which the fate of Europe may at the moment be stated to depend."[19]

In these circumstances, Nelson hoisted his flag at the mizzen of HMS *Vanguard* as Rear Admiral of the Blue and on 1 May 1798 joined St. Vincent's fleet off Cadiz. A week later he entered the Mediterranean in command of a reconnaissance force of three 74-gun sail of the line, the *Vanguard* (Captain Berry), *Orion* (Saumarez), and *Alexander* (Ball), and three frigates, charged to observe French activities in Toulon. Initially, the frigates performed well. The *Terpsichore* captured a French corvette whose crew confirmed that Bonaparte was in the port and that troops were embarking daily, but no one would admit to knowing their destination. Nineteen sail of the line were observed in harbor, of which fifteen appeared to be ready for sea.[20] Then, on 20 May, near-disaster struck Nelson. Driven south by northwest gales, the *Vanguard* lost her foremast and her other two topmasts. In a truly Nelsonian gesture, Captain Ball refused to obey the admiral's order to leave the flagship to her fate. Despite a dangerous lee shore, the *Alexander* took the *Vanguard* in tow and shepherded her to shelter off Saint Peter's Island on the Sardinian coast. Thus, in similar fashion to the incident the previous year when Nelson had risked the frigate *Minerve* in order to save Hardy from capture by the Spanish, bonds of trust and affection were cemented between Nelson and one of his captains.[21] Within four days the *Vanguard* had jury masts rigged. More serious was the disappearance of the frigates. Their senior commander, Captain Hope, assumed that the *Vanguard* would have to dock for repairs and took the vital scouting ships back to Gibraltar. For the rest of the campaign Nelson suffered from the lack of frigates, "the eyes of the fleet," and had to rely on suspect information garnered from intercepted vessels, mostly French and Italian, from consular and other officials in foreign, often hostile, ports and on the invaluable dispatch services of HM brig *La Mutine* commanded by Captain Thomas Hardy.

By the time Nelson returned to watch Toulon the harbor was empty. Bonaparte's massive armada of some one hundred troop and supply ships escorted by thirteen ships of the line and seven frigates, with Vice Admiral Brueys's flag in the 120-gun *Orient,* had sailed unobserved in the wake of the storm. Knowing no more than he had when he left St. Vincent's fleet, with only three battleships and without scouting vessels, Nelson had to find an enemy who had vanished beneath the horizon and who might be heading west into the Atlantic or east to southern Italy, Egypt, or the Levant. The choice made by Nelson would be critical to the whole course of the war. If he searched eastward and was wrong, the enemy would break out into the Atlantic and might even elude St. Vincent's fleet off Cadiz.

Meanwhile, St. Vincent had received a directive from the Admiralty that twelve line-of-battle ships were to be sent into the Mediterranean to "de-

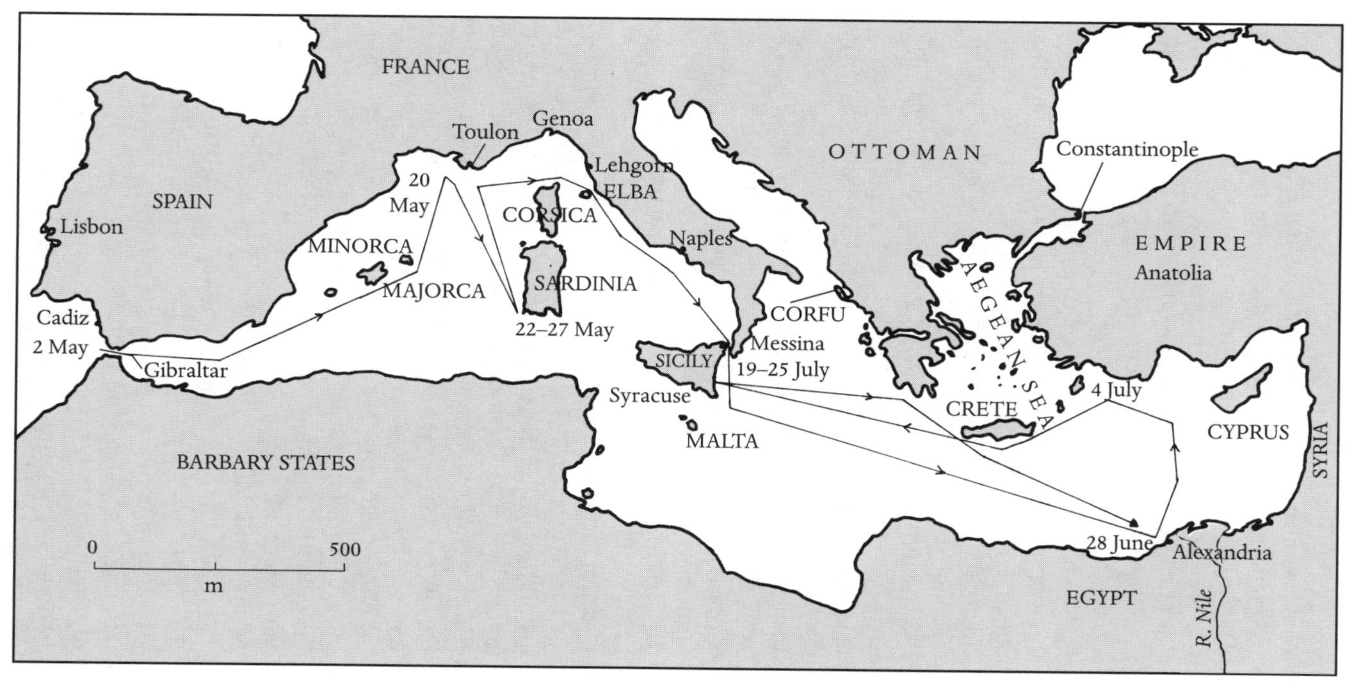

13. Nelson's Pursuit of the French Fleet, 1798.

feat the purpose of the Toulon Armament, whatever it might be." St. Vincent himself could command the fleet or put it under "some discreet Flag-Officer." An accompanying private and confidential letter from Lord Spencer added that if St. Vincent did not command the expedition himself, "I think it almost unnecessary to suggest to you the propriety of putting it under the command of Sir H. Nelson, whose acquaintance with the part of the world, as well as his activity and disposition seem to qualify him in a peculiar manner for that service."[22]

On 5 June, the *Mutine* joined Nelson off Cape Sicié near Toulon with the news that a force of eleven battleships was on it way. Two days later, Captain Troubridge arrived with the reinforcements. Nelson now commanded a fleet consisting of the thirteen 74-gun ships: the *Vanguard, Orion, Alexander, Culloden* (Troubridge), *Theseus* (Miller), *Minotaur* (Louis), *Swiftsure* (Hallowell), *Audacious* (Gould), *Defence* (Peyton), *Zealous* (Hood), *Goliath* (Foley), *Majestic* (Westcott), and *Bellerophon* (Darby), the 50-gun *Leander* (Thompson), and the 16-gun brig *Mutine*. But Captain Hope and the frigates remained in Gibraltar.

Orders from St. Vincent instructed Nelson to seek and "to take, sink, burn, or destroy" the French fleet. St. Vincent's assessment that the enemy's objective was "either an attack upon Naples and Sicily, the conveyance of an Army to some part of the Coast of Spain, for the purpose of marching towards Portugal, or to pass through the Straits, with the view of proceeding to Ireland," added nothing that Nelson did not know. There was no mention of Egypt. The admonition that he should "take especial care to prevent" the enemy's escape to the west made Nelson's choice even more difficult.[23]

There was nothing to be done but hunt for news of the enemy. The *Mutine* was sent to look into Telamon Bay, on the Italian coast, which Nelson thought a likely rendezvous for the French out of Toulon and those that had gathered in Genoa, but drew a blank. Already half convinced that Bonaparte's objective was Egypt, Nelson took the fleet southward toward Naples. On 14 June, off Elba, intelligence was received that seemed to confirm Nelson's suspicions. A Tunisian cruiser reported that a Greek vessel had seen the French fleet on the fourth steering southeastward off northwestern Sicily. That slim piece of evidence suggested to Nelson that the French would pass to the south of the island. "If they pass Sicily," he wrote to Earl Spencer, "I shall believe they are going on their scheme of possessing Alexandria. . . ."[24]

On the seventeenth, Troubridge sped to Naples in the *Mutine* in an attempt to obtain frigates, pilots, and supplies for the fleet from the king.[25] Troubridge rejoined Nelson off Ischia without frigates but with authorization to revictual in Neapolitan ports and a report from Sir William Hamilton, the British minister in Naples, that the French had gone toward Malta.

Immediately, expecting to catch the French off Malta, Nelson dispatched a letter to the Grand Master, asking him to assemble his warships to join the British the moment they appeared off the island.[26] Off Messina on the twentieth, he found local authorities frightened, of no assistance, and unwilling to provide even information. "On the contrary," he wrote in anger and frustration to Sir William Hamilton, "the French Minister is allowed to send off Vessels to inform the Fleet of my arrival, force, and destination, that instead of surprising them, they may be prepared for resistance."[27] To compound the problems, the British consul brought news that Malta had surrendered to Bonaparte. Two days later, about thirty-five miles southeast of Cape Passaro, on the southeast tip of Sicily, the *Mutine* spoke to a Genoese brig whose master reported that the French fleet had left Malta on the sixteenth, "as was supposed, for Sicily."[28]

Once again, the French had disappeared. On meager information, all of it secondhand, Nelson had to make a judgment that might decide the fate of Pitt's alliance overtures and, hence, the outcome of the war. Officials in Naples and Sicily had made it clear to him that the kingdom was at peace with the French republic and that no practical help would be forthcoming. With Malta in French hands, it was unlikely that he would obtain useful information there. Unaware that *Mutine*'s information was incorrect and that the French had not sailed from Malta until 19 June, Nelson felt certain that if Sicily was the French objective he would have received word of sightings before now and that the king of Naples would have called on him for aid. It was also clear that the huge enemy armada, which Nelson now estimated at 40,000 troops in 280 transports, had not been assembled simply to take Malta. If the French were destined for the Atlantic, he thought it unlikely that they would have gone southeast to Malta, from whence seasonal west-northwesterly winds would make it almost impossible to sail the transports to the west.

On the other hand, if the French destination was to the east, the winds were right and Malta made an excellent base. Assuming, then, that they were heading eastward, their objective could be Corfu, in which case it was probably too late to catch them at sea; or to topple the Ottoman Porte, which would involve taking the armada through the Aegean or landing in Syria to march into Anatolia from the south; or, as Nelson was almost sure, to seize Alexandria and move the army via the Red Sea to India. "Three weeks, at this season," he wrote to St. Vincent, "is a common passage to the Malabar Coast."[29] Of these alternatives, Egypt would be the easiest to take and pose the greatest threat to Britain, Constantinople would be the hardest nut to crack, with Syria strategically the most unlikely target.

Immediately after receiving the *Mutine*'s news, Nelson signaled for Saumarez, Darby, Ball, and Troubridge to come on board the *Vanguard* for a conference. Weighing their information and the options, his captains agreed with Nelson that Egypt was almost certainly the French target and that the fleet should make haste for Alexandria. Accordingly, the squadron crammed on all sail and, without frigates to scout ahead and on its flanks, passed the slower and cumbersome French force during the night. At daylight on 23 June, the fleets were out of sight of each other. Brueys was steering toward Crete in an effort to confuse any merchantmen who might observe him. For five days, Nelson received no word of the enemy. On 26 June, he sent the *Mutine* ahead with dispatches for the British consul in Alexandria, where the fleet arrived two days later to find the port devoid of enemy activity. In despair that his judgment had failed him, Nelson swung his ships north toward Cyprus. The massive French convoy lumbered into Alexandria harbor unscathed on 1 July. Nelson had missed the opportunity of destroying Bonaparte's *armée d'Orient* at sea and perhaps Bonaparte himself.

Nelson has been criticized for not realizing that he had overtaken the enemy. There was no reason why such a possibility should have entered his mind. On the contrary, he had every reason to push the squadron as fast as he could to Egypt. Had the report from the Genoese merchantman that the French had left Malta on the sixteenth been correct, the British squadron could not have overtaken them. Nelson's arrival off Alexandria probably would have found the enemy in harbor. His assessment of the information available to him had been correct. He had no way of knowing that one critical piece of that information was faulty.

For almost four fruitless weeks, Nelson scoured the northeastern Mediterranean. On 20 July, he was back in Syracuse, "as ignorant of the situation of the Enemy as I was twenty-seven days ago."[30] But it was clear that the French had not gone westward; indeed, Nelson felt sure that he would have heard if they were anywhere to the west of Corfu. Despite "scandalous" treatment from the governor of Syracuse, who refused to allow more than four ships in the harbor at a time, the fleet victualed and watered. It sailed from Syracuse on the twenty-fourth for a second cast to the east. At last Nelson's luck changed and his initial judgment was confirmed. Troubridge, who had been sent on the twenty-eighth to scout the Gulf of Coron in the Peloponnesus, returned the next day with a captured French brig and information that the enemy fleet had been seen steering southeast from Crete about four weeks earlier. This intelligence was corroborated the same day by a vessel that passed close by Ball's *Alexander*. Immediately, Nelson made full sail southeastward for Alexandria. At about four o'clock on the afternoon of 1 August, the *Zealous* (Captain Samuel Hood) signaled that the enemy were in sight, seventeen men-of-war, of which thirteen or fourteen were anchored in line of battle across Aboukir Bay some fifteen miles east of Alexandria.

The fleet that bore down on Brueys's men-of-war was ready and eager for battle. Nelson's strategical insight had proved correct. Now his tactical skills would be put to the test. His captains were thoroughly versed in what they had to do. The crews had been honed to a knife-edge by constant drills during the long, frustrating weeks at sea. Morale was high. "The utmost joy," Captain Berry later remarked, "seemed to animate every breast on board the Squadron, at sight of the enemy."[31] This was certainly true of Nelson, whose reaction was of elation mixed with relief at having found the French. Without ado, he made the prearranged signal to attack the enemy van and center. Then, while the *Vanguard*'s decks were being cleared for action, he sat down at the first hearty dinner he had eaten in weeks. As his officers rose from the table to go to their battle stations, Nelson predicted that "Before this time tomorrow, I shall have gained a Peerage, or Westminster Abbey."[32]

The French position appeared impregnable. Anchored by the bow about five hundred feet apart across the mouth of the bay with shoal waters to landward and at either end of the line, their line-of-battle ships faced the British squadron with a solid wall of guns. Theoretically, their weight of metal was vastly superior. Opposed to Nelson's thirteen 74s and one 50, Brueys had his 120-gun flagship, the *Orient,* four 80-gun ships and eight 74s, plus a 40 and two 36-gun frigates, together with several bomb ketches and gunboats. A gun-battery had been placed on Aboukir Island just to the west of the French van. As it turned out, Nelson's firepower was reduced considerably for much of the battle. The *Swiftsure* and *Alexander* had been sent to reconnoiter off Alexandria and did not join the battle until eight o'clock that evening. The *Culloden* ran onto the Aboukir shoal to become the only British ship not to fire a shot during the battle. The French advantages were somewhat offset by the condition of their fleet. Admiral Brueys himself was sick, as were many of his officers and men. Watering parties were ashore and could not return to their ships once fighting commenced. The ships themselves were cluttered from being in harbor for so long and consequently could not rapidly clear for action. They swung to anchor, some without the springs or bower cables that would have enabled them to avoid being raked from stern to stem. Expecting that an attack would be directed at his rear, Brueys had positioned his most powerful ships at that end of the line. In addition, some ships had only their seaward guns run out in firing position.

Nelson surprised the French admiral on two accounts. First, by attacking as darkness fell. Second, by risking the shoals to attack from both sides of the line. Not until almost the last moment, when he saw the British forming into line ahead and astern of the *Vanguard,* did Brueys believe that Nelson would attack in the final hour of daylight. It was a reasonable assumption. The bay was not well charted and the British ships would have

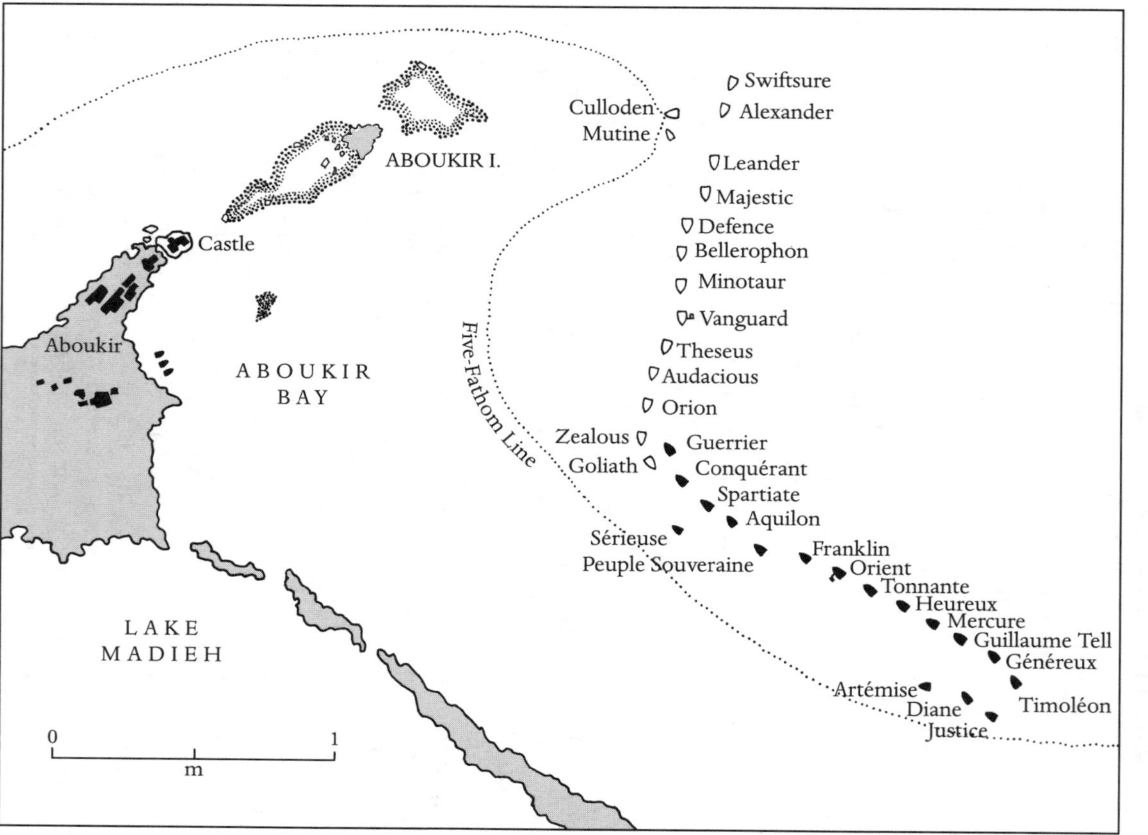

14. The Battle of the Nile, 1 August 1798: the approach of Nelson's fleet.
Based on a map published in Paris in 1838.

7. The Battle of the Nile, 1–2 August 1798. Nicholas Pocock's contemporary painting shows the situation at approximately six o'clock in the afternoon, when Nelson's fleet had rounded Aboukir Island shoal. The *Goliath* has already crossed in front of the *Guerrier* at the head of the French line. (The National Maritime Museum, Greenwich, England.)

constantly to take soundings. The French could concentrate on their gunnery while the British would also have to maneuver their vessels in dangerous waters. A night action appeared to be suicidal for the attacker. Brueys thought that, at most, the British would send one or two vessels to observe and take soundings in the bay. He confidently expected to have the whole night to prepare for battle; instead, he had about forty-five minutes.

At half-past five, as the fleet was almost abreast the Aboukir Island shoal, Nelson made the signal for close action; the sun set at half-past six, by which time the battle had begun. In the steady waters of the bay, to have attacked the enemy line of battle in the conventional fashion would have been like bombarding shore fortifications, with all of the advantages on the side of the defenders. Nelson never intended to do this. His plan was straightforward and did not require elaboration to his captains. They had discussed every conceivable possibility, including that of attacking the French fleet in harbor. Seeing that where there was room for an enemy ship to swing, there must be room for a British ship to slide between it and the shoal, they would split the enemy van and center, attacking from both sides. Each British captain would seek a position that would allow for mutual and maximum concentration of firepower. They would then anchor by the stern with bower cables bent forward so that the ships could maneuver to keep their broadsides bearing on the enemy. By attacking the van and moving down the line as the enemy were reduced to rubble, the British would reverse the French advantage of firepower. With the approaching darkness, Nelson ordered his ships to go into battle flying the White Ensign, more easily seen than the Blue Ensign to which he was entitled, and three lanterns horizontally at the mizzenheads.[33]

Shortly after half-past five, Nelson asked Hood whether he thought there was enough water to clear the shoal if they bore up. Hood replied that he did not know but would like to find out. Nelson assented and the *Zealous* cautiously led the fleet around the head of the shoal. The way in to the awaiting French was clear. Within the hour, as the sun set and under fire from the leading French ships, the *Guerrier* and *Conquérant,* both 74s, and the ineffective Aboukir battery, the *Zealous,* with *Goliath* on her port bow, followed by the *Orion, Audacious,* and *Theseus,* sounded the way across the head of the French line. The *Goliath* opened the action for the British with a raking broadside as she passed under the *Guerrier*'s forefoot. She then anchored between the *Conquérant* and the 36-gun frigate *Sérieuse* as the other four British ships inside the line selected their targets.

Meanwhile, Nelson took the *Vanguard* and the rest of his ships down the seaward side of the French. The last vessel in the British line, Troubridge's *Culloden,* hit the shoal, where she stuck fast, her only service during the battle being to act as a beacon to the *Alexander* and *Swiftsure* as they arrived just before eight o'clock in darkness to join the fight. Within half an hour, the five leading French ships were battling eight British, five on their port, or landward, side and three to their starboard. Resistance was fierce and it was more than two hours before all five were taken and the British 74s could move down the line to assist the *Bellerophon* and *Majestic,* which were being badly battered by Brueys's *Orient, Tonnant,* and *Heureux* at the center. As the *Bellerophon* drifted totally disabled from the fight, her place was taken by the *Alexander* and *Swiftsure.* Shortly thereafter, Brueys was killed and his flagship caught fire. At about ten o'clock the *Orient* blew up. From then on, the outcome of the battle was never in doubt.

The fighting continued until well after dawn. Only Rear Admiral Villeneuve's flagship, the 80-gun *Guillaume Tell,* together with the 74-gun *Généreux* and two frigates at the rear of the French line escaped. Taking advantage of the British ships being fully engaged at the center, they set sail and slipped their cables. Hood, in a magnificent attempt to hold the enemy until help could come up, for a few minutes engaged the four ships single-handed.

With no ships fit for pursuit, Nelson recalled the *Theseus* and the French vessels made their way safely out of the bay.

Although his ships had been severely mauled, Nelson's victory was complete. Of a total complement of 8,068 men, British losses amounted to 218 killed and 677 wounded. There is no firm record of French casualties; the best estimate is that of a total of 8,930 men actually aboard the French vessels during the battle, 5,225, almost 60 percent, were killed, drowned, or taken prisoner.[34] Nelson's tactical judgments had been correct. His willingness to delegate authority, reinforced by the frequent discussion on board the *Vanguard* during the long search, had paid off, as had the daily sail and gunnery exercises that maintained morale and efficiency. Nelson's offensive spirit seems to have infected every man in the squadron. These factors came together at the Nile as captains and crews did exactly what Nelson expected of them. The scale of the resultant massacre emphasized how much Nelson had changed the idea of naval battle, using the same instruments as his predecessors but bold tactics that aimed at annihilation of the enemy rather than simple defeat.

At Aboukir Bay another episode was added to the growing legend of Nelson's fame. Early in the action Nelson sustained a nasty head wound. Carried semiconscious to the cockpit, he refused immediate treatment, exclaiming "No, I will take my turn with my brave followers."[35] Convinced that he was dying, Nelson asked the chaplain to convey his regards to his wife and to send for Captain Louis of the *Minotaur* that he might thank him for coming to the *Vanguard*'s assistance. Typically, in his report to Lord St. Vincent, Nelson mentioned the wound only to stress the services of Edward Berry: "I was wounded in the head, and obliged to be carried off the deck; but the service suffered no loss by that event; Captain Berry was fully equal to the important service then going on." Nelson did not include his own name on the official casualty list drawn up after the battle.[36] Quick to acknowledge the vital part played by every man in the squadron, his public praise of his subordinates and his ultimately successful attempt to gain prize money for them further endeared him to officers and men alike. On 3 August, the captains of the squadron formed the Egyptian Club in commemoration of the victory and presented Nelson with a sword. Some months later, Benjamin Hallowell, captain of the *Swiftsure,* presented Nelson with a coffin made from the *Orient*'s mainmast. "You may look at it, Gentlemen, as long as you please," he told his officers, "but, depend on it, none of you shall have it."[37]

Nelson's willingness to depart from the conventions of the Fighting Instructions and to take calculated risks reflected a changing attitude toward warfare and toward the political situation of Europe. The French Revolution threatened the very bases of the European state system. No longer were monarchies with essentially similar political and social structures struggling with one another. In the 1790s the conflict with France was one against a new kind of enemy, an ideological battle of monarchy against a revolution-exporting republic. In all previous wars, the British had been fighting to retain imperial holdings or to gain strategic or mercantile advantages. Now they were faced with a fundamental threat to the whole European system of monarchy. As well as a contest for territorial gain, warfare had become a contest for the minds of men. Accompanying this beginning of the decline of the Continental empires and the first signs of the ideological clashes that were in the twentieth century to divide Europe into two armed camps, was the dawning of the age of mass warfare, conscript citizen armies, and rapid technological change. The Nelsonian battle for annihilation was a small but significant indication of what was to come.

Nelson himself saw the struggle with France very much in ideological terms. He hated the French for their godlessness and for their republicanism, principles that attacked everything he believed in. In the short run, the victory at the Nile helped to alleviate the threat. By the time the Second Coalition collapsed and the Peace of Amiens was signed in 1802, Bonapart had become First Consul and the French Republic was an imperial power. When, in 1803, Napoleon crowned himself Emperor of the French, the way to a Bourbon restoration was already opening and revolutionary republicanism was temporarily shunted aside. Nelson's last great victory, off Cape Trafalgar on 21 October 1805, confirmed Britain's mastery of the seas.

That mastery had not been obtained simply by Nelson's genius at handling men and his tactical insight, crucial though they were. Nelson himself was the first to acknowledge that he owed his success to others—to Spencer, Barham, and St. Vincent, who supplied the grand strategy that he helped to implement and, always uppermost in his expressions of gratitude, the captains and men who sailed under his command. He recognized that without them there could have been no Nelson. Between Nelson and the officers and sailors there operated a mutual admiration and respect that was crucial in securing the eclipse of French naval power.

NOTES

1. John Keegan, *The Price of Admiralty* (London: Hutchinson, 1988), p. 8, points out that the major naval victories of the late eighteenth century were British—Rodney at the Battle of the Saints in 1782, Howe at the Glorious First of June in 1794, and Duncan at Camperdown in 1797, together with Nelson's three.

2. Horatio Nelson, "Sketch of My Life," written in October 1799 for John McArthur, the editor of the *Naval Chronicle,* quoted in Geoffrey Rawson, *Nelson's Letters* (London: Dent, 1960), p. 1.

3. Ibid., pp. 58–59.

4. Letter, Nelson to Captain Locker, 12 July 1783, Sir Nicholas Harris Nicolas, ed., *The Dispatches and Letters of Vice Admiral Lord Viscount Nelson,* 7 vols. (2nd ed., London: Henry Coburn, 1845; 1st ed., 1844), I:76.

5. "Lives of Nelson," *Quarterly Review,* vol. 3 (February 1810), p. 230.

6. *Naval Chronicle,* 1799, quoted in Nicolas, op. cit., III:49.

7. Keegan, op. cit., pp. 49–59.

8. Geoffrey Bennett, *Nelson the Commander* (New York: Scribner's, 1972), p. 267.

9. Rawson, op. cit., p. 155.

10. Letter, Nelson to Captain Locker, 12 July 1783, Nicolas, op. cit., I:76.

11. Message from Nelson to the Captains of the Ships of the Squadron, 2 August 1798, ibid., III:61.

12. Letter, Nelson to Lord Spencer, 7 September 1798, Rawson, op. cit., pp. 200–201.

13. Letter, Nelson to Dr. Moreley, 11 March 1804, Nelson Papers, British Library, Additional MSS. 37076.

14. Quoted in Joshua White, *Memoirs of the Professional Life of the Right Honourable Horatio Lord Viscount Nelson, Vice-Admiral of the White . . .* (London: Albion Press, 1806), pp. 337–39.

15. Many years later, the SPCK distributed to ships Southey's *Life of Nelson,* along with the Bible.

16. *Soldiers' and Sailors' Magazine,* vol. 35 (December 1852), p. 419, and vol. 39 (April 1859), p. 165.

17. Letter, Nelson to Captain Sir Robert Calder, 9 July, Rawson, op. cit., p. 160.

18. Nelson, serving under Hotham as captain of the 64-gun *Agamemnon,* was dismayed at the order to break off action on 14 March 1795. "My disposition cannot bear tame or low measures," he wrote to Mrs. Nelson on 1 April. "Sure I am, had I commanded our Fleet on the 14th, that either the whole French Fleet would have graced my triumph, or I should have been in a confounded scrape." Ibid., p. 102.

19. W. H. Richmond, ed., *Spencer Papers* (London: Navy Records Society, 1923), II:437.

20. Letter to Lord St. Vincent from Nelson, *Vanguard,* off Cape Sicié, 17 May 1798, Rawson, op. cit., p. 179.

21. Nelson's refusal to leave Hardy to his fate is recounted in almost every book about the admiral. While the *Minerve* was being pursued by two Spanish ships of the line, a British seaman had fallen overboard. Hardy, the first lieutenant, took a longboat to his rescue and was in danger of being captured. Exclaiming, "By God, I'll not lose Hardy!" Nelson ordered Captain Cockburn to back the *Minerve*'s topsails. Fortunately, this so confused the Spanish captains that they too backed their sails and the rescue of Hardy and his crew was made without untoward problem.

22. Letters of 2 May and 29 April 1798, Rawson, op. cit., pp. 183–84.

23. Instructions from St. Vincent to Nelson, 21 May 1798, delivered by Captain Troubridge on 7 June, ibid.

24. Nelson to Lord Spencer, 15 June 1798, in Nicolas, op. cit., III:31.

25. The events of 17 June 1798 are murky. Lady Hamilton's own account, retold in J. Harrison, *The Life of the Right Honourable Horatio, Lord Viscount Nelson* (London:

C. Chapple, 1806) and repeated in many works since, is that the king and General Acton, the prime minister, would do nothing to offend the French and that Emma Hamilton went to the queen and obtained a letter from her ordering the governors of ports in Naples and Sicily to admit and provision Nelson's fleet. Nelson endorsed this view in 1800 and, no doubt, would have liked to believe it. There is nothing to support it in any of the correspondence. Sir William Hamilton wrote to Lord St. Vincent the same day that General Acton had given him a written order "to the Commanders of all the Ports of Sicily to supply our ships with provisions. . . . Troubridge was perfectly satisfied with this." See Jack Russell, *Nelson and the Hamiltons* (London: Penguin, 1972), pp. 46–47.

26. Letter, Nelson to the Grand Master of Malta, 20 June 1798, Nicolas, op. cit., III: 34.

27. Letter, Nelson to Sir William Hamilton, 20 June 1798, ibid., pp. 34–36.

28. Letter, Nelson to St. Vincent, 29 June 1798, ibid., p. 39.

29. Ibid., p. 40.

30. Letter, Nelson to Sir William Hamilton, 20 July 1798, ibid., pp. 43–44.

31. Berry's narrative of the battle, ibid., p. 49.

32. Ibid., p. 55.

33. The idea did not originate with Nelson. St. Vincent had foreseen the likelihood of confusion and had issued a general order to the fleet that the White Ensign should be flown during an action in addition to the usual battle flags.

34. Nicolas, op. cit., III: 54–55.

35. Ibid., p. 55. By some accounts Nelson used the word "fellows"; see, for example, Bennett, op. cit., p. 138.

36. Letter and reports from Nelson to Lord St. Vincent, 3 August 1798, Nicolas, op. cit., III: 56–60.

37. Ibid., p. 89. Nelson was buried in the coffin on 9 January 1806 in the crypt of St. Paul's Cathedral.

NOTE ON SOURCES

The materials on Nelson are legion. Only a minute portion can be mentioned here. Major collections of papers devoted entirely or in part to Nelson are in the National Maritime Museum, Greenwich, England. Letters and papers of Nelson, Lady Hamilton, Lady Nelson, and other members of the family are described in volumes I and II of R. J. B. Knight's *Guide to the Manuscripts in the National Maritime Museum* (London: Mansell, 1977, 1980). Useful notes on the provenance of some of the papers are in K. F. Lindsay-MacDougall, "Nelson Manuscripts at the National Maritime Museum," *The Mariner's Mirror,* vol. 41 (1955), pp. 227–32. The bulk of Nelson Letter Books are in the Manuscripts Room of the British Library. Other collections of "Nelsoniana" are in the Nelson Museum, Monmouth, the McCarthy Collection at the Royal Naval Museum, Portsmouth, at Lloyd's of London, and at the Nelson Museum on Nevis, W.I.

Many of the documents relevant to Nelson's life have been printed. The most complete source is Sir Nicholas Harris Nicolas, *The Dispatches and Letters of Vice-Admiral Lord Viscount Nelson,* 7 vols. (London: Henry Colburn, 1844–46). A handy collection of the major letters, with a little commentary, is Geoffrey Rawson, *Nelson's Letters* (London: Dent, 1960; paperback edition, 1971). Thomas Pettigrew, *Memoirs of the Life of Vice-Admiral Lord Viscount Nelson,* 2 vols. (London, 1849) and *The Hamilton and Nelson Papers* collected by Alfred Morrison, 2 vols. (London, privately printed, 1893–94), contain some material not found in Nicolas. The Navy Records Society has issued several volumes of documents. G. P. B. Naish, *Nelson's Letters to His Wife and Other Documents, 1785–1831* (London: Navy Records Society, 1958), and H. C. Gutteridge, *Nelson and the Neapolitan Jacobins* (London: Navy Records Society, 1903), are among the most useful; they should be supplemented with the collections of papers of Spencer, Barham, St. Vincent, and Keith, also published by the NRS.

There are myriad biographies, some excellent, some less so. It would be invidious to draw comparisons. The best known, and the longest-lived, are those by Robert Southey (1813), Alfred Thayer Mahan (1897), and Carola Oman (1947). The latter is the most comprehensive. The most recent biography (1988), by Tom Pocock, deals sketchily with the campaigns but tries with some success to get under the skin of Nelson. Unfortunately, like most Nelson biographers, Pocock does not detail his sources.

Books that deal in part with Nelson often contain the most valuable discussions of his character and leadership qualities and the conditions of life and battle in the wooden walls. John Horsfield, *The Art of Leadership in War: The Royal Navy from the Age of Nelson to the End of World War II* (Westport, Conn.: Greenwood Press, 1980), tries to fit Nelson into what he sees as a tradition of confident leadership that developed in the eighteenth century. On a different tack, the opening chapter of John Keegan's *The Price of Admiralty* (London: Hutchinson, 1988) is a vivid evocation of the Battle of Trafalgar that places Nelson's victory in the context of the technology of the day. Christopher Lloyd's brief *The Nile Campaign: Nelson and Napoleon in Egypt* (New York: Barnes and Noble, 1973) is a more conventional treatment but contains translations of some important French documents. Dudley Pope, *The Great Gamble* (New York: Simon and Schuster, 1972), is a full and well-documented study of the events leading up to and the consequences of the Battle of Copenhagen. A fast-paced narrative by Peter Padfield, *Nelson's War* (London: Hart-Davis MacGibbon, 1976), makes a splendid introduction to the general topic.

Several works put the war at sea into its full context. The most ambitious is Paul Kennedy's tour de force, *The Rise and Fall of British Naval Mastery* (London: Allen Lane, 1976), which is essential reading for anyone interested in British maritime power. Dealing in more detail with the French Revolutionary and Napoleonic wars are G. J. Marcus, *A Naval History of England: The Age of Nelson* (London: Allen and Unwin, 1971), the same author's *Heart of Oak: A Survey of British Sea Power in the Georgian Era* (Oxford: Oxford University Press, 1975), and C. Northcote Parkinson, *Britannia Rules: The Classic Age of Naval History, 1793–1815* (London: Weidenfeld and Nicolson, 1977).

9

Andreas Miaoulis
From Pirate to Admiral
(1769–1835)

Konstantinos Varfis

IN THE MINDS OF MODERN GREEKS, THE NAME ANDREAS Miaoulis is synonymous with courage and successful endeavor. The ten-year-old boy who became a sailor and grew up to be a pirate and a merchant before embracing the cause of Greek independence would be remembered as one of the most remarkable figures in Greek history and the symbol of devotion to the ideal of an independent Greek state. The navy recalls him as the first admiral of the Greek fleet, the man who turned a small number of merchant ships into a force that defied the combined Turkish and Egyptian fleets and who made the Aegean once more a Greek sea.*

The life of Andreas Miaoulis can be understood only in the context of the island that shaped it. Hydra, a lonely piece of rock in the Aegean with an area of barely sixty-four square kilometers, was settled mainly by refugees fleeing the Turkish persecution that followed the wars between Venice and Turkey (1640–1715) and an unsuccessful uprising in the Peloponnesus during the Russo-Turkish War of 1768. Unable to wring a living from the island's barren soil, the Hydriotes turned to the sea as their sole means of survival. They built their own ships, primitive at first, and began making a living by transporting merchandise to nearby ports and islands. Gradually they became merchants, without ceasing to be the owners and crewmen of their vessels. The responsibility they showed in their transactions and the speed of their ships, improving from year to year, led them to substantial profits. Soon word spread that Hydriote mariners were the best in the eastern Mediterranean.[1]

Hydra's prosperity stemmed in part from its special relationship with the Turkish Empire (or, more formally, the Ottoman Porte), which had ruled Greece since the fifteenth century. In 1770, the Russian Admiral Alexander Orlof destroyed the Ottoman fleet at the Battle of Chesme and gained control of the Aegean. Almost all the Greek islanders were ready to take part in the struggle against the Turks, hoping to achieve independence. Hydra was an exception: its people were *forced* to collaborate with the Russians, a circumstance they did not hesitate to make known to the Porte. As a reward for the Hydriotes' loyalty, the Turks later granted them passes that allowed their ships to conduct business while the Ottoman fleet suppressed the trade

* The author gratefully acknowledges the valuable assistance of Mr. George Fassoulakis, attorney at law and member of the bar of Athens, Greece, in preparing the English translation of this paper.

of other islands. This policy enabled Hydra to become a major maritime power and perhaps the wealthiest part of Greece. Its privileges were perpetuated by the Treaty of Kioutsouk-Kainartzi (1774),[2] one of whose provisions granted Hydra the right of self-administration; others, facilitating the Greek carrying trade, made it possible for the islanders to take full advantage of a fall in European maritime commerce. It is said that until 1815 the financial boom was such that, having run out of safes and other storage places, at times wealthy Hydriotes used their water cisterns to hold their ever-increasing hoards of gold coins.[3] During the same period, the need to defend their ships against the pirates with whom the Mediterranean swarmed and the compulsory service to which they were subject in the Ottoman fleet introduced the Hydriotes to the techniques of war at sea. Some of their trading vessels were more heavily armed than British warships of the same size.[4]

Like most of Hydra's well-to-do citizens, Dimitrios Vokos was the owner of a *latini,* a sailing ship of less than two hundred tons. Moody, violent at times, and intensely religious, the captain had eight children by three successive wives. Andreas, the future admiral, was the fifth. He was born in 1769, the same year in which Napoleon Buonaparte came into the world on another Mediterranean island. Also in that year Hydra was shaken by a series of earthquakes, which would later be interpreted as an omen of the decisive role Dimitrios Vokos's son was to play in Greek history.

Andreas's childhood was far from calm. The Vokos household often shook from violent conflicts among the brothers, while the narrow streets and whitewashed walls of the island's houses echoed the moans of refugees from the Peloponnesus, fleeing the massacres that followed their unsuccessful rebellion against Ottoman rule. Homeless and in despair, these unfortunate people could be seen everywhere in Hydra.

Dimitrios followed a Hydriote tradition when he sent his son to sea before the boy was ten. Most of his crewmen were relatives or friends. During four to six years' cruising in the capricious Mediterranean, Andreas learned not only how to be an efficient mariner but also to evade or, failing that, fight off pirates. He also demonstrated an exceptional ability to memorize the position of stars and the location of landmarks used by seamen of the era as a means of orientation. Soon his skill as a navigator earned him the respect of Hydriote crews and the reputation of a capable captain.

Yet Andreas's record was not altogether stainless. Stories were told of a violent temper and his taste for alcohol. The young seaman justified his reputation for impatience when, at the age of sixteen, he demanded to be given command of his father's ship. When Dimitrios rebuffed him, the ambitious adolescent decided to fulfill his aspirations through the practice of piracy. Helped by a friend equally desirous of taking over a paternal ship, he found sailors seeking adventure and easy money and simply sailed away!

Information available on young Andreas's piratical activities is not clear: there are grounds to believe that for some time he fought on the side of the notorious Guillaume Lorenzo, alias "the Maltese," before starting his own operations along the Egyptian coast.[5] He may also have cooperated with Captain Lambros Katsonis, a Russian naval officer of Greek origin who combined forces with many of the area's leading pirates to dominate the Aegean during the new Russo-Turkish War that began in 1788. His biographers are doubtful of this, however, as Hydra's political conservatism made Katsonis anything but friendly toward its sons. What is certain is that some time later Andreas reappeared in Hydra, penniless and dejected, perhaps having himself been victimized by a more powerful pirate.[6] In these straits, he was obliged to accept work as member of the crew of his father's vessel, now commanded by his older brother.

Circumstances may change, characters hardly. On the very first trip to Chios, Andreas had a fight with his brother and beat him unconscious. He then proceeded to commit embezzlement against his father's interests, selling the cargo himself and using the proceeds to buy his first ship. *Miaoulis* was the name of the vessel, and from this moment Andreas ceased to be called by his family name and was referred to as "Miaoulis," a sobriquet that was to follow him for the rest of his days and by which he is known to history.

Craving independence, Miaoulis was soon in pursuit of new goals. No longer content with the ownership and command of a vessel, he desired the wealth and prestige of a well-to-do merchant. This was the Hydriote conception of success in life. Ironically, it was again through embezzlement that he would achieve it. The victim was, once more, his father, one of whose cargoes Miaoulis misappropriated to sell for himself. The profit provided the capital with which he set himself up in business. His father, understandably in despair over Andreas's deeds, soon abandoned worldly things for the life of a monk in a monastery in the Dodecanese. Long afterward, Miaoulis, by then admiral of the Greek fleet, visited him and begged for his forgiveness.

The turmoil of the Napoleonic wars gave the Greeks the chance to take over a significant portion of the Mediterranean carrying trade. Enterprising merchants and daredevil seamen, among them Miaoulis, frequently broke through the blockade that Nelson's fleet maintained to deprive France, Spain, Portugal, and Italy of maritime commerce. They reaped great profits—providing, of course, that they escaped the occupational hazards of Mediterranean shipping, such as capture and enslavement by North African pirates.[7] To survive such expeditions required daring, quickness of decision, and seafaring skills—qualities Miaoulis possessed in full measure.

Nevertheless, impunity has its limits, as Miaoulis soon discovered. In 1802, the weather failed him while he was trying to outrun a British blockader. Captured off Cadiz, Miaoulis was interrogated by Admiral Nelson himself. His unexpected release is attributed mainly to the fact that he was brave and frank in answering the admiral's questions; furthermore, both were reportedly Freemasons, and Nelson was reputed to be sympathetic toward the Greeks in general.[8]

That same year, Miaoulis acquired the largest and swiftest ship in Hydra, a corvette displacing five hundred tons at a time when other Hydriote vessels did not exceed two hundred tons at most. She also carried 22 guns. Yet his pride of ownership was to be shortlived; on one of her first voyages, the corvette ran aground on a reef somewhere off Cadiz—an unlucky place for the Greek seaman. Rumor held that the wreck was due to Miaoulis's stubbornness in refusing to change course despite warnings from some of his sailors. Exaggerated and unproven as such stories may be, they indicate Andreas's resolution and headstrong character. It is to his credit that the crew escaped the accident unharmed and was safely transported to Italy to man a smaller ship, the *Heracles,* which Miaoulis purchased with a loan.

Flourishing commerce gave Hydriotes the opportunity to build considerable fortunes. The sudden influx of cash and material wealth brought with it an unprecedented wave of violence, moral decadence, and crime. These circumstances contributed to the already explosive social unrest on Hydra, whose leading citizens were regarded by the majority as unduly inclined to cooperate with the Turks. Following a petition by these notables, the Porte appointed George Voulgaris governor of the island in 1802. Voulgaris, one of Miaoulis's best friends, was known for his authoritarian views and the harshness of his character. Nevertheless, no one could question his administrative efficiency. No sooner had he set foot on Hydra than he imposed order.[9] The arrival of a Russian squadron at Hydra aggravated the division already existing between those who were pro-Russian and those who identified with the Ottoman Empire. A clash between the two parties became inevitable. Finally, the pro-Russian faction prevailed, which led to the ouster of Governor Voulgaris, Miaoulis, and the other conservatives, who had acquired the stigma of being pro-Ottoman.

The Turks, as was to be expected, took a dim view of these proceedings. Plans were made for an incursion to punish their restless subjects. At the last moment, the threatened massacre was averted by Voulgaris's diplomacy. He successfully petitioned the Turks to delay the operation, and in the respite Miaoulis managed to restore order. This was a terrible moment for the members of the pro-Russian party, many of whom, fearing retaliation, thought of leaving the island, which would have been a serious blow to its economy. In the end, they were persuaded to remain and Voulgaris exerted his influence to convince the Porte to pardon most of the dissidents.

Next to Voulgaris, who returned to the island in triumph, Andreas Mia-

15. The Greek War of Independence, 1821–29.

oulis was now the most powerful man on Hydra. Yet politics were not his domain. The sea never ceased to call him back to new adventures. Soon Hydriotes began to hear new tales of his exploits. In 1811, a French frigate intercepted and attempted to search his ship somewhere off Sardinia. Miaoulis responded by firing a broadside. The ensuing action extended over two days. The outcome, incredibly enough, was the withdrawal of the French warship, with casualties of forty dead and seventy-five wounded. Miaoulis lost only one man killed.[10]

By 1816 Miaoulis's success as an entrepreneur was attested by his ownership of three vessels. He spent the five years that elapsed before the beginning of the revolution quietly, leading the life of a respectable family man in the company of his six sons (all of whom became officers of the Greek navy) and his only daughter. Vokos was a name only a few remembered and no one used: more than a sobriquet, Miaoulis was now a name—and an honor.

Today most historians agree that the Greek revolution (1821–29) against Ottoman rule owed its survival to the ability of Greek vessels to dominate the Aegean. Turkish coastal fortresses, even though besieged by Greek troops, could still be used as bases of operations, especially if reinforced by seaborne transport. Besides, the revolutionary forces, cut off from overland communications by the Turkish occupation of the Balkans, had to be supplied by friendly ships. To maintain control of the sea lanes, the protection of the Greek islands from invasion was an absolute necessity. If the advanced naval bases on the islands were lost, nothing would stand in the way of the movement by sea of Ottoman forces from Constantinople to the Peloponnesus, which constituted the cradle of the revolution.

In 1820, virtually the entire Greek merchant fleet was owned by the inhabitants of three islands: Hydra, Spetses, and Psara. The first two are situated off the eastern Peloponnesus, well placed to defend its own coast, while the third neighbors Asia Minor. Psara's position made it an important advanced base as well as an obstacle to Ottoman communications between Constantinople and the southern ports of the empire.

The revolution broke out on 25 March 1821. Spetses and Psara were the first islands to make their vessels available to the Greek cause and use them to spread the spirit of revolt to coastal towns and villages, as well as to attack Ottoman ships. Reluctant to lose the privileges the Porte had granted them, Hydra's notables were not exactly eager to follow the example of the revolutionary islands. The people of Hydra felt otherwise. In April 1821, they rebelled against their leaders and forced them to adhere to the Greek cause. The support of the upper classes was crucial because they possessed the wealth needed to finance the struggle.

Soon the Greeks established the so-called Three-Island Fleet, with a strength often reaching sixty to eighty ships of two to five hundred tons each. Its activities were dictated by the leaders of Hydra, Spetses, and Psara, so to reach a unanimous decision was far from easy.[11] In addition, the islands reserved the right for their respective squadrons to act independently, as a result of which elements of the Greek fleet sometimes withdrew in the midst of an operation because of personal rivalries, disagreements, and localism. As a rule, however, such discords were put aside when the danger became acute.

At the age of fifty-one—considered old at that time—Miaoulis found it hard to believe that small Greek vessels with independent-minded crews could ever dominate the Aegean. At first he was content merely to watch the developments of events, which included the first Greek victories[12] as well as several mutinies by crews who were left unpaid or found themselves unemployed once their contracts expired. The intervention of Hydra's governor, Lazaros Kountouriotis, finally persuaded him to join the revolution.[13] The contents of a long private conversation that took place between the two men remain unknown, but after the meeting Miaoulis's attitude changed drastically. One of his first actions was to offer the use of his three ships to the Greek fleet and his fortune to finance the revolutionary struggle. As if to emphasize the seriousness of the new phase of his life, he stopped drinking, a touching demonstration of self-abnegation, since Miaoulis's fondness for spirits was well known. At first one of Hydra's several admirals, he later became the first admiral of the island and of the Greek combined fleet. From the moment that Miaoulis committed himself to the revolution, his biography becomes the history of the war at sea from 1822 to 1827, for he did not miss a single campaign.

In material terms, the Greeks' improvised sea forces were much inferior to those of the enemy. Their converted merchantmen faced an Ottoman fleet consisting of seventeen ships of the line carrying 80 to 100 cannons each, plus numerous frigates and smaller craft. Furthermore, the Turkish navy was eventually reinforced by Tunisian and Algerine squadrons of light vessels[14] and, beginning in 1824, with a number of heavy Egyptian warships. Thereafter the Greeks had to face two fleets, one based in the north at Constantinople, and the other in the south at Alexandria. Greek squadrons were superior to their adversaries in speed, maneuverability, seamanship, and experience in local waters. Yet, sluggish though they were, Ottoman frigates and ships of the line, armed with cannons ranging up to 64-pounders, were all but invulnerable to small ex-cargo vessels carrying at most 18-pounders.

Miaoulis overcame these disadvantages by the use of a weapon that was to prove decisive in the war at sea: the fireship. Although fireships had played a part in naval warfare throughout the Age of Sail, never before had they been employed so consistently or to such effect. Miaoulis seldom undertook an operation without them. Through his aggressive use of fireship tactics, which he studied and improved throughout the conflict, Miaoulis transformed this outmoded weapon into the terror of an empire.

Fireships were first employed against ships at anchor. The procedure, though simple, had to be carried out swiftly and smoothly. Her crew would make the fireship fast to the vessel they were to destroy before escaping in a boat they had in tow for that purpose. The threat of such attacks compelled Ottoman squadrons to avoid as much as possible using the Aegean naval bases and to stay in port only for the length of time strictly necessary for quick repairs and resupply, which reduced their crews to exhaustion.

Subsequently, fireship operations were extended to the open sea. In offensive battles, fireships moved through a blanket of powder smoke from the guns of the opposing forces until they found their target. Their intervention was equally advantageous in defensive engagements, particularly when Greek squadrons were cornered by the enemy. Billowing flames, the fireships would sail toward the hostile line. The mere sight of them usually led to a loosening of the pressure, for fire was a wooden ship's worst enemy,

8. The Battle of Andros, June 1825. The effect of a successful fireship attack is graphically illustrated in this contemporary French lithograph of the destruction of a Turkish frigate in the Battle of Andros. The action resulted when Miaoulis's fellow Hydriote, Admiral Sachtouris, attacked a strong Turkish squadron en route to Crete. In the same encounter, his fireships sank two Turkish corvettes. (The Beverley R. Robinson Collection, U.S. Naval Academy Museum.)

and the object of their attentions often chose to withdraw. The use of fireships in this manner anticipated one of the classic roles of destroyer formations in the world wars.

Wrote Miaoulis: "In order to destroy a frigate by fire, two fireships have to be sent against it, that is one fireship to each side of the vessel. Should a single fireship be used, the frigate might escape the first by simply maneuvering, thus distancing itself from peril."[15] These are conclusions Miaoulis reached after long experience. Obviously, the use of such tactics required the crews to be expert shiphandlers, not to mention extremely brave. The enemy gunfire into which they sailed was only one of the perils the men aboard a fireship had to face. They were for practical purposes traveling on a bomb about to explode, for every part of their vessel, including the masts, was covered with flammable material. For these reasons, Miaoulis often insisted on selecting fireship crews himself.

Thirty-nine successful fireship attacks are known to have taken place against the Ottoman fleet during the Greek revolution. Another nineteen or so attacks were ineffectual. Konstantinos Kanaris, a native of Psara, personally conducted four successful operations. Miaoulis had recruited him to serve in the Hydriote squadron, despite the mistrust with which Hydra's own sailors viewed the outsider. In June 1822, a month after the Turkish massacre of the population of Chios,[16] Kanaris managed to destroy the flagship of the Ottoman fleet—a deed that Thomas Gordon, an Englishman who served as a general in the Greek forces, characterized as one of the most extraordinary exploits in military history.[17] Yet, in fairness, it must be added that, though Kanaris carried out the mission with exemplary courage and skill, it was Miaoulis who conceived the plan.

Miaoulis's leadership was as forceful as his tactics were aggressive. To command a fleet consisting mainly of private vessels belonging to individuals whose localistic mentalities had never risen above the pursuit of profit was a formidable achievement. By strength of character and heroic example, he succeeded in imposing order on undisciplined crews who, accustomed to the practice aboard Greek merchant ships, expected to have a voice in important decisions. When members of his crew called on him to withdraw from a difficult engagement, Miaoulis leveled his pistol at them and shouted, "For my deeds I answer only to God!" On another occasion, surprising some seamen praying to the Virgin for salvation, he exclaimed with a grin: "If I were the Holy Mary I would drown you all, cowards that you are!"[18]

In the summer of 1822, European opinion doubted that the Greek revolution would survive another autumn. The Porte made no secret of its plans to crush the uprising, starting with the Greek naval bases. A fleet of ninety-four Turkish vessels was soon launched under the command of Mohammed Ali, with the mission of leveling Hydra and Spetses and supplying the Turkish fortress at the Peloponnesian city of Nauplia, whose besieged garrison was facing starvation.

If undertaking such a campaign was no great problem for the Ottomans, the same cannot be said for the Greeks' efforts to counter it. Neither the Central Revolutionary Administration—the Greek provisional government—nor its supporters could readily bear the financial burden the situation imposed. Miaoulis, put in charge of the Greek squadron, complained that "although we have managed to gather 50 ships, [dissention is so widespread that] we have never been able to assemble all at once. At times there were 5 vessels, then 10 or 20, sometimes just 3. . . ."[19]

Meanwhile, the Ottoman fleet approached the Gulf of Nauplia. The news produced a wave of fear throughout the area. Many Spetsian families, anticipating a massacre, fled to Hydra. For his part, Miaoulis planned to repeat the ruse through which more than two thousand years earlier another Greek admiral, Themistocles, had led a mighty Persian fleet to destruction. He would lure the enemy to sail through straits in which the superior force

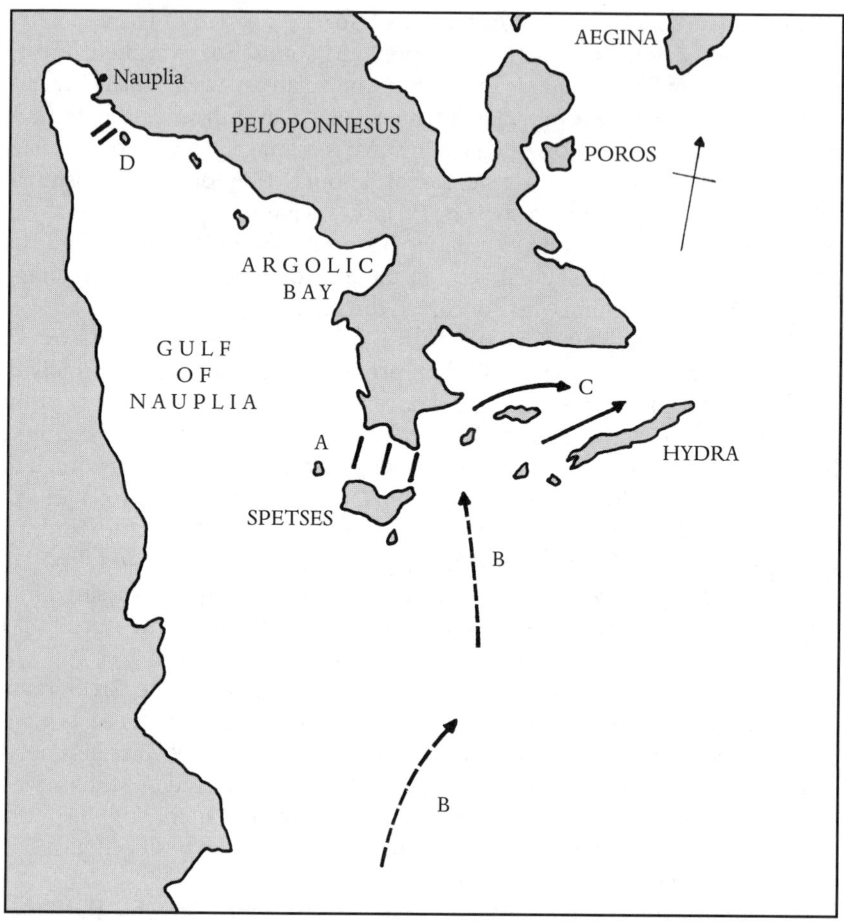

16. The Battle of Nauplia, 8 September 1822. (A) Main body of the Greek fleet in three echelons of six ships and two fireships each. (B) Approach of the Turkish fleet. (C) Planned withdrawal of the Greek decoy squadron. (D) Third Greek squadron.

would lose its freedom of maneuver. Miaoulis disposed of sixteen fireships and fifty-six vessels, the best of which he placed in a central position between Spetses and the Peloponnesus, where they would be able to defend whatever site the Turks had chosen for their landing, up to that moment unknown. Farther east, another Greek squadron received orders to withdraw toward the straits as soon as the enemy ships appeared and lure them on until the hidden fireships made their attack. Finally, a third squadron was ordered to wait in the Gulf of Nauplia with the mission of surrounding the Turkish force after letting it sail deep into the bay.

Miaoulis was also foresightful enough to make contingency plans in case the Turks moved forward in more than one wave. In that event, an equal number of Greek squadrons from the forces stationed between Spetses and the Peloponnesus would immediately advance and try to encircle them.

On 8 September, the Ottoman fleet sailed toward the Greek central squadron waiting north of Spetses. The eastern squadron found itself unable to withdraw into the straits because of a total lack of wind. Thus the battle took place in relatively calm waters, which put the Greeks in a less than ideal position. After six hours of heavy gunfire and the unsuccessful burning of two Greek fireships, the Turks chose to retire and regroup. Two days later, they attempted to sail directly into the bay. Miaoulis's squadron was careful to closely follow the Ottoman forces so as to be able to encircle them in the innermost part of the bay, while the Greek vessels in the central position had orders to attack if reinforcements sought to join the enemy fleet. Suddenly, however, the Turks realized that they were being drawn into a trap, reversed course, and sailed away, still without having resupplied their besieged compatriots.

On 13 September, the Turks made a third attempt to enter the bay. The destruction of a brig with her entire crew by a fireship spread fear through the Ottoman fleet and convinced Mohammed Ali that the time had come to return to Constantinople. Kanaris seized the opportunity offered by the enemy's retreat to successfully attack a Turkish corvette. In Constantinople the vice admiral of the Ottoman forces was beheaded, while Miaoulis received a hero's welcome from the people of his island. The Hydriotes had every right to celebrate the victory. Had Hydra and Spetses fallen, the revolution would have failed.

Following the departure of the Ottoman fleet, the starving defenders of Nauplia capitulated to the Greeks. As a result of these victories on land and sea, many historians consider the Battle of Nauplia to be the greatest of Miaoulis's contributions to the Greek cause.

Victories notwithstanding, in the following months the Central Revolutionary Administration continued to be wracked by political disputes and private quarrels among its stubbornly shortsighted members. On the other hand, the Turks had problems of their own. A terrible fire broke out in the navy yards at Constantinople, causing great damage and disrupting preparations for a landing on the Greek mainland. The consequences of this catastrophe were, however, overcome by the recruitment of foreign seamen and the modernization of the fleet through the replacement of sluggish, older ships with swifter, modern types. Algiers, Egypt, and Tripoli joined in the effort by providing the Turks with a considerable number of high-quality vessels and experienced crews. The Ottoman fleet was also given a new admiral, Hosref Pasha, renowned for his diplomacy. After resupplying many

Turkish forts in the Peloponnesus (1823), he began to cruise through the Aegean, avoiding contact with the Greek squadrons and overawing the inhabitants of various islands, some of whom chose to declare their loyalty to Ottoman rule.

Faced with this critical state of affairs, the revolutionaries had to react rapidly and efficiently; this was easier said than done. After many difficulties, ten ships were fitted out from Spetses. It was another story trying to meet the conditions that the crews of fourteen Hydriote vessels laid down. To abandon their profitable work on the quays and board ship, they demanded wages that were beyond the capacity of the revolution's finances to pay.

What long hours of fruitless negotiations failed to achieve, Miaoulis accomplished by personal example. Bedridden with a severe attack of rheumatism, he had himself carried to the harbor on a litter. The sight of this brave man, defying illness for the struggle for independence, appealed to the seamen's better nature. In no time, the Hydriote ships were at sea.[20]

The ensuing engagements proved inconclusive and the Turkish fleet returned to Constantinople. By then, new antagonisms were rocking the Greek fleet. Miaoulis accused the leaders of the Spetses squadron of disloyalty and refused to give the Psaran contingent a share of the spoils of an action to which he deemed its contribution was minimal. This created still more ill-will. Subsequently Miaoulis sometimes burned captured ships and booty when it appeared that their division would give rise to resentments.

In 1824, such dissent led to a civil conflict among the revolutionaries. Miaoulis organized a naval blockade of Nauplia to isolate his political adversaries. On two occasions, the Peloponnesians experienced the fire of his guns. Fortunately, some semblance of order was soon restored to the revolutionary ranks.

While the Greeks were busy trying to sort out their internal differences, Sultan Mahmud II kept seeking a way to extinguish the revolution of his ever-rebellious subjects. Finally he turned to Mohammed Ali, the virtually independent viceroy of Egypt, with a promise to grant him sovereignty over the Peloponnesus and Crete in return for his assistance. Mahmud had made a wise choice. Mohammed Ali possessed a sizable navy organized by Europeans and realized that to crush the Greek revolt he had simply to gain control of the sea lanes. Captain Drouault, the pro-Turkish commander of the French Levant Squadron, helped in the planning. Together they masterminded a project to seize the bow formed by the Greek islands lying close to the coast of Asia Minor. This would secure undisturbed communications between Turkey, Egypt, and Syria. Mohammed Ali's next step was to assemble his landing forces in Crete for an invasion of the southern Peloponnesus.

No sooner was the plan conceived than it was put into execution. That summer the islands of Kasos and Psara, both major Greek naval bases, suffered the consequences of Ottoman fury. The savagery of the attack became legendary. When the smoke lifted, the Greeks had twenty thousand dead to mourn, along with the loss of their advanced bases.

Despite these tragic setbacks, the Greek forces were not disheartened. Miaoulis arrived off Psara with a fleet of sixty vessels on 15 July and in barely five hours succeeded in annihilating an enemy squadron of twenty-five ships caught at anchor. In the shore battles that followed, two thousand of the Turkish troops that, days before, had been responsible for the devastation of Psara were killed.

Encouraged by this victory, Miaoulis proceeded toward the island of Mytilini, where the bulk of the Turkish fleet was based. He had not counted upon the internal differences that continued to plague the Greek cause. Result: while cruising around Mytilini in search of the enemy fleet, Miaoulis found himself deserted by a sizable number of his vessels, which sailed away without bothering even to consult him. Realizing that it would be quixotic to pursue his plans to attack with the force remaining at his disposal, he returned to Hydra.[21]

Threatened by the imminent junction of the Egyptian and Turkish fleets, Hydra and Spetses began feverishly to prepare to meet the crisis. Fortunately, a British loan gave the revolutionary administration enough money to finance the naval preparations of the two islands. The danger arising in the wake of the disaster at Psara and Kasos and the possibility of more joint Turco-Egyptian operations left Hydra and Spetses no alternative but to put Miaoulis in charge of the organization of the Greek fleet.

Miaoulis was convinced that the enemy should be intercepted as far as possible from the Peloponnesus. He justified this view by arguing that even if the Greek forces were defeated, they would inflict enough damage to compel the enemy to withdraw to make repairs before continuing the operation; besides, the guerrilla troops on shore would still present a serious obstacle to a Turkish landing. These delays would give the revolutionaries time to pull themselves together.

Miaoulis's first action as admiral of the combined fleet was to send a squadron of twenty-two ships under his friend, the Hydriote Admiral George Sachtouris, to protect the island of Samos from invasion. The balance of the Greek force readied itself to engage the Egyptian fleet, which was making preparations to sortie from Halicarnassus (now Bodrum), on the coast of Asia Minor.

The first Greek victory occurred on 5 August 1824, when Sachtouris's squadron attacked the Turkish fleet near Samos. Three Turkish vessels were blown up by six Greek fireships and two thousand enemy seamen perished.[22] The Turkish admiral's rage was such that he had his second-in-command and the commander of a frigate beheaded before hastily starting—still harassed by Sachtouris's squadron—for Halicarnassus to join the Egyptian fleet.

Miaoulis made for the same point and united with Sachtouris off Halicarnassus. Between 17 and 29 August, the Greeks managed to assemble 70 ships with 800 guns and 5,000 men, plus a number of fireships. The Turco-Egyptian fleet numbered 3 ships of the line, 16 frigates, 14 corvettes, 70 brigs, and a number of smaller vessels, in all amounting to 133 warships with 2,500 guns and 9,500 men. Also present were 150 transports carrying 16,900 troops and 150 artillery pieces.[23]

In a council of war, the Greeks adopted Miaoulis's proposal to make an immediate attack on Halicarnassus Bay, where the massed enemy vessels were having difficulty avoiding collisions in their hurried efforts to sail. In the beginning, the Greek operations met little success. On 25 August, six fireships were burned, without effect because of unfavorable weather conditions. That night there was a lull, which gave Miaoulis the opportunity to withdraw to Gerontas Bay in order to cover the routes to Samos, ready to intervene should the enemy attempt a landing there. Discord was again so acute, even at such a critical moment, that some squadrons chose to leave Miaoulis's main body and sail closer to Samos, while others preferred to wait farther west.[24]

On 29 August the enemy fleets took the offensive. The Turks sailed westward to engage the scattered Greek vessels, while the Egyptians steered toward Miaoulis's force. As if the dispersion of their ships did not make things difficult enough for the Greeks, an almost dead calm badly limited Miaoulis's ability to react. Resourceful as ever, he lowered boats filled with oarsmen to tow his ships toward the other Greek vessels, which were strung out in a line fifteen miles long.[25]

Meanwhile, firing began as the Turkish and Egyptian forces made their twin attacks, impeding Miaoulis's efforts to join his dispersed ships. For the Greeks there was only one hope: the fireships. As soon as the first gust of wind made the calm surface of the Aegean shiver, Miaoulis began giving orders to his ships, orders that were to become history:

> Get ready to attack the enemy and when I make signal to you, launch your attack with God's help and do your best to stick to [the enemy's] prow.
>
> Go and stick on the enemy's side with all your bravery as you have been ordered.
>
> Launch your attack bravely and I'll pick you up.[26]

Four fireships cost the Turks a brig and drove them toward the Egyptians, giving the Greek vessels the opportunity to unite at last. Still, the enemy had the advantage of the wind. Guns grew literally red-hot from

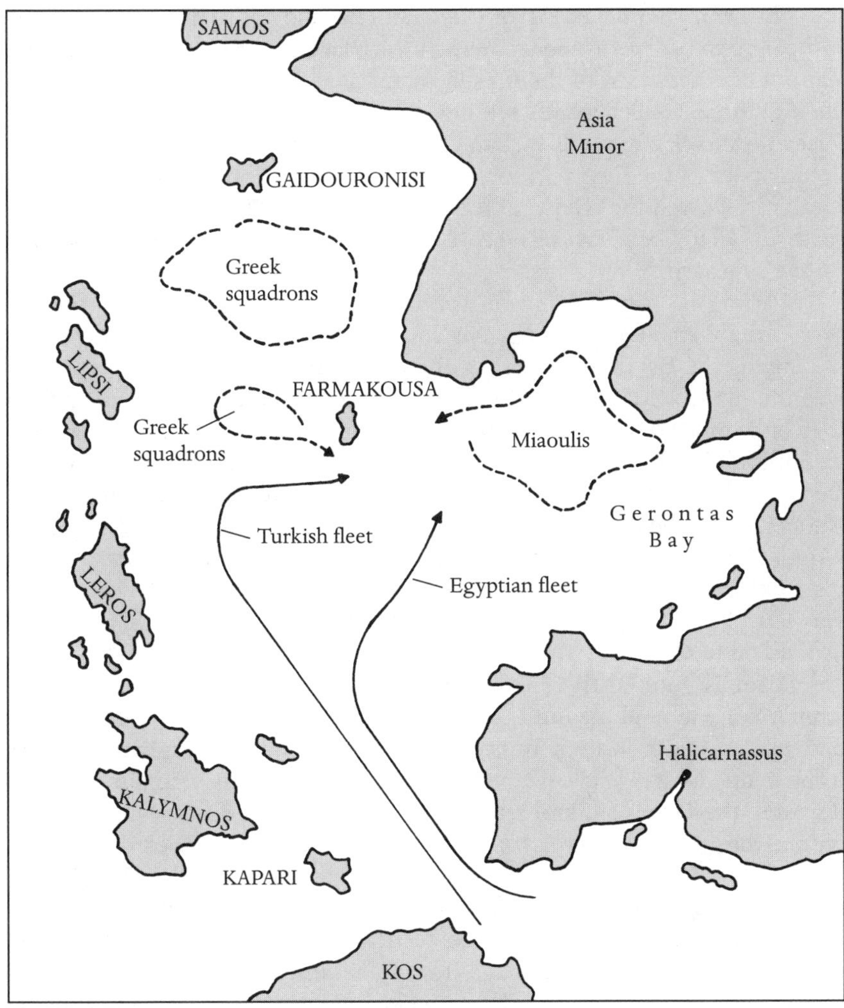

17. The Battle of Gerontas Bay, 29 August 1824.

constant firing as the air filled with the smell of burned powder. Miaoulis now directed a general attack by his fireships. Five of them broke the enemy line, blowing up a Tunisian frigate with 1,300 sailors and soldiers aboard. This decisive thrust into the heart of the enemy formation caused the Turco-Egyptian forces to break off the engagement and retreat to the south. Thus ended the action in reference to which the French naval historian Admiral Jurien de la Gravière wrote, "in the pages of naval history, there are perhaps few of equal interest to the seaman."[27]

The enemy withdrawal from Gerontas Bay did not signify the end of the campaign. Subsequent engagements took place around Samos and Chios. Kanaris directed most of the fireship operations, in which an Egyptian frigate and three smaller vessels were destroyed. These new losses left Hosref Pasha no choice but to fall back to Constantinople, while Ibrahim Pasha, the commander of the Egyptian forces, returned to Halicarnassus. Once there, Ibrahim followed the advice of the French Captain Drouault and was soon ready to sail to Crete, where he could make better preparations for a landing on the southern Peloponnesus.

Wasting no time resting on the laurels of his latest victory, Miaoulis immediately steered for Crete. His small but efficient squadron succeeded in denying the Egyptians access to the coastal town of Chania. So effective was the night attack he launched against the Egyptian fleet off Heraklion (1–2 November 1824) that soon Ibrahim made the following signal: "Prepare to sail for salvation."[28] His language was understandable: twenty Egyptian ships had been destroyed[29] and the rest were scattered in the direction of Rhodes, Karpathos, and Alexandria. This was too bad for Ibrahim's captains, who had to suffer their commander's rage at having been defeated again: ten to fifteen of them were stripped of their rank and executed, while what was left of the Egyptian squadron quickly began to reorganize for a new expedition to Crete.

Miaoulis guessed the enemy's plans and awaited developments in the Cretan Sea. He used the intermezzo to talk his exhausted crews into having patience and faith in their mission, harshly upbraiding them at times and using gentle language at others. Apart from the recurrent threat of insubordination, the Greek admiral still had to face the dire effects of the disunity within the revolutionary administration. He was hardly heard when he pleaded for more fireships and funds to continue the struggle. The government's scandalous lack of unanimity once more forced Miaoulis to return to Hydra, thus leaving the court free for the Egyptians. Ibrahim seized the opportunity, landed on Crete, and from there, undisturbed, quickly covered the eighty miles of sea to the Greek mainland. On 24 February 1825, the first Egyptian troops landed in the southern Peloponnesus. The Greek administration was taken by surprise. Panic-stricken, it tried in haste to finance a new campaign with Miaoulis—whom else?—in command of the entire undertaking.

Faithful to the offensive, Miaoulis tried to attack the Egyptian base at Crete, but strong winds frustrated his plans. Immediately following this disappointment he sailed to the Peloponnesus and engaged an Egyptian squadron—to no effect. This time luck seemed to be on the enemy side. It was not until 30 April that Miaoulis finally managed to strike a blow: with six fireships he attacked a strong Egyptian squadron in the small Peloponnesian port of Methoni. With nightmarish speed, the flames spread from one ship to another, consuming two frigates, four corvettes, six brigs, and thirteen to twenty transports. The explosion of a number of coastal storage installations added to the damage inflicted on Ibrahim's forces.[30]

Unfortunately, the lack of either additional fireships or a landing force prevented Miaoulis from capitalizing on his success. Moreover, the emergence of the Turkish fleet from the Dardanelles obliged the Greek forces to separate into two squadrons, one in the north and the other in the south. These events caused Miaoulis to fear for his success of the revolution. Gravely preoccupied, he could not enjoy the celebrations grateful Hydriotes organized in his honor after the action at Methoni. His thoughts were centered on the terrible drama unfolding at Missolonghi.

Missolonghi, a picturesque town built on a lagoon with an exit to the sea, was a center of resistance to the Turkish conquest of mainland Greece. Besieged by land and sea, the town's defenders were to write an epic page in Greek history. Soon reduced to starvation, they chose to eat dogs, cats, and other pets rather than surrender to the superior forces outside their walls.

Determined not to abandon the people of Missolonghi in their ordeal, Miaoulis gathered a force of fifty ships to supply the town with munitions and food. On 22 July 1825 he engaged fifty-six Turkish vessels, including eight frigates, off Missolonghi. His objective was not so much to damage the enemy as to push him away from the area, thus opening a passage for the supplies. Restraining his usual impetuosity, he used clever tactics to draw the enemy off, enabling five of his vessels to reach Missolonghi. Thus it is no wonder that the grateful defenders named the town's bastions and batteries in honor of the Greek admirals: Miaoulis, Sachtouris, Kanaris. . . .

Despite the increase of the enemy blockading fleet to a strength of 135 to 145 vessels, Miaoulis persisted in his effort to maintain a flow of food and munitions into Missolonghi throughout the siege. At the end of January 1826, he succeeded in landing provisions enough to last the defender for two months. By the time of his return in early April, Ibrahim's forces had captured the Greek positions defending the lagoon that led to Missolonghi and cut the town off from the sea. Dispatching a request to the Central Revolutionary Administration to send him shallow-draft vessels, Miaoulis laid plans to force a passage through the lagoon. Before he could put this project into execution, however, hunger forced the inhabitants of Missolonghi to a desperate decision. On the night of 22 April the whole population, civil and military, attempted to break through the enemy lines. Only a handful lived to see the sunrise.

The fall of Missolonghi and the extension of Ottoman power throughout the Peloponnesus cast the future of the revolution in doubt. At the same time, however, the growth of Philhellenic movements abroad—stimulated by the heroic defense of Missolonghi—increased the encouraging possibility of foreign intervention. The granting of loans by British banks to the revolutionary administration contributed to the creation of especially strong bonds between Greece and Great Britain, and in June 1825, the chiefs of the revolution had issued a declaration expressing their desire to entrust the freedom and independence of the Greek nation to King George IV. (As commander of the Greek sea forces, Miaoulis was one of the signatories of this document.) Although the king declined the offer, it left the revolutionary leaders no room to object when British lenders put pressure on them to engage Admiral George Cochrane, Lord Dundonald, a British sailor-of-fortune, to command the Greek fleet. Arriving in Greece in February 1827, Cochrane was named admiral in chief with complete control of naval operations.

And Miaoulis? The former chief of the Greek naval forces would now have to be content with command of the *Hellas* (Greece), a new 2,200-ton frigate built in the United States. An American who served as a volunteer officer in the Greek navy recorded that "I personally overheard Admiral Miaoulis saying he would gladly concede the command to his brave ally Cochrane and that, for his country's benefit, he could even be a ship's boy."[31]

Cochrane's contribution to the revolutionary struggle did not have a major influence on its outcome. The decisive development was the intervention of the Great Powers. Under strong pressure from public opinion, the governments of Great Britain and Russia joined in calling on the Ottoman Empire to grant Greece autonomy. The sultan's refusal to do so led to the formation in July 1827 of an alliance between Britain, France, and Russia aimed at securing the independence of Greece. At the same time, a combined fleet under Admiral Sir Edward Codrington was dispatched to the Aegean "to prevent the spread of hostilities." When on 20 October Codrington's force began to enter the western Peloponnesian port of Navarino, where the Turco-Egyptian fleet lay at anchor, an outbreak of firing for which each side later blamed the other precipitated the last great battle between wooden warships. At the end of the day, the Ottoman squadrons had been annihilated and the eventual independence of Greece was assured. Shortly thereafter, Cochrane abandoned his position and returned to England.

In the meantime, Count Ioannis Kapodistrias, a Corfu islander who had gained distinction in the Russian diplomatic service, had been chosen to become the first governor of Greece. In 1828 he disembarked at Nauplia to the cheers of an exultant crowd and assumed the formidable task of governing the turbulent new state. Much of the cheering died into ominous muttering when the chief executive, with the consent of the National Assembly, suspended certain provisions of the constitution, but Kapodistrias put his soul into the organization of a Greek government. The assistance that the Protecting Powers (Britain, France, and Russia) had promised him proved to be ambivalent. Because each of the powers wished to exert paramount influence, their attitude toward Greece would change from helpful to hostile to benevolent once more. Kapodistrias also met opposition from local notables, who found their privileges and powers severely curtailed when he began to establish a powerful central government.

Kapodistrias recognized the decisive role that Andreas Miaoulis had played in the war for independence. The brave Hydriote was granted the highest naval rank and his every ambition fulfilled. The other great naval hero of the revolution, Konstantinos Kanaris, received equal honors in what many viewed as a covert effort by Kapodistrias to sow the seeds of discord in the naval world, which, united as it mostly was, represented an important political nucleus that might eventually challenge his authority.

Miaoulis kept a low political profile during the opening months of the Kapodistrias regime. He had undertaken to suppress piracy in the central Aegean, which he patrolled in command of a squadron with his flag in the *Hellas*. His abilities were again demonstrated by a fast-paced campaign in which he attacked the pirates' bases and captured eighty ships. He made another contribution to the survival of the new state at the liberation of Chios, during which his experienced gunners sank a Turkish frigate. Later, he established a blockade that forced the Turkish garrison of Missolonghi to surrender, restoring the martyred town to Greek rule. This event marked the last of the operations conducted by Miaoulis for the independence of his country after four hundred years of oppression.

Amazing as it seems, throughout the course of the revolution Miaoulis had hardly lost a ship. A vessel from Spetses was taken by the Turks when the wind failed during a chase in September 1821, but its crew still found time to escape. In the same year a second Greek ship mysteriously disappeared at sea. A final unpleasant event was the accidental explosion of a fireship at anchor.[32] As for personnel casualties, no official data exist, but they are estimated not to have exceeded one hundred dead.[33] What happened on the other side was a different story. Kanaris's fireships alone destroyed four major Ottoman vessels, bringing about the loss of approximately three thousand lives. The remainder of the fireship attacks and assorted other actions raised the number of Turco-Egyptian dead to at least 25,000.

Although Greece achieved independence in 1830, Kapodistrias found himself in an increasingly difficult position. France and Britain were secretly encouraging the dissatisfaction with his administration that already existed in certain elements of Greek society. The ouster of government representatives from many areas provoked the inevitable retaliation by those loyal to Kapodistrias, and soon the persecution of political opponents began to occur.

In 1831, the island of Hydra began behaving like a small state in itself, defying the directives of the central government. Miaoulis, convinced that Kapodistrias's policies would be disastrous for Greece, supported this movement. Kapodistrias was at first willing to seek a compromise, generously offering to forget Hydra's rebellious behavior if the islanders abandoned their opposition to his administration. Finding that his conciliatory efforts had no appeal, Kapodistrias chose to make a show of strength by ordering Kanaris to fit out the ships of the Greek fleet at the navy yards on Poros and blockade the refractory islands. The governor failed to reckon on Miaoulis. Anticipating the government's action, the admiral arrived in Poros at the head of two hundred men, seized control of the ships in a bloodless coup, and sent Kanaris away empty-handed.

Tension mounted steadily in succeeding days. The opposition demanded the convocation of a national assembly with the object of putting the entire constitution in force and limiting Kapodistrias's powers. The latter sought the help of the commander of the Russian squadron in the Aegean, Admiral Ricord, urging him to sail to Poros and crush the insurgency. Ricord soon concluded that it was pointless to negotiate with Miaoulis and decided to resort to force. Meanwhile, the commanders of the British and the French eastern squadrons sailed to Poros to join the Russians, having themselves condemned the Hydriotes' rebellious activities.

A meeting between the foreign officers and the insurgents produced no agreement. The British and French commanders elected to return to Nauplia to notify Kapodistrias of the islanders' intransigence and try to convince him to accept a compromise. Ricord indignantly accused them of breaking the alliance and immediately proceeded to undertake offensive operations against Poros. Miaoulis did not hesitate to return his fire, inflicting severe damage and heavy casualties on two Russian ships and forcing Ricord to withdraw.

Miaoulis's exchange of shots with the Russian squadron, defensive though it was, nevertheless shocked a great many people—including some of the insurgents—as a major offense against the flag of one of the Protecting Powers. Ricord informed the French Captain Vaillant, through whom he communicated with Miaoulis, that he intended to renew the attack. In reply, the fearless Hydriote declared that he was ready to destroy every ship in Poros the moment the Russian squadron made a hostile move. Any hope that these were mere words vanished on 13 September 1831, when, upon his orders, the *Hellas,* the pride and flagship of the Greek fleet, and the corvette *Hydra* were blown up. Ricord, compelled to retaliate, duly attacked. The sixty-one-year-old Miaoulis had a narrow escape, sailing through heavy Russian fire to reach Hydra. There he was acclaimed by his compatriots, who heartily approved of their admiral's deeds. On the other hand, in his report to Kapodistrias, Kanaris wrote: "Miaoulis burnt *Hellas* and *Hydra;* may his name be damned forever. . . ."

The situation rapidly deteriorated. Hydra soon found itself in the grip of a blockade by the vessels of the Protecting Powers. Kanaris, now commander in chief of the Greek navy, undertook another effort to reason with the insurgents, while Hydriote ships slipped through the blockade to the mainland in an effort to encourage unrest and finance operations intended to overthrow the governor.

The peak of the crisis came and quickly passed with the assassination of Kapodistrias at Nauplia on 9 October 1831. The unity of the administration that he had tried to establish collapsed and two separate Greek governments emerged, both claiming sovereignty. Miaoulis's party, the Constitutionalists, prevailed, and when the Protecting Powers chose Prince Otto of Bavaria to become king of Greece, Miaoulis was among the delegation that traveled to Munich to greet the new sovereign in August 1832.

Miaoulis's loyalty to the king was not unrewarded; he received the rank of vice admiral of the Greek navy. Those who met him during this period speak of a calm, gentle man whose modesty made him reluctant to talk about his achievements during the revolution.

Andreas Miaoulis, the ambitious Hydriote sailor to whom Greece was deeply indebted for its independence, died quietly in his sixty-seventh year, on 11 June 1835. His tomb is beside that of the ancient Greek admiral Themistocles, victor of the Battle of Salamis, on the grounds of the Naval Cadets School in Piraeus, near the sea he loved and dominated.

NOTES

Editor's note: Titles followed by an asterisk are available only in Greek.

1. *Voyages dans l'Asie Mineur et en Grèce faits au dépens de la Société des Dilettanti dans les années 1764, 1765, 1766 par le Dr. R Chandler (Traduit de l'Anglais par M. M. Servoir et Bocage),* 3 vols. (Paris: Arthus Bertrand [et] Buisson, 1806), II:291–93. See also Samuel G. Howe, *Diary of the Struggle, 1825–29* (Greek translation, Athens: Notas Karavias, 1971), p. 5: "An American Navy officer assured me they are the best sailors he had ever seen."

2. The Treaty of Kioutsouk-Kainartzi allowed free traffic between Turkish and Russian ports and the use of the Russian flag by Greek ships, which could sail with either Turkish or Russian papers, depending on the political situation.

3. Spiro Melas, *Andreas Miaoulis* (3rd ed., Athens: Biris, 1972),* pp. 92ff.

4. Chandler, op. cit., II:293.

5. A. N. Sachinis, *A Brief Biography of Admiral Andreas Miaoulis* (Nauplia: Sotirios Vigas, 1882),* p. 11; and Melas, op. cit., p. 54.

6. Eugène Yemenitz, *La Grèce Moderne: Héros et Poètes* (Paris: Michel Lévy Freres, 1862), p. 124; J. Lazaropoulos, *The Greek Navy* (Athens: The Naval Review, 1936),* p. 49. Miaoulis's ship was rammed by Maltese pirates somewhere off the southern Peloponnesus.

7. In 1811 alone, fourteen Greek vessels (ten from Hydra, two from Spetses, and two from Galaxidi) fell into Algerine hands; see K. A. Alexandris, *The Revival of Our Sea Force during the Years of Turkish Occupation* (Athens: Greek Navy Historical Service, 1960),* p. 268.

8. K. N. Rados, *Miaoulis before the Revolution* (Athens: P. Leonis, 1898),* pp. 40ff.

9. Melas, op. cit., p. 103: "Voulgaris was considered 'the best sailor of the Orient' and the Turks had granted him the highest title ever enjoyed by a Christian seaman."

10. G. D. Kriezis, *History of the Island of Hydra before the Revolution of 1821* (Patras: A. S. Agapitos, 1860), p. 167; French edition, *Histoire de l'île d'Hydra, jusqu'à la Révolution de 1821,* trans. Théodore Blanchard (Marseilles: Imprimerie H. Chassetière fils, 1888).

11. For details on this complicated administrative system, as well as on the relations between officers and men, see Tryfon Konstantinides, *Ships, Captains and Sailors (1800–1830)* (Athens: Greek Navy Historical Service, 1954),* and Howe, op. cit.

12. These included the destruction by fireship of a two-masted Turkish ship at anchor and the frustration of the enemy's plans for a landing on Samos.

13. Kontouriotis was one of the most respected figures of the Greek revolution. On some islands the old adage "Lazaros said so" is still used to affirm that a statement is true.

14. Jurien de la Gravière, *History of the Greek Struggles (Especially Those of the Navy) for Freedom* (Greek translation by K. N. Rados, Athens: Ioannis Notaris, 1894).

15. A Lignos, ed., *Archives of Hydra* (Piraeus: various publishers, 1930),* X:24 September 1824.

16. M. Simpsas, *The Navy in Greek History,* vols. 1–4 (Athens: Greek Navy General Staff, 1982),* IV:26. After these massacres, the Greek population was reduced from 113,000 to barely 15,000; 23,000 Greeks were slain and another 48,000 taken prisoner. The remainder sought refuge on other islands.

17. Thomas Gordon, *History of the Greek Revolution,* 2 vols. (Edinburgh: William Blackwood, 1844), I:366.

18. Melas, op. cit., pp. 185, 65.

19. *History of the Greek Nation* (Athens: Athenian Editions, 1971–78),* XII:281.

20. Melas, op. cit., pp. 92ff.

21. This disgraceful situation is described by Miaoulis in the *Archives of Hydra,* XII:26 and 30 September and 3 October 1826.

22. Durand-Viel, *Les campagnes navales de Mohamet Ali et d'Ibrahem* (Paris: Imprimerie Nationale, 1835), pp. 263–64. Kanaris conducted his third successful fireship attack, destroying a Turkish frigate.

23. Simpsas, op. cit., IV:45.

24. As a result, at the Battle of Gerontas the Greek force consisted of nine different squadrons under the command of nine independent admirals.

25. This formidable task inspired folk artists and popular paintings of the era that depict Miaoulis giving orders to the boats.

26. Excerpts from signal books of the era; see Simpsas, op. cit., IV:344.

27. De la Gravière, op. cit., p. 145.

28. K. Alexandris, *The Greek Navy in the Struggle for Independence 1821–1829 and the Activities of the Fireships* (Athens: Greek Navy Historical Service, 1968),* pp. 116ff.

29. Durand-Viel, op. cit., p. 280.

30. Ibid., pp. 299–300.

31. Stephen A. Larabee, *Greece 1775–1865, As Seen by the Americans* (Athens: 1961), p. 117.

32. A. A. Anargirou, *Spetsiotika,* vols. 1–3 (Athens: D. A. Mavrommatis, 1861; reprint, Athens: The Greek Historical and Ethnological Society, 1979),* p. 38.

33. Selection of data on casualties from various archives.

Note on Sources

Despite the vast literature on the Greek Revolution, a truly scholarly biography of Miaoulis has yet to appear. The most recent treatment is Spiro Melas, *Andreas Miaoulis* (3rd ed., Athens: Biris, 1972),* a dramatized but responsible work utilizing a wide range of sources. K. A. Alexandris, *Where Was Andreas Miaoulis Born?* (Euboic Studies, 6, 1959)* offers a detailed examination of the question its title poses. Miaoulis's contribution to the revolution is minimized in two controversial volumes focusing on the history of Spetses, A. A. Anargirou, *Spetsiotika* (Athens: D. Mavrommatis, 1861; reprinted, Athens: The Greek Historical and Ethnological Society, 1979),* and Anastasios Orlando, *Nautica,* vols. 1–2 (Athens: H. N. Philadelpheas, 1869).* K. N. Rados attempted, not without success, to refute their criticism in *Miaoulis before the Revolution* (Athens: P. Leonis, 1898).* His work was based largely on the *History of the Island of Hydra before the Revolution of 1821* (Patras: A. S. Agapitos, 1860)* by G. D. Kriezis, a Hydriote contemporary of Miaoulis. A. N. Sachinis, *A Brief Biography of Admiral Andreas Miaoulis* (Nauplia: Sotirios Vigas, 1882),* contains valuable information furnished by the admiral's relatives. The effort to idealize its subject leads to a number of historical errors in V. N. V. Vounisseas, *A Brief Biography of Andreas Miaoulis* (Athens: Vassilios A. Kokotas, 1889).* Miaoulis's role in the post-revolutionary period is examined in K. Varfis's *The Greek Navy in the Kapodistrias Period: The Years of Adaptation* (Athens: Society for the Diffusion of Useful Books, 1994).*

Among the unpublished materials consulted, particularly in regard to Miaoulis's post-revolutionary activities, were the following records in the General Archives of Greece: Mavrokordatos Archives, files 14–18; State Secretariat on Military and Naval Affairs, files 1–4; and State Secretariat on Naval Affairs, files 9–11, 13–20. Equally important information was extracted from the Lyon's Archive, MS B/65 and B/84/1, at the British Public Record Office.

Helpful published documentary collections include *Papers Relative to the Affairs of Greece, 1826–1832* (London: M. H. Stationary Office, 1835); A. Lignos and K. Diamandis, eds., *L. and G. Kountouriotis Archive,* vols. A–E (Athens: P. D. Sakellariou, 1920–27 and 1966–69);* A. Lignos, ed., *Archives of Hydra,* vols. 1–17 (Piraeus: various publishers, 1930);* *Documents on Greek History: Foreign Office Document Collection, General Correspondence/Greece,* vol. a, parts 1–2 (Athens: Greek Academy, 1975);* and Y. Vlachoyannis, ed., *Archives of Chios,* vols. 1–4 (Athens: n.p., 1910–24).* Editions have also appeared of the logs of a number of Greek revolutionary warships.

For a modern English-language overview of the Greek Revolution, see Douglas Dakin, *The Greek Struggle for Independence* (London: B. T. Batsford, 1973). An early but still useful English work by a veteran of the struggle, emphasizing naval and military events, is Thomas Gordon, *History of the Greek Revolution,* 2 vols. (Edinburgh: William Blackwood, 1844). A team of leading Greek historians reviews the revolutionary era in volume 12 of Athenian Editions' *History of the Greek Nation* (Athens: 1975).*

The naval aspects of the conflict are described in detail in volumes 3 and 4 of M. Simpsas, *The Navy in Greek History* (Athens: Greek Navy General Staff, 1982).* K. A. Alexandris, *The Naval Operations in the Struggle for Independence, 1821–1829* (Athens: The Naval Review, 1930),* is a scholarly study of the same subject. Another well-researched work, highlighting the problems and mentality of the revolutionary navy, is Tryfon Konstantinides, *Ships, Captains and Sailors, 1800–1830: An Introduction to the History of Greek Revolutionary Naval Operations* (Athens: Greek Navy Historical Service, 1954).* The illustrated *Memorandum on the Construction of a Fireship* (Athens: D. A. Mavrommatis, 1862)* by K. Nicodimus, once a fireship captain, is the best description of its kind.

Three other interesting works are R. Matton, *Hydra et la guerre maritime* (Athens: The Athens French Institute Collection, 1953); Durand-Viel, *Les campagnes navales de Mohamet-Ali et d'Ibrahem* (Paris: Imprimerie Nationale, 1835), which was based on research in Egyptian archives; and Admiral Jurien de la Gravière, *History of the Greek Struggles (Especially Those of the Navy) for Freedom* (Greek translation by K. N. Rados, Athens: Byron Editions, 1988), in which the leading nineteenth-century French naval historian sometimes allows his sympathy for the Greek cause to carry him away.

Survey III
The Machine Age at Sea
(1830–1866)

Although the success of Miaoulis's fireships constituted the most dramatic naval development of the Greek revolution, its influence on the evolution of sea warfare was nil. The conflict's lasting significance lay in its juxtaposition of two other events: the Battle of Navarino, the last fleet action of the Age of Sail, and the deployment of the *Karteria* (Perseverance), the first steamer to enter high-intensity combat. A 400-ton sidewheeler armed with eight 64-pounders, the *Karteria* owed her existence and her fame to Captain Frank Abney Hastings, a British Philhellene and former Royal Navy officer who had been an eleven-year-old midshipman at Trafalgar. It was upon Hastings's recommendation that the Greek Revolutionary Committee in London had her built, and it was under his command from September 1826 to May 1828 that she performed outstanding service in engagements with Turkish forces afloat and ashore. The initiative that had distinguished her operations disappeared after Hastings was mortally wounded while attacking an enemy coastal fortification. By then, however, the *Karteria* had provided the first major demonstration of the naval potential of steam propulsion, the earliest of the innovations, all products of the Machine Age—shell guns, armor, and iron ships—that in little more than thirty years would transform the world's combat fleets.

The *Karteria* was not the first purpose-built steam warship. Pride of place belonged to a 24-gun, 120-horsepower floating battery designed during the War of 1812 by the brilliant American marine engineer Robert Fulton to help defend New York Harbor in the event of a British attack. Fulton called her the *Demologos* (Voice of the People). When he died prior to her completion, she was renamed in his honor. Unlike the *Karteria,* the *Fulton* never entered action. She had not been completed by the time the war ended, and, in any case, the British omitted to attack New York. A sailor brought her quiet career to a resounding close late one afternoon in June 1829 by carrying a lighted candle into her magazine in search of a powder charge to fire her evening gun.

Meanwhile, two other, originally civilian steamers, a Hudson River ferry and a tiny tug, had preceded the *Karteria* into combat. Beginning with her recapture of a merchant schooner in February 1824, the USS *Sea Gull,* formerly the ferry *Enterprise,* actively participated in the suppression of West Indian piracy, and a few months later the tug that had become HMS *Diana* routed native warcraft on the Irrawaddy during the First Burmese War. Their appearance did not signify an outburst of institutional interest in steam warships, however. Both had been acquired through the initiative of individual officers: Commodore David Porter and Captain Frederick Marryat, respectively, who foresaw the value of shallow-draft, self-maneuverable vessels in these particular campaigns, and the little steamers' adventures ended upon their conclusion. In the course of the decade, the Royal Navy acquired a number of auxiliary steamers—tugs, dredgers, and the like, some mounting a few guns—and the French navy launched its first, the *aviso* (dispatch boat) *Sphinx,* in 1829, but as of 1830 there was not a major steam warship in commission in any navy.

In view of the fact that by that date twenty-nine years had passed since William Symington built the first practical steamship, the paddlewheel tug *Charlotte Dundas,* and literally thousands of civilian steamers were at work throughout the world, the lack of enthusiasm navies manifested for steam propulsion has been attributed to the reflexive conservatism of which the naval profession is often accused. No doubt there is something in this interpretation. Spending one's career on things that can sink conduces to a preference for the proven.

Yet naval establishments had legitimate reasons, tactical and technological, to delay their embrace of steam power. Tactical, in that seagoing steamers were propelled by sidewheels that extended over at least a third of the length of a ship's hull, reducing the space available for her broadside battery by a corresponding extent, and that those sidewheels would be vulnerable to enemy fire. Technological, in that early steam engines were prone to break down and so inefficient that no ship could carry enough coal to last more than a few days; on long voyages, steamers spent most of their time under sail. Fulton had addressed the tactical problem in the design of the *Demologos.* His solution had been to center a single, broad paddlewheel in the channel between twin catamaran hulls, but this imaginative arrangement, satisfactory for a floating battery, was not suitable for a blue-water warship.

As time went by, improvements in the reliability and performance of marine engines gradually overcame the technological difficulties that had delayed their introduction into naval service. The British and French navies built a number of steam sloops, smallish craft carrying two to six guns, in the early 1830s, and later in the decade these navies and the U.S. Navy as well began laying down steam frigates. These sizable ships gave good value. The USS *Mississippi,* for example, a 3,250-ton vessel launched in 1842, served as Commodore Perry's flagship in the Mexican War and the opening of Japan and twice circumnavigated the globe before being lost on the Mississippi during the Civil War. Still, the tactical liabilities of steam-powered warships remained as great as ever.

They were dispelled by the advent of the screw propeller, a device that left the whole of a ship's broadside free for her guns and could not readily be disabled by even the hottest fire. The idea of screw propulsion dated back for centuries. By 1830 a number of inventors—most notably Josef Ressel, an Austrian navy forester who built the first serviceable screw steamer—had demonstrated that the application of steam power could make it a practical reality, but none managed to arouse the support of the maritime community. That achievement, a triumph of showmanship as well as technology, was shared by Francis Pettit Smith, an English gentleman farmer, and Captain John Ericsson, a Swedish engineer and erstwhile army officer who eventually settled in the United States. Ericsson was principally responsible for the design of the first screw warship, the USS *Princeton,* a 954-ton corvette commissioned in September 1843. Smith convinced the British Admiralty that propellers were practical and supervised the installation of one he designed in HMS *Rattler,* a 1,115-ton sloop that began her trials in October of that year. The system's performance fully satisfied its supporters' expectations, and in 1845 the Admiralty pitted the *Rattler* against HMS *Alecto,* a sidewheeler of virtually the same size and horsepower, in a series of contests staged to convince the still skeptical. The competition climaxed in a tug-of-war in which the *Rattler* dragged her opponent backward at a speed of 2.5 knots.

That same year, the French navy became the first to launch a screw frigate, the *Pomone,* a 2,010-ton vessel with machinery for which Ericsson furnished the plans. The Royal Navy followed with the *Amphion,* converted from a purely sail-powered ship before completion, in 1846, and the *Dauntless,* planned as a screw ship, in 1847; the U.S. Navy, with the *San Jacinto* in 1850. The French navy was also first to produce a purpose-designed steam ship of the line, the 90-gun *Napoléon,* a screw-driven vessel of 5,080 tons laid down in 1848 according to plans prepared by the gifted young naval architect Dupuy de Lôme. The Royal Navy, which had earlier converted four old two-deckers into steam-powered floating batteries, responded to reports of her start by beginning work on its first full-power steam line of battle ship, the 91-gun *Agamemnon.* She was ready for sea in 1853. By then, the days of sailing warships had ended, at least in a technological sense, and those of sidewheel steam warships were numbered. Aside from the gunboats the U.S. Navy more or less mass-produced for coastal and riverine operations during the Civil War, no combatant sidewheelers were put under construction after 1853.

Their limitations notwithstanding, paddle ships had made a major contribution to the triumph of steam by their performance in the campaigns and expeditions of the preceding decade, repeatedly demonstrating the advantages inherent in the ability to maneuver independently of wind and tide. None of the conflicts involved much distinctly naval combat, and for the most part steamers performed supporting roles, such as towing sailing ships into position to deliver shore bombardments, but on two occasions they held center stage. The first occurred in November 1845 off the Rio Parana port of Obligado, Argentina, where three steamers belonging to an Anglo-French force of eleven small vessels played a key part in breaking the boom, silencing the batteries, and sinking the three gunboats that the dictator Rosas had expected to close the river to foreign shipping. The second took place off Veracruz, Mexico, in March 1847, when the little U.S. steamers *Spitfire* and *Vixen,* each with two sailing gunboats in tow, closed to six hundred yards to attack the Castillo San Juan de Ulloa and remained there, virtually untouched, for more than an hour after Commodore Perry, alarmed by their temerity, signaled them to withdraw. Afterward, the Mexican gunners complained that their cannons could not be depressed sufficiently to bear on ships that close.

By the outbreak of the Crimean War in 1853, screw ships, including the *Napoléon* and the *Agamemnon,* could join sidewheelers in displaying the utility of steam power, on an immensely greater scale than in any previous conflict, in attacks on Russian coastal fortifications in the Black Sea and the Baltic. Three years later, summing up the lessons to be drawn from the struggle, the French minister of the marine, Vice Admiral Baron François Hamelin, who had commanded the French fleet in the Black Sea in 1854, expressed what had become a naval truism: "Any ship that is not provided with a steam engine cannot be considered a warship."[1]

The Crimean War also provided dramatic proof of the effectiveness of another agent of change in the texture of naval combat: the explosive shell. Shells themselves were nothing new. Special-purpose "bomb vessels" mounting one or two mortars had been used to deliver high-angle shell fire against shore targets ever since the French included five *galiotes à bombes* in a fleet sent to bombard Algiers in 1682. Owing to the considerable danger shells presented of fire and accidental detonation, however, they had seldom found a place in the armament of ships intended to fight other ships, and their influence on fleet operations had been negligible.

The exponential increase in that influence was chiefly due to a French artillery officer, General Henri-Joseph Paixhans. A graduate of the Ecole Polytechnique and veteran of nine Napoleonic campaigns, then-Major Paixhans had never served a day at sea but his interest in naval warfare was long-standing when in 1822 he published his *Nouvelle Force Maritime.* In this work, he argued that France could overcome Britain's wooden walls by building swarms of small, iron-armored steamers mounting one or two shell guns. "Cannon balls," he wrote,

> can fall on a ship by the hundreds without putting her in danger of being lost. . . . But a shell will shatter, shake, and spring an enemy ship's sides by a terrible shock. If the shells are arrested by the thickness of the wood, their explosion will have the effects of a mine, opening large breaches from which irregular cracks extend below the waterline and allow water to enter as through an abruptly broken dike. . . . If the shells penetrate the ship's side . . . they will produce their effect between the decks, in the midst of the combatants, the guns, the munitions, where they will vomit deadly iron splinters, incendiary materials, and unbearable billows of smoke.[2]

Swarms of armored steamers were too much for the French navy in 1822, but it did authorize the experimental production of a flat-trajectory shell gun Paixhans had designed. Years of tests, including one in which shells wrought havoc on a decrepit ship of the line, and numerous committee reports followed. (Frank Hastings did not await the outcome; shell guns contributed to the *Karteria*'s success.) Finally, in April 1838, the Ministry of the Marine decreed that a specified proportion of the new guns would be included in the armament of all French ships. Only seven months later, the French navy used those guns in action for the first time to bombard the Castillo San Juan de Ulloa at Veracruz in an intervention ostensibly incited by the sack of a French bakery. The Royal Navy added shell guns to its armory the following year, and other navies began to do so shortly thereafter.

The acceptance of shells as a general-purpose weapon had been inhibited in part by the facts that, though undeniably very destructive, they were shorter ranged and less accurate than solid shot. The remedies to these defects appeared in the form of the first breech-loading, rifled guns in 1846 and aerodynamically efficient, elongated shells in 1855. Depending upon their locking mechanism, early breechloaders were liable to blow off their breechblocks, and most navies, after giving them a try, temporarily reverted to muzzleloaders. But none of these innovations had been necessary to show what shells could do to wooden ships; thirty-eight Russian muzzle-loading smoothbores firing spherical projectiles sufficed.

The display occurred off Sinope, a Turkish port on the southern shore of the Black Sea, on 20 November 1853. At 1:30 that afternoon, a Russian squadron consisting of six ships of the line, two frigates, and three steamers attacked a Turkish squadron of seven frigates, three corvettes, and two steamers anchored in the roadstead. By 3:30, every Turkish ship but a single steamer had been blown up, sunk, or beached. No Russian vessel suffered significant damage. The Turks lost approximately 2,960 dead; the Russians, 37. What stunned both naval and public opinion was not so much the completeness of the Russian victory—given the odds, that was scarcely surprising—but the terrible inequality of the contest, for which the use of shells was believed chiefly responsible. Old General Paixhans wrote a newspaper article lauding his protégés' performance.

In the aftermath of Sinope, Britain and France, anxious to uphold Turkey as a barrier to Russian expansion into the eastern Mediterranean, intervened on her behalf in what then became the Crimean War. This raised the disquieting prospect that their wooden fleets would be called upon to attack shell-firing Russian forts. Emperor Napoleon III, a trained artilleryman with a passionate interest in ordnance matters, conceived the idea of constructing ironclad floating batteries to bear the brunt of such engagements, and it was agreed that each power would build five. Only three, all French, the *Dévastation, Lave,* and *Tonnante,* reached completion in time to take part in the war. Ungainly steamers of 1,650 tons displacement, they mounted 18 guns and wallowed along at 4 knots. Their distinctive feature, of course, was their armor: 4.0 inches of iron over 17 inches of teak along their sides and 4.5 inches over the same thickness of teak in a waterline belt. On 17 October 1855, these *batteries flottantes cuirassées* led an allied fleet into action against the Russian fortress at Kinburn on the Black Sea. Anchoring to engage the fort at a range of approximately three-quarters of a mile, they fired, on average, slightly more than a thousand shot and shell in a four-hour bombardment that ended in the Russian surrender. During the same period, each of them sustained about sixty hits. None penetrated their armor.

The next step was obviously to construct a seagoing ironclad, and the French took it. Dupuy de Lôme, who had proposed building an armored frigate a decade earlier, masterminded the project. Commissioned in August 1860, the *Gloire* measured 266 feet in length and displaced 5,618 tons. She was therefore about 20 percent longer and of roughly the same displacement as recent three-decker ships of the line, but her battery was concentrated in a single tier of 36 rifled guns, and her wooden sides were covered by forged iron plates from 4.4 to 4.8 inches thick. On trials her 2,600-horsepower engines gave her a top speed of 13 knots. At the date of her completion, the *Gloire* was incontestably the most formidable ship afloat.

That distinction proved short-lived. Upon learning of the French decision to build the *Gloire,* the British began planning a vessel that has been called the first modern warship, HMS *Warrior.* She entered commission a year to the month after the *Gloire.* Iron-hulled as well as iron-armored, the *Warrior* was 380 feet in length, displaced 9,137 tons, attained a speed of 14.3 knots with 5,290-horsepower engines, and mounted a single-tier battery of 40 guns including ten 7-inch shell-firing rifles. So sizable a vessel, far exceeding the potential of even the best-braced wooden frame, could only have been built of iron, a material that had furnished hulls for big civilian steamers as early as 1832, but which prejudice and once-reasonable doubts of its ability to withstand cannon fire had previously confined to minor naval vessels. Its use in the *Warrior* also enabled her to be provided with underwater compartmentation—that is, to have her lower decks partitioned by watertight bulkheads, another instance of naval innovation imitating civilian practice. The largest, swiftest, and most powerfully armed fighting ship ever built, she combined all the advances in naval technology since the War of 1812.

Indeed, the only major structural element of the battleships of the world wars missing from the *Warrior* was the turret, and it soon became available in different designs independently produced by John Ericsson and Captain Cowper Coles, RN. Coles had become intrigued by the idea of axial fire during the Crimean War. In March 1861, after prolonged agitation, he persuaded the Admiralty to install an experimental revolving turret in the floating battery *Trusty*. Its trials proved entirely satisfactory, and in February 1862 the Admiralty scheduled the construction of a six-turreted, iron coast-defense ship, the *Prince Albert*. Two weeks later, on the other side of the Atlantic another turreted ship entered combat.

The ship was Ericsson's *Monitor*, the famous "cheesebox on a raft"—the cheesebox being her turret. Ericsson had sought to interest Napoleon III in plans for just such a vessel in 1854, but all he had got for his trouble was a thank you note from an aide-de-camp. President Lincoln proved more receptive, and the *Monitor* began to become a reality in October 1861. Spurred by the knowledge that the Confederate navy had already begun building a casemated ironclad ram on the wooden hull of the former-U.S. frigate *Merrimack*, her construction was rushed to completion in four months. Nonetheless, the *Merrimack*, reincarnate as the CSS *Virginia*, narrowly beat her into action, emerging from the James River on 8 March 1862 to sink the wooden sloop-of-war *Cumberland*, 32 guns, by ramming and the frigate *Congress*, 52 guns, by shell-fire in the opening day of the Battle of Hampton Roads. The *Monitor* reached the scene that evening, and the next day she and the *Virginia* fought the first battle between ironclads. Tactically, their four-hour-long action ended in a draw. Strategically, the *Monitor* had won, since she prevented the *Virginia* from completing the destruction of the Union blockading squadron.

The U.S. Navy, understandably elated, ordered sixty-three more monitors during the war and retained a sentimental attachment to the type for half a century. But the good service they rendered in Southern waters notwithstanding, monitors were a technological dead end. The extremely low freeboard that was among their most distinctive characteristics (the original *Monitor's* measured less than two feet) made them unsuitable for employment in seagoing fleets. The future belonged to the high-freeboard turreted ship, but in the ferment into which the ironclad's advent had plunged naval architecture, many years would go by before that became clear.

Two other mid-century developments, less dramatic than the mechanization of navies but likewise destined to affect their operations, were the perfection of the electric telegraph—the beginning of a communications revolution that continues to the present—and the introduction of mine warfare. Overland telegraph lines had been strung on an increasing scale ever since Samuel Morse patented his system in 1840, and short undersea cables began to be laid in the 1850s. The British and French commanders in the Crimea were the first to be in more or less immediate communication with their governments while waging a foreign war. The link ran from London across the English Channel to Paris and then to the Turkish (now Bulgarian) port of Varna, from which a cable laid during the conflict extended beneath the Black Sea to the Allies' headquarters at Balaklava; messages spent from twelve to twenty-four hours in transit. From the onset of the American Civil War, the Union and Confederate governments routinely employed the telegraph to communicate with their armies in the field and naval forces in domestic ports. Ships at sea and—the initial attempt to lay a transatlantic cable ending in failure in 1858—in ports outside their own continental waters remained as isolated as ever from home authorities, but even under these limitations, the new technology demonstrated the capacity to influence events. In June 1864 a telegram from the U.S. minister to France alerted the USS *Kearsarge,* then at anchor off Flushing in the Netherlands, that the Confederate cruiser *Alabama* had entered port at Cherbourg, thereby setting the stage for the duel in which the latter was destroyed. Two years later a report sent by undersea cable that the Italian fleet was attacking the island of Lissa led to the Austrian sortie that climaxed in the first fleet action fought on the open sea since Trafalgar.

Floating explosive charges, the precursors of sea mines, had been set adrift against ships and bridges as early as the sixteenth century. Robert Fulton and others began experimenting with true mines around the time of the American Revolution, and between 1839 and 1842 an Englishman, a Swede, and an American (Colonel Samuel Colt, inventor of the six-shooter) independently developed command-detonated electrical mines exploded by a current from a storage battery. Prussian forces laid mines of this type to defend Kiel harbor against the Danish fleet during the Schleswig-Holstein War of 1848–51, but they were never tested. The first ships actually mined were three British vessels that struck a total of four Russian contact mines in the Baltic in June 1855. Following the last of these incidents, boat parties swept up thirty-three of the "infernal machines." In fact, they were not especially infernal, as none of the ships sustained major structural damage; nor, for that matter, did Rear Admiral Michael Seymour, the Baltic Fleet's incautious second-in-command who had a mine he was examining blow up in his face. Seymour returned to duty in two months without lasting injury aside from the loss of an eye. Less than a decade later, however, the mines (then called torpedoes) Confederates sowed to augment the defenses of their ports and rivers achieved impressive results, sinking twenty-nine Union vessels, among them four monitors, and damaging another fourteen. One of these successes, the destruction of the gunboat *Commodore Jones* on the James River, Virginia, was attained by a command-detonated mine designed by the Confederate navy's Torpedo Division; the remainder were the work of contact mines laid by local military authorities. At least on coastal and inland waters, naval warfare had acquired a subsurface dimension.

The Civil War also witnessed the earliest successful submarine attack, the sinking of the wooden steam sloop USS *Housatonic* by the CSS *H. L. Hunley* off Charleston, South Carolina, on the evening of 17 February 1864—albeit that the *Hunley* was surfaced at the time. The idea of undersea craft had intrigued the inventive for centuries. Leonardo da Vinci's sketchbooks show that he envisioned submarines as well as tanks and aircraft, and there is a strange story that in the 1620s King James I crossed the Thames in an oared submersible boat built by a Dutchman named Cornelius Drebbel, an act that would have been wholly out of character for that prudent prince. During the War of the Revolution, David Bushnell, a Yale man, produced a hand-cranked, single-seater submarine, the *American Turtle,* and Continental Army Sergeant Ezra Lee took her into New York Harbor in 1776 to attack the 64-gun ship of the line *Eagle.* Alas for ingenuity, the British vessel's sturdy hull frustrated Lee's attempts to attach the *Turtle*'s time-bomb to it. Several other more or less functional submarines appeared in the ensuing decades, but none engaged an enemy warship before the *Hunley.*

By the time Horace L. Hunley and his associates put their craft under construction in the spring of 1863, most of the key features of the modern submarine had been identified, and the *Hunley* incorporated them all: diving planes, ballast tanks, a rudimentary conning tower, a propeller and rudder aft, and a cylindrical shape with tapering ends. Unfortunately, two elements absent from this inventory—a mechanical propulsion system and the torpedo, neither as yet available—were necessary to make the submarine a practical man-of-war. The *Hunley* was powered by eight volunteers turning a deformed crankshaft and her projected armament consisted of a floating contact charge towed on two hundred feet of line. Leaving harbor under cover of darkness, she would dive beneath a blockader anchored for the night, surface on the other side, and continue on her way until the charge bobbed into her victim. After three crews, one captained by Hunley, perished in training accidents, the general commanding at Charleston ordered the *Hunley* to remain on the surface and relinquish her towed charge for a spar torpedo—that is, a contact charge at the end of a wooden shaft projecting from her bow, the weapon used by the little steam-powered "torpedo-boats" the Confederates called Davids, after the giant-killer. It was with a spar torpedo that the *Hunley* surprised and sank the *Housatonic*. She herself was mysteriously lost with all hands while returning to harbor. Years would pass before such craft posed a significant threat to surface vessels, but a fateful precedent had been set.

Naval tactics in the Age of Sail had been limited to maneuvers that could be performed by ships that depended on wind to propel them. The advent of steam-powered warships, easily able to do many things sailing ships could not, obviously opened new possibilities. Forward-looking officers did not hesitate to address these possibilities, a British captain's consideration of tactics appropriate to steam navigation appearing as early as 1828,[3] and by the approach of mid-century of the progressive view, carefully set out in a treatise by another captain, held

> [t]hat steam vessels, from the precision with which they can be steered on any given course; the rapidity of their rate, and the regularity with which both course and rate may be sustained, are capable of effecting combinations which cannot be accomplished with certainty by sailing vessels; and that a system of tactics commensurate with these powers is indispensable to their most effective use.[4]

Between 1855 and 1870, similar works appeared in Britain, France, Russia, and the United States on an international average of once a year. What most excited their authors was the prospect that for the first time since the days of galley warfare, a fleet could be maneuvered with equivalent exactitude and in much the same way as an army. Commodore Foxhall Parker, whose *Squadron Tactics under Steam* (1864) and *Fleet Tactics under Steam* (1870) served as manuals for the U.S. Navy, assured his readers that "through the agency of steam, war has become not less a science at sea than on land," in consequence of which "The naval officer will . . . do well in the future to make a close study of military tactics. . . ."[5] Like their competitors, though, Parker's books had a great deal more to say about evolutions than about tactics. Their reticence reflected the prevailing uncertainty as to whether, with the coming of armored steam warships, ramming would not replace the exchange of fire as the dominant means of naval combat.

The damage civilian steamers did when they ran into other vessels, as they would from time to time, had not escaped naval attention. Enthusiasts had been attempting to interest navy departments in building steam-driven rams ever since the 1820s, but their proposals were pigeonholed until the Crimean experience of the French floating batteries indicated that armored ships would be virtually impervious to gunfire. This cast the matter in an entirely new light, and beginning with the French *Couronne,* an iron-hulled half-sister to the *Gloire* laid down (but not completed) prior to the *Warrior,* most European ironclads built after 1859 had reinforced bows suitable for ramming or protruding spur rams. Confederate authorities, though handicapped by a grossly inadequate industrial base, made the majority of the ships they built or bought for home defense capable of ramming, and placed secret orders for five state of the art armored rams with British and French yards. Diplomatic complications kept any of the latter from entering action under the Stars and Bars, but ships outfitted in the South sank or drove ashore seven Union vessels by ramming in engagements during which their gunfire destroyed only one.

Granted that these encounters usually occurred on rivers and sounds that favored ramming tactics by cramping the combatants' maneuvering room, their results could be interpreted to vindicate the concept. Upon assuming command of the French ironclad squadron of evolution in August 1864, Vice Admiral Count Bouët-Willaumez told his captains that he proposed to develop maneuvers "appropriate to [their ships'] *strength,* which is the *bow;* [and] to their *weakness,* which is the *side,* pierced for gunports, against which the blow of a ram struck perpendicularly must lead to disaster."[6] In short, naval tactics as well as technology appeared to be in flux.

Yet for all the tactical confusion they created, the only major immediate change mid-century innovations imposed on naval combat was an acceleration of its tempo. In port, an admiral's intelligence surround might cover a continent through the agency of the telegraph, but at sea it remained restricted to the twenty-mile radius visible from the mastheads of his fleet or its scouts. This meant that steam fleets moving toward one another at, say, twelve knots would close to eight hundred yards, by 1860 the effective range of shipboard guns, in approximately forty-five minutes after coming into view, and a fleet advancing on an enemy awaiting its approach would do so in an hour and a half. The time between contact and combat could therefore be reduced to roughly one-sixth to one-third of that which, depending upon winds and seas, would have elapsed under sail.

In none of the battles fought during the 1860s, however, did the range hold at eight hundred yards. Ships and formations intent on ramming naturally sought to reduce it to no yards at all, but even in the two high-seas gunnery actions of the period the adversaries edged toward the 350 yards that Nelson's navy had considered point-blank. The small Austro-Prussian and Danish squadrons that clashed off Heligoland in May 1864 did so at ranges decreasing from 1,200 to 500 yards, and a month later the *Kearsarge* and the *Alabama,* which began their pas de deux at 1,750 yards, gradually closed to the same range. Thus the battle area of navies in the Machine Age initially increased very little beyond that of their predecessors in the Age of Sail. Naval combat remained close combat.

The administrative and logistical support upon which these navies depended was supplied by bureaucracies whose efficiency, if not necessarily generosity, would have excited the envy of any seventeenth-century admiral. The organization of these bureaucracies varied from country to country, but generally it consisted of a number of departments embracing one or, more frequently, several kindred categories of naval matériel, plus another for personnel. Those comprising the "Bureau System" adopted by the U.S. Navy in 1845, for example, were yards and docks; ordnance and hydrography; construction and repair—irreverently, "destruction and despair"; provisions and clothing; and medicine and surgery, each headed by a uniformed bureau chief. With some modifications—the creation of bureaus of engineering, equipment and recruiting, and navigation (later renamed personnel) in 1862 and aeronautics in 1921, and the amalgamation of the bureaus of construction and repair and engineering into a Bureau of Ships in 1940—this system bore the strain of two world wars. Indeed, it remained essentially intact until the 1960s, as did similar machinery established at the British Admiralty in 1832. As yet, no institutional arrangements were made for long-term planning or the formulation of naval policy and strategy. These responsibilities remained an additional duty of a few very senior people, in some cases a navy secretary alone, assisted by whatever informal advisers or ad hoc committees he chose to consult. Functional naval staffs would not take shape until the eve of World War I.

The final defeat of France's bid for European hegemony left a victorious Britain the world's preeminent naval, colonial, maritime, mercantile, industrial, and financial power. In none of these respects would her supremacy be challenged until century's end. The number of technological firsts that the French navy (never quite reconciled to Trafalgar) attained around mid-century might appear to contradict that statement so far as naval power is concerned, and several of them did indeed affright the British public, but there was really no cause for alarm. To Admiralty officials, it seemed foolish to have the largest navy in the world pioneer developments that would devalue ships in inventory (as decades later critics accused Jacky Fisher of having done with his *Dreadnought*). The Royal Navy could afford to leave innovation to others, certain of the capacity of British industry to overtake and outperform any rival whenever it was asked. The manner in which, as a *Punch* cartoon portrayed it, the *Warrior* trumped the *Gloire* provided a case in point. With an annual defense expenditure amounting to no more than 2 to 3 percent of the national income, mostly spent on the army, Britannia not only ruled the waves, she did so almost effortlessly.

The Crimean War, about which much has already been said, was the only European conflict in which Britain indulged between the end of the French wars and the start of World War I. In it, the British and French fleets, for once allied, carried the war to the enemy's coasts unopposed in either the Black Sea or the Baltic by Russian fleets that declined to leave port. A few years later, in the American Civil War, the U.S. Navy also carried the war to an enemy coast. Its intrusions were far from uncontested, however, and in addition to the Battle of Hampton Roads and a number of lesser actions, major engagements took place on the Mississippi below New Orleans and at the mouth of Mobile Bay. Much as the two wars differed in this regard, command of the sea was critical to the prosecution of both. That was not true of the four wars of German and Italian unification fought between 1859 and 1871, on the outcome of which naval operations exercised no influence. Nevertheless, the third of those struggles included the Austro-Italian fleet action off Lissa, a battle that would bemuse naval tacticians for more than thirty years.

NOTES

1. Philippe Masson, Michèle Battesti, and Jacques C. Favier, *Marine et constructions navales, 1789–1989* (Paris: Charles-Lavauzelle, 1989), p. 43.

2. Thomas Adams, "Artillerie et Obus," in *Marine et technique au XIXe siècle* (Paris: Service Historique de la Marine / Institut d'Histoire des Conflits contemporains, 1988), pp. 192–93.

3. Captain John Ross, RN, *A Treatise on Navigation by Steam; Comprising a History of the Steam Engine, and an Essay towards a System of the Naval Tactics Peculiar to Steam Navigation. . . .* (London: Longman, Rees, Orme, Brown, and Green, 1828).

4. Captain C. R. Moorsom, RN, *On the Principles of Naval Tactics; with Exemplifications of the Practice; and also Tables for Facilitating the Evolutions; with an Appendix Containing the Demonstrations* (Birmingham: Wrightson and Webb, 1846), p. 17.

5. Captain Foxhall A. Parker, USN, *Fleet Tactics under Steam* (New York: D. Van Nostrand, 1870), pp. 219, 238.

6. H.G., Officier de Marine, *Analyses des diverses tactiques navales publiées en europe depuis 1855* (Paris: Arthus Bertrand, [1870]), p. 16 (original italics).

10

David Glasgow Farragut

Deliberate Planner, Impetuous Fighter

(1801–1870)

Edward L. Beach

BORN JAMES GLASGOW FARRAGUT ON 5 JULY 1801, THE FIRST full admiral in the U.S. Navy experienced one of the most unusual childhoods on record. His father, a very young Spanish sea captain, was from the island of Minorca. At the age of twenty-one, George Farragut emigrated to America at the call of the Revolutionary War adventure. After the revolution, he settled in Tennessee, married a frontier woman of part Irish descent and great courage, and begot five children in quick succession. James Glasgow, who later changed his first name to David, was the second child, second son. There were two younger sisters and another brother, and their ties, from "Glasgow's" side at least, were always close.[1]

One of young Glasgow's earliest recollections was of his mother standing off a group of Indians who were demanding whiskey and threatening her with a knife at the door of their home. She had seen them coming, quickly sent her children into the loft of the separate kitchen, where they might not be found, bade them be quiet, and stood at the door of her principal building with a brandished axe. There was a terror-stricken moment of close contact with the knife-wielder, but the mother retained control of the axe and her composure and the discomfited Indians slunk away. Young James was five years old at the time, and he and his older brother, William, watched the entire encounter through cracks between the logs of the kitchen cabin wall. Sadly, he was to lose that stand-up mother only three years later.

In 1808, George Farragut brought home a friend, David Porter, also a retired sea captain, also making a somewhat scanty living partly from a land grant for his Revolutionary War service and partly from what may have been a sinecure appointment as warrant officer in the navy. (George Farragut was in the identical situation.) The two had been fishing on Lake Pontchartrain, near the Farragut home—the family had moved to the New Orleans area—and Porter had suffered a sunstroke in the blazing Louisiana sun. He was unable to walk, temporarily had lost the power of speech, and as has been suggested, may have been already in the last stages of tuberculosis. In any case, he needed round-the-clock care. In the frontier tradition, Mrs. Farragut generously provided for him in addition to her many household and family duties, even after she herself took sick with yellow fever. To what extent her strong constitution might have been weakened by the burdens suddenly fallen upon her is beyond determination. What is known is that Sailing Master Porter and Farragut's mother died on the same day, in the same house (in June 1808), and were buried in the same cemetery, two days later.

Porter's son, the later famous David Porter of the War of 1812, was at the time a Master Commandant* in the U.S. Navy and had just arrived at New Orleans to command the naval station there. The tremendous debt of gratitude he must have felt to his father's benefactors caused the twenty-eight-year-old David Porter, junior, to take an interest in the unfortunate Farragut family. Within the year, growing awareness of George Farragut's distress, with five little children to care for, impelled Porter to offer more assistance. This he did by supporting the application of the older brother for an appointment as a midshipman in the navy, and taking the second son, Glasgow, and one of the girls into his own home.

Probably no thought was given at the time to the possible duration of the arrangement, and apparently no formal adoption procedure ever took place. The girl ultimately lived with one of Porter's sisters, and the young Glasgow—as he was always called by his intimates—stayed in the Porter home. The lad was evidently a very appealing child, clearly delighted with his new family and the promise of a naval career that went with it.

Sometime during this first year with Porter, the young Farragut, most likely to honor his friend and protector, changed his first name to David. Again, there is no evidence this was done by legal action. Things were less formal in those early frontier days. What is known is that the gold watch Porter gave to Farragut upon his entry into the naval service (it may be viewed at the U.S. Naval Academy Museum) is inscribed, "D.G.F., 1810."

Glasgow Farragut's final separation from his own family took place when Porter was detached from New Orleans. This occurred in 1810, and Farragut lived for a time at the Porter home in Pennsylvania while his mentor was awaiting orders to command the 32-gun frigate *Essex*. Deep affection was already growing between the volatile Porter and his worshiping ward, and this could only have been greatly strengthened when Porter secured a midshipman's warrant for him. Thus, when he became ten years old, Glasgow Farragut "entered upon a man's estate," in the quaint saying of the time. He was an officer of the navy and, despite his extreme youth, was entitled to be addressed as "Mr. Farragut," which must have been a source of pleasure to the lad. Porter was known as a disciplinarian, and there is evidence he insisted on punctilious observance of this old naval custom wherever he had the authority.

But a ten-year-old child still needs parental guidance, and one can imagine the discussions that must have been held in the Porter household before the final decision that he should accompany Porter aboard the *Essex*. This

* Equivalent to the present-day rank of commander, by which it was replaced in 1837.

took place in the summer of 1811. War clouds that were to culminate in the War of 1812 were gathering; command of a frigate, even a rather small one like *Essex,* was sought after by all ambitious officers. Porter, combative and personally aggressive, was already marked among his contemporaries as a man to watch. Some of this aura must have affected young Glasgow, too.

One must also think about Farragut's position as a ward and protégé of a dominating skipper. He could so easily have become disliked, sneered at behind his and Porter's backs, supported on the surface but actively sabotaged in the many small ways available to disgruntled subordinates. In the event, the reverse of this happened. Although only ten, he had already received considerable tutelage in small boats by his real father, and had voyaged in a merchantman with his foster father. He would therefore have been able to impress his shipmates as not altogether unknowing about the sea. At the same time, he obviously took to a naval career like the proverbial duck to water, no doubt earning approval as a good shipmate, if a small one.

Apparently he had been outfitted in full naval uniform for a midshipman, rather a ridiculous necessity for a little boy, but his unaffected manner and uncomplicated seriousness of purpose overcame whatever prejudice his exalted status might have produced. Perhaps his very small stature aroused the protective instincts of the hard-bitten sailors whom his duties required him to order about. Instead of making enemies, he became a general favorite. As midshipman, one of his duties was occasionally to be in charge of a ship's boat. Illustrative of the feeling he evoked is the story of the reaction of his boat's crew to an instance of ridicule to which he was subjected because of his youth and fancy outfit. The entire boat's crew leaped ashore with him and had a high old time cleaning up on his tormentors until the police put a stop to the fight by arresting everyone in sight, including the little ringleader. When Porter learned of the fracas, he was delighted.

David Porter's command of the *Essex* is one of the classic tales of the War of 1812. His was the first action with the enemy: *Essex* captured the sloop-of-war *Alert* in an eight-minute fight. The action, minimized by Porter in his official report, was nevertheless Farragut's first experience under fire. Then came the great adventure. The *Essex* was ordered as part of a three-ship squadron to go on a commerce-destroying cruise in the South Atlantic. If feasible, the ships were to proceed around Cape Horn into the Pacific to disrupt the British whaling industry. The other two ships were the *Constitution,* 44 guns, and *Hornet,* 18 guns. At the beginning of the projected cruise, the *Constitution* captured HBM Frigate *Java,** 38 guns, and *Hornet* took the

* "His Britannic Majesty's Frigate" was officially correct in those days. The *Java,* though a three-masted square-rigger, was a frigate, not a "ship of the line." Hence, she was usually referred to as His Majesty's Frigate or "HM Frigate." More often than not, the adjective

brig *Peacock,* 18 guns. Both victors then returned to port. Only the *Essex* was left to carry out the ambitious plan of invading the Pacific.

After touching at all the previously selected points of rendezvous but one, finding no word of any sort and unaware that his consorts had already terminated their cruises, Porter resolved to carry out the remainder of the original plan and turned the *Essex*'s bows to the south. It was an audacious decision, but typical of him. The passage through Drake's Strait, south of Cape Horn, was a severe trial, but early in 1813 the ship was coasting northward along the shores of Chile, repairing storm damage and searching for British whaling ships.

Porter's account of the adventures of his ship during her ensuing year in the Pacific is one of the fascinating pieces of naval adventure reading.[2] He dealt the whalers a blow from which they did not recover for many years, capturing nearly all of their ships in the area, converting the best ones into an impromptu naval force and some of the others into support vessels. During this period Farragut, then twelve years old, was put in charge of one of the captured ships with orders to sail her to Valparaiso, in company with several others, to be sold as a prize. The *Barclay,* thus Farragut's first command, was actually an American whaler that had been captured by a British warship and recaptured by the *Essex.* By the prize laws of the time, her recapture did not restore the status quo; since the ship would otherwise have been a total loss, a variation of the salvage laws applied.

Porter was looking out for his own crew members, himself included, and the U.S. government as well. The *Barclay*'s insurance company, if the policy still held despite the state of war with England, would have to make appropriate restitution to her owners. On the other side of the ledger, her cargo remained aboard; all her equipment was exactly as it had been, her crew and officers themselves were also still on board. She was in no way changed for her short period under British capture, and one can sympathize with her captain, who no doubt had a pecuniary as well as a proprietary interest in his ship. Porter nonetheless had the law on his side, and he refused to listen to the protestations of the *Barclay*'s master. So far as he was concerned, the prize courts would decide the issue.

When *Barclay*'s original captain found his place usurped by a twelve-year-old boy, he decided to reassert command as soon as his ship was clear of the others and present Porter with a fait accompli that, if he was fortunate, might never be tested. Young Farragut would be too frightened to frustrate his game, and in any event could hardly constitute an obstacle.

Britannic was inserted, thus: "HBM Frigate *Java.*" HMS did not enter general use until mid-century. The *Peacock,* correspondingly, was "HBM Brig *Peacock.*"

However, the whaling captain had underestimated his young opponent, and he had not reckoned with the caliber of his small prize crew. Porter, perhaps, should be criticized for having overly exposed his young ward, although as events developed, it might also be said that he thought the experience would be beneficial.

The *Barclay* was to follow a former British whaler that had been converted to an auxiliary renamed *Essex Junior.* As the distance between the ships began to increase, Farragut directed the *Barclay*'s sails set in order to follow. The captain shouted he would do no such thing, and went below to get his pistols. Once he was out of sight, copying as well as he could the tone the redoubtable Porter would have used, Farragut ordered the burly boatswain's mate who was his second in command, "I'll have those sails set and the yards braced around, if you please!"

Porter had well set the stage. The boatswain's mate had been one of the boat's crew in the earlier encounter with the dock toughs and was known for his protective instincts toward the child officer. "Aye, aye, sir!" he shouted. He blew his pipe, stamped his feet, and waved his arms. The customary routine, set in motion by a man long accustomed to doing just that, often with recalcitrant or resentful sailors, sent both the prize crew and the whaler's original crew running into the rigging to take the familiar action. The yards swung around, the sails filled, and when the captain regained the deck he found the ship moving in the ordered direction, his own crew helping, and a much bigger person, who had received his orders and intended to carry them out, with whom to deal.

David Porter may already have guessed that little Midshipman Farragut had the right qualities to go far in the navy, and no doubt got a degree of pleasure out of each time this instinct was proved right. The year in the Pacific was in a sense the making of the future admiral. Even its disastrous end at Valparaiso, with the *Essex* outmatched two to one in number of guns and badly outranged besides by the British *Phoebe* and *Cherub,* was good for the midshipman's personal future. It was a terrible battle and a bloody defeat. Porter fought his ship until there was absolutely nothing more to be done, her casualties greater than those suffered by any other American vessel in any battle of the war. By good fortune, Farragut was not among the injured nor was Porter, and Glasgow Farragut was ever after to look back on this day as one of the climactic ones of his career, despite that he was not yet thirteen. In the two years just past he had experienced more of fighting, seamanship, leadership, shiphandling—and all other naval arts—than most officers accumulated in a lifetime.

Farragut was a small child, and became a small, slender man. His father was short and stocky, and the son's maximum height has been given as five feet, six inches. Only in his later years did his slim figure begin to add weight. Another inheritance from his father was his swarthy complexion, augmenting years of facing extremes of weather. He spoke Spanish fluently, and perhaps because he began in a bilingual family, never had any difficulty with foreign languages, ultimately becoming proficient in several. He became a magnificent shiphandler, and in this was helped by a stentorian voice rather surprising from such a small figure. Stories of his early career make reference to his ability to handle sail from the quarterdeck with nothing but a speaking trumpet and his uncanny understanding of wind, sea, and sail.

As Farragut grew older, he was in great demand as an aide to senior officers because of his dependability, willingness to exert himself, and clear-cut awareness of how to accomplish the duties assigned. There was only one thing in which he was deficient. Possessing an extraordinary practical education in ships and the sea, he had little formal schooling. There is evidence that for a time he considered this lack to be of little moment, but one of his inherent characteristics was that of attracting warm friendships among quality people. One of the young men thus attached to him was Charles Folsom, chaplain of the ship of the line *Washington,* in which Farragut served from 1816 to 1819. Folsom, only a few years older than Farragut and later to become librarian at Harvard University, was dismayed at the uncultivated state of the younger man's otherwise superior mind and set himself to correcting it.

One of the chaplain's duties in a big ship was that of "schoolmaster" to the midshipmen, usually a thankless job. Although Farragut was by this time about eighteen and still only a midshipman, he had been at sea almost continuously since he was ten, and was already a very successful young officer. No doubt he also had begun to entertain doubts as where his lack of formal education would lead, for he was receptive to Folsom's efforts, and the dedicated teacher soon discovered that he had found the greatest of prizes, an apt pupil. He awakened the young sailor's interest in literature and mathematics, led him on tours of ancient ruins near Tunis, and continued to stimulate him by correspondence for years after their careers had drifted apart. To Folsom for his broadening influence, and to David Porter for his training in the naval profession, Farragut owed most of the development during his formative years.

Following the War of 1812, the U.S. Navy entered upon a period of stagnation and decline. Aside from a few exploring expeditions, its principal activities consisted of showing the flag in various areas of the world. The war with Mexico provided a moment of excitement, but Mexico had no navy and it was mostly a land war. Ambitious and energetic officers found time hanging heavily, with little to do. Many went on half-pay—inactive duty—because of no employment, and the first "retiring board" sat in judgment and recommended that many of its fellow officers be discharged. Glasgow's older brother, William, physically disabled because of rheumatism, was one. Glasgow, however, despite a few bouts with yellow fever, a near fatal encounter with cholera, and a severe case of sunstroke to which he attributed the eye weakness that troubled him in later years, was in good physical condition. He had gained an excellent service reputation, causing senior officers to request his assignment. Although he had periods of half-pay for reasons to be explained, a lack of need for his services was rarely one of them.

Promotion was slow during the years before the Civil War. Farragut was fourteen years a midshipman, sixteen a lieutenant, and fourteen more a commander before receiving his commission as captain in 1855. During this period, however, he commanded ships in each of his ranks, and it was said of him that no damage from any navigation hazard ever occurred to any ship under his command.

Early in his career, Farragut developed an interest in gunnery and became known as something of an ordnance expert. His principal expertise, however, was as a shipboard officer, in which his reputation grew steadily. Not only was he an expert shiphandler, skilled in conducting evolutions under sail in any sort of weather, he had grown up with steam power as well, and was accomplished in its employment—although there were some who claimed he never believed steam could take the place of sail. His Irish heritage gave him, apparently, a sort of doggedness of objective; once he had determined on a course of action, his temperament drove him to see it through. His Spanish impetuousness, on the other hand, caused him to move quickly, sometimes, it was said by his occasional detractors, too quickly, before there had been time for full consideration of all aspects of whatever problem existed. With one characteristic everyone agreed: whatever Farragut was into, action could be predicted, and this extended into his personal life.

His first marriage provided an early illustration. Susan Marchant and he married in September 1824, in Norfolk, her hometown. Less than two years later she began suffering from the illness that ultimately killed her, at the time diagnosed as neuralgia. Young Farragut's career of that period is studded with references to his need to go on half-pay in order to be with her. He took her to specialists wherever they could be identified, requested frequent changes of duty to facilitate whatever program they were trying to follow at the time, and in general neglected his own professional interests to tend to her needs. She died late in December 1840, having borne, in his words, sixteen years of unparalleled suffering. The care he had devoted to her caused a local lady to announce, "When Captain Farragut dies, he should have a monument reaching to the skies, made by every wife in the city contributing a stone."[3]

Farragut's second marriage took place three years later, to another Norfolk woman, Virginia Loyall. Their son Loyall was born late the following year. This marriage was blessed with good health, and it is evident that Farragut was a devoted father and that his son fully returned the affection. Loyall was at one point of the Civil War privileged to sail with his father in his flagship, much as his parent had years before with Porter. Loyall's tales of his experiences as an unofficial aide have added much to history's understanding of his father.

Nothing so clearly demonstrates Farragut's devotion to duty and his oath of loyalty to the United States—in which he never wavered—than his action as his state considered and finally adopted the Ordinance of Secession, passed by the Virginia legislature on 17 April 1861. Although born in Tennessee, his home of record was Norfolk. He was there "awaiting orders" while the Virginia legislature was debating secession and, like everyone, engaged in many discussions with friends over the advisability of this drastic step. Over the exciting weeks sentiment gradually swung toward leaving the Union, a trend he argued against. He began to notice growing coolness toward him as "not loyal to Virginia."

He had made it clear to all his friends, and also his wife, that he would remain loyal to the Union, but the suddenness with which the secession ordinance was passed caught Farragut by surprise. Norfolk burst into a fervor of excitement. The friends with whom he discussed events, many of them fellow officers also living in Norfolk, had earlier greeted with derision his defense of Lincoln's decision to support Fort Sumter and the obligation they all had taken to support the Constitution. In so many words, they now told him he must either resign from the navy or leave Norfolk. At this juncture he told his wife that he must leave immediately, that very day, and she, too, must decide what her course would be.

Virginia Farragut was more of a "Norfolkian" even than her husband, but her answer was ready: she would follow him wherever it led her. Without doubt it was an emotional moment, followed straightaway by one of great activity as, without notice, they broke up their home of so many years and bade good-bye to family and friends. They departed Norfolk by steamer for Baltimore that same afternoon.

The Farraguts were very religious, their ties to their home very strong. This was one of the lowest points in their lives. As they stood on the deck of the steamer carrying them from Norfolk, they must already have begun to sense the tragedy that was facing the country. The effect on themselves was bad enough: loss of their entire way of life, so far, and there would surely be more. Deep among their feelings must have been the realization that from this point there was to be no turning back, ever.

Reaching New York without incident, the Farraguts quickly moved on to the little town of Hastings-on-Hudson, where they rented a small house. This was to become the family home base for the duration of the war, and is, in fact, the village with which the name of Farragut is most closely associated. Immediately upon arriving there, Farragut wrote to inform the Navy Department of his new domicile, the reason for the change, and to request active duty. For a combination of reasons, nothing happened for some time. Washington was understandably in a state of great flux, not to mention anxiety. Secretary of the Navy Gideon Welles was a newspaperman, not a navy person. Although he had served in the Navy Department for a short time during the Mexican War, he had only minimal background in the problems suddenly landing upon him. Among the great questions, as he perceived the situation, was the loyalty of the members of the naval service.

Sure of no one, Welles had caused a new oath of allegiance to be required of all officers, and even then felt insecure for a time. Farragut executed the new oath as soon as he was aware of the requirement, but he was a very senior officer, with fifty years of service, and had not only been born in the South but had married two Norfolk women. Until very recently he had considered Virginia to be his home state. Welles and the navy establishment were simply not ready to trust anyone with Farragut's antecedents.

Shortly after his sixtieth birthday, Farragut traveled to Washington to plead his case for active duty, but without tangible result. It was the Union's decision for what was called the "Anaconda" policy that finally turned events in his favor. By Anaconda was meant the slow strangling of the South by blockading—and, eventually, seizing—all its coastal ports and capturing the vital Mississippi River. The South would then have no way of obtaining capital by selling its produce (principally cotton and tobacco) or of importing the vitally needed sinews of war that were procurable only in Europe. All suitable inlets and harbors, whether the site of a port city or not, had also to be blockaded against possible improvised use. It was a massive program, and it would obviously require many relatively small independent commands, interrelated as necessary by war exigencies and geography, to put it into effect.

The Mississippi was an entirely different problem. If the river could be itself captured by a naval force, all the ports fronting on it would be useless to the South no matter which side held them. Initial plans visualized a combined campaign by army and navy forces downstream from a base at Cairo, Illinois.

There is some confusion as to just where the plan originated to direct the Gulf Squadron to mount a second, simultaneous, campaign to capture

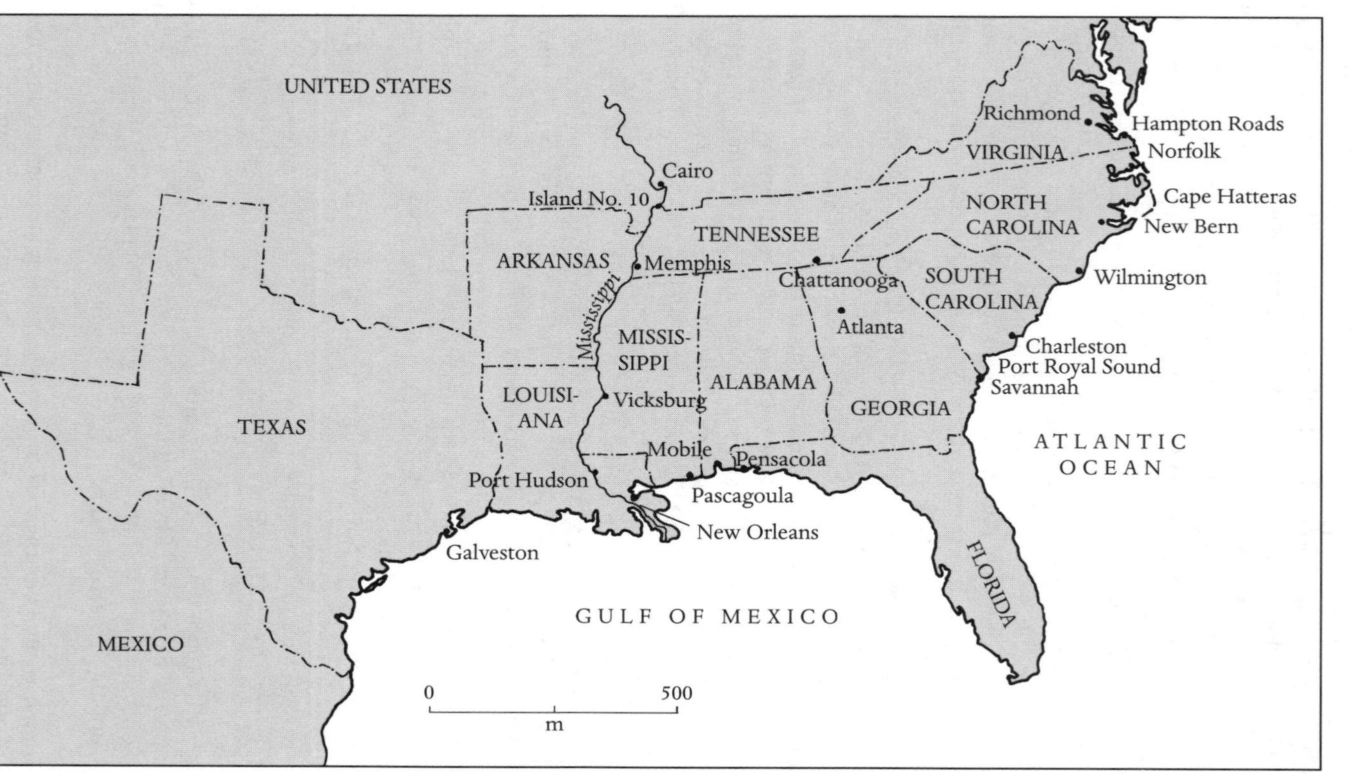

18. The Confederate States of America.

the Mississippi River from its southern end and link up with the Union forces coming downstream. The preponderance of evidence suggests it was Secretary of the Navy Welles himself who initially advocated it, but Gustavus V. Fox, Welles's ambitious assistant and a former naval officer, later claimed the honor. So did Commander David Dixon Porter, second son of David Porter of *Essex* renown, an officer of some talent but totally unscrupulous and given to much bluster and brag. The most important thing was the decision to set a separate force specifically to capture New Orleans as soon as possible, thereby blocking the river and all traffic on it from access to the sea.

Selection of a suitable commander for the effort was the next order of business. Later Welles wrote that he had his eye on Farragut from the beginning, and although he had not responded earlier to Farragut's plea for active service, he had noted with favor the uncompromising nature of his immediate move out of his seceded home state.[4] There were some preliminaries, for selection of the commander of the squadron to be tasked with capture of New Orleans was of obvious importance. All indications pointed to Farragut, however, and the command was confirmed as his near the end of 1861.

Until this moment the forces of bureaucracy had moved in their imponderable slow ways. Now it was to be up to the man of action. Here it was that Farragut showed that other part of his character that was, perhaps, less well appreciated. Impetuous he was reputed to be, but he was also a man of careful and thorough preparation, in personal makeup the antithesis of the planner who cannot himself take action. Early in 1862 he was on his way to the Gulf of Mexico. Despite carping criticism from David Dixon Porter, his subordinate who was writing confidentially to Assistant Secretary Fox, in a few weeks he got his ships across the mud bars at the entrance to the Mississippi for the attack on New Orleans itself.

The principal defense of the city consisted of two forts, Jackson and St. Philip, one on either side of the river, roughly one-third of the way from the delta to the city. Under orders from Secretary Welles (probably written by Fox) to "reduce" the two forts by mortar fire from Porter's gunboats before passing them, Farragut spent a week waiting for the promised results. When Porter was unable to deliver, Farragut at last gave signal for his ships to advance and pass the forts. This they did on 24 April 1862, in the process receiving a terrific bombardment, described by Farragut as "a fire such as the world has scarcely known."[5] All the ships were damaged, some severely, and all had suffered some losses in personnel, though not so great as the most pessimistic predictions. The fleet then went on upriver, brushing aside the little Confederate river defense flotilla and exchanging fire with improvised batteries a few miles below the city. Finally, with all the Union ships before New Orleans, a delegation of Farragut's senior officers went ashore to demand surrender of the city. This they received, amid tumultuous mobs of hostile citizenry.

Years earlier, during the Mexican War, Farragut had submitted a careful thought-out plan for the capture of the fort of San Juan de Ulloa at Vera Cruz. Nothing came of it. Farragut's research as to the fort's vulnerability was discounted on the theory that wooden ships could never "stand" against fortresses of thick masonry and great numbers of heavy, long-range cannon. Welles, in his encomiums of Farragut written afterward, stated that he was present at the briefing when Farragut submitted his plan, and had been favorably impressed; so that from the beginning he had thought of Farragut as a naval leader not afraid of combat with forts. This, he wrote, had been one of the factors disposing him to support the selection of Farragut for the formidable task of passing Forts Jackson and St. Philip and attacking New Orleans.[6]

The campaign is known to U.S. naval history as "Passing the Forts of New Orleans." It is also sometimes referred to as the "Battle of New Orleans," despite the earlier battle of the same name in 1815, when Andrew Jackson's troops repulsed a British attempt to capture the city. Farragut's battle was actually against the forts, and he did not capture them, or even "reduce" them, but merely bypassed them at close range and under very strong opposition. A principle of naval warfare was thereby beautifully illustrated: that a land-based, immovable installation not supported by a chain of interlocking bases can be bypassed by mobile forces and thereby rendered useless, ultimately to surrender ignominiously. This was the fate of the two Confederate forts, which capitulated within days after the Union fleet had passed. The lesson was thoroughly studied by the U.S. Naval War College during the years prior to World War II, and formed the basis for Admiral Nimitz's preeminently successful campaign to bypass the Japanese island strongholds as the Pacific Fleet drove toward the mainland of Japan.

The importance of the capture of New Orleans was even greater than anticipated. Professor Charles L. Lewis, in his carefully researched biography of Farragut, says:

> There is good evidence that the failure of Napoleon III to recognize the Confederacy and take some positive step towards bringing the war to a close even without English cooperation was due to Farragut's capture of New Orleans. If Farragut had failed, it is not unlikely that, a few months later after McClellan's army suffered such a crushing defeat in Virginia, England too would have taken steps towards bringing about peace with the establishment of the Confederate States of America as an independent nation.[7]

New Orleans, it will be remembered, had been Farragut's home as a child. It was the site of his mother's death, the breaking up of his father's home, and the fortuitous meeting with David Porter. His two sisters still lived there, one in the city itself and one in the vicinity of Pascagoula, and both had husbands and sons fighting for the Confederacy. Fresh from the furious battle passing the two forts below the city, their brother's first move after establishing the occupation was to call on his sisters and assure himself of their well-being. In the circumstances, the visit by their brother was at best a difficult one, and there is little evidence either sister actively returned his solicitude.

Very much on Farragut's mind at this juncture were two antithetical objectives. His instructions for the campaign against New Orleans were to push upstream as soon as possible after taking the city and join his force with that of Flag Officer Andrew Foote, commanding in the Cairo-based downstream campaign. At this stage of the war, the authorities in Washington had no appreciation of the tremendous difficulties being faced by both commanders. The Union army had been directed to work its way downstream with Foote—and this, too, turned out to be a much bigger order than anyone had anticipated, for an aroused countryside contested every foot of ground. The campaign was to cost many lives, including that of Andrew Foote, dead of infection after injury in battle, and months of arduous fighting. In the North it would eventually produce the winning general Lincoln had been looking for: Ulysses S. Grant. In the South it brought Farragut to national prominence.

At the same time he was campaigning before New Orleans, Farragut had received separate orders to capture Mobile Bay and the city of Mobile as soon as possible, because that was one of the prime alternatives to New Orleans as a base for blockade runners. Moreover, the South had reputedly begun building a very powerful ironclad warship at Mobile, more powerful even than the *Merrimack,* or *Virginia* as that ship had been renamed, of whose tremendous combat potential the Battle of Hampton Roads, only a few weeks before, had been an electrifying example to the world. This new ironclad he was asked to capture, destroy, or neutralize. There was evident uncertainty in Farragut's own mind as to which of the two objectives, up the Mississippi or the diversion to Mobile, should be pursued first. That both would involve heavy fighting he was positive.

The decision finally was made to go upstream first. Just as Farragut's superiors in Washington had begun to appreciate the difficulties in the way of successful passage upriver and to repose more trust in his judgment, he took his fleet upstream to an anchorage immediately below Vicksburg, but remained there only a short time for fear of the river becoming more shallow with the approach of summer. Additionally, coal was not available, and there was real danger that these two factors might trap his ships in the Mississippi until the water level rose again in the late fall.

Totally lost on Washington was the fact that Farragut's seagoing warships were not suited for shallow-water river fighting. Foote's ships coming downstream from Cairo were mostly river steamers converted by addition of armor and guns. With shallow draft and broad flat bottoms, they had no worries about falling water and little concern from running aground—a contingency for which they had been built. Returning to New Orleans, Farragut made special preparations for the conditions he would face below Vicksburg, particularly the batteries on the bluff facing the river, which his own guns could not reach because they could not be sufficiently elevated. Early in June 1862 he was back before Vicksburg, and this time passed the fortifications with his fleet, effecting juncture with the northern Union forces, now under Flag Officer Charles H. Davis, poor Foote's relief.

Bypassing the Vicksburg batteries was not the same as bypassing the delta-isolated forts below New Orleans, for the New Orleans forts had no inland supporting structure, whereas Vicksburg was surrounded by an entire countryside occupied by the Confederate army. In consequence, it was still necessary for the naval forces continuously to run the gauntlet of the Confederate batteries at Vicksburg until final surrender of the city to General Grant on 4 July 1863.

There was much, much, more in the campaign for control of the Mississippi. Farragut was constantly the butt of disparaging reports sent secretly by his subordinate, David Dixon Porter, to Secretary Welles and (more viciously worded yet) to Welles's assistant, Fox. Flag Officer Davis came in for his share of such letters as well, some of them from another Porter in his own force, David Dixon's older brother, William, an even looser cannon. Fortunately, the Porter brothers overreached themselves, the navy secretary began to see through their self-aggrandizement as a collection of half-truths and occasional outright falsehoods, and Farragut's steady star began to shine in its proper light. This was the situation when Farragut's promotion from "flag-officer" (captain commanding of a squadron or fleet, with courtesy rank of commodore) to the newly created rank of rear admiral was authorized by Congress, effective in 1862, with date of rank in January 1863. He was the first officer of the U.S. Navy to wear that rank on active duty.[8]

Once control over the Mississippi River had been achieved, Farragut returned to his basic command, the Union forces in the Gulf of Mexico. It was now 1863, and he harbored firm intentions of proceeding as soon as possible to the next job at hand, capture of Mobile Bay and termination of its employment as a blockade-runners' haven. In this purpose he never wavered, but other exigencies intervened, and Washington did not find it possible to provide the Gulf command with the force necessary (so Farragut was informed by letter from Fox). At the same time, he was enjoined to strengthen the Gulf blockade, which had been unavoidably neglected during his effort to capture the great river. The year 1864 dawned in this vital and yet desultory duty. In the meantime, he had kept himself informed as well as possible as to conditions at Mobile, in particular the state of construction of the great ironclad, *Tennessee,* and had passed along all pertinent information to Washington.

Farragut knew, for example, that the *Tennessee*'s commander, a brother officer from the prewar years, was to be Franklin Buchanan, a Marylander who had "gone South."[9] Buchanan had commanded the converted *Merrimack* (*Virginia*) and destroyed the Union fleet blockading Norfolk. Wounded in the leg by a rifle bullet fired from the shore, he had missed the second day's battle when the hastily built little *Monitor* inaugurated a new era of naval warfare as she stood off his great ironclad. After his recovery, Buchanan had been promoted to rear admiral and given command of Confederate forces in Mobile Bay, with the new and very powerful *Tennessee* as his flagship. In mid-1864, Farragut knew the *Tennessee* was complete, but blocked by shallow water from crossing the bar at the mouth of the Mobile River, where she was built, and entering Mobile Bay. He also knew of Buchanan's scheme to get her over the bar with loaded barges placed under heavy beams run through her gunports so that, when unloaded, their buoyancy would lift the bigger ship.

Farragut did not know, however, that Buchanan planned to have other ships following with the ironclad's ammunition and equipment, so that his flagship could become battle-worthy within hours. Crossing the bar at night, she would load instantly, and immediately run the blockade. Buchanan would appear at Pensacola, destroy or capture the Union ship-repair facilities there, then head for New Orleans, where the news of his coming would spread fright among the Union ships and exultation among the populace, and almost assuredly restore the city to its rightful Confederate control.

Such were Confederate expectations for the new ship—the most powerful Southern ironclad of the war—that they believed could break the blockade of the Gulf ports. Farragut, in the meanwhile, had studied the reports of the Battle of Hampton Roads, and had experience of his own from fighting the ironclads of the Mississippi. Sailing ships were finished, but steam-powered ships, even if made of wood, could, he thought, if aggressively handled, hold their own. Their guns would probably not be powerful enough to have much effect on the greased slopes of the ironclad's armor (even a point-blank hit at short range would merely glance off), but if they could strike the low-lying enemy vessel at high speed, ten knots or so, they might ride up on top of her slanted sides and force her down to where water would pour into her through gun-ports and other openings and thus, in a few moments, sink her.

Watertight reserve buoyancy was the key, and the Confederate ironclad design contained very little such buoyancy, none of it watertight. Reports from the *Cumberland*'s commander at Hampton Roads indicated that as his ship sank, with the *Merrimack*'s ram embedded in her side, she very nearly carried the Confederate warship down with her; only at the last moment had the ironclad wrenched free. From this Farragut formulated his scheme of attack. His wooden ships would remain under way at all costs and seize every opportunity to hurl themselves upon the enemy ironclad. Iron straps were bolted to their stems to strengthen them and provide a contact surface on which the spoon-shaped bows of the wooden sailing steamers could slide high upon the low-lying sloped sides of the Confederate ship and bear her down by their weight. The *Merrimack* would clearly have been sunk could this have been done. The *Tennessee* was much better built, much stronger, and with much more reserve buoyancy. Nonetheless, Farragut believed she could be "ridden down," and laid his plans accordingly.

In addition, there was the lesson that at Hampton Roads only the little *Monitor* could stand up to the *Merrimack*. With the prospect of battle against a far stronger ship, Farragut urgently demanded at least a few of the many later-model monitors the North had been building. Until 1864 there had been no monitors available for the Gulf forces, but now that was changed. Four were ordered to report to him: two light, double-turreted types and two very heavy, single-turreted ones mounting monster 15-inch guns that had hardly been thought of before the war began.

The Union commander's reputation as a fighting admiral had been confirmed by New Orleans and other Mississippi River battles. Washington knew him for a man given to the most careful preparation it was possible to make, but then, like Horatio Nelson, whose aphorisms he often quoted, he could be depended on to fight. Many officers were (and are still) born bureaucrats, able at administration but not possessed of the spirit of combat. Farragut, to the contrary, was appreciated as eager enough for victory to risk all on the outcome. Washington knew that the monitors being sent to Farragut would shortly have all the employment they could desire.

Buchanan got the *Tennessee* over the bar in May, but failed in his attempt to get her loaded and off the same night, and thus lost the tactical surprise he hoped to achieve by a sudden foray. He did not, however, have the imagination to take his ship to sea anyway, because he still possessed strategic surprise, as Farragut would undoubtedly have done in his place. He waited, instead, while Farragut gathered his forces, made his plans, got army troops to join in order to occupy Forts Morgan and Gaines at the entrance to Mobile Bay, and Fort Powell (guarding the less important Grant's Pass into the bay), and, finally fully ready, brought the battle to him. Farragut attacked in the early morning of 5 August 1864, in a pattern he was making routine. His objective was to pass Fort Morgan, which guarded the channel left open at the end of the Confederate minefield. Having got behind Morgan, he would have control of the bay, and in good time land his army troops to capture the fort from the rear where its guns could not bear.

Probably Farragut's greatest personal deficiency lay in excessive thoughtfulness of the feelings of others when more important considerations should be controlling. Putting Captain James Alden in command of the *Brooklyn,* one of his most powerful ships, was an example of this. Permitting Alden to lead his fleet into battle past Fort Morgan was a second; he had intended to lead himself, in his flagship, the *Hartford,* but yielded to pleas of his staff that as overall commander he ought not so to hazard himself. Alden had proved himself lacking in any Farragut-like ardor for battle as early as April 1861, when Welles sent him and Engineer-in-Chief Benjamin F. Isherwood to rescue the new steam frigate *Merrimack* from the Norfolk Navy Yard just before Virginia seceded. The ship was ready to sail, Isherwood having accomplished a miracle of improvisation, but the yard's senile commander, Captain Charles McCauley, refused to let her go. Isherwood begged Alden to ignore McCauley and carry out the secretary's order, but he would not.[10] In the instant case, with his ship in the channel passing the fort under fire, Alden again lost his nerve.

Disregarding Farragut's explicit order to stay in the middle of the channel, Alden instead remained as far from Fort Morgan as he could steer, far to the left of where he had been ordered to go. The result was that the buoys marking the Confederate "obstructions," a line of submerged mines intended to force the attacking fleet to keep close to Fort Morgan, appeared to starboard instead of to port as had been specified in Farragut's operation order. The newly arrived monitor *Tecumseh,* one of those with the big 15-inch guns, was guiding on the *Brooklyn.* She consequently crossed the line of obstructions on the wrong side of the end buoy, detonated a mine, and sank instantly. Signaling frantically, Alden ignored Farragut's order to "go ahead" and, with the Union fleet under heavy bombardment from Fort Morgan, began backing and twisting his ship to turn around and go back the way he had come. The result was that he put the *Brooklyn* broadside across the channel, blocking advance of all those following her, bunching them exactly where the fort's guns could do the most damage.

The only way into the bay, now, was across the marked line of "obstructions," accepting the risk of explosion of another mine. This was the purport of Farragut's famous order, given with the full power of the magnificent voice that had been handling sail for fifty years: "*Damn* the torpedoes! Drayton! Four bells! Jouett! Full speed ahead!"[11] Drayton was captain of the *Hartford.* "Four bells" was the signal for full engine power. Jouett was skipper of the gunboat *Metacomet,* lashed alongside to lend her motive power to

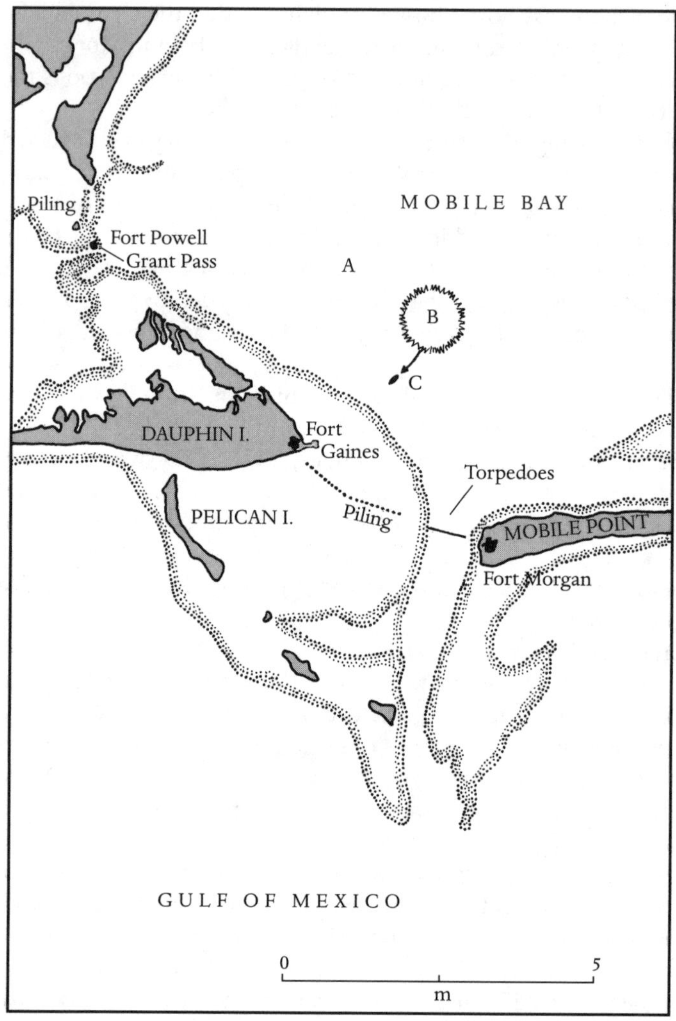

19. The Battle of Mobile Bay, 5 August 1864. (A) Position in which Farragut's fleet anchored after passing the forts. (B) Melee with the CSS *Tennessee.* (C) Surrender of the *Tennessee.*

the flagship; each of the big ships had a gunboat lashed alongside, although Alden had cut his loose.

Gathering speed, the *Hartford* swept ahead, passed the dithering *Brooklyn,* and led the fleet past the fort and into the bay. No more mines exploded, although there were reports that primers were heard detonating as the ships crossed the line where they had been placed—and one can imagine the disaster caused by Alden had they performed as intended. Considerable damage had been received from Fort Morgan's heavy guns, however, mostly during the time while the invading fleet was temporarily immobilized under the fort's guns. Once inside the bay, Farragut signaled his ships to anchor and prepared to implement the second part of his plan, the attack on the forts protecting the bay. All except one had, in fact, anchored when the *Tennessee* was seen coming out from the protection of Fort Morgan.

Farragut knew Buchanan well enough to believe he would see more of him before the adventure of Mobile Bay was over, but most accounts indicate he hardly expected the Confederate ship would offer solitary battle, and so soon. She had already been in combat, had fired on and been fired upon in turn by each ship in the Union fleet as it passed. She had apparently tried to ram each in succession, but without being able to make contact. Her engine was underpowered, and having only a single propeller she had very little maneuverability unless making reasonable speed. Now, however, Buchanan had apparently resolved to do all the damage of which he was capable in a glorious fight to the finish. In his words, he intended to expend all his small supply of ammunition and coal and then retire under the guns of Fort Morgan to be of what assistance he could in its defense.

In any case, if the battle between the *Monitor* and the *Merrimack* presaged a new era in naval warfare, the much bigger contest in Mobile Bay between the *Tennessee* and the whole Union fleet conclusively proved that the future of all navies lay in the steam-powered iron-armored battleship, even though the numerically very superior wooden ships won.

The battle was a regular melee, without formation, all Union ships moving about as rapidly as they could, maneuvering to ram the slow-moving Confederate ship, firing broadsides or single guns at her whenever they would bear, getting in each other's way, and more than once actually colliding with each other. Farragut had well infused his captains with his attack plans. All his ships except James Alden's *Brooklyn* tried to ram and "ride down" the *Tennessee,* some of them more than once, heedlessly suffering more damage to themselves than they were able to inflict. This was not, however, what finally forced Buchanan to surrender. Instead, the chink in the Confederate ram's armor was a design flaw: although her 26-inch-thick yellow-pine-and-oak sides, covered with 6 inches of iron, were essentially impervious to normal shot, *Tennessee*'s rudder was controlled by chains in plain view on deck aft.

Recognizing this, the monitor *Chickasaw* ranged alongside and began shooting exclusively at the chains. Ultimately she cut them, and the Confederate ram became unmanageable. Buchanan had been injured; he could do no more, and so authorized surrender.

9. The Battle of Mobile Bay, 5 August 1864. This engraving depicts the surrender of the CSS *Tennessee* at the battle. (From Robert Underwood Johnson and Clarence Clough Buell, eds., *Battles and Leaders of the Civil War,* 4 volumes [New York: The Century Company, 1884–88].)

At Mobile Bay Farragut had won the hardest fought and by all odds the greatest naval battle in American history to date. Fort Morgan was isolated, and in a few days the giant battery defending Mobile Bay's entrance surrendered. Farragut's half-century of active service had culminated in a resounding victory, at precisely the right time for the Union. The presidential election was due in exactly three months, and Lincoln's chances seemed low. Mobile Bay, followed by Sherman's march through Georgia, made a great difference. Farragut had changed the course of history, for had either of his two big victories not taken place, it is entirely possible that the outcome of the Civil War might have been different.

Farragut's work was done. Now remained only graceful acceptance of the plaudits of a grateful country. Congress created the rank of vice admiral for him in late December 1864, and made him the U.S. Navy's first full admiral in January 1865. Still on active duty, he went to Europe in the new steam frigate *Franklin* to take command of the European Squadron in 1867, where he was everywhere received like a conquering hero. The account of his travels aboard his flagship reads more like a grand social tour than naval duty, although the conscientious Farragut did his best to accommodate both sets of obligations. In the meantime, the physical strains endured during his years of service at last began to tell, and his sturdy heart finally gave out on 14 August 1870, not quite two years following return from his triumphant European cruise and barely a month past his sixty-ninth birthday.

Definite evaluation of any man is difficult, even from the vantage point of a century. Farragut was made by the times in which he lived. Much of the opportunity that fell to him was unquestionably pure happenstance, but the outcome was clearly the result of his character. He was manifestly the man of action the navy and the nation needed at a crucial point in history. He had many critics, mostly ambitious brother officers who would predictably have failed in his place, and all were proved wrong. Farragut's greatness lay in his thorough planning, the visceral courage with which he followed through, and his personal stability. His biographers give much credit to his religious life; born a Catholic, he later attended the Episcopal Church when he could, and held prayer meetings on board his flagship—causing the strength of his almighty *Damn!* at Mobile Bay to be far greater, and remembered much longer, than a whole string of stronger expletives would have been from most other commanders.

He was always thoughtful of others, particularly those serving him. The enlisted men of his various ships swore by him. From his earliest service, as a child midshipman aboard the *Essex,* he was trusted and liked. This was because he trusted and liked the men working for him: a perfect example of leadership.

There were those who thought he became overly excited during battle—"impetuous" was the word they used—because their ideal, somehow, was the man whose pulse did not beat faster under the stimulation of danger, as if such a quality were praiseworthy, instead of dangerous to himself and those dependent on him. Anyone who has been in combat, particularly combat with command responsibility for the result, knows that the excitement clears the brain, firms the resolve, improves the performance. So was it with Farragut. First the careful preparation, in which he always excelled, then the execution of what he had planned, as nearly as possible the way he had planned it. Finally the excitement of doing it, seeing things develop as expected, holding to himself those always necessary adjustments to accommodate the unexpected. During the Mississippi campaign he was referred to as "old woman," "doddering old fool," "great talk but little action."[12] This from the same envious group calling him too impetuous. Farragut answered the calumnies only when he felt them destructive of the business at hand. The fact was that he was the right man for the job. Very few others could have done as well. Selected for important service, he turned in a magnificent performance, and for this the nation reveres his memory.

NOTES

1. Charles Lee Lewis, *David Glasgow Farragut,* 2 vols. (Annapolis: U.S. Naval Institute, 1941–43), I:1–8.

2. David Porter, *Journal of a Cruise Made to the Pacific Ocean by Captain David Porter in the United States Frigate* Essex *in the Years 1812, 1813 and 1814,* eds. Robert D. Madison and Karen Hamon (Annapolis: Naval Institute Press, 1986); for a scholarly modern account, see David F. Long, *Nothing Too Daring: A Biography of Commodore David Porter, 1780–1843* (Annapolis: Naval Institute Press, 1970).

3. Loyall Farragut, *The Life of David Glasgow Farragut, First Admiral of the U.S. Navy* (New York: D. Appleton, 1879), p. 136.

4. Gideon Welles, *The Diary of Gideon Welles, Secretary of the Navy under Lincoln and Johnson,* 3 vols. (Boston: Houghton Mifflin, 1913), II:134.

5. Farragut, op. cit., p. 234.

6. Welles makes this point several times in his diary. Because of early criticism of his appointment of Farragut he felt obliged to defend it, and when it was crowned with success he gloried in his part in it, particularly in his spirited defense of the man.

7. Lewis, op. cit., II:77.

8. Three other active officers, including the unfortunate Foote, were also promoted to the new rank, as well as nine officers on the retired list. Ibid., II:116, 439.

9. For details, see Charles Lee Lewis, *Admiral Franklin Buchanan, Fearless Man of Action* (Baltimore: Norman, Remington, 1929).

10. The fiasco at Norfolk is more fully described in Edward L. Beach, *The United States Navy: 200 Years* (New York: Henry Holt, 1986), pp. 143–48.

11. Lewis, *Farragut,* II:269, 469–70.

12. Culled, generally, from letters of David Dixon Porter to Assistant Secretary Fox, to his brother, William, and to Mrs. Porter.

NOTE ON SOURCES

The definitive biography, upon which this essay has relied for details of its subject's life, is *David Glasgow Farragut,* vol. 1: *Admiral in the Making,* and vol. 2: *Our First Admiral,* by Professor Charles L. Lewis, a member of the U.S. Naval Academy faculty (Annapolis: U.S. Naval Institute, 1941–43). Loyall Farragut's *The Life of David Glasgow Farragut, First Admiral of the U.S. Navy* (New York: D. Appleton, 1879) is a typical product of nineteenth-century filiopiety but should by no means be ignored for that reason. Another older work, more interesting for its authorship than its contents, is Alfred Thayer Mahan's *Admiral Farragut* (New York: D. Appleton, 1892). Like it, four other biographies published between 1866 and 1905 were superceded by Lewis's work.

The literature, both primary and secondary, on the U.S. Navy in the Civil War is extensive. Notable among the memoirs is the *Autobiography of George Dewey, Admiral of the Navy* (New York: Charles Scribner's Sons, 1913, and Annapolis: Naval Institute Press, 1983, ed. Eric McAllister Smith); Dewey served with Farragut at New Orleans and on the Mississippi and ever afterward regarded him as the ideal naval officer. Excellent accounts of Farragut's battles by men who fought for and against him appear in the classic *Battles and Leaders of the Civil War* edited by Robert U. Johnson and Clarence C. Buell, 4 vols. (New York: The Century Company, 1884–88). The most detailed scholarly treatment of the naval war as a whole is Virgil Carrington Jones's *The Civil War at Sea,* 3 vols. (New York: Holt, Rinehart and Winston, 1960–62). Readers seeking a reliable overview of Union operations will find it in *Mr. Lincoln's Navy,* by Richard S. West, Jr. (New York: Longmans, Green, 1957). West also wrote the first scholarly biography of Farragut's would-be rival, *The Second Admiral: A Life of David Dixon Porter* (New York: Coward-McCann, 1937). A new study by Chester G. Hearn treats *Admiral David Dixon Porter: The Civil War Years* (Annapolis: Naval Institute Press, 1996). Porter's own *The Naval History of the Civil War* (New York: Sherman, 1886) is a better indicator of how he remembered things than of how they happened. Farragut's reports and correspondence are included in the multivolume series of *Official Records of the Union and Confederate Navies in the War of the Rebellion* (Washington, D.C.: Government Printing Office, 1894–1922).

For what went on behind the scenes at the Navy Department, see Robert Means Thompson and Richard Wainright, eds., *Confidential Correspondence of Gustavus Vasa Fox, Assistant Secretary of the Navy, 1861–1865,* 2 vols. (New York: The Navy History Society, 1918–19); *The Diary of Gideon Welles, Secretary of the Navy under Lincoln and Johnson,* 3 vols. (Boston: Houghton Mifflin, 1913); and R. S. West, Jr., *Gideon Welles: Lincoln's Navy Secretary* (Indianapolis: Bobbs-Merrill, 1943).

Chester G. Hearn's *Admiral David Glasgow Farragut: The Civil War Years* (Annapolis: Naval Institute Press, 1997) appeared too late to be consulted before this book went to press.

II

Wilhelm von Tegetthoff
Admiral of the Unexpected
(1827–1871)

Helmut Pemsel
Translated by Jack Sweetman

WILHELM VON TEGETTHOFF WAS DESCENDED FROM AN OLD military family. His forefathers made their home in Westphalia. His great-grandfather entered the service of the Holy Roman Emperor, fought as a captain of cavalry in the Seven Years War (1756–63) and was raised to the hereditary nobility by Empress Maria Theresa. One of the admiral's great-uncles won the knight's cross of the Military Maria-Theresa Order, the monarchy's highest military decoration, in the war with France in 1799. Tegetthoff's father, Karl, joined the Imperial Army in 1805, the year before Napoleon dictated the dissolution of the Holy Roman Empire and the lands ruled by the House of Habsburg became known as the Austrian Empire.[1] Karl von Tegetthoff fought in the War of Liberation against Napoleon (1813–14) and finally entered garrison at Marburg-an-der-Drau in the province of Styria (now Maribor, Slovenia). Tegetthoff's mother was the daughter of a civil servant in Prague. Wilhelm, the second of five sons, was born on 23 December 1827.

When the boy was three years old, his father was temporarily detailed to the garrison at Piacenza in northern Italy, then under Austrian rule. Wilhelm therefore spent his early, most impressionable years under his mother's loving care. Throughout his life, he never again experienced love and affection in like measure. During his long shipboard service he scarcely had the opportunity to find someone else prepared to give him such devotion, and the love and warmheartedness of which he was capable would be expressed solely in letters to his mother. On each of his rare leaves, he endeavored to spend most of his time with her.

Following his father's return from Italy in 1836, young Tegetthoff underwent the fair but extremely strict military upbringing then customary in many officers' families. Self-discipline and modesty, together with studiousness and industry, were prerequisites for a member of the petty nobility or the middle class to establish himself in the officer corps.

In accordance with his own wishes, on 28 November 1840 Tegetthoff entered the five-year course at the Naval Cadets College (*Collegio di Cadetti di Marina*) in Venice. The Imperial Austrian Navy was at this time completely under the influence of its Italian component. The fleet base and naval arsenal were also located at Venice, and Tegetthoff had prepared for his career by learning Italian, the navy's language of command. He served aboard ship for the first time in the summer of 1841, when his class made a training cruise in the Adriatic and Ionian seas.

On 21 July 1845, Tegetthoff graduated from the cadet school with distinction. Of the thirteen members of his class, only two completed the course. After five years away from home, his dearest wish was to take a well-deserved leave to see his beloved mother and his stern but revered father. Unfortunately, his family could not afford both the expense of outfitting a cadet, to which the navy made no contribution, and the cost of a trip home. So, with a heavy heart, he had to forgo leave and begin his service with the fleet as a naval cadet on 16 August.

On 28 September Tegetthoff sailed in the brig *Montecuccoli* on a cruise to Corfu, where he first made the acquaintance of his contemporaries in the British and French navies. Through them he became aware of the material and geographical limitations of the Austrian navy. He used his meager time for further study, especially of English and French. In 1846 the *Montecuccoli* proceeded into the Aegean to protect Austrian merchant ships from pirates. After a few months Tegetthoff was transferred to the corvette *Adria,* which also cruised in Greek waters. In January 1848 he was promoted midshipman and returned to Austria.

That spring a tide of liberal revolution swept across the Continent. Austria's multinational empire was rocked by virtually simultaneous uprisings in Prague, Budapest, Venice, Milan, and Vienna itself. Tegetthoff's mind was firmly closed to liberal ideals. Although both before and after 1848 he often complained of the navy's shortcomings in technology and training, there is no indication that he was affected by the liberal currents that were certainly present in it. Like most of the technical services, the engineers in particular, the navy was receptive to the new spirit. From his personal perspective, however, Tegetthoff viewed the revolt of the empire's Czech, Hungarian, and Italian inhabitants not as a social and political upheaval but as a conflict of nationalities, in which he stood firmly on the side of the Austrian imperial house and thereby of reaction. In this sense he was an ardent German nationalist, who hoped that the course of events would promote the unity of all German-speaking peoples, naturally under the leadership of Austria rather than Prussia. Though it was destined for disappointment, this hope did not appear unreasonable in 1848: until then, Austria had unquestionably dominated the German Confederation loosely organized at the close of the Napoleonic Wars, and many nationalists aspired to the unification of a "Big Germany" that would include the German population of the Austrian heartland.

The empire's most pressing agenda, however, was the suppression of the revolutions that imperiled its very existence, a task completed late in the summer of 1849. So far as the navy was concerned, the most threatening uprising occurred in Venice, as a result of which about half of the Austrian fleet fell into the hands of the revolutionaries. To make matters worse, the Italian kingdoms of Sardinia and Naples intervened on the rebel side. The remaining Austrian vessels were concentrated at Trieste, the majority of the Italian officers and men were discharged, and the crews filled out with marines and merchant seamen.

In May 1848 Tegetthoff was present at Trieste when the handful of Austrian ships there were blockaded by the combined naval forces of Sardinia, Naples, and the provisional government of Venice. By that time, the Austrian army was ready to take the offensive and in July Field Marshal Radetzky won a brilliant victory over the Sardinians at Custoza. Following another Austrian victory at Novara in March 1849 Sardinia was forced out of the war; Naples had already withdrawn, so the way was now open for an Austrian blockade of Venice. Meanwhile, on 14 September, Tegetthoff was appointed adjutant to the commander in chief of the navy, Vice Admiral von Martini, whom he accompanied on a voyage to Naples to purchase new ships. During an official visit to Vienna he was able to see his mother for the first time in eight years. He underwent his baptism of fire in the *Adria* during the blockade of Venice in May 1849 and on 28 August he entered the conquered city on the staff of the navy's new commander, Vice Admiral Birch von Dahlerup, a Dane.

From then on, the navy's German element was placed in the foreground. German became the language of command, and the main fleet base was moved from Venice to Trieste and then Pola (now Pula), at the time an insignificant fishing village. This transition gave industrious young officers an opportunity that the ambitious Tegetthoff knew how to use. His outstanding ability soon attracted the attention of the navy's leaders and consequently he almost always received sensitive missions and was entrusted chiefly with commands at sea, where his talents could come into full play.

In September 1849 Tegetthoff was appointed executive officer of the paddlewheeler *Marianne,* in which he made cruises to Tunis and in the Aegean. From February 1851 he was executive officer to Commander Bernhard von Wüllersdorf-Urbair in the *Montecuccoli,* in which he received his promotion to lieutenant, junior grade. In November he went to the corvette *Carolina* in the same capacity. This ship belonged to the Levant Squadron and during his months aboard her Tegetthoff learned first-hand of the political circumstances that would lead to the Crimean War (1853–56).

In April 1854 Tegetthoff, already a full lieutenant, was detached from the *Carolina* in order to assume his first command, the schooner *Elisabeth,* on 13 July. In this vessel he cruised mostly in the Adriatic and Ionian seas, with a side trip to Beirut. Upon relinquishing command in November 1855 he was given an outstanding fitness report by the chief of the Levant Squadron. During this period he also occupied himself with the study of the Turkish language.

Next Tegetthoff received command of the paddlewheeler *Taurus,* with the mission of representing Austrian interests at Sulina, a Turkish Black Sea port at the mouth of the Danube. Anything affecting the navigation of the great river was of vital importance to the Austrian economy, and the impact of the Crimean War had created a situation approaching anarchy at Sulina. As station commander from January 1856 through January 1857, Tegetthoff acted energetically and without regard for ceremony, making a decisive contribution to the normalization of conditions there. This was favorably noted by his superiors at naval headquarters. He also obtained the Turkish Order of the Medjidie, but his hope of taking part in the round-the-world cruise by the frigate *Novara* was not fulfilled.

Upon his return from Sulina, Tegetthoff made a detailed report to the fleet commander, Archduke Ferdinand Maximilian, the twenty-four-year-old brother of Emperor Franz Joseph, and was entrusted with another sensitive assignment. Following the brief leave, Tegetthoff set out to look for a suitable fleet base on the Red Sea, for a great increase in trade with Asia was expected upon the completion of the Suez Canal. The first stage of the journey, made in company with Vice Consul von Heuglin, took him up the Nile to Luxor and then across the desert to Koser on the Red Sea. There the two men chartered a sailing ship and proceeded to Aden, where von Heuglin remained. Continuing on alone, Tegetthoff visited the island of Socotra (which seemed to him most suitable for a fleet base) and Berbera before returning to Aden. In March 1857 he was back in Trieste. Because of the confidential nature of this reconnaissance he could not be awarded a decoration, but he was promoted to lieutenant commander and made chief of the first section of naval headquarters. This section, the largest of the headquarter's three subdivisions, was responsible for operations, personnel, justice, medical services, education, and the marines.[2] As its chief, Tegetthoff was also deputy to the commander in chief of the navy.

Tegetthoff's shore duty did not last long. On 24 October 1858, he assumed command of the corvette *Erzherzog Friedrich,* in which he made a cruise to Morocco. As a result of the growing danger of war he was recalled in February 1859. Once again, the enemy was Sardinia, this time in alliance with France. Against their greatly superior forces the young Austrian fleet was condemned to inactivity. Narrowly defeated in the war on land, Austria surrendered Lombardy, one of its two Italian provinces, and the Kingdom of Italy was proclaimed in 1860. Italian unification remained incomplete, however, for Austria still held the province of Venetia.

After the war Tegetthoff was briefly reassigned to naval headquarters and then accompanied Archduke Ferdinand Max on a botanical expedition to Brazil. They sailed from Trieste in the naval steamer *Kaiserin Elisabeth* in November 1859 and reentered the Adriatic at the end of March 1860. Tegetthoff then took his first months-long leave, during which he was promoted to commander.

On his return to duty, Tegetthoff assumed command of the screw frigate *Radetzky,* in which he proceeded to the coast of Syria to represent Austrian interests amid the unrest prevailing there. Following a yard overhaul in Pola, the *Radetzky* was based on the Bay of Cattaro (Boka Kotorska) and cruised in the southern Adriatic to interdict arms' smuggling from Italy to the unruly Balkans. She returned to Pola in October 1861 and Tegetthoff lay down his command. A month later he was advanced to captain. He spent most of 1862 at naval headquarters and played an important role in Ferdinand Max's reorganization of that office.

In October 1862 Tegetthoff took command of a division consisting of the screw frigate *Novara,* of which he was simultaneously appointed captain, the corvette *Erzherzog Friedrich,* and the gunboats *Veleblich* and *Wall.* The division sailed for Greece to protect Austrian interests in the turmoil attending the overthrow of King Otto. Tegetthoff's precise reports of developments met with the complete approval of Archduke Ferdinand Max. Throughout his career, Tegetthoff's reports showed the deep insight into political, social, and economic realities possible only to a man who understood how to master a subject and draw the correct conclusions.

When the *Novara* had to enter the yard in November 1863, Tegetthoff shifted to the command of the screw frigate *Schwarzenberg.* In December he began a cruise through the eastern Mediterranean, visiting Alexandria, Aboukir, and the work in progress on the Suez Canal. Shortly thereafter, a long-simmering dispute between Denmark and the German Confederation over the status of the border provinces of Schleswig and Holstein came to a head. Tegetthoff learned of the crisis at Beirut and turned toward home. Off Corfu he received orders to proceed to Lisbon and await the arrival of an Austrian squadron being formed for service in the North Sea.

On 1 February 1864, German and Austrian troops had marched across the Eider to secure the attachment of the contested provinces to the German Confederation. Denmark immediately imposed a blockade of the German coast. As the German fleet was too weak to challenge the Danes, the decision was made to send an Austrian squadron under Tegetthoff's old captain, Baron von Wüllersdorf-Urbair, to the theater of war.

In the meanwhile, Tegetthoff hastened to Lisbon in the *Schwarzenberg.*

The *Radetzky* joined him at the beginning of April 1864. As the outfitting of the squadron was delayed, Tegetthoff was authorized to advance into the North Sea with his two frigates alone. After brief layovers to take on coal at Brest and the Downs, he reached Cuxhaven on 4 May.

Precisely informed by British sources of the Austrian ships' strength and movements, the Danes awaited the enemy with a force composed of the steam frigates *Niels Juel* and *Jylland* and the steam corvette *Heimdal* under Commodore Suenson. Learning that this squadron was present in the vicinity of the island of Heligoland, Tegetthoff immediately put to sea with both his frigates and three Prussian gunboats. The resulting Action off Heligoland was fought on 9 May. The two Austrian ships resolutely engaged the enemy's superior squadron for several hours before the *Schwarzenberg*'s foremast caught fire, forcing Tegetthoff to break off the action. After the blaze was extinguished he returned to Cuxhaven. The Danes also left the North Sea, having learned that an armistice had been concluded. The blockade of Germany was lifted.

A day later the emperor promoted Tegetthoff to the rank of rear admiral and decorated him with the Order of the Iron Crown, Second Class. Despite the honors that came to him, however, Tegetthoff retained his modesty and insisted that his valiant officers and men were chiefly to thank for his success.

In the middle of May Wüllersdorf-Urbair's squadron entered the North Sea, where it remained until September. Despite an interruption of the armistice that summer, the opposing naval forces did not again come to blows. Defeated on land, Denmark sued for peace on 1 August and on 21 September Tegetthoff sailed for home. By the terms of the treaty signed a month later, Denmark conceded Schleswig and Holstein to the German Confederation. In course of the conflict Tegetthoff had displayed an eagerness to accept responsibility and always interpreted orders from naval headquarters in such a way as to leave him the greatest possible freedom of action. Even if tactically the Action off Heligoland was not a victory, combined with the subsequent arrival of the main Austrian squadron, it safeguarded German commerce in the North Sea. Thus Tegetthoff became the first German naval hero of modern times, not only in Austria but throughout northern Germany.

By then, Tegetthoff had lost his patron, Archduke Ferdinand Max, who had accepted the throne of Mexico in April 1864—a mistake for which he would pay with his life. It had been Tegetthoff's good fortune to have such an understanding commander in chief. Tegetthoff was not an agreeable subordinate. He defended his opinions vigorously and tenaciously even against his superiors and was not disposed to deviate from his conclusions once he was convinced that they were correct. Recognizing his ability, Ferdinand Max overlooked the offense that the high-tempered Tegetthoff not infrequently gave. The archduke often remarked after fierce debates with him that if it had been anyone except Tegetthoff he would have long since thrown him out, because his thick skull was almost intolerable. Unfortunately, Ferdinand Max's successor, Archduke Leopold, was a friend of neither the navy nor Tegetthoff. He made his attitude clear by promoting his favorite, Captain Friedrich von Pock, to rear admiral with seniority to Tegetthoff.

Following a short tour of duty in Vienna, Tegetthoff was named to command the Levant Squadron, consisting of the *Schwarzenberg* and *Radetzky* and five gunboats. On 28 August 1865, he encountered his opposite number at Heligoland, Commodore Suenson, off Corfu. The squadron then proceeded to Greece, Beirut, and Alexandria. Tegetthoff again inspected the progress of work on the Suez Canal and sent a detailed report to Vienna. The squadron then returned to Pola.

The higher Tegetthoff advanced in rank, the more isolated he became. His self-discipline and dedication made him a constant critic of the navy's many deficiencies. Few of his superiors had any love for this troublesome fault-finder, although they could hardly overlook him for difficult missions. Most of his comrades of the same rank were jealous of his advancement; only the junior officers and enlisted men were enthusiastic about him. Despite his stern and often stormy manner, he was fair and won the support of subordinates by taking an interest in their problems, a quite unusual practice at the time.

A passage from the memoirs of then-Naval Cadet Rottauscher describing an inspection Tegetthoff made of SMS *Saida* in 1863 may be quoted in illustration of this characteristic. Rottauscher wrote that

> in his warm blue eyes there was a respect for the individual. . . . Tegetthoff was the first person to speak to us as well brought-up young people since our entry [into the navy]. Tears of gratitude and love came into the eyes of the cadets, who had to clean the ship's guns and scrub decks. We would gladly have shielded him with our bodies from any foe. We grew up a year during the hour in which Tegetthoff drew us under his sway and into his navy. It was as though previously we had served somewhere else entirely.[3]

Once a cadet whom Tegetthoff had reprimanded too harshly lodged a complaint. Tegetthoff was then commodore of the squadron as well as captain of the flagship. The complaint against himself as the ship's captain had therefore to be handled by himself as commodore. Summoning the cadet, he said: "I've conferred with the captain of the *Schwarzenberg* and he regrets the excessively harsh words he used, but I advise you not to irritate the fellow again, he seems to be a really rough customer."[4] This episode shows clearly that Tegetthoff had not only a sense of humor but, in addition to a capacity for self-criticism, a strong sense of justice.

Tegetthoff also possessed a fitting measure of personal bravery. During the blockade of Venice in 1849 he was not shy of exposing himself to enemy fire, and after a seaman beside him was literally torn to pieces by a cannonball he wrote that the event only aroused his curiosity, as it was the first time he had been sprayed with blood. It did not prompt him to take cover, however. Later, during his Brazilian travels with Archduke Ferdinand Max, he spied a snake in a freshwater stream and decided to capture it for the imperial collector. When Tegetthoff lifted the snake into his boat on an oar, the poisonous reptile unexpectedly attacked him; with great presence of mind, he killed it with the oar.

Early in 1866 preparations for a projected East Asian cruise by the *Schwarzenberg* and *Erzherzog Friedrich* under Tegetthoff's command had to be abandoned because of the threat of war with Prussia and Italy. The former wished to eliminate Austrian influence in northern Germany, the latter to expel Austria from the province of Venetia. Their alliance placed the empire in the highly undesirable position of having to fight a war on two fronts.

In Vienna Tegetthoff's efforts to put the fleet promptly on a war footing were frustrated, mainly by the unresponsiveness of the central administration. Finally, at the end of April, orders were given to mobilize every available ship. Archduke Leopold, who was also inspector of army engineers, went to the northern front. Rear Admiral von Pock became the naval adviser on the staff of the commander in chief of the southern front, although according to rank he could have claimed command of the fleet. This command, in which it was generally believed that no laurels would be won against Italy's more powerful fleet, went to Tegetthoff.

The latter threw himself furiously into fitting out every remotely serviceable ship. The unfinished ironclads *Erzherzog Ferdinand Max* and *Habsburg* were rapidly completed. As Tegetthoff wished to lead the fleet into action at the earliest possible moment, he contented himself with material that was not the latest model, but took care that it was in good condition and that, as a result of intensive training, the crews had complete confidence in it. As the modern guns on order from Krupp in Germany for the two new ironclads would obviously not be forthcoming, he had the vessels armed with old smoothbores. The wooden ships received an improvised

20. The War in the Adriatic, 1866.

armor of chains and railroad rails. In contrast, at the last moment the Italian Admiral Count Carlo di Persano had some of his ironclads equipped with new Armstrong guns. No real advantage resulted, however, as there was not enough time for his crews to become accustomed to the use of these guns.

Thanks to the dedication of everyone involved, Tegetthoff achieved the unexpected and the Austrian fleet became operational before the Italian. When the Italian declaration of war came on 20 June, Tegetthoff was ready for action. Persano's much stronger fleet moved from Taranto, on the instep of the Italian boot, to Ancona, on the northern Adriatic. On 24 June, the Austrian Southern Army defeated the Italians at Custoza, but then had to transfer troops to help meet the Prussian threat on the northern front.

Even before the war began, Tegetthoff received orders from naval headquarters to defend the coast, cover the flank of the Southern Army where it touched the Adriatic, and in the event of offensive action, not to endanger his ships! This typical order would have crippled the activity of any fleet commander, for to achieve victory without accepting losses is for practical purposes an impossible requirement. Nevertheless, upon the outbreak of war Tegetthoff asked the High Command of the Southern Front under Archduke Albrecht, to whose orders he was subject, for more freedom of action. He then received permission to take offensive as far south as the Austrian-held island of Lissa (now Vis) on his own responsibility (!) and without exposing the flank of the Southern Army.

Tegetthoff recognized clearly that the best way to defend the Austrian coast was to eliminate the Italian fleet. In view of the Italians' distinct superiority in number and quality of guns, he had to devise an appropriate tactic for the anticipated engagement. He chose the ram as his principal weapon and had his crews especially trained in close combat. For the sake of simplicity, the order of sailing was arranged so that it was also the order of battle and the fleet could enter action without further commands or changes of formation. As in the time of the Greek triremes, the ship herself would be the weapon and whenever possible destroy the enemy by ramming.[5]

Hardly had Tegetthoff obtained operational freedom than on 27 June he sailed for Ancona, where the Italian fleet was assembling, with six ironclads and seven large wooden ships. The Italians were not ready for action, however, and when at length the first ships raised steam and put to sea but made no move to accept the battle being offered, Tegetthoff sailed back to the harbor of Fasana, near Pola. The result of this demonstration was a perceptible rise in Austrian morale and a corresponding cooling of Italian ardor.

Through the sortie against Ancona Tegetthoff learned that the Italian fleet was not yet fully operational, for a few vessels in process of changing guns had not even raised steam. But he also saw that there was no thirst for action on the Italian side. For although a few of the enemy's ironclads were not combat ready, the relative strength off Ancona would have been in approximate balance. In a battle off their base the Italians would have been able to bring in every damaged ship, whereas Tegetthoff would have had to reckon on the loss of all his cripples.

Finally, the threat of being relieved of command caused Admiral Persano to undertake an offensive operation. On 18 July, the Italian fleet began shelling the island of Lissa, defended by two thousand Austrian troops, in preparation for a landing. At first Tegetthoff could not believe that the action was seriously intended, for he regarded the elimination of the opposing fleet as prerequisite to secondary operations of this sort. After satisfying himself that the attack on Lissa was not a feint, he ordered all combat-ready ships to sea on 19 July.

The Austrian fleet sailed from Pola around one o'clock that afternoon. It was organized in three divisions, whose order of sailing was also the tactical formation for battle. The first division, led by the flagship *Erzherzog Ferdinand Max,* was composed of Tegetthoff's seven ironclads. The second division contained the seven large wooden ships, headed by the screw ship of the line *Kaiser.* The third division consisted of seven wooden gunboats. Dispatch boats for relaying orders were posted in the intervals. All three divisions proceeded in a wedge-shaped formation, with the armored vessels in the lead. In the aggregate, the force under Tegetthoff's command—7 ironclads and 20 unarmored vessels—displaced 57,300 tons, mounted 532 guns, and carried 7,870 men. The Italian fleet consisted of 12 ironclads and 11 large and 8 small unarmored ships, displaced 86,000 tons, mounted 645 guns, and carried 10,900 men.

The Austrian fleet appeared off Lissa on the morning of 20 July. As the enemy came in sight, Tegetthoff had the following signals hoisted:

Dispatch boats to their posts.
Clear for action.
Close up.
Full speed ahead.
Run into the enemy to sink him.[6]

On account of the nearness of the enemy, there was no time to hoist the prepared signal, "There must be victory at Lissa." Furthermore, like Nelson before Trafalgar, Tegetthoff had so thoroughly acquainted his captains with his tactics that he did not have to give another order throughout the entire battle. His next signal to the fleet was a single word at its close: "Assemble."

10. The Battle of Lissa, 20 July 1866. C. Fredrik Sörensen's dramatic painting shows the ironclad *Re d'Italia* sinking after being rammed by Tegetthoff's flagship, the *Erzherzog Ferdinand Max*. (Heeresgeschichtliches Museum, Vienna.)

At the approach of the Austrian fleet, the Italians ceased preparations for landing. Eleven of their ironclads began to form a column; the wooden ships and, on account of damage sustained during the bombardment, the ironclad *Formidabile* did not take part in the action. Attacking at a right angle, Tegetthoff broke through the Italian line and immediately sought close combat; even the wooden ships became hotly engaged, the *Kaiser* ramming the *Re di Portogallo*. At the height of the battle, Tegetthoff's flagship succeeded in ramming and sinking the Italian ironclad *Re d'Italia*. After the ironclad *Palestro* exploded, Persano gave up the fight and withdrew to Ancona.

Tegetthoff had not only saved the island of Lissa and thus deprived the Italians of a bargaining chip at the peace table, but with an inferior fleet inflicted a decisive defeat on the enemy, who lost two ironclads and command of the Adriatic. His victory was the first battle between oceangoing armored vessels in the history of war at sea. The tactic he had adopted for the action exercised an unholy influence on naval constructors and tacticians for the next three decades, during which every major warship was built with an armored ram. In any event, Tegetthoff, with a clear grasp of existing circumstances, had achieved his objective through the optimal utilization of modest means.

Tegetthoff was promoted to vice admiral by Emperor Franz Joseph the day after the battle and, upon his solicitation, awarded the commander's cross of the Military Maria-Theresa Order. To bypass the knight's class of this prestigious order, all of whose members received the title of baron

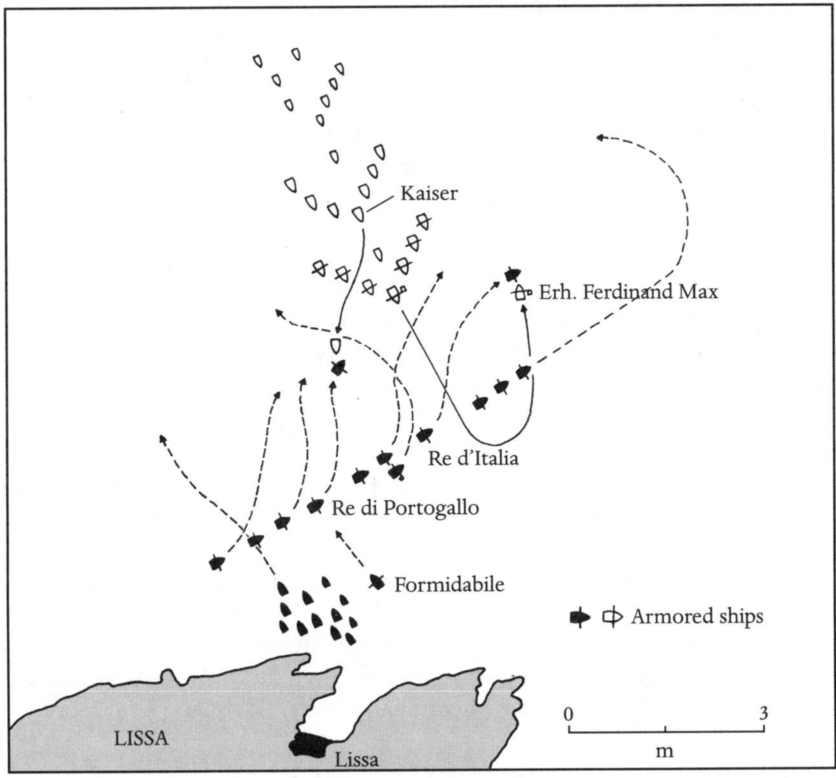

21. The Battle of Lissa, 20 June 1866. Based on the map in the author's *A History of War at Sea* (Annapolis: Naval Institute Press, 1977).

(*Freiherr*), was a most unusual distinction. Subsequently Tegetthoff was made an honorary member of the Academy of Science and an honorary citizen of Vienna.* Hearty congratulations on his victory reached him from, among others, his former commander in chief, Emperor Maximilian of Mexico, as well as retired Vice Admiral von Dahlerup. On 13 August the commander of the Southern Front, Archduke Albert, inspected the fleet and praised its high degree of combat readiness so soon after the battle.

Though in the south Austria was victorious on land and sea, in the north its army had been defeated by the Prussians at Königgrätz (Sadowa) on 3 July. By the terms of peace, signed on 23 August, she was compelled to withdraw from German affairs and give up Venetia. By right of her victories at Custoza and Lissa, however, she was able to avoid the embarrassment of surrendering the province directly to Italy. Instead, an arrangement was made whereby she ceded Venetia to neutral France, which transferred it to the Italian kingdom.

Following the cessation of hostilities the fleet was ordered to demobilize and Tegetthoff relinquished command of the active squadron. No suitable command then stood available for the thirty-nine-year-old vice admiral. As he was viewed as a future commander in chief of the navy, it was decided to send him on a professional tour of the great sea powers. After a visit to his mother in Graz, he set out on his journey on 27 September 1866. Proceeding through Salzburg, he reached London on 3 December. He visited various naval installations, saw the gigantic steamer *Great Eastern* in Liverpool, and sailed for New York on 19 December. In the United States he visited Niagara Falls, Philadelphia, Washington, Annapolis, Charleston, Mobile, New Orleans, Pittsburgh, and Norfolk. During these travels he saw the effects of the recently concluded Civil War. In April 1867, he returned to Europe.

While attending the Paris Universal Exposition in June, Tegetthoff received a telegraphed order to return home at once. The Emperor Maximilian had been executed by his Mexican captors at Queretaro. Franz Joseph gave Tegetthoff the delicate mission of bringing Maximilian's remains back to Austria.

Accompanied by his brother, a colonel in the army, Tegetthoff set out for Mexico on 10 July and arrived in that country on 26 August. At first the Mexicans refused to surrender Maximilian's body. Following lengthy nego-

* In contrast, the luckless Persano was tried by the Italian senate, found guilty of negligence and incompetence, broken in rank, dismissed from the navy, and to top it off, required to pay the costs of his trial.

tiations, which he conducted with great diplomatic skill, Tegetthoff obtained its release. At the end of the year the mortal remains of the former commander of the navy were brought back to his homeland in the *Novara*. Tegetthoff returned in the same ship.

Reaching Vienna on 17 January 1868, Tegetthoff was called upon to develop a plan for the reorganization of the navy. As his desire for a separate Ministry of the Navy was frustrated by the opposition of Hungary, the landlocked half of the Dual Monarchy into which the empire had been transformed in 1867, he recommended a fully responsible Navy Section within the Ministry of War. His proposals were accepted and on 25 February 1868, Tegetthoff was appointed to head the Navy Section and carry out the reorganization. He was granted the right of direct access to the emperor (*Vortragsrecht*), which made him immediately responsible to the latter, rather than to the minister of war, for the effectiveness of the navy. But it was the minister of war who represented the navy to the parliamentary delegations of the two halves of the empire, especially in regard to budgetary matters. This most unfortunate system, in which Tegetthoff was without direct influence in budgetary questions but nevertheless completely responsible for the efficiency of the fleet, contributed greatly to the inner tension that drew heavily on his mental stamina and undermined his physical strength. The navy's succeeding commanders also suffered greatly under this arrangement.

Despite these obstacles, Tegetthoff pushed through important reforms. The organization of the navy still stemmed wholly from the Age of Sail, with boarding parties from naval infantry regiments and a separate corps of naval gunners. Tegetthoff simplified this organization and abolished many special-service personnel. In the future, the guns would be served by seamen who were trained in a gunnery school ship, usually an old ironclad. He also eliminated the diffusion of responsibility for important decisions. Formerly, a whole row of signatures from the departments concerned often had to be placed on a single ordinance, as a result of which none bore final responsibility for it. Now, in almost every case, only one department was authorized to issue a particular order. The "flight from responsibility" was thus checked and only conscientious individuals ready to stand by their decisions had a chance of advancement.

In debates over the reorganization of the empire's defenses, Tegetthoff vigorously advocated a reduction of coastal fortifications and an emphasis on a strong mobile fleet. He agreed only to fortifying the central naval base at Pola and installing long-range coastal batteries to defend the harbor of Fasana. Through his reforms, in which he proved himself to be an economical as well as a capable administrator, Tegetthoff was able to reduce the peacetime manning level of the navy by almost two thousand men. Nevertheless, he was denied the credits to build the navy up to a projected strength of fifteen ironclads. He could not overcome the opposition of the army, which preferred to base itself on fixed coastal fortifications and despite the lesson of Lissa, failed to grasp the advantage of a mobile coast defense.

The constant skirmishing over the budget and the manifold difficulties arising from the division of the empire into two parts noticeably embittered Tegetthoff. A last pleasure for the increasingly lonely admiral came in 1869, when he accompanied Emperor Franz Joseph to Egypt for the opening of the Suez Canal. On the return home he hauled down his vice admiral's flag for what would be the last time in Trieste on 7 December. In the winter of 1870–71, already in threatened health, Tegetthoff caught cold on the way home from a social gathering. He died in Vienna at seven o'clock in the morning of 7 April 1871.

The Tegetthoff Memorial, reminiscent in its artistic conception of the Nelson Monument in Trafalgar Square, stands at the Praterstern in Vienna. On it are inscribed the words that his emperor dedicated to Tegetthoff:

FIGHTING BRAVELY AT HELIGOLAND
TRIUMPHING GLORIOUSLY AT LISSA
HE WON DEATHLESS FAME FOR
HIMSELF AND AUSTRIA'S SEA POWER.

The Imperial Navy honored Tegetthoff's memory by always naming one of its newest ships after him, and even today a passenger ship on the Danube bears his name.

Notes

1. When Napoleon was proclaimed emperor of the French in 1804, the Holy Roman Emperor Franz II reacted by assuming the additional title of Emperor Franz I of Austria. He renounced the crown of the Holy Roman Empire on 6 August 1806, following Napoleon's victory at the Battle of Austerlitz, and thereafter reigned solely as emperor of Austria.

2. It existed in this form only from August 1856 to (with minor modifications) August 1859. See Walter Wagner, *Die obersten Behörden der k. und k. Kriegsmarine, 1856–1918*, supplementary volume VI of the *Mitteilungen des Osterreichischen Staatsarchiv* (Vienna: Ferdinand Berger, 1961).

3. Paul Rohrer (pseudonym), *Als Venedig noch österreichisch war* (Stuttgart: Robert Lutz, 1913), pp. 97–98. Rottauscher used a pseudonym because his book was in part very critical of the Imperial Austrian government still in power at the time of its publication.

4. Peter Handel-Mazzetti and Hans H. Sokol, *Wilhelm von Tegetthoff* (Linz: Oberösterreichischer Landesverlag, 1952), pp. 161–62.

5. Whether Tegetthoff's decision to adopt ramming tactics was influenced by the fact that they had been used with some success in the American Civil War (1861–65) is not known.

6. Josef Fleischer, *Geschichte der k. k. Kriegsmarine während des Krieges im Jahre 1866* (Vienna: Gerold, 1906), p. 193.

NOTE ON SOURCES

The English literature on the navy of the Habsburg monarchy is less than voluminous. The first scholarly study is Lawrence Sondhaus's recent *The Habsburg Empire and the Sea: Austrian Naval Policy, 1797–1866* (West Lafayette, Ind.: Purdue University Press, 1989). This well-researched and reliable work traces the policies that guided the navy's evolution from its origins through the War of 1866. *The Imperial and Royal Austro-Hungarian Navy* (Annapolis: U.S. Naval Institute, 1968), by Anthony E. Sokol, who served in it as a junior officer in World War I, is a beautifully illustrated, concise history. The 1866 campaign is described by Admiral Sir Reginald Custance's "The Campaign of Lissa," in *The Ship of the Line in Battle* (London and Edinburgh: W. Blackwood & Sons, 1912) and by H. W. Wilson in *Ironclads in Action,* 2 vols. (Boston: Little, Brown, 1896) and *Battleships in Action,* 2 vols. (Boston: Little, Brown, 1928).

Only one full-length life of Tegetthoff has appeared to date and, like all the other works listed below, is available only in German: Peter Handel-Mazzetti and Hans H. Sokol, *Wilhelm von Tegetthoff* (Linz: Oberösterreichischer Landesverlag, 1952). C. von Wurzbach, *Biographisches Lexikon des Kaiserthums Osterreich,* vol. 43 (Vienna: Hof-und-Staatsdruckerei, 1881), contains a biography and genealogy of the admiral, a description of his funeral ceremonies, and a list of his honors and awards, including the ships and streets named and monuments erected in his memory. For brief treatments, see Helmut Pemsel, "Wilhelm von Tegetthoff," in *MARINE—Gestern, Heute,* vol. 4 (1977); the entry on Tegetthoff in the same author's *Biographisches Lexikon zur Seekriegsgeschichte: Seehelden von der Antike bis zur Gegenwart* (Koblenz: Bernard & Graefe, 1985); and P. Handel-Mazzetti, "Tegetthoff und der Einsatz der Flotte im Urteil der Armee," in *Reichsoffiziersblatt,* 1941.

Key works on Austrian naval history include J. Ch. Allmayer-Beck, W. Wagner, and L. Hobelt, *Die bewaffnete Macht,* vol. 5 of *Die Habsburgermonarchie, 1848–1918,* edited by A. Wandruska and P. Urbanitsch (Vienna: Osterreichische Akademie der Wissenschaften, 1987); F. Ritter von Attlmayr, *Der Krieg Osterreichs in der Adria 1866* (Pola-Vienna: Gerold' Sohn, 1896); J. Freiherr von Benko, *Geschichte der k. k. Kriegsmarine während der Jahre 1848 and 1849,* part 3, vol. 1, of the official history of the Imperial and Royal Navy (Vienna: Gerold' Sohn, 1884); Josef Fleischer, *Geschichte der k. k. Kriegsmarine während des Krieges im Jahre 1866,* part 3, vol. 3, of the official history (Vienna: Gerold, 1906); G. Hamann, "Die österreichische Kriegsmarine im Dienst der Wissenschaften," in *Osterreich zur See,* vol. 8 of the Papers of the Army Historical Museum, Vienna (Vienna: Osterreichischer Bundesverlag, 1980); and M. Freiherr von Sterneck, *Erinnerungen aus den Jahren 1847–1897* (Vienna-Pest-Leipzig: Hartleben, 1901). The navy's active operations are surveyed in Helmut

Pemsel, *Seeherrschaft: Eine maritime Weltgeschichte von den Anfängen der Seefahrt bis zur Gegenwart,* 2 vols. (Koblenz: Bernard & Graefe, 1985).

The principal documentary sources for Tegetthoff's career are located in the Osterreichischen Staatsarchiv / Kriegsarchiv, Vienna. They include the *k. k. Marine-Grundbuchsheft,* giving dates of assignments, promotions, and decorations; the Tegetthoff Archiv, containing his personal notes and letters; his travel diaries; and the files including his official reports. Also at the Kriegsarchiv is Peter Handel-Mazzetti's unpublished biography, "Wilhelm von Tegetthoff," a manuscript of 650 pages tracing the admiral's career to 1864.

Survey IV
The New Steel Navies
(1866–1905)

In the decades following the Battle of Lissa, the technological transformation of navies continued at an accelerating pace. Wooden-hulled ironclads gave way to iron-hulled vessels protected by steel-faced iron, which were in turn replaced by steel ships armored with face-hardened nickel-steel. Muzzle-loading, wrought-iron, smoothbore guns yielded to breech-loading steel rifles; roundshot and spherical shells to ballistically superior cylindrical shells; and traditional black powder to comparatively slow-burning, smokeless cordite—gun-cotton impregnated with nitroglycerin—which increased a projectile's muzzle-velocity and, thereby, its range, accuracy, and impact. Hydraulic mechanisms were developed to absorb the recoil of even the largest gun, and armor-piercing ammunition appeared in the form of steel-capped shells that penetrated the surface they struck rather than exploding on contact. Higher steam pressures made possible by improved boilers and the introduction of double- and triple-expansion engines complemented the increases in ships' offensive and defensive capabilities with equally dramatic advances in their efficiency, speed, and endurance.

The challenge navies confronted was to combine the elements of the new technology into the best possible ships. Of the vessels that fought at Lissa, all except the Italian double-turreted ram *Affondatore* carried their guns in the broadside configuration that had prevailed for almost three centuries. The need for another arrangement soon became evident, as weight considerations precluded swaddling an entire ship in steel from stem to stern. Weight also established the limitations of every alternative, positive buoyancy being perhaps the only design characteristic upon whose desirability everyone agreed. Granted that only so many guns and so much armor could be floated, how should they be apportioned and where should they be positioned? Answers abounded, and most of them became ships. The pair of circular coast-defense battleships built by the Imperial Russian Navy between 1872 and 1877 were only the oddest among many curious craft. For two decades the world's navies constituted what a wag called a collection of experiments in naval architecture. Little by little, however, consensus emerged, and by the 1890s the ship types that would comprise the battle fleets of World War I—and, with the addition of the aircraft carrier, World War II—had assumed recognizable form. These were the battleship, the cruiser, and the destroyer.

Battleships succeeded the Age of Sail ships of the line (of battle), by which their name was inspired, as the decisive instrument of war at sea. In the more or less standard design that crystalized late in the century, their main armament consisted of four 12- or 13-inch guns mounted in two centerline turrets fore and aft. They also carried extensive secondary batteries in smaller turrets, broadside casemates, and bulges (technically, sponsons) in their hulls. The ordnance suite of the three U.S. *Indiana*-class battleships commissioned in 1895–96 included four 13-inch, eight 8-inch, and four 6-inch guns, plus twenty-six smaller pieces. A pattern also developed in the placement of armor. The contest between steel and shells having ended in a draw unchanged through World War II, with every inch of shell caliber representing an inch of penetrating power, protection had to be relative rather than absolute. Turrets and casemates were usually clothed in armor equal in thickness to the caliber of the guns they mounted. Armored belts connected by transverse bulkheads and topped by an armored deck shielded a battleship's waterline and provided a degree of protection to her interior spaces. Finally, a conning tower sturdy enough to withstand any but a heavy-caliber hit cloaked her command in time of battle. Such vessels might displace as much as 15,000 tons and the swiftest could attain speeds slightly in excess of 18 knots. For the next half-century, the conventional measure of a nation's naval power would be the number of its battleships.

Cruisers inherited the roles performed by Age of Sail frigates as scouts and, in smaller navies, substitutes for capital ships. First on the scene were protected cruisers, so-called because their hull spaces were "protected" by an armored deck (only). Otherwise, armor was limited to their turrets, gun emplacements, and conning towers. The majority carried 6-inch or smaller guns in their main batteries, although a few, including the USS *Olympia,* Dewey's flagship at Manila Bay, had 8-inch turrets. The largest protected cruisers displaced approximately 5,600 tons and could make 20 knots. In the 1890s they began to be replaced by armored cruisers. These were much more formidable vessels, ranging from half to virtually the same size as battleships and carrying the same suit but a lesser thickness of armor. Their big guns topped out at 9.2 inches, and their maximum speed reached 24 knots.

Destroyers, swiftest and most fragile of the new ships, came into being to combat a weapon of which, ironically, they became a primary means of delivery. This was the locomotive or "fish" torpedo developed by Robert Whitehead, an English marine engineer working together with an Austrian naval officer, Commander Johann Luppis, between 1865 and 1867. Although

Whitehead's early torpedoes had ranges of no more than four hundred yards, they were soon added to the armament of ships of all sizes, and around 1880 seagoing torpedo boats designed especially for their employment began to appear. The first vessel indisputably sunk by a torpedo, the 3,370-ton armored ship *Blanco Encalada,* fell victim to one of these little craft, the *Almirante Lynch,* during the Chilean Civil War of 1891. In France, the Jeune Ecole of naval strategy had already concluded that in future conflicts swarms of such boats would scour the seas, eradicating an enemy's merchant marine in an irresistible *guerre de course* and overwhelming its big ships by force of numbers.

The disappointment in store for this anticipation resulted from three defensive developments. The earliest, dating from the late 1870s, was the introduction of searchlights—the first shipboard application of electricity—an innovation expressly intended to pierce the cover of darkness under which torpedo boats were to be most feared. In the following decade came the advent of quick-firing 4.7- and 6-inch guns, the former capable of hurling fourteen aimed rounds per minute, a single one of which could transform a torpedo boat into charred flotsam. Lastly, the 1890s witnessed the appearance of what was originally and very explicitly denominated the "torpedo-boat destroyer," a fast, low-lying craft, slightly larger than a torpedo boat, armed with small quick-firing guns and torpedoes of her own. Entirely unarmored, destroyers, as they were soon abbreviated, displaced between 230 and 500 tons, and raced along at speeds ranging from 27 to 30 knots. By century's end, these fierce little ships had combined the offensive role of the torpedo boat with the defensive function for which they had been conceived.

In this way the torpedo, which the Jeune Ecole believed would revolutionize naval warfare, was accommodated within its existing format. Increases in the new weapon's accuracy, range, speed, and payload resulting from the installation of gyroscopic steering and the adoption of improved propellants and explosives did not alter the balance. Big guns in big ships remained decisive, but after 1900 big ships were screened by friendly destroyers, and the threat of unfriendly destroyers suddenly emerging from the night or fog, torpedo tubes at the ready, joined an admiral's concerns. The reality of this threat was demonstrated shortly past midnight on 9 February 1904, when an attack (without benefit of a declaration of war) by ten Japanese destroyers disabled two battleships and a protected cruiser at anchor in the Russian Far Eastern fleet base at Port Arthur.

Submarines, destined to become the most destructive of all torpedo carriers, made a serious debut on the naval scene about the same time as destroyers. The first boat moved by anything other than muscle, Charles Bruns's compressed air-powered *Plongeur,* had appeared in 1863. Since then a number of more or less experimental craft had been built with a variety of mechanical propulsion systems, including steam engines, but none performed satisfactorily both above water and below. The answer was a dual propulsion system, and in 1898 the Irish-American inventor John P. Holland installed one in the *Holland,* the U.S. Navy's first submarine, which ran on a gasoline-fueled internal combustion engine while surfaced and electric batteries when submerged. Unfortunately, other Holland boats soon purchased by the U.S. and European navies showed this pairing to be an imperfect solution, as their gasoline engines emitted intoxicating fumes and were inclined to catch fire or explode. Nevertheless, by 1905 the British, French, Russian, and U.S. navies each had several boats in commission. As of that date, however, their technological limitations and tactical doctrine consigned submarines to the role of coast defense, and they did not enter combat until the eve of World War I.

The other underwater weapon, mines, had become an important instrument of coast and harbor defense. In 1898, Dewey weighed and shrewdly rejected the possibility that the Spanish had mined the entrance to Manila Bay, but at Santiago de Cuba minefields in the channel separating the U.S. North Atlantic Squadron from the Spanish cruiser squadron blockaded there enforced a stalemate that endured until the landing of an American army propelled the latter into a suicidal sortie. The first high seas minelaying took place in the Russo-Japanese War, during which both sides sowed fields in waters the other was known to frequent off Port Arthur. In little more than a month in the spring of 1904, one Russian and two Japanese battleships went down in them.

At least as important in their impact on war at sea as improvements in hardware were the advances in electronic communications. The Atlantic cable was successfully laid in 1866, and by the 1880s an undersea network connected most of the world's principal ports. No longer did an exchange of messages between an admiral on a distant station and his government depend on ships that might be months in transit; now virtually instantaneous contact with home authorities was as near as the closest cable office. Dewey received the momentous order to attack the Spanish squadron in the Philippines via a cablegram sent from Washington to Hong Kong.

Of greater tactical significance was the introduction of wireless communications, a development resulting primarily from research undertaken by the Italian engineer Guglielmo Marconi around 1895. The use of two of his sets aboard ship and another ashore during British fleet maneuvers in 1899 demonstrated that naval radio had become a practical reality, and despite its relatively limited range—then less than one hundred miles—within a few years every major navy had begun installing wireless equipment produced by Marconi or his competitors in its big ships and coastal signal stations. For the first time, vessels could talk across the horizon. Their earliest opportunity to do so in wartime came during the Russo-Japanese conflict. Admiral Togo relied on radio reports from scouts to notify him of the First Pacific Squadron's sorties from Port Arthur and, later, to relay the news of the Second Pacific Squadron's sighting. For their part, the Russians initiated the practice of electronic countermeasures by jamming Japanese transmissions and often detected the approach of enemy ships or formations by eavesdropping on their signals traffic. To prevent the Second Pacific Squadron from betraying its position by the same means, its commander, the unfortunate Admiral Rozhdestvenski, imposed radio silence as it neared Japanese waters. The blessings of wireless were not unmixed.

How future battles would be fought long remained a matter of conjecture. The mighty blow the *Erzherzog Ferdinand Max* struck the *Re d'Italia* reverberated through three decades, during which many tactical theorists held that the coming of steam-driven, armored ships had inaugurated a golden age of ramming. That no further fleet actions occurred for more than a quarter-century after Lissa only added to the uncertainty. As late as the mid-1890s, tactical treatises included detailed discussions of ramming, and navies continued to lay down battleships and cruisers with projecting ram bows until 1906.

By that date, however, three battles—the Yalu in 1894, and Manila Bay and Santiago in 1898—had revealed that the ram was a weapon whose time had come and gone. Tegetthoff had exploited a window of technological opportunity before ships' guns had become powerful enough to disable an ironclad charging bows-on. At the Yalu, a Chinese squadron arrayed in a wedge-shaped, Lissa-like line abreast was mauled by a Japanese force divided into two line-ahead components; at Manila Bay, Dewey's ships fought in line ahead; and at Santiago, the Spanish squadron was gunned down in a spontaneous general chase. The course of these engagements made it clear that gunfire delivered from the traditional line-ahead formation would remain dominant in naval combat.

The reaffirmation of the superiority of gunfire made the determination of the guns by which and ranges at which that fire could best be delivered matters of utmost importance. Toward century's end, the 12- and 13-inch guns in a battleship's main battery had attained—theoretically—an effective range of approximately 10,000 yards (5.7 miles).* Because the resources available to the turret officer who controlled their fire consisted of his eyeballs and experience alone, however, there was no way these guns could be aimed

* The miles cited in this and subsequent surveys are statute miles of 5,280 feet.

accurately enough to hit a moving target at more than a fraction of that distance. In recognition of this limitation, the Royal Navy routinely conducted battle practice at a range of 1,500 yards (0.85 mile), well within the reach of the many smaller guns in a battleship's secondary battery. Furthermore, 12-inch guns could fire at most one round per minute, whereas 6-inch quick-firers threw from eight to twelve. Conventional thought therefore envisioned relatively close actions in which the enemy would be smothered by the sheer volume of fire from the gradiation of guns every big ship carried. This was exactly what took place at Manila and Santiago. In both actions, U.S. vessels closed to within 2,000 yards (1.1 miles) or less of their opponents—and scored approximately 3 percent hits.

Even before these embarrassing performances, a handful of energetic young officers in the British and American navies had concluded that vast improvements could be made in long-range fire control and begun developing the techniques and technology to bring them about. Beginning in the late 1890s, progress was so rapid that by 1905 the Japanese and Russian navies, both equipped with identical, British-built Barr & Stroud optical rangefinders, could fight the Battle of Tsushima at the then-remarkable range of 5,000 yards (2.8 miles). In a few years, such a range would be regarded as virtually point-blank.

In contrast to the evolution of tactical doctrine, naval strategy received what was universally acclaimed as its definitive exposition at one stroke when in 1890 an obscure American naval officer, Captain Alfred Thayer Mahan, published his study of *The Influence of Sea Power upon History, 1660–1783*. Based on lectures he had delivered at the newly established U.S. Naval War College, the book used the seven wars England had waged between the given dates against the Dutch Republic and France as test cases to investigate the historical significance of sea power—that is, a nation's aggregate maritime resources—and the strategic principles underlying the effective conduct of war at sea. As Mahan acknowledged, he did not discover anything startlingly new; most of his findings had been foreshadowed in professional publications during the previous quarter-century, but never before had they been marshaled in a grand synthesis.

Although a succession of publishers improvidently rejected Mahan's manuscript, the reception accorded the work when it finally appeared was nothing less than phenomenal. The direct and compelling correlation Mahan drew between sea power, naval power, and national greatness seized the attention of naval establishments, political leaders, educators, and editors throughout the world. In Britain, where he received honorary degrees from Oxford and Cambridge and an invitation to dine with the queen, Mahan's message served as confirmation of the wisdom of a course steered for centuries. In Germany and Japan, where translations of his book were disseminated under government auspices, as well as in the United States (which he viewed as a mighty sea power in embryo), it furnished both a rationale and a focus for the naval buildups launched later in the decade.

Of paramount operational interest was Mahan's conclusion that the classic French strategy of *guerre de course,* to which the U.S. Navy adhered, had proven to be a formula for defeat. No naval war had ever been won by sinking merchantmen. The reason Britannia ruled the waves was that its navy always sought to destroy or, failing that, bottle up the enemy fleet in order to achieve "command of the sea"—a prize whose possessor could use the world ocean for its own military and commercial purposes while preventing its antagonist from doing the same. Any and every other exercise of naval power, including the elimination of enemy trade, would thereby be assured, and assuming that it was challenged by more than fugitive raiders, command of the sea could be secured only by a navy capable of winning fleet actions. Obviously, to fulfill that function it must possess vessels as powerful as any it might be called upon to engage. In 1890, that meant battleships. Thus the Mahanian synthesis not only prescribed the elimination of the opposing fleet as the ultimate tactical objective of naval operations, but dictated the capital-ship configuration necessary to carry it out. Within a few years, these postulates had become the orthodoxy of the naval world.[1]

Throughout the century's closing decades the Royal Navy retained the naval mastery upon which Nelson had set the seal at Trafalgar. Indeed, that mastery may be said to have reached its apogee in 1889, when the specter of a Franco-Russian alliance led to the adoption of the "two-power standard," according to which the Royal Navy must be maintained at a strength equal to that of the two most powerful foreign navies combined—although this was actually nothing more than a formal declaration of a policy already being pursued. Subsequently, the standard was tacitly expanded to two powers, plus 10 percent. Perhaps the greatest discrete display of British naval majesty occurred in 1897 at the Diamond Jubilee fleet review celebrating Queen Victoria's sixty years on the throne, when thirty miles of warships passed in review before the royal yacht, and not a single vessel had been recalled from overseas to join in the festivities. Yet in retrospect it would become evident that this was an autumnal grandeur. Before another ten years went by, the status quo that had seemed frozen in Britain's favor was overturned by the emergence of the three vigorous new naval powers. Germany signaled its entry into the lists by the passage of long-range naval appropriations guaranteed to produce a great fleet. The other two powers heralded theirs by victory in battle: the United States at Manila Bay, Japan at Tsushima.[2]

NOTES

1. Shortly before World War I, some of Mahan's arguments were convincingly qualified by the great British naval historian Sir Julian Corbett, who emphasized that in the final analysis events at sea are important only to the extent they affect events ashore. Since World War II, his entire thesis has been challenged by several critics on several grounds, the principal being that: (1) the historical interpretations from which Mahan derived his theories are sometimes suspect; (2) Mahan mistakenly imputed universal significance to circumstances that were, in fact, peculiar to the period he studied, and that improvements in land transport and communications have eliminated the relative advantage he ascribed to sea power; and (3) the appearance of the submarine, a vessel impervious to blockade, made "command of the sea" a meaningless concept. There is more than a little truth in these charges. Command of the sea, for example, would never again be quite so commanding once it became possible for a submarine to sink a capital ship unaware of its proximity. Yet in the century since Mahan published his work, no one has presented a comprehensive refutation of his basic conclusions. Both world wars were won by navies imbued with his doctrine, and the combat role foreseen for the carrier battle groups to which the U.S. Navy remains committed is not to attack merchant shipping.

2. For a thorough examination of the erosion of British preeminence, see Paul M. Kennedy, *The Rise and Fall of British Naval Mastery* (New York: Charles Scribner's Sons, 1976), Chapters 7–8.

12

George Dewey
His Father's Son
(1837–1917)

John F. Wukovits

GEORGE DEWEY WAS BORN IN THE LITTLE TOWN OF Montpelier, Vermont, on 26 December 1837, the youngest of three sons. Little is known of his mother, Mary Perrin, who succumbed to tuberculosis when Dewey was five. His father, Dr. Julius Dewey, formed the main influence of his son's life. A pillar of the community, Dr. Dewey epitomized the Puritan spirit of discipline, hard work, and perfectionism.[1] Dewey later gave much credit for his success to his father, asserting that "To my father's influence in my early training I owe, primarily, all that I have accomplished in the world. From him I inherited a vigorous constitution and an active temperament."[2]

That active temperament was not always under control during Dewey's childhood. Dr. Dewey worried that his rebellious son would become a failure and constantly prodded young George to make something of himself. Later, Dewey would admit that his father's discipline was "necessary to a nature . . . inclined to rebel against sedate surroundings," but at the time his father's concern had little effect.[3]

Dewey could be particularly troublesome at school, where he earned the nickname "the black-eyed cuss." One new teacher, ninety-pound Z. K. Pangborn, quickly discovered that Dewey "was ever looking for trouble, and . . . he resented authority and evinced a sturdy determination not to submit to it unless it suited him."[4]

Other teachers had been intimidated by Dewey but, with help from a stout cowhide whip, the frail-looking Pangborn quickly brought him into line. This audacity so impressed Dewey that when he met Pangborn during the Civil War he confessed, "I shall never cease to be grateful to you. You made a man of me. But for that thrashing you gave me in Montpelier, I should probably ere this have been in state prison."[5]

In 1852 Dr. Dewey sent his high-spirited son to Norwich University, a military school. In 1854, Dewey attempted to enter the U.S. Military Academy, but since all appointments from Vermont were filled, he enrolled with fifty-nine other hopefuls in the Naval Academy. Accompanying his son to Annapolis, Dr. Dewey remarked, "George, I've done all I can for you. The rest you must do for yourself." Years later Dewey wrote that "This advice I have always tried to keep in mind."[6]

Dewey chafed under the monotonous, rigid system at the academy and sought relief from the "endless grind of acquiring knowledge" with pranks, earning 113 demerits in his first year. At its end, he ranked thirty-third of his thirty-five remaining classmates. At the same time, another side of Dewey appeared. In his free time he conducted Bible classes for local children, a seeming contradiction in his character but a sign that the mature Dewey was emerging. A more studious Dewey also managed to graduate from the academy on 18 June 1858, rising to fifth in the class of fifteen survivors.

A graduate of Annapolis in those years was required to complete a two-year cruise before receiving his commission. Dewey's first assignment was on the steam frigate *Wabash*, the flagship of the Mediterranean Squadron. Dewey relished the experience. Since young naval officers were eagerly sought as escorts for the daughters of ambassadors and court officials, Dewey was assured of pleasant company wherever the *Wabash* anchored. He always believed that these early years constituted "the happiest period that comes to a naval officer's career."[7]

Upon completion of the cruise, Dewey returned to the academy to take the examination required for promotion to the rank of lieutenant. He passed handily and received his commission in April 1861, at the age of twenty-three. Dewey rejoiced that this accomplishment would show his father that he had, indeed, "done 'the rest' reasonably well."[8] He would continue to be driven to higher achievements by the words and memory of his father.

Dewey's post-commissioning leave was cut short when Confederate shells over Fort Sumter threw the nation into the Civil War. Dewey was aboard the old steam frigate *Mississippi* as executive officer when she joined the Northern blockade in the Gulf of Mexico in May 1861.

Dewey first saw action at New Orleans, where he served under sixty-year-old Captain David Farragut. New Orleans was rumored to be impregnable. Below the city, two imposing forts, Jackson and St. Philip, commanded the Mississippi at a bend in the channel. Brigadier General J. O. Barnard, who had constructed Fort St. Philip, warned Farragut that he must take both works before he could assault New Orleans. Farragut decided to ignore this advice and lead his fleet directly past the forts to New Orleans itself.[9]

This bold decision left an abiding impression on the youthful Dewey. "Like Grant, Farragut always went ahead," wrote Dewey later. "Instead of worrying about the strength of the enemy, he made the enemy worry about his own strength."[10]

On the night of 24 April 1862, Farragut led his ships up the river to victory. During the battle Dewey noticed an irregular-shaped object bearing down on the *Mississippi*. It was the Confederate ram *Manassas*. With no time to consult the captain, Dewey immediately ordered the helm hard astarboard. The ram struck her a glancing blow, but major damage was avoided by Dewey's adroit handling of the ship.[11]

Dewey had found in Farragut his role model, "my ideal of the naval officer." He learned from Farragut to become immersed in every aspect of a battle, in both its planning and its execution. Farragut's personal bravery enthralled Dewey, particularly when he saw Farragut standing in his ship's rigging, barking out orders to other ships, "his face eager with victory . . . and his eyes snapping. . . . I shall never forget that glimpse of him." When Farragut ignored rumors of powerful enemy defenses near New Orleans, Dewey learned to be skeptical of reports of enemy strength. As Dewey recalled, "as so often happens, the enemy in reality was not anything like so powerful as rumor had made him."[12] This was true of New Orleans. It would be true in Manila thirty-six years later.

Farragut always took the initiative, a trait implanted in Dewey when a young officer failed to ram an escaping Confederate ship because he was "waiting orders." In Dewey's presence, Farragut stared at the unfortunate officer and slowly replied, "Young man, you had the opportunity to make a great name for yourself in your profession, but you missed it. I doubt that you will ever get another."[13]

Farragut set such an example that Dewey wrote in his *Autobiography*: "Whenever I have been in a difficult situation, or in the midst of such a confusion of details that the simple and right thing to do seemed hazy, I have often asked myself, 'What would Farragut do?' . . . Valuable as the training of Annapolis was, it was poor schooling beside that of serving under Farragut in time of war."[14]

On 14 March 1863, Dewey participated in the action off Port Hudson, a Confederate stronghold on the Mississippi. The *Mississippi* ran aground through a river pilot's error and had to be abandoned under heavy fire. To ensure that the crews of three lifeboats returned through the fire to gather more survivors, Dewey jumped into one of the boats and, at gunpoint, forced the terrified sailors to row back and forth until everyone had been saved.

Although Dewey earned high praise from his captain, he was concerned that his actions might have been misinterpreted. As executive officer, he was supposed to remain at his post until all but the captain and he were safely off. Had he been killed while in the lifeboat, others might think "I had left my ship in distress. . . . This would not be pleasant reading for my father up in Vermont. He would no longer think that I had done the 'rest' reasonably well." Dewey considered this "the most anxious moment of my career."[15]

A different type of job awaited Dewey in the fall of 1864 when he was assigned executive officer of the *Colorado,* a ship plagued with inefficiency, lack of discipline, and low morale. Dewey's task was to form her crew of seven hundred men into a cohesive unit.

When he arrived, more than one hundred of the *Colorado's* crewmen were in irons for disciplinary reasons and officers were being verbally abused by the remainder. After much of the crew failed to appear at "all hands" the first morning, Dewey stormed below, tipping the sleepers out of their hammocks. Most of them joined their shipmates on deck, but a small group led by an enormous seaman named Webster ignored Dewey's orders.

Dewey realized that "It was a case of my being master, or the rough element being master," and decided the group would collapse if its strongest member was eliminated. He ordered Webster put in irons and kept below.[16]

A few days later Webster broke free and began smashing bottles against the bulkheads, swearing that he would kill the first man who descended the ladder. Dewey grabbed a revolver, stepped to the ladder, and shouted, "Webster, this is Mr. Dewey, the executive officer. I am coming down, and Webster you may be sure of this: if you raise a finger against me, I shall kill you." Before Webster could reply, Dewey raced down the ladder and forced him to surrender. Dewey wrote that this "soon brought a change over the ship."[17] Like his ninety-pound teacher, Mr. Pangborn, Dewey eliminated a problem by attacking its core.

Dewey profited from his Civil War experiences. He served as executive officer of six different ships and participated in four major campaigns, earning a promotion to lieutenant commander by the age of twenty-eight. More importantly, Dewey had scrutinized officers in combat and learned from both the superb and the inept.

George Dewey now entered into a thirty-year span that was largely filled with personal and professional frustrations. On 27 October 1867, he married Susan Boardman Goodwin, the daughter of New Hampshire Governor Ichabod Goodwin. The Deweys spent three happy years at Annapolis, where Dewey supervised the fourth classmen. Shortly before Christmas, 1872, Susan gave birth to George Goodwin Dewey, but she never recovered from a difficult labor and died five days later. Her loss demolished Dewey. For the rest of his life, he carried her picture in his watch case.[18]

The years between the Civil War and the Spanish-American War were frustrating for ambitious young naval officers. The powerful Civil War navy quickly faded into insignificance. Naval innovations were largely ignored until the 1880s and U.S. naval power plunged to twelfth in the world, below Chile. Moreover, the huge surplus of officers generated by the Civil War made promotion agonizingly slow. Some officers chose to leave the navy, but Dewey stayed on, taking hope from the knowledge that "While you are on the active list there is always a chance for action."[19]

Long periods of lighthouse inspections and monotonous map surveying were broken by a few moments of excitement during which Dewey gave glimpses of the leader he was becoming. On his first cruise as commander of his own ship, Dewey steamed the *Narragansett* into the Gulf of California for survey work. While there, Spanish authorities seized the American-registered ship *Virginius* for smuggling guns into Cuba. When three American crew members were executed, war fever spiraled in the United States. Dewey's officers moaned that they were stuck on the Pacific coast while any possible action would occur in the Atlantic, but Dewey quickly brushed aside their complaints. "On the contrary, we shall be very much in it. If war with Spain is declared, the *Narragansett* will take Manila."[20] His bold words became mute when Spanish authorities agreed to indemnify the American families.

The United States emerged from its naval doldrums in the 1880s to begin work on a new navy. Congress appropriated funds for the first modern ships built since the Civil War, three steel-hulled cruisers and a dispatch boat, in 1883. Sixteen battleships and armored cruisers followed in the late 1880s and early 1890s.

Right in the middle stood Dewey. As the chief of the Bureau of Equipment (1889–93) and president of the Board of Inspection and Survey (1895–97), he was near the centers of rebuilding and the people behind the navy's growth. Since the Board of Inspection and Survey tested and approved all new construction, Dewey acquired firsthand knowledge of the most advanced ships. The lean years that had followed the Civil War appeared to be ending, and Dewey, who had slowly advanced to commander in 1872 and captain in 1884, finally reached the permanent rank of commodore on 23 May 1896.[21]

Yet, as the new commodore traveled with an old classmate through the hills of his beloved Vermont in the summer of 1896, serious doubts weighed on his mind. He remarked that while his classmate, a judge, had achieved prominence, he had worked hard in the navy for an entire career with little to show for it. He then bared his soul.

> I don't want war, but without it there is little opportunity for a naval man to distinguish himself. There will be no war before I retire from the Navy, and I'll simply join the great majority of naval men, and be known in history only by consulting the records of the Navy Department, as "George Dewey, who entered the Navy in 1854 and retired as rear admiral at the age limit."[22]

Only four years remained until his retirement, yet events were transpiring that would thrust the unknown George Dewey into worldwide recognition. What appeared to be the twilight of his career would turn out to be its highlight.

American sympathy for the revolution against Spanish colonial rule that broke out in Cuba in 1895 had produced a steady deterioration in the relations between the United States and Spain. As conditions worsened, creating the possibility of war, command of the Asiatic Squadron appealed to a number of officers, since it would conduct any attack on Spain's other great island colony, the Philippines. One influential figure believed that Dewey would be ideal for the post. Assistant Secretary of the Navy Theodore Roosevelt wanted an aggressive commander on the scene, and in his opinion Dewey "was a man who could be relied upon to prepare in advance and to act fearlessly and on his own responsibility when the emergency arose."[23] Roosevelt and Dewey, with the assistance of Vermont Senator Redfield Proctor, applied pressure on President William McKinley, who, in October 1897, ordered Secretary of the Navy John D. Long to appoint Dewey as commander of the Asiatic Squadron.

Dewey wasted no time preparing for his departure. Finding the information on the Philippines in Naval Intelligence files outdated, he gathered every bit of reading material he could find. To alleviate a severe ammunition shortage that was not due to be corrected for six months, he arranged for ammunition to be loaded on the gunboat *Concord,* scheduled to join the Asiatic Squadron in February, while additional munitions were earmarked for the cruiser *Baltimore,* set to join him in March. Since the *Baltimore* actually arrived in the Far East a mere forty-eight hours before news of war reached Dewey, his farsightedness in arranging speedier delivery of ammunition proved of vital importance. Even with it, Dewey's ships steamed into battle with their magazines half empty.[24]

After crossing the Pacific Dewey boarded his flagship, the protected cruiser *Olympia,* in Yokohama on 2 January 1898. The next month, as soon as munitions from the recently arrived *Concord* had been transferred to his flagship, Dewey steamed to Hong Kong to be closer to the Philippines.

A telegram from Secretary Long awaited him when he arrived in Hong Kong on 17 February, informing him of the destruction of the battleship *Maine* in Havana, Cuba. Eight days later a bolder telegram followed from Roosevelt, who was running the Navy Department in Long's absence, ordering Dewey to concentrate his squadron in Hong Kong and prepare for offensive operations.

By 22 April, when the *Baltimore* and *Raleigh* arrived, Dewey's squadron was assembled. It consisted of six naval vessels—the protected cruisers *Olympia, Baltimore, Boston,* and *Raleigh,* and the gunboats *Concord* and *Petrel*—plus the lightly armed revenue service cutter *McCulloch,* which had been attached as an auxiliary. Together, the six warships displaced 19,098 tons and carried 1,456 officers and men. The *Boston,* commissioned in 1887, was the only vessel more than ten years old. To carry supplies, Dewey purchased the col-

11. The USS *Olympia* in 1899, with Dewey's pennant at the main. "Protected cruisers" such as this were unarmored except for a deck at the waterline to shield their interiors from plunging fire. Commissioned in 1895, the *Olympia* displaced 5,586 tons, carried a crew of 411, and had a speed of 20 knots. Her main battery consisted of four 8-inch guns. Today she is preserved at Philadelphia, Pennsylvania. (Library of Congress photograph, U.S. Naval Institute Photographic Collection.)

lier *Nanshan* and steamer *Zafiro,* and cleverly registered them as unarmed American merchant vessels. This enabled the ships to enter neutral ports during wartime to purchase coal and other necessities. Dewey's attention to seemingly minor details, in emulation of Farragut, guaranteed supplies for his force. Dewey then ordered each ship drydocked, overhauled, and painted dull gray.[25]

Dewey enlisted the aid of Oscar F. Williams, the American consul in Manila, to acquire information about Spanish preparations to defend the Philippines. Before leaving his post for Hong Kong on 23 April, Williams informed Dewey that six new guns had been installed on the island of Corregidor. Eager for further information, Dewey ordered his aide to dress in civilian clothes and, posing as a traveler interested in nautical affairs, visit ships as they arrived in Hong Kong from Manila.[26]

Whatever information Dewey received was shared with his staff. Ensign Hugh Rodman, who admired Dewey's thoroughness much as Dewey admired Farragut's, stated that "every contingency which might arise was considered and studied, and plans made to meet each one, so that when the time actually came to engage the enemy's fleet, we had a prearranged plan which fitted the case perfectly."[27]

Attacking Manila would not be easy. Because Dewey was seven thousand miles from the nearest American dockyard, damaged vessels would be as good as sunk, while the Spanish could easily make repairs at their own base facilities. Simply entering Manila Bay could be disastrous. The small islands of Corregidor and Caballo divide the ten-mile-wide entrance to the bay into two channels. The channel, two miles in width, north of Corregidor was called Boca Chica; the passage south of Caballo was known as Boca Grande. A rock formation named El Fraile halfway between Caballo and the shore further narrowed the southern channel. The Spanish placed powerful guns at Corregidor, and less potent batteries at Caballo and El Fraile. Dewey's force would have to steam directly past these guns.[28]

Rumors flooded Hong Kong that the Spanish had mounted powerful guns at Manila and laid extensive minefields in the mouth of the bay. Consul Williams reported that the Boca Grande was mined, but Dewey discounted the rumors as a bluff by his foe. He was convinced the deep water and strong currents would make mining impractical, while the tropical waters would rapidly corrode the wiring of any mines. Remembering Farragut, Dewey decided to ignore the threat. His country expected him to attack, and attack he would.[29]

Manila stood thirty miles beyond the bay's entrance. The strongest Spanish batteries were emplaced there. They included four 9.4-inch guns that could outrange Dewey's 8-inchers. Six miles southwest of Manila, Sangley Point jutted into the bay, forming the smaller Cañacao Bay. Where Sangley Point and the mainland met stood the arsenal of Cavite.

Spanish authorities had long known that Dewey's objective was Manila. The Spanish naval commander, Admiral Don Patricio Montojo y Pasarón, would have preferred to await Dewey in Subic Bay, thirty miles to the north, where fire from his ships could envelop Dewey's fleet as it entered the narrow channel. Fortunately for Dewey, the Spanish administration was slow to develop base facilities there, forcing Montojo to make his stand in Manila Bay.[30]

Montojo's only advantage lay in the big guns near Manila, but he discarded it before the battle by positioning his squadron in Cañacao Bay. Convinced that he had little chance of defeating Dewey with the weak force at his disposal, he hoped to spare Manila an American bombardment. He also believed that the relatively shallow waters off Cavite would improve his men's chances of saving themselves after their ships went down.[31]

Montojo arranged his seven ships—the unprotected cruiser *Reina Christina* (flag), the elderly wooden cruiser *Castilla,* the small cruisers *Isla de Cuba, Isla de Luzon, Don Antonio de Ulloa,* and *Don Juan de Austria,* and the gunboat *Marqués del Duero*—in a crescent-shaped line, from east to west inside Cañacao Bay. Four other gunboats, some of whose guns had been landed, were placed behind Cavite, out of harm's way. At a total of 11,689 tons, his squadron's displacement was approximately one-half that of Dewey's. Montojo's force was also greatly inferior in firepower, mounting only thirty-one guns above 4.7-inch, and none longer than 6.2-inch, against Dewey's fifty-three, which included ten 8-inchers.[32]

On 24 April, Secretary Long telegraphed Dewey that "War has commenced between the United States and Spain. Proceed at once to the Philippines. Commence operations against the Spanish squadron. You must capture or destroy. Use utmost endeavors." That same day the governor of Hong Kong requested that, since the United States was now at war with Spain, Dewey remove his ships from the harbor. As Dewey led his squadron to sea, few observers gave the Americans much of a chance. One British official remarked, "A fine set of fellows, but unhappily we shall never see them again."[33]

Dewey steamed for Mirs Bay, thirty-five miles north of Hong Kong, where he put his men through additional training and distributed ammunition from the recently arrived *Baltimore.* When Consul Williams arrived from Manila on 26 April, he informed Dewey that guns had been mounted near Manila and at Cavite, Corregidor, and Caballo, and that the channel between Corregidor and the mainland was mined. Dewey decided to attack at once, for "the more aggressive and prompt our action the smaller would be our losses and the sooner peace would come." The next day, traveling in two columns at a speed of 8 knots, Dewey's squadron set out for Manila, 620 miles away.[34]

Battle and damage-control drills kept the crews busy as the force slowly moved toward the Philippines, and sailors searched their ships to throw overboard anything made of wood to reduce fire and splinter hazards. To boost morale, Dewey asked Williams to address the *Olympia*'s crew. The consul delivered a fiery speech in which he recounted Spanish threats to his life and insults to the American flag. He also read from a proclamation issued by the Spanish military governor on 23 April disparaging Dewey's squadron for "possessing neither instruction nor discipline" and predicting that Spain "will emerge triumphantly from this new test, humiliating and blasting the adventurers from those States." According to witnesses, this

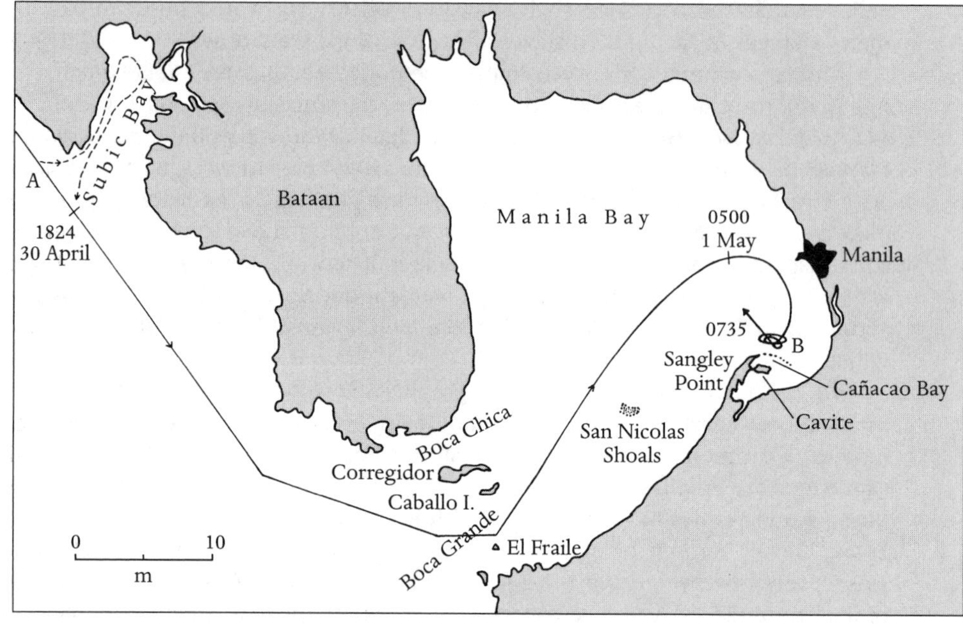

22. The Battle of Manila Bay, 1 May 1898. (A) The *Boston* and *Concord* are detached to reconnoitre Subic Bay. (B) Dewey discovers and engages the Spanish squadron anchored off Sangley Point.

was greeted with a "roar of derisive laughter," and when Williams finished, "every mother's son of us cheered and cursed the Spaniards."[35]

His fleet was ready; his men were in fighting trim. But as Dewey inched closer to his objective unsettling questions nagged at him. Because he was so far from American base facilities, he could ill afford to lose or even eke out a marginal victory. A triumph was required. Though Dewey was confident, he conceded that "The prevailing impression among even the military class in . . . [Hong Kong] was that our squadron was going to certain destruction."[36]

As the squadron neared the Philippines, Dewey detached the *Boston* and *Concord* to scout Subic Bay. At 3:30 P.M. on 30 April they signaled that no enemy force was present there, causing a relieved Dewey to exclaim, "Now we have them!"[37]

Ahead lay Manila Bay. Dewey could not count on surprise, because the Spanish knew when he left Hong Kong and could estimate the time of his arrival. This meant the seventeen Spanish guns guarding the bay's entrance could pose serious problems. Particularly worrisome were the six guns on

Caballo and El Fraile, which would be able to fire on Dewey's force for fifteen agonizing minutes as it steamed by, a mere mile and a half away.[38]

Dewey announced his final plans at a captains' conference on board the *Olympia*. Rather than wait for daylight, he would lead the fleet through the entrance that very night, hoping to catch the Spanish off guard. He surmised the Spanish would act on the basis of what they would do if they were in his situation, and he believed that they would never consider entering an unlighted, unfamiliar fortified bay at night.[39]

Dewey planned to head the line in the *Olympia*. When his nephew, Lieutenant William Winder, suggested a supply ship lead the way to detonate any possible mines, Dewey brushed aside the notion. "Billy, I have waited sixty years for this opportunity. Mines or no mines, I am leading the squadron in myself." He ended the conference with one simple order: "Follow the motions and movements of the flagship."[40]

Admiral Farragut was very much with Dewey as the Asiatic Squadron approached Manila Bay. In his *Autobiography,* Dewey admitted that he asked himself what Farragut would do if he were in his place. "In the course of preparations for Manila Bay I often asked myself this question, and I confess that I was thinking of him the night that we entered the Bay, and with the conviction that I was doing precisely what he would have done."[41]

At 9:45 P.M., the crews were called to quarters. All lights were extinguished except for a small stern beacon for the ships following. Wearing a tropical white uniform and golf cap, Dewey assumed the position on the *Olympia*'s flying bridge that he would maintain throughout the battle. Correspondent Joseph L. Stickney, a former naval officer whom Dewey had taken along as an unofficial aide, noted that "the quiet man on the bridge . . . was as unmoved, apparently, as though he were sailing into a peaceful harbor."[42] Around midnight, the American force entered the Boca Grande in a single column one-half mile north of El Fraile and two miles south of Caballo. Everyone tensed, waiting for the black stillness to erupt in a flurry of Spanish shells.

The first ships passed through safely, but at 12:17 A.M. on 1 May the last two, the *Concord* and *Boston,* drew fire from 4.7-inch guns on El Fraile. Three shells splashed harmlessly in the water, and the ships' return fire silenced the enemy position.

Dewey's surprise move had succeeded. His ships had entered the bay and were free to search for the Spanish fleet. The force continued slowly toward Manila so as to arrive at daylight. Except for two mines that exploded ahead of the *Olympia,* the journey was uneventful. Around 4:00 A.M., crews downed coffee and hardtack at their stations. Shortly after, Dewey headed for Sangley Point when he saw that the Spanish fleet was not anchored near

Manila and its 226 guns. His final order before the battle sent the *Nanshan, Zafiro,* and *McCulloch* to a remote section of the bay to avoid damage.[43]

The *Olympia* was followed into battle by the *Baltimore, Raleigh, Petrel, Concord,* and *Boston,* in that order. The initial Spanish shells boomed out at 5:15 A.M., causing Dewey to close up his column. Moving steadily at eight knots toward Cavite, he tightened the formation to two hundred-yard intervals between ships as Lieutenant C. G. Calkins, the *Olympia*'s navigator, called out the rapidly decreasing range.[44]

For almost thirty minutes Spanish batteries blasted away while Dewey headed directly toward them. They scored no hits, but according to a correspondent "the strain on the nerves of the crew during this time was intense; at any moment a dozen or more men might be scattered about the decks, dead or dying."[45] When the range fell to five thousand yards, Dewey turned his ships to the west to parallel the shore line. Leaning over the pilothouse, he uttered a phrase that has been celebrated in American history. At 5:40 he calmly told Captain Charles V. Gridley, "You may fire when you are ready, Gridley." An 8-inch shell from the *Olympia* signaled the squadron to open fire.[46]

The American ships began the first of five two-mile runs across the front of the Spanish squadron. After the first pass, Dewey decreased the range to three thousand yards. The three leading cruisers concentrated their fire on Montojo's flagship, the *Reina Christina.* Huge geysers erupted around each American ship as Spanish guns attempted to find the range. Though one shell splashed water on the *Olympia* and ripped a chunk of wood from the deck near Dewey, the Spanish fire was ineffectual. Lieutenant Bradley Fiske compared the squadron's maneuvers to "a performance that had been very carefully rehearsed. The ships went slowly and regularly, seldom or never getting out of their relative position. . . ." The hours of rigorous training Dewey put his men through in Hong Kong were paying dividends.[47]

Around 7:00 A.M., the *Reina Christina* charged the *Olympia,* hoping to swing the battle toward Spain. American fire quickly stopped this futile move. By 7:30 the ship was a battered wreck with half her crew wounded or dead, forcing Montojo to transfer his flag to another vessel.

On the fourth pass Dewey learned the bay was deeper than his charts showed, so he closed to under two thousand yards. Although this brought him within range of additional Spanish guns, he was willing to take the risk in order to inflict maximum damage with his limited ammunition.[48]

At 7:30 Captain Gridley informed Dewey there were only fifteen rounds of ammunition remaining for the *Olympia*'s 5-inch guns. This news, "as startling as it was unexpected," staggered Dewey, since he had no resupply. The Spanish, though taking a serious beating, still seemed to be firing shells in quantities "as ample as ours was limited." Dewey had little choice but to order all ships back for an assessment of the situation. Stickney gazed at the surprised looks about him. "I do not exaggerate in the least that as we hauled off into the bay, the gloom on the bridge of the *Olympia* was thicker than a London fog in November."[49] To mask the real reason for the withdrawal, the crews were told the squadron was moving back for breakfast. Most men wanted to continue the battle. One pleaded with his commander, "For God's sake, Captain, don't let us stop now! To hell with breakfast!"[50]

Dewey soon discovered the low ammunition reports were erroneous. Fifteen was the number of 5-inch rounds that the *Olympia* had fired, not the number she had left. Eighty-five remained to resume the fight. Captains reported they had suffered little damage to their ships, and only eight men, all on the *Baltimore,* had been wounded.

When Dewey returned to action at 11:16 A.M., only the *Ulloa* and the Sangley Point batteries were able to fight back. While the *Baltimore* concentrated on the shore batteries, the rest of the forces targeted the *Ulloa* and quickly sank her. Since the guns at Sangley Point could not be depressed to bear at a range of under two thousand yards, the American ships cruised safely by the point, pummeling the batteries until a white flag appeared at Cavite at 12:15 P.M. By 12:30 the battle was over.[51]

Dewey's squadron had won a crushing victory. All seven of Montojo's ships had been destroyed, 161 of their crewmen killed and 210 wounded. No American vessels had been seriously damaged and only nine men wounded. With the war less than one week old, Spanish naval power had been eliminated from the Pacific. When Dewey assembled his officers in his cabin to thank them afterward he added, "Gentlemen, a higher power than we has won this battle today."[52]

The very one-sidedness of the victory led a few skeptics to question Dewey's achievement. Dewey encountered this attitude shortly after the battle and commented, "I suppose it would have been a greater victory if, when I drew off for breakfast during battle, I had concluded, 'Nobody killed yet—must have somebody killed or people won't think we were in a fight,' and I had sent in one ship as a target unsupported by the fire of others." The purpose of battle is to win while minimizing casualties. Dewey succeeded in doing both. Sustaining heavier losses would not have made him a greater admiral, simply a bloodier one.[53]

Because Dewey ordered the Manila–Hong Kong cable cut to sever Spanish communications, word of his victory did not reach the United States until 7 May. The American people erupted in wild displays of patriotism, elevating Dewey and his sailors to instant hero status. Children were named "Dewey" and Dewey hats, canes, spoons, paperweights, and chewing gum called "Dewey's Chewies" flooded store shelves. Congress honored Dewey on 16 May, increasing the authorized number of rear admirals from six to seven specifically to allow for his promotion. Ten months later it appointed him Admiral of the Navy, a unique rank never before or since bestowed upon an American naval officer, with the right of either remaining on active duty until death or retiring at full salary.[54]

In the Philippines Dewey had little time to celebrate, for although Montojo's squadron had been destroyed, the Spanish still held Manila. Dewey could take the city at any time, but he informed Washington that he needed more men to hold it. On 2 May he moved his squadron to a protected anchorage at Cavite, outside the range of Manila's guns, where he remained for the rest of his campaign.

In mid-June Washington informed Dewey that a fleet under Rear Admiral Manuel de la Cámara had sailed from Spain for the Far East. At least on paper, this force was superior to Dewey's, but whatever threat it posed soon passed. In July, the U.S. North Atlantic Squadron destroyed the cruiser squadron Spain had sent to the Caribbean at the Battle of Santiago de Cuba and Cámara's fleet was recalled to defend Spanish home waters against the eventuality of an American attack.[55]

The Germans posed another problem for Dewey. Hoping to fill part of the power vacuum in the Philippines, Germany sent a force under Vice Admiral Otto von Diederichs to Manila. From May to August, the stronger German squadron flouted international customs pertaining to blockaded ports. Dewey was so enraged that one correspondent found him preparing plans "if we should have to fight the Germans."[56]

In June and July a total of six thousand American soldiers arrived to occupy Manila. Dewey now felt strong enough to assert his rights as blockade commander and told a German officer in blunt terms that "if Germany wants war, all right, we are ready." When no other foreign power present in Manila supported von Diederichs, he agreed to a compromise that defused the situation.[57]

For all intents and purposes, Dewey's role at Manila ended when American troops took possession of the city on 13 August 1898. He remained at his post while peace negotiations dragged on, but on 20 May 1899, one year and twenty days after he arrived, an exhausted Dewey finally left the Philippines, telling a reporter, "I am not sorry to leave. I could not stand the care and responsibility much longer."[58]

A spectacular reception awaited America's greatest war hero at New York. More ammunition was expended to welcome Dewey than he had fired at Manila Bay. The city's newspapers collected 70,000 dimes from schoolchildren to melt into a huge loving cup. Poems appeared in hundreds of newspapers memorializing the admiral's exploits. The festivities culminated on 30 September with a tumultuous parade in which 35,000 marchers, led by President William McKinley, swept down Fifth Avenue. Seats at building windows providing a panoramic view sold for $500.00.[59]

Dewey disliked the fuss made over him, writing his son that he planned "to get out of everything I can." But one experience pleased him. Stepping ashore from the *Olympia* at New York, Dewey happily noticed many of his relatives in the crowd. He turned to correspondent Frederick Palmer and gleefully said, "Now I know they think George has cut some figure in the world."[60]

Dewey's popularity plunged when he married Mildred McLean Hazen, a widowed Washington socialite, on 9 November 1899. The public idol was now someone else's private companion, and as a popular chronicler of the times wrote, "it was as if the American public had elected itself to be Admiral Dewey's bride; and as if the admiral had committed bigamy."[61]

Public displeasure increased when the press disclosed that a beautiful Washington home, purchased for the admiral through popular subscription, had been willed by Dewey to his new wife. Dewey only wanted to ensure that his son received the home upon his death, but local laws required he first will it to his wife. By the time a correction was printed, Dewey's image had been further tarnished.[62]

At the same time speculation persisted that Dewey would run for president in 1900. Had a convention been held immediately after his return from the Philippines, he might have been nominated by acclamation. But Dewey was not as imposing now. He added to his woes on 3 April 1900, when he told a reporter that "I am convinced that the office of the President is not such a very difficult one to fill, his duties being mainly to execute the laws of Congress." Heavy criticism swamped Dewey for what a correspondent called "one of the most naive declarations ever given out by any man who had even the briefest part in American politics." When he stuck his other foot in his mouth on 6 May by admitting he had never voted, Dewey's short-lived candidacy collapsed.[63]

For the rest of his life Dewey fortunately returned to the area where he had exhibited greatness—naval command. Except for a brief stint of sea duty during the Venezuelan crisis in 1902–1903, Dewey spent the remainder of his career behind a desk. On 13 March 1900, he became the first president of the General Board of the Navy, the first organization set up to plan for war during peacetime and an influential factor in shaping future naval policy. His name and prestige lent weight to its work.[64]

Dewey's health declined in 1913 when he suffered a minor stroke. Although he recovered, he was never the same. On 11 January 1917, piercing chest and back pains struck the admiral. On 16 January, he addressed his father in delirium, "I hope, father, you think I have done well. I hope you are proud of me, father." At 5:36 P.M., Dewey passed away.[65]

Dewey's body lay in state under the Capitol dome, an honor accorded few public figures. Pinned to the breast of his uniform was a single decoration—the first campaign medal authorized by the U.S. Congress. Inscribed around a picture of a gunner stripped for action it bore the simple words,

IN MEMORY OF THE VICTORY OF MANILA BAY.[66]

NOTES

1. Ronald Spector, *Admiral of the New Empire: The Life and Career of George Dewey* (Baton Rouge: Louisiana State University Press, 1974), p. 4; Laurin Hall Healy and Luis S. Kutner, *The Admiral* (New York: Ziff Davis, 1944); George Dewey, *Autobiography of George Dewey* (reprint, ed. Eric McAllister Smith, Annapolis: Naval Institute Press, 1987), p. 16.
2. Dewey, op. cit., p. 14.
3. Ibid., pp. 16, 18; Healy and Kutner, op. cit., p. 29.
4. Richard S. West, Jr., *Admirals of American Empire* (Indianapolis: Bobbs-Merrill, 1948), p. 16; Healy and Kutner, op. cit., p. 26.
5. Healy and Kutner, op. cit., pp. 26–27.
6. Dewey, op. cit., p. 23.
7. Ibid., p. 30.
8. Ibid., p. 41.
9. Spector, op. cit., pp. 12–13.
10. Dewey, op. cit., pp. 50–52, 72–73.
11. Ibid., pp. 64–70; Spector, op. cit., pp. 14–15.
12. Dewey, op. cit., pp. 59, 68–69, 97–98.
13. Healy and Kutner, op. cit., pp. 67–68.
14. Dewey, op. cit., pp. 50–52.
15. Ibid., pp. 88–90, 95.
16. Ibid., pp. 111–14; Healy and Kutner, op. cit., pp. 82–83.
17. Dewey, op. cit., p. 114.
18. Spector, op. cit., pp. 19–21.
19. Healy and Kutner, op. cit., pp. 99–100.
20. Dewey, op. cit., pp. 128–29.
21. Spector, op. cit., pp. 30–32; Allen Johnson and Dumas Malone, eds., *Dictionary of American Biography* (New York: Charles Scribner's Sons, 1930), V: 269–70.
22. Healy and Kutner, op. cit., pp. 127–28.
23. Theodore Roosevelt, *Theodore Roosevelt: An Autobiography* (New York: Macmillan, 1915), p. 86.

24. Spector, op. cit., p. 42; Dewey, op. cit., p. 152.

25. Spector, op. cit., pp. 47–48; Dewey, op. cit., p. 170.

26. G. J. A. O'Toole, *The Spanish War* (New York, W. W. Norton, 1984), p. 176.

27. Healy and Kutner, op. cit., p. 171n.

28. Spector, op. cit., pp. 50–52.

29. Ibid., pp. 49–50; Murat Halstead, *Life and Achievements of Admiral Dewey* (Chicago: H. L. Barber, 1899), p. 164; Dewey, op. cit., pp. 175–76.

30. David F. Trask, *The War with Spain in 1898* (New York: Macmillan, 1981), pp. 68–69, 96–97.

31. Ibid., p. 97.

32. French E. Chadwick, *The Relations between the United States and Spain: The Spanish-American War,* 2 vols. (New York: Charles Scribner's Sons, 1911), I: 169.

33. Spector, op. cit., pp. 2, 49, 51.

34. Dewey, op. cit., p. 185.

35. Mark Sullivan, *Our Times,* 6 vols. (New York: Scribner's, 1927), I: 315; Lawrence Conlan, "Dewey's Two-Round Victory at Manila Bay," *Annals of War,* vol. I, no. 1 (September 1987), p. 40.

36. Dewey, op. cit., pp. 168–70.

37. Spector, op. cit., p. 56.

38. Trask, op. cit., pp. 98–99.

39. Joseph L. Stickney, "With Dewey at Manila," *Harper's Magazine,* XLCII (February 1899), p. 478.

40. Healy and Kutner, op. cit., pp. 174–75.

41. Dewey, op. cit., pp. 50–52.

42. Joseph L. Stickney, *Admiral Dewey at Manila* (Philadelphia: American Library, 1899), p. 37.

43. Conlan, op. cit., p. 40; Dewey, op. cit., pp. 188, 263.

44. Healy and Kutner, op. cit., p. 179; West, op. cit., pp. 58–59.

45. Stickney, "With Dewey at Manila," p. 479.

46. Dewey, op. cit., p. 191; West, op. cit., p. 203.

47. Spector, op. cit., pp. 59–60; Frank Freidel, *The Splendid Little War* (New York: Bramhall House, 1958), p. 22.

48. Conlan, op. cit., p. 41.

49. Stickney, "With Dewey at Manila," p. 476.

50. Ibid., p. 477.

51. Trask, op. cit., p. 103; Spector, op. cit., p. 62.

52. Healy and Kutner, op. cit., p. 191.

53. Frederick Palmer, *With My Own Eyes* (Indianapolis: Bobbs-Merrill, 1933), pp. 127–28.

54. Spector, op. cit., pp. 67.

55. Trask, op. cit., pp. 372–76.

56. Spector, op. cit., pp. 72–76.

57. Ibid., pp. 78–82.

58. Ibid., pp. 91–101.

59. Healy and Kutner, op. cit., pp. 248–52.

60. Spector, op. cit., p. 104; Palmer, op. cit., p. 125.
61. Sullivan, op. cit., 332.
62. Spector, op. cit., p. 109.
63. Sullivan, op. cit., pp. 309–11; Healy and Kutner, op. cit., pp. 266–73.
64. Spector, op. cit., pp. 122–27, 175–78.
65. Healy and Kutner, op. cit., pp. 309–10.
66. Spector, op. cit., p. 203.

NOTE ON SOURCES

Any examination of George Dewey must start with the three major volumes covering the admiral's life. Along with correspondent Frederick Palmer, Dewey wrote the *Autobiography of George Dewey* in 1913 (reprint, ed. Eric McAllister Smith, Annapolis: Naval Institute Press, 1987). As with any autobiography, the story presented by Dewey must be balanced with more objective works. In 1944, Laurin Hall Healy and Luis S. Kutner produced the first serious biography, *The Admiral* (New York: Ziff-Davis). Ronald Spector followed it in 1974 with *Admiral of the New Empire* (Baton Rouge: Louisiana State University Press), a more critical assessment of Dewey's career. Richard S. West, Jr.'s *Admirals of American Empire* (Indianapolis: Bobbs-Merrill, 1948) provides a useful short biography of Dewey.

Two books on the Spanish-American War that contain excellent chapters on Dewey at Manila are David F. Trask's *The War with Spain in 1898* (New York: Macmillan, 1981) and G. J. A. O'Toole's *The Spanish War* (New York: W. W. Norton, 1984). These volumes have been supplemented by Charles H. Brown's *The Correspondents' War* (New York: Charles Scribner's Sons, 1967), which examines the action in Manila Bay through correspondents' eyes, and by two general studies of the war, Frank Freidel's *The Splendid Little War* (New York: Bramhall House, 1958) and Alan Keller's *The Spanish-American War: A Compact History* (New York: Hawthorn Books, 1969). Lawrence Conlan's "Dewey's Two-Round Victory at Manila Bay," *Annals of War,* vol. 1, no. 1 (September 1987) also proved helpful.

Contemporary accounts, if used with caution, can yield excellent observations on Dewey's maneuvers at Manila. French E. Chadwick's two-volume *The Relations between the United States and Spain: The Spanish-American War* (New York: Charles Scribner's Son's, 1911) remains an important source. Particularly valuable are the article "With Dewey at Manila," *Harper's Magazine,* XLCII (February 1899) and book *Admiral Dewey at Manila* (Philadelphia: American Library, 1899) written by Joseph L. Stickney, the correspondent who accompanied Dewey throughout the battle. Mark Sullivan sheds much light on America's wild Dewey celebrations after Manila in *Our Times,* vol. 1 (New York: Charles Scribner's Son's, 1927). Also helpful are Louis Stanley Young's *Life and Heroic Deeds of Admiral Dewey* (Bay City, Michigan: H. H. Taylor, 1899), Murat Halstead's *Life and Achievements of Admiral Dewey* (Chicago: H. L. Barber, 1899), and Frederick Palmer's *With My Own Eyes* (Indianapolis: Bobbs-Merrill, 1933).

The development of the U.S. Navy between the Civil War and the Spanish-American War receives fine treatment in Dudley W. Knox's *A History of the United*

States Navy (New York: G. P. Putnam's Sons, 1936) and Donald W. Mitchell's *History of the Modern American Navy* (New York: Alfred A. Knopf, 1946). William Reynolds Braisted's *The United States Navy in the Pacific, 1897–1909* (Austin: University of Texas Press, 1958) focuses on naval strategy in the Far East.

Foster Rhea Dulles's *America's Rise to World Power: 1898–1954* (New York: Harper & Brothers, 1955) and Walter LaFeber's *The New Empire* (Ithaca: Cornell University Press, 1963) present a look at America's vault onto the world stage. Bradford Perkins's *The Great Raprochement: England and the United States, 1895–1914* (New York: Atheneum, 1968) and Page Smith's *The Rise of Industrial America* (New York: McGraw-Hill, 1984) were also useful.

Three books depicting Theodore Roosevelt's relations with Dewey are the superb biography by Edmund Morris, *The Rise of Theodore Roosevelt* (New York: Ballantine Books, 1979), as well as Henry F. Pringle's *Theodore Roosevelt* (New York: Harcourt, Brace & World, 1956), and William Henry Harbaugh's *The Life and Times of Theodore Roosevelt* (New York: Collier Books, 1963).

13

Heihachiro Togo

Japan's Nelson

(1848–1934)

E. Stuart Kirby

ADMIRAL HEIHACHIRO TOGO[1] PLAYED A GREAT PART IN JAPAN'S transition from feudal seclusion to the status of a modern great power. Revered in his own country, esteemed worldwide for his naval competence, purposefulness, and highmindeness, he has been dubbed "the Nelson of Japan." That tag is far from unmerited, but it must be qualified. The two men were of different epochs: Nelson of the Age of Sail, of the "wooden walls of Old England" and its "hearts of oak," Togo of that of steam and steel, of the Industrial Revolution that brought Japan preeminence in the Far East. In this latter process Togo waged and won the first major war at sea on modern lines. The circumstances in which the two men acted and the patterns of their campaigns were thus fundamentally different.

So were their characters and temperaments—except for common standards of professional ability and ethical values. Certainly, Togo regarded Nelson as his greatest model for strategy and organization. But Nelson figures, in contemporary terms, romantically; for the novelist or moviemaker, as a real-life Horatio Hornblower, colorful, dashing, inspirational. Togo was contrastingly staid, conformist not only in personal life but in political and service outlook, and very much a family man. He was a paragon of thoroughness and persistence, a sea dog primarily by virtue of doggedness. He was always fully prepared as to training, alertness to technical and other alternatives and opportunities, their optimal utilization, and the collection and use of intelligence; as well as being chivalrous, humane, beloved by his men and all his people. Finally, it must be noted that the designation of Togo as "Japan's Nelson" is of British, not Japanese, provenance. Indeed, a Japanese text on European history would explain that Nelson was "the Togo of England."

Togo's career, unlike that of many men at arms, contains no dramatic turning points. It was, in present-day terminology, more of an exponential rise. This, too, is a generalization that must be qualified. As will be seen below, he erred on occasion, at least in the sense of failing to follow up tactical openings, but he was quick to learn from such mistakes. And, per contra, in his greatest victory he took a spectacular, original, and decisive turn (in the literal sense of the word). Also, he was not lacking in "dash," and did in fact exercise on occasion such a Nelsonian touch as turning a blind eye to ill-advised signals—metaphorically, of course, as Togo was full-sighted. Basically, however, his posture was complete preparedness and full planning. A crowning illustration is that of the time when a second Russian fleet was approaching Japanese waters in 1905. Togo had a detailed plan, anticipating all possible contingencies, to intercept the Russians at five possible points between southwestern Japan and their final destination, Vladivostok. The first two of these proved unsuitable, owing to the disposition of the enemy ships, and their slowness, which put them at target points mainly at night. At the third, Togo had his smashing success, rendering the fourth and fifth superfluous.

It is in those perspectives that the biography must be presented. And in one more: namely, that while Togo is world-renowned for his destruction of the czarist fleet, this was actually only the third of four phases in his long career, each of which has historical importance. The first was that of his origins and setting in the fateful emergence of Japan as a modern nation. The second was his rapid rise and experience in naval service. And a fourth was to follow: Togo continued to serve his country as an elder statesman for practically a quarter of a century after the defeat of Russia. It is tempting to invoke again the comparison with Nelson by imagining him returning alive from Trafalgar and—another extreme assumption—being morally and otherwise acceptable enough to the Establishment to be entrusted with great affairs of state. The realistically cynical historian might well conclude that Nelson would have done as badly as Wellington actually did. Togo, on the other hand, was deemed eminently suitable and rendered solid service, though in his last years (1931–34) he was very old and unable to counter the disastrous course on which Japan was embarked. The factual record is as follows.

Togo was born in 1848 into a lower-middle samurai family in Satsuma in southernmost Japan, an area of strong maritime traditions and antecedents. The country was still closed to foreign ideas or devices, except for those held by a secret government bureau. The construction of oceangoing vessels had long been prohibited. The feudal system was, however, in deep decay. Provinces such as Satsuma were in the hands of lords, feudatory to the military autocracy (Shogunate) in Edo (now Tokyo), organized as clans. By the 1850s the Satsuma clan was acquiring its own fleet, purchasing warships abroad. In 1853–54, when Togo was five and six years old, America's Commodore Perry appeared to demand the opening of Japan to the Western world. His "black ships," including steamers belching smoke, were particularly impressive. In 1860 Togo, aged only twelve (but that was considered a coming-of-age), was appointed a "copyist" in the clan service. He also underwent musketry training. Martial pursuits were, of course, inherent to the samurai class. Togo at age eight was wielding his sword—to kill fish in a pond! As a small boy, his behavior was unruly by the standards of his grade, but he was a logician already. He stole candy from his mother's cupboard, and when taxed with this said he had asked for some but the mother had told him there wasn't any. So how could he have stolen what wasn't there?

In 1863 a British squadron bombarded the Togos' hometown of Kagoshima in retaliation for the assassination of some foreigners. British gunnery was impressive, Japanese defenses relatively weak. For the locals, it was a traumatic experience. In 1866 a Naval Bureau was established by Satsuma, and Togo and his two brothers entered naval service—in which he was to be involved for nearly seventy years. He was posted to sentry duty at the Imperial Palace in Kyoto. This represented a sacred task, the emperor being the spiritual ruler, though at that time without temporal power. In 1868, however, the Shogunate collapsed and the restoration of the emperor was effected, opening the Meiji era, which means Enlightened Government. The emperor was only sixteen, four years younger than Togo, but supported by able ministers committed to modernization. Confusion continued, instanced by the slogan combining "exalt the emperor" with "expel the barbarians." This was only gradually replaced, after further civil wars, by the advocacy of "strong forces and a prosperous country." At the beginning of that great year 1868, Togo was appointed third officer of the paddle frigate *Kasuga.*

The extraordinary fact is that the Japanese navy began with mutiny. The feudalist Admiral Enomoto removed the best ships to Hokkaido to join the anti-Imperials there. The *Kasuga* was damaged in an unsuccessful attempt to prevent the defectors from leaving Tokyo Bay. By the spring of 1869, however, the rebel vessels were all wrecked or captured. The *Kasuga* and three other loyalist ships with transports carrying 6,500 soldiers went to Hokkaido to finish quelling the rebellion. Enomoto surrendered that summer; he was soon pardoned and gave many years of distinguished service to the country. Togo's own brothers supported the Shogunate, but family relations were not impaired.

This affair concluded, Togo was sent to Yokohama to study, especially to learn English. He did so, by dint more of diligence than brilliance, in about one year. Early in 1871 he became a cadet on a training ship and was soon sent to England in a group of cadets for further training. The shade of Nelson traveled with them; after their ship passed Gibraltar, the young Japanese mustered on deck and demanded to be shown the exact location of the Battle of Trafalgar. Togo studied in a school at Portsmouth, lodging with a British family. He and his comrades gazed worshipfully at the *Victory,* which at this time was used for gunnery and small arms practice. Her employment may actually have heightened his interest, as he had always a sharp eye for military procedures. He then served on HM Training Ship *Worcester*. Thenceforward throughout his long life he remained a convinced Anglophile. In 1875 he served as an ordinary seaman on the sailing ship *Hampshire*, proceeding from Australia back to England round Cape Horn, observing everything most carefully. After further study at Cambridge, he was appointed by the Japanese government to monitor the construction of three armored warships it had ordered in Britain.

Togo returned to Japan in 1878 in one of these vessels, the corvette *Hiei*. Promoted to first lieutenant, he continued aboard that ship before going to the ironclad battleship *Fuso* and then back to the *Hiei*. At the end of 1879 he became a lieutenant commander and first officer of the much smaller *Jingei*, a wooden paddlewheeler, which was, however, important for having been built in Japan and as being the emperor's yacht. Early in 1881 he married and bought the house in Tokyo that was his until his death. In the great earthquake of 1923 his house stood when all around it fell, which was popularly considered a special omen.

At the end of 1881 Togo was made first officer of the wooden screw sloop *Amagi*, and in the following year he entered for the first time an arena of international conflict. Serious nationalist disturbances, including anti-Japanese incidents, erupted in Korea, nominally a vassal of China. The *Amagi* convoyed troops to Chemulpo (Inchon) and order was quickly restored. After surveying the whole area, she proceeded to Shanghai to protect Japanese interests there. In the summer of 1884 French naval forces won a conflict with China and attacked Taiwan (Formosa). Togo, with the cooperation of the dour French Admiral Courbet, observed this closely.

In 1885 Togo was promoted commander and transferred to the Naval Construction Bureau. The Yokosuka Yard, under the direction of eminent French engineers, was then operating at a high standard. Promoted to captain in 1888, the following year Togo was made chief of staff of the newly established Kure Naval Station. A major event of 1890 was the visit of a Chinese squadron showing off some powerful modern ships. At first these vessels impressed everyone—except Togo, who, going in mufti to inspect them, thought them not so powerful as they looked. Later others were disillusioned by evidence of Chinese untidiness, such as hanging out laundry on the gun barrels.

The year-end usually marked a step for Togo; in December 1891 he was posted to command the protected cruiser *Naniwa* and dispatched to Hawaii to protect Japanese settlers there, then numbering about 22,000. The queen of Hawaii had been deposed by American settlers who had formed a provisional government not recognized by Japan. Togo acted in a mildly Nelsonian way. He refused to give the provisional government the regular gun and flag salute, though all the other foreign ships accorded them. Then a Japanese escaping from prison ashore came aboard the *Naniwa*. Orders came from Tokyo to hand him over to the Hawaiian authorities. Togo did not comply and gave him to the Japanese consul, saying, more like a Pontius Pilate than a Nelson, "Do with him as you will, but not where I can see it."

In May 1893 the *Naniwa* cruised with a Japanese squadron visiting Vladivostok. This was Togo's first direct contact with the Russians. He thoroughly surveyed the coasts of Siberia and northern Japan. Fresh troubles erupted in Korea in the summer of 1894 and the *Naniwa* convoyed troops to Chemulpo, in which area the Chinese also landed soldiers. As relations between China and Japan worsened, Togo's ship was assigned to the Japanese First Flying Squadron. In July, prior to a declaration of war, this force came upon some Chinese warships in the northern Yellow Sea and attacked them. One of China's finest ships ran herself aground and a smaller one fled to China. A remarkable incident followed; a British merchantman in Chinese service under British officers, the *Kowshing* of Jardine Matheson and Company, appeared carrying more than a thousand Chinese soldiers, as well as a German major. The Chinese troops prevented the British captain from complying with Togo's signal, "Raise anchor and follow me." Togo, standing no nonsense, took off the Europeans and sank the *Kowshing* with gunfire—British flag and all, though that was the most respected ensign in the world and dear to Togo's own heart. The only aspersion ever cast on Togo's character was that Chinese survivors were machine-gunned in their boats or in the water, but in his defense it is asserted that some firing came from the Chinese, that the fugitives had not surrendered, and the Japanese were still menaced by Chinese vessels presumed to be in the vicinity.

This initiation of hostilities against China before a declaration of war was, of course, notoriously repeated later—most spectacularly at Pearl Harbor, but at the same time against Hong Kong, Malaya, and the Netherlands East Indies, as it had been previously against China, French Indochina, and Thailand, without, in these cases, even a post hoc declaration. The consciousness of Westerners is indelibly scarred by those acts of treachery, but it behooves historians to consider the whole setting, the circumstances in a long train of events, and the outlook of the times. As for Togo, he made no demur on moral grounds. He was interested, even expertly, in international law, but philosophically, on an intellectual rather than an ethical basis. The need to advance the fashionable plea of post-1945, that one was "only following orders," would never have crossed his mind. More generally, in addition to the prevalence of fatalism in Oriental attitudes, that was how the world was in that epoch—a state, it may be remarked, of rather widespread free-booting. Let us consider what the devil's advocate might have to say on this issue: Japanese jurists could—and did—adduce a large number of cases in which hostilities had begun prior to the delivery of a formal notice, both between Western powers and in the expansion of their colonial spheres of influence. Others can—and did—stress that this is not a simple matter of black and white, with the former turning at a stroke into the latter by a specific act and/or declaration, but a large and protean "gray area." To vary the metaphors: a worldwide and many-sided operational field, on the map of which there is no particular Rubicon, to cross which means to go from peace to war (both of which are relative terms). A long and wide Great Game had been going on, not a single roll of the dice, winner-take-all. This was a spectrum, a succession of events from the lighter end, peace and negotiability, through disputation and provocation to, at the darkest end, the final arbitrament of arms. By 1894, the world was far past the era of sending heralds to arrange when, where, and how overt hostilities were to begin. It had progressed (?) into the continuum of agitation, vituperation, boycotts, and acts of violence. So who, in hindsight—the devil's advocate might conclude—cast the first stone, and which stone was it? With this digression, the present account may, like history itself, pass on.

The *Kowshing* incident made a profound impression on Togo, impelling his direct interest in international law and relations. Later, as an instructor at the Staff College, he taught that ship management and training were essentials, but another was diplomacy: a commander will constantly have to face decisions with possible consequences far beyond those immediate to him, which he must appraise not merely instantaneously but fully. That aspect certainly loomed large in the final part of this phase in Togo's development, his rise to the highest competence in the naval profession.

On 17 September 1894, the Chinese fleet was located at sea between the mouth of the Yalu River and Chinese-held Port Arthur, precipitating what became known as the Battle of the Yalu. The Chinese fleet—two modern battleships, eight cruisers, and three destroyers—was drawn up in line abreast or echelon. The Japanese squadron under Admiral S. Ito consisted of eight cruisers, the old ironclad *Fuso,* and three smaller units. It approached in line ahead, with Togo's ship the fourth in the leading Japanese group. The Japanese column swung around the starboard (western) flank of the Chinese—who failed, surprisingly, to redeploy or try to cross the T—and broke them up from the rear. Five of the Chinese cruisers were sunk and the remaining vessels put to flight, while the Japanese suffered relatively slight damage.[2] Chinese errors were serious, the Japanese operation almost like clockwork.

Togo's predilections were confirmed: full preparedness and sheer persistence. And he was always learning; ten years later he applied the same "hooking" maneuver against the Russians, but with a bold variation, despite much heavier enemy fire. In 1894–95 he also learned effective cooperation with land forces, which would distinguish Japanese operations against the Russians in 1904–05. The Chinese surrendered in 1895, but Russia, France, and Germany induced Japan to give up the Liaotung area (Dairen and Port Arthur) seized by its forces. Japan was, however, free to annex Taiwan. Togo was promoted to rear admiral. In both this war and the one with Russia, the Japanese navy gained in strength, not only materially and psychologically but in acquiring detailed knowledge of the whole Far East, together with training and experience. Togo valued all those things, in fairly equal measure.

At the end of 1895 Togo was appointed a member of the Council of Admirals and president of the Council on Naval Techniques and a few months later president of the Higher Naval College. Now "top brass" indeed, he headed the Naval College for nearly three years, revising and modernizing the curriculum. In January 1899 he became commander in chief of the Sasebo Naval Base and was operationally in place when serious trouble developed in China in the shape of the anti-foreign Boxer Rebellion of 1900. The powers organized a combined expeditionary force, which Togo joined as commander in chief of Japan's Standing Squadron.

In just over a year the revolt was crushed. Japanese troops made a great impression, both for bravery and for refraining from the extensive looting that contributed so much to museums and collections in the Western world. Togo, it goes without saying, observed and noted everything—particularly the Russians, who had not only contributed the largest contingent but used the occasion to occupy most of Manchuria, including the great natural fortress of Port Arthur, which they proceeded to strengthen. Togo was as unimpressed with the Russians as he had been a few years earlier with the Chinese. He said their discipline was slovenly and their disposition to use warships to carry supplies was fatally unsound. This reminded him of the concept that guided Chinese naval operations in 1894–95—that the navy's function was to deliver the army at landing points. He believed that the navy should sweep the seas to sustain as well as initiate the war on land.

Togo was alarmed when Russians failed to withdraw from Manchuria as they had promised and rivaled Japan for the control of Korea. China had been dealt with, but still had to have an imperial eye kept on it. Clearly,

Russia had now to be reduced if the Far East in general was to be serene and the safety and progress of Japan, in particular, assured. At the turn of the century he pondered this, training himself and his forces, storing and sifting information. Navigation received special attention. The modern maritime history of Japan shows a high incidence of wrecks and strandings; small wonder, given the stormy and reef-strewn character of the region. Full surveying and charting therefore proceeded, also meteorological work and other aids to navigation.

On the plane of grand strategy, in 1902 an alliance was made with Britain, then the world's paramount naval power and in other ways "number one" in Japanese eyes. France broadly supported Russia, Germany was self-assertive. When the inevitable war with Russia came in 1904, it had to be in two stages. The Russian empire had in the Far East a fine Pacific Squadron, with two naturally strong harbors—Vladivostok and Port Arthur—well fortified and fairly well equipped. Nevertheless, this was a force the Japanese navy could match. Far away in Europe, however, the Russians had other units of the same or greater size—principally the Baltic Fleet, with possible additions from the Black Sea Fleet. When or if this second Russia armada reached the Far East, Japan's situation would become more perilous. It was vital therefore to destroy the Russian Pacific Fleet before the Baltic Fleet could be brought to bear, and then to be in full readiness to meet the latter. It was with this task that in February 1904 Togo, appointed commander in chief of the Japanese Combined Fleet in October 1903, sailed in his flagship *Mikasa* toward Port Arthur following the emperor's order to "prepare for war."[3]

Despite the increasing friction between the two countries, Japan had yet to declare war and the Russian ships were lying at anchor, fully illuminated, when Togo's three destroyer flotillas attacked Port Arthur.[4] In this engagement a Russian battleship was grounded and a second holed below the waterline. Another Japanese destroyer flotilla went to Dairen Bay, but found no Russian vessels there. (As Japanese intelligence was excellent throughout, it may be that the enemy's absence was expected, but it was deemed worthwhile to make a reconnaissance and show the flag.) Concurrently, effective action was taken against a cruiser and gunboat at Chemulpo, Korea. This was a ticklish situation, because they were in port among ships of neutral Western countries. The Russians were, however, induced to come out—a striking application of Togo's "diplomacy"—and did so bravely, with colors flying, only to scuttle themselves. Russian crews never lacked in courage, often manning their guns until their ship sank beneath them, but the incapacity of their superiors beggars description.

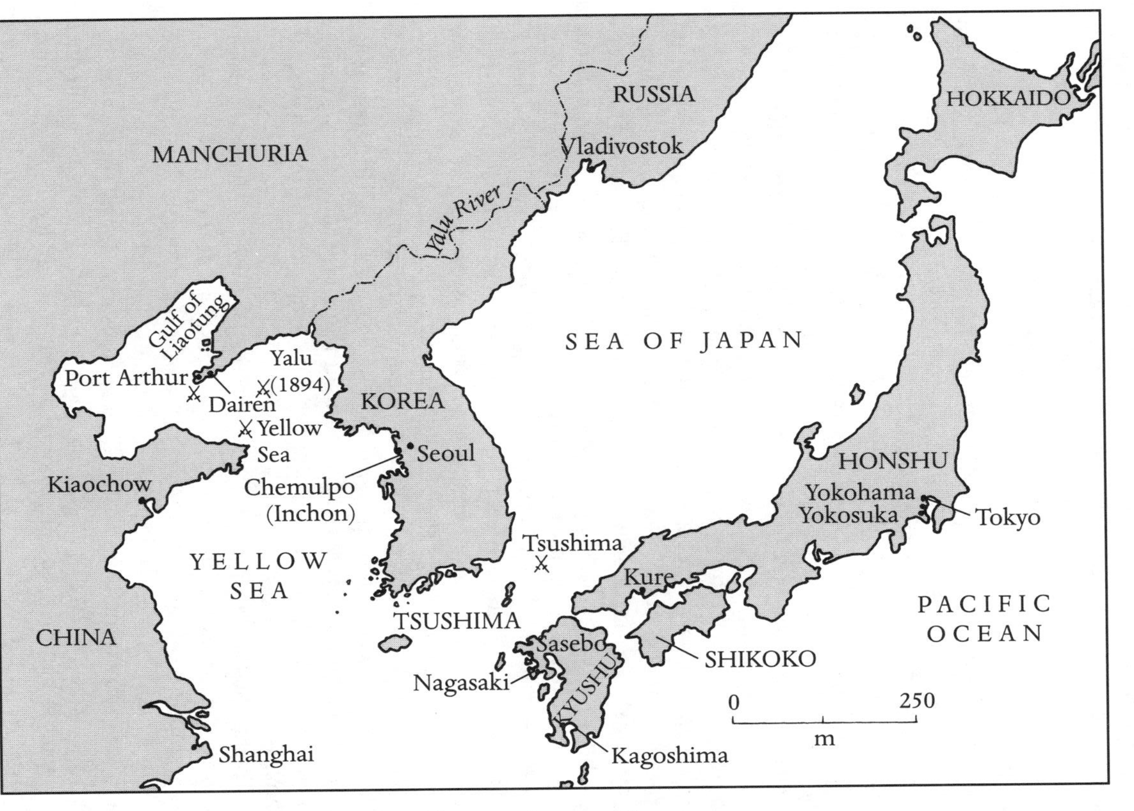

23. The Russo-Japanese War, 1904–1905.

The ship categories used in some accounts can be confusing. Battleships averaged around 14,000 tons displacement each for the six on the Japanese side and 11,000 tons for the seven on the Russian, with speeds of 17 to 18 knots. Vessels in lower categories were relatively small by later standards. The Japanese had eighteen cruisers averaging less than 4,000 tons each, with speeds of 18 to 21 knots. The Russian Pacific Squadron had twelve cruisers, some with slightly less speed, some with slightly more. Seven of these, similar in size to the Japanese cruisers, were at Port Arthur. Five larger ones, averaging over 5,000 tons displacement, were based at Vladivostok, where there were no battleships, all those being at Port Arthur. In the category of destroyers, Japan had fifteen, of between 247 and 375 tons each; the Russian Pacific Squadron had twenty-seven, similar in size, all at Port Arthur. In this class, the Japanese had the edge in speed: 27 to 30 knots against the Russians' 24 to 27. The Japanese mustered five 600-ton gunboats, one of 1,300 tons, and one of over 2,000 tons; the Russians, two gunboats of as much as 1,500 tons, capable of only 11 to 14 knots, plus two little 400-ton but 20-knot ones at Port Arthur and a fifth offstage at Shanghai. It is striking that the Japanese list no minelayers or minesweepers, but the Russians had two of the former at Port Arthur, each of 2,600 tons, 18 knots. At Vladivostok the Russians held a swarm of no less than seventeen tiny torpedo boats—from 140 tons down to 22 tons—but could mount no such mosquito fleet in the Yellow Sea. The Japanese had, of course, to keep "coast defense" capability for their territories and the Russians for theirs around Vladivostok, yet the latter, unlike the Japanese, had no ships specifically designated for that purpose. Last but not least, Japan had many auxiliaries (nineteen merchant vessels "attached for special service," totaling more than 54,000 tons), the Russians almost none. All this, plus massive cooperation with Japanese land forces advancing from Korea into Manchuria, illustrates the complexity of the analysis that Togo faced.

To resume the chronological account: the Japanese, with great gallantry, made five unsuccessful attempts to sink blockships at the entry to Port Arthur and nine naval attacks on that citadel. In the process, they lost several ships to Russian mines, but gradually Japanese persistence and courage began to wear down the Russians, inflicting losses that, for all their valor, they could not replace. Togo proved his obduracy, but also his farsightedness. The Japanese had methodically acquired great knowledge and experience of the area, while the Russians at Port Arthur and in their Far East territory (navally Vladivostok) had always had a fortress complex.

Objectively and subjectively, all the advantages lay with the Japanese. Their homeland and heartland was nearby. It was industrializing rapidly:

witness the helpful presence of a substantial Japanese merchant marine. The masses in Japan were literate and directly conditioned to a martial tradition. Their government, administration, and command (at all levels) were competent and fairly democratic. They were Asians, able to merge with other Orientals, sometimes to pose as such people, and certainly to recruit them as agents or informants, since their patterns of thought and behavior had much in common. As for morale, in 1904–1905 the Japanese were as elated as they have ever been, even in 1941–42.

The Russians' situation was in all respects the opposite. Their center of gravity was far away, west of the Urals. Russia was industrializing, too, but almost solely at its European end; its springboard in this war was its own underdeveloped Far Eastern region, connected to European Russia only by the just-completed and rather inefficient Trans-Siberian Railroad. Its masses were largely illiterate; its autocratic government, administration, and officer corps grossly inefficient and strictly hierarchical. As for mixing with Orientals or using them in any confidential capacity, this was corporeally impossible and emotionally unacceptable to anything more than a very slight extent. At the outset the Russians disdained the Japanese—until they learned, the hard way, to revise their estimate.

In sum, in a classic service phrase, the Russian sailors and soldiers were bewildered and far from home, and so were all their superiors, whose relations with each other were bad. The errors and ineptitudes of the Russian high command would take a whole volume to enumerate. If the present writer may interpolate his own philosophy in this connection, it is that (as adduced by Tolstoy in *War and Peace*) wars are not only won by the superior cerebral capacity of the victor, but lost by the greater stupidity of the adversary.

Togo did not attain his full historic standing in 1904, though he was rapidly gaining eminence; the apotheosis was his victory at Tsushima in 1905. In March 1904 the czar sent a man of ability to command the fleet at Port Arthur, the only person of high caliber to appear on the Russian side. And he was soon to perish. This was Admiral S. O. Makarov, a considerable thinker on naval strategy. Togo greatly admired his works, had them translated, annotated them in his own hand, and kept them near him. On 12 April 1904, Makarov led his ships out to sea, but they turned back when his flagship, the *Petropavlovsk,* struck a mine and Makarov himself drowned. His successor, Admiral Vilgelm K. Vitgeft, made another sortie late in June with six battleships and five cruisers. They were repulsed but were able to return to Port Arthur, anchoring outside the harbor, as the inner roadstead was being shelled by Japanese land forces besieging the city.

In early August, St. Petersburg ordered its Pacific Squadron to move to Vladivostok. It set out at daybreak on 10 August and was met by Togo—who had been promoted to full admiral in June—in what is called the Battle of the Yellow Sea. Vitgeft's flagship *Tsarevitch,* damaged the preceding day by gunfire inside Port Arthur, was hit in the steering gear and careened into her formation, creating massive confusion. Vitgeft and his whole staff were killed by a single shell. Otherwise, the Russians might have gotten through; as it was, they fled—the flagship and some destroyers to German-held Kiaochow, one cruiser to Shanghai and another to Saigon, all to be interned and disarmed. Another cruiser made it to Sakhalin, but was sunk there. Five battleships and four smaller vessels returned to Port Arthur.

Togo has been blamed for not thrusting ahead to demolish the fleeing Russians. Japanese reports counter by claiming that the light was failing (though later there was moonlight) and that the coup de grâce was to be administered by destroyers and torpedo boats, in which the Japanese had a strong preponderance (but that was not achieved). Moreover, the noose was tightening around Port Arthur; the Russian ships might be captured or at least neutralized there.

The Russians at Vladivostok also became more aggressive, but they too were defeated, one of their cruisers being sunk, another and a destroyer damaged. Bitter land fighting continued round Port Arthur for the rest of 1904. Early in December the Russian squadron at Port Arthur was devastated by gunfire from land and sea. Japanese commentators said that by returning there it had "mounted its own scaffold." Three battleships, two cruisers, a minesweeper, and a gunboat were sunk. There were, of course, Japanese losses throughout the war, but they were much fewer than the Russians' and far less telling. The death-trap perspective was fulfilled on New Year's Day 1905: Port Arthur surrendered. The news rang round the world. In Russia it sparked the First Revolution, which broke out later in January.

Round One having thus been completed, Japan geared up nimbly for Round Two, training and planning for almost a year before the Russian Baltic Fleet arrived in the Far Eastern arena. The latter, formally constituted as the Second Pacific Squadron at the end of April 1904, displayed the level of Russian efficiency by taking five-and-a-half months to leave the Baltic, which it did on 15 October. It proceeded forthwith to bring itself into general obloquy by firing on some British fishing trawlers in the North Sea, imagining that they were Japanese torpedo boats. The only slight justification was that Britain was so closely supportive of Japan as to be suspected of letting the Japanese use British harbors and even joining them in operations. The threat arose of war with Britain, and an indemnity had to be paid.

12. The Battle of Tsushima, 27–28 May 1905. Togo on the bridge of the *Mikasa,* his flagship, at the beginning of the battle. The admiral is holding the sword presented to him by the emperor and his Zeiss binoculars. At left, a seaman is hoisting the "Zed" flag conveying Togo's famous message to the fleet. The hammocks abundantly in evidence have been rigged as splinter shields. (*Mikasa* Preservation Society photograph by William M. Powers, U.S. Naval Institute Photographic Collection.)

At Tangier, on the Atlantic coast of Morocco, the Baltic Fleet split, its lighter units proceeding via Suez, the heavier ones round the Cape of Good Hope: both conscientiously refraining from firing on native craft. They rejoined at Madagascar, vainly awaited some reinforcements (which were finally left to catch up), and steamed across the Indian Ocean. At the beginning of April they passed Singapore and entered the China Sea, where they anchored in Camranh and Vanfong bays, off French Indochina. En route, the Baltic sailors learned that there were strikes and actual armed uprisings back home in Russia, including a mutiny on the battleship *Potemkin* in the Black Sea.

This fleet was slow-moving, containing a number of supply ships and its own colliers. Every movement of its odyssey, from start to finish, was observed closely and in detail by Japanese agents. Although the evidence for the following report is only anecdotal, it is illustrative. The name of the Russian commander, Admiral Z. P. Rozhdestvenski, baffled all non-Russian writers, who were unable to spell it correctly in any of the various modes of transliteration. All except, it is said, Japanese intelligence. In Russian "Rozhdestvenski" implies "the man of Christmas," and Japanese agents reported continuously on the approach of "le père Noël," how many reindeer and sledges he had, and how they were loaded. The Russians had no such information on the Japanese and their communications were so poor that many key messages from Port Arthur were cabled via Nagasaki, where the Japanese read them before passing them on to St. Petersburg.

The Russian fleet was sighted southwest of Japan at daybreak on 27 May. The Japanese had already acted to seal its final destination, Vladivostok, with 715 mines. Rozhdestvenski's force was stronger than the Pacific Squadron of which the Japanese had already disposed, especially in the weight of its eight battleships, averaging 12,100 tons each, of 15 to 18 knots, and three each coast defense "battleships" and armored cruisers averaging approximately 5,900 tons, plus five protected cruisers and nine destroyers. Then there were eight "special service" auxiliaries, and now, significantly, two hospital ships.

The fleet under Togo's command consisted of four battleships (the other two with which Japan began the war having been sunk by Russian mines off Port Arthur), eleven armored cruisers, fourteen cruisers, and twenty-one destroyers, plus a number of torpedo boats and miscellaneous craft. Its inferiority in capital ships was more than offset by its homogeneity and training. The main force fell on the Russian fleet at 2:00 P.M. on the same day eastward of the island of Tsushima, which lies in the middle of the strait between Japan and Korea. There is the famous tableau of Togo hoisting a signal echoing Nelson's at Trafalgar. Its wording may be rendered, "the fate of the Empire depends on this one engagement: let each man do his fitting part." Here again some qualifications are in order. The signal was not absolutely new in the Japanese navy. A similar message, only slightly less graphic, had been made by Admiral Ito at the Yellow Sea the year before. Togo's was in Chinese characters, a more classical format. The Japanese sailors were generally literate and would have understood it, but a more vernacular rendering was actually circulated for them.

The Russians were heading from south to north, intent on reaching Vladivostok; the Japanese approached on the same line but in the other direction, from north to south, determined to destroy the Russians before they got any further. In textbook terms, Togo would likely intercept either by crossing the T or hooking into the enemy formation. Here, however, Togo made his most original and unorthodox move, which may be counted among the critical decisions with which this book is especially concerned. If

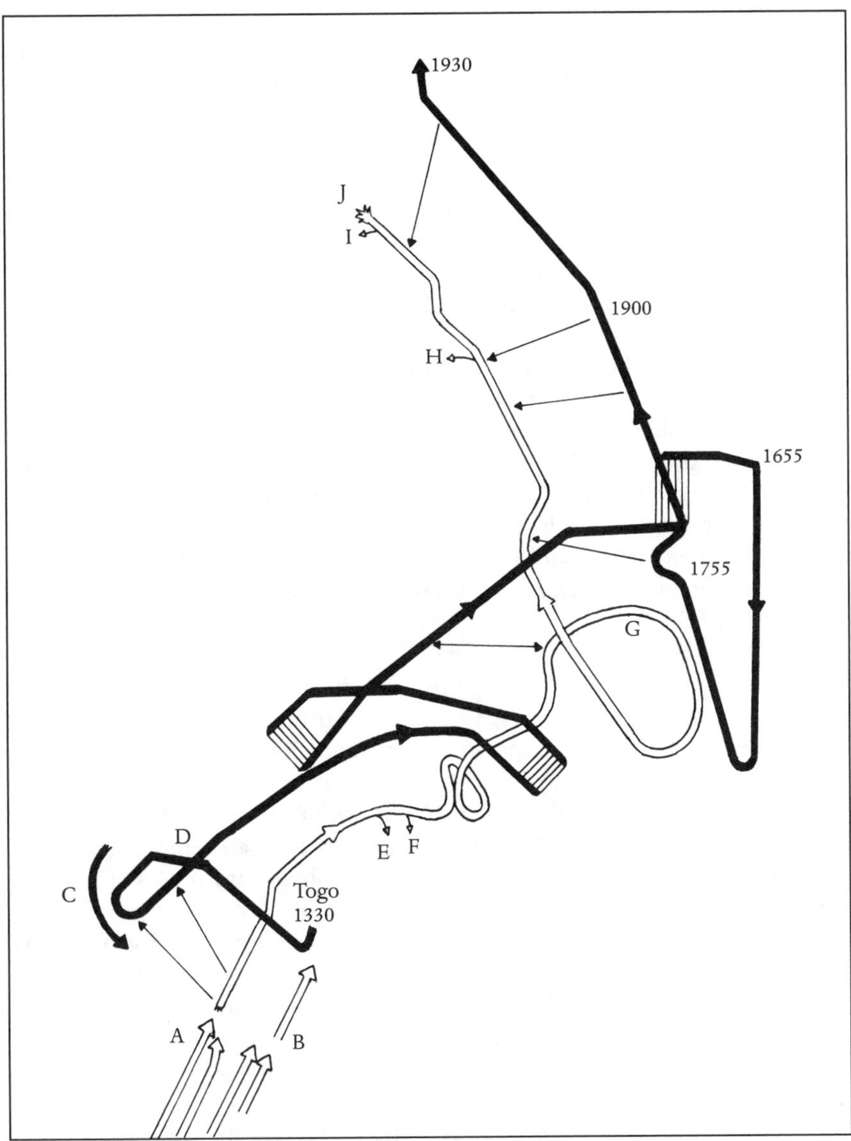

24. The Battle of Tsushima, 27 May 1905. (A) Russian battleships form line ahead. (B) The Russian fleet train, escorted by cruisers and destroyers; in the interests of clarity, the action between this formation and the Japanese cruiser divisions that intercepted it is not shown. (C) Japanese cruisers. (D) Togo's turn under fire. (E) At 1450, the Russian flagship *Suvorov* is disabled and sheers out of line. (F) The *Osliaba* sinks at 1515. (G) The *Suvorov* sinks at 1730. (H) The *Alexander III* sinks at 1900. (I) The *Borodino* sinks at 1920. (J) At 1930, the Russian column disintegrates.

he had continued on course the two fleets would have passed each other in a short, sharp encounter, after which at least some of the Russian ships would continue to Vladivostok. If so, Japan's situation might become parlous, with a sword of Damocles hanging over the Sea of Japan.

Togo therefore had his main fleet execute a U turn to take the same course as the Russians, alongside them. This meant taking very heavy fire during the upturn of the U, running south to north parallel to the Russians on their port side, while the leading Japanese ships masked the fire of those that were still on the downturn going north to south. Togo was confident that they could stand that grueling test and proceed to destroy the enemy. If Togo had not done this, he would have had to turn somewhere farther south and pursue the Russians on an unfavorable bearing. Underlying this bold stroke was, besides the element of courage and endurance, the basic psychological difference that the Japanese were determined to eliminate the Russian fleet there and then and were confident, especially after their signal victory the preceding year, of their ability to do so. The Russians, in contrast, saw their salvation in reaching the bastion of Vladivostok, the only place from which they could continue the war. It was also a place of the highest subjective importance to them, its very name in Russian meaning "possessor of the East."

That was the Battle of Tsushima. The details have been extensively discussed in the international literature, and there is no room here for any special recapitulation. The first phase, off Tsushima, was indeed a killing time. Four Russian battleships were sunk and the remainder of the fleet broken up and cast into deep dismay. Its surviving ships dispersed throughout the northern part of the Sea of Japan, so the second phase represented Japanese actions for mopping up the scattered Russian remnants in quick succession. A Japanese historian divided this phase into no less than nine separate "encounters," each ending in the capture or destruction of one or more Russian vessels. By noon on 28 May it was over. Of the Russians' fourteen battleships and armored cruisers, none escaped. Only three vessels, the armed yacht *Almaz* and two destroyers, succeeded in reaching Vladivostok. A few others found sanctuary in Shanghai and Manila. The cost to the Japanese of this crushing victory was three torpedo boats. For czarist Russia, the war was indeed fini.

At that apotheosis Togo was aged fifty-seven and still had nearly thirty years to live. His triumphant return to Japan was marred only by an accidental explosion on his flagship, the *Mikasa,* which sank only five days after the signing of peace between Japan and Russia at Portsmouth, New Hampshire. She was subsequently raised, to be used as a naval museum and (like the *Victory*) a national shrine. Togo reported to the Shrine of the Imperial Ancestors at Ise, then to the emperor himself, and was given an enormous reception in Tokyo. Ticker tape was not in vogue, but there were floral adornments and great marches-past, with a detachment of His Britannic Majesty's Royal Marines in a place of honor, expressing the Japanese regard for Britain as not only a great ally but virtually an elder brother.

Togo himself was heaped with honors: made a count (eventually, on his deathbed, a marquis) and decorated with the First Class of the Order of the Golden Kite, Japan's foremost military distinction. Could a citizen fly any higher? Yes, he was elevated with the Grand Cordon of the Supreme Order of the Chrysanthemum—to which a Collar was added in 1925. Britain conferred a rare honor in the shape of the Order of Merit, presented by a delegation of princely status. Photographs of Togo in full rig from then onward show him as bemedaled as dignitaries of the erstwhile Soviet Union.

The tenor of the war of 1904–1905 was in general impressively chivalric. It extended into sentimentality, with which in that era such devoted militarists as the Germans and the Japanese appeared to be deeply imbued. Togo's respect for Makarov has been mentioned. "Father Christmas" Rozhdestvenski, Russian commander in chief at Tsushima, was shown great courtesy when he was captured, badly wounded, in the destroyer to which he and his staff transferred after the flagship was disabled. Togo visited him in the hospital in Japan and delivered a short homily on defeat and capture being part of the destiny of the fighting man. They exchanged expressions of mutual respect, clasped hands, and—according to Japanese reports, which may be exaggerated—looked into each other's eyes for some minutes. Russian prisoners were paraded in Japan—but with dignity. The enemies saluted each other. It is startling to juxtapose the knightliness of this era with the Japanese bestialities in World War II, from Bataan to the River Kwai. Togo would not have tolerated such things. Had he been living, he might have slashed his own entrails in protest.

Most Japanese were disappointed with the peace treaty. Russia appeared to be let down lightly by the "good offices" of the Western powers, including the great ally Britain (et tu, Britannia?), while Japan had to relinquish some conquered territory. The Westerners' patronizing air was also resented; for example, habitual references, especially in Britain, to the "gallant little Japs." How would they like to be called the "brave hulking Brits"? The germs of reciprocal unease were already present. For the first time, Orientals employing thoroughly modern methods and equipment—and displaying startling bravery and self-sacrifice—had defeated a Western (-type) Power. The militarists who seized control of the Japanese government three decades later found this a bracing precedent. Togo himself would never go beyond being a strong nationalist, in the best sense of the term, demanding fair play for Japan and honorable relations among nations according to their merits rather than their physical strength, viewing the latter as coming normatively from the former. On the other hand, as regards the terms of peace, he must have been among well-informed people who realized that Japan's resources had been severely strained by the war, to the extent of being almost as incapable as Russia of carrying it on much longer.

For the remaining, fourth, part of his career Togo was cast essentially in the role of a man of peace. His personal name, Heihachiro, rather subtly suggests that classification. It may be translated "eighth son of peace," a reference to the classical Sino-Japanese concept of the "eight corners" of the world coexisting under "one roof." Less philosophically and in day-to-day functioning, Togo became something of an elder statesman. He also fulfilled the ceremonial duties that are characteristic of and essential to monarchical states, such as the especially emulated Britain. With the army commander in Manchuria with whom he had collaborated so well, General Nogi, he planned in 1907 and inaugurated in 1909 a war memorial, the "Tower of Loyalty," at Port Arthur. Just before the dedication he had been relieved of his posts as chief of the Naval General Staff and member of the Council of Admirals, though appointed to an overall body of equal or higher standing, the Supreme Military Council.

From April through July 1911 Togo escorted the imperial prince and princess to England to represent the emperor at the coronation of King George V. Among the festivities he attended were the annual navy review, dinners with British admirals and other dignitaries, and an inspection of Boy Scouts. Possibly relevantly, sixteen years later a Togo's Boys Association was formed in Japan.

There was also an Old Boys' reunion aboard the training ship *Worcester*. (The Japanese are no less prompt than the British to recognize and foster "Old School" ties.) One of the guests was a Captain Galbraith, whom Togo did not recognize but who eventually related that he had been the captain of the *Kowshing* in the awkward incident noted above during the Sino-Japanese War. Togo was moved to marvel at the inscrutability of the British character; this man had not divulged, at the time of the incident or in all the subsequent years, that they had been *Worcester* alumni.

From Britain, Togo proceeded to the United States, where he was guest of honor at receptions in New York, at the White House, Annapolis, and elsewhere, to be home again via Niagara Falls and the Pacific Coast in September. In July 1912 the great Emperor Meiji died. The funeral, with Togo a prominent mourner, was extremely impressive. General Nogi and his wife chose to follow their sovereign in death by committing suicide in the traditional samurai manner. Not so Togo, who continued in his duty.

As one of the World War I Allies, Japan rendered many services—and acquired dominance in China as well as some German territories in the

Eastern Hemisphere. Togo had no direct part in the operations but must have been influential behind the scenes. Before the war began he was appointed to a task of positively sacred importance: head of the Office for the Education of the Crown Prince. This very high function he performed until 1921, when the Crown Prince came of age. It was a most responsible commission and one that provides a significant connection of Togo with our day and age, because that Crown Prince was none other than the Emperor Hirohito, who was crowned in 1926. The liberal propensities of that monarch, comparative or stifled by the military dictatorship as they may have been, can accordingly be credited to some extent to Togo's tutelage.

The next decade, when Japan invaded China and established the puppet Empire of Manchukuo, embarking on the course to disaster, was a very painful time for Japan. While the skies darkened abroad, at home there was economic boom and bust. A great rise in Japanese exports—in those days to less developed countries—brought recriminations, boycotts, and tariff measures. All around the Pacific Basin, Japanese immigration was disliked and feared, with hostile public demonstrations and official obstacles. In the navy sphere, the Washington treaties of 1922 restricted Japan's capacity and ambitions. Britain opposed Japan: their grand alliance came to an end. Togo was tightlipped about all this, in illustration of which the present writer may mention his own experience. The only time he had a personal conversation with Togo, at the very end of the 1920s, the old admiral completely refused to be drawn on any such issue, insisting instead on sounding out the reaction of a young Englishman born in Japan to current developments there.

In the early 1930s Japanese politics took a violent turn to the far right. Political assassinations by fanatical young officers counted among their victims some of Togo's friends and even comrades in arms. It was a sad world for Togo in his last years. Finally his health failed. He had undergone an operation for bladder stones in 1907. His health has not been mentioned above; for the most part he was well and strong. In the 1880s he was sorely afflicted with rheumatism, which lasted intermittently for years, requiring frequent sick leaves, but he suddenly threw this off sometime before the war with Russia. At the end of 1933 he fell into his final illness—this time, cancer of the throat. At the beginning of 1934 he took to his bed. By 27 May he was critically ill and on the thirtieth he died.

Some people write their own epitaphs, either on purpose as such or in phrases that may be quoted from their writings or sayings. It would have been most unlike Togo to do the former, and he was too economical with words to provide much in the way of the latter. There is, however, an ode that he composed while president of the Office for the Education of the Crown Prince, which may be deemed appropriate:

A dull man I may be
But all my duties I fulfill
in all sincerity.
Look on my work, O gods above,
And just my honesty approve.[5]

The world, besides respecting Togo for his professional competence, also admired his integrity and steadfastness. In 1937 Admiral Bradley A. Fiske, USN, made an interesting comparison. "A counterpart of Togo . . . in point of modesty and gentleness and loyalty," he wrote, "was General Ulysses S. Grant."[6]

Notes

1. The pronunciation of the surname is simply as in English, "toe go," each o being in this case long—i.e., slightly dipthongated in almost the British manner.

2. In this action Commander Philo McGiffen, a U.S. Naval Academy graduate serving in the Chinese navy, became the first American to command a battleship in action when the captain of the *Chen Yuen* fled the bridge.

3. The same expression (*junseji*), which may be rendered either as "war-preparation period" or "semi-wartime," was regularly and officially used in Japan in the 1930s.

4. An interesting point arises in this connection. Both sides in this war distinctly feared the torpedo. It was the latest in new weaponry, and there is always a tendency to exaggerate the striking power of an innovative device, at least to begin with. Nervousness about possible torpedo attacks continued all through the war on both sides, although this first salvo by the Japanese had limited success, some torpedoes sinking before reaching their targets. A more basic technological innovation of the war was, perhaps, that wireless telegraphy had become available. And there was one technical advantage—held by the Japanese—in the shape of a new gunsight of British provenance.

5. The main citation on which this wording is based is in the concluding pages of N. Ogasawara's *Life of Admiral Togo* (Tokyo: Seito Shorin, 1934), on which the present author has drawn at various points. He should perhaps add that, as a poem, it is not a gem of Japanese literature, and its sentiments need not be taken too literally given the Japanese propensity for self-deprecation, which may become an act of ritual upon receiving a high appointment.

6. In the foreword to Edwin A. Falk, *Togo and the Rise of Japanese Seapower* (London: Longmans, Green, 1937), p. vii.

Note on Sources

The rise of Japanese naval power has attracted a voluminous international literature, focusing mainly on the Russo-Japanese War. Works have appeared in various languages: principally Japanese, English, Russian, French, and German, in something like that in order of both quantity and concern. The present writer draws here on all these, plus his own lifetime's experience in East Asia, to offer a summary digest—with special reference to the character, conditioning, and motivation of Admiral Togo. That more personal aspect is largely submerged in the general historiography, so that there are not many publications that can be recommended as specially relevant to the subject of this essay—Togo as Togo.

The judicious reader must further be advised that, broadly speaking, there are difficulties regarding the treatments in the different languages. The extensive material in Japanese is most varied and most difficult to transpose into terms of other cultures. Western writers, with very few exceptions, are insufficiently versed in the languages, usages, or other features—in some cases, even the topography—of the Far East. For example, the area of Tamshui in Taiwan is described by one writer as "steaming jungle." It is in fact savannah, and happens to be the site of one of the best golf courses in the Far East. In addition, proper names, as well as concepts and emphases, are sometimes imperfectly rendered (over and above the vagaries of transliteration). Few Russian writings are impressively cogent, widely perceptive, or lucidly readable. Czarist material tends to be ponderous, while Soviet authors were doctrinaire and sadly schizophrenic in their attempt to combine denunciation of czarist rottenness with the New Soviet Patriotism, in which all things Russian were intrinsically good. Consequently, only a few references will be cited here. The listing is selective also in referring only to items reasonably accessible to the reader of English. Explanatory footnoting on every point would be very cumbersome: notes on the text have therefore been held to a minimum.

Practically the only book that is entirely and exactly to the same purpose as this essay is the *Life of Admiral Togo* by Vice Admiral Viscount N. Ogasawara, well translated into English by J. Inouye, a close colleague of Togo's, and his son T. Inouye (Tokyo: Seito Shorin, 1934). This is detailed, meticulous (except for Russian names), and well illustrated. It has been drawn upon in this essay for various personal details concerning Togo, as it gives a clear picture of those aspects for the reader of English. Naturally, a close view is given by Admiral Togo's nephew Kichitaro Togo in his *The Naval Battles of the Russo-Japanese War* (Tokyo: Gogakukyokwai, 1907). The works of Edwin A. Falk, *Togo and the Rise of Japanese Seapower* (London: Longmans, Green, 1937) and *From Perry to Pearl Harbor: The Struggle for Supremacy in the Pacific* (New York: Doubleday, Doran, 1943; reprinted Westport, Conn.: Greenwood Press, 1974), are useful and accurate.

Also to be recommended, with special reference to the war of 1904–1905, is a most readable work of the highest-grade journalism, David Walder's *The Short Victorious War: The Russo-Japanese Conflict, 1904–1905* (London: Hutchinson, 1973), vividly depicting the ineptitudes on the Russian side. Georges Blond's *Admiral Togo,* translated by Edward Hyams (London: Macmillan, 1960), is good on naval aspects but not in local knowledge. *The Emperor's Sword: Japan vs. Russia in the Battle of Tsushima,* by Noel F. Bush (New York: Funk & Wagnalls, 1969), also merits mention. In the fictional or semifictional category there are two interesting Russian works—exceptions to the general dullness of the Russian treatment—namely, A. Novikoff-

Priboy's *Tsushima* (London: George Allen and Unwin, 1936) and V. Semenov's *Rasplata* (*The Reckoning*), 2nd rev. ed. (London: John Murray, 1909–10).

The foregoing comprises a "short list" for the general reader. The historian will obviously find heavier ammunition in the official histories. The British one is the *Official History of the Russo-Japanese War* (London: H.M. Stationary Office, 1910–20). There are also the Admiralty's *Reports on Technical Subjects,* attaché reports, and other materials of the kind. The French official history has also been published in English translation.

Survey V

The Dreadnought Revolution

(1905–1916)

Less than a decade separated the end of the Russo-Japanese War from th beginning of World War I, but by the onset of the latter every capital sh afloat during the former had been rendered obsolete. The agent of the antiquation, laid down in October 1905 and rushed to completion a ye later, was HMS *Dreadnought,* the first of the "all-big-gun" battleships th would be categorized by her name. Of course, neither she nor her prog eny were literally *all*-big-gun battleships. Some precaution had to be take against torpedo boats or destroyers that might slip close inboard, and th original *Dreadnought* mounted more than two dozen little quick-firers to de with them. Her distinction lay in her main battery, for in contrast to th assortment of ordnance her predecessors carried, she mounted a unifor armament of 12-inch guns in five double turrets: one fore, two aft, and on on each beam. This arrangement gave her a broadside of eight big guns twice as many as any other battleship in commission. Furthermore, th *Dreadnought*'s revolutionary quality did not end with her armament. She wa also the first battleship to be powered by steam turbines, which had made their maritime debut only eight years earlier. More reliable than comparably powerful reciprocating engines, which tended to shake themselves to pieces, they also averted the design and protection problems posed by the growing height of the latters' huge pistons.

The idea of an all-big-gun battleship had been in circulation since the 1890s, but its fruition was brought about largely by one man, Admiral Sir John Fisher. Dynamic, irascible, deliberately outrageous, Jacky Fisher had assumed the duties of First Sea Lord in October 1904. By then the Anglo-German naval race was well under way, and Fisher believed that Britain's security depended on enhancing the Royal Navy's fighting power without increasing its already alarming demands upon the treasury. Sponsoring the *Dreadnought* was among the numerous initiatives he took in pursuit of those goals.

Although a few mixed-caliber battleships were started after the *Dreadnought*'s appearance, every other major navy soon began designing dreadnoughts of its own. The most important innovation to ensue was "superfir-

ing"—stepping a pair of centerline turrets so that the one in the rear could shoot directly over its twin—a system introduced in the U.S. *South Carolina* class in 1906–1908 and subsequently adopted worldwide. By the summer of 1914, the three leading naval powers—Britain, Germany, and the United States—had a total of forty-seven dreadnoughts in commission, and seven lesser powers had thirteen more. Each generation of these vessels was larger, swifter, and more powerfully armed than the last. The *Dreadnought* displaced 18,000 tons, could make 21 knots, and mounted ten 12-inch guns positioned as described above. The five *Queen Elizabeth*–class "super-dreadnoughts" laid down in 1912–13 and completed in time to fight at Jutland displaced 27,500 tons, made 24 knots, and mounted eight 15-inch guns in superfiring twin turrets fore and aft. Of these increases, the most significant was in firepower. Because one of her amidships turrets was always odd man out, the *Dreadnought* and the *Queen Elizabeths* could bring the same number of guns to bear in broadside, but there the similarity ended. The difference in weight between 12-inch and 15-inch shells (870 to 1,920 pounds) enabled the *Queen Elisabeths* to throw approximately two and a quarter times as much explosive as the *Dreadnought,* making them more superior to her in that respect than she was to a pre-dreadnought.

Traditionally, historians have viewed the dreadnought as the centerpiece of Fisher's matériel reforms. Recent research has revealed that this was not the way he viewed it.[1] Except for a professional consensus that not even he could ignore, Fisher would not have built any manner of battleship. His weapon of choice was the battle cruiser, the first three of which, the *Invincible* class, were authorized at the same time as the *Dreadnought*. An even greater departure from conventional design, battle cruisers carried the same all-big-gun armament as dreadnoughts and displaced as many or more tons, but they were more powerfully engined, significantly faster, and to keep their cost remotely within reason, much less heavily armored.

These characteristics reflected Fisher's credo that speed and firepower were a warship's most important attributes. Convinced that recent improvements in the quality of naval gunnery had made it possible for future battles to be fought at ranges inaccessible to all except the biggest guns, Fisher reasoned that the battle cruiser's combination of high speed and heavy armament would enable her to dictate the terms of an engagement, holding and hitting an enemy at ranges that would virtually immunize her from being hit in return. The strength of her armor was therefore unimportant. That the battle cruiser would excel at catching and killing armored cruisers was obvious, but Fisher had bigger game in mind. He believed she would be equally adept at eliminating dreadnoughts. "She is," he exulted, "a battleship in disguise!!!"[2] Unlike the dreadnought, however, the battle cruiser did not inspire widespread imitation. At the coming of war, Britain had nine and

Germany five battle cruisers in commission, but Russia and Japan were the only other powers to have begun building them.

Afterward, the abstainers could congratulate themselves, for the battle cruiser, at least in her British format, did not prove a success. Three of the nine engaged at Jutland blew up, and a quarter-century later HMS *Hood*, the last and largest battle cruiser ever built, did the same in action with the *Bismarck*. In fairness, it is necessary to add that two of the problems that contributed to the disasters at Jutland had nothing to do with the battle cruiser concept per se. One was the tendency of British cordite charges to explode rather than merely burn if ignited. The other was the absence of adequate baffles in British shell hoists, which allowed the flash from turret explosions to shoot down the shaft into the shell-handling room at its base and from there to the adjacent magazine. The testimony of survivors and witnesses leaves no doubt that this is what occurred aboard the battle cruisers lost at Jutland. It was also true that, as Fisher grumbled, they had not been used to fight in the manner he had foreseen, although it was less than realistic to expect they always would. Yet none of this would have mattered had they worn enough armor to keep shells out. Four of the five better-protected German battle cruisers at Jutland were heavily damaged, but only the *Lützow* went down, and she had limped to within sixty miles of home.

There was still another reason why the battle cruiser failed to fulfill Fisher's expectations. His confidence in naval gunnery had been to an extent misplaced. In the virtually point-blank battles still fought within living memory, gunners could aim directly at their target. As advances in ordnance and propulsion increased the range and speed at which battles took place, this ceased to be possible; the target would have moved before shells could reach it. For example: at 8,800 yards (5 miles) a ship making 20 knots would travel 120 yards during the 12 seconds a projectile would spend in flight. Thus it became necessary for gunners to aim, not at their target, but at the empty ocean surface they expected it to occupy when their shells arrived. It also became necessary for them to make allowance for their own ship's roll, pitch, and yaw, which could throw off the most expert aim.

Between 1898 and 1907, improvements in training methods and gunlaying techniques pioneered by Admiral Sir Percy Scott overcame most of the difficulties posed by a firing ship's motions. There remained the infinitely more complex problem of calculating the degree of deflection required to compensate for her target's movement. To solve it demanded determining not merely the target's range and bearing, the latter being obtained by the triangulation of sights taken from the fore and after parts of the firing ship, but the rate at which the range was changing, as it must unless the two vessels were steering parallel courses in the same direction at the same speed. Further to complicate matters, the change of range rate was not necessarily constant; depending upon their relative motion, it might itself be changing. So long as such a computation could be made solely on the basis of observation and experience, the prospect of getting it right was remote.

Commencing around the turn of the century, a number of instruments and systems were developed to help deal with this problem. In 1902, a Royal Navy lieutenant, John S. Dumaresq, invented a trigonometric slide rule that became known by his name, on which the user set his ship's speed and course and the target ship's bearing and estimated speed and course. Subject to the accuracy of these estimates (a very considerable qualification) the resultant reading showed the change of range rate and the appropriate deflection. Two years later, the Admiralty began trials that led to the adoption of a mechanical range indicator, the Vickers Clock, designed by one of Britain's leading armaments firms. This instrument consisted of a clockwork motor that moved a pointer around a dial calibrated in thousands of yards. The pointer was set at a starting range and the motor adjusted to run at a speed reflecting a change of range rate obtained from either stopwatch observations or a dumaresq. So long as that rate was constant or changing at a constant rate, the pointer would indicate the range at any given moment. Even though its mechanism could not deal with a rate of change that was itself changing, the Vickers Clock greatly reduced the element of guesswork in gunnery. It became even more helpful after 1906, when the odds of obtaining an accurate starting range were improved by the introduction of a new Barr & Stroud rangefinder capable of measuring distances up to 7,000 yards (4.0 miles) with an error not exceeding 1 percent and up to 10,000 yards (5.6 miles) with little more.

A year earlier, Sir Percy Scott had begun developing director firing, a concept that dated from the 1880s but had remained impractical until electric circuitry permitted shipboard communications to become instantaneous. The idea was to concentrate control of a ship's big guns in the hands of a "director" (her first gunnery officer) who, together with his enlisted assistants, would occupy a "director tower" high up the foremast. From this eyrie, excellently situated for observation with the director's "master sight," cables ran to a central "transmitting station," from which he received firing data, and to the turrets, to which he relayed it. When the guns were laid, the director fired one or all by closing the appropriate circuits, and waited to spot the fall of shot. In the event the director tower was disabled, turrets would revert to local control. The Admiralty, where Scott was regarded as an obstreperous fanatic, long resisted adopting the director system, but reluctantly relented after a highly successful trial in November 1912. Unfortunately, it relented slowly, and at the outbreak of war only a third of Britain's dreadnoughts had been fitted with director towers.

Meanwhile, Arthur Hungerford Pollen, a well-to-do businessman with a profound grasp of technology, had produced a fire control system—in effect, an early analogue computer—that might have given British battle cruisers the gunnery advantage Fisher had assumed they possessed. By 1912, seven years after Pollen secured the Admiralty's support for its development, his system's salient components included a greatly improved rangefinder, a range clock with a variable-speed mechanism that, in contrast to its predecessors, gave an accurate indication of the change of range rate even if the rate was changing, and an automatic plotting table that maintained a continuous real-time record of the courses and relative positions of the firing and target ships.

Pollen's was not, however, the only such system available to the Royal Navy. Ever since 1908, his innovations had been consistently countered by an alternative method or mechanism devised by Lieutenant (later Admiral Sir) Frederick C. Dreyer, a gunnery specialist in whom he had once confided. Dreyer's efforts eventuated in the appearance of the Dreyer Table Mark I, a Rube Goldbergesque apparatus that plotted observed rates of change in a target's range and bearing. The result, put through a built-in dumaresq, indicated the target's speed and course and provided a mathematical change of range rate. Like all of Dreyer's inventions, his table was—to an extent, deliberately—less sophisticated, and, except under ideal conditions, less reliable than the corresponding Pollen product. On the other hand, it was much less expensive and performed to its users' satisfaction in some simple trials. That Dreyer was a naval officer in good standing, whereas Pollen was not only a civilian but, in the eyes of some senior officers, a pushy, grasping civilian, may also have influenced matters. In any case, in 1912 the Admiralty decided that the Dreyer Table was adequate to the navy's needs and allowed its relationship with Pollen to lapse. Four improved models followed up to 1914, but none could equal the performance of the Pollen system.

Whether the adoption of that system would have improved the Royal Navy's shooting sufficiently to make a difference in World War I must remain a matter of conjecture. One recent student has argued that it would not: accurate fire at very long ranges was simply beyond the bounds of technological possibility prior to the appearance of radar and electronic computers.[3] Still, there is no question that the developments outlined above, most of which were duplicated in other major navies, greatly extended the effective reach of ships' guns. In 1904, long range meant upwards of 5,000 yards (2.8 miles); in 1914, it meant upwards of 10,000 yards (5.6 miles).

Yet as the ranges at which hits became frequent lengthened, those at which battles were fought increased. At the Battle of the Falklands in December 1914, the only battle-cruiser action that followed Fisher's scenario, the *Invincible* and the *Inflexible* exploited their superior speed to hold the hopelessly outgunned armored cruisers *Scharnhorst* and *Gneisenau* at ranges varying from 12,000 to 16,000 yards (6.8 to 9.0 miles) and sank both with negligible damage to themselves, but it took them four and a half hours and 1,180 shells, and they scored approximately 6 percent hits. Six weeks later, the five British battle cruisers engaged at Dogger Bank achieved less than 1 percent hits at 16,000 to 18,000 yards (9.0 to 10.2 miles).

Neither of the battle cruisers present at the Falklands and only one of those at Dogger Bank were equipped with director firing, although all carried some sort of Dreyer Table. All except two of the dreadnoughts and battle cruisers engaged at Jutland in mid-1916 had received directors, however, and their shooting showed little improvement. Overall, at ranges of 7,000 to 21,000 yards (4 to 12 miles), their main batteries expended 4,598 shells to score approximately 100 hits, a rate of 2.17 percent. German ships shot better, hitting with 120 of 3,574 shells (3.33 percent) fired by director systems using apparatus comparable to that aboard British vessels except for the absence of any type of plotter. The disadvantage this deficiency seemingly imposed had been more than offset by three factors: the superiority of the German navy's stereoscopic rangefinders, especially in poor visibility; the realism of its training, which accustomed German gunnery officers to cope with sudden and sharp changes in range, course, and bearing; and the manifestly limited utility of the Dreyer Table.

In short, the gunnery revolution remained incomplete. As of 1914, consistent hitting still could not be achieved at the ranges guns could reach, but capital ships equipped with directors could attain a reasonable number of hits up to perhaps 12,500 yards (7.2 miles). At Jutland, for example, the Grand Fleet's flagship, HMS *Iron Duke,* hammered the light cruiser *Wiesbaden* with seven of forty-three shells fired in a five-minute period at approximately that range. And if, on the whole, the fleets engaged in that battle scored about the same small percentage of hits as the U.S. forces at Manila Bay and Santiago, they did so under considerably more difficult conditions and at up to ten times the range.

The battle cruiser's debut signaled the armored cruiser's demise. Only one was laid down after its advent, Germany's *Blücher,* and she was sunk at Dogger Bank. Those already in inventory took part in the war, but they were a dying breed. Light ("scout") cruisers, descendants of the protected cruisers of the late nineteenth century, emerged as the outriders of the fleet. Those in service in the Royal Navy in 1914 displaced from 3,300 to 5,440 tons and could attain speeds of 25.5 knots. All except the earliest mounted 6-inch guns. Their slightly smaller German counterparts were equipped with 4.1-inch guns until 1912 and 5.9-inch thereafter.

Like every other category of combatant, destroyers gained in size during the prewar decade. They also became much more dangerous. This they owed to the invention of the heater torpedo, which used hot gas rather than simple compressed air to power its engine and could run twice as far as preceding types: in its German 1906 version, up to 6,000 yards (3.4 miles) at 36 knots and for shorter distances at greater speeds. At the start of the war, the latest British destroyers, built according to a design philosophy that emphasized their defensive function—that is, the destruction of other destroyers—displaced about 1,000 tons, carried three 4-inch guns and two torpedo tubes, and had a top speed of 29 knots. The latest German destroyers, built according to a philosophy that emphasized their offensive function—the destruction of big ships—displaced at most 800 tons and had only 3.5-inch guns, but mounted four torpedo tubes and could make 33 knots. Both types soon acquired the additional responsibility of screening their battle lines from hostile submarines.

Submarines, the other principal beneficiary of the heater torpedo, had made great strides since 1904, when the French had solved the propulsion problem that compromised the performance or safety of earlier boats by the introduction of the diesel (surface)/electric (submerged) system that powered submarines throughout both world wars. In 1914, recent models had an operational radius of nearly four thousand nautical miles and the ability to travel up to eighty nautical miles underwater before the need to recharge their batteries compelled them to surface. By then, Britain and France each had about seventy-five boats in commission. Germany, the last major power to begin building submarines—the first *Unterseeboot* was not launched until 1908—had twenty-eight. At the close of a prewar VIP briefing extolling the capabilities of the new craft, Saxony's notoriously plainspoken King Friedrich August III had posed a very good question: "Well, then, why don't we have more of them?"[4]

The answer was that, its progress notwithstanding, the submarine's potential remained generally unrecognized. A Greek boat, the *Delfin,* had fired a dud at a Turkish cruiser during the First Balkan War (1912–13), but a ship had yet to be hit, much less sunk, by a submarine-launched torpedo. Despite the Royal Navy's use of one of its boats in conjunction with the battle fleet in the 1910 maneuvers, submarines continued to be regarded primarily as instruments of coast defense.

How seriously they had been underestimated was revealed in the war's opening months. When the British fleet declined to appear in German waters, the Imperial Navy sent its U-boats out looking for trouble. On 5 September 1914, *Kapitänleutnant* Otto Hersing's *U-21* became the first submarine to destroy an enemy vessel, dispatching the light cruiser *Pathfinder* with a single torpedo, and one afternoon later that month *Kapitänleutnant* Otto

Weddigen's *U-9* sank an entire squadron of armored cruisers, HMS *Aboukir, Cressy,* and *Hogue,* off the Dutch coast. Weddigen's success proceeded in part from his victims' faulty reactions (the first ship hit assumed she had struck a mine and the second was preparing to take off survivors when he torpedoed her), but it forever established the submarine as a major factor in war at sea.

During the next four years, U-boats would account for more than sixty other warships. With a very few exceptions, however, these sinkings were the results of chance encounters. In 1915 and 1916, both sides made repeated attempts to integrate submarines into fleet operations, principally by establishing patrol lines across which the enemy was to be enticed, but somehow something always went wrong: either destroyers held the submarines at arm's length or the enemy force passed through the patrol line without being sighted or it steered another course, after all. The great submarine ambush that seemed so plausible in planning never took place. In a sense, that scarcely mattered. After Weddigen's exploit, it was not necessary for a submarine to be anywhere in the vicinity to complicate the conduct of surface operations. The mere possibility that one might be sufficed.

Moreover, by the turn of the year 1914–15 the German navy had decided its U-boats could be most productively employed to respond to the British surface blockade of Germany by establishing a counter-blockade of Britain; that is, by *guerre de course.* This was a task for which they were superbly suited in all respects save one. A submarine is armored in invisibility. When it becomes visible, it becomes vulnerable, and international prize law required it to become visible. According to prize law, a commerce raider could not sink a merchant ship without confirming that her cargo included war material (contraband), which necessitated sending an officer to examine her papers, and making provision for the safety of her passengers, if any, and crew. To observe this etiquette, a U-boat had to come to the surface, and although some did, the practice was fraught with peril, especially after the British Admiralty began arming merchantmen and sending out decoys called Q-ships bristling with hidden guns. The alternative, to sink noncombatant vessels without warning, struck prewar sensibilities as so barbarous that in January 1914 Britain's First Lord of the Admiralty, Winston Churchill, scorned the idea that a civilized power would ever adopt such a policy.

In February 1915 the Imperial Navy's leaders did not perceive this to be a problem. The proclamation of a precisely delineated "ocean war zone" around the British Isles expressly warned that vessels, even neutrals, found inside it were liable to be sunk on sight. Intimidation was part of the program; moreover, from a German perspective the British blockade, including as it did foodstuffs, appeared no less inhumane. Six weeks later, the *U-20* sank the British liner *Lusitania,* with the loss of 1,198 lives, including 128 Americans. President Woodrow Wilson responded with angry protests implying that unless Germany abandoned unrestricted submarine warfare, the United States would declare war. The problem then became fully apparent. To respect international law forfeited the U-boats' chief operational asset. To violate it risked adding the United States to Germany's already daunting list of enemies. After months of haggling, the Imperial government acceded to the president's demands, but the final reckoning had merely been postponed.

Mines, the other concealed weapon in the naval arsenal, also played an influential part in the world war. Indeed, their influence predated its outbreak. In 1912 the extent of the minefields girding the German coast, coupled with the threat of surface and subsurface torpedo attacks, led the British to conclude that in the event of war it would be too costly to maintain a coastal blockade of the sort traditionally imposed on France. Instead, they decided to establish a "distant blockade" of the exits from the North Sea, thereby conceding the German navy unimpeded access to a body of water that lapped the British Isles. In the course of the conflict, some 247,000 mines were laid, 11,000 from specially configured German submarines. Altogether, mines sank approximately 140 warships—more than submarines' torpedoes, more than other warships' guns—including seven battleships (six predreadnought) and, in an impromptu demonstration of the danger the Admiralty had apprehended, seven of eleven German destroyers that ran into Russian minefields in the Gulf of Finland one night in 1916.

While mines and submarines created a new dimension of naval warfare under the sea, aircraft and airships opened one above it. Powered flight, made practical by the development of the relatively lightweight internal combustion engine, was achieved by Count Zeppelin's rigid airship in 1900 and the Wright brothers' heavier-than-air craft in 1903. The interest with which admiralties began to monitor the progress of both technologies quickened after the French aviator Henri Fabre built the first seaplane in 1910, and despite the usual skeptics, by 1914 at least eight navies had instituted air services. Three even made provision to take a few aircraft afloat, converting existing vessels into seaplane carriers: the French the cruiser *Foudre* in March 1912, the British the cruiser *Hermes* in May 1913, and the Japanese a former merchantman, renamed the *Wakamiya,* in November 1913. In the meantime, the Royal Hellenic Navy became the first to use an aircraft in combat when in February 1913 one of its seaplanes dropped four small bombs, all misses, on Turkish warships in the Dardanelles during the Second Balkan War.

These pioneering activities notwithstanding, as of 1914 naval aviation remained embryonic. Upon its detachment from the Royal Flying Corps that July, Britain's Royal Naval Air Service, then the world's largest, numbered 50 officers, 550 men, 91 aircraft, and 7 nonrigid airships. Following the outbreak of war, the belligerent navies rapidly and repeatedly increased the strength of their air forces. At the time of its incorporation into the Royal

Air Force in April 1918, the Royal Naval Air Service, still the world's largest, numbered 5,000 officers, 43,000 men, 3,000 aircraft, and 100 nonrigid airships.

The most important mission foreseen for both aircraft and airships was reconnaissance. In the crucial North Sea theater, the Imperial German Navy's Zeppelins performed this task about as well as weather permitted—it kept them grounded three days out of four—during the war's opening years, when their high ceiling and rate of climb safeguarded them from interception by aircraft not airborne upon their approach. In 1917 advances in heavier-than-air technology put an end to their inviolability, but by then they had logged 568 scouting flights and reported observations of tactical value to the High Seas Fleet on several of its sorties. Fortunately for the British, high winds prevented five Zeppelins from carrying out a scheduled reconnaissance before the fleets made contact in Jutland.

A prewar attempt by the Royal Navy to build a rigid airship having ended in ignominy, the Grand Fleet initially relied on aircraft flying from coastal bases or embarked in seaplane carriers. The results were disappointing. Shore-based planes lacked the range to accompany the fleet far from land, and at sea weather conditions more often than not made it impossible for seaplanes to take off. At Jutland the *Engadine,* a seaplane carrier assigned to the British Battle Cruiser Fleet, succeeded in getting one of her four planes into the air early in the action. This aircraft, the first to participate in a fleet engagement, made a potentially helpful sighting report, but the message did not get through to the fleet flagship, and after a flight of thirty-nine minutes a broken fuel pipe forced it down. The British nonetheless persisted in the aim of incorporating aircraft into the fleet, and in 1917 they began to develop true carriers, an initiative examined in the following survey.

In addition to reconnaissance, naval aircraft essayed most of the other missions they would perform between 1939 and 1945, attacking and defending land and sea targets, harrying submarines, and correcting fire in shore bombardments. The major difference was that between 1914 and 1918 they could not carry big enough bombs or deliver them with sufficient accuracy to endanger surface vessels of any size. When in January 1918, the Turkish battle cruiser *Yavuz Sultan Selim* (formerly the German *Goeben*) spent five unhappy days aground in the Dardanelles, a sitting duck 612 feet long, British single-engine bombers showered her with fifteen tons of explosives during more than two hundred sorties and scored two trifling hits. Thus, despite the importance aircraft achieved in other contexts, their influence on high-seas surface operations was marginal.

The limitations imposed by the use of low frequencies notwithstanding, radio played a vital role. By 1914 signals sent by very high-power transmitters could carry almost three thousand miles, and the colonial powers had begun building relay stations to link their overseas possessions. British forces quickly severed Germany's global communications net, but that did not affect operations in the North Sea, where both sides were within easy reach of home stations. Shipboard wireless equipment also had increased in range and reliability. Initially installed only in big ships, wireless had been added to destroyers and submarines well before the war, and soon became standard equipment in observation planes and airships.

At the onset of hostilities, flag hoists and signal lamps remained a faster means of making tactical signals. "Repeated" by designated ships, a practice dating from the Age of Sail, they could be carried out in two or three minutes, while because of time lost in handling, wireless signals took ten to fifteen minutes. By 1916, however, improved procedures allowed them to be executed with equal alacrity and the great advantage that they did not depend upon visual recognition. This was especially important in the North Sea, where pervasive fogs and mists deepened the obscurity in which coal-burning fleets firing cordite charges were apt to enshroud themselves. The forces engaged at Jutland could hardly have been maneuvered as effectively as they were without radio communications.

But the capacity of the electronic envelope in which naval warfare now occurred exceeded the conduct of communications between friendly forces; it could be exploited to disseminate disinformation and plundered to gather intelligence. The first radio deception, unless Rozhdestvenski's imposition of radio silence as his fleet neared Japanese waters can be considered such, was practiced by Vice Admiral Count Maximilian von Spee's German East Asia Squadron in October 1914. Arriving off the coast of Chile after an undetected voyage across the South Pacific, it restricted its wireless traffic to the light cruiser *Leipzig* to give the impression that only a single German ship was in the vicinity. Rear Admiral Sir Christopher Cradock's much weaker squadron was therefore surprised to encounter five of von Spee's cruisers off Cape Coronel, where it went down to the first serious defeat the Royal Navy had suffered in more than a century. Later in the war, the Germans routinely transferred the High Seas Fleet flagship's DK call sign ashore before the fleet sortied to preserve the appearance that it remained in port. Before Jutland, they even sent the flagship's regular wireless operator ashore, so that British eavesdroppers would not detect the "touch" of an unfamiliar hand on the key.

If intercepted messages might mislead, they could also be extremely enlightening. During the Russo-Japanese War, all that the antagonists had been able to learn from one another's signals was that the sender was somewhere within range of their receivers. Since then, the development of radio direction finding enabled two or more stations taking cross-bearings on the same transmission to pinpoint the position of senders hundreds of miles away. The operational implications were obvious, and by the spring of 1915 the Royal Navy had built five stations to sweep the North Sea; later, other stations were positioned to reach into the North Atlantic. These facilities' reports proved of great value to British forces in the surface campaign against the High Seas Fleet, and, together with the shipboard rangefinders the U.S. Navy began installing in its destroyers in 1917, helped to defeat the second unrestricted U-boat offensive. The Germans also established direction-finding stations on the North Sea, but the extreme reticence the British observed in wireless communications limited their productivity.

Given that being able to determine the enemy's whereabouts in the course of his operations was a great advantage, the advantage of being able to anticipate those operations was greater still. This was made possible by signals intelligence, the practice of analyzing the enemy's radio traffic to detect changes in the pattern of his transmissions and breaking the ciphers in which he had veiled them. No navy had prepared to conduct such activities prior to the war. Very soon after its outbreak, however, accidental intercepts of enciphered enemy messages inspired the British and German navies to institute signals intelligence services. The British became noncommittally known as Room 40, the office assigned it in the Admiralty Old Building in November 1914; the German, situated at Neumünster, south of Kiel, was forthrightly entitled the Deciphering Service (*Entzifferungsdienst* or *E-Dienst*).

Before the end of 1914, Room 40 received an incredible windfall in the form of no fewer than three German naval code books: two retrieved from sunken warships and one seized aboard an interned merchantman. Although in time the Germans changed their ciphers, the insight that had been gained into their methods and their relatively unrestrained use of wireless allowed Room 40 to read their signals almost without interruption throughout the war, even after the cipher began to be changed daily. Because the Germans customarily transmitted their operations orders in writing, limiting most of Room 40's intercepts to consequential communications, such as instructions to minesweepers to clear a certain channel by a certain time, British cryptographers could seldom discover exactly what the High Seas Fleet was up to, but they could deduce that it was up to something. Of the sixteen sorties it made after November 1914, Room 40 gave advanced notice of fourteen and reported the others while they were in progress. As the war wore on, the obvious excellence of British intelligence provoked the Germans to look for a source of leaks. They concluded that their ciphers could not be broken (a mistake destined to be repeated in World War II) and focused their suspicions on espionage and treason.

German signals intelligence lacked the luck that facilitated its rival's success. Whereas in 1916 Room 40 obtained still a fourth German code book from a Zeppelin downed over England, the *E-Dienst* never gained access to one of their British equivalents. Furthermore, British reserve denied the *E-Dienst* more than a fraction of the material with which German garrulity regaled Room 40. That its achievements were modest does not seem surprising.

The cumulative effect of the systems and technologies, electronic and otherwise, that had begun to appear in the Machine Age upon the conditions of World War I naval combat was profound. It was true that despite the intervention of the aircraft and the submarine, big ships mounting big guns remained supreme. It was also true that those ships fought in the traditional line ahead, so that all their heavy turrets could traverse to bear in broadside. But if the style of battle had not changed fundamentally, its dimensions and tempo had increased dramatically.

Thanks to improvements in wireless and the introduction of direction finding, a fleet's intelligence surround, tactical as well as strategic, might embrace an entire theater of war. In any event, it would extend as far in any direction as that fleet's most distant component. The potential extent of the battle area also underwent a considerable though much less extreme expansion. This was most notable in the North Sea arena, where the effect of the advances in naval gunnery was compounded by the size of the opposing fleets. In the great clashes of the Anglo-Dutch Wars it had not been unusual for 80 to upwards of 100 vessels to be present on each side, but the strategic circumstances of the Anglo-French Wars were such that neither belligerent brought such numbers into any action after Barfleur, and except for Navarino, the battles fought since 1815 had involved lesser naval powers. There were, in all, 57 fighting ships at Quiberon Bay; 37 at the Nile; 69 at Trafalgar; 22 at Mobile Bay; 58 at Lissa; 26 at the Yalu; and, excluding torpedo boats, gunboats, and fleet auxiliaries, 78 at Tsushima. At Jutland there were 249: 150 British and 99 German. Although by the time the British battle line came into action patchy visibility limited the area in which ships were actually exchanging fire to approximately 25 square miles, the two fleets occupied at least 60 square miles, and immediately after the last exchange of fire prior to nightfall they extended over roughly 130 square miles. Even with the assistance of the staffs fleet commanders had acquired since the turn of the century—Jellicoe's numbered sixteen officers[5]—to exercise effective control over forces engaged in operations on this scale was a difficult undertaking.

Of still greater consequence to the conduct of battle than the expansion of its area was the acceleration of its pace. In the Age of Sail, the combined closing speed of two well-ordered lines of battle did not exceed four to six knots; that of two dreadnought battle squadrons was about forty knots. The hours that the fleets of years past had spent in visual contact before they could commence firing were compressed into minutes, and sometimes less: in poor light, hostile formations might not catch sight of one another until they were near enough to open fire the instant they did. Such circumstances placed the power of decision at a premium. During the long approach to Trafalgar, Nelson had six hours to dispose his fleet. At Jutland, where insufficient information as to the bearing of the enemy battle squadrons forced him to delay his deployment to the last possible moment, Jellicoe did not have many more than the twenty seconds he actually took.[6]

In 1914, as in 1814, the Royal Navy was incomparably the strongest in the world. True, the German naval challenge—that most counterproductive attempt at coercion, which almost guaranteed that in the case of a general war Britain would intervene on the side opposed to Germany—had led to an apparent lessening of the margin of naval superiority the British government pledged itself to uphold. In 1912 the two-power standard formally in effect since 1889, stipulating that the Royal Navy should be maintained at a strength equal to that of the next two strongest navies plus 10 percent, was abandoned in favor of a one-power standard requiring it to be maintained at a strength equal to that of the next strongest navy plus 60 percent. While some observers interpreted the change as a retreat, the Admiralty calculated that should the second strongest navy (the German) substantially outbuild the third (that of the United States), the new standard would actually provide a greater margin of superiority than the old. In fact, if applied to modern capital ships at the outbreak of war, it would have produced exactly the same result. In July 1914, Germany had thirty in commission or under construction, and together Germany and the United States had forty-four. The maintenance of either the one-power or the two-power standard would have given Britain forty-eight. Construction having fallen below formula, she actually had forty-two, which were immediately reinforced by the requisition of three being built for foreign powers. The augmented total, though still short of the magic number, gave the Royal Navy a commanding capital-ship superiority of exactly 50 percent.

How these ships compared to their German opposites is a question that still exercises historians. German vessels were beamier and their underwater compartmentation was more minute. The former made them steadier gun platforms and allowed for better protection against mine and torpedo hits; the latter, achieved at the expense of crew comfort, facilitated damage control in the event of flooding. (These were advantages for which the Royal Navy was unable to compete. The beam of its ships was constricted by the breadth of docks dating from Victorian times, and as a global force faced with the prospect of distant deployments, it could not sacrifice habitability with such abandon as one intended to operate close to home in the North Sea and the Baltic.) Finally, German ships carried more and thicker armor, which, together with the features described above, made them highly resistant to damage and extremely difficult to sink.

On the other hand, British capital ships were faster and more heavily armed. The first two classes of German dreadnoughts, eight vessels in all, had reciprocating engines that gave them a maximum speed of 19.5 knots, against the earliest British dreadnoughts' 21 knots, and their turbine-powered successors remained 1.5 to 2 knots slower than British contemporaries. Inferiority in firepower was the price German ships paid for their durability, since every ton of displacement allocated to armor meant one less for guns and munitions. Of the thirty-seven British dreadnoughts and battle cruisers at Jutland, twenty-two mounted 13.5- to 15-inch guns and none less than 12-inch; of the twenty-one German, none mounted more than 12-inch and six only 11-inch. Even had the 12-inch-gunned British ships not been present, the remainder would have hurled almost twice the weight of metal as the German. Unfortunately for the Royal Navy, the benefit it might have derived from this imbalance was largely vitiated by the gunnery problems already examined and the propensity of its armor-piercing shells to burst on impact.

Which side's ships were the better overall can be argued either way. Jellicoe expressed his opinion in a memorandum of 14 July 1914, warning that "assuming equality in design it is dangerous to consider that our ships as a whole are superior or even equal fighting machines."[7] Whether that was true, it cannot have been a comforting thought to a man who would shortly assume command of the Grand Fleet.

Notes

1. For a detailed account, see Jon Tetsuro Sumida, *In Defence of Naval Supremacy: Finance, Technology and British Naval Policy, 1889–1914* (Boston: Unwin Hyman, 1989).

2. Ibid., p. 58.

3. Robert L. O'Connell, *Sacred Vessels: The Cult of the Battleship and the Rise of the U.S. Navy* (New York: Oxford University Press, 1991), pp. 118–19.

4. Friedrich Kracke, *Friedrich August III: Sachsens volkstümlicher König* (Munich: Studiengruppe für Sächsische Geschichte und Kultur, 1965), p. 138.

5. To wit: a chief of staff and three "war staff" (plans and operations) officers; a "captain of the fleet" responsible for logistics and drills; a fleet navigation officer; a signals officer with two assistants; a wireless officer with an assistant; a fleet coaling officer; a flag secretary and an additional secretary; and a flag commander and flag lieutenant.

6. For this comparison and a detailed discussion of the situation that inspired it, see Admiral Sir R. H. Bacon, *The Life of John Rushworth, Earl Jellicoe* (London: Cassell, 1936), pp. 264–68, 301–2.

7. Correlli Barnett, *The Swordbearers: Supreme Command in the First World War* (Bloomington: Indiana University Press, 1975), p. 116.

14

John R. Jellicoe

Technology's Victim

(1859–1935)

James Goldrick

HIS FINAL STYLE AND TITLES DESCRIBED HIS ACHIEVEMENTS. When John Rushworth Jellicoe died in 1935 at the age of seventy-five, he was an Admiral of the Fleet, an Earl, a Knight Grand Cross of the Order of the Bath and of the Royal Victorian Order, and a member of the Order of Merit.

He had come far. Born at Southampton on 5 December 1859, son of a Royal Mail Line captain, Jellicoe was the product of the Victorian English middle class and the traditions of service and self-improvement it cherished. In this he was also an exemplar of the Royal Navy's tendency to derive its greatest leaders from that same middle class.

Jellicoe was a marked man from the start. Described as "one of the cleverest cadets" ever to enter the training ship *Britannia*,[1] he did equally well as a midshipman and in his examinations for lieutenant, gaining First Class certificates at every opportunity. Jellicoe's academic abilities were accompanied by sporting skills and a flair for practical work, notably in seamanship. A natural leader, he was clearly destined for the top.

Jellicoe was admired not only by his seniors and subordinates but by his contemporaries, that most critical audience. But courteous, friendly, and apparently unassuming as he was, Jellicoe was very sure of himself and determined to succeed. Before his entry to the Royal Navy, he did not conceal his ambition to become "Admiral Sir John Jellicoe."[2]

Yet the ability to inspire both affection and admiration at all levels while sustaining an absolute conviction in his own rectitude means that Jellicoe represents a paradox for the historian, for that conviction hardened as he aged. Invariably tactful with mistaken superiors, he became unwilling to bear subordinates whom he thought to be speaking out of turn. Those who enjoyed Jellicoe's confidence always declared that he was receptive to new ideas and lent his staff a sympathetic ear.[3] In truth, his record of handling those zealous for reform was never good[4] and he suffered from an inability to delegate. This tendency was magnified by the inadequacy of the Admiralty's bureaucracy, which found him having to occupy senior appointments in Whitehall with scant technical or clerical support. Doing everything himself left little space for other views.

Jellicoe was not alone in this failing. Social commentary on the Royal Navy of his era is unanimous on the extent of "Very Senior Officer Veneration."[5] But his restrictive ideas as to how the Grand Fleet should be fought and his lack of sympathy with any alternative confined the potential of his command within even tighter bounds than Jellicoe himself conceived. Because his subordinates expected to have little to do on their initiative, that initiative atrophied; because uncontrolled aggression could put the Grand Fleet at risk, there would be no aggression at all; because there was little to gain from night fighting, in the event even less would be gained. As Admiral Sir Herbert Richmond was later to observe, "The tactical doctrine was the reflex of [Jellicoe's] whole attitude. Safety was at the bottom of his mind throughout, not destruction of the enemy."[6]

In two ways, Jellicoe's career served to reinforce his natural caution. A gunnery officer closely associated with the early reforms of John Fisher, he was later not only a member of the committee that developed the design for the first all-big-gun battleship, the *Dreadnought,* but director of Naval Ordnance and Controller. Between 1884 and 1914 there were few technical weapon developments with which he was not concerned. This involvement instilled in Jellicoe a belief that the Royal Navy possessed as many weaknesses as strengths. Essentially practical in his outlook, but neither engineer nor scientist, he was eventually overwhelmed by the ever-increasing complexity of the navy's matériel problems. He would make do instead—but cautiously.

Such technical judgments were congruous with Jellicoe's seagoing experience. The ability to make the best out of the material at hand was and is the hallmark of the successful executive officer of big ships. In this, as commander in the battleships *Sans Pareil, Victoria,* and *Ramillies,* Jellicoe was superlative. He gave further evidence of his ability to improvise when he served as chief of staff for the international naval force sent to relieve Peking during the Boxer Rebellion in 1900. His combination of tact in dealing with the foreign naval contingents and personal courage were sorely missed after his evacuation with a bullet in his left lung.

It is important to note that Jellicoe saw little independent service until his command of the Atlantic Fleet in 1910. He did not even command a private ship—that is, one without a flag officer embarked—until the cruiser *Drake* as a forty-four-year-old captain. Jellicoe was a "company" man in every sense of the term.

To ensure that he would be in command of the Grand Fleet, the newly assembled principal battle force in home waters, Jellicoe was sent posthaste to sea in August 1914 on the eve of war, with the warning that he must be prepared to take over as commander in chief from the incumbent, Admiral Sir George Callaghan.

Jellicoe did not relish the prospect of peremptorily relieving an old friend, but the Admiralty was convinced that he was the only man to manage the war at sea. Early in the morning of 4 August the change was made. As an acting admiral, Sir John Jellicoe was now commander in chief of the Grand Fleet.

The situation was not an easy one. The key to the British strategy was the distant blockade, by which the passages to the Atlantic were shut to German shipping. In theory, Germany was thus closed off to maritime commerce, but the definition of contraband of war had become so narrow by 1914 that it took many months and ruthless action in the face of neutral protests before the Allies could be sure that this economic weapon was having real effects.

Distant, as opposed to close or observational, blockade was the result of the realization that steam power, the mine, and the torpedo had between them rendered impossible a constant watch upon the enemy in his ports. Successive prewar exercises had demonstrated not only how easily a hostile force could slip past a blockade but also the facility with which the blockading force could be worn down.

Sensible as the distant blockade was, it did little to protect the British east coast, which lay open to German raids. Jellicoe himself admitted that without adequate warning "it must be realised that the fleet cannot stop [a raid]."[7] The increasing vulnerability of surface ships to submarines made matters worse. The CinC was forced to abandon the battle fleet sweeps into the southern North Sea that he had initiated at the start of the war.[8]

The lack of bases on the east coast added another dimension to the problem. Plans to develop Scapa Flow as a fleet base and Rosyth as a dockyard were little advanced in 1914 and neither they nor any other northern anchorage possessed realistic protection against submarines or mines. Much of Jellicoe's energy in the first months of the war was consumed by his frantic efforts to improve these bases and to keep the Grand Fleet safe in the meantime. Despite the strain on men and machinery, the CinC was able to maintain both morale and efficiency throughout his squadrons[9] while pushing the pace of improvements to harbor defenses as hard as he could.

By 1916 there would be more than enough defended anchorages but they were concentrated in the north. No matter how well protected, no harbor south of Rosyth could take more than a squadron of heavy ships in all conditions of tide.

Jellicoe's approach to the raid problem was simple. He would do all that he could to get the German ships if they were to attempt any attacks upon the long and ill-protected east coast. But such raids could have little more than propaganda value. The most effective British reply would be destruction of the perpetrators, which could practicably be achieved only after the event. This may have held little comfort for the inhabitants for the east coast towns, but it was the only choice.

Jellicoe was also concerned with the risk of a defeat in detail. The loss of a single battle squadron would reduce the Royal Navy's margin of superiority in the North Sea to nothing. This danger also applied to the battle cruisers under Vice Admiral Sir David Beatty that were stationed at Rosyth from late 1914. As Jellicoe wrote to Beatty in March 1915, "It is quite all right if you keep your speed, of course, but it is the reverse if you have some ships with their speed badly reduced in the fight with the [German] battle cruisers, or by submarines."[10]

In the process of impressing his ideas upon the Grand Fleet, Jellicoe began to develop comprehensive orders for its operations. His book, *The Grand Fleet 1914–1916: Its Creation, Development and Work,* is an indispensable reference in any consideration not only of this evolution of doctrine but of Jellicoe's performance as a commander. Yet it is an apologia that must be treated with care. Jellicoe naturally sought to justify his actions as CinC and he tended to give the impression that his analysis of the strategic and tactical situation on assuming command was more coherent than was in fact the case. *The Grand Fleet* must therefore be studied in conjunction with the steadily developing *Grand Fleet Battle Orders* to gain a complete picture of Jellicoe's intentions.

In the first place, Jellicoe had an absolute belief in the reliance of the Germans upon "submarines, mines and torpedoes" and in "their actual superiority" in these arms.[11] Conversely, although he was equally convinced of the superiority of the Grand Fleet in heavy guns, he was conscious that this could be sustained only under certain conditions. The first of these was visibility. If this were to be reduced in the course of an action, the British would not only face a concomitant increase in the danger of a torpedo attack but the advantage of the heavier armament of their capital ships would be lost.

Jellicoe extended this view to the subject of night actions, remarking that "night actions between heavy ships must always be largely a matter of *chance,* as there is little opportunity for skill on either side."[12] His idea was that preservation of the British battle line was paramount and to this effect he intended that the Grand Fleet flotillas first act in their destroyer role to neutralize any torpedo attack, only then themselves moving against the enemy heavy ships.

Jellicoe went further. So convinced was he of the superiority of German night-fighting techniques that he was inclined to think that any encounter would have few benefits for the British, because "we were bound to suffer serious losses with no corresponding advantage."[13]

The second factor derived from the inability of the Grand Fleet to sustain accurate fire while maneuvering. The gunnery fire control problem has been exposed at length in recent years in the debate over the relative merits of the Pollen and Dreyer systems.[14] The fact is that the equipment operational in 1916 was not helm free—that is, it could not maintain an accurate solution while the firing ship was in the turn or for some time afterward, even when only one turn was involved, let alone multiple alterations in short succession. The fire control systems were also incapable of dealing with the high rates of change of range rate that were implicit when firing at a maneuvering target.

The Grand Fleet could expect to achieve an effective number of hits at long range only if the engaged forces were meeting in the classical line of battle artillery duel. In but one other instance, that of crossing the enemy's T, in which the geometry of the situation would place the least strain upon predictive systems, could the Grand Fleet have any confidence that it would be effective.

Whatever Jellicoe's part was in the decision to eschew Pollen in favor of the inferior Dreyer system, he was acutely aware of the limitations of British technology. Despite the naïveté suggested by Jellicoe's plaint that "only I want to fight them fairly,"[15] his plans of action reflected not so much the wishful thinking suggested by some[16] as that awareness.

Apart from the obvious problems of command, it is likely that these same limitations in fire control prejudiced Jellicoe absolutely against divided tactics, whereby subordinate admirals could maneuver their squadrons independently in order to exploit some local advantage. Implying as they did frequent turns at decreasing ranges to the enemy, there existed the danger that squadrons so engaged would be open to a concentration of fire from nonmaneuvering opponents while themselves unable to shoot with any accuracy.

Jellicoe also faced a dilemma over the use of armor-piercing shell as opposed to high explosive. Despite his subsequent protestations over the discovery of the inferiority of armor-piercing shell at Jutland,[17] it is likely that he was aware of the problem from prewar experiments.[18] He himself favored the use of high-explosive shells, believing that the "weight of bursting charge"[19] would disable an opponent's fire control and command arrangements, leaving him helpless.

Gunnery was not the only difficulty. Jellicoe faced unprecedented problems in maneuvering the Grand Fleet. The largest steam-powered tactical formation in history, it had to be handled at higher speeds and in more extreme conditions than had ever been attempted. In order to reduce his battle line to practical dimensions, Jellicoe ordered a standard distance of only five hundred yards for his dreadnoughts.[20] Even so, with twenty battleships in company the line was more than five miles in length.

Given his need to place the two hundred guns of the battle fleet in the most favorable position, the tactical integrity of the big ships represented Jellicoe's overweening preoccupation. Overcautious the CinC may have been, but the practical difficulties involved in any maneuver in a sea in which the visibility was not often sufficient for him to encompass all his command cannot be underestimated. The German "battle turns together" (*Gefechtskehrtwendung*) at Jutland demonstrated what could be done in an emergency, but Jellicoe regarded the risks of such tactics as unacceptable. He felt that he had to confine himself to maneuvers that were safe in any visibility or sea state.[21]

Jellicoe's unwillingness to take risks resulted principally from his preoccupation with his concept of the "chosen moment." He was convinced that the Germans could organize an assault at the time of their greatest strength, with no important units detached from the High Seas Fleet, and at the weakest moment for the British. Since Jellicoe had to accept a regular program of refits in the interests of his fleet's long-term efficiency, he was the more certain to set his face against any "operation tending to weaken [the] Grand Fleet."[22] In reality, the Germans had their own problems with dockyards and they were sometimes willing to act with an incomplete order of battle.

The most extraordinary thing about Jellicoe as commander in chief is the extent to which he accepted the technological limitations of the Grand Fleet as they were when he took command. To some extent this was only proper. Responsibility for technical development rested in Whitehall, although the Grand Fleet's record of innovation was not unimpressive.[23] But Jellicoe always felt that he could not devote time to experiments at the expense of current operational standards. This was one of his objections to attempting divided tactics.[24] Because Jellicoe believed that the High Seas Fleet could sortie with little or no warning he felt that he had to keep the fleet trained in what he knew it could do, not what it might achieve.

Yet it is clear that Jellicoe adhered too closely to his self-imposed restrictions as time passed. The dangers of simply accepting what he found and minimizing risks were as much psychological as material because they did not encourage that eye for the main chance that was essential if the Grand Fleet were to achieve substantial success against the Germans. In particular, Jellicoe did not make sufficient use of the wealth of operational experience that became available as the war went on.

This information was directly utilized in only one significant area. As well as the *Magdeburg*, a series of fortunate encounters[25] placed all the German basic cyphers in British hands by the end of 1914 and the Admiralty was able to develop a highly effective system on this foundation. Known as "Room 40 Old Building," it was by 1916 capable of decrypting the majority of German transmissions within a few hours—soon enough to be of real tactical as well as strategic value. Unfortunately, the organization lacked the understanding necessary between signal analysis and operations staff if decryptions were to be properly interpreted. Jellicoe himself sought to create a decryption cell aboard his flagship but a security-conscious Admiralty would not permit it.

The danger signs for Jellicoe's ideal of fighting the enemy were there to be seen well before Jutland in the few abortive encounters that did take place between units of the Grand and High Seas Fleets.

During the Battle of Heligoland Bight on 28 August 1914, British communications were poor and operations ill-coordinated. The Admiralty made the error of ordering a sweep by light cruisers and destroyer flotillas deep into German waters without thought of the risks to which these ships would be exposed if they met heavier German metal so far from their own ports. Jellicoe's dispatch of Beatty's squadrons as reinforcements and the latter's speedy intervention saved the day. The Germans lost three light cruisers and a torpedo boat; the more thoughtful officers in the Royal Navy had been badly frightened.

Although Jellicoe was able to ensure that command arrangements would never again be so muddled, there was insufficient close analysis of the affair for equally serious problems to become manifest. Few of the light cruisers or destroyers had been able to maintain an adequate navigational reckoning; there were discrepancies on such a scale that each squadron was hard put to reconstruct a coherent picture of events, let alone maintain one in "real time." To compound this shortcoming, there had been no systematic efforts to relay sufficient enemy contact reports. Herein lay the seed of Jellicoe's greatest but least comprehended difficulty at Jutland.

Jellicoe was later to quip, "Never imagine that the CinC sees what you see"—after a tactical floor reconstruction of the Battle of Jutland. Yet even he does not seem to have comprehended the extent of the shortcomings until it was too late. The truth was that there was no idea of an action information organization at sea in 1914–16. Not even flagships went so far as to have an officer designated for signal-writing duties at action stations.[26] Manning did not allow operation of a tactical plot except in the most senior flagships. Sir Arthur Wilson, a former First Sea Lord, put the problem in a nutshell when he complained in December 1914 that "very few Admirals have the 'mooring board mind'! They steer for where the enemy is, not where he will be."[27]

It was a vicious circle. Because they had no adequate methods for displaying, processing, and transmitting tactical information, the British commanders had little chance of developing a comprehensible tactical picture. Without such a picture, sensible instructions could not be initiated nor assessments distributed to subordinate commands. With little or no knowledge of what was going on, the chance sighting could not be placed in perspective and its significance comprehended by these subordinates. Schooled to keep their traffic to a minimum (and the signal system had a very limited capacity), they were too quick to assume that their seniors must be seeing what they themselves saw.

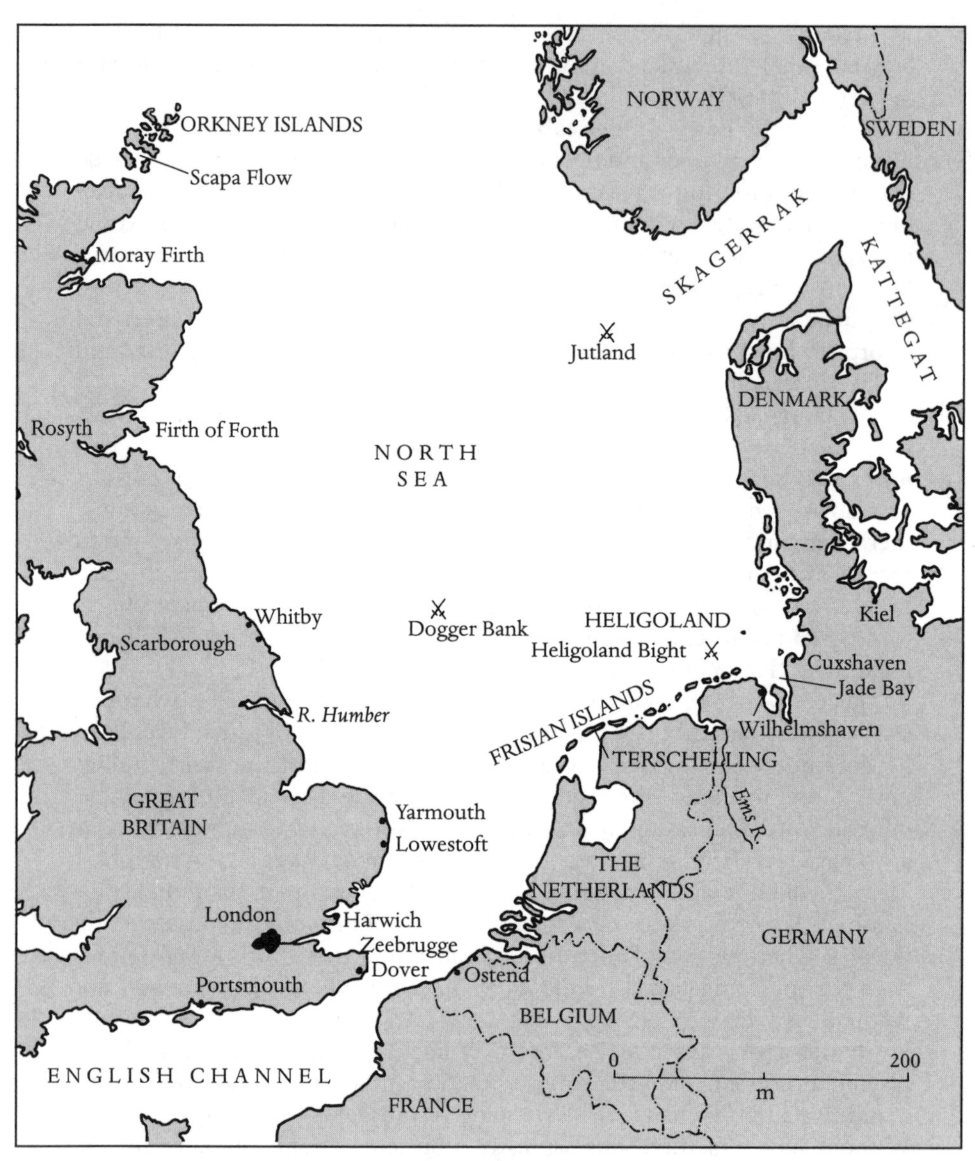

25. The War in the North Sea, 1914–18.

The engagement between detached British squadrons and the German scouting groups that raided Scarborough and Whitby on 16 December 1914 sounded a further warning. Because of a confusion of signals and positions in restricted visibility, cruisers actually in contact with the Germans thought that a signal directing the remainder of the British force to concentrate on the flag was meant for them and broke off the engagement.

Beatty's signals officer bore a measure of guilt for this error through his vague wording of the signal, but he was right to say that the withdrawal "broke elementary tactical principles." Equally valid was his comment: "That this should have been so is not surprising, since no elementary tactical instructions existed. Special instructions were issued by the CinC . . . dealing with the particular mistakes made, but the lack of cohesion and confusion of tactical thought were not to be remedied in a moment."[28]

Yet it was the lack of aggression implicit in this incident that should most have concerned Jellicoe and that demanded action of some kind, action that was not forthcoming. While he was rightly slow to dismiss subordinates for errors made in the heat of action, the CinC failed to put his squadron admirals under pressure to perform.

The Battle of the Dogger Bank on 24 January 1915, the real rehearsal for Jutland, found the British claiming a victory but a vastly incomplete one. Yet another breakdown in signaling, poor teamwork, and, once more, a lack of aggression meant that the British forces failed to catch a German squadron already weakened by the near destruction of the flagship of the First Scouting Group, the battle cruiser *Seydlitz*. In the midst of a headlong pursuit, Beatty's flagship, the *Lion*, was hit hard and began falling astern. But Rear Admiral Sir Archibald Moore in the *New Zealand* became confused by an unexplained turn that Beatty had ordered to evade a chimerical submarine periscope. Moore was further confused by a new and poorly composed signal from Beatty to attack the enemy in the rear—which happened to be the crippled armored cruiser *Blücher*. Instead of continuing after the German battle cruisers, Moore led the remaining British capital ships against the wretched *Blücher*.

Moore was later quietly removed from command. If the battle cruiser officers took notice of his fate, however, the lesson did not percolate to the Grand Fleet proper. That the command might be unable to give direction at the moment of crisis was completely missed.

The Battle of the Dogger Bank was followed by more than a year of inactivity, largely due to the extreme caution of the ailing German commander in chief, von Pohl, but his relief by Vice Admiral Reinhard Scheer in January 1916 saw the war enter a wholly new phase. Determined that the struggle had to be "waged far more energetically,"[29] Scheer embarked upon a campaign of coordinated measures against the British in home waters.

For its part, the Royal Navy resumed a program of seaplane attacks against the German Zeppelin bases to draw the High Seas Fleet out. Scheer would not take the bait; his entry into the North Sea would be on his own terms. He sortied once in March and twice in April; on the last occasion the German scouting groups attacked Lowestoft. Each time, Jellicoe sailed in an attempt to make contact, but weather and the considerable speed-time-distance problems that were still apparent, even with the benefit of cryptographic warnings, combined to defeat his intent. Nevertheless, with the two fleets set upon some kind of encounter, the North Sea was too small to sustain their indefinite separation.

Scheer sought to capitalize on the British practice of sortieing to meet any German movement by stationing U-boats as "trip wires" outside the Grand Fleet anchorages while his heavy squadrons made a cautious thrust north against Allied shipping in the Skagerrak. The Germans sailed in the early hours of 31 May 1916. Ironically, the British—in response to the increase in German radio traffic—had left their own harbors several hours before.

First contact came at 1420 on 31 May between light units of the German scouting groups and Beatty's cruisers. Neither battle-cruiser admiral hesitated to close and within less than ninety minutes Beatty's and Hipper's heavy ships were exchanging fire.

The duty of each commander was clear, Beatty to press home his reconnaissance and, if possible, cripple or destroy Hipper. The latter's task was to entrap Beatty, whose six battle cruisers and four battleships (the Fifth Battle Squadron was temporarily attached to his fleet) represented exactly the powerful but vulnerable force that Scheer sought to isolate and annihilate.

In what became known as the "Run to the South," Hipper led Beatty toward the High Seas Fleet. In doing so, he destroyed the battle cruisers *Indefatigable* and *Queen Mary* at little cost to himself. It was only when the Fifth Battle Squadron came within range that the Germans began to suffer, but by this time Hipper had achieved visual contact with Scheer.

At 1638, the light cruiser *Southampton* broadcast the critical information that she had sighted the enemy fleet. Beatty followed with his own signal to Jellicoe as he wheeled the battle cruisers around to the north with the aim, in his turn, of drawing the Germans on to the Grand Fleet.

Up to this point, Jellicoe had no intimation that Scheer was at sea. In fact, he had been misled by a report from the Admiralty that had placed Scheer's flagship still in her anchorage. But there could be no doubt about the reports he was now receiving. The Grand Fleet had already cleared for action. Jellicoe increased the formation speed successively to 17 and 18 and then to 20 knots, the practical maximum. The three battle cruisers under Rear Admiral Hood he sent on ahead.

Jellicoe had one advantage, unknown to him, as well as one problem of which he was acutely aware. His advantage lay in the fact that Scheer, overconfident in his intelligence and outlying U-boats, did not believe that the Grand Fleet was at sea. Jellicoe's problem was that the action would take place too late in the day to allow a decisive result before dark. Because of the geography of the situation a late afternoon encounter was almost inevitable and he had long feared it.[30]

By 1705 a signal from Beatty reported that he was facing the entire enemy fleet, some "26–30 battleships probably hostile"[31] to the south-southeast. This estimate confirmed Jellicoe's expectation that this was the Germans' "chosen moment"—"not so great a disparity of force when the issues at stake were borne in mind."[32] He could not assume he was facing an inferior enemy.*

The Grand Fleet was disposed in a cruising formation of six four-ship columns with the leading ships in line abreast. The columns were 2,000 yards apart from each other; with the battleships at 500-yard intervals there was thus the space, with care, for what is termed an equal speed maneuver. This would involve a selected wing column steering in the direction of the deployment and the remainder falling in astern to form a single line.

Despite the CinC's efforts to create a reference system to reduce positional inaccuracies, the anomalies within the signals coming into Jellicoe's flagship, the *Iron Duke,* made it impossible to determine where within a southeast to southwest arc the High Seas Fleet lay. The most critical problem concerned Beatty's *Lion*; the cumulative discrepancy between her reckoning and that of the *Iron Duke* was some ten miles. When the position of the *Lion* was finally confirmed, Jellicoe discovered that the High Seas Fleet was both farther north and farther west than he had believed—and thus closest to his starboard wing columns.

While Jellicoe assessed that a deployment to starboard would bring the Grand Fleet most quickly into action and was his "first and natural impulse,"[33] it would mean that the oldest and weakest ships could be heading toward a formidable torpedo-gun trap. Furthermore, the Grand Fleet units would be exposed to gunfire while themselves still in the turn and thus at their most vulnerable and least effective.

Deploying in the other direction, to port, would keep the battle line clear of the enemy during the maneuver. It was likely to cross the T if the High Seas Fleet continued its advance north. Arthur Marder has noted an-

* German capital ship strength at Jutland actually consisted of five battle cruisers, sixteen dreadnought and six pre-dreadnought battleships; British strength consisted of nine battle cruisers and twenty-eight dreadnoughts. In all, 99 German and 151 British ships were present.

13. The Battle of Jutland, 31 May 1916. The dreadnought *Bellerophon,* a unit of Jellicoe's fourth battle division, maneuvers into line ahead during the deployment of the Grand Fleet in "Windy Corner," by Charles Dixon, RI. Light cruisers race up on the fleet's unengaged side. (The Elder Brethren of Trinity House.)

other advantage; the positioning of the two forces would silhouette the German units against the evening light while concealing the British in the gloom to the east.[34]

But by far the most important benefit of the deployment to port was the fact that the movement east meant that Jellicoe could cut Scheer off from his bases. This is precisely what happened after Jellicoe gave the order, "Very well. Hoist equal-speed pendant SE by E."[35]

The deployment was not a simple one, with Beatty being forced to cut across the front of the battle line to take up his proper position in the van and many battleships having to reduce speed to keep clear of each other. Nevertheless, by 1830, fifteen minutes after execution of the signal, the Grand Fleet was in action and hitting the Germans hard.

This could not last and Scheer took the drastic step that was, in retrospect, the only one open to him. The rapid *Gefechtskehrtwendung,* the turn together 180 degrees to starboard, was ordered at 1833 and completed in twelve minutes.

It was left to Jellicoe himself to decide that the Germans had turned away. He thought at first that their disappearance was due to a reduction in visibility,[36] because none of his subordinates thought to report. In any case, Jellicoe would not willingly pass over the same ground as the Germans because of the danger of torpedoes and floating mines. There was nothing in the German actions to suggest a trap, but he dared not risk his battleships in conditions that so much favored the enemy light forces.

At this point the merit of the port wing deployment became apparent. The Grand Fleet was obviously between the High Seas Fleet and its bases. If Jellicoe could maintain the line the Germans would be forced to come to him. If on 31 May he had missed the early start that he believed essential for a decisive victory, there was still 1 June. Jellicoe edged the fleet around to the southeast and shortly afterward to the south. No sooner had he done so than he found that Scheer had reversed course again in a second thrust at the Grand Fleet. The British dealt severely with Hipper's battle cruisers and the battleships of the van, so much so that in minutes Scheer was once more attempting to withdraw, this time under cover of smoke and supported by a torpedo attack on the British line.

Met by heavy fire from the battleships and an advance by the British destroyers, the German attack was not pressed as far as it might have been. The majority of torpedoes were fired at over seven thousand yards, effectively their maximum range. Although the attack was focused on his center and rear, Jellicoe nevertheless turned his entire line away, in accordance with Grand Fleet doctrine and as he had always said he would.

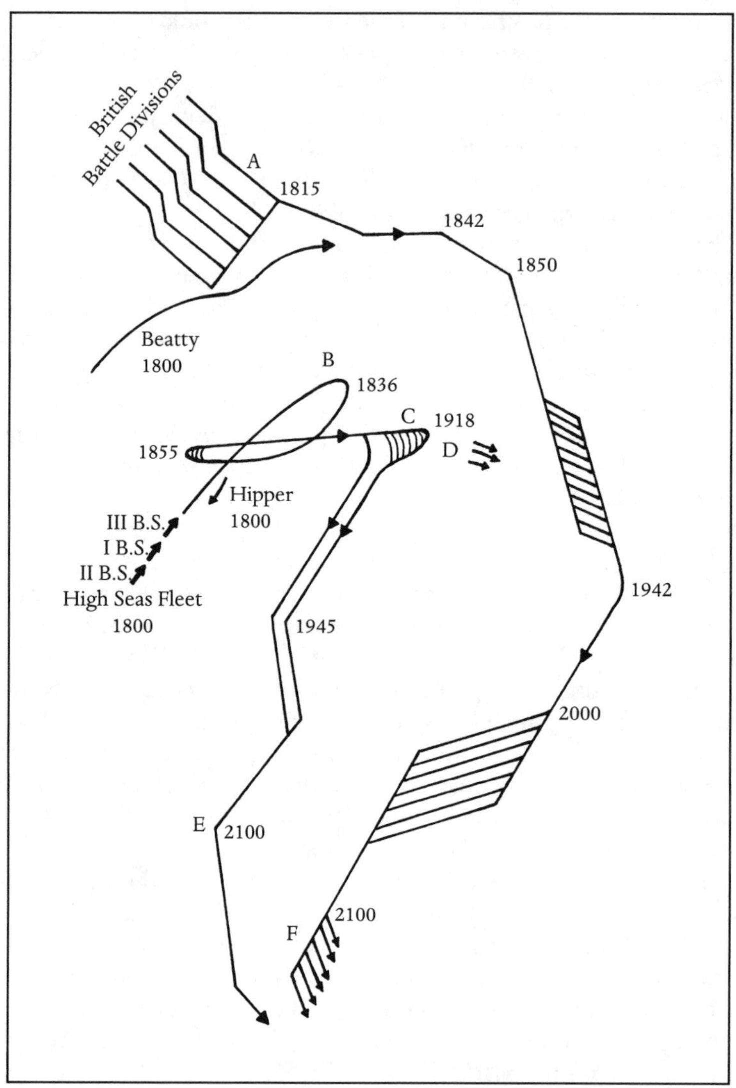

26. The Battle of Jutland, 31 May 1916. (A) Jellicoe deploys into battle line to port. (B) Scheer's first battle turn. (C) Scheer's second battle turn. (D) German destroyer attacks. (E) Scheer turns south. (F) Jellicoe takes up night cruising formation. *Note:* in the interests of clarity, after the initial contact only the tracks of the opposing battle squadrons are shown. The battle cruiser squadrons followed roughly parallel tracks.

The loss of time and distance was small—about twelve minutes and little more than a mile—but it was enough for the Grand Fleet to lose touch with the High Seas Fleet. For this decision as much as any other, Jellicoe has been greatly criticized.

That is not entirely fair. Scheer would have adopted desperate measures to shake off the British. The result would have been a pell-mell action that might have been in the Nelsonic tradition but which would have evened the odds considerably. Even after their attacks on the British battle line the German torpedo boats had nearly two hundred torpedoes between them, twice as many as had been fired.[37] With much reduced ranges they must have achieved some success, particularly since the British defenses would have been operating piecemeal, with separate divisions of battleships and the destroyer flotillas struggling to keep up with the heavy units.

Jellicoe, however, once more did not know that the Germans had turned away. His natural priority was to maintain the integrity of the battle line and thus the concentration of force that had already dealt so hardly with Scheer.

In the event, by a little after 2000, the Grand Fleet was steering west at 17 knots, with Beatty and his scouting forces southwest of the battleships, searching for the enemy's van. When Beatty did meet the Germans again, a sharp but inconclusive action followed, significant because it forced the High Seas Fleet still farther to the west while Jellicoe turned southwest toward the gunfire he could hear. Light cruisers supporting the battle fleet then went into action at 2045, just after Beatty had lost sight of his opponents, the pre-dreadnoughts of the Second Squadron. With very little information trickling into the *Iron Duke,* however, Jellicoe could not be sure that these light cruisers to the west had correctly identified their opponents. Even if they were really engaging the enemy and not their own side, Beatty's activities indicated that the High Seas Fleet was disposed across an arc running west to southwest, heading south. In this case, a turn to the west might close the distance temporarily but it would also open the German avenue of escape. Jellicoe stood on.

But the encounter itself was not well handled by his subordinates. The Germans were repeatedly misidentified and British destroyers hesitated to attack because of the range and the uncertainty of heavy support. Personal culpabilities aside, what strikes the historian is the extent to which subordination within the Grand Fleet had damped down both curiosity and aggression.

There was now no chance of a daylight action. After 2100 visibility was decreasing every minute, within an hour it would be measurable in hundreds of yards. Since "nothing would make [him] fight a night action," Jellicoe "never had a harder task" than to decide on his line of action during the night and "it was a most anxious time."[38]

Jellicoe determined to maintain a north-south barrier, steering the Grand Fleet initially south, his battleships in four columns with cruisers ahead and to the west. He disposed the destroyer flotillas astern to "protect the fleet from destroyer attack and at the same time be favourably situated for attacking the enemy's ships."[39] As events proved, this was a well-conceived disposition. With Beatty's ships to the west-southwest, the trap seemed shut.

But the Germans were prepared to risk night action. Jellicoe's conviction that Scheer would not seek a general action at night, or even one against his unsupported flotillas, betrayed him into assuming that his blocking position would force the Germans into a long run south to the mine-free approaches to the Ems River or toward a gap in the British Heligoland Bight minefields that led to the Jade and Weser Rivers. This, too, entailed a lengthy transit for the High Seas Fleet and left sufficient daylight hours for the Grand Fleet to do its work.

Scheer could not risk another day's battle, particularly as he feared that the Grand Fleet might be reinforced by other units (such as the light cruisers and destroyers of the Harwich Force) the next morning. He turned his battle squadrons toward the east, directly for the Horns Reef, marking the nearest and most northerly of the passages to the inner bight.

The polemic *Riddle of Jutland* described the events of that night. The two fleets

> steamed down the sides of a very long and slender V, and it was one of the most curious circumstances in history that they did not come together at the V's point . . . the V became an X—the courses of the two fleets crossed, neither side was conscious of what was happening—and from then onward, from the hour of midnight onward, they began to draw apart.[40]

What the Germans met was not the British battle line but the destroyer flotillas. In the series of brief but brutal encounters that followed, the superiority of the High Seas Fleet's battle squadrons' night-fighting techniques was clearly demonstrated. Fixated as they were upon the prospects of a dawn engagement, the British heavy ships displayed a total unfamiliarity with night fighting. Careless with their challenge and reply signals, slow to suspect that unidentified contacts might be hostile, and all too ready to assume that their superiors knew more about a fast-changing situation than they, the British missed many opportunities, despite the gallant performance of the destroyer flotillas.

Between 2148 and 0248 German heavy ships, both within Scheer's main body and detached from it, were seen repeatedly by major and minor British units. As often as not, they were eventually correctly identified. But at no time was Jellicoe warned that his subordinates had come into contact with heavy forces. Worn out by the previous twenty-four hours, he and many others made the assumption that the activity in his rear came from German torpedo boats that had encountered his destroyers.

The High Seas Fleet suffered in its push to the east but, well before dawn at 0310, the Germans were clear of the Grand Fleet. They did not loiter. Too late, Jellicoe was informed by the Admiralty that decrypted signals reported the High Seas Fleet approaching the Horns Reef lightship. This put the Germans well to the northeast of the Grand Fleet. All Jellicoe could do was conduct a sweep to ensure that the High Seas Fleet had not left any stragglers behind. By noon on 1 June the Grand Fleet was withdrawing to the north.

There were a few immediate footnotes to the battle. U-boats, upon which Scheer had placed such hopes, made abortive attacks on a number of heavy ships. One German battleship was damaged by a mine laid a month earlier by the *Abdiel.* Ironically, Jellicoe had despatched the minelayer to the Horns Reef late on 31 May as insurance, however inadequate, against the Germans attempting the shortest route home.

Capital ships were not to meet each other in the North Sea again, despite another German sortie in August. It was not in Scheer's interest to risk further encounters, the more so as it became clear that his submarines were not consistently effective against fast-moving and heavily escorted surface ships.

In tactical terms, the Germans could and did claim victory. The statistics appeared to support them. Although outnumbered, they had sunk fourteen British ships of 111,980 tons at a cost of eleven ships of 62,233 tons to themselves. Their advantage was, however, less striking if the comparison was continued, for no fewer than seventeen of the High Seas Fleet's capital ships had suffered substantial damage, whereas only seven of the Grand Fleet's had done so.

But, in strategic terms, such comparisons were irrelevant. The essential fact was that the outcome simply confirmed the status quo in the North Sea. Mortifying as this may have been to British professional and public opinion, it meant that the blockade remained in effect. Strategically, the victory at Jutland belonged to the Grand Fleet.

The depth of Jellicoe's feelings in the wake of the battle is difficult to gauge. Certain as it is that he was "desperately" disappointed[41] by the failure to bring the German fleet to a decisive action and however much he deplored the missed opportunity in private,[42] he neither surrendered to despair nor refused to admit the defects within his organization.

On 4 June he established committees to examine the action, with particular emphasis on gunnery, protection, communications, and night fighting. The quantum improvements made by war's end attest to their success, even though Jellicoe's selection of his flag captain, Dreyer, to head the gunnery team was a dubious one in view of the latter's vested interest in fire control.

Although protective of subordinates, Jellicoe did not equivocate when he reported on the fleet's inadequacies. He did not attempt excuses, admitting especially that "under night conditions we have a good deal to learn."[43]

Setting in train the work of reconstruction, while at the same time sustaining morale within the Grand Fleet when it became apparent that the presumption that "they *must* come out before the end"[44] no longer held true, was Jellicoe's greatest achievement as commander in chief. The tragedy was that he did not make the improvements in 1915.

Jellicoe hauled down his flag in November 1916, going ashore as First Sea Lord with the task of combating the U-boat menace to merchant shipping. Overtired, still tending to overcentralize and, perhaps because of these two factors, now almost a pathological pessimist, he found himself in increasing conflict with the government. Slow to introduce the convoying of merchant ships, Jellicoe lost credit with the prime minister and the War Cabinet. Matters came to a head after the new First Lord, Sir Eric Geddes, insisted on the replacement of the admiral commanding at Dover, one of Jellicoe's oldest friends. The First Sea Lord could not agree to the change, and this brought about his own dismissal on Christmas Eve 1917.

After this Jellicoe remained in effective retirement until 1919, when he was dispatched on a tour of the empire. His brief was to report upon the future of imperial naval forces. The tour lasted just under a year, during which he was promoted to Admiral of the Fleet.

Already a viscount, Jellicoe had reached the pinnacle of his profession; the promotion was sweetened by a parliamentary grant of £50,000. The fly in the ointment was that Beatty, who had succeeded him in command of the Grand Fleet, had been created an earl (a higher title), promoted to Admiral of the Fleet, and granted £100,000.

Jellicoe's reports from abroad were well conceived for the long term. His recommendations, centering as they did on the Pacific, were realistic in their estimate of the conflicts of interest that would arise with Japan. Inevitably, however, disarmament and economy combined to reduce his proposals to a shadow of their intent. Nevertheless, Jellicoe's emphatic recommendations and his insistence on the need for a collective empire effort were largely responsible for the renascence of an Indian navy and the eventual creation of the Royal New Zealand Navy.

Jellicoe was able to cap this tour with a highly successful appointment as governor-general of New Zealand from 1920 to 1924. Having married late but very happily in 1902, his years in that country allowed him to devote much time to his wife and five children. On his return he was made an earl. An active decade in Britain followed, which Jellicoe devoted to charitable work. His retirement was overshadowed by the "Jutland Controversy," but Jellicoe was impatient with might-have-beens. He had produced two lengthy apologia in his books on the Grand Fleet and the U-boat crisis but, while ensuring that what he conceived to be the facts of the Jutland battle were not misrepresented, was wisely content to leave their interpretation to others. He died, greatly mourned, on 20 November 1935.

It was said of Jellicoe that he possessed every Nelsonic virtue save that of insubordination. He was an admirable chief of staff but as an independent commander he had an absolute lack of originality. Although he could execute policy superbly, he was fatally weak at innovation. The authoritarian methods and overcentralization prevalent in the Royal Navy of his day magnified his defects and, to this extent, Jellicoe was not so much the villain of Jutland as a victim of the system.

That the Grand Fleet was capable of much more than it achieved at Jutland was clearly demonstrated by the extraordinary advances in fighting efficiency that were achieved in the months after the battle. Jellicoe had clung too closely to the concepts of operations that he viewed as being the practical limits when he took command. No one could have led the Grand Fleet more capably during the first months of the war. The pity was that Jellicoe could not encourage his subordinates to capitalize on his early work. The talent was there but he failed to use it.

Yet it must be understood that the crushing victory of Nelsonic tradition was never really a possibility unless the Germans not merely sought battle but remained to fight it out. Where the British could have done more was in exploiting every opportunity and thereby inflicting the maximum possible damage on the High Seas Fleet. If this had been done at Jutland, for example, few of the German battle cruisers would have made harbor. The tactical victory that the Germans claimed Jutland to be would have been at least a draw.

It was all in the eye for the main chance that was so conspicuously absent from the Grand Fleet in 1916. More than 120 years earlier Nelson had written of a CinC's decision to rest content with limited results: "Now, had we taken ten sail, and allowed the eleventh to escape when it had been possible to have got at her, I could never have called it well done."[45]

Jellicoe would have been the first to admit the truth of this statement. His tragedy was that, before 31 May 1916, he could not see *how* it could be done.

NOTES

1. Rear Admiral Sir William Jameson, *The Fleet That Jack Built: Nine Men Who Made a Modern Navy* (London: Hart-Davis, 1962), p. 171.

2. Ibid., p. 170. See also John Winton, *Jellicoe* (London: Michael Joseph, 1981), p. 9.

3. Rear Admiral Roger Bellairs, "Obituary of Jellicoe: The Grand Fleet," *The Naval Review*, vol. XXIV, no. 1 (February 1936), pp. 12–16.

4. See particularly Arthur Marder, *From the Dreadnought to Scapa Flow: The Royal Navy in the Fisher Era, 1904–1919*, vol. IV, *1917: Year of Crisis* (London: Oxford University Press, 1969), pp. 170 ff.

5. See, for example, Commander Stephen (later Lord) King-Hall, *My Naval Life* (London: Faber, 1952), pp. 97 ff. Dr. Andrew Gordon's studies of the rival schools of tactical thought within the Royal Navy have cast much light upon the issue and culture of centralized control.

6. Arthur Marder, *Portrait of an Admiral: The Life and Papers of Admiral Sir Herbert Richmond* (Cambridge: Harvard University Press, 1952), p. 356 (Richmond diary, 4 August 1919).

7. Jellicoe to Secretary of the Admiralty, 14 November 1914, A. Temple Patterson, ed., *The Jellicoe Papers: Selections from the Private and Official Correspondence of Admiral of the Fleet Earl Jellicoe of Scapa* (London: Navy Records Society, 1966), p. 90.

8. Jellicoe to Churchill, 30 September 1914, ibid., p. 72.

9. James Goldrick, *The King's Ships Were at Sea: The War in the North Sea, August 1914–February 1915* (Annapolis: Naval Institute Press, 1984), pp. 173 ff.

10. Jellicoe to Beatty, 23 March 1915, Patterson, op. cit., I: 152.

11. Jellicoe to Secretary of the Admiralty, 30 October 1914, ibid., p. 75.

12. Admiral of the Fleet Viscount Jellicoe of Scapa, *The Grand Fleet 1914–1916: Its Creation, Development and Work* (London: Cassell, 1919), p. 373.

13. Ibid.

14. See Anthony Pollen, *The Great Gunnery Scandal: The Mystery of Jutland* (London: Collins, 1980); Jon T. Sumida, *The Pollen Papers: The Privately Circulated Printed Works of Arthur Hungerford Pollen, 1901–1916* (London: Navy Records Society, 1984); and Jon T. Sumida, *In Defence of Naval Supremacy: Finance, Technology and British Naval Policy, 1889–1914*, 2nd ed. (London: Routledge, 1993).

15. Jellicoe to Prince Louis of Battenberg, 18 August 1914, Patterson, op. cit., I: 52.

16. Marder, *From the Dreadnought to Scapa Flow*, vol. III, *Jutland and After: May 1916–December 1916*, 2nd ed. (London: Oxford University Press, 1978), pp. 29 ff.

17. Jellicoe, op. cit., p. 69.

18. Goldrick, op. cit., p. 41.

19. Jellicoe to Churchill, 14 July 1914, Patterson, op. cit., I: 38.

20. Grand Fleet Battle Order 2 dated 18 August 1914, ibid., p. 52.

21. For example, the battleships *Conqueror* and *Monarch* collided in December 1914, at a particularly unfortunate time for the Grand Fleet. The *Barham* and *Warspite* hit each other in December 1915, *Warspite* and *Valiant* in August 1916. The *New Zealand* and *Australia* collided in April 1916, as a result of which the latter missed Jutland. See Oscar Parkes, *British Battleships* (London: Seeley Service, 1957).

22. Jellicoe, op. cit., p. 39.

23. Ibid., pp. 60–62.

24. Marder, *From the Dreadnought to Scapa Flow,* III: 33.

25. Patrick Beesly, *Room 40: British Naval Intelligence 1914–1918* (New York: Harcourt, Brace, Jovanovich, 1982), pp. 21–23.

26. Goodenough to Jellicoe, 5 June 1916, Patterson, op. cit., I: 270.

27. Fisher to Jellicoe, 21 December 1914, A. J. Marder, ed., *Fear God and Dread Nought; The Correspondence of Admiral of the Fleet Baron Fisher of Kilverstone,* vol. III, *Restoration, Abdication and Last Years, 1914–1920* (London: Jonathan Cape, 1959), p. 102.

28. Lady Seymour, *Commander Ralph Seymour, RN, CMG, DSO* (Glasgow: privately published, 1926), p. 151: "Tactical Reconnaissance: Lecture to RNSC Greenwich, 4 November 1919."

29. Admiral Reinhard Scheer, *Germany's High Seas Fleet in the World War* (London: Cassell, 1920), p. 96.

30. Jellicoe to Jackson, 12 April 1916, Patterson, op. cit., I: 232–33.

31. Julian S. Corbett and Henry Newbolt, *Naval Operations* (London: Longmans, Green, 1923), III: 349n.

32. Marder, *From the Dreadnought to Scapa Flow,* III: 95.

33. Jellicoe, op. cit., pp. 348–49.

34. Marder, *From the Dreadnought to Scapa Flow,* III: 102.

35. Admiral Sir Frederick Dreyer, *The Sea Heritage: A Study of Maritime Warfare* (London: Museum Press, 1955), pp. 146–47.

36. Marder, *From the Dreadnought to Scapa Flow,* III: 120–21.

37. Ibid., pp. 130–31.

38. Jellicoe to Jackson, 5 June 1916, Patterson, op. cit., I: 271.

39. Dispatch on the Battle of Jutland, ibid., pp. 301–2.

40. Langhorne Gibson and Vice Admiral J. E. T. Harper, *The Riddle of Jutland* (London: Cassell, 1934), pp. 219–20.

41. Jellicoe to Jackson, 5 June 1916, Patterson, op. cit., I: 271.

42. Marder, *From the Dreadnought to Scapa Flow,* III: 237.

43. Confidential Despatch on the Battle of Jutland, Patterson, op. cit., I: 286.

44. Keyes to his wife, 6 June 1916, Paul G. Halpern, ed., *The Keyes Papers: Selections from the Private and Official Correspondence of Admiral of the Fleet Baron Keyes of Zeebrugge,* vol. I, *1914–1918* (London: Navy Records Society, 1972), p. 360.

45. Robert Southey, *The Life of Nelson* (London: The Folio Society, 1956), p. 72.

NOTE ON SOURCES

Of purely biographical treatments, the best recent work is John Winton's *Jellicoe* (London: Michael Joseph, 1981), a thorough but sympathetic study that canvasses most of the major issues. Professor A. Temple Patterson produced a useful but circumspect study in *Jellicoe: A Biography* (London: Macmillan, 1969). Admiral Sir Reginald Bacon's *The Life of John Rushworth, Earl Jellicoe* (London: Cassell, 1936) verges on hagiography but was effectively the official biography, written immediately after the admiral's death. Jellicoe's own *The Grand Fleet 1914–1916: Its Creation, Development and Work* (London: Cassell, 1919) and *The Crisis of the Naval War* (London: Cassell, 1920) are comprehensive and generally honest apologia. His papers and autobiographical notes are in the British Museum; selections have been published as *The Jellicoe Papers* in two volumes, edited by Professor A. Temple Patterson, by the Navy Records Society in London in 1966 and 1968.

Professor Arthur J. Marder's monumental five volumes *From the Dreadnought to Scapa Flow: The Royal Navy in the Fisher Era, 1904–1919* (London: Oxford University Press, 1961–70) remain a basic source for the period although their conclusions, notably in tactical and technical matters, have been overtaken by more recent research. The last word on Jutland has yet to be written. John Campbell's *Jutland: An Analysis of the Fighting* (Greenwich: Conway Maritime Press, 1986) is a comprehensive study of the details of the action, especially when dealing with gunnery and damage reports, but it does not treat tactics or personalities. Some understanding of the fundamental fire control problem can be gained from *The Pollen Papers*, edited by Jon T. Sumida (London: Navy Records Society, 1984), and still more from his study *In Defence of Naval Supremacy: Finance, Technology and British Naval Policy, 1889–1914*, 2nd ed. (London: Routledge, 1993). Dr. Sumida's work has been in the vanguard of a long overdue emphasis on the critical part played in naval operations at every level by technology.

In addition to the revised third volume of Marder's study *Jutland and After: May 1916–December 1916*, 2nd ed. (London: Oxford University Press, 1978), much light is cast on Jutland operations by Stephen Roskill's *Admiral of the Fleet Earl Beatty: The Last Naval Hero* (London: Collins, 1980). The official history of the battle, written by Sir Julian Corbett in the third volume of *Naval Operations* (London: Longmans, Green, 1923), remains a basic reference, although its pro-Jellicoe approach was not well received by the postwar Admiralty under Beatty. Less academic but nevertheless useful are Geoffrey Bennett's *The Battle of Jutland* (London: Batsford, 1964) and Donald Macintyre's *Jutland* (London: Evans, 1957). Both suffer to some extent from lack of access to all the official material but they are written by distinguished RN officers of great practical experience in naval operations (Macintyre was one of the most successful convoy escort commanders of World War II). They are shrewd and engaging commentaries. Another professional work much more critical of Jellicoe and of the Royal Navy is *The Battle of Jutland* by Commander Holloway H. Frost, USN, published in London by B. F. Stevens & Brown in 1936 and in America by the Naval Institute. Vice Admiral K. G. B. Dewar produced a much less well known, three-part study of Jutland in the British service journal *The Naval Review* (January, April, and July 1960, vol. XLVIII). Very anti-Jellicoe, Dewar had been jointly responsible for the official *Naval Staff Appreciation* of the battle in the 1920s. This had taken such a critical line that the Admiralty was forced to order its withdrawal from circulation. Dewar's 1960 study reflects on the points raised within the *Appreciation*.

Finally, Dr. Andrew Gordon's monumental study, *The Rules of the Game: Jutland and British Naval Command* (London: John Murray, 1996), was published as this book went to print. This work will shed new light on the development of British tactics and other professional and cultural issues that underlay the Grand Fleet's difficulties.

15

Reinhard Scheer

Intuition under Fire

(1863–1928)

Gary E. Weir

FULL OF ANTICIPATION, REINHARD SCHEER BOARDED THE cadet training ship of the Imperial German Navy, the sailing frigate *Niobe,* on 22 April 1879. With his sixteenth birthday only five months away, the sharp memories of Oberkirchen near Bückeberge, his birthplace, and of his home in Hanau on the River Main had not yet given way to the romantic intimacy with the sea that would hold him fast for the rest of his life. His long career with the kaiser's navy would witness the creation of the High Seas Fleet by Admiral Alfred von Tirpitz and its long-awaited confrontation with the British Grand Fleet. But those developments lay far in the future on that April morning when nothing seemed more important to this adolescent than his impending voyage.

The cruise lasted from June to September 1879 and provided Scheer with some of his first and deepest impressions of life at sea. Almost a half-century later he recalled this voyage in his autobiography and stressed the importance of the lessons he learned about precision, practice, and professional experience. Night work on the masts and yards and navigation by the stars formed habits, instilled confidence, and shaped an officer's invaluable professional intuition.[1] He particularly singled out the duties of the watch officer for the qualities and the strength of character this responsibility demanded of every cadet. In this role he learned shiphandling, the necessity of always remaining alert and vigilant, and the determination to overcome the unexpected.[2]

The voyage in the *Niobe* added instruction and practical experience in navigation, engineering, and stoking to the basic infantry training he received before the cruise began. Upon his return home, Scheer and his fellow cadets proceeded to the Naval School in Kiel as the next step in their forty-two-month training program as prospective officers in the Imperial German Navy. After entering the navy in 1879 with only a "satisfactory" on the cadet evaluation, in Kiel he posted the second highest grade on the Sea Cadet's Exam in the Crew of 1880.*

As far as Scheer was concerned the navy saved the best of the training experience for last. After the Naval School, he underwent six months' special instruction in gunnery, torpedo warfare, and infantry field practice after which he reported to the artillery school-ship SMS *Renown,* and later served

* The term "crew" was employed as the equivalent of the American term "class," which would denote the year of graduation.

briefly on the armored frigate SMS *Friedrich Karl.*[3] All midshipmen spent the last year of their education with the fleet, and Scheer drew a billet on board SMS *Hertha,* an armored corvette scheduled to participate in a voyage around the world. Before Scheer received his commission as an ensign, he honed his newly acquired skills on a trip that took him to Melbourne, Yokohama, Shanghai, Kobe, and Nagasaki.

Soon after graduation, Scheer served two tours with the Imperial Navy's East African Cruiser Squadron, the first between 1884 and 1886, and the second from May 1888 to the early summer of 1890. Besides the experience he gained, the most profitable result of these assignments proved to be the contacts he made. During his first tour, spent on board SMS *Bismarck,* Admiral Eduard von Knorr's squadron flagship, Scheer was befriended by Lieutenant Henning von Holtzendorff. A few years later Lieutenant Scheer served under von Holtzendorff in the cruiser SMS *Prinzess Wilhelm* on a trip to the Orient with a naval team interested in the Sino-Japanese War of 1895–96. This relationship proved personally and professionally rewarding when von Holtzendorff became commander in chief of the High Seas Fleet in 1909 and asked then Captain Scheer to take over as his chief of staff.[4]

After his first African tour, Scheer, now promoted to lieutenant (jg), spent the next four years acquiring expertise in torpedo technology and warfare. He passed through the torpedo course in the navy's training ship, SMS *Blücher,* from January to May 1888. In his second tour on the east African station he served as torpedo officer in the light cruiser SMS *Sophie,* and upon his return to Germany in June 1890 assumed the post of instructor at the Torpedo Research Command in Kiel.

During the years 1888 to 1897, interrupted only by two short tours at the Naval Academy in 1894 and 1896 and his voyage to Asia in 1895–96, Scheer built a reputation as a torpedo and navigation specialist.[5] In this capacity he came into contact with the other most significant individual in his professional life, Admiral von Tirpitz. Scheer first attracted Tirpitz's attention at the Torpedo Research Command in Kiel. With the admiral's appointment to the post of state secretary of the Imperial Naval Office (*Reichsmarineamt*—RMA)* in 1897, Scheer found himself transferred to Tirpitz's direct command in the RMA Torpedo Section.[6]

Tirpitz molded the Imperial German Navy to his own design with the full support of his patron, Kaiser Wilhelm II. To the kaiser's delight, the admiral skillfully extracted a long-term commitment to fleet construction from the German Reichstag in the form of the Fleet Laws of 1898 and 1900. With this political coup, Tirpitz became the father and principal architect of the German High Seas Fleet. For the next eighteen years he governed the

* A position roughly equivalent to the U.S. secretary of the navy.

RMA and remained the navy's chief politician and one of its most important strategic thinkers.

The state secretary based his construction plans and his choice of the types of vessels to join the fleet upon his grand strategy, the "Risk Theory." This view held that Germany could defeat or at least restrain Great Britain by building a fleet of modern capital ships that would remain a permanent threat in the Baltic and North Seas. The British would not dare to oppose Germany's emergence as a major naval power because the cost of prevention in money and lives would be too great to contemplate.

But what if the impossible happened? Could Germany expect to engage the Royal Navy and succeed? The German Admiralty, conscious of the overwhelming British superiority in numbers, systematically trained its officers to develop tactical alternatives for use by the High Seas Fleet, assuming the possibility of a decisive battle against a quantitatively superior opponent.[7] Tirpitz supported this effort, and when the Naval Academy fell under the control of the RMA after 1907, he revised the curriculum for sea cadets to include a more thorough technical education as part of an officer's professional training. This would provide his new navy with strategically competent officers who were entirely comfortable with the technology at their fingertips.[8]

Scheer spent the crucial middle years of his career working with Tirpitz and learning from the master. From his first billet in the RMA in the Torpedo Section in 1897 to his appointment as chief of the Central Division of the RMA in 1903, Scheer absorbed the Tirpitz doctrine, as did most of his contemporaries.[9] Naturally, he supported Tirpitz's efforts to expand fleet construction via amendments to the existing Fleet Laws, but he was not himself politically active. Scheer's careful professional and nonpolitical attitude typified the outlook of the educated German middle class, which formed the backbone of the Imperial Navy's officer corps.[10]

While under Tirpitz at the RMA, Scheer rose quickly to lieutenant commander in 1900 and commander in 1904. He made captain in 1905, a full two years before leaving the RMA to take command of the battleship SMS *Elsass*.

In the absence of any personal papers, Scheer's fitness reports—annual evaluations written by his superiors throughout his career—provide valuable indicators of his ability and personality. The report filed on 1 December 1907, the year he left the RMA, gives an excellent insight into the new commander of SMS *Elsass*. Scheer's superiors at the RMA focused on his high sense of duty, selflessness, and technical competence. They believed that Scheer would make an excellent line officer because his men would respect him as an individual as well as an able commander. The RMA, always reluctant to lose a competent torpedo specialist, recommended him for the post of director of the Torpedo Inspectorate.[11]

Scheer remained captain of SMS *Elsass* for two years, from the autumn of 1907 until 1909, when von Holtzendorff offered him the position of fleet chief of staff. While he served in the *Elsass*, one of Scheer's fitness reports prophetically read: "Filled the position well, very accomplished in gunnery. Should be well suited for a high staff position."[12]

The Admiralty confirmed these estimates in its evaluations covering the period of Scheer's transition from SMS *Elsass* to the staff of the High Seas Fleet. Recommending Scheer for greater responsibility without reservations, the report for 1 December 1909 went on to characterize him as energetic, sure, clear-headed, reliable, and adept at handling warships. While his friendship with the commander in chief of the High Seas Fleet certainly helped, these repeatedly confirmed personal qualities surely impressed the promotion board, for Scheer achieved flag rank less than six months after taking charge of von Holtzendorff's staff.[13]

A rear admiral at the age of forty-seven, Scheer had the textbook career pattern for a German naval officer. Ever since his promotion to ensign in 1882, all of his tours in administrative positions had propitiously alternated with valuable assignments at sea. In the Imperial German Navy the latter played the determining role in a promotion board's deliberations.[14]

At sea Scheer's character came to the fore and his colleagues and subordinates felt the force of his personality. He entered into the life of his ship's company with great zest. There he found the best in his crew and in himself, for the sea tested loyalty, friendship, and professional skills. On board ship, his crew and staff saw him as a joyful and spirited senior. Baron Ernst von Weizsäcker, his flag lieutenant at Jutland, recalled that "He was of cheerful disposition and had a quick mind, and was a man without pretensions."[15] His optimistic nature always recovered quickly from a setback. Natural fighting instincts led him to address problems energetically with new solutions as opposed to old formulas. His vigor led him to discover his own answers and take the initiative in important situations. As von Weizsäcker wrote after the war, "Scheer had no use for rigid schemes. He was always ready to look at a problem from a new angle. Someone on his staff once called him the *primesautier,* which is a person who reacts on the first stimulus."[16] From his earliest days in the navy, Scheer freely voiced his opinions when he felt he could make a contribution, exhibiting the self-confidence and willingness to accept responsibility that characterized his whole career.[17]

He displayed this confidence and earned the trust of his colleagues and subordinates in administrative assignments as well as operational command. After directing von Holtzendorff's staff until the autumn of 1911, Scheer returned to work for Tirpitz in the RMA as the chief of the General Naval Department for little more than a year.[18] He then rejoined the High Seas Fleet as commander of the six battleships of the Second Squadron. His fitness report of 1 December 1915 described him as an energetic and accomplished officer with a high sense of duty. At one point the authors of this report commented that Scheer "possessed the trust of his commanders and officers."[19] Scheer's subordinates trusted him no less than he trusted himself. He relied heavily on his training and a refined instinct developed over the nearly forty years since he boarded SMS *Niobe* in 1879. In his account of the High Seas Fleet in World War I, Scheer reflected on the nature of leadership and the split-second decisiveness expected of a naval commander in battle. He realized all too clearly that the correct choice relied completely on sound instinct and training, because long deliberation was a luxury reserved for the armchair strategists on the day after the battle. He admitted to himself and demonstrated by his actions that strategies had limits, commenting that "the art of leadership consists in securing an approximately correct picture from the impression of the moment, and then acting in accordance with it."[20]

The key to Scheer's valuable instinct was the repeated and varied experiences that he gained in fleet exercises and during many years of service at sea.[21] Textbook scenarios would not win battles, skill and experience would. These conclusions led him to place a high premium on his intuition and the absolute necessity of retaining the initiative. This would give him the advantage of choreographing an encounter, and keeping his opponent on the defensive, even if the opponent had the numerically superior force.

Scheer went to the Second Squadron of the High Seas Fleet in January 1913 and was promoted to vice admiral on 9 December. He remained at this post until January 1915, six months after the assassination of Archduke Franz Ferdinand had touched off the world war. Scheer then assumed command of the Third Squadron, which he held until January 1916. From the beginning of the war he advocated the use of the fleet, supported by airships and submarines, in limited engagements or bombardments that might draw the British piecemeal out of their bases. He knew that a decisive battle against the entire Grand Fleet invited disaster, but believed that a meeting between the High Seas Fleet and a portion of Admiral Jellicoe's formidable force could end profitably for Germany.

Thus he criticized Admiral Friedrich von Ingenohl, the first wartime commander of the High Seas Fleet, for his precipitate withdrawal from the Dogger Bank on 24 January 1915 after Rear Admiral Franz Hipper's bombardment of Scarborough and Hartlepool indeed drew Admiral Beatty's cruiser force into battle.[22] Hipper, left to his own devices, crippled Beatty's flagship, HMS *Lion,* while losing SMS *Blücher.* Scheer felt that Ingenohl "had robbed us of the opportunity of meeting certain divisions of the enemy according to the prearranged plan, which was now seen to have been correct."[23]

Ingenohl's withdrawal left an indelible impression upon Scheer. He would never offer his back to the enemy. An action of this sort implied cowardice, abdicated the responsibility of a commander to engage the enemy if possible, and immediately granted the initiative to his opponent.

By 1915 the admiralty had discarded the decisive battle against the Grand Fleet required by Tirpitz's prewar strategic dogma. Like Scheer, its leaders believed that the only realistic course of action open to the Imperial Navy was to divide the Grand Fleet and defeat its component parts. A general engagement under circumstances favorable to Germany seemed unlikely.

Ingenohl lost his command in February as a direct result of his performance at Dogger Bank and the kaiser's reaction to the loss of the *Blücher*. His successor, Admiral Hugo von Pohl, held the post for only a year before resigning due to ill health. During that year the German battle fleet remained at anchor, a witness to the kaiser's reluctance to risk the High Seas Fleet and the government's desire to preserve it as a diplomatic bargaining tool.

In July 1915, the chief of the kaiser's Naval Cabinet, Admiral Georg Alexander von Müller, noted in his diary that the considered wisdom in Berlin cast Scheer in the role of the dark horse candidate to succeed the ailing Pohl as chief of the High Seas Fleet.[24] Admiral von Tirpitz first emerged as the prime candidate, supported by the chief of the admiralty staff, Vice Admiral Gustav Bachmann.[25] However, Tirpitz's reputation as a crafty politician worked against him. Many members of the officer corps, while pleased with Tirpitz's legislative success on behalf of the navy, distrusted anyone who meddled in politics. In addition, Tirpitz's vacillation on the issue of taking the initiative with the fleet early in the war after years of proclaiming the doctrine of the "decisive battle" severely damaged his credibility.

On 18 January 1916 Vice Admiral Reinhard Scheer became the commander in chief of the High Seas Fleet. For Erich Raeder, later Hipper's chief of staff at Jutland and the first chief of Hitler's navy, Scheer was the best possible selection. It pleased the officer corps to have a chief who had the extensive experience at sea that Tirpitz lacked. Scheer "not only had great practical common sense and a keen sense of perception, but he also possessed that rare commodity, a delight in responsibility."[26] Von Weizsäcker recalled: "We knew that Scheer was made of different stuff from Pohl. There were many stories of his exploits as a young lieutenant. His old friends had given him the odd nickname of 'Bobschiess' [Shooting Bob], on account, it was said, of his likeness to his fox terrier, which he was fond of provoking to bite his friends' trousers."[27]

Scheer chose a well-balanced and competent team of friends to work at his side. The calm and deliberate Captain Adolf von Trotha took over as chief of staff while the brilliant and impulsive Captain Magnus von Levetzow directed operations.[28] Both the German navy and the British knew that the High Seas Fleet would not remain dormant for very long if Scheer retained both his post and the support of the kaiser.[29]

German naval strategy underwent a series of changes between 1890 and 1916, emphasizing the offensive from 1900 until 1912 and the defensive from 1912 into the war. Initially, the anticipation of a close blockade by the British fleet prompted leaders of the German naval staff to propose offensive strategies designed to challenge the Royal Navy's control of the North Sea coast and the Skagerrak area at the northern tip of the Danish peninsula. This offensive viewpoint prevailed through 1912, fueled by Tirpitz's political successes and the RMA's propaganda machine, which generated amazing public support for fleet expansion. The activities of the RMA guaranteed the navy increased budgets and supported the very ambitious construction program needed to sustain an offensive strategy against a British blockade or attack.

Tirpitz's political success came to an abrupt halt in 1912, when Reichstag financial priorities shifted back to the army as the best defense in an ever more unstable international situation. In these circumstances, the nature of the navy's strategy changed as well. With the prospect of a dramatic slowdown in the growth of the fleet, the admiralty staff, under Vice Admiral August von Heeringen, came to view the prospect of war with a numerically superior British fleet in a different light.[30] Thereafter it planned not only to conduct operations close to German shores, but also to employ submarines, mines, and quick sorties by small task forces in actions designed to reduce British fleet strength to a level roughly commensurate with the High Seas Fleet.[31]

As the war progressed, Scheer supported the most aggressive variation on this defensive strategy. In his operations order for 31 May 1916, Scheer made it abundantly clear that he wanted to deal with the British in a piecemeal fashion. His Scouting Force, under Vice Admiral Hipper, was to act as the bait. Hipper would threaten any advanced British patrol forces around the Skagerrak and along the southwestern coast of Norway as well as any merchant shipping in the vicinity. Scheer earnestly hoped that this would prompt the British to pursue Hipper, who would then draw his foe into the approaching main body of the High Seas Fleet. To cover both forces, Scheer ordered airship reconnaissance, and directed his submarines to take up offensive patrol positions off Scapa Flow, Moray Firth, the Firth of Forth, Terschelling Bank, the Humber, and the coast of Flanders.[32]

At 3:48 P.M. (GMT) on the afternoon of 31 May 1916, Hipper's Scouting Force opened fire on the British Battle Cruiser Fleet under Vice Admiral Sir David Beatty, the advanced guard of Admiral Sir John Jellicoe's Grand Fleet, and the Battle of Jutland began.[33] The range between the two opposing battle lines quickly decreased to approximately 16,000 meters and a gunnery duel began as both forces ran parallel to the southeast at speeds approaching

25 knots. For the outnumbered Hipper it was imperative to draw Beatty into Scheer's main force approaching from the south. Beatty's best intelligence placed the High Seas Fleet at anchor in the Jade Basin and his aerial reconnaissance suffered from the same poor weather that had hampered Scheer's efforts to employ airships to his own advantage.

The initial phase of the battle belonged to Hipper. The British Fifth Battle Squadron damaged the *Moltke, Von der Tann,* and *Seydlitz.* But thanks to the antiflash safeguards implemented after the Dogger Bank encounter in 1915, Hipper's force suffered little compared to the losses it inflicted. Two minutes after the battle began, the Germans struck the center turret of HMS *Lion,* inflicting enough damage to warrant flooding the turret magazines. SMS *Von der Tann* sent HMS *Indefatigable* to the bottom of the North Sea with 1,000 men, and the *Derfflinger* and *Seydlitz* destroyed HMS *Queen Mary* at approximately 4:30 P.M. with the loss of 1,300.

Shortly after the *Queen Mary*'s demise, Beatty's cruisers sighted Scheer's main force on the horizon. Instead of facing an overwhelmingly superior foe in Beatty's Battle Cruiser Fleet, Hipper now joined with Scheer to turn the tables on the British. Without the Germans realizing it, the tables had indeed turned completely, for now Beatty assumed Hipper's role and, at 4:40, the British Battle Cruiser Fleet turned northwest and then north, leading the Germans toward Admiral Jellicoe and the Grand Fleet only sixteen miles away.

At 6:15 P.M., shortly before the two fleets came into contact, Jellicoe ordered the Grand Fleet to deploy from its four columns-abreast formation into a single line of battle to port. This inspired choice not only crossed Scheer's T as the High Seas Fleet approached from the southeast, but also silhouetted the German ships against the western sky and allowed the Grand Fleet to take up a position between Scheer and his base.[34]

Despite further success, notably the sinking of the British battle cruiser *Invincible,* Scheer realized, upon meeting the larger British force, that he had to extricate his fleet or face annihilation. Hipper's flagship, SMS *Lützow,* had to withdraw from the battle line after suffering repeated hits and soon the entire High Seas Fleet began to feel the power and numerical superiority of the Grand Fleet. Scheer therefore ordered a *Gefechtskehrtwendung,* or battle turn away to starboard at 6:36 P.M. In just a few minutes, every ship in Scheer's force simultaneously completed this radical 180-degree change in course and steamed off to the east under the cover of smoke and a daring torpedo attack.

At this juncture Scheer made the decision that has confounded analysts and historians to the present day. When Jellicoe did not pursue him, Scheer had the opportunity to assess the condition of his force. Because damage

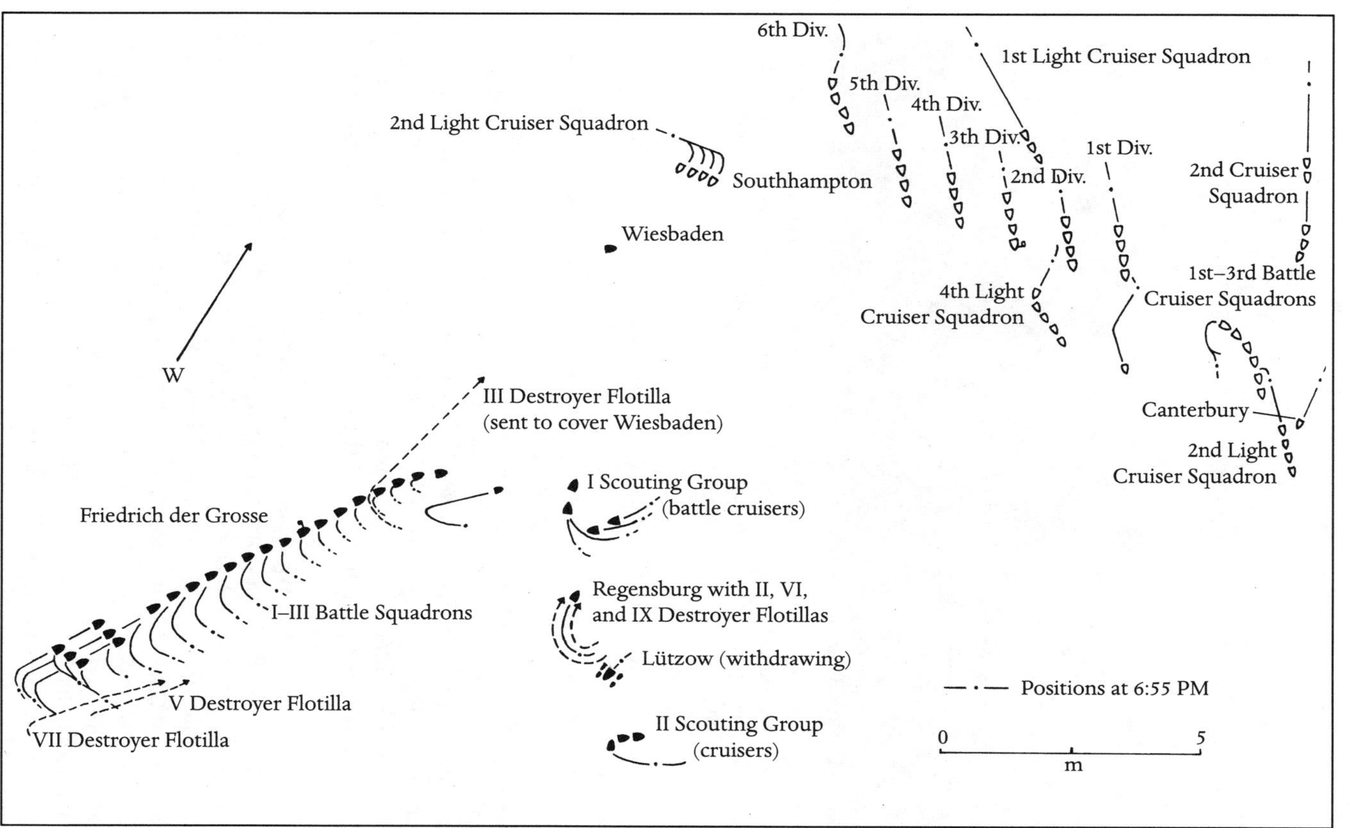

27. Scheer's Second Battle Turn, 6:55 PM, 31 May 1916.

14. SMS *Friedrich der Grosse* was Scheer's flagship at Jutland. Commissioned in 1913, she displaced 24,330 tons, had a top speed of 19.5 knots, and mounted a main battery of ten 12-inch guns. In 1916 her complement numbered approximately 1,250 officers and men. (Imperial War Museum, London.)

seemed minimal and the fleet was still battleworthy, he decided to order another battle turn to starboard at 6:55 P.M. Placing Hipper's battle cruisers in the van, Scheer made straight for the center of the Grand Fleet in such an apparently reckless manner that the decision became the subject of endless investigation and debate after the battle.

At 6:55 Scheer knew the approximate British position from a report sent ten minutes earlier by SMS *Moltke* placing Jellicoe's force east by south of the High Seas Fleet. Actually, only HMS *Canterbury,* which the Germans had located by radio direction-finding, and the 2nd Light Cruiser Squadron lay in this direction; the true bearing of the Grand Fleet was northeast. Given the poor quality of his intelligence, caused by the weather and Jellicoe's very conservative use of the wireless, it is not surprising that some confusion existed about the British position. Indeed, the possibility exists that Scheer did not yet know that he faced Jellicoe's whole fleet. Otto Groos, the author of the German official history, and the American strategist Commander H. H. Frost suggest that only after Scheer's flagship, SMS *Friedrich der Grosse,* received a message from the commander of Destroyer Flotilla IX at 7:48 giving the approximate size and power of the opposing force did Scheer have firm evidence that the entire Grand Fleet lay before him.

Scheer's intuition and practical experience now took command. His instincts told him to seize the initiative at all costs. Forcing the British to react to the unexpected appeared the only way both to help the light cruiser *Wies-*

baden, crippled by the British Third Battle Cruiser Squadron, and to exhaust the hours until darkness might offer the High Seas Fleet an opportunity to escape.[35]

Many historians have tried to attribute motives and insights to Scheer that the smoke, mist, rapid movement, and poor intelligence available at Jutland would never have permitted. For the German commander, this attack on the British seemed the most natural choice to make. He was a seaman and a fighter. He would never consider showing his back to the British the way he felt that Ingenohl had done at Dogger Bank. Furthermore, the battered *Wiesbaden* needed help. Scheer would not abandon a crew to its fate if he saw an alternative.

He took pride in the way his command had executed the battle turn and extricated itself from Jellicoe's grasp, but breaking off the engagement also meant losing the initiative. Thus far Scheer had kept Jellicoe guessing and had to a large degree determined the actual course of the battle despite the British numerical advantage. He felt that only by retaining that initiative could he hope to keep the British at bay until nightfall.[36]

The withering fire from the Grand Fleet that his battle cruisers encountered shortly after 6:55 did not catch Scheer by surprise. When he ordered the third and final battle turn away in order to save his ships at 7:18 he had not achieved his object of aiding the *Wiesbaden.* But he did force Jellicoe to take evasive action, in conformity with standing British battle orders, by turning two points away from the audacious torpedo attack that covered the German withdrawal. Again, Scheer retained the initiative and the High Seas Fleet escaped ruin.

The Grand Fleet's one-knot advantage in speed and a belief that Scheer would run south for the Frisian Islands, seeking safety in the Ems Estuary on his way to Wilhelmshaven, led the British to feel confident that the battle would resume at daybreak. Jellicoe proceeded on that assumption, hoping he could remain between Scheer and his base until dawn offered him a chance to renew the engagement on his own terms. Scheer instead chose the eastward route to Horn's Reef. In a series of night actions with the light forces at the rear of the Grand Fleet, he broke through the British line and made good his escape, via the Amrum Channel and Heligoland to Wilhelmshaven.[37]

In the avalanche of scholarship on Scheer's performance at Jutland, historians have virtually discarded Otto Groos's evaluation of the second battle turn. Most scholars dismissed his acceptance of the explanation Scheer offered as far too simplistic. Yet for Scheer, maintaining the initiative, saving the *Wiesbaden,* avoiding the appearance of a retreat, and disrupting the enemy's plans for the remaining daylight hours adequately explained his bold decision at 6:55 on 31 May.[38]

For many who examined this last great clash between battleships, the thirst for resolution and a clear victor has demanded a more involved and intricate explanation. This explains the intense and acrimonious debate in Britain over the course of the battle after 1 June 1916 and the rush in the years since to propose more comfortable formulas for the failure of the Royal Navy to capitalize on a rare opportunity. A half-century later, the incomparable Arthur Marder, rushing to offer his own interpretation, condemned Otto Groos and the German official history for comparing Scheer's tactics to those of Nelson. Unfortunately, Marder did not linger over Groos's work long enough to realize that the German author actually rejected the view that Scheer had Nelson's style of command in mind.[39] Like Commander Frost, Groos correctly perceived that on "the English side there has been, therefore, a tendency to underrate the fundamental reasons for the decision of the German commander."[40] Scheer accomplished his limited objective of engaging and inflicting considerable damage on a portion of the Grand Fleet. But the British saw a second Trafalgar slip through their fingers. The apparently casual and simple reasoning behind Scheer's decision at 6:55 only compounded their frustration.

In his 1936 examination of the battle, Commander Frost came closer to understanding the confusion about Scheer's decision when he commented that his "motives were so simple that naval critics the world over seem unable to credit them."[41] Scheer trusted his impressions and his judgment and, as Frost put it, "He was willing, contrary to Jellicoe, to leave something to chance." He believed strongly in taking the initiative, acting boldly, and using surprise to his advantage, and there is every indication that he would have done so even if, as Churchill said of Jellicoe, he had been in a position to lose the war in an afternoon. His actions in the most critical hours of the battle were guided, not by a strict preconceived plan, but by the impulse of the moment that faithfully reflected decades of experience and a seasoned intuition.[42] In his memoirs von Weizsäcker recorded a conversation in which Scheer discussed the second battle turn with his old friend, Admiral von Holtzendorff:

> Scheer, who was already in a mellow frame of mind, said: "My idea? I had no idea. I wanted to help the poor *Wiesbaden*. And then I thought I had better throw in the cruisers full strength. The thing just happened—as the virgin said when she got a baby." To which Holtzendorff replied: "But you must admit, Scheer, that one has to give the virgin some of the credit for what happened."[43]

Hailed as a hero upon his return from Jutland, Scheer was promoted to admiral on 5 June and awarded the Order *Pour le Mérite*, Prussia's highest military decoration, on the same day. He retained control of the High Seas

Fleet until August 1918, when he assumed command of the newly created combined naval staff, or *Seekriegsleitung*. After the war ended, he retired from the navy, living another decade to write his memoirs of the wartime High Seas Fleet (1919) and his autobiography (1925). In 1928, Admiral Reinhard Scheer died in Marktredwitz, Bavaria, at the age of sixty-five.

NOTES

1. Reinhard Scheer, *Vom Segelschiff zum U-boot* (Leipzig: Quelle und Meyer, 1925), p. 3.

2. Ibid., pp. 7–8.

3. For an excellent description of the training program for officers in the Imperial Navy, see Holger Herwig, *The German Naval Officer Corps: A Social and Political History 1890–1918* (Oxford: Oxford University Press, 1973), especially p. 63.

4. Friedrich Forstmeier, "Zum Bild der Personlichkeit des Admirals Reinhard Scheer (1863–1928)," *Marine Rundschau,* 58: (April 1961): 75.

5. Fall 1894 = Naval Academy
February 1895–Summer 1896 = Holtzendorff's navigation officer in SMS *Prinzess Wilhelm*
Winter 1896 = Naval Academy
Spring–Fall 1897 = navigation officer in the flagship of the First Squadron, SMS *Kurfürst Friedrich Wilhelm*
Fall 1897 = Torpedo Section of the RMA.

6. Forstmeier, loc. cit., p. 75.

7. Kapitänleutnant W. Diercks, "Der Einfluss der Personalsteuerung auf die Seekriegfuhrung, Eine Untersuchung zur seestrategischen Konzeption und operativen Planung in der Kaiserlichen Marine 1914–1918 anhand der Organization und Stellenbesetzungen der oberen Führungsstabe," *Unveröffentliche Jahresarbeit an Führungsakademie der Bundeswehr,* Hamburg, 1979, p. 12.

8. Ibid., p. 10.

9. The Central Division of the RMA was responsible for a variety of matters directly affecting fleet expansion, viz., political issues and complications, organization, and ship construction and weapons technology.

10. Forstmeier, loc. cit., p. 76.

11. Diercks, loc. cit., Scheer Fitness Report, 1 December 1907, Anlage #2.

12. Ibid.

13. Ibid.

14. Diercks, ibid., pp. 5–6, 12.

15. Ernst Heinrich Freiherr von Weizsäcker, *Memoirs of Ernst von Weizsäcker,* trans. J. Andrews (London: Victor Gollancz, 1951), p. 31.

16. Ibid., pp. 30–33.

17. Forstmeier, loc. cit., pp. 75–78; Scheer, *Segelschiff,* pp. 168–69. While captain of SMS *Elsass* Scheer acquired two friends who would prove very important, Lieutenant Commander Moritz von Egidy (later commander of the battle cruiser

Seydlitz at Jutland) and Lieutenant Commander Adolf von Trotha (Scheer's chief of staff at Jutland).

18. The General Naval Department of the RMA concerned itself with the military organization of the navy, mobilization matters, development of ship types, and the preparation for the naval appropriation and fleet law supplement debates in the Reichstag.

19. Diercks, loc. cit., Scheer Fitness Report, 1 December 1915, Anlage #2.

20. Reinhard Scheer, *Germany's High Seas Fleet in the World War* (New York: Peter Smith, 1934), pp. 135–36.

21. Scheer, *High Seas Fleet,* p. 7.

22. Ingenohl was commander in chief of the High Seas Fleet from February 1913 to February 1915.

23. Tobias R. Philbin, *Admiral von Hipper: The Inconvenient Hero* (Amsterdam: B. R. Grüner, 1982), p. 100.

24. The Naval Cabinet performed the same advisory function for the kaiser on naval affairs in peace and war as the Military Cabinet did for matters relating directly to the army.

25. Walter Görlitz, *Regierte der Kaiser?* (Göttingen: Musterschmidt Verlag, 1959), p. 116 (diary entry for Pless, 19 July 1915).

26. Erich Raeder, *My Life,* trans. H. W. Drexel (Annapolis: Naval Institute Press, 1960), pp. 59–61.

27. Von Weizsäcker, op. cit., pp. 30–31.

28. The adjectives describing these two officers are Raeder's words in *My Life,* pp. 59–61.

29. Forstmeier, loc. cit., p. 78. Churchill noted Scheer's daring and aggressiveness and his tendency to take action see *The World Crisis* [New York: Scribner's, 1927], III:113–14, 152–53).

30. Von Heeringen was chief of the admiralty staff from March 1911 to February 1913.

31. "Evolution of German Naval War Plans" by Captain Weniger, German Imperial Navy (Ret.), translated for the *ONI Monthly Information Bulletin,* December–January 1930–31, Box 932, F-6-g, CNO Intelligence Division Naval Attaché Reports, Record Group 38, National Archives (NA); Gary E. Weir, *Building the Kaiser's Navy: The Imperial Naval Office and German Industry in the Tirpitz Era, 1890–1919* (Annapolis: Naval Institute Press, 1992).

32. Operations Order No. 6 (in accordance with O-Plan II, 5.), 28 May 1916, Commander in Chief of the High Seas Fleet, Box 944, ZO5 Battle of Jutland, Naval Records Collection Subject Files, 1911–1927, Record Group 45, NA.

33. Depending on the account, the time used in descriptions of the Battle of Jutland can vary dramatically. Therefore, it is important to realize that the Germans were not only one hour ahead of the British, but had already shifted to summer time or daylight saving time, which would add yet another hour to the difference. Thus, when Sir Julian Corbett, in the British official history, sets the first battle turn away at 6:35 he is using Greenwich mean time (GMT). Rear Admiral Paul Behncke, commander of Squadron Three of the High Seas Fleet, noticed that the fleet was

making a 180-degree turn at 8:40 (his Z or main communication antenna was malfunctioning so he would periodically lose direct communication with Scheer). This showed him that Scheer had ordered the turnabout with which Behncke immediately complied. The order was actually given at 8:36 German time, 6:36 GMT. In this chapter, Greenwich mean time is used throughout. Sir Julian Corbett, *History of the Great War: Naval Operations,* vol. 3 (London: Longmans, Green, 1923), p. 369. Squadron Three Battle Report Concerning the Battle on 31 May 1916 by Rear Admiral Paul Behncke, 6 June 1916, Box 944, ZO5 Battle of Jutland, Naval Records Collection Subject Files 1911–27, Record Group 45, NA.

34. Holger Herwig, *Luxury Fleet* (Atlantic Highlands, N.J.: Ashfield Press, 1987), chap. 9.

35. Philbin, op. cit., p. 49. N. J. M. Campbell, *Jutland, an Analysis of the Fighting* (Annapolis: Naval Institute Press, 1986), pp. 162–63. Commander H. H. Frost, *The Battle of Jutland* (Annapolis: Naval Institute Press, 1936), pp. 384–87. Otto Groos, *Der Krieg in der Nordsee,* vol. 5 (Von Januar bis Juni 1916) (Berlin: E. S. Mittler und Sohn, 1925), p. 531. The German official history employs central European standard time, so this entry appears as 8:48 in Groos's list of messages sent by the German forces during the battle.

36. For the reasons given by Scheer for the battle turn at 8:55, see his *High Seas Fleet,* p. 155, and *Segelschiff,* pp. 228–31.

37. Herwig, *Luxury Fleet,* chap. 9.

38. Groos, op. cit., V: 310–11; Frost, op. cit., pp. 340–49.

39. A. J. Marder, *From the Dreadnought to Scapa Flow, The Royal Navy in the Fisher Era, 1904–1919,* vol. 3 (New York: Oxford University Press, 1966), pp. 110–22.

40. Groos, op. cit., p. 311.

41. Frost, op. cit., p. 343.

42. For interesting and largely positive evaluations of Scheer's style of command, see *Théories Stratégiques, The German Operations in the North Sea,* vol. 2, chap. 6 and 7, by Admiral Raoul Castex, September 1932 (Naval War College translation), Box 992, Naval Records Collection Subject Files 1911–27, Record Group 45, NA; *The Battle of Jutland, A Strategic and Tactical Study* by Captain C. C. Gill, USN, 18 October 1935, Box 9, Chief of Naval Operations Intelligence Division Naval Attaché Reports 1886–1939, Record Group 38, NA.

43. Von Weizsäcker, op. cit., p. 33.

Note on Sources

Admiral Scheer is a difficult figure to assess because there is a bare minimum of primary source material that explores his personality and background.

Friedrich Forstmeier's article in *Marine Rundschau* provides a good secondary framework for a discussion of Scheer's personality and its effect on the way the admiral fought at Jutland. He also calls the reader's attention to the most valuable published sources and thereby furnishes an excellent point of departure for the historian just beginning research on Scheer.

The Bundesarchiv-Militärarchiv, now in Potsdam outside Berlin, has the Fitness

Reports, or *Qualifikationsberichte,* covering Scheer's career, but the admiral left behind no personal papers to help the historian probe his personality, motives, and attitudes. Therefore, next to these reports on his professional life, the best primary sources are Scheer's autobiography, *Vom Segelschiff zum U-boot* (Leipzig: Quelle und Meyer, 1925), and his operational history of *Germany's High Seas Fleet in the World War* (London: Cassell, 1920; New York: Peter Smith, 1934; original German edition, Berlin: A. Scherl, 1920).

The best primary supporting materials on Scheer are the memoirs left by those who knew and worked with him. Both the von Weizsäcker and the Raeder memoirs are available in English and German and contribute helpful insights into his character, habits, and nature.

The Battle of Jutland (Skagerrak) has inspired mountains of analytical literature offering a variety of viewpoints on Scheer's performance. The works by Corbett, Campbell, Marder, Frost, and Groos are the best and most complete. In addition, the National Archives and Records Administration in Washington, D.C., holds a great deal of material on the battle and a number of excellent international evaluations of the performance of both sides. The Chief of Naval Operations Intelligence Division Naval Attaché Reports in Record Group 38 and the Naval Records Collection Subject Files (ZO5–Battle of Jutland) in Record Group 45 also proved valuable in the preparation of this chapter.

Survey VI

The Advent of Air-Sea Warfare

(1916–1945)

It is sometimes said that the High Seas Fleet never came out after Jutland. That is incorrect. Scheer took his battle squadrons back to sea in August and again in October 1916. On both occasions, British signals intelligence intercepted his orders for the German fleet to sail. In August, with the benefit of this information, the Grand Fleet nearly succeeded in springing another Jutland-style surprise, but in the outcome neither sortie brought the opposing forces into contact.[1] Even before these operations, however, Scheer had concluded that promising as it appeared in theory, in reality the chance that the High Seas Fleet could whittle its enemy down to size was impossibly remote; Germany's surface strategy had failed. Accordingly, on 4 July 1916 he submitted a memorandum to the kaiser advocating the resumption of unrestricted submarine warfare.

The problem Germany faced in unleashing its U-boats was that to do so would almost certainly bring the United States into the war on the Allied side. Blistering notes from President Woodrow Wilson following the sinking of the *Lusitania* in May 1915 had been responsible for the cancelation of the first unrestricted submarine campaign. Under these circumstances, Chancellor Theobald von Bethmann-Hollweg and the German Foreign Office took a dim view of launching another. The navy's leaders dismissed civilian fears, insisting that Britain could be starved into submission before American intervention became militarily meaningful. Their calculations showed that the U-boats could accomplish this goal by sinking a monthly average of 600,000 tons of merchant shipping for five consecutive months, an achievement they guaranteed. The army high command endorsed the admirals' arguments, and in January 1917 the kaiser gave the navy its head.

Although the United States did indeed declare war, on 6 April 1917, for a time it seemed that Germany's gamble would pay off. Between the beginning of February and the end of July 1917, the U-boats actually exceeded expectations, sinking a monthly average of 658,000 tons of Allied and neutral shipping. By the end of April, a despondent Jellicoe had become convinced that the war was lost. He and the Germans erred on two counts. The first was by overestimating the effect that such losses, awesome as they were, would have on the flow of supplies to Britain. The second was by failing to foresee the possibility and consequences of the adoption of convoy, the Age of Sail practice of sending merchantmen to sea in groups under naval escort rather than letting them take their chances sailing alone.

For months, Jellicoe resisted recommendations from Admiralty staff officers to implement convoy, convinced that it was infeasible. Finally, late in April, he decided to give it a try. By the end of August, convoy systems had been organized for both homeward- and outward-bound ocean shipping, and thereafter sinkings declined by almost 50 percent, though not on account of what might seem the self-evident reason. The convoys' success did not derive so much from their ability to fight off U-boats as to elude them, for the swarm of independently routed vessels that previously blanketed the North Atlantic had been drawn into knots the raiders seldom sighted. The U.S. Navy's Cruiser-Transport Force carried a million American soldiers to Europe without losing a ship or a man to enemy action. The German *guerre de course* had failed.

The events and aftershocks of 1914–18 shaped the postwar naval order. Victory's terrible cost so weakened the British economy that the Royal Navy was compelled to abandon its traditional preeminence and accept parity with the U.S. Navy. Two other major navies fared far worse. The Russian navy virtually disappeared amid the chaos of war, revolution, and civil war, and the terms of the peace imposed at Versailles reduced the German navy to little more than a coast guard.

The relative strength of the five remaining great navies was reflected and regulated by the Washington Naval Treaty of February 1922. This instrument established a ceiling on battleships and battle cruisers of 525,000 tons each for the United States and Great Britain, 315,000 tons for Japan—the 5:5:3 ratio that so offended many Japanese, to whom it translated as "Rolls-Royce: Rolls-Royce: Ford"—and 175,000 tons each for France and Italy. Limitations were also placed on aircraft carriers, the United States and Britain being allowed 135,000 tons, Japan 81,000, and France and Italy 60,000. In addition, no new capital ships were to be laid down during the treaty's ten-year term.

The big three powers agreed to extend these arrangements for five years at the London Naval Conference of 1930. By the time the Second London Conference convened to renegotiate them in December 1935, the tide had turned against arms limitations. Japan demanded equality with the United States and Great Britain. Upon being rebuffed, Japan withdrew from the conference. The English-speaking powers and France then concluded a treaty consisting primarily of escalator clauses. For practical purposes, naval arms limitations came to an end with the expiration of the First London Treaty on 31 December 1936. Between that date and the outbreak of war in

Europe thirty-two months later, the five powers that had signed the Washington Treaty laid down sixteen battleships and ten aircraft carriers.

A sixth, nonsignatory power also began building big ships. In 1935 Adolf Hitler announced that Germany would no longer abide by the Treaty of Versailles. By the end of 1936 he had authorized the construction of four battleships and an aircraft carrier, and in March 1939 he approved a major building program, Plan Z, designed to produce a powerful, balanced fleet by 1948. Fortunately, the war into which he rushed six months later left this project in limbo. In contrast to the *Kaiserliche Marine* of 1914, the *Kriegsmarine* of 1939 could not even dream of challenging the Royal Navy for command of the sea. *Guerre de course* was its only offensive option. Once again, the German submarine arm threatened to depopulate the sea lanes upon which Britain's survival depended, but once again, it went down to defeat. The difference was that this time there were no great battles in the North Sea. The fleet actions of World War II took place in the Mediterranean, where the concentrated strength of Italy's regional navy compared favorably to the forces its global commitments allowed Britain to assign to that theater, and, on a vaster scale, in the Pacific, where at the onset of hostilities the Imperial Japanese Navy was substantially superior to the U.S. Asiatic and Pacific Fleets.

Technological innovations of the interwar years profoundly influenced the format of the new war at sea. The most spectacular was the development of the aircraft carrier, a weapon system destined to supplant the battleship as the ultimate instrument of sea power. The supremacy that carrier aviation quickly asserted came as a surprise to most admirals, who had believed that big guns would determine the outcome of engagements in which carriers acted as auxiliaries to the battle line. Their failure of imagination has been the subject of considerable and, in part, undue criticism, for that failure was far from complete.

As noted in the preceding survey, navies were quick to sense the potential applications of aircraft to sea warfare. Although in World War I the great majority of naval aircraft flew from shore bases, the Royal Navy pointed the way to the future by taking some of its machines to sea. Several of its seaplane carriers had short flying-off decks forward for launching land planes, as did HMS *Furious,* a light battle cruiser modified by the removal of her fore turret, which joined the Grand Fleet in July 1917. The only way any of these vessels could recover an aircraft once it had become airborne, however, was to hoist it back aboard with cranes. This time-consuming procedure made it impossible for a carrier operating seaplanes to keep up with a fast-moving fleet and meant that unless they could reach shore, land planes were obliged to ditch in the sea.

The answer to these difficulties appeared in August 1917, when Squadron Commander E. H. Dunning succeeded in landing his Sopwith Pup on the flying-off deck of the *Furious* while she was under way. Eugene Ely, an American civilian aviator, had landed on a temporary platform aboard an anchored U.S. cruiser in 1911, but never before had a plane touched down on a ship in motion. The Admiralty quickly recognized the operational possibilities this opened. Procurement of seaplane carriers halted; the *Furious* was sent back to the yard to have her after turret removed and a separate landing deck installed; and the conversion in process on the unfinished liner that emerged as HMS *Argus* was altered to include a continuous flight deck.

The *Furious* rejoined the fleet in March 1918. She was not a success. Her battle-cruiser superstructure had been retained, dividing her flight deck into fore (flying off) and aft (landing) segments, and swirling funnel gases that made the after deck almost unusable. It therefore fell to the *Argus*, completed in September 1918 with an uninterrupted flight deck 565 feet in length, to confirm the practicality of recovering as well as launching aircraft aboard ship. Plans to use her to attack the High Seas Fleet in harbor were overtaken by the signing of the Armistice, but she had already earned a niche in naval history as the prototype of the modern carrier.

The idea of employing a ship to stage aircraft into battle was in itself not new. Between 1914 and 1916 British seaplane carriers had attempted ten raids on German Zeppelin bases on the North Sea coast. Seven of the these operations were aborted because of fog or rough seas, and none managed to put more than a single seaplane over its target, to which it did no harm. The reappearance of the *Furious* encouraged another try, and on 19 July 1918 she launched seven Sopwith Camels that destroyed two Zeppelins in their sheds at Tondern in the first real carrier air strike.

Impressive as the range of wartime activities in which naval aircraft engaged may appear, in the final analysis they had not accomplished very much. No battle or campaign had been determined or decisively influenced by aviation, and no surface combatant larger than a coastal motorboat had been destroyed by aerial action. Probably the most fruitful naval application of aircraft was to counter the second unrestricted U-boat offensive by standing patrols and, to the extent their range allowed, convoy escort. In 1917 and 1918, British aircraft and airships sighted 361 boats and were able to attack 237. Their primitive depth bombs sank only one, but their intrusions inhibited the others' operations.

That the multiengine bombers built late in the war could destroy big ships—at least, under ideal conditions—was proven in the summer of 1921 by a series of tests held by the U.S. Navy to explore the survivability of surface vessels under air attack. Surrendered German warships served as the targets. The U.S. Army Air Service responded to an invitation to participate in their immolation by contributing a "provisional air brigade" that flamboyant Brigadier General "Billy" Mitchell organized for the event. The climax came on 21 July, when the old dreadnought *Ostfriesland,* badly damaged the preceding day, went down after being hit by seven specially designed, two-thousand-pound bombs dropped in rapid succession from an altitude of two hundred feet.

Mitchell and other air power advocates proclaimed that the *Ostfriesland's* annihilation heralded the ascendancy of the aircraft over the battleship. Most naval officers heatedly rejected this conclusion, asserting that airmen could not replicate the destruction wreaked on the helpless *Ostfriesland* on a ship that was manning her guns, repairing her damage, and maneuvering to throw off their aim. They were probably right. The state of aviation technology in 1921 makes it unlikely that Mitchell's bombers could have inflicted much woe on a dreadnought in condition to defend herself.

Overall, then, at the time the Washington Conference convened in November 1921, the employment of aircraft in naval operations had demonstrated great promise and little else. If scarcely an officer outside the aviation community listened seriously to Sir Percy Scott and a handful of other distinguished old iconoclasts who insisted that the aircraft had made surface warships obsolete, the majority realized that it could become an important element of sea power. By the close of the decade, four of the five treaty navies had carriers afloat.

Its wartime conversions gave the Royal Navy an early lead. As of 1921 it had two true carriers in commission, the *Argus* and *Eagle*; the interrupted-deck *Furious* awaiting modification; and a new *Hermes,* the first purpose-built carrier, under construction. The U.S. Navy finished converting the fleet collier *Jupiter* into the carrier *Langley* in 1922. The *Hosho,* designed and built with the assistance of a British technical mission, joined the Japanese fleet later that same year. The French navy completed the *Béarn* in 1927, making Italy's *Regia Marina* the only treaty navy that, to its subsequent discomfit, chose not to acquire a carrier between the wars. Between 1927 and 1930, the United States commissioned the largest carriers of the prewar period, the *Lexington* and *Saratoga,* 37,000-ton sister ships that had begun life as battle cruisers canceled by the Washington Treaty, and Britain and Japan each completed two carriers, also built on hulls originally intended for capital ships. More were authorized in the following decade, especially after the collapse of the treaty system, so that by the resumption of war in September 1939 the Royal Navy had seven carriers in commission and six under construction, and both the U.S. and Japanese navies had five in commission (excluding a Japanese training carrier) and two under construction. The most commodious of these vessels could carry upwards of ninety aircraft, as many as today's supercarriers.

By then, great progress had been made in mastering the complex techniques of launching, recovering, and servicing aircraft at sea. Much thought and many exercises had also addressed the role of carriers in future conflicts. Orthodox opinion held that the battleship remained the weapon of decision, but that the carrier had become its most helpful handmaiden. The Royal Navy took the most conservative approach. Its carriers, more heavily gunned and armored than their U.S. and Japanese counterparts but embarking at best only two-thirds as many aircraft, were intended to be tied more tightly to the battle line and used within range of land-based air. U.S. carriers sometimes slipped the leash during the navy's annual fleet problems, with startling results. In 1929, the *Saratoga* executed an end-run that enabled her to "bomb" the Panama Canal, and in 1932 she and the *Lexington* launched a surprise attack on Pearl Harbor, an exceedingly pregnant precedent repeated in several subsequent games. Nevertheless, the four missions that U.S. Navy doctrine assigned its carriers at the time of the real attack on Pearl Harbor were all in support of the battle line: reconnaissance and observation; correcting ships' fire; defense against enemy aircraft and submarines; and attacking retiring enemy formations to reduce their speed so that the battleships could catch up. In a fleet engagement, carriers were to position themselves prudently on the battle line's disengaged side. Admiral of the Fleet Sir Ernle Chatfield, Britain's First Sea Lord from 1933 to 1938, summarized every navy's official position in the last years of peace when he declared that as an element of naval power, aircraft were second in importance only to gunnery.

The events of 1939–45 would prove this position mistaken; yet it was less wrongheaded than slightly out of date. Not until the mid-1930s, with the experience gained from the second generation of carriers, did the U.S. and Japanese naval air arms attain the operational competence prerequisite to tackle heavy surface units. The British took even longer, and high-performance monoplanes of the type that would fight the great Pacific air-sea battles did not reach any fleet until 1937. After a long adolescence, carrier aviation came of age quickly.

Almost equally revolutionary in their impact on naval combat were two electronic innovations: the invention of radar and the adoption of high-frequency radio. Radar proved to be the most important in fleet engagements. Scientists had known since 1886 that electromagnetic waves can be reflected from metal objects and in 1922 Marconi suggested that radio waves could be used for long-distance detection. During the following decade three navies secretly and independently set out to investigate that possibility: the United States in 1930, the German in 1933, and the British in 1935.

The Germans were the first to get radar to sea, beginning trials on a range-finding set called *Seetakt* in 1935. Both their competitors installed experimental sets aboard ship two years later. *Seetakt* went into production in

1939, but its reach did not extend more than eleven miles, and subsequently German research languished. The British and Americans, in contrast, forged steadily ahead. By the end of 1940 a number of ships in both navies, including every U.S. carrier, had been equipped with air-search radar; a U.S. surface-search radar was about to enter service; and the British had developed an airborne search radar and a fire-control microwave radar. They shared these technologies with the Americans, whose own versions of them appeared in 1941. Ironically, the U.S. Type 79 fire-control set was superior to the British model, giving not only range and bearing but spotting the fall of shot. Its introduction completed the gunnery revolution that had begun early in the century. Now ships could deliver accurate fire on a target the human eye could not see.

Anglo-American radar capabilities continued to improve in succeeding years. By 1944, U.S. air-search radar had achieved a range of 150 miles. Together with voice radio, an American invention dating from World War I, it was the key to the almost choreographic precision that distinguished U.S. carrier flight operations in the last two years of the war. Furthermore, the advantage of radar remained virtually an Allied monopoly. Aside from a radar detector that registered the receipt of waves from a sender set, German developments subsequent to *Seetakt* were negligible. The major battles in the Mediterranean had already been fought by the time the Italian navy received its first satisfactory shipboard radars in October 1942. The Japanese navy began to install air-search radar in big ships in mid-1942 and also produced a radar detector, but the sum of its efforts remained insignificant in comparison to those of its American adversary.[2]

Navies converted from low-frequency to high-frequency radio, capable of reaching any corner of the globe, during the 1920s. For the first time, worldwide communications became independent of undersea cables. This and other advances in radio technology, however, remained subject to compromise by enemy traffic analysis, direction finding, and worse yet, codebreaking. The accomplishments of the British Admiralty's Room 40 had become widely known in the interwar years, and by the eve of World War II every major navy had established signals intelligence activities to attack enemy transmissions.

To safeguard the security of their own communications, the German, Italian, Japanese, and U.S. navies acquired cipher machines of such sophistication—the permutations and combinations possible with the German Enigma eventually reached 10^{17}—that messages emanating from them were confidently assumed to be unbreakable. This assumption proved unwarranted. Allied operations benefited immensely from "Ultra" intelligence gathered by breaking enemy machine ciphers as well as by the penetration of lesser codes and the more prosaic practice of traffic analysis. The flow of information was never continuous. Changes in codes could cause months'-long blackouts, and some signals defied decryption until the usefulness of their contents had been overtaken by events. Even after the codebreakers had done their best, a degree of guesswork was usually necessary, but their best often proved invaluable. It was, for example, thanks to the U.S. Navy's Operation Magic that before the Battle of Midway Admiral Chester W. Nimitz, commander in chief of the U.S. Pacific Fleet, had the privilege of reading 85 percent of the operations order issued by Admiral Isoroku Yamamoto, commander in chief of the Japanese Combined Fleet. Not that the flow of information was wholly one way. Although Axis signals intelligence produced nothing approaching the importance of Ultra, the success the German navy's *B-Dienst* (*Funkbeobachtungsdienst* or Radio Surveillance Service) enjoyed in breaking British naval codes until the summer of 1943 made a substantial contribution to the effectiveness of U-boat operations prior to that date.

Of other interwar innovations, the most important in its operational consequences was every fleet's completion of the change, begun shortly before World War I, from coal to oil fuel. The use of oil enabled ships to refuel through hoses passed from oilers steaming beside them, a procedure pioneered by the U.S. Navy. Such "under-way replenishment," impractical in the days of coal, significantly increased a fleet's flexibility and endurance. In 1944 the U.S. Pacific Fleet carried this concept to its logical conclusion by organizing a huge fleet train of support vessels—oilers, tenders, store ships, ammunition ships, repair ships, even an ice cream ship—that made it virtually independent of shore bases during the last phase of the war against Japan.

Improvements in the design and capabilities of surface ships other than aircraft carriers were evolutionary. Compared to the dreadnoughts that fought at Jutland, the battleships launched after 1936 were from 35 to 50 percent faster, considerably larger—at 57,540 tons full load, the USS *Iowa* displaced practically twice as much as Jellicoe's *Iron Duke*—better protected against bomb and torpedo hits, and on the average, somewhat more powerfully armed, but they were not fundamentally different. What most distinguished the new generation of dreadnoughts was the quality of their gunnery, which radar direction and electromechanical computers enabled to hit targets at unprecedented ranges, regardless of visibility, and whether day or night. Yet their guns rarely trained on the targets that, more than any other, they had been designed to hit. Between 1939 and 1945 there were only six occasions—four in the European theater and two in the Pacific—on which battleships fired at their own kind on the high seas.[3]

Cruisers and destroyers, too, grew larger and faster, and both branched into two types, light and heavy. Heavy cruisers—in a sense, the second coming of the armored cruisers of the pre–World War I period—were an unplanned product of the Washington Naval Treaty, which allowed cruisers to displace up to 10,000 tons, almost twice as much as the light cruisers that fought in World War I, and to mount 8-inch guns. Especially in view of the freeze on battleships, it was inevitable that numbers of big cruisers would be built up to these limits. Prewar light cruisers generally displaced from 5,200 to 7,500 tons and carried 5- or 6-inch guns in their main batteries. (There were, as always, exceptions. For various reasons, both the Royal Navy and the U.S. Navy put 6-inch guns in some 10,000-ton platforms, which were referred to as light cruisers.) American and British cruisers had top speeds of 30 to 33 knots; their less well-protected Japanese and Italian opposites were up to 4 knots faster.

Nearly all World War II destroyers displaced between 1,350 and 2,650 tons, and mounted 4- or 5-inch guns. They could make from 35 to 38 knots. "Light destroyers" appeared while the war was in progress. The Royal Navy, which originated the type, called them escort destroyers; the U.S. Navy, destroyer escorts. Used to screen convoys and escort small carriers, they had displacements of 1,000 to 1,450 tons and miniature main batteries of 3- or 4-inch guns. Their best speeds ranged from 20 to 23 knots in the U.S. Navy up to 27 to 28 knots in most others.

The development of submarines was also evolutionary. The diesel / electric boats of World War II were more reliable, dove deeper, and handled better underwater than their World War I predecessors. They were also more formidable, firing larger salvos of more destructive torpedoes from a greater number of tubes. On the other hand, their speed and endurance (surfaced and submerged) had not changed much, and until the appearance of the German *Schnorkel* in 1944 they remained submersible boats rather than true submarines, obliged to surface to recharge their batteries and take on air for their crews. The major improvement in their performance came about through the application of electronic technologies. Electromechanical computers produced immediate solutions to fire-direction problems; surface-search radar (used by the Allies) located ships at night; and most important of all, radio enabled headquarters ashore to assemble all the submarines within reach into a wolfpack to attack a convoy sighted by a single boat, a German inspiration that came close to bringing the *Kriegsmarine* success in the Battle of the Atlantic.

The improvements in radio also gave promise that submarines could be integrated into fleet operations. In the Pacific, the Japanese and U.S. navies repeatedly sought to capitalize upon this possibility, but the difficulty of positioning submarine forces in the right place at the right time no less repeatedly frustrated their efforts. The first success came at the Battle of the Philippine Sea in June 1944, when U.S. boats reported the approach of the

Japanese Mobile Fleet and in the action itself penetrated its screen to sink the carriers *Shokaku* and *Taiho*. Four months later, at Leyte Gulf, Pacific Fleet submarines again furnished early warning of the Japanese advance, during which they destroyed two heavy cruisers and crippled a third. In neither case, however, was their intervention decisive; carrier aviation determined the outcome of both battles. Although the considerable number of warships they picked off on patrols affected the naval balance, submarines' most productive role continued to be war on trade.

What all this meant was that at the outbreak of World War II two generations of admirals who had spent their careers in the expectation that future fleet actions would take the form of great gunnery duels à la Jutland abruptly found themselves engaged in a mode of combat in which the big gun, for centuries the dominant weapon in war at sea, was eclipsed by the aircraft. Surface engagements did not cease to be fought—indeed, ten of the eighteen admirals killed in action afloat died in them—but all except a handful occurred at night, when existing technology precluded effective air operations against sea targets, and capital ships were seldom engaged. The new Jutland never took place.

The curtain raised on the Age of Air-Sea Warfare on 11–12 November 1940, the night twenty-one obsolescent, open-cockpit, canvas-covered Fairey Swordfish torpedo planes from the British carrier *Illustrious* surprised the Italian fleet at anchor in its base at Taranto, sinking one battleship and putting two others out of commission for months. Any idea that this event had been an aberration was dispelled on 7 December 1941, when the Imperial Japanese Navy staged its own super-Taranto at Pearl Harbor. Ironically, by eliminating the Pacific Fleet's battle line, the Japanese left the Americans no choice but to begin using their carriers as capital ships. The first encounter between U.S. and Japanese carrier forces, the Battle of the Coral Sea in May 1942, was also the first engagement in which the opposing vessels traded blows by proxy. Carrier aircraft played the decisive role in each of the five great fleet actions to follow—Midway, the Eastern Solomons, Santa Cruz, the Philippine Sea, and Leyte Gulf.

The nature of these battles differed radically from that of their predecessors in the Age of the Gun. In a sense, naval combat had come full circle. No longer did ships fight ships. The aircraft carrier was an assault ferry, like the galleys and cogs of the Age of Shock Action, except that in place of the marines they had borne into battle it embarked aircraft. Of course, it can be argued that those aircraft were simply flying artillery, a means of delivering projectiles to ranges beyond the reach of the heaviest guns, but even granting that proposition, the enormous quantitative change they brought to the practice of sea warfare imposed an immense qualitative change, as well.

Perhaps the most striking aspect of this change was the expansion of the battle area. The longest range at which a battleship's big guns could reach an enemy with reasonable consistency was about twenty miles.[4] U.S. carrier aircraft could do so comfortably at two hundred miles; Japan's less sturdy, longer-legged models at three hundred. Arbitrarily assuming that its attack squadrons would make their flights within a 60-degree arc opening toward their target, a Japanese fleet launching at 300 miles would be conducting operations over an area slightly in excess of 47,000 square miles—half the size of the United Kingdom. Throughout most of their time aloft these squadrons would be unopposed, but as they neared the U.S. fleet they would encounter its combat air patrol. If the interception took place at a conservative 60 miles from the U.S. carriers, and assuming that the ensuing action occurred within a 60-degree arc extending from them, the actual battle area would encompass approximately 1,880 square miles.

Imposing as they are, these figures would apply only to straightforward battles such as Midway and the Philippine Sea, in which the opposing forces were organized in relatively compact formations—although in those cases one side's attacks on enemy airfields ashore made the actual field of combat larger than that hypothesized above. Even so, their dimensions paled in comparison to those of Leyte Gulf, the naval war's most complex battle, involving three Japanese task forces (one in two echelons) operating up to eight hundred miles apart, Japanese land-based aviation units, and two U.S. fleets. The tactical theater of this vast action, embracing virtually the entire Philippine Archipelago, measured some 10 degrees in longitude and 12 degrees in latitude, or 432,000 square miles, and the battle area extended over 110,000 square miles—more than 7,000 times the area of the last major engagement fought in Philippine waters, the Battle of Manila Bay in 1898.[5]

Paradoxically, the new mode of combat caused both a lessening and a quickening of the tempo of naval battle. By the outbreak of World War I, ships had attained a speed and their guns a range that allowed mutually inclined formations to begin exchanging fire in something like a quarter-hour after establishing tactical (visual) contact. After a carrier force established contact with an adversary, generally by aerial reconnaissance, and commenced launching, two to three hours might elapse while its air groups assembled overhead and proceeded toward the enemy before their leading elements engaged him.

Once attackers closed with the enemy's ships, combat was compressed into a relatively few minutes of extreme violence. The fate of the *Shoho,* the first Japanese carrier sunk, anticipated the brevity and intensity of the conflicts to come. Jumped by two U.S. carrier air groups at the Coral Sea, she was struck by thirteen bombs and seven torpedoes in the twenty-five minutes she remained afloat. In the morning's action at Midway, the Japanese First Carrier Striking Force was under attack by U.S. carrier aircraft for fifty-three minutes—longer than it should have been, for in the confusion that enveloped the U.S. air groups after launching, their torpedo squadrons delivered three almost inevitably unsuccessful, independent attacks—but the climax of the battle occurred in a five-minute period during which two dive-bomber squadrons destroyed three Japanese carriers. At the Philippine Sea in June 1944, the Mobile Fleet's four strike waves kept the ships of the U.S. Fifth Fleet actually under attack for little more than an hour. By that stage of the war, however, the exponential expansion of the U.S. carrier force—from the three platforms that could be mustered for Midway to the seventeen at Leyte Gulf—enabled its commanders to stage serial raids that greatly increased their air groups' time over target. In the Cape Engaño component of the Battle of Leyte Gulf in October 1944, six strikes mounted by two U.S. task groups over a span of eleven and a half hours spent some three hours in contact with the Japanese Northern Force, sinking all four of its bait carriers. At the Battle of the East China Sea in April 1945, three waves totaling 386 U.S. aircraft subjected the super-battleship *Yamato* and her screen to a virtually uninterrupted assault for two and a half hours before she rolled over and sank, having been hit by a number variously estimated at from nineteen to thirty-four bombs and torpedoes.

The complexity naval operations had now attained made it necessary for fleet commanders to be assisted by substantial staffs. As commander of the Grand Fleet, Jellicoe had had a staff of sixteen officers. As commander of the Fifth Fleet, Spruance, who sought to keep his staff as small as practical, had about twenty—a chief of staff, operations, logistic, communications, assistant communications, navigation, air, and intelligence officers, a flag secretary, a flag lieutenant, a meteorologist, Marine Corps and Army liaison officers, a Japanese linguist, and eight junior communications and plotting officers. When Halsey commanded the same force (redesignated the Third Fleet), he had more than forty.

The admirals of World War II received the advice and relied upon the expertise of such staffs in planning and conducting the operations of the sophisticated fleets under their command, but as the following essays make clear, they did not necessarily accept their staffs' counsel. If Andrew Cunningham had done so on the evening of 28 March 1941, for instance, there probably would not have been a Battle of Cape Matapan. As in the past, the responsibility for and power of decision rested on the admiral alone. In this respect, despite the myriad changes the centuries had brought to war at sea, it had not changed at all.

Notes

1. The High Seas Fleet's only subsequent sortie, in April 1918, proved equally unproductive.

2. Another electronic innovation of the interwar era was the submarine detection system the Royal Navy, which began work on it in World War I, called Asdic (probably after the Admiralty's Anti-Submarine Division) and the U.S. Navy, sonar (for Sound Navigation and Ranging). This device, similar in principle to radar, emitted a note of supersonic sound from an underwater oscillator that produced an echo upon coming into contact with a submarine's hull. Its range was less than a torpedo's, limiting its utility to very close combat.

3. In the European theater: the Action off Calabria, between elements of the British Mediterranean fleet and the Italian fleet, 9 July 1940; the Battle of the Denmark Strait, in which the *Bismarck* destroyed HMS *Hood,* 24 May 1941; the sinking of the *Bismarck,* 27 May 1941; and the sinking of the *Scharnhorst,* 26 December 1943. In the Pacific: the battleship night action in the Naval Battle of Guadalcanal, 14–15 November 1942, and the Battle of Surigao Strait, 24–25 October 1944. In addition, battleships were engaged on both sides in the actions fought by British and American forces, respectively, with Vichy French fleet units in port at Oran, 3 July 1940, and Casablanca, 8 November 1942.

4. In the Action off Calabria in July 1940, the British battleship *Warspite,* not yet equipped with radar, scored a single, lucky hit on the Italian battleship *Giulio Cesare* at a range of thirteen miles. This appears to be the greatest distance across which a ship's shell ever found its way to a sea target.

5. For all except the last of these figures, see Giuseppe Fioravanzo, trans. Arthur W. Holst, *A History of Naval Tactical Thought* (Annapolis: Naval Institute Press, 1979), p. 203.

16

Andrew Browne Cunningham

The Best Man of the Lot

(1883–1963)

Eric J. Grove

THE TIME WAS 2225 ON 28 MARCH 1941, THE PLACE THE eastern Mediterranean off Cape Matapan, Greece, about 35°30′N, 21° E. Three old but powerful British battleships, all veterans of the Battle of Jutland, were sliding purposefully through the calm sea. Each carried eight 15-inch guns, which were trained to port in the expectation of an imminent meeting with the Italian enemy. On the crowded bridge of HMS *Warspite,* the leading ship, Captain Douglas Fisher had just been joined by the commander in chief and his staff. On the left breast of the admiral's immaculate Number 5 blue uniform were four rows of ribbons, among which an expert might have noted the red and blue of the Distinguished Service Order, a coveted gallantry award second only to the Victoria Cross. Two small rosettes on the ribbon showed that the admiral had been awarded the DSO three times. Admiral Andrew Cunningham's zest for action was clearly undiminished as he paced the side of the bridge nearest the expected position of the enemy and anxiously scanned the darkness with his binoculars. Then Commodore John Edelsten, his newly appointed chief of staff, spotted three dark shapes ahead, crossing from starboard to port. Cunningham soon had them in the binoculars, too, and Commander Power, the Staff Officer Operations, used his submariner's skills of ship recognition to identify two of them as enemy 8-inch gun cruisers of the *Zara* class. Cunningham was an old destroyer man and he had drilled his battle squadron to act like destroyers; on a wireless signal the three ships swung to starboard and lined their guns and searchlights up on the target.[1]

Cunningham never forgot that moment; as he wrote a few years later:

> The battlefleet were turned back into line ahead and in the dead silence in the ship, a silence that could almost be felt, one heard only the voice of the gun control personnel getting the guns onto the new target. One heard the orders repeated in the director tower behind and above the bridge and saw the 15″ guns swing round until they pointed at the enemy cruisers. I do not know that I have experienced a more thrilling moment than when I heard from the director tower "Director layer sees the target[,]" a sure sign that all was ready and that his finger was itching on the trigger.[2]

Captain Fisher ordered his chief yeoman to challenge the ships now only about two miles away, but "A.B.C." would have none of it; according to the yeoman the admiral snapped, "Challenge my foot—shoot!"[3]

Cunningham had always been impatient to get to grips with his opponent. In the training ship *Britannia,* where bullying was almost always a problem, the small, intelligent Scot, with his strange accent and slightly alien culture, soon found that a certain capacity for physical violence was vital. "Fight you on Sunday" was the accepted way of settling scores. Although his memory was of not being "particularly quarrelsome as a boy," his nickname "Meat Face" told of many bare-fisted Sunday meetings in local quarries or on the playing fields.[4]

A willingness to fight for what they considered to be the right was a long-standing Cunningham family trait. Andrew's first known ancestor was a minister of strong Covenanting views ejected in 1662 from the parish of Ettrick for refusing to conform to the compromise Restoration Scottish religious settlement. The Cunninghams combined this strength of will with considerable intellectual gifts. Andrew's grandfather, the Very Reverend Dr. John Cunningham, was a classic success story for the egalitarian and meritocratic Scottish tradition of progress through education. The son of an ironmonger, he became one of Scotland's most distinguished churchmen. Andrew's father was Professor Daniel Cunningham, who, while still in his early thirties, in 1882 received the Chair of Anatomy at the Irish Royal College of Surgeons. Thus it was in Dublin on 7 January 1883 that Daniel's wife, Elizabeth (née Browne), gave birth to their third child, Andrew Browne.

Professor Cunningham was soon appointed to the Anatomy Chair at Trinity College, Dublin, and became a leading member of the scientific community in Ireland. The Cunningham children saw little of their workaholic father and Andrew less than most, as he was sent to live with aunts in Edinburgh so that he could attend the academy there. The little boy from Dublin found it "rough going" at first and it was probably here that Andrew first honed his skills with his fists. Andrew "had always liked boats and the sea" and received a telegram from his father one day: "Would you like to go into the Navy."[5] Encouraged by his aunt, Andrew telegraphed by return, "Yes, I should like to be an admiral."[6] So, after three happy years at Fosters, a specialized "crammer" at Stubbington House Fareham, he sailed through the demanding entrance examination into the *Britannia,* the static training ship moored just above Dartmouth. Cadet Andrew Cunningham joined with the term that entered on 15 January 1897; he was a week over fourteen years of age.

From his Cunningham ancestors Andrew inherited a number of traits that provided the foundation for his successful naval career and his development into a great leader of men: an excellent intellect, a determined individualism, an ambitious self-confidence, and enormous energy. His mother provided a leavening of kindness, Scots common sense, cheerfulness, and a sense of humor, all of which combined to make Cunningham a magnetic and likable as well as respected character. Cunningham's relationship with his remote and rather formidable father also gives a clue to another feature of his character that was to have a great influence on his career—his attitude to discipline. This was in part a reflection of his Calvinist background—"discipline" has been a central tenet of the Scottish church since the days of John Knox—but one feels that Andrew's later passion for pleasing difficult, authoritarian superiors, something in which he achieved considerable success, had much to do with the deep psychological desire to prove himself to his distinguished father, whose capacity for hard work he knew he did not share, at least when the subject matter did not interest him. As he later wrote, in a passage that was toned down in the published version of his autobiography:

> I think I developed very young, I was usually top of my class and got several prizes at Fosters. Mathematics came easily to me and I was pretty good at Euclid's propositions. On the other hand Latin, French and English I could not abide and was quite useless at. I never found I had to work hard in fact I have always been lazy.[7]

Cunningham used his native ability and training at Fosters to cope more than adequately with the mathematical gymnastics of the *Britannia* course: he came third in the half-term examinations that were purely mathematical, but his impatience with foreign languages brought down his final passing-out result. Cunningham's disciplinary record reveals a boy of high spirits prone to "skylarking" who was in trouble a little more than most, especially when his patience toward the end of the fifteen-month course began to wear a little thin.[8] But Andrew was careful not to push his rebellion too far. He was always able to judge the boundary between individualism and indiscipline. When he passed out on May 1898 Cadet Cunningham's conduct was considered "Very Good" overall, the top grading. "Much" as opposed to "Very Much" application to study had achieved tenth place on the list, with Firsts in Mathematics and Seamanship but only a Second in French and Extra Subjects.[9]

Cunningham now continued his training at sea. At his own request he was posted to the Cape Station and on the way out in the liner *Norman* demonstrated his precocity by sitting at Cecil Rhodes's table in the saloon and beating the great man in the ship's chess tournament. With the coming of the Boer War in 1899 Cunningham wished to serve with the naval artillery ashore and was eventually forced to wake his formidable and notorious flag captain "Prothero the Bad," asleep in his cabin, to obtain permission. It was, he later said, "the bravest act" of his life, but it was an initiative crowned with the usual Cunningham success.[10] He saw action near Pretoria, but "Dan" Cunningham had used influence with his friend Lord Roberts, the

British commander in chief, to get the young midshipman to the front. This, and Cunningham's being summoned to join his distinguished father when the latter came out on a medical commission of investigation, had not gone down well with someone in authority. Cunningham was the only surviving midshipman from his ship who had seen combat with the brigade not recommended for early promotion, despite a certificate from the brigade commander commanding his "coolness, endurance and energy."[11]

Cunningham completed his midshipman's time in a battleship of the Channel Squadron, a boy ratings' training brig, and a large cruiser. This gave good experience and helped him attain a First in Seamanship, but little in the way of a theoretical professional foundation. Except in the first few months, Cunningham had "practically never . . . been under a proper naval instructor" at sea and his war service had not given him much time for study.[12] He paced himself to settle for only a Second Class Pass in the Sub-lieutenants' Navigation Course at Greenwich but was genuinely shocked to receive only a Second in Pilotage and was not able to do any better at the Gunnery School at Whale Island. Cunningham always found HMS *Excellent* and its apparently mindless drills and bullying staff "detestable," and when his "mutinous" feelings for once got the better of him, he received a "not satisfactory" conduct rating.[13]

Cunningham was happier at the torpedo school at HMS *Vernon* and obtained another First, which at least meant that he did not lose seniority, but the classical ladder to the top had been shut off, distinction in the sub-lieutenants' courses and specialist training, especially in gunnery. Cunningham chose a different path, one that made him a rather different kind of officer. He began it in 1903 after only a few weeks in his first appointment as a fully commissioned sub-lieutenant, the smart Mediterranean battleship *Implacable*, whose routine the young man found "rigid and irksome."[14] Then Cunningham heard that the destroyer *Locust* needed a new second in command: "I was tired of having no responsibility and too little to do so I asked the commander to ask the captain to apply for me to go. I had the feeling that they were quite glad to see the back of me so I got the job right away."[15]

The *Locust*'s commanding officer, Lieutenant A. B. S. Dutton, was notoriously difficult to please but gave Cunningham considerable independent responsibility to keep the little ship clean and efficient—a professional challenge that had proved too much for some of Cunningham's predecessors. The new sub-lieutenant thrived on it and earned his CO's approbation; Cunningham, Dutton wrote, was "a hard working and able officer well up in his work and always to be relied upon."[16] Dutton became something of a role model for Cunningham, who consolidated his self-confident disdain for service bureaucracy with which he was unsympathetic. He shocked his next captain in the destroyer *Orwell* by consigning an unwelcome official letter to the wardroom fire. There were no repercussions.

Acquiring his second stripe as a lieutenant at the end of March 1904, Cunningham next spent a happy couple of years in training cruisers, consolidating his own professional knowledge by teaching, a responsibility that he enjoyed and performed with "zeal and ability."[17] In 1906 he once more joined Dutton, who was now first lieutenant of the armored cruiser *Suffolk*. Her commanding officer was "Rosy" Wemyss, later to become a distinguished First Sea Lord. Cunningham observed with care his new captain's judicious mix of courtesy blended with bursts of fiery but just severity. Wemyss noted Cunningham's qualities, too, and arranged for his next appointment to be command of a new "coastal destroyer," *Torpedo Boat No. 14*, part of the Reserve Fleet with only a "nucleus crew." This first exercise in command was a great success, and Cunningham was next appointed to command an old coal-burner in the same flotilla, the *Vulture*. He had the temerity to inform the flotilla commander, Captain Reginald Tyrwhitt, that he considered his new command inferior to the little "oily wad." Tyrwhitt was "rather annoyed" but he regarded Cunningham as a "most capable and keen destroyer officer" and, when he could, gave him a newer destroyer, the *Roebuck*.[18] This little ship soon developed boiler trouble and it looked as if Cunningham might have to return to a battleship or cruiser, as the Admiralty preferred for officers after two or three years in torpedo craft. Cunningham hated this idea and enlisted the aid of Tyrwhitt's replacement to help arrange a more attractive appointment. Cunningham could not have achieved a better result: command of one of the newest destroyers in the navy, the *Scorpion* of the First Flotilla, which he joined at the beginning of 1911.

Cunningham was once more, very much to his taste, having to please a rigid disciplinarian, as his new captain (D—destroyer) was that most pathological of martinets, Sir Robert Arbuthnot. The two got on well; Cunningham later wrote of Arbuthnot: "I learned to like and admire him and he taught me a lot about discipline. He was hardhearted and inhuman but he expected nothing of one that he was not fully prepared to exact from himself."[19] Arbuthnot in his turn appreciated Cunningham's efficiency and ability to make his ship come up to his exacting and sometimes unreasonable standards.[20] Arbuthnot helped Cunningham avoid most of the necessary command examinations and did not demand his head when the *Scorpion*'s officer of the watch made an error and collided with a sailing ship during a night exercise in the channel. Cunningham was perhaps the only man in the flotilla sorry to see Arbuthnot go in mid-1912.

Cunningham's flotilla, by then commanded by Captain Cecil H. Fox, was ordered to the Mediterranean in 1913. Fox was, in Cunningham's words, "a fine destroyer officer, a most pleasant man and a good disciplinarian." Fox thought equally highly of his young subordinate, writing that Cunningham was "a most able destroyer commander. Strongly recommended for promotion."[21] This did not come straightaway, however, and Cunningham became a lieutenant commander in 1914 when all senior lieutenants were thus redesignated.

The *Scorpion* was still in the Mediterranean when war broke out that year and "A.B.C.," as he was to become affectionately known, was to spend almost the entire war in this theater. He thus avoided the boredom of Scapa Flow and the frustration of Jutland, experiences that would dominate the perceptions of his contemporaries. Instead, Cunningham took part in the unsuccessful chase of the German battle cruiser *Goeben* and was involved in the Dardanelles operations from beginning to end, the *Scorpion* being engaged in minesweeping and bombardment operations. Her captain won his first DSO and was promoted to commander. After the withdrawal from Gallipoli, Cunningham operated off the Turkish coast in the Dodecanese with his own small force, exploiting every opportunity to lead picket-boat assaults on small harbors himself. After taking his ship home for a refit in 1916 he went back to the Mediterranean to the destroyer *Rattlesnake*. On the *Scorpion*'s return Cunningham, whose reputation for efficiency and going through first lieutenants was now second to none, had the challenge of raising her new "hostilities only" crew to the ship's previous standards of smartness and effectiveness. One of the arrivals was Sub-Lieutenant R. V. Symonds Tayler, DSC, who later as a flag officer himself described the Cunningham style of leadership:

> A.B.C. expected nothing but the best and yet he was most patient in training me, an inexperienced youngster. "Oh *miserable* Sub what *are* you doing!" was a common cry. . . . After a few months, the then First Lieutenant left, and I became A.B.C.'s 13th First Lieutenant.
>
> From then onwards, instead of "miserable Sub" the cry was "First Lieutenant, what *do* you think you're doing!" when things were not as he wished them to be. He helped, advised and guided me in the running of the ship, which was extremely clean and efficient.
>
> Life was strenuous, discipline was very strict, and one had to be on one's toes all the time. He had an eye like a hawk and the "balloon" went up frequently. Having delivered a "rocket," usually on the quarter-deck, I well remember him saying: "Right, come and have a drink." Down we would go to the Wardroom and the incident was never mentioned again, I never heard him admonish anyone in the wardroom, where all was jolly and cheerful.

> Occasionally, after a particularly bad "rocket," I was sent to my cabin under arrest! There I remained, sometimes for several hours, till I was sent for and released. In spite of all this, I knew that A.B.C. was a friend who trusted me and who, if need be, would stick by me through thick and thin.[22]

The *Scorpion* suffered a collision shortly after her return and following repairs spent some months escorting convoys. Cunningham found this work dull. He therefore turned down the job of command of all destroyers at Malta when offered it and wrote to a previous flotilla commander now on the Naval Staff in London to arrange a transfer to see some action with the Harwich Force or the Dover Patrol. The *Scorpion* was duly called home at the end of 1917 and Cunningham, who considered ships "expendable," was untypically sad to leave the "staunch little vessel" that had been his home for seven years.[23] He was sent temporarily to the Grand Fleet destroyer *Ophelia* in the Firth of Forth and his disappointment at having his plans confounded was not improved by his shock at the ship's appearance and the slackness of her crew. His solution was to keep his men busy and he persuaded his flotilla commander to adopt a more demanding daily routine. His superiors were sorry to see Cunningham go when he obtained the first available vacancy in the Dover Patrol, command of the powerful destroyer *Termagant*—which he at once proceeded to try to smarten up.

To his disgust, Cunningham's only part in the attempt to block the U-boat base at Zeebrugge was screening monitors, and a boiler defect kept *Termagant* out of the Ostend blocking operation. His frustrations continued in May 1918 when he went off in pursuit of some German destroyers. He turned a Nelsonic blind eye to recall signals from the monitor *Terror,* whose screen he commanded, but all to no avail, as Cunningham's aggression was not matched by his ship's gunnery. Fortunately, the commodore at Dunkirk, who had known Cunningham in the Mediterranean, disregarded *Terror*'s complaints. Next Cunningham was sent to Chatham to organize an operation to use the obsolete battleship *Swiftsure* to block Ostend. This was eventually called off, much to Cunningham's disappointment, and he returned to the *Termagant.* For his activities in the Dover Patrol, Cunningham obtained the first bar to his DSO.

Happily for Cunningham, the end of the war did not bring an end to action. His new ship, the destroyer *Seafire,* was ordered to join Rear Admiral Walter Cowan's squadron backing the newly independent Baltic states against the Bolsheviks and the Germans. Cowan was another martinet, under whose peppery authority Cunningham thrived. He had the confidence and willpower to stand up to Cowan when he thought the admiral was being unreasonable. After some tricky moments in a most sensitive diplomatic situation, Cunningham returned in the spring of 1919 with glowing reports; Cowan assured the Admiralty that Cunningham was as "as good an officer as he could remember."[24] On 1 January 1920, A.B.C. was duly informed that he had been selected for early promotion to the rank of captain: he was thirty-seven years old. The war had done Cunningham a lot of good; he was the kind of officer whose qualities of practical leadership were best displayed in real combat situations.

His first appointment in his new rank was president of the subcommission charged with demolishing the German fortifications on Heligoland, a task that, carried out with the usual Cunningham energy, was finished early. After rapidly updating his naval knowledge in the first part of the Senior Officers Technical Course at Portsmouth, Cunningham found himself given a welcome "pierhead jump" to the command of the Sixth Destroyer Flotilla. This was in reserve but Cunningham was able to squeeze the maximum sea time out of his limited supplies of men and fuel. A few months later, at the end of 1922, he was appointed to a fully operational destroyer flotilla, the First, on loan to the Mediterranean Fleet because of the Chanak crisis with Turkey. Morale was not high and Cunningham was in his element smartening up the flotilla. As one of its officers later wrote, "For a month after he took over the 1st Flotilla wondered what had hit it."[25] Cunningham was far from well, with internal problems eventually diagnosed as a grumbling appendix, which did not improve his temper, but his sense of humor and real generosity of spirit made his subordinates endure the constant pressure and occasional fits of emotion. Soon the First Flotilla was taking pride in its reputation for impeccable seamanship, an image it retained when it rejoined the Home Fleet.

Cunningham was appointed captain of HMS *Columbine*, the Firth of Forth destroyer base in 1924, but moved from the destroyer world two years later when offered a appointment that would have daunted lesser men, flag captain and chief of staff to the dreaded Sir Walter Cowan. The old fire-eater wanted to take Captain Cunningham with him to command his new flagship on the America and West Indies Station, where Cowan was to become the new CinC. This was the light cruiser *Calcutta* and she remained the standards both of admiral and captain—who was now hoping for better health minus his appendix. Cunningham's secret was his instinct to respect in others those qualities of originality, courage, and initiative that he expected of himself. His subordinates sensed, as Cunningham did of Cowan, that "His ideals and duty and honor were of the highest and never sparing himself he expected others to do the same."[26] Based on this mutual respect, Cunningham and Cowan built up not only a professional relationship of "intimate trust and confidence" but a very close and sincere friendship.[27]

The main duty of the America and West Indies Squadron was "showing the flag," making friends and influencing people and maintaining local perceptions of British power and prestige. It was a significant station in this period, although its social demands posed a hazard to the hardiest constitution. In 1927 the *Calcutta* was replaced by the slightly larger *Despatch,* and the following year the exhausting social round finally came to an end. Cunningham had been a great success in a role that exploited the softer side of his character. The Chilean newspaper *Mercurio De Antofagasta* referred to him approvingly as an "excessively affable sailor" who "had a smile on his lips the whole time."[28]

Cunningham had never received any formal command training and the Admiralty took advantage of his having no better potential appointment to send him on two successive courses, the army's Senior Officers Course at Sheerness and the Imperial Defence College (now the Royal College of Defence Studies) in London. Cunningham surprised himself by liking the intellectual broadening he thus obtained. He also took the opportunity to acquire a wife, a vital social attribute for an officer at this stage of his career.

At the end of 1929 Cunningham took command of the new battleship *Rodney,* a novel experience for the destroyer man but a vital prerequisite for advancement to flag rank. The officers and ship's company of the battleship found their captain not quite the "frightening" and ferocious "tiger" they had expected, and put it down to his recent—and very happy—marriage.[29] Nevertheless, the *Rodney*'s commanding officer's commitment to excellence and competitive success was as strong as ever, which appealed to Admiral Sir Ernle Chatfield, the fleet commander. Chatfield was beginning to explore the possibilities of fleet action at night. Despite the lesson of Jutland, night action was still anathema to some officers, including Vice Admiral Sir Howard Kelly, second-in-command of the Mediterranean Fleet, whose unwillingness to fight after dark ruined the spring maneuvers of the combined fleets. Cunningham found night fighting second nature, as destroyers were already expected to attack after dark to "produce opportunities for obtaining decisive results in a subsequent attack by capital ships."[30] He was later to exploit with consummate skill the expertise in handling the fleet at night built up in the 1930s.

In the prevailing atmosphere of economy, captains being groomed for promotion were being limited to a year's sea time and Cunningham left *Rodney* at the end of 1930 to become commodore of the Royal Navy Barracks at Chatham. He was in this key post when the Invergordon Mutiny occurred in 1931. This brought out Cunningham's basic generosity of spirit. In his memoirs he took his share of responsibility for not having sufficiently recognized the financial hardship pay cuts would bring to the men. Cunningham kept a firm grip on his barracks but tempered this with humanity and understanding, spending day after day in five hundred interviews having his eyes opened to the everyday financial problems of the 1931 naval rating. There was little trouble at Chatham.

In 1932 Cunningham was informed that he was to become a rear admiral. After senior officers' technical and tactical courses at Portsmouth, he was granted his perfect appointment, rear admiral (D) in the Mediterranean in charge of the navy's three premier destroyer flotillas. Since 1930 the Mediterranean Fleet had been working at the night action problem; Chatfield, appointed that year as CinC, had been determined "to continue the investigation of the problem whenever opportunity offers as it is without doubt a problem of pressing importance and of great opportunities."[31] He had been strongly supported by his able second-in-command, the awesome W. W. Fisher, who took over the Mediterranean command in October 1932 and kept up the good work. Cunningham thus inherited a destroyer force whose night-fighting abilities were second to none; his job was to improve them still further. Fisher was also keen to explore the possibilities of using battleships at night. In the combined fleet exercises of March 1934, shortly after Cunningham's arrival, the Mediterranean Fleet soundly "defeated" the Home Fleet thanks to a surprise night encounter in which Cunningham's destroyers made a preliminary torpedo attack in heavy seas that allowed Fisher's battleships to engage on favorable terms.

The Mediterranean Fleet's Battle Instructions that in Kelly's day had stated that night action between ships was to be avoided were amended to state that such action was to be positively welcomed.[32] Cunningham was exactly the right kind of admiral for these tactics that required decisiveness, initiative, courage, imagination, and a willingness to take risks, and for every ship to be handled with a verve traditionally reserved for destroyers. Certainly the new, mature, healthy, and slightly mellower Cunningham seemed to his destroyer captains to be the perfect commander for the Mediterranean flotillas at this critical time, when as a result of the Abyssinian crisis war with Italy was a real possibility.

Cunningham left the Mediterranean in 1936 and "this final severence from the destroyer service" was a wrench after almost three decades in the little ships.[33] What made it worse was that the Admiralty had no immediate employment for him, especially after he became a vice admiral in July and thus too senior for courses. At the beginning of 1937 employment came in the shape of chairmanship of a committee on the accommodation and ventilation of HM's ships, where reform was overdue. More active work was on the way, however, as the navy began to suffer that series of losses to ill health that almost decapitated it just before the outbreak of World War II.

The exhaustion and strain caused by World War I, then very stringent economy, then rearmament and international crisis, compounded by a professional style not to delegate and to take far too much work on oneself, tested even the strongest constitution; the result was sickness, premature retirement, and early death. Cunningham had never had quite the leadership style of his "big ship" and gunner contemporaries and his enforced rest, irksome though it was, did him a great deal of good. He was thus able to emerge in the right place in the seniority lists to provide precisely the combat leadership skills the navy needed.

W. W. Fisher, who had become CinC at Portsmouth, was the first to go; a sad Cunningham attended his funeral. The news from the Mediterranean was that Admiral Sir Geoffrey Blake, commander of the Battle Cruiser Squadron, was also seriously ill and Cunningham was offered the job of temporary stand-in. Blake was eventually diagnosed as too ill to continue in the service and Cunningham's appointment turned out to be longer than expected. He rushed to Malta and hoisted his flag in the pride of the Royal Navy, HMS *Hood*. The rest of the squadron was made up of the smaller battle cruiser *Repulse,* the carrier *Glorious,* and the repair ship *Resource,* and Cunningham was effectively second-in-command of the entire fleet. The CinC was Sir Dudley Pound, who got on well with Cunningham and encouraged him to speak his mind. Cunningham had an able flag captain in A. F. Pridham and was soon handling his squadron with all his usual style. The *Glorious* tended to operate on her own, but a British carrier could not keep enough aircraft in the air to do this safely, as was proved on exercise, and Cunningham learned the apparent lesson that a carrier needed to operate as an integral part of the battle fleet and under its cover. This was not the way of the future, but such apparently old-fashioned attitudes were more than just a natural response from a destroyer man jealous of the potential subversion of important destroyer roles by aircraft. For a number of reasons, Britain could not deploy naval air power in the quantity that the United States and Japan were beginning to do; in these circumstances, limited numbers of aircraft tied to the battleships could achieve a great deal and were far too important to throw away.

It was still a delicate time in the Mediterranean with the Spanish Civil War and the necessity for naval patrols to prevent the Nationalist navy and air force from enforcing unrecognized belligerent rights—and to deter Italian submarines from sinking ships on sight. The *Hood* sailed around the Spanish coast and Cunningham spent a great deal of time negotiating firmly but amicably with the Nationalist naval commander. He also helped entertain the Italian fleet at Malta when it visited in June 1938 as part of the attempted rapprochement between Britain and Italy.

Cunningham's next job would also demand political skills. In February, Pound had told A.B.C. that he had been selected by the retiring First Sea Lord, Chatfield, and his successor, Sir Roger Backhouse, to become deputy chief of the Naval Staff in London. Cunningham would have preferred to have stayed in the *Hood* and in an interview with his boss-to-be claimed to be untrained and inarticulate on paper. Backhouse knew better and just smiled; Cunningham was one of the exceptional men whose innate abilities made lack of formal staff training unimportant.

Cunningham could not know it, but he was to become not just a deputy but acting First Sea Lord: Backhouse was struck down with a fatal tumor in March 1939. At the same time the Third Sea Lord also had to resign through ill health—and all this the same month that Hitler marched into Czechoslovakia, causing Britain's policy of appeasement of Germany to be transformed into a policy of confrontation! Much devolved on Cunningham, who had to stand in for his chief in the Chiefs of Staff Committee and the Committee of Imperial Defence. Unlike Backhouse, Cunningham could delegate and was a great success in this first, brief essay at the top of his profession.[34]

The growing crisis in Europe put serious question marks over the accepted British Far Eastern naval priority and the idea of sending the main fleet to Singapore. It is possible that Backhouse, who seems to have had a more Eurocentric view than Chatfield, chose Cunningham as his deputy partly for this reason. Certainly, it was natural for Cunningham, with his long experience of the area and his lack of exposure to staff convention, to throw his weight behind a new emphasis on Mediterranean concerns. A fleet fully committed to war with Italy could not be quickly withdrawn to be sent east. On 5 April 1939 Cunningham produced a paper that announced the change in blunt terms: "there are so many variable factors which cannot at present be assessed that it is not possible to state definitely how soon after Japanese intervention a fleet would be dispatched to the Far East. Neither is it possible to enumerate precisely the size of fleet it is proposed to send."[35]

Cunningham also liked the new idea of attacking Italy first as the weakest of the Axis partners. The attempt to detach Mussolini from Hitler had apparently failed; indeed, Mussolini's hostility was confirmed by the invasion of Albania only two days after Cunningham signed the above paper. A week later, on 13 April, Cunningham was a member of the key C.I.D. Committee considering the chiefs of staff "Appreciation" of European strategy, which produced an interim report that endorsed the potential of operations to "knock out" Italy.[36]

Having helped define this new strategy, the aggressive Cunningham was the obvious man to put it into effect. In May, Pound was called home to relieve the dying Backhouse, and Cunningham, now Sir Andrew following the award of a K.C.B.* in February, was chosen to replace him as CinC Mediterranean Fleet in the acting rank of admiral. He hoisted his flag in HMS *Warspite* on 6 June 1939.

Soon, however, Cunningham was dismayed to find that in his absence and with the increase of friction with Japan, more traditional priorities had reasserted themselves in London. On 24 July, Pound wrote to Cunningham to tell the new CinC his doubts about any early attempt to knock out Italy, and to restate the old dilemma of interwar British naval strategy; fighting someone somewhere might lead to insoluble complications elsewhere. Throwing the battle fleet prematurely against the Italian coast would expose it to losses, especially from air attack, which, "if Japan was wobbling," might encourage it to enter the war.[37]

Pound had always told Cunningham to be frank, and so he did not hide his feelings. He replied that he had been both "worried" and "most depressed" by the First Sea Lord's note and that his "views were at variance with some of those expressed therein."[38] Cunningham argued that there was little point in restraining the battle fleet, as it was more vulnerable in its poorly protected harbors than it was at sea; much better to use it to the full against the Italians and perhaps force the enemy fleet to sea. As he wrote, "I could see no point in holding back the battleships from doing their utmost against a power we were at war with in case we should have to fight another in the future."[39]

Alas for Cunningham, Italy did not join Germany when war came in September 1939 and the Royal Navy's finest fighting admiral had to watch his fleet be run down to support the campaigns in the Atlantic. Even before the German invasion of France, however, it was felt prudent to build up Cunningham's fleet and in May 1940 the CinC hoisted his flag again in the *Warspite*, returned from the Atlantic. This gave Cunningham four capital ships with which to begin operations against Italy when it finally came into the war in June. He had already decided that he would use his fleet to command the eastern Mediterranean and cut off the Dodecanese, with only periodic sweeps into the central Mediterranean. This made the most of his limited assets but paid due regard to his shortage of light forces and aircraft. When he communicated these intentions to London, he received a signal from Pound, for which the latter subsequently apologized by private letter, that Churchill considered them too "defensive." This "astonished" and "infuriated" Cunningham, especially in the context of the exchange of letters of the previous year.[40] Cunningham signaled the Admiralty that "my chief

* Knight Commander of the Order of the Bath.

fear is that we shall make contact with little or nothing except aircraft and submarines and I must get the measure of these before attempting sustained operations in the Central Mediterranean."[41]

This kind of "backseat driving" was anathema to Cunningham's concept of higher command. His fury still showed when he came to draft his memoirs. He had imbued his men with a healthy sense of superiority over the Italian fleet:

> whatever the number of their capital ships and the reports varied from 3–5 to 7 we were quite confident that the fleet we had at the outset could deal with them. Our difficulty as we realized but those at home particularly the PM did not, was how the devil to find them with the reconnaissance we had, practically nil, secondly when we had found them how to fix them until we could get near enough. . . . It was in that type of signal that the PM was so bad. It couldn't possibly do any good. If the C in C who knows all the chances was not prepared to get at the enemy on every possible occasion he just ought not to be there. To make "buck up" signals to him was just an insult.[42]

The fall of France saw Cunningham demonstrate both his moral courage and diplomatic skills in fighting off pressure from London to take violent action against the French ships at Alexandria and achieving their peaceful demilitarization. Then, in an action fought off Calabria during one of his sweeps in July 1940 he asserted a superiority over the Italian fleet, notably in long-range gunnery, that inhibited Italian movements for the rest of the war. Yet Cunningham's fears about air capability proved sadly justified: the available carrier, HMS *Eagle,* was unable to fix the fleeing enemy or do much against the disturbingly efficient Italian high-altitude bombers. When the *Eagle* was supplemented by the more modern *Illustrious,* however, Cunningham was able to put into effect the long-nurtured Mediterranean Fleet ambition to make an attack on the Italians in their base. The Taranto raid in November 1940 effectively halved the strength of the Italian battle fleet, sinking two battleships and disabling a third. The only unfortunate effects of this success from Cunningham's point of view were that it made a fleet action even less likely and it brought to the Mediterranean the Luftwaffe's Stuka dive-bombers, which came close to sinking the *Illustrious* in January 1941.

Cunningham pursued a vigorous operational program covering convoys and conducting bombardments and air raids, but like Nelson or Jellicoe, he could not induce an inferior fleet to come out and be defeated. He got his chance when the British reinforcement of Greece by sea in March 1941 stimulated the Germans to goad the Italians into making a move with their still powerful fleet. On 26 March "Ultra" code-breaking intelligence provided warning of the Italian sortie, which allowed Cunningham to move the troops out of danger, "to clear area concerned and so endeavor to make enemy strike into thin air while taking all action possible damaging him while he is doing so."[43] Cunningham was concerned that if the Italians got wind of a movement by his fleet in the direction of the planned operation they would simply stay in harbor until shortage of fuel forced the British back to base. It was thus vital to take them by surprise and Cunningham organized a deception plan on 27 March, playing a part himself by going ashore at Alexandria to play golf and carrying a suitcase to suggest that he planned to spend the night there. He was back on the *Warspite* to lead his fleet out of harbor at 1900 that evening. An RAF flying boat had confirmed that an enemy force of cruisers and destroyers was at sea moving toward Crete. Indeed, there were three separate Italian forces at sea, one including the new battleship *Vittorio Veneto*. Flying his flag in her and in command of the whole operation was Admiral Angelo Iachino, CinC of the Italian fleet.

Part of the British fleet, a force of four light cruisers and four destroyers, was already at sea covering the troop convoys and under the command of Vice Admiral Light Forces, Mediterranean Fleet, Vice Admiral Henry Pridham-Wippell, who had been a destroyer captain in the same flotilla as Cunningham's *Scorpion* in World War I. V.A.L.F. was ordered to rendezvous with Cunningham off Gavdhos (Gaudo) Island southwest of Crete on the morning of 28 March, but before he could do so, aircraft from Cunningham's new carrier, the *Formidable,* spotted an Italian surface force in the same area. All uncertainty was removed when Pridham-Wippell's cruiser *Orion* sighted one of the Italian cruiser-destroyer groups. He immediately turned to draw the enemy into the guns of the three battleships of the First Battle Squadron. His force was slowed by engine problems in the *Gloucester,* its most powerful ship, but luckily for the British, the more heavily armed Italian cruisers were hampered by poor rangefinders.

To support his old colleague, Cunningham sent *Valiant,* his fastest capital ship, ahead together with his two most powerful *Tribal*-class destroyers. Before they could arrive, the Italians tried the lure trick and turned back toward their battleship. Cunningham reconcentrated his force and pressed on at the partially modernized battleship *Barham*'s best speed of 22 knots. He had held back his air strike as long as he dared so as to allow his relatively slow battleships the maximum opportunity to exploit any damage inflicted but the danger to V.A.L.F.'s cruisers was such that first he ordered in Swordfish based in Crete and then the *Formidable*'s Albacores. His instinct was vindicated when the British cruisers spotted the Italian battleship and came into serious danger. They were saved only by the timely arrival of the Albacores, which caused Iachino to retire northwestward.

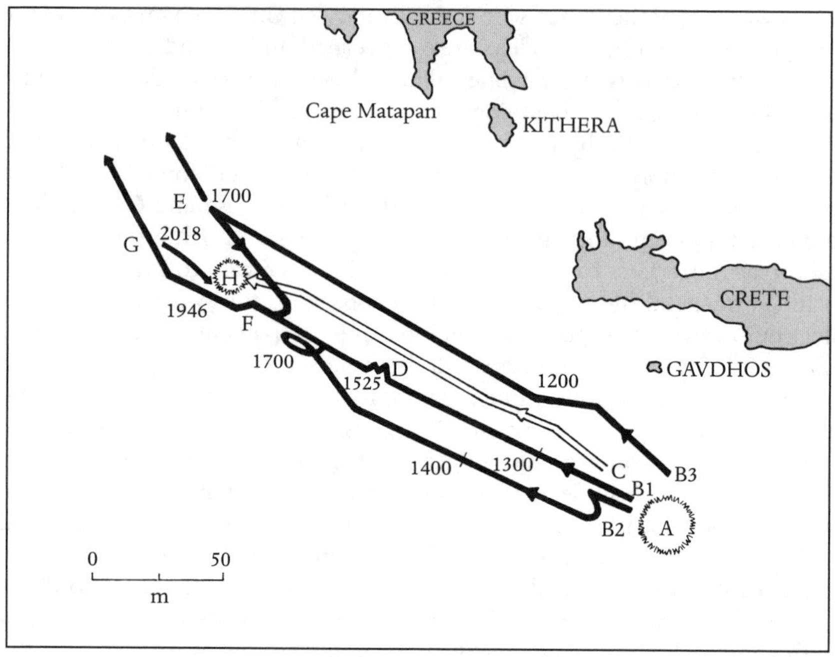

28. The Battle of Cape Matapan, 28 March 1941. Following its morning action with the British cruiser force (A), the Italian fleet (B) retires in three formations: (1) The *Vittorio Veneto* and four destroyers; (2) the 3rd Cruiser Division (three ships) and three destroyers; and (3) the 1st and 8th Cruiser Divisions (five ships) and six destroyers. It is pursued by Cunningham's 1st Battle Squadron (C) and cruiser force (track not shown) and subjected to air attacks from Greece and Crete. The *Vittorio Vento* is damaged by a strike from the *Formidable* (D), but soon regains way. An hour and three-quarters later, Iachino concentrates his fleet, ordering the 1st Cruiser Division (*Zara, Fiume,* and *Pola*) (E) to join the main body. The *Pola* is subsequently disabled (F) by a strike from the *Formidable.* Soon thereafter, Iachino deatches the *Zara* and *Fiume* and three destroyers (G) to assist her, leading to the night action with the British fleet (H).

Cunningham's worst fears of provoking a premature turn away had been realized, and the British tried desperately to fix the fleeing foe with air strikes. At 1519, four Albacores and two Swordfish from the *Formidable* put a torpedo into the Italian battleship's stern. The successful Albacore was shot down, but the *Vittorio Veneto* lay dead in the water. Because of conflicting aircraft reports, the situation appeared confused to Cunningham, who sent Pridham-Wippell to find out what was going on. This also allowed the available carrier aircraft to be concentrated for one last strike in the early evening. Iachino had deployed his forces in a protective ring around his stricken battleship. She had been coaxed back into movement by the time the British torpedo-bombers arrived. The defenders held off the carrier planes, but a Swordfish from Crete torpedoed the heavy cruiser *Pola,* which the retreating Italians had to leave behind. At 2018 Iachino, who had not received a vital sighting report that would have told him of Cunningham's presence, sent back the rest of the *Pola*'s group, the cruisers *Zara* and *Fiume,* and four destroyers to look after their crippled companion.

Cunningham was also making a difficult decision, one of the key decisions of his life. At long last, in the late afternoon a report from an experienced observer flying in one of the *Warspite*'s Swordfish gave him a good idea of what lay ahead, but the news that there were at least six cruisers and no less than eleven destroyers skillfully concentrated around the damaged battleship made pressing on seem foolhardy. Any British officer in such a situation would have welcomed the opportunity to lay a destroyer-torpedo trap for his pursuers.[44] Cunningham's staff members counseled caution, especially as the fleet had not had much recent practice in night action. Reportedly, about 2000, with "the well known steely blue look in [his] eye," A.B.C. called them "a pack of yellow-livered skunks" and, as it was his customary supper time, said that he was going off to eat alone and "see after supper if my morale isn't higher than yours."[45] Over the meal Cunningham weighed a number of factors. He knew that British night-fighting techniques were second to none in Europe and far superior to the Italians' techniques.[46] Waiting for the morning would be even more dangerous than pressing ahead, as it would bring the fleet well within range of German Stukas. "The question was whether to send the destroyers in now to attack this difficult target or wait until morning in the hope of engaging at dawn but with the certainty of exposing the fleet to a heavy scale of air attack. The decision was taken to attack with destroyers and follow up with the battlefleet."[47]

Given Cunningham's style and background, no other decision was possible. His blend of instinctive aggression leavened by a brilliant intellect and years of experience and training directed toward this very moment came up with the right answer. Certainly his men, with their "healthy contempt" for the Italian foe, expected no less.[48] At 2037, Cunningham sent eight destroyers forward under Captain Philip Mack to engage the enemy with torpedoes while he followed with the battleships. The result was described at the beginning of this chapter; the *Fiume* and *Zara* were blown out of the water by Cunningham's battleships and the *Pola* was finished off by Mack's destroyers. Two Italian destroyers were also sunk, and all for the loss of a single Albacore in the attack on the battleship.

Regrettably, Cunningham let the adrenalin go to his head and at 2332 made a signal, "All forces not engaged in sinking the enemy, retire north east."[49] This was intended to get as many ships as possible "clear from the

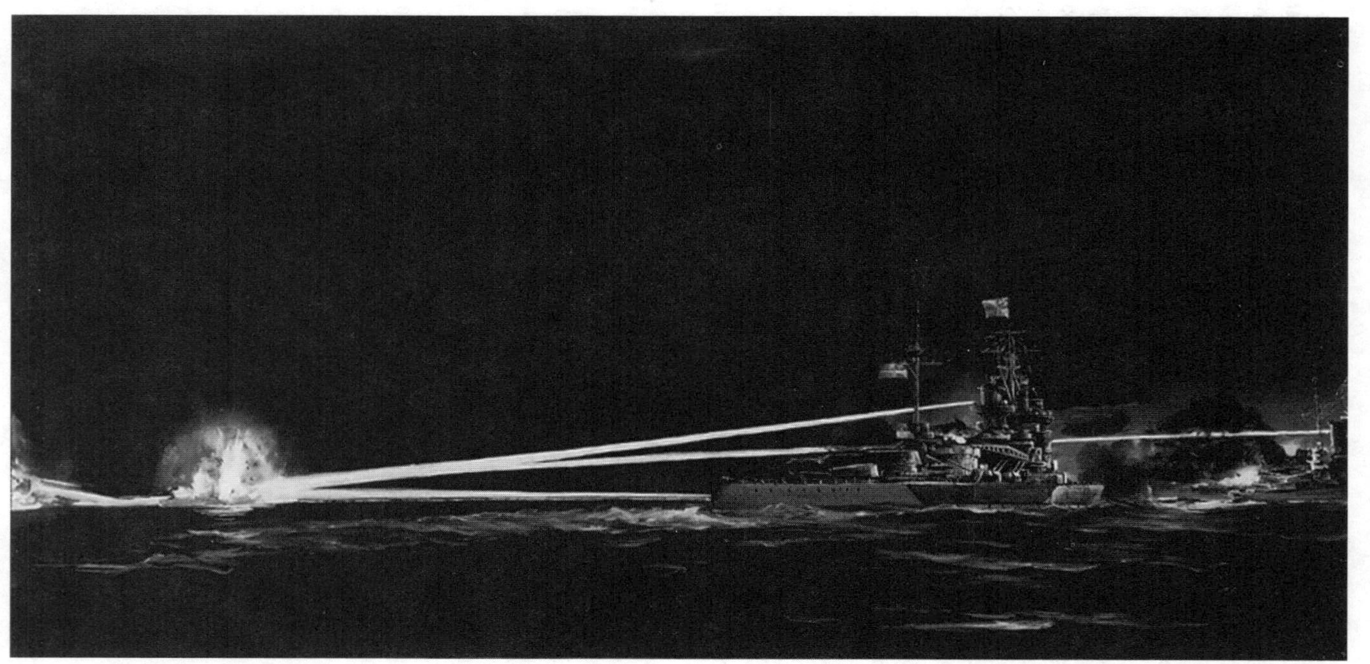

15. The Battle of Cape Matapan, 28–29 March 1941. The Italian cruiser *Fiume* is illuminated and eliminated by the British battleships *Warspite* and *Valiant* in a John Hamilton painting of the opening of the night action. (Imperial War Museum collection, the artist's estate.)

destroyer melee and was made under the impression that cruisers and striking force were in contact with the enemy."[50] Sadly, however, they were not directly engaged and Pridham-Wippell interpreted the "extremely bad" signal literally and withdrew. As Cunningham was also taking his battle force eastward out of danger, the remainder of the Italian fleet was able to escape.

Perhaps more formal staff training would have produced a signal that could not have been misunderstood. Cunningham was a big enough man to admit his error.

> Looking back one is conscious of several things that might have been done better but it is a very different matter sitting in an armchair and thinking calmly and being on the bridge of a ship at night. In no other circumstances as in a night action does the fog of war completely blot out one's knowledge of what is taking place. But still, looking back I cannot find the reason for deciding to steer a course with the battlefleet so far to the East after the action with the cruiser, nor yet a good and sufficient reason for ordering forces not engaged in sinking the enemy to withdraw.[51]

Cunningham's enthusiasm had, however, secured far from insignificant results before it went over the top. The destruction of the three heavy cruisers removed a menace to the much less powerful British cruiser force. More importantly, the Italian navy had received yet another lesson in its inferiority, one that kept it in harbor until autumn. In Cunningham's own words, the successful British evacuation from Greece and Crete "may be said to have been conducted under the cover of the Battle of Matapan."[52] The threat from the air was bad enough and the CinC's maintenance of morale in these travails was a masterpiece of leadership in adversity.

Never again would Cunningham lead his fleet in a major surface action. It was his diplomatic, political, and policy-making skills that would be relied on for the rest of the war. In April 1942 Cunningham became head of the British Admiralty delegation in Washington. This led to his return to the Mediterranean as naval CinC of the Allied Expeditionary Force that invaded North Africa in November 1942. Promoted to Admiral of the Fleet early in 1943, he resumed the post of CinC Mediterranean, oversaw the Sicily and Salerno landings, and had the satisfaction of taking the surrender of the Italian fleet in September 1943.

The following month another brain tumor, this one Sir Dudley Pound's, took him back to London as First Sea Lord. Given their previous conflicts, Churchill had opposed Cunningham's appointment and the latter continued to prove "impervious to Churchill's spell," which was a welcome change after the Pound era.[53] Because of his undoubted bravery in action, Cunningham was one of the few admirals whom Churchill respected, a feel that was reciprocated by A.B.C. This mutual respect made Cunningham a successful

First Sea Lord. No other "fighting admiral" had A.B.C.'s intellect and, therefore, perhaps only Cunningham could combine ability and full confidence of the prime minister. Created a Knight of the Thistle in 1945, Lord Cunningham in Churchill's resignation honors list, and Viscount Cunningham of Hyndhope in the New Year's Honours of 1946, A.B.C. finally left the Admiralty in June of that year. After an active "retirement," he died in 1963 and was buried at sea from the new guided missile destroyer *Hampshire.*

Despite his success at the very top, Andrew Cunningham's real forte remained leadership at sea. The peak of his career was 1940 and 1941 in the Mediterranean, when Britain stood alone against the Axis powers. The charismatic Cunningham, "fiery, aggressive and intolerant . . . scintillating, successful and inclined to be schoolboyishly boastful," a "champion charger" who had on occasion to be reined in by his staff, was what the desperate situation demanded.[54] In May 1940, just as that crucial period began, Sir Walter Cowan had sent one of his numerous letters to his friend Cunningham. "Ned," the formidable old martinet wrote, "I think when it's all triumphantly over you'll have proved yourself the best man of the lot."[55] He did.

NOTES

1. Oliver Warner, *Cunningham of Hyndhope, Admiral of the Fleet* (London: John Murray, 1967), pp. 126–39, contains an account of Matapan with memories of participants upon which the opening paragraph of this chapter has been largely based. See also Cunningham's dispatch, "The Battle of Cape Matapan," Public Record Office (PRO) ADM 199/781, his published autobiography, *A Sailor's Odyssey* (London: Hutchinson, 1951), pp. 326–35, and the photographs opposite p. 341.
2. The original holograph draft of the autobiography in the Cunningham Papers, British Museum, Additional Manuscripts, 52581A, f. 85.
3. Chief Yeoman E. J. Freestone's recollections reported in Warner, op. cit., p. 138.
4. Cunningham, op. cit., p. 13. Interestingly, there is no mention of Cunningham's pugilistic skills in the original draft.
5. Cunningham Papers, 52580A, f. 18.
6. Ibid.
7. Ibid.
8. Captain S. W. C. Pack, *Cunningham the Commander* (London: Batsford, 1974), pp. 13–14.
9. *Britannia* Certificate, Cunningham Papers, 52568, f. 1.
10. Draft autobiography, ibid., 52580A, f. 24.
11. Certificate of service, ibid., 52568, f. 7.
12. Cunningham, op. cit., p. 35.
13. Ibid., p. 36.
14. Ibid., p. 37.

15. Draft autobiography, Cunningham Papers, 52580A, f. 35.

16. Dutton's Certificate of 10 November 1903, ibid., 52568, f. 36.

17. Certificates from *Northampton* and *Hawke,* ibid., ff. 35–36.

18. Cunningham, op. cit., p. 46.

19. Draft autobiography, Cunningham Papers, 52580A, f. 46.

20. Arbuthnot's Certificate of 30 July 1912, ibid., 52568, f. 44.

21. Cunningham, op. cit., p. 52, and Fox's Certificate, Cunningham Papers, 52568, f. 37.

22. Quoted in Warner, op. cit., pp. 31–32.

23. Cunningham, op. cit., p. 87.

24. Excerpt of letter from Cowan to Rear Admiral R. W. Bentinck, 1 May 1919, written from the Baltic and on Bentinck's death returned to Cowan and sent on to Cunningham; Cunningham Papers, 52562, f. 95.

25. Vice Admiral Sir James Troup, quoted in Pack, op. cit., p. 46.

26. Cunningham, op. cit., p. 137.

27. Cowan to Cunningham, 10 June 1940, Cunningham Papers, 52562, f. 7. The tone of the extensive correspondence contained in this file attests to the real affection the normally irascible Cowan had for his old subordinate.

28. Cunningham Papers, 52568, f. 89.

29. Vice Admiral Sir Dymock Watson's memories, quoted in Pack, op. cit., p. 50.

30. Naval War Manual 1925, PRO ADM 186/66.

31. Chatfield's comments on Exercise "OX," 29 October 1930, in "Exercises and Operations 1930," PRO ADM 186/148.

32. "Battle Instructions Mediterranean Fleet," 1928 and 1934 editions, PRO ADM 186/106.

33. Cunningham, op. cit., p. 178.

34. Stanhope to Cunningham, 24 May 1939, Cunningham Papers, 52568, f. 126.

35. Memorandum SAC 16 in, PRO CAB 16/209.

36. SAC 13, ibid.

37. Pound to Cunningham, 24 July 1939, Cunningham Papers, 52560, ff. 9–10. This reflects the view expressed at a C.I.D. meeting of a few days before, see C.I.D. meeting 309, 19 July, PRO CAB 53/10.

38. Cunningham to Pound, 26 July 1939, ibid., ff. 16–17.

39. Draft autobiography, Cunningham Papers, 52580B, f. 90.

40. Ibid., 52581A, f. 3.

41. Telegram of 7 June 1940, ibid., 52566.

42. Ibid., 57581A, ff. 3–4.

43. Signal, CinC Mediterranean to Vice Admiral Light Forces, 1728, 26 March, "Admiralty Use of Special Intelligence in Naval Operations," PRO ADM 223/28, p. 326.

44. Draft autobiography, Cunningham Papers, 52581A, f. 81.

45. Memory of Commander (late Vice Admiral Sir Geoffrey) Barnard, fleet gunnery officer, quoted in S. W. C. Pack, *The Battle of Matapan* (London: Batsford, 1961), p. 115.

46. Draft autobiography, Cunningham Papers, 52581A, f. 88.

47. Cunningham's dispatch, "covering remarks," paragraph 14, PRO ADM 199/781.

48. Draft autobiography, Cunningham Papers, 52581A, f. 11.

49. Despatch, PRO ADM 119/781, "covering remarks," para. 17.

50. Ibid.

51. Draft autobiography, Cunningham Papers, 52581A, f. 11.

52. Despatch, PRO ADM, 119/781, para. 22.

53. John Colville, *Footprints in Time,* quoted in Stephen Roskill, *Churchill and the Admirals* (London: Collins, 1977), p. 216. Cunningham kept a diary in 1944–46 that is a very useful source with its frank and pungent comments. Cunningham Papers, 52577–79.

54. Admiral Sir Manley Power, who as a commander and Cunningham's Staff Officer Operations at Matapan won a ten shilling bet that the Italians would indeed come out, to Stephen Roskill, quoted in *Churchill and the Admirals,* p. 217.

55. Letter, Cowan to Cunningham, 10 May 1940, Cunningham Papers, 52562, f. 6.

NOTE ON SOURCES

There is as yet no proper scholarly biography of Viscount Cunningham. The fullest account of his life is his autobiography, *A Sailor's Odyssey,* first published in 1951 by Hutchinson of London and New York. This excellently written book was actually the work of Captain Taprell Dorling, who wrote under the pseudonym "Taffrail." Cunningham provided Dorling with a handwritten draft that he recast into a more formal and elegant form, while retaining the spirit of the original. Dorling also looked up facts that the admiral only partially remembered and added quotations from signals, etc. It should be noted that radio signals were deliberately reworded for security reasons (see the original draft and related correspondence in the Cunningham Papers). The autobiography is usefully supplemented by Oliver Warner's memoir, *Cunningham of Hyndhope, Admiral of the Fleet* (London: John Murray, 1967), and Captain S. W. C. Pack's *Cunningham the Commander* (London: Batsford, 1974). Although both these books are somewhat hagiographical, they contain fascinating reminiscences by Cunningham's former subordinates and other valuable material. Also of great use for an assessment of Cunningham is Stephen Roskill's *Churchill and the Admirals* (London: Collins, 1977).

Captain Pack wrote two books on Matapan, *The Battle of Matapan,* published in Batsford's "British Battles" series in 1961, and *Night Action off Cape Matapan,* No. 2 in the "Sea Battles in Close-Up" series published by Ian Allan of Shepperton, England, and the Naval Institute Press of Annapolis in 1972. Both cover much of the same material in the same way and sometimes in the same words. The latest updated account of the battle in English appears in *Sea Battles in Close-Up: World War II,* by Martin Stephen and edited by Eric J. Grove, published by Ian Allan and the Naval Institute Press in 1988. The classic exposition of the Italian side of the story is given in Admiral Iachino's *Gaudo e Matapan* (Milan: Mondadori, 1946); there is a typewritten translation in Cunningham's papers. The latest Italian account is *Il Giallo di Matapan: Revisione di Giudizi,* by Francesco Mattesini, published in two volumes by

Edizioni dell'Ateneo, Rome, 1985. Another useful non-British source is "Matapan" by Marc Benoist, *La Revue Maritime,* March and April 1948 (consulted in the translation produced for the Royal Naval Staff College, Greenwich, London, and now in the keeping of Professor Till). The secret intelligence aspects of Matapan are covered in *British Intelligence in the Second World War* (London: H.M.S.O., 1979), I: 403–6.

The most important original sources of Cunningham's life are the twenty-eight volumes of Cunningham Papers in the British Museum, Additional Manuscripts 52557–84. These are in process of rearrangement and the folio numbers cited in the Notes may be changed. The Public Record Office contains Cunningham's long Matapan dispatch in the War History Cases and Papers, "The Battle of Cape Matapan," references ADM 199/781. This must be supplemented by Chapter XXII on Matapan in "Admiralty Use of Special Intelligence in Naval Operations," a once "Top Secret Ultra" study by Captain G. E. Colpoys, RN, kept in the PRO at ADM 223/28. Perhaps the best source of facts on the battle is the Naval Staff History, Battle Summary No. 44, "The Battle of Cape Matapan, 28th March 1941," written in 1950 and numbered BR1736(35) in the Official Publications series. It is available for public consultation at the PRO at ADM 186/795.

17

Isoroku Yamamoto

Alibi of a Navy

(1884–1943)

H. P. Willmott

THE ROLE OF INDIVIDUAL COMMANDERS IN TWENTIETH-century warfare presents obvious problems of interpretation and evaluation. Warfare in modern times has assumed a complexity and scale beyond the capacity of any single intelligence to control and direct, and the development of staff and doctrine necessarily supplies the elements of constancy and continuity in the never-ending processes of personnel change and technological development. The commander is clearly important, but the extent to which any individual, irrespective of rank or position, can provide leadership and direction is an open question. Assessing the role and leadership of Fleet Admiral Isoroku Yamamoto, commander in chief of the Japanese Combined Fleet from September 1939 to April 1943, thus presents a problem of separating the man from the system.

This task is further complicated by difficulties of historiography and methodology. Though warfare in the present age is fought between societies and systems in a manner distinctly different from that in previous times, Anglo-American historiography remains heavily influenced by Carlyle's "great men" approach that presents war in terms of a gladiatorial contest between national champions. Such an interpretation demands the naming of Yamamoto as the Japanese entry in the lists, as *Time* magazine presented him in its first issue after Pearl Harbor. The conceptualization of history in these terms, questionable at best, is especially dubious in light of the diffusion of power within the Japanese decision-making process, which makes the identification of personal responsibility highly problematical. Moreover, any analysis of the Japanese performance in World War II is conditioned by the reality of defeat, the fact that Japan's bid for supremacy in the Far East was in the nature of a national kamikaze effort. This being so, the limits of individual culpability are hard to define when set against the conclusion that defeat was unavoidable.

Even more difficult in an assessment of Yamamoto is the fact that for the better part of four decades a very simple and persuasive picture of the admiral has found uncritical acceptance in the West. The picture has provided Japan and the Imperial Navy with alibis in the examination of a record that otherwise would do neither any credit. In its general outline, the view of Yamamoto that has gained currency in the postwar world is of a moderate nationalist and patriot who vainly tried to stem a headlong rush into war spurred by the Imperial Army, but who was determined, when war became inevitable, to wage it to the full in an attempt to secure a victory that, privately, he recognized to be beyond Japan's reach. His often-quoted prediction that Japan could command success for a year or eighteen months in a war with the United States, but that thereafter problems would multiply,[1] is cited as proof of realism and foresight, which by implication is associated with the Imperial Navy as a whole.

This picture of Yamamoto is very convincing—after forty years it could hardly be anything else. Whether it is accurate is another matter. The Imperial Navy, as its activities at Shanghai in the 1930s clearly demonstrated, was hardly a model of restraint and moderation. It was the navy, not the Imperial Army, whose eyes were fixed on the Asian mainland, that pressed for war in southeast Asia in 1941; and it was Yamamoto, not the Navy Ministry or the Naval General Staff, that insisted that war in southeast Asia had to include war with the United States. And the Battle of Midway, the Guadalcanal campaign, and the Japanese air offensive in the southwest Pacific in April 1943 hardly represent stunning strategic or tactical successes on the part of "the greatest admiral since Lord Nelson."[2] With such a track record, one wonders where the likes of Jellicoe and Nimitz stand in the all-time pecking order.

Similar problems beset any attempt to evaluate Yamamoto's prewar career and his personality. There is little in the way of English-language literature about Yamamoto. Much of the Japanese material is trivial and laudatory, and the fatalism that attaches itself to Japanese accounts avoids the posing of searching questions. What emerges in and between the lines written about Yamamoto as a person is not altogether attractive. His treatment of wife and family passed beyond mere neglect. A womanizer, he was given to personal indulgence and was an obsessive gambler. To have risen to the top of a service wracked by intrigue required a well-developed instinct for survival, and he was ruthless toward personal rivals and disdainful of those of lesser abilities.[3] In his last years he became increasingly autocratic. He made no attempt to argue the merits of his Midway plan, and used his prestige to overcome reasoned criticism from superiors and subordinates alike. After Midway, when qualities of resilience and foresight were at a premium, he appears to have lost much of his former self-assurance. On the other hand, he had a very strong sense of duty, was not moved by desire for material possessions, and disliked the extravagances of the cult of personality. Moral courage was an important ingredient in his makeup, and though small in stature, he had an immediate and intimidating presence.

Yamamoto, born Isoroku Takano at Nagaoka, Niigata Prefecture, on 4 April 1884, was to occupy the post of commander in chief of the Combined Fleet for longer than any other admiral in the history of the Imperial Japanese Navy. The son of a schoolteacher, he graduated from the Etajima naval academy in the Class of 1904 and served in Togo's fleet at the Battle of Tsushima, in which he was wounded in the right leg and lost two fingers of his left hand. Both his parents had died by the time he reached twenty-nine and he was adopted into the Yamamoto clan, adult adoption being a common practice in Japan. In 1919 he was sent to study English in the United States, where he remained until mid-1921, living in the Boston suburb of Brookline. Following his promotion to captain, he returned to the United States to serve as Japanese naval attaché, 1926–28. Yamamoto was popular among his American acquaintances, although he formed a poor opinion of their navy, which he dismissed as "a social organization of golfers and bridge-players."[4]

After his return from the United States, Yamamoto, whose career had begun in the gunnery branch, progressed from command of a fleet carrier in 1928 to flag rank in 1929 and command of a carrier division in 1933. Nevertheless, it was in a series of administrative and political posts that Yamamoto marked himself as "the coming man": as a member of the Japanese delegation at the London naval arms limitations conferences of 1930 and 1935, as head of the Technical Division of the Aeronautics Department and later of the department itself, and then as vice minister of the navy in four successive governments between 1936 and 1939. He first came into public prominence, both domestic and international, as a result of the London conferences. His standing within the navy itself was not enhanced by the fact that throughout the 1930s he was identified with three causes that were opposed by mainstream service opinion. The first was his general adherence to the principle of naval limitations that had begun with the Washington Naval Treaty of 1922, through which the ratio of capital-ship strength between the United States, Britain, and Japan was set at 5:5:3. The second was the development of carrier aviation, which in the Japanese as in other navies was opposed by traditionalists convinced of the continuing supremacy of the dreadnought. The third was resistance to Japan's alignment with the European Axis powers, a course of action strongly favored by many officers in both the army and navy, especially the army. Despite the myths that developed after his death, Yamamoto did not command the loyalty and affection of the fleet at the time of his appointment as its commander in chief. To the contrary, the reputation by which he was known within the fleet was far from flattering. He had made many enemies, and one of the main reasons for his appointment was his superiors' desire to place him beyond the reach of assassins from the various patriotic associations that bedeviled Japanese public life.

The outcome of the issues in which Yamamoto made himself controversial was mixed. Although by late 1941 Japan had more carriers in commission, ten of all classes, than any other power, on the two critical questions of foreign policy—naval limitations and association with Germany and Italy—the moderates were worsted. Neither defeat occurred while Yamamoto held a position of responsibility, however. On the matter of naval limitations, which was crucial to Japan's relations with the United States, Yamamoto was too junior to have had a major influence in shaping policy, and Japan's commitment to the Axis camp came after he had left Tokyo for the fleet. Given the divisions between the Navy Ministry, the Naval General Staff, and the Combined Fleet, between the pro- and anti-limitation factions that had persisted since 1922, and a command structure that "necessitated [senior officers] having a number of protégés who could be used in various ways . . . to bring about their rivals' early downfall,"[5] Yamamoto, Navy Minister Mitsumasa Yonai, and like-minded colleagues faced a monstrous challenge. Perhaps the most they could do was to see that the manipulation of senior officers by middle-ranking subordinates did not become as pervasive in the navy as it had in the army. That, and at least the postponement of Japan's alignment with Germany, may have been the limits of the power of those nominally responsible for the navy. Under the circumstances, these would have been no mean achievements.

Yamamoto went to the fleet base at Hashirajima with a status, apparently conceded by his opponents, as an extremely able commander, closely associated with carrier aviation. These two strands form the basis of his reputation as a great admiral of the twentieth century. The fact remains, however, that Yamamoto had never commanded one of Japan's subordinate fleets before 1939, and his period as commander of a carrier division between October 1933 and May 1934 hardly constituted sufficient time to learn the practical aspects of this new dimension of naval warfare, still less to demonstrate competence, flair, and powers of innovation. Indeed, this whole aspect of Yamamoto's career and reputation is puzzling to the Western observer; not only was there a lack of sea time between 1929 and 1939 in which Yamamoto could have demonstrated tactical ability, but he does not seem to have had any obvious personal impact upon the development of Japanese naval doctrine either before or after 1939. His reputation as an innovator and pioneer of Japanese naval aviation also seems to have little basis in reality. In his thinking Yamamoto was outpaced by Vice Admiral Shigeyoshi Inoue by a very considerable margin, and although it is true that the Japanese aviation industry made very great advances in the time that Yamamoto filled various posts in the Navy Ministry, his personal contribution to a much bigger process of industrial development is hard to discern. It is sometimes asserted that during his service at the Aeronautics Department Yamamoto was instrumental in the development of the Mitsubishi Zero, the world's premier naval fighter in 1941, but while he undoubtedly supported the Zero, so did many others. There is no firm evidence that he should be considered its sponsor or in any way especially responsible for it.

The question of Yamamoto's strategic and operational ability is best considered, not in terms of the operation with which he is most closely identified, the attack on Pearl Harbor, but the Battle of Midway. A careful examination of the Combined Fleet's doctrine, organization, and procedure in the planning and conduct of the Midway campaign, the only occasion when Yamamoto commanded the Combined Fleet in battle, shows that Japanese method in 1942 had scarcely changed from that of a decade earlier. The same careful examination must preclude Yamamoto's being considered one of the great captains of naval warfare.

Like Pearl Harbor, Midway was an operation mounted on Yamamoto's insistence: he imposed it upon a reluctant and skeptical Naval General Staff and he decided its timing. The staff favored prosecuting the offensive in the southwest Pacific, with the strategic objective of isolating Australia from the United States. Yamamoto, in contrast, was resolved upon a return to the Central Pacific. By the occupation of Midway Island, only a thousand miles from Honolulu, he intended at one fell swoop to force the Pacific Fleet's carriers to give battle and be destroyed, thereby completing the task left unfulfilled in December 1941, and to secure an advanced outpost that would, among other things, reduce the prospect of a repetition of the American air raid on the home islands in April. In the end, a fatal compromise was reached. An amphibious assault would be made on Port Moresby, the base for Australian operations in eastern New Guinea, in May; the Midway operation would follow in June. The need to prepare the Combined Fleet for the latter venture precluded the covering forces allocated to the Port Moresby operation being adequately invested. This was a major factor in the outcome of the Battle of the Coral Sea (7–8 May 1942), in which the Japanese invasion force was turned back with the loss of one light carrier sunk and a carrier division too badly mauled to be made available in time for the Central Pacific offensive.

In the case of Midway itself, Yamamoto approved plans that were flawed on a number of counts. He endorsed a submarine reconnaissance plan with scouting lines that consisted mostly of gaps that could not be covered by eye and available search equipment. With eight carriers available, and a ninth if he had been prepared to wait a month, Yamamoto accepted a division of his force that resulted in the reduction of Japanese strength at the point of contact to four carriers tasked with two contradictory objectives—neutralization of Midway and the defeat of the American fleet—and with no real margin of superiority over an enemy with just three carriers. The overall Japanese deployment involved a dispersal of force throughout the western Pacific, from Midway to the Aleutians, that ensured that no single formation could be supported when subjected to attack and defeat. The major part of the air formation that was to be moved to Midway to provide a critically important shore-based air capability in the battle expected to develop when the Americans responded to the occupation of the island was embarked in

29. The War in the Pacific, 1941–45, showing the locations of the major carrier battles: (1) Coral Sea, 4–8 May 1942; (2) Midway, 4–6 June 1942; (3) Eastern Solomons, 23–25 August 1942; (4) Santa Cruz Islands, 26–27 October 1943; (5) Philippine Sea, 19–20 June 1944; (6) Leyte Gulf, 24–25 October 1944.

the two carriers directed to the Aleutians. By no standard can the Japanese plan of campaign, for which Yamamoto bore sole responsibility since it was conceived, prepared, and finalized by the Combined Fleet staff, be considered even competent. Perhaps the most telling comment on the Japanese arrangements for Midway is the fact that in the course of a battle that saw the Combined Fleet deploy 24 submarines, 109 surface units, and 433 aircraft, the Japanese managed to attack exactly one American warship while losing four fleet carriers and a heavy cruiser.[6]

In terms of doctrine and operational procedures, what is most remarkable about the Japanese plan for Midway is that the majestic clockwork whereby the Japanese were to establish themselves in the Central Pacific and annihilate the Pacific Fleet was no advance over the elaborate and unreal concept of "the decisive battle" that had been developed in the interwar period. Centered around the gun and night torpedo attacks, this schema could trace its pedigree back to Tsushima[7] and made no serious attempt to integrate the fleet carrier within a balanced organization. There was the obvious concession to the proven ability of carrier aircraft to sink warships, yet after six months of war, during which Yamamoto had been at Hashirajima watching and presumably studying American and Japanese carrier operations, apparently neither he nor his staff attempted to resolve the divergence of objectives. Furthermore, they failed to recognize and rectify the most serious single weakness of their plan—the fact that the vanguard had only a minimal reconnaissance capability, while the main battle force, hundreds of miles astern, had a surplus.

The inherent weakness of such arrangements is obvious, and indeed as Yamamoto's staff completed the Midway plan there was sufficient contemporaneous evidence of the risks run by carrier formations in attacking shore-based targets without adequate reconnaissance to provide against the presence of enemy naval forces in position to counterattack. Off Ceylon (Sri Lanka) in April the Japanese had found British units at sea only after their initial attack on shore and port facilities, and at the Coral Sea in May the Japanese plan came apart as formations operating independently of one another proved unable to overcome shore-based air power supported by a carrier force. On both occasions, and particularly at the Coral Sea, the Japanese fleet carriers thus committed had been fortunate to escape the full consequences of cursory reconnaissance, but such warnings went unheeded by commanders and staffs seemingly impervious to the dictates of common prudence, much less the rigorous demands that staff training should have imposed. Those experiences notwithstanding, in May 1942 the Combined Fleet sailed with a plan of campaign that never even addressed basic tactical problems and with reconnaissance provisions that can best be characterized as pathetic. Under Yamamoto's overall supervision, the staff played war games that were fixed to ensure a Japanese victory rather than tackle the problems that these games were intended to reveal, as in fact they did.

The First Carrier Striking Force was defeated off Midway on 4 June 1942 by an outrageous combination of circumstances—the compromise of Japanese naval codes, the unfortunate order in which events unfolded, and a luck that favored the Americans—but a lack of professionalism and competence on the part of the Combined Fleet command exposed its vanguard to defeat in detail, despite what should have been an overwhelming numerical advantage. Once the vanguard had been destroyed there was nothing that Yamamoto, flying his flag in the super-battleship *Yamato* in the main battle force, could do to retrieve this situation. For all the very considerable strength that remained to the Combined Fleet, at 0015 on 5 June he was compelled to turn his force to the west to avoid being caught within range of enemy aircraft at daybreak even before learning that the American fleet's movements eliminated any possibility of engaging it in a night surface action. The general verdict of history upon the Battle of Midway has been that responsibility for the Japanese defeat lay with the breaking of Japanese codes by U.S. naval intelligence and operational errors on the part of Vice Admiral Chuichi Nagumo, commander of the First Carrier Striking Force.[8] The fact of the matter is that fundamental errors of doctrine, organization, and planning exposed the Striking Force to defeat, and even if this force did not fight the most skillful of battles, its commanders had at least recognized the tactical problems they faced, only to have their reservations preemptorily dismissed by none other than Isoroku Yamamoto.[9]

If an objective examination of the Battle of Midway must preclude Yamamoto's being considered a master of sea power, much the same can be said about the attack on Pearl Harbor. Despite the suggestions that he conceived the idea for this operation in early 1941, Yamamoto was not its author,[10] but he was certainly its sponsor and he forced it upon the Naval General Staff. The plan was prepared under his auspices, and the carriers trained for it under his supervision. The contrast between the plans made for Pearl Harbor and for Midway, less than a year later, is so striking that it is hard to believe that the difference of peacetime and wartime routine was wholly accountable. The main cause seems to have been the casual assumption of the Combined Fleet in 1942 that success was guaranteed irrespective of what plans were prepared, whereas in 1941 the absence of "victory disease" bred by past successes had ensured proper attention to detail.

The Pearl Harbor attack represented a soaring achievement in terms of strategic imagination. The largest carrier raid to date in the European war had involved only a single carrier. At Pearl Harbor, the Japanese committed no fewer than six fleet carriers to a strike against the enemy's main base some 3,900 nautical miles from Tokyo. In matters of detail as well as its wider context, however, the Pearl Harbor attack raises questions—most obviously whether it was the operation with which the Japanese should have begun hostilities. Yamamoto's insistence upon an attack on Pearl Harbor as the essential prerequisite for the conquest of southeast Asia was prudent and correct from a purely military perspective. It made little strategic sense for the Japanese to attempt to breach the Malay Barrier while leaving the Philippines unreduced in their rear, the U.S. Pacific Fleet intact on their flank, and a hostile United States poised to make its move at a time of its own choosing. Moreover, behind the rationale for an attack on Pearl Harbor were decades of animosity between Japan and the United States and the self-fulfilling belief they shared that war between them was inevitable. Yet in 1941 Admiral Osami Nagano, chief of the Naval General Staff, opposed Yamamoto's proposal for an attack on Pearl Harbor on the grounds that the seizure of British and Dutch possessions in the Far East did not have to involve war with the United States. It appears hard to fault Nagano's assertion that President Roosevelt could not have taken the United States into a war in defense of European colonies.[11] There is a fine irony in the fact that the historiography of Pearl Harbor has paid so much attention to Yamamoto's having devoted so much effort to an operational plan for a war that he did not want and so little to the effort he dedicated to overruling his nominal superior when the latter attempted to defend the very views that Yamamoto is supposed to have held. There is another aspect of these proceedings that has commanded but little historical attention. In order to get his way over the Pearl Harbor operations, and again in 1942 over Midway, Yamamoto used his official position and personal influence to overcome opposition: he never used that same position and influence to oppose Japan's final alignment with Germany and Italy in 1940.

In the argument within the Japanese high command about the Pearl Harbor operation, Nagano was certainly correct in one sense: a war along the Malay Barrier did not have to involve war with the United States in December 1941, and Roosevelt would have faced great, probably insurmountable, congressional opposition to any attempt to go to war except in defense of the Philippines or American national territory. Acceptance of this premise would suggest that Yamamoto's determination that war must begin with an attack on the Pacific Fleet in order to destroy American capacity to interfere with Japanese operations in southeast Asia condemned Japan to fight a war that it could have avoided and, indeed, the only war that it could have lost. By such reasoning, Yamamoto's relentless insistence upon beginning hostilities with an attack on Pearl Harbor would appear to have been an act of the grandest folly.

Yet the premise of this argument may well be invalid, in that by 1941 the deeper tides of history ensured that a clash between Japan and the United States was unavoidable and that Yamamoto, not Nagano, was in tune with reality. In 1941 the Imperial Navy had to face the consequences of its attitudes and actions of two decades. It could not escape the situation created by singling out the United States as its hypothetical enemy when that enemy became real. It could not escape the situation created by its insistence upon the deregulation of navies when the United States embarked upon a building program guaranteed to reduce the Imperial Navy to an irrelevance within three years. It could not escape the situation that arose when its attempt to free itself from the perceived ignominy of the naval limitation treaties threatened to lead only to the real ignominy of being rendered powerless even in waters it considered its own. When its attempt to secure the means whereby Japan could insure itself against American power and malevolence provoked the American embargo, Japan really had no recourse other than a trial by arms. Given the convergence of these developments in 1941, Nagano's defeat may well have been inevitable and Yamamoto's plan to attack Pearl Harbor quite possibly the best option open to Japan.

Be that as it may, the attack itself demands attention on a number of counts. First, although the Japanese were unlucky in that no American carriers presented themselves for destruction on the day of infamy, even if the entire U.S. Pacific Fleet had been destroyed at Pearl Harbor on 7 December 1941 and if the Japanese had completed their remaining construction program without losing a single ship in the meantime, by mid-1944 the Imperial Navy would still have been outnumbered two to one by the U.S. Navy. Second, the Combined Fleet's plan for the attack did not set out the need for follow-up strikes, and it did not assign Nagumo's carrier force the task of destroying vital base facilities. Moreover, no attempt was made to seize Oahu, an omission recognized by the Combined Fleet in the aftermath of the attack to have been a major error. This lapse cannot in fairness be laid at Yamamoto's door, for the original decision not to attempt landings on Oahu was the result of commitments elsewhere. The failure to include follow-up operations against base installations was more serious. With six fleet carriers available for the attack, the Japanese had the physical means to stand off Oahu for four or five days and pound base and fleet into ruination, not merely content themselves with a tip-and-run raid. The latter took courage; the former demanded real imagination. Third, the idea of a preemptive strike that would divide and demoralize American society represented a profound and fatal misreading of American psychology. If nothing else, the attack on Pearl Harbor ensured Japan's defeat, because, once at war, the United States faced all-or-nothing alternatives: the United States could not make peace without total victory or total defeat, and it was beyond Japan's resources to totally defeat the United States.

Yamamoto's admirers have noted that he was appalled to learn that a Sunday morning staff shortage at the Japanese Embassy in Washington had delayed the delivery of the Japanese note of 7 December 1941 until after his aircraft had devastated Battleship Row. "It does not do to cut a sleeping throat," he is reported to have remarked.[12] Yet as early as November 1940 Yamamoto had identified his priority as the destruction of the American fleet, "in order to demoralize the U.S. Navy and people decisively,"[13] and ex post facto doubts about timing would seem to be utterly irrelevant when set against a mistaken rationale that had been thirteen months in gestation. The note finally presented to the State Department by the Japanese envoys was not technically a declaration of war, and in the final analysis whether the Japanese attacked Pearl Harbor before or after its delivery was immaterial, because American opinion was not likely to make fine distinctions when confronted with the reality of the attack. Yamamoto's observation may have been appropriate, but it was late in the day for such rectitude.

Taken together these considerations point to one, seemingly incontrovertible, conclusion: that the Imperial Japanese Navy did not understand the nature of the war it initiated in 1941. Great industrial powers can be defeated only in protracted struggles, yet the Imperial Navy sought to cripple American naval power and demoralize the American people at the outset of hostilities and then to break American resolve by fighting a defensive campaign in the western and Central Pacific over the next three years. With the exception of Inoue and a few like-minded colleagues, not including Yamamoto, the Imperial Navy had no inkling of how an air war in the Pacific would be fought. It had no idea of how the Americans might set about the reduction of Japan's positions in the Central Pacific. It had no appreciation of the importance of trade defense to Japan's ability to wage war, and in adhering to the concept of "the decisive battle" it showed that it had no real understanding of naval history. Even at the height of its naval mastery, Britain's supremacy at sea had never been the product of a single battle, and never had victory in battle automatically conferred that supremacy. The British ability to exercise command of the sea in successive wars was ensured by victories in fleet actions, but even the most conclusive of these victories had not eliminated the need to continue blockade and trade defense operations. The Imperial Navy was selectively imitative and esoteric in the evolution of its doctrine, and its success in local wars with China and Russia around the turn of the century provided it with the basis of a concept of sea control and denial that otherwise was belied by historical experience. From the absence of evidence suggesting that Yamamoto recognized the flawed nature of Japanese naval doctrine, it would seem that he shared the conventional wisdom of his time and service. Put most simply: for all its undoubted technical and tactical qualities, the Imperial Navy did not understand the business of war, and Yamamoto did not possess the strategic insight to rise above the system of which he was a product.[14]

What was on Yamamoto's part at best a questionable performance on the strategic plane was matched by an indifferent record at the tactical level in the course of the Guadalcanal campaign from August 1942 to February 1943 and the air offensive in the southwest Pacific in April 1943. Although the main cause of the Japanese failure in the struggle for Guadalcanal was strategic rather than tactical, the Combined Fleet was slow to respond to the situation that developed and its handling of the two carrier actions during the campaign, the Eastern Solomons in August and Santa Cruz in October, was flawed. In both, the Japanese persisted with the dispersal of force that had proved so disastrous at Midway, with the result that they sacrificed the chance of attaining important results even when, as at Santa Cruz, they had the better of the exchanges. The recasting of organization by the employment of surface-action forces in the vanguard to absorb punishment that would otherwise be directed against the carriers was no more than a palliative: it could not be a substitute for effective screens of the scale needed in 1942.

An inability to revise doctrine and organization extended beyond Yamamoto. The continuity of policy and doctrine throughout the closing years of the Imperial Navy's existence testifies to a corporate failure to learn operational lessons in the course of the war. If, once again, Yamamoto does not seem to have had the capability to rise above the system, this same conformity was equally apparent in another aspect of command. One of the most curious features of the Pacific conflict is what seems to have been a lack of feel for a battle on the part of most Japanese commanders—the ability to sniff out the enemy, discern his intentions, to interpret the true course of events, and to recast plans during action in order to turn defeat into victory.

The Japanese air offensive in April 1943 appears to indicate that Yamamoto himself did not have the ability to read a battle and provides an interesting insight into the Combined Fleet's conduct of operations in the middle phase of the war. The Japanese objective was to neutralize American air power in the southwest Pacific and to cripple or at least delay the buildup of Allied power in this theater. After the Guadalcanal campaign, which had lasted six months, cost the Japanese 893 planes[15] and ended in defeat, this offensive took the form of four raids, none mounted with more than 180 aircraft, against Allied bases at Guadalcanal, Oro Bay, Port Moresby, and Milne Bay between 7 and 14 April. How such an offensive, with its dispersal of effort and relatively small scale, was supposed to achieve results that had eluded the Japanese for the past nine months is not readily evident. Nevertheless, Yamamoto uncritically accepted his airmen's vastly inflated claims of the results that had been obtained. His death on 18 April was a reflection on Yamamoto's conduct of the offensive: the aircraft in which he was flying was shot down by American fighters operating from Guadalcanal, supposedly neutralized on 7 April.

Any evaluation of Yamamoto's leadership must concentrate upon those years when he exercised command of what was in 1941 the largest and most powerful single naval force in the world. In these years Yamamoto emerged as the arbiter of strategic policy within the navy, his position as fleet commander and the immense prestige he enjoyed after Pearl Harbor allowing him to override the Naval General Staff. This division of authority and the ability of the fleet commander to dictate policy to the supposedly superior level of command are only two aspects of the cultural difference between

Japan and the democracies that makes an appraisal of Yamamoto so difficult for a Westerner. The manner in which the Imperial Navy conducted itself on occasions seems beyond belief. When told that his carrier division would not take part in the attack on Pearl Harbor, Rear Admiral Tamon Yamaguchi, much the worse for drink, physically assaulted the force commander, Nagumo, who was rescued by subordinates and the promise that Yamaguchi's division would indeed be allowed to participate in the raid.[16] This was the same Nagumo who in the 1930s had tried to intimidate Inoue with a thinly veiled threat of assassination because of Inoue's moderation.[17] At all levels of command there was a manipulation of superiors by subordinates and an extraordinary deference by senior commanders to juniors, particularly to staffs, which would never have been forthcoming from the likes of Cunningham and Nimitz. With whom—if anyone—the power of decision rested within the Imperial Navy is a question that is crucial to any balanced assessment of Yamamoto, but one that defies a ready answer.

Yamamoto was lucky in one respect: he died at the right time. His period as commander in chief of the Combined Fleet witnessed Japan's greatest victories, and he vanished from the scene before the reality of defeat became apparent. Responsibility for that defeat was to fall upon his successors, although there is no reason to assume that Yamamoto would have been more successful than they in trying to stem the advance of American power across the Pacific. His record as commander in chief of the Combined Fleet was a reflection of Japan's record in the Pacific war: it contained elements of brilliance and imagination, but little of the steadiness needed to underpin and give substance to these qualities. The brittleness of Yamamoto's wartime performance stands in sharp contrast to his effectiveness as vice minister to Yonai, when the latter's dogged determination and stubbornness complemented his more brilliant subordinates's mercurial talents.

Nevertheless, Yamamoto's historical reputation remains secure. His is the name all but synonymous with the Japanese dimension of the Pacific war. Herein, perhaps, lay his most enduring service both to the Imperial Navy and to a state that did not see fit to grant him the posthumous ennoblement that might have been expected. Of the fifteen defendents on whom the Tokyo war crimes tribunal passed judgment between 4 and 11 November 1948 only one, former Navy Minister Shigetaro Shimada, was a naval officer; the Imperial Navy, in the form of ten of its senior officers, took responsibility for the outbreak of the Greater East Asia War. At a time when the United States sought Japan's rehabilitation as an ally in an uncertain postwar world, Yamamoto's name and credentials as an opponent of the alliance with Germany, as a moderate who wished to avoid first a breach and then a war with the United States, and as a realist who recognized the certainty of defeat in a conflict with the democracies, was politically convenient in the cultivation of the idea of a Japan frog-marched into war, despite the resistance of a temperate navy, by a power-crazed military clique. The truth was very different. Yamamoto's credentials are not all that they appear, and the manner in which they have been presented would seem at best selective and at worse mendacious. In either case, the record has been written in a way that has ensured that in death Isoroku Yamamoto provided an alibi for the Imperial Japanese Navy.

NOTES

1. Hiroyuki Agawa, trans. John Bester, *The Reluctant Admiral: Yamamoto and the Imperial Navy* (Tokyo: Kodanasha International, 1979), pp. 232–33.

2. Advance review comment by William Manchester in reference to the Agawa biography.

3. Agawa, op. cit., pp. 32, 127.

4. Roger Pineau, "Yamamoto," in Field Marshal Sir Michael Carver, ed., *The War Lords: Military Commanders of the Twentieth Century* (Boston: Little, Brown, 1976), p. 393.

5. Agawa, op. cit., p. 46.

6. H. P. Willmott, *The Barrier and the Javelin: Japanese and Allied Pacific Strategies, February to June 1942* (Annapolis: Naval Institute Press, 1983), pp. 87–109. (In the course of the battle the Japanese accounted for two American warships, the fleet carrier *Yorktown* and the destroyer *Hamman*. The *Hamman*, however, was sunk by a torpedo aimed at the *Yorktown*.)

7. Stephen E. Pelz, *Race to Pearl Harbor: The Failure of the Second London Naval Conference and the Onset of World War II* (Cambridge: Harvard University Press, 1974), pp. 29–32, 35–39; Mark R. Peattie, "Akiyama Saneyuki and the Emergence of Modern Japanese Naval Doctrine," U.S. Naval Institute *Proceedings*, vol. 103, no. 1 (January 1977), pp. 60–69.

8. See, for example, Mitsuo Fuchida and Masatake Okumiya, ed. Clarke H. Kawakami and Roger Pineau, *Midway: The Battle That Doomed Japan* (Annapolis: Naval Institute Press, 1955), pp. 176–77.

9. Willmott, op. cit., pp. 109–12; Fuchida and Okumiya, op. cit., pp. 92–93.

10. Japanese Self-Defense Agency, War History Office, *Senshi Sosho. Hawaii Operation* (Tokyo: Asagumo Shimbun, 1967), p. 81.

11. Willmott, op. cit., p. 11.

12. Pineau, loc. cit., p. 390.

13. Letter from Yamamoto to Admiral Shigetaro Shimada, November 1940, quoted in Kiyoshi Ikeda, trans. Ian Nish, "Germany and the Capture of the Automedon Documents (1): A Japanese Appreciation in German-Japanese Relations in the 1930s," *International Studies*, 1986/3.

14. For a comprehensive analysis of the evolution of Japanese naval doctrine, see David C. Evans and Mark R. Peattie, *Kaigun: Strategy, Tactics, and Technology in the Imperial Japanese Navy, 1887–1941*, forthcoming in 1997 from the Naval Institute Press.

15. Adrian Stewart, *Guadalcanal: World War Two's Fiercest Naval Campaign* (London: William Kimber, 1985); see also Samuel B. Griffith II, *The Battle for Guadalcanal* (Philadelphia: J. B. Lippincott, 1963), pp. 244, 272.

16. Gordon W. Prange, with Donald M. Goldstein and Katherine V. Dillon, *At Dawn We Slept: The Untold Story of Pearl Harbor* (New York: McGraw-Hill, 1981), p. 281.

17. Agawa, op. cit., p. 130.

NOTE ON SOURCES

Yamamoto and indeed virtually all matters Japanese in World War II present formidable problems to Western historians. English-language material is sparse, and Japanese sources offer not merely the obvious linguistic problem but ones of methodology. Thus the Japanese official histories reflect the differences between the Imperial Army and the Imperial Navy that so beset the direction of the war effort, and the volumes are not provided with indexes. The naval volumes, moreover, are written by theater rather than time, and there are "official lines" that are followed. In the case of Yamamoto, for example, there is virtually no critical examination of the planning and conduct of the Midway operation, whether in the official histories or other accounts, merely a fatalistic interpretation that sees the Japanese defeat as one that was meant to happen or puts the blame for defeat on Nagumo's alleged indecisiveness in the course of the battle. In short, Yamamoto seems to have been raised to a status that denies critical analysis and reproach, but, of course, the Japanese are not alone in the propagation of national myths.

The Library of Congress has many Japanese-language works on Yamamoto, though all accounts suffer from the fact that the whereabouts of the papers of Yasuji Watanabe, the officer closest to Yamamoto on the Combined Fleet planning staff, which could cast much light on our subject, remain unknown. In the English language there are but three works that demand consideration. James Deane Potter's *Yamamoto: The Man Who Menaced America* (New York: Viking, 1965) was for long the only English-language biography, but it is dated and of very limited value. Hiroyuki Agawa's *The Reluctant Admiral*, trans. John Bester (Tokyo: Kodanasha International, 1979) is peripheral, undisciplined, and fails to address obvious questions of Yamamoto's exercise of command. Roger Pineau's sketch of Yamamoto in Field Marshal Sir Michael Carver, ed., *The War Lords: Military Commanders of the Twentieth Century* (Boston: Little, Brown, 1976) is perhaps the best single account, but by the nature of things it is not comprehensive and leaves much unanswered. In short, Yamamoto awaits a serious biographer.

18

Raymond A. Spruance
The Thinking Man's Admiral
(1886–1969)

John B. Lundstrom

FOR A COMMANDER, SUCCESS IN WAR RESTS UPON A GREAT number of factors. Some are inherent in the man himself, his intellect, character, and the other attributes of leadership. Others arise from the situation in which he finds himself, and the strength and situation of the opposing forces. Still others are random. The so-called fortunes of war often come down simply to being in the right place at the right time. One of the most important aspects of command is the opportunity to exercise it in the first place. Raymond A. Spruance made the most of his opportunity.

As the first six months of war in the Pacific neared an end in late May 1942, the strategic situation confronting the United States appeared bleak. Admiral Chester W. Nimitz, commander in chief of the Pacific Fleet (CINCPAC), had learned on the basis of radio intelligence that powerful forces of the Japanese Combined Fleet were about to descend upon tiny Midway Island. Midway was only 1,150 miles northwest of the U.S. fleet base at Pearl Harbor on Oahu in the Hawaiian Islands. For the first time since the surprise carrier attack that devastated the American battle line on 7 December 1941, the Japanese were challenging the Pacific Fleet to decisive battle.

To meet this challenge, Nimitz relied primarily on his own carrier force led by the senior aviator in the Pacific Fleet, Vice Admiral William F. Halsey. With two of the three available carriers—the *Enterprise* and *Hornet*—Halsey's Task Force 16 was the single most powerful element in the fleet. On 26 May, however, Nimitz was shocked to learn that Halsey was too ill to retain command. Without hesitation, Halsey recommended the commander of his cruiser screen, Rear Admiral Raymond Spruance, as his replacement. Nimitz concurred.

From this unforeseen opportunity, Spruance emerged as the chief architect of victory in the Battle of Midway (4–6 June 1942) and thereby entered the first rank of naval leaders. Midway proved to be the first decisive encounter in a wholly new type of naval warfare, combat between opposing aircraft carriers. As a result of his performance at Midway, Spruance earned further opportunities at high command and led the amphibious offensives that comprised the Pacific Fleet's greatest contribution to victory over Japan.

What was Spruance's professional background and how did it reflect the personal qualities that engendered so much confidence in him on the part of Nimitz, Halsey, and others? Born in Indianapolis on 3 July 1886, Spruance came from a middle-class family with no ties to the military. A 1903 congressional appointment to the U.S. Naval Academy (USNA) at Annapolis was a way for him to obtain a college education. Midshipman Spruance was a thoughtful, quiet, and reserved young man, but also independent and strong-willed. He did not care for the horseplay and cliquishness of academy life, nor was he particularly impressed with the quality of academic instruction. Spruance stood well up in the Class of 1907, which was graduated early in September 1906. His final ranking was 25 of 209.

Spruance's first duty assignments were in the capital ships of the growing U.S. Fleet. The greatest event of his early naval service was the 1907–1909 circumnavigation of the globe by the sixteen battleships of the "Great White Fleet." Serving in the *Minnesota,* Ensign Spruance was delighted by the experience. According to his biographer Thomas Buell, this voyage very likely helped Spruance decide once and for all to make the navy his career.[1] He soon demonstrated definite talents in engineering, gunnery, and other technical subjects. Early in 1913 he received his first command, the old destroyer *Bainbridge,* operating out of Subic Bay in the Philippines.

During World War I Lieutenant Commander Spruance spent most of his time at home ashore as a technical specialist. He had no opportunity to see combat—as was true of most U.S. naval officers. His only sea duty came in late November 1918, when he served as executive officer of the troop transport *Agamemnon,* formerly the German liner *Kaiser Wilhelm II.*

In 1920 Spruance received a position much to his pleasure, command of the new destroyer *Aaron Ward* in the Pacific. Under Rear Admiral Henry A. Wiley and later Captain William Veazie Pratt, the Pacific Fleet destroyer force emerged as an elite unit renowned for its seamanship and tactical skills. Spruance stood out as a fine destroyerman among the best in the navy. His division commander was none other than Bill Halsey (USNA 1904). So different in personality, the two became lifelong friends.

The remainder of the 1920s offered Commander Spruance few chances for sea duty. For a time he continued to specialize in turboelectric propulsion systems, but soon realized that his future was as a line officer. Staff duty in Europe and a tour as skipper of the destroyer *Osborne* were followed in 1926 by enrollment at the Naval War College at Newport, Rhode Island. It was an interesting time to attend the college. The new superintendent, Rear Admiral W. V. Pratt—Spruance's former commanding officer—worked vigorously to upgrade the curriculum and stressed its importance in qualifying graduates for higher command. Spruance completed the senior course, then spent two unremarkable years as assistant director of the Office of Naval Intelligence.

In 1929 Spruance became executive officer of the battleship *Mississippi,* where he again demonstrated his fitness for command. Two years later he returned to the Naval War College, this time as a member of the faculty. In

1933 Captain Spruance was appointed chief of staff to the Commander of Destroyers, Scouting Force. Two years later he found himself unwillingly assigned again to the Naval War College. At first head of the Tactics Section, he later took charge of the Operations Department. This tour gave him the opportunity to work with some of the navy's prominent younger strategists, among whom he became known as an undemonstrative and rather conventional character, but a careful thinker. Certainly, he was not an unsung prophet of air power. Spruance's strength as a strategist and tactician was his deeply logical, unemotional approach to problem solving. He displayed great flexibility and adaptability in reaching solutions.

In the spring of 1938 Spruance received an assignment that pleased him greatly, command of the *Mississippi*. Even though his performance was flawless, Spruance—never one to politic for promotion—believed he would be passed over for admiral. Fortunately, his superiors recognized his competence and in 1940 selected him for advancement. Rear Admiral Spruance's first flag duty was as commander of the newly created Tenth Naval District, with headquarters at San Juan, Puerto Rico. There he oversaw the buildup of U.S. bases in the Caribbean, threatened by the growing European war.

In September 1941 Spruance returned to sea. At Pearl Harbor he assumed command of the Pacific Fleet's Cruiser Division 5 with four heavy cruisers: the *Northampton, Pensacola, Salt Lake City,* and *Chester*. Disappointed not to be in battleships, Spruance could not know that under the circumstances there were few better positions from which to see the fleet into war. Admiral Husband E. Kimmel divided the fleet into three task forces, each containing battleships, cruisers, destroyers, and one carrier. Spruance's division was part of Vice Admiral Halsey's Task Force 2. In the years since they last served together, Halsey had turned to naval aviation, earning his wings of gold in 1935 at the age of fifty-two. Commander, Aircraft, Battle Force, Pacific Fleet, he was the navy's senior carrier commander.

On 28 November 1941, Halsey's Task Force 2 sailed from Pearl Harbor on what appeared to be a routine deployment. At sea, however, it was mysteriously split into two parts. The battleships soon returned to port, but the newly designated Task Force 8, consisting of the *Enterprise,* three of Spruance's cruisers and nine destroyers, steamed westward on a secret mission. It was bound for Wake Island, only seven hundred miles north of Japanese bases in the Marshalls. Privy to a "war warning" message from Washington, Halsey expected a fight and issued his "Battle Order Number One." On 4 December, twelve Marine fighters flew off the *Enterprise* to establish a modest air defense for the exposed American outpost. The voyage back to Pearl Harbor was uneventful except for heavy seas, which delayed the force's return until the evening of 7 December. Only by accident did it escape the debacle of the Japanese strikes against Oahu.

Spruance remained the cruiser screen commander of Halsey's carrier task force for nearly six months. December was frustrating in the extreme. Shocked by the crippling surprise attack on Pearl Harbor, the Pacific Fleet looked for some way to retaliate. Spruance himself took the lesson of the destruction of the battleships to heart and recognized the growing importance of air power more quickly than most. Wake Island fell after a glorious defense on 23 December because a caretaker CINCPAC was unwilling to risk the loss of precious carriers in order to relieve the besieged island. For the navy the most positive events of the month were the appointments of Admiral Ernest J. King (USNA 1901) as commander in chief of the U.S. Fleet (COMINCH) and Chester Nimitz (USNA 1905) as the new CINCPAC.

Spruance's first taste of combat occurred on 1 February 1942, during Halsey's raid against the northern Marshall Islands. This was the Pacific Fleet's first counterpunch. In concert with air strikes from the *Enterprise,* the cruisers of Task Force 8 bombarded enemy installations on two atolls. At Wotje Spruance's warships dueled with shore batteries and tried hitting naval auxiliary vessels in the lagoon. Attacking Taroa, the *Chester* also had to endure several air attacks, as did the *Enterprise.* Understandably, given the inexperience of the crews and the disappointing performance of some of the matériel, the results were not particularly satisfying. Spruance himself displayed a calm, careful demeanor in the face of these adversities and acted fearlessly under fire. He knew that the efficiency of his division, if barely adequate at the moment, was something he could improve.

On 24 February, Halsey's task force conducted another coordinated air-ship bombardment of a Japanese base, this time Wake Island. Spruance showed he was willing to innovate by adopting a plan proposed by his chief of staff. During the night, Spruance took his task group of two heavy cruisers and two destroyers around to the west of Wake. He hoped to surprise its defenders at dawn by emerging out of the western darkness. Things did not work as planned; the Japanese were not surprised, and the glare of the rising sun adversely affected Spruance's fire control. To top off the morning's misadventures, the *Enterprise*'s aircraft were late in attacking. Fortunately, the Japanese lacked the strength to do any real damage. Even so, Spruance learned a valuable lesson about the difficulty of coordinating carrier air operations.

On Halsey's next two operations, the Marcus Raid (4 March) and Task Force 16's celebrated Tokyo Raid (18 April) by army B-25 medium bombers flying off the carrier *Hornet,* Spruance was pretty much a spectator. He felt that the Doolittle Raid, despite its importance to morale, was a waste of effort in that it tied up the services of two of the Pacific Fleet's four carriers for a month. Events proved him correct, for by mid-April radio intelligence was pointing toward a major Japanese amphibious movement against Port

Moresby, the Allied base of supply in eastern New Guinea, in early May. To counter the threat Nimitz sent Rear Admiral Frank Jack Fletcher's Task Force 17, with the carriers *Yorktown* and *Lexington,* to the Coral Sea. On 30 April Halsey's Task Force 16, with the *Enterprise, Hornet,* and Spruance's cruisers, departed Pearl Harbor to join Task Force 17 in the southwest Pacific. There Halsey would take overall command. Nimitz had deployed his entire carrier force to meet the advancing enemy head-on.

From 4 to 8 May, Fletcher fought the Battle of the Coral Sea. At the cost of the *Lexington* and two smaller ships, he sank the light *Shoho,* damaged the big carrier *Shokaku,* and most importantly, turned back the Port Moresby invasion force. However, the *Yorktown* was also damaged, and it was not known whether she could be repaired swiftly at Pearl Harbor. During this battle, the first between opposing aircraft carriers, Halsey and Spruance were bitterly disappointed to be distant spectators, still nearly a thousand miles away. American and Japanese forces both withdrew from the Coral Sea. On 15 May, at Nimitz's express orders, Halsey allowed Task Force 16 to be spotted by the Japanese, which caused the enemy to cancel invasions of Ocean and Nauru Islands. The next day Halsey received orders to return to Pearl Harbor. There Task Force 16 ended its frustrating cruise on 26 May. Big surprises were in the offing.

After his own flagship docked, Spruance went to the *Enterprise* to make the customary arrival call on his old friend Halsey. He was surprised that the admiral was not on board. Suffering from a severe case of dermatitis aggravated by stress, Halsey had reluctantly followed doctor's orders to enter the hospital. Informed of the impending Midway operation, he unhesitatingly recommended that Spruance be given command of Task Force 16. In this case, Spruance was the man on the spot. Having served the past eight months with Halsey, he knew the task force and the capabilities of its captains. Nimitz left word on the *Enterprise* for Spruance to come to headquarters.

Dismayed by Halsey's inability to exercise command in what was shaping up to be the decisive carrier battle of the war, Nimitz reviewed his options. What about Ray Spruance? Although he had never served with Spruance, Nimitz well knew his character and reputation. Nimitz had been chief of the Bureau of Navigation (later Naval Personnel) when Spruance was selected for admiral. He had already indicated his confidence in Spruance by choosing him as his next chief of staff.

Regarded as highly intelligent by fellow officers, Spruance was known for his "cold and careful calculation" both at sea and in solving problems at the Naval War College. Logical, calm, and deliberate, Spruance could act decisively once he had made up his mind, but he did not allow himself to be swayed by emotion. He remained unshaken in adversity and never raised

16. The USS *Enterprise,* Spruance's flagship at Midway, photographed in Pearl Harbor in May 1942. The "Big E" was probably the most famous American carrier of World War II, during which she earned the remarkable total of twenty battle stars. Commissioned in 1938, she displaced 19,800 tons, could make 33 knots, and carried a complement of 2,919, including aviation personnel. At Midway her air group consisted of 79 aircraft: 27 fighters, 38 dive-bombers, and 14 torpedo-bombers. (National Archives photograph, U.S. Naval Institute Photographic Collection.)

his voice. A reserved and modest man, he shunned self-advertisement, prefering to let his deeds speak for him. He had the ability to work with a staff, listen to the ideas of others, and delegate authority. Physically, Spruance was tough, renowned for taking very long walks in any kind of weather. Yet despite his generally serious mien, he had an understated, dry sense of humor.

There is no evidence that Nimitz seriously considered anyone else to command Task Force 16. Probably the only other candidate was Rear Admiral Leigh Noyes (USNA 1906), a naval aviator who had just come from Washington to be Halsey's administrative deputy, but who lacked combat experience. Spruance was a member of the "gun club" of battleship and cruiser admirals, not a naval aviator. To the displeasure of the aviation community, however, his appointment was not unusual. Of the five flag officers who had led Pacific Fleet carrier task forces since the outbreak of the war, three were nonaviators. Indeed, next senior to Halsey was Frank Jack Fletcher (USNA 1906), the cruiser specialist who commanded Task Force 17 in the Battle of the Coral Sea. Spruance was told to bring only his flag lieutenant with him to the *Enterprise.* For advice in aviation matters, Spruance would rely on Halsey's aviation staff, headed by the temperamental Captain Miles R. Browning.

That afternoon Spruance learned of his new command and the reason for all the concern. After a swift turnaround in port, Task Force 16 was to sail on 28 May to defend Midway from a major Japanese invasion force that could include four big carriers. Nimitz expected the enemy to strike early in June. If the *Yorktown* could be made battleworthy in time, Fletcher's Task Force 17 would follow. In that event, Fletcher would assume command of the three carriers; otherwise, Spruance would make do with his two. Another carrier, the *Saratoga,* was at San Diego following repairs and a refit. She was to proceed to Pearl Harbor as soon as possible, but only if the Japanese were considerably delayed would she be in time to fight at Midway. The Pacific Fleet battle line of seven old battleships, organized as Task Force 1, did not even figure in the plans to defend the island. Convinced that the elderly dreadnoughts were too slow and too vulnerable to air attack, Nimitz had sent them to safer waters off the West Coast.

Nimitz stressed to Spruance the need for taking calculated risks to inflict as much damage as possible on the enemy without unduly endangering the American carriers. That was like being told to jump into the water but try not to get wet. The carriers depended heavily upon Midway's land-based air strength for long-range reconnaissance and attack on enemy forces. Nimitz emphasized that Midway could be recaptured, which would be preferable to holding the island but losing the carriers.

On the morning of 27 May Spruance attended an important conference with Nimitz and the top army commanders in the Central Pacific. The staff discussed the intelligence that underlay the estimates of the imminent Japanese moves against Midway and the Aleutians. Its source was the decryption and analysis of enemy radio messages. Nimitz expressed confidence in his decoders and intelligence personnel. The Japanese were to precede the Midway attack a day or two by carrier strikes against American bases in the Aleutians. Decrypts pointed to 5 or 6 June as "N Day," when the Japanese main body, steaming east from Saipan, would land troops at Midway. Indications were that the enemy's striking force, built around the four big carriers *Akagi, Kaga, Soryu,* and *Hiryu,* operated in advance of the main body or support force. It seemed likely that about N–2 Day the enemy carriers would conduct air strikes to destroy Midway's defenses. Put on the spot by a direct question from Nimitz, Lieutenant Commander Edwin T. Layton, the fleet intelligence officer, forthrightly gave his opinion that the Japanese carrier force would be sighted about 0700 on 4 June at a point bearing 325 degrees and 175 miles from Midway.[2]

Whether or not such a precise statement could be sustained, the fact that the Japanese carriers would be launching a powerful dawn strike against

Midway offered a real opportunity for American carriers lurking on their left flank to surprise them. Thus Nimitz desired his carriers to take a position 350 miles northeast of Midway and wait for the enemy to appear, ideally on schedule.

In the afternoon of 27 May, Task Force 17 arrived at Pearl Harbor after an unprecedented 101 days at sea. A quick inspection of the battle-scarred *Yorktown* determined that after emergency repairs she could sail for Midway on 30 May. Frank Jack Fletcher would therefore command the American carrier force. Time for the two admirals to coordinate their planning was limited, because Task Force 16 would soon depart. However, Spruance knew that once the enemy carriers were located, his two carriers were to attack with their full strength. Captain Browning and the rest of the aviation staff undertook detailed planning and preparations based on that premise.

Task Force 16 put to sea on the morning of 28 May. It consisted of 2 carriers (150 operational aircraft), 5 heavy cruisers, 1 light antiaircraft cruiser, and 9 destroyers. Spruance set course north of the Hawaiian Islands, away from enemy submarines. Secrecy was paramount. He even ordered that the radio keys on the airplanes be secured so that no transmissions could be sent inadvertently. On 1 June, after fueling, Task force 16 moved into position northwest of Midway. The next afternoon, Fletcher's Task Force 17 appeared on the horizon at "Point Luck," 325 miles northeast of Midway, with 1 carrier (71 operational planes), 2 heavy cruisers, and 6 destroyers. Fletcher brought the two task forces together, but he did not combine them into a single formation. Instead, he ordered Spruance to operate ten miles southeast of Task Force 17—within visual signaling range, to preserve radio silence—and conform to its movements. To avoid an accidental encounter with the Japanese should they be early, Fletcher steered northeast away from Midway during the day, reversing course at night to remain within the assigned area. From now on, Spruance held his aircraft in reserve, ready to launch the main strike, while the *Yorktown* conducted the necessary searches. Once battle was joined, her air group would act as the reserve.

On the morning of 3 June, while the American striking force maneuvered northeast of Midway, the first real confirmation was received of the elaborate intelligence framework upon which Nimitz had based the entire operation: there had been a Japanese carrier strike against Dutch Harbor in the Aleutians. Just before noon, Fletcher and Spruance learned that Midway-based search planes had sighted enemy ships seven hundred miles west of the island. From Pearl Harbor, Nimitz quickly warned all commanders this was the main body with the transport force, not the enemy carriers. Presumably the latter were already considerably closer to and northwest of Midway, preparing to strike at dawn. Throughout the day, the storms that covered the American carriers also hid the enemy flattops from the Midway search.

During the night Fletcher's task forces steamed southwest at a leisurely 13.5 knots. At dawn on 4 June, the *Yorktown* sent ten dive-bombers northward on a precautionary search, then reversed course according to plan. Spruance's *Enterprise* and *Hornet* were on full alert. Midway was ready to do its part to repulse the Japanese. Twenty-two PBY flying boats departed on search and sixteen Boeing B-17 heavy bombers took off to attack the Japanese main body closing from the west. Thirty-seven dive-bombers, torpedo planes, and medium bombers were ready to depart once Midway's radar detected incoming enemy planes. The feeling of anticipation was terrifically intense.

Totally unaware that the enemy was fully aroused against it, Vice Admiral Chuichi Nagumo's *Kido Butai* (Striking Force) with four carriers, two fast battleships, two heavy cruisers, one light cruiser, and eleven destroyers had arrived on schedule. At dawn (0430, Zone plus 12, Midway local time) this formation was 240 miles northwest of Midway and only 200 miles west of Fletcher's striking force. The four carriers had a total of 228 flyable carrier fighters, bombers, and attack planes, plus 21 additional fighters destined for the new Midway garrison. Nagumo promptly launched a strike of 108 planes against Midway and prepared a second wave of 108 planes in the rather unlikely event that his own search located any American ships in the area. The Japanese were supremely confident that they had achieved surprise.

At 0534 the American carriers intercepted a PBY voice radio transmission: "Enemy carriers." Eleven minutes later another plane reported: "Many planes heading Midway bearing 320, distance 150 miles."[3] Thus the anticipated Midway strike was inbound, but where were the carriers? Fletcher decided to detach Spruance and send him out on his own in the probable direction of the enemy carriers. The *Yorktown* began blinking a message to Task Force 16: "Proceed southeasterly and attack enemy carriers as soon as definitely located. I will follow as soon as planes recovered."[4]

While this order was being signaled, at 0603 the long-awaited sighting report sounded on the radio: "Two carriers and battleships bearing 320 from Midway, distance 180 miles, course 135, speed 25 knots."[5] There they were, at least two of the Japanese flattops. At 0607 Task Force 16 logged Fletcher's orders authorizing Spruance to go after the enemy. These two messages set the stage for the first of Spruance's three crucial decisions in the Battle of Midway.

In the flag shelter, Spruance and the staff swiftly plotted the reported enemy position, 247 degrees and 175 miles from Task Force 16. From their location and course, it appeared that the enemy carriers would continue steaming toward Midway in order to recover the strike they had already sent against the island. Browning wanted nothing more than to deliver the attack after these carriers had recovered their aircraft and before they could get off a second strike. Spruance's primary concern was, as he later wrote, "the urgent need for surprise and a strong desire to hit the enemy carriers with our full strength as early as we could reach them."[6] Satisfied that the enemy was within range, he gave the order: "Launch the attack."[7] Two carriers were about all Task Force 16 could handle at one time; it would have to worry about the other flattops later.

The staff examined the situation in detail before implementing Spruance's order. Complicating matters was the fact that 175 miles was close to the maximum effective range of the torpedo-bombers and escort fighters. The launch could begin immediately. Fletcher had dispatched attacks from that distance during the Battle of the Coral Sea. Indeed, the *Hornet*'s Captain Marc A. Mitscher expected such an early departure. He soon ordered his pilots to man their planes. However, in order to launch, the carriers had to steam southeast into the wind at high speed on a course that sharply diverged from the target. This lengthened the mission and permitted less time for search if their targets were not where the strike groups expected to find them.

Consequently, Browning recommended that the launch be delayed for forty-five minutes while the carriers closed the enemy. Deferring to Browning's aviation expertise, Spruance agreed. At 0614 Task Force 16 turned left to course 240 degrees and increased speed to 25 knots. If the enemy carriers maintained their reported course and speed, at 0700 they would bear 239 degrees and 155 miles from Task Force 16. Should the launch take another forty-five minutes, as expected, the planes would still have about 175 miles to go to reach the target.

The delay also allowed Midway to authenticate in code the original voice contact. This message reached Spruance at 0634. Four minutes later the strike orders drawn up by Spruance's staff were transmitted to the waiting *Enterprise* and *Hornet* air groups. Along with giving the position, course, and speed of the two enemy carriers as of 0600, they specified 0700 as launch time. Each group was to attack one carrier. The orders revealed the intended Point Option course—used to tell the pilots where their carriers should be when they returned—by noting that Task Force 16 would continue closing to about one hundred miles from the enemy. Given the state of American carrier doctrine at the time, the staff did not try to combine the groups or provide any particular course for the strike groups to follow to the targets. That was left up to the individual carrier captains and their air group commanders. As events transpired, the *Enterprise* and *Hornet* leaders had radically different ideas as to where to find the enemy carriers.

At 0656 Task Force 16 split into two groups and turned southeast into the wind and began launching aircraft at 0700. In line with his assigned role, Spruance was sending every strike plane he had, sixty-seven SBD dive-bombers and twenty-nine torpedo-bombers, escorted by twenty out of fifty-four available fighters. Not all of these aircraft could be spotted on the flight decks at the same time. It was necessary to launch the first "deck load," then bring up the rest from the hangar deck. So that the squadrons within individual air groups could proceed to the target together and execute a coordinated attack, the initial deck load had to circle overhead until the second batch got away.

The launch turned out to be a lengthy process, longer than Spruance expected. He grew more and more impatient at the delay. At 0742 the last *Hornet* plane lifted off. Inexplicably, the *Enterprise* was much slower. Only the thirty-three SBDs were aloft; her second deck load of ten fighters and fourteen torpedo-bombers still was being spotted aft on her flight deck. It was about ninety minutes since Spruance had given Browning the order to launch the strike. Now the event he feared had come to pass. It appears that the *Enterprise* intercepted a voice radio message from a Japanese search plane reporting the sighting of American ships northeast of Midway. Spruance quickly ordered the *Enterprise* SBDs to "proceed on mission assigned" without waiting for the other planes. To get at least some of the Big E's planes pointed toward the enemy without further delay, Spruance had to sacrifice the integrity of the group attack.[8]

The *Enterprise* completed her launch at 0806, when Task Force 16 finally resumed the base course of 240 degrees to close the enemy. By that time Spruance's strike force had fragmented into three separate groups flying out of sight of each other (and would split again before discovering the enemy carriers). Departing at 0746 to the west (265 degrees) were thirty-four *Hornet* dive-bombers and ten fighters under the group leader, Commander Stanhope C. Ring. The *Hornet* brain trust deduced that the Japanese carriers either had or soon would turn away from Midway. Trailing Ring were the fifteen planes of the *Hornet*'s Torpedo Squadron Eight and the ten *Enterprise* escort fighters, which had latched onto them by mistake. Following the admiral's orders, Lieutenant Commander Clarence Wade McClusky, the *Enterprise* air group commander, gathered his thirty-three SBDs and left at 0752. He assumed the enemy carriers would continue closing Midway and took a southwesterly course (231 degrees) in order to intercept them. The *Enterprise*'s Torpedo Squadron Six followed the Task Force 16 base course (240 degrees) and thus flew between the other two groups.[9]

Spruance soon had confirmation that the Japanese had indeed sighted Task Force 16. At 0815 the *Northampton*'s radar detected an enemy search plane lurking thirty miles to the south. Now Spruance had to hope that his

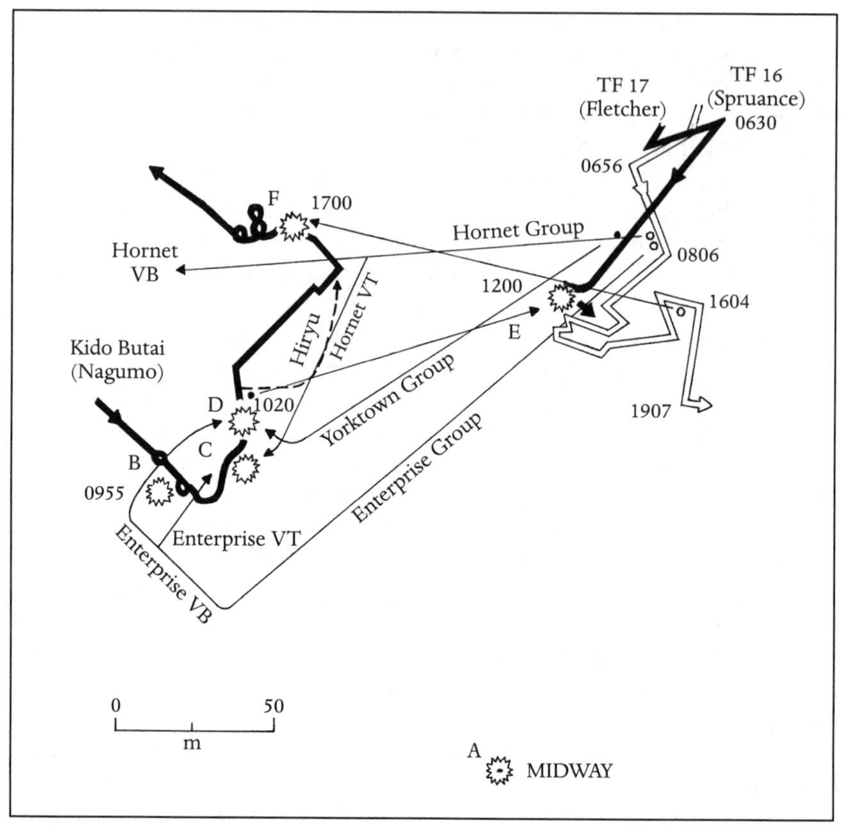

30. The Battle of Midway, 4 June 1942. The action opens at 0634 with a Japanese air strike on Midway (A). Between 0705 and 0900 the *Kido Butai* beats off counterattacks by Midway-based aircraft (B), recovers its strike force, and emerges unscathed from a succession of virtually suicidal runs (C) by three U.S. torpedo-bomber squadrons (VT). Before it can launch against the U.S. carriers, however, dive-bomber squadrons (VB) from the *Enterprise* and *Yorktown* deliver an attack (D) that reduces the *Akagi*, *Kaga*, and *Soryu* to flaming wrecks. The remaining Japanese carrier, the *Hiryu*, then gets off a strike that damages the *Yorktown* (E). The *Hiryu* hits the *Yorktown* with a second strike (not shown) at 1445, but a little over two hours later the *Enterprise*'s dive-bombers bring her opeations to an end (F).

strike would knock out the enemy carriers before they could counterattack the American flattops.

At 0857 Spruance learned that someone else was giving the enemy's striking force a rough time. A Midway-based flight reported damaging a Japanese carrier. More encouraging word came at 0914, when another combatant entered the lists. Now over the horizon north of Task Force 16, Fletcher radioed that the *Yorktown* had dispatched three-fourths of her strike group. He had waited as long as he dared for additional sighting reports to locate the other two Japanese carriers should they not be with the force already sighted. Finally, he sent seventeen dive-bombers, twelve torpedo planes, and six fighters against the same targets sought by Spruance's aircraft. For follow-up attacks or searches, he retained seventeen SBDs in reserve.

Not until later did Spruance learn of the valiant, if unsuccessful, actions of the Midway-based planes. The Japanese strike virtually destroyed Midway's defending Marine fighters. From 0705 to 0820, a total of six navy torpedo planes, four torpedo-carrying army medium bombers, twenty-seven Marine dive-bombers, and sixteen army heavy bombers had attacked the Japanese carrier force. These Midway flyers sustained heavy losses, totaling eighteen aircraft, but failed to achieve a single hit. Midway had shot its bolt; everything depended on the success of the carrier air groups.

Ranged around the radio receiver in the flag shelter on the *Enterprise*'s island, the staff grew increasingly nervous as the time passed 0930, when they had expected the strike groups to find the enemy carriers. After this point, fuel became a vital consideration. No contact reports emerged from the static. Undoubtedly there were some, but poor radio communications plagued the combatants the whole day. Deciding that the Japanese carriers must have turned away from Midway, at 0954 Spruance changed course 20 degrees right to 260 degrees.

Finally at 0956 came the first word vouchsafed Spruance from his strike groups. The *Enterprise* intercepted two radio messages from the commander of Fighting Squadron Six, Lieutenant James S. Gray, Jr., who led her ten escort fighters. Gray reported he was flying over two enemy carriers, two battleships, and six destroyers. He then repeated the enemy's strength, gave their course as "about north," and advised that he would have to return because of dwindling fuel. On the *Enterprise* Browning mistakenly thought that Wade McClusky had sent the message. Infuriated, he grabbed a microphone and shouted, "McClusky attack, attack immediately!"[10]

To match the enemy's northerly course, Spruance turned northwest. At 1014 he informed Fletcher of the sighting report, gave the enemy's course and advised that Task Force 16 was on course 285 degrees. A few minutes later the radio relayed snippets of excited messages from carrier pilots ordering attacks and assigning targets. Exactly what they were doing and where could not be ascertained, but things sounded favorable, especially since a Japanese attack on Task Force 16 had yet to materialize.

Meanwhile, the *Enterprise* and *Hornet* proceeded with routine air operations for the combat air patrol (CAP). Gray's escort fighters had a swift trip back from the target area and landed around 1100. While Gray was being debriefed, Fletcher radioed Spruance for the position, course, and speed of the enemy carriers once they could be ascertained from the returning planes. *Yorktown* had another squadron of dive-bombers and escorts ready to go. At 1110 Spruance replied with the enemy position as learned from Gray. He suggested to Fletcher that the *Yorktown* planes be used to find and track the carriers already hit by the strike groups of the two task forces, and that they search the northwest quadrant for any other enemy carriers that might be operating separately. This was excellent advice. Spruance added that his own groups upon their return would be readied to attack again.[11]

Up to this point, both Fletcher and Spruance had worked in a near vacuum of outside information as to the progress of the battle. As they circled the *Yorktown*, Fletcher's returning dive-bombers happily informed him at 1115 that they had sunk one enemy carrier. Deciding that he had finally been sighted by the enemy, Fletcher assigned ten dive-bombers to search two hundred miles to the northwest, as Spruance had suggested. They began taking off at 1133 and freed the *Yorktown*'s flight deck so she could land her strike planes.

About the same time, the *Enterprise* and *Hornet* began landing their attack groups, which had straggled back in small groups. Their losses were staggering. Talking with a wounded Wade McClusky and some of the other surviving pilots gave Spruance and the staff an idea of the great triumph and tragedy that had taken place 150 miles to the west. Only fourteen of the thirty-two *Enterprise* SBDs that had made it to the target area returned. Most were lost trying to find their way back home.[12] They had fought a force of four enemy carriers with battleships, cruisers, and destroyers spread out across a wide expanse of ocean. McClusky's planes had bombed two carriers, flight decks crowded with aircraft, and left both as raging infernos, certain to sink. They saw the *Yorktown* dive-bombers deal a death blow to a third enemy flattop. This left the fourth apparently untouched. Only four of Torpedo Squadron Six's fourteen aircraft came back to the *Enterprise*. Their crews told of a lone charge right through the enemy task force fiercely defended by Zero fighters. They were bitter that their own fighters had not protected them.

The *Hornet* discovered tragedy rather than triumph. Of the fifty-nine planes she launched, only Ring with twenty dive-bombers returned. They had not sighted the enemy at all. Thirty-nine planes were missing. Midway soon reported that eleven *Hornet* SBDs had sought sanctuary there, but that meant that all fifteen torpedo planes, ten fighters, and three dive-bombers had been lost.

It has taken years for researchers to piece together the events of the attack that destroyed three Japanese carriers and gave victory to the United States at Midway. Even after learning that the Americans had at least one carrier within range, Vice Admiral Nagumo procrastinated over organizing a strike. He wanted to recover and rearm the planes he had sent against Midway. The last of these aircraft landed at 0918, at which time Nagumo changed course left to 030 degrees. He would head northeast toward the American ships readying a second, massive strike to destroy them.

Two minutes later the *Kido Butai* sighted the first planes from Task Force 16, the fifteen aircraft of Lieutenant Commander John C. Waldron's Torpedo Squadron Eight from the *Hornet*. From low level Waldron had followed Ring's dive-bombers westward for about forty minutes, when he decided they were going too far west. In a rather acrimonious radio exchange with Ring, Waldron gave his opinion of the group commander's plan and turned his squadron southwest. From high altitude Lieutenant Gray's *Enterprise* escort fighters followed the torpedo planes. Waldron's change in course uncannily took him directly toward the Japanese carriers, while Ring continued west. Not until he returned to the ship did Ring realize his error. At 0920 Torpedo Eight gallantly attacked alone, but scored no hits. Zeros swiftly shot down all fifteen. Clouds hid their plight from Gray's escort fighters circling overhead waiting for McClusky's dive-bombers to arrive.[13]

Next to find the Japanese carriers was the *Enterprise*'s Torpedo Squadron Six, led by Lieutenant Commander Eugene E. Lindsey. It sighted the enemy ships about 0940 from the southwest and spent the next thirty to forty minutes pressing its attack west to east through the center of the *Kido Butai*. Zero fighters shot down nine of fourteen aircraft (another ditched later), and the squadron made no hits on the enemy carriers. Overhead but again unaware because of the clouds, Gray's escort fighters circled until after his two messages to the *Enterprise*, then he set course for home.

McClusky, leading the *Enterprise* dive-bombers, had flown too far ahead of the Japanese task force. By 0935 he realized he had missed the target. Unlike Ring, he alertly flew a systematic "box" search to cover the area to the north before dwindling fuel would force him to return to the *Enterprise*. At 0955 he spotted the rooster-tail wake of a lone destroyer (the *Arashi*) steaming northeast at high speed. McClusky took her course and at 1000 was gratified finally to sight the enemy thirty-five miles to the northeast.

Before McClusky could reach the target, the *Yorktown* strike group of seventeen dive-bombers, twelve torpedo planes, and six fighters appeared on the scene. Launched over an hour after Task Force 16's strike, the Yorktowners flew an almost straight line to the target. Lieutenant Commander Lance E. Massey's Torpedo Squadron Three spotted the Japanese ships at 1003 and turned the group northwest in their direction. Cloud cover and radio difficulties again prevented a coordinated effort. Covered by the six fighters, the twelve torpedo planes made for the nearest enemy carrier at about the same time that the remnants of Torpedo Six completed their valiant attack. Together the two squadrons and the *Yorktown*'s fighters drew the

17. The Battle of Midway, 4 June 1942. Douglas SBD Dauntless dive-bombers from the *Enterprise* and *Yorktown* attack the Japanese carriers *Kaga, Akagi,* and *Soryu* in R. G. Smith's painting of the climax at Midway. (R. G. Smith.)

defending Zeros down to low level. Torpedo Three lost ten of its twelve aircraft during the fight.[14]

The sacrifice of Lindsey's and Massey's crews unwittingly cleared the way for McClusky, approaching from the southwest, and for Lieutenant Commander Maxwell F. Leslie's Bombing Squadron Three to the east. At 1020 the stage was set for a most dramatic reversal of fortune. Having beaten off numerous attacks in the past hour, Nagumo's carriers were ready to launch their strike against the American carriers. They were too late. By 1030 McClusky's SBDs had mortally wounded the *Kaga* and *Akagi,* while Leslie's squadron devastated the *Soryu.* Only the *Hiryu* had escaped attack.

Shortly after 1200, even as Spruance was being advised of her presence, the fourth enemy carrier struck Task Force 17. Fighters from the *Enterprise* and *Hornet* raced to help her own planes defend the *Yorktown,* now visible on the horizon to the northwest. Task Force 16 could see the distant flashes and black dots of her antiaircraft fire, then a pall of black smoke over the *Yorktown.* She lost power after sustaining three bomb hits from *Hiryu* aircraft. Fletcher had to shift his flag to the heavy cruiser *Astoria*. For the time being, control of the Striking Force tacitly passed to Spruance. Unbidden, Spruance at 1230 dispatched two heavy cruisers and two destroyers from his screen to assist Task Force 17. At 1313, after completing more air operations he turned Task Force 16 northwest to close the stricken *Yorktown*, whose aircraft aloft were taking refuge on the *Enterprise* and the *Hornet*.

Heavy on Spruance's mind was the location of the undamaged Japanese carrier. His own air groups, in a shambles after their heavy losses, were busy absorbing the *Yorktown* dive-bombers and fighters to fill the gaps. Spruance felt that he did not have the strike planes to spare to launch another search unless it became certain that the planes sent by Fletcher at 1145 would not find the target. He rejected the advice of Browning, who proposed dispatching some sort of search-and-attack mission in hopes of turning up the enemy carrier.

At 1445 two significant events transpired. One of the *Yorktown* search planes radioed the location, course, and speed of the remaining enemy carrier. As reported, she was 130 miles northwest of Task Force 16. At almost the same instant, Task Force 17 came under attack again. The *Yorktown*, which had gallantly worked back up to 19 knots, was hit twice by *Hiryu* torpedo planes. Now totally without power, she took a steep list to port and threatened to capsize. The order was given to abandon ship, and the other vessels of Task Force 17 began taking on the survivors.

On the basis of the report so providentially provided by the *Yorktown* plane, Spruance ordered an immediate air strike. Because it was necessary to relieve the CAP, it took nearly an hour for the *Enterprise* to complete the launch of twenty-five SBDs (including fourteen *Yorktown* planes). The *Hornet*, operating separately, did not get the word from Browning in time and belatedly dispatched her strike of sixteen SBDs at 1604.

Spruance at 1611 took the opportunity to advise Fletcher in the *Astoria* that his two air groups were attacking the fourth enemy carrier. His intention was to steam westward until he recovered the strikes. He concluded: "Have you any instructions for future operations?" Realizing that he could not run the battle from his present location, Fletcher responded: "Negative. Will conform to your movements."[15] Command now officially passed from one admiral to the other.

On their flight westward toward the setting sun the *Enterprise* and *Yorktown* dive-bombers flew past the three sinking carriers they had plastered that morning. At 1650 they caught sight of the *Hiryu* and her escorts. Within fifteen minutes the SBDs had hit her four times and left her burning as fiercely as her three sisters. The *Hornet* strike did not even waste any more bombs on the *Hiryu*, but attacked her screen without success.

With the *Hiryu* fatally damaged, the Japanese were no longer in a position to win the Battle of Midway, but Spruance still could lose it. That evening as his two carriers recovered their strike groups, he made his second key decision of the battle. Task Force 16 would withdraw eastward for five hours, then retrace its course and close Midway from the northeast. The next morning it would then be in position to support the island in the event the Japanese continued with the invasion. Spruance knew that nearby the enemy had powerful surface forces, including fast battleships, which outgunned his cruisers. Directed by float planes that had shadowed Task Force 16 until dark, these forces could attack him that night if he continued westward in pursuit. Such an action could benefit only the Japanese, for the American carrier planes could not participate. Besides, the enemy might have a fifth carrier, a possibility indicated by pre-battle intelligence, or one of the crippled flattops might have become operational again. At 1915 Spruance changed course to 090 degrees, speed 15 knots, and temporarily disengaged his forces. Fletcher with Task Force 17 (minus *Yorktown* and a destroyer) soon appeared ten miles to the east.[16]

Spruance's reasoning was correct, if not very popular with those who wanted Task Force 16 to charge after the enemy. Unbeknownst to anyone on the American side, Admiral Yamamoto was at sea with a strong force of battleships backstopping the fleets attacking Midway. He tried to orchestrate a night surface attack against the American carriers by Nagumo and most of Vice Admiral Nobutake Kondo's Second Fleet. By 0300, 5 June, a total of four battleships, six heavy cruisers, three light cruisers, and nineteen destroyers were to have converged on a position that Task Force 16 could have reached had Spruance pressed westward that evening. At the same time a submarine, to be followed by four heavy cruisers and four destroyers, was to bombard Midway. However, from his search plane reports, Nagumo wrongly deduced the Americans had three or four carriers. Faced with such overwhelming air power, after midnight Yamamoto canceled the Midway Operation and began withdrawing all his ships.

Not privy to the intentions of the enemy commander, Spruance still had reasons to believe the Japanese threatened Midway. After 0300, 5 June, Task Force 16 learned of a report by the U.S. submarine *Tambor* of "many unidentified ships"[17] only about ninety miles west of the island. Spruance thought the Japanese might still try to invade and swung southwest toward Midway. Actually the ships sighted by the *Tambor* comprised the erstwhile bombardment force of four heavy cruisers and four destroyers. The most exposed element of the Japanese fleet, they were already retiring. Adding to their woes was a collision between the cruisers *Mogami* and *Mikuma*.

Spruance spent the morning of 5 June determining that Midway was safe from attack. From the island's morning search, he learned that the enemy had mostly cleared out. Only two groups were sighted. One to the northwest included what was reported as a burning carrier, while to the west were two "battleships" (actually the damaged *Mogami* and *Mikuma*). Spruance finally decided to chase the carrier withdrawing to the northwest. He did not know that she was the *Hiryu,* which had already slipped beneath the waves.

During the afternoon no new information reached Spruance, so he finally decided to launch a long-range search-and-attack mission by his dive-bombers. Browning directed that 1,000-pound bombs be carried by the SBDs. The pilots immediately protested. They thought the bomb load was too heavy for the distance they would have to fly. Wade McClusky, their spokesman, confronted Browning in the flag plot. Spruance ended the fierce argument by declaring, "I will do what you pilots want."[18] He delayed the proposed launch for an hour and ordered only 500-pound bombs to be used. Shocked and enraged by the admiral's rebuff, Browning descended to the *Enterprise*'s bridge, raised havoc with his ranting, and retired to his cabin. Later he somewhat sheepishly returned to duty.

Beginning at 1512 the two carriers sent fifty-seven dive-bombers in three groups to the northwest. They went as far as 315 miles and sighted nothing but a lone enemy destroyer, which most of them attacked without success. The late launch and long mission brought the planes to their flattops after dark. To enable them to land, Spruance risked submarine attack by ordering the carriers to turn on their deck lights. The maneuver was eminently successful. Despite many inexperienced pilots, only one SBD had to ditch. After debriefing the crews, Spruance still did not know for certain whether the enemy carrier had sunk. However, he felt the enemy force would turn west, and decided to follow at a more sedate pace, 15 knots. This would conserve fuel, which for his destroyers was becoming a real problem, and prevent any surprise night encounters with the enemy.

At dawn on 6 June, Task Force 16 launched its own search for the first time during the battle and quickly located the Japanese "battleship" group only 128 miles southwest. That morning and afternoon three strikes from the *Hornet* and *Enterprise* plastered the enemy force of two heavy cruisers and two destroyers and ultimately sank the hapless *Mikuma.*

During the day Spruance drew closer to Wake Island and to a decision as to whether he would continue westward overnight. If he did so, the next dawn would see him well within range of enemy bombers from Wake. Counterbalancing the desire to continue harrying the fleeing enemy were a number of factors. Spruance knew his aviators were tired and that the squadrons desperately needed a chance to regroup. Dwindling fuel had compelled him to detach all but four of his destroyers. Underlying all was the sense that Task Force 16 had already done everything it could to harm the enemy without taking undue risks: "I just had the feeling that we had pressed our luck to the westward about far enough."[19] At 1907, a triumphant, exhausted Task Force 16 changed course to 050 degrees for a fueling rendezvous north of Midway.

Spruance's third major decision, to break off the battle, was undoubtedly correct, for Admiral Yamamoto was desperately hoping that Wake's land-based bombers could reach Task Force 16 on 7 June. His surface forces would then deliver a night attack. The Japanese even resorted to radio deception by transmitting, in the clear, fake calls for help by a supposedly crippled battleship. Spruance was having none of it. Like his decision to withdraw to the east on the night of 4 June, his refusal to pursue after 6 June drew criticism from those who thought he should have been more aggressive. It was the one question about the battle that bothered Spruance. Later in 1942 Commander Layton obtained information on Japanese intentions and movements on those two occasions. They clearly demonstrated the dangers that Spruance's swift action had adverted. When Layton told him, Spruance gratefully replied: "The weight of a score of years has been lifted from my shoulders."[20]

The United States had won an enormous victory at Midway. The enemy's only success during the battle came on 6 June, when the submarine *I-168* torpedoed the damaged *Yorktown* before she could be towed to safety; she sank at dawn on 7 June. The loss of four big carriers crippled the Imperial Navy's offensive power. On 13 June, Task Force 16 returned to Pearl Harbor, and Spruance went ashore as Pacific Fleet chief of staff. The victors' elation was tempered by the knowledge that Japan remained strong, the war had just begun, and soon it would be their turn trying to burst through enemy defenses. There was no time to rest on laurels. Within a few weeks the Pacific Fleet was committed to an offensive to prevent Japan from consolidating its hold on the Solomon Islands.

Spruance's reputation was greatly enhanced as a result of his success in the Battle of Midway. It was only the first of an unbroken series of brilliant victories. His performance on Nimitz's staff, which brought out his strategic talents, ultimately earned him the highest operational command in the fleet. Vice Admiral Spruance led the Central Pacific amphibious offensive that captured the Gilbert Islands (November 1943) and the Marshalls (January–February 1944). As a full admiral commanding the Fifth Fleet, he invaded the Marianas in June 1944, in response to which the Japanese fleet came out in force for the first time since late 1942. The ensuing Battle of the Philippine Sea—also known as the Marianas Turkey Shoot—was the second of Spruance's great carrier air victories. Although, once again, some members of the aviation community criticized him for excessive caution, the end of the action found the enemy fleet in retreat toward home waters, having lost three carriers and virtually its entire air crew. Subsequently, Spruance commanded the Fifth Fleet in the invasions of Iwo Jima (February–March 1945), and Okinawa (March–June 1945). After the victory over Japan, he briefly served as CINCPAC. Until his retirement in July 1948 he was president of the Naval War College. From 1952 to 1955, he served as U.S. ambassador to the Philippines. He died on 13 December 1969.

Admiral Nimitz, his old commander, summed up the virtues Spruance demonstrated at Midway and elsewhere: "Spruance has excellent judgment. He was the type who thought things through very carefully after a thorough examination of all the facts, and then when he decided to strike, struck hard."[21] Nimitz added, "I sorely needed commanders of that type." Well could he say that, for admirals of the quality of Raymond Ames Spruance have only very rarely appeared in the annals of naval history.

Notes

1. Thomas B. Buell, *The Quiet Warrior: A Biography of Admiral Raymond A. Spruance* (Boston: Little, Brown, 1974), pp. 19–21. This is the most important source for details on Spruance's life.

2. Rear Admiral Edwin T. Layton, with Roger Pineau and John Costello, *"And I Was There," Pearl Harbor and Midway—Breaking the Secrets* (New York: Morrow, 1985), pp. 429–30.

3. Task Force 16 (Commander, Carriers, Pacific Fleet) War Diary, 4 June 1942, in Operational Archives, Naval Historical Center, Washington, D.C.

4. Ibid. Most authors believe that Fletcher sent this message after the 0603 position report, but I think the evidence demonstrates that it was sent before. Fletcher's role as overall commander of the Carrier Striking Force has been downplayed in most accounts of Midway. A welcome exception is Gordon Prange's *Miracle at Midway* (New York: McGraw-Hill, 1982).

5. Ibid.

6. In Admiral Spruance's foreword to Mitsuo Fuchida and Masatake Okumiya, *Midway: The Battle That Doomed Japan* (Annapolis: Naval Institute Press, 1955), p. v.

7. Buell, op. cit., p. 131. The respective roles of Spruance and Browning concerning the launch of the Task Force 16 strike have been a matter of great controversy. Most studies of Midway follow Rear Admiral Samuel Eliot Morison's *History of United States Naval Operations in World War II,* vol. 4, *Coral Sea, Midway and Submarine Actions, May 1942—August 1942* (Boston: Little, Brown, 1949), p. 113. Morison stated that Spruance originally wanted to delay the launch for three hours until he had closed to one hundred miles of the target, but was dissuaded by Browning. In *The Quiet Warrior* (pp. 130–31, 459–61), Buell vigorously and effectively rebutted this error. See also my introduction to a reissue of *The Quiet Warrior* in the series "Classics of Naval Literature" (Annapolis: Naval Institute Press, 1987), pp. ix–xv, where the likely reasons behind Morison's error are discussed in detail.

8. Rear Admiral C. Wade McClusky, "Historical Commentary," in *Midway Battle Manual* (Baltimore: Avalon Hill, 1964), p. 18.

9. For the deployment of the Task Force 16 strike groups and particularly with a new interpretation of the flight of the *Hornet* Air Group, see my *The First Team: Pacific Naval Air Combat from Pearl Harbor to Midway* (Annapolis: Naval Institute Press, 1984), pp. 332–36.

10. The text of Gray's message is given in "Fighter Director," 4 June, 1942, enclosure with the report of Commander, Cruisers, Task Force 17 (12 June 1942); Browning's order is in Fighter Director School, Navy Yard, Pacific Fleet, "The Battle of Midway Island" (3 April 1943). Both documents are in the Operational Archives. From the Task Force 16 War Diary, it is evident that McClusky's contact report was either not copied by the *Enterprise* or furnished to the Task Force 16 staff.

11. Task Force 16 War Diary, 4 June 1942.

12. Buell (pp. 134–35) blames Browning for not recommending that the *Enterprise* broadcast her position to her returning pilots. Only her SBDs had trouble getting back, and the problem was that Task Force 16 had not advanced as far to the southwest as they expected.

13. For new information on Torpedo Eight, see *The First Team,* pp. 341–43.

14. Most treatments of Midway fail to note the length of the attack by Torpedo Six and that Torpedo Three pressed its assault before, during, and after the SBDs bombed the three Japanese carriers. See *The First Team,* pp. 344–64.

15. Task Force 16 War Diary, 4 June 1942.

16. Spruance's reasoning can be found in his Midway action report: Commander, Task Force 16 to CINCPAC, "Battle of Midway" (13 June 1942).

17. U.S. Naval War College, *The Battle of Midway, Including the Aleutian Phase, June 3 to June 14, 1942, Strategical and Tactical Analysis* (Newport: U.S. Naval War College, 1948), pp. 157, 165.

18. Buell, op. cit., p. 142. His treatment of this incident on pp. 141–43 is very important for an understanding of Browning's personality and role in the battle.

19. Letter, Spruance to Captain W. J. Holmes, 23 January 1959, in "Admiral Spruance on Midway," *Pull Together: Newsletter of the Naval Historical Foundation and the Naval Historical Center,* 26:1 (Spring 1987), p. 3.

20. Buell, op. cit., pp. 158–59. See also Layton, op. cit., pp. 445–46.

21. Prange, op. cit., p. 386.

Note on Sources

For Spruance's life, the indispensable source is Thomas B. Buell's *The Quiet Warrior: A Biography of Admiral Raymond A. Spruance* (Boston: Little, Brown, 1974). With a new introduction by this author, it was reissued in 1987 by the Naval Institute Press, Annapolis, in its series "Classics of Naval Literature." A professional naval officer like his subject, Buell made use of his extensive contacts with Spruance's family and associates to paint a remarkably detailed and appealing portrait of this brilliant but modest and unassuming fighting man. Professor E. B. Potter has written biographies of two of Spruance's great contemporaries: *Nimitz* (Annapolis: Naval Institute Press, 1976) and *Bull Halsey* (Annapolis: Naval Institute Press, 1986).

Although increasingly dated by more recent research, the basic source on the

Pacific naval war remains Rear Admiral Samuel Eliot Morison's *History of United States Naval Operations in World War II:* vol. III, *The Rising Sun in the Pacific, 1931–April 1942* (Boston: Little, Brown, 1948) and vol. IV, *Coral Sea, Midway and Submarine Actions, May–August 1942* (Boston: Little, Brown, 1949). An excellent recent overview of the Pacific war is Ronald H. Spector's *Eagle Against the Sun* (New York: Free Press, 1986). My two books also cover the early campaigns of the U.S. Pacific Fleet: *The First South Pacific Campaign: Pacific Fleet Strategy, December 1941–June 1942* (Annapolis: Naval Institute Press, 1976) and *The First Team: Pacific Naval Air Combat from Pearl Harbor to Midway* (Annapolis: Naval Institute Press, 1984).

The literature on the Battle of Midway is extensive and growing, but the definitive study of this classic action has not yet appeared. Therefore it is necessary to consult a wide variety of sources, many of which remain unpublished. The early classic accounts include the U.S. Naval War College, *The Battle of Midway, Including the Aleutian Phase, June 3 to June 14, 1942, Strategical and Tactical Analysis* (Newport: U.S. Naval War College, 1948); Mitsuo Fuchida and Masatake Okumiya, *Midway: The Battle That Doomed Japan* (Annapolis: Naval Institute Press, 1955); and Walter Lord, *Incredible Victory* (New York: Harper and Row, 1967). Another book based on extensive interviews is Gordon Prange's *Miracle at Midway* (New York: McGraw-Hill, 1982), which draws heavily on the excellent doctoral dissertation of one of his students, Robert E. Barde's "Decision at Midway" (University of Maryland, 1971). The Japan Maritime Self-Defense Force's War History Office has issued a volume on Midway in its official War History Series, *Senshi Sosho,* vol. 43, *Middowe Kaisen* (Midway Sea Battle) (Tokyo: Asagumo Shimbun, 1971). In *"And I Was There," Pearl Harbor and Midway—Breaking the Secrets* (New York: Morrow, 1985), Rear Admiral Edwin T. Layton, former Pacific Fleet intelligence officer, offered important new insights about radio intelligence and the Midway campaign. Also worthy of note is Robert J. Cressman et al., *A Glorious Page in Our History: The Battle of Midway, 4–6 June 1942* (Missoula, Mont.: Pictorial Histories, 1990).

19

William F. Halsey, Jr.

The Bull

(1882–1959)

Clark G. Reynolds

"A REAL OLD SALT" IS HOW "WILLIE" HALSEY'S CLASSMATES described him in their 1904 U.S. Naval Academy yearbook, adding that he "looks like a figurehead of Neptune." He had at least as much salt water in his veins as any American naval officer of his generation, having descended from a long line of seafaring men. His formidable head continued to evoke images of the Roman god of the sea as he matured, leading his midshipmen students at Annapolis a dozen years later to regard him as "the Bull"—a nickname reinvented by reporters during World War II. Aside from his looks, however, Halsey consciously acted and performed in the manner of the sea dogs of old—the last in any navy before naval warfare passed into the nuclear war–managerial age.[1]

William Frederick Halsey, Jr., was the most famous American admiral of World War II, a renown based primarily on his flamboyant personality and command achievements in the Pacific during 1942–43. Controversial decisions made later in the war never diminished his public image; he was the only flag officer to adorn the cover of *Time* magazine twice—November 1942 and July 1945.[2] Quite simply, Halsey personified the layman's vision of swashbuckling sea fighters like Drake and Nelson—or John Paul Jones and David Farragut of his own navy. It was an accurate impression, uncomplicated as the man himself—in contrast to his calculating, businesslike, and relatively reserved contemporaries of the managerial style: Ernest J. King, Chester W. Nimitz, Raymond A. Spruance, and John H. Towers, to name but a few.

Halsey inherited the tradition of the aggressive, independent naval commander embodied in the meleeist school of eighteenth-century naval tactics. That is, he aimed to seek out, engage, and destroy the enemy fleet by decisive action. He gathered the necessary intelligence on enemy movements but exploited opportunities whenever they presented themselves, rather than waiting for more complete data, as did peers like Spruance in similar situations. He tended to throw caution to the winds in a manner reminiscent of the "general chase" option of the Royal Navy's Fighting Instructions in the Age of Sail, if a calculated risk seemed to offer immediate victory. And like the meleeists of the Nelsonian era, when this style succeeded, as at Guadalcanal, he was applauded. When it was less successful, as at Leyte Gulf, he was roundly criticized within the navy. And since the risks increased with the complexities of modern warfare, his seemingly impulsive tactics became ever more questionable.

Born in Elizabeth, New Jersey, on 30 October 1882, Halsey was the son of a naval officer, Lieutenant William F. Halsey, a graduate of the Naval Academy Class of 1873, and Anne Brewster Halsey, a descendant of William Brewster of the early Massachusetts Bay Colony. The family, which included a younger sister, moved frequently as the father changed duty stations. Though young Willie was consequently shunted between schools, he always desired to follow his father in a naval career. After repeated failures for appointment to Annapolis, however, he enrolled at the University of Virginia in 1899, hoping to enter the navy via a medical degree. The following year he finally gained admission to the Naval Academy, where he played football and participated in numerous extracurricular activities. No scholar, he graduated forty-third in the Class of 1904's sixty-two men. He married Fanny Grandy of Norfolk in 1909; she bore him first a daughter, then a son. This small family became a source of satisfaction to him, especially when his son, Willam F. Halsey III, also entered the navy. Sadly, on the eve of World War II Fanny developed serious emotional problems, which remained a great concern to the admiral thereafter.[3]

Schooled in the art of ship command, Halsey devoted the first thirty years of his career to the surface line, not only in gunnery but especially torpedo warfare. After preliminary service in two battleships and a gunboat, he spent nearly two decades aboard destroyers, practicing surface torpedo tactics as well as antisubmarine operations and general escort duties—plus one year as executive officer of the battleship *Wyoming*. As commanding officer of single destroyers (ten times!), destroyer divisions (twice), and a destroyer squadron (once), Halsey profited from the experience of independent leadership so conducive to his style of command. Long interested in aviation, he managed to obtain a waiver for his corrected vision to enter flight training in 1934 and earn his wings the following year—at age fifty-two! He immediately assumed command of the aircraft carrier *Saratoga* and further honed his tactical skills during the fleet problems of 1935–37. Though no talented pilot himself, he quickly learned to appreciate the offensive possibilities of carrier aviation, at which he became a proficient tactician.[4]

Even when assigned for a year each at the navy and army war colleges in the early 1930s, Halsey related all of his thinking to command. In his thesis at the Naval War College in 1933—entitled "The Relationship in War of Naval Strategy, Tactics and Command"—he concluded:

> Command is the nerve center that directs, controls, and coordinates the strategic and tactical. They are command's right and left hands. As command controls these hands, so command controls the war. Strategy, tactics, and command may be called the trinity of war; and the greatest of these is command.[5]

A warm, friendly, and popular captain, Halsey—known to his friends simply as Bill—always produced "happy" ships, the supreme accolade for a successful skipper. Thus he was a natural choice for selection to rear admiral in 1938 and command of a carrier division, making him one of only five flag officers with an aviation designator at the time. He refined his tactics in the fleet's war games of 1938–40 at the head of a two-carrier division, amply displaying his talents aboard his flagships *Yorktown* and *Saratoga*. By then, he had carefully managed to obtain mostly seagoing billets, with only an occasional tour of duty ashore. His experience afloat led to his elevation in mid-1940 to the most coveted aviation billet, the "Carrier Command"—Commander Aircraft, Battle Force—in the rank of vice admiral.[6]

With the U.S. Fleet concentrated in the Pacific to deter Japan, Halsey's task was to develop its four carriers into an effective component of the Battle Force. The tactical problems of the preceding years had led to sharp disagreements between the battleship admirals and the aviation community over the proper tactical role of the carriers in war. Repeated mock air attacks on Pearl Harbor, the Panama Canal, and "enemy" fleet formations had convinced the aviators that the carriers must exploit their tactical mobility by operating independently of the battle line. Halsey was no exception and steadfastly opposed the battleship men who wanted to tie the carriers to the battle line as defensive insurance.

But Halsey also knew that the airmen's arguments had a hollow ring until improved aircraft could extend the striking range and attacking power of the carriers. In July 1940, immediately upon assuming the Carrier Command, he complained to Rear Admiral John H. ("Jack") Towers, chief of the Bureau of Aeronautics, that his carrier planes were "seriously deficient from a modern standpoint, both in performance and in numbers available." The Grumman biplane fighters and assorted scout-bombers were obsolescent and the new Douglas TBD monoplane torpedo-bomber only "mediocre." He begged for more new monoplane fighters and scout-bombers, namely the Brewster F2A Buffalo fighter and Douglas SBD Dauntless dive-bomber, and even went so far as to suggest that the Douglas company be forced to cut back production of its DC-3 commercial airliner in favor of the SBD. Justifiably anxious, he admitted his ignorance of the overall production picture, to which Towers quickly enlightened him: the newer Grumman F4F Wildcat was even better than the F2A, SBD deliveries would soon increase, and ever more modern planes were already in the experimental stage. But such zeal was what impressed Halsey's superiors; he wanted to fight, and fight to win.[7]

Until better and more planes became available, Halsey spent 1940–41 sharpening carrier tactics with existing equipment for the war with Japan that seemed only a matter of time. His selection of tactical officers for his staff revealed much about Halsey. Rejecting the officers recommended by the Bureau of Aeronautics, he picked Commander Miles R. Browning, a brilliant air tactician but an abrasive, unpredictable individual.[8] Halsey simply overlooked Browning's personality quirks in his zeal to exploit the man's considerable talent. He was interested in results and soon elevated Browning to be his chief of staff. Browning no doubt appealed to Halsey as a fighter, not unlike himself, a preference clearly reflected in Halsey's wartime relations with scrappers like John S. ("Slew") McCain and Frederick C. ("Ted") Sherman. Despite McCain's recklessness and Sherman's bombast, Halsey enjoyed the rough-and-tumble give-and-take with men of their ilk. Needless to say, such confidence generated a mutual loyalty, and Halsey fiercely defended his subordinates, notably Browning, who was later removed from the war zone for personal indiscretions and errors of professional judgment.[9]

As war suddenly seemed imminent to Halsey, on 1 December 1941 he took the extraordinary and officially questionable step of placing his flagship *Enterprise* and escort on a war footing when they departed Pearl Harbor to deliver Marine Corps planes to Wake Island. His initiative was vindicated six days later when the Japanese struck Pearl Harbor, and he was immediately sent to prowl around Hawaii in search of the enemy fleet. Halsey's fighting image and pronouncements acted as an elixir for the stunned Pacific Fleet, making him the obvious choice to lead the first carrier raids on Japanese island outposts—the Marshalls, Wake, and Marcus—in late January, February, and March 1942. "Bill Halsey is a grand man to serve under, especially at a time like this," reported his escort commander, Rear Admiral "Ray" Spruance, to his wife during these strikes. A month later Spruance applauded Halsey as "a splendid seaman [who] will smack them hard every time he gets a chance."[10]

Halsey's initial exploits caught the attention of the public, but only the high command and the participants knew of the top secret mission he was assigned to lead in April 1942—the bombing of Tokyo by Army Air Force (AAF) bombers launched from the carrier *Hornet*. The operation required audacity, and Halsey provided it. "I am not kicking so long as I can go to sea with Bill Halsey," wrote Spruance at the beginning of the month. "Things will happen, and happen well, wherever he goes and is allowed some initiative."[11] Spruance was right. With his flag in the *Enterprise,* Halsey took the two carriers to a point 620 miles from the Japanese coast and launched sixteen B-25 Mitchell bombers under Lieutenant Colonel James H. Doolittle that struck Tokyo on 18 April and crash-landed in China.

Not surprisingly, Halsey's continuous combat duty since the Pearl Harbor attack took its toll on him physically. Late in May he came down with a severe case of shingles, an irritating skin rash that caused such discomfort he was unable to get enough sleep. Admiral Nimitz, the Pacific Fleet commander, had no choice but to order him to the hospital—on the eve of the epic Battle of Midway! Unable to command the carriers in that action, Halsey selected Spruance—a nonaviator—to do so in his stead with the support of his well-honed staff, including Miles Browning. The exact credit due Halsey's staff for that monumental victory is impossible to measure, but its role was indisputably vital.

Following his recovery and recuperation in the States, Halsey returned to the Carrier Command in October, expecting to lead the *Enterprise* and *Hornet* in the desperate defense of the Marines' toehold at Guadalcanal in the southwestern Pacific. Upon his arrival there, however, Halsey received unexpected orders to relieve Vice Admiral Robert Lee Ghormley as commander of the South Pacific Forces. His fighting tenacity made him a natural choice to overcome the sense of despair that had enshrouded Ghormley's command. Elevation to a theater command took him ashore—to Nouméa, New Caledonia—and out of a seagoing billet. Before long, all surviving American carriers were either sunk or immobilized by battle damage, forcing Halsey to depend on shore-based air.[12]

With no time to spare, Halsey succeeded in turning the tide, at the cost of many ships and lives lost in the Battle of the Santa Cruz Islands and the titanic Naval Battle of Guadalcanal, both waged during his first month in command. Carefully weighing the stakes, he assembled and committed all available men and material to decide the issue for Guadalcanal. "If I have any principle of warfare burned within my brain," he later wrote, "it is that the best defense is a strong offense. Lord Nelson expressed this very well: 'No captain can do very wrong if he places his ship alongside that of an enemy.'"[13] It was this offensive spirit that inspired the confidence of the South Pacific Forces. Although the Allies had not yet won the campaign for Guadalcanal, the victory in the Naval Battle of mid-November foreshadowed its outcome.

Halsey's reward was immediate promotion to the rank of full admiral. It was his finest hour; Nimitz's faith in him had been fully justified. Halsey exploited the situation to heighten the morale of his forces by rashly predicting that Japan would be defeated during 1943 and visiting units of his command to make a famous speech that consisted of just one line: "Kill Japs, kill Japs, kill more Japs!"[14]

Halsey's tenacity proved crucial in consolidating the Allied hold on the southern Solomons, particularly after the enemy evacuated Guadalcanal early in 1943. Air battles raged daily and nightly, with the Japanese sending planes down the Solomons from their big airdrome at Rabaul in the Bismarck Archipelago. Shorn of carrier strength, Halsey minimized the exposure to land-based air of his two repaired fleet carriers *Saratoga* and *En-*

terprise and three *Sangamon*-class escort carriers—a tactical caution that became fundamental to his thinking—and depended on his own land-based air forces (navy, army, marines, and New Zealand) to wrest control of the air from the Japanese. It was an exhausting campaign of attrition in which American tactics, equipment, airmanship, and the policy of rotating tired veteran pilots home proved ultimately superior.

As commander of the South Pacific Area and Forces, Halsey was charged with planning and leading one of the three prongs of the American counteroffensive against Japan. Beginning in the summer of 1943, his forces would advance up the Solomons toward Rabaul, while General Douglas MacArthur's forces leapfrogged along the coast of New Guinea and Nimitz's moved into the Central Pacific. Because this theater-size Solomons campaign required careful interservice coordination, Admiral King, commander in chief of the U.S. Fleet and chief of naval operations (CNO), wanted Halsey to have a less contentious chief of staff than Captain Miles Browning. King and Halsey finally agreed upon Rear Admiral Robert B. ("Mick") Carney, who was promoted to the post from command of a cruiser after the initial assault on New Georgia Island in June. Carney was the complete opposite of Halsey in personality—a steady, careful thinker who could provide a counterweight to his exuberant boss. Carney became so essential as Halsey's chief of staff that when he tried to obtain a sea command later in the war Admiral King told him, "You'll stay there as long as Halsey can fight."[15]

The success of the Solomons campaign demonstrated Halsey's strategic flexibility. After six weeks of heavy fighting secured New Georgia, Halsey took his staff's advice and fooled the Japanese by bypassing his next ostensible objective, Kolombangara, to seize Vella Lavella against only light opposition in mid-August. Similarly, in order to avoid a long and costly campaign for the heavily defended island of Bougainville in the northern Solomons, Halsey decided to neutralize the southern end of the island by air attacks while landing at Empress Augusta Bay on the west coast. Like the bypassing of Kolombangara, the idea for this maneuver originated with the staff "dirty tricks department" that Halsey had created to think of ways to keep the Japanese off balance. The risks of a heavy Japanese air and sea counterattack from Rabaul were accepted.

Halsey's assault troops went ashore at Bougainville on 1 November 1943, and his covering gunships drove off four Japanese cruisers and six destroyers that tried to interfere. Then, learning that six enemy cruisers had assembled at Rabaul to threaten his amphibious shipping, Halsey followed his staff's thinking to order Rear Admiral Ted Sherman to attack the Japanese base with all his planes from the *Saratoga* and new light carrier *Princeton*; the carriers were protected by land-based fighters. The gamble paid off when Sherman's planes so damaged the cruisers at Rabaul on 5 November that they withdrew to Truk in the Carolines. Thereafter, only Japanese planes attacked the landing forces—without success.[16]

Halsey's style of command worked well in the Solomons because of his tactical flexibility and his ability to work with MacArthur, who respected him as a fighting leader. The neutralization of Rabaul as a naval base enabled Halsey to extinguish it as an airdrome by seizing surrounding islands for airfields between December 1943 and February 1944. All of this was accomplished despite the vague command relationship in which he operated under the strategic direction of MacArthur as commander in chief of the southwest Pacific but with naval forces provided by Nimitz as commander in chief of the Pacific Fleet and Pacific Ocean areas. Rarely did MacArthur and Halsey disagree, however. The only time they differed was over whether Nimitz or MacArthur should have jurisdiction over the base development of the Admiralty Islands. When Halsey accused MacArthur to his face of wanting control for political reasons—to reach the Philippines ahead of Nimitz—MacArthur backed down, but the Joint Chiefs of Staff (JCS) soon gave him jurisdiction anyway.[17]

The Halsey-MacArthur dual push from the south reflected credit on both men for having neutralized Rabaul, making an invasion unnecessary. Simultaneous victories by Spruance's Central Pacific Force in the Gilberts and Marshalls culminated in a decision by the JCS in March 1944 to bypass mighty Truk, neutralizing it by air attacks in the same way as Rabaul. MacArthur had advocated concentrating all American forces in the Pacific for a concerted drive from the south toward the Philippines, with himself in overall command and Halsey as his naval commander. Though eschewing the command role, Halsey had agreed with MacArthur's proposal, as had most of Nimitz's key advisers. But Admiral King's strategy prevailed in the March 1944 JCS decision—to continue the dual drives by MacArthur's SoWesPac and Nimitz's CenPac forces toward Luzon and Formosa (Taiwan) to keep the Japanese off balance.[18]

Correct as events proved King's strategy to be, the decision was a fateful one for Halsey, for it perpetuated the theater command divided between MacArthur and Nimitz. In June 1944, with the SoPac theater now a rear area, Halsey received a new assignment. He was designated Commander Third Fleet, the very same "big blue fleet" battle force then operating under Spruance as the Fifth Fleet. Spruance retained command during the conquest of the Marianas in the summer of 1944, while Halsey and his staff were at Pearl Harbor with Nimitz, planning the next operation. That operation would be the liberation of the Philippines, during which the fleet would simply change numbers. Unlike Spruance, who operated directly under Nimitz's command, Halsey would resume his dual role, in this instance providing strategic cover for MacArthur's forces while operating under Nimitz's authority. And Nimitz and MacArthur were responsible only to the JCS in Washington. That the division continued was due to the singular fact that the navy did not trust MacArthur to use its new Fast Carrier Task Force without undue risk—a feeling that MacArthur reciprocated by denying the navy control of his ground forces.

An additional wrinkle loomed that might affect Halsey's ability to perform effectively during the Philippine campaign. Although he held the title of Commander Third Fleet, he was not to have control of the amphibious forces, as he had in the Solomons. In fact, for the first time in more than two years, Halsey was to have direct command of the fleet's carriers. When he had left the old seagoing Carrier Command in 1942, he had had charge of only two—the *Enterprise* and *Hornet*. Now, in late August 1944, he returned to sea at the head of no fewer than sixteen—the new *Essex*-class carriers, plus his beloved "Big E." Since the amphibious responsibilities belonged to the Seventh Fleet under MacArthur's authority, the Third Fleet was for all intents and purposes the Carrier Command. Administratively, it was known as Task Force 38, and it had its own tactical commander, Vice Admiral Marc A. Mitscher, who had held the same position under Spruance. Mitscher would rotate back to Pearl Harbor with Spruance as soon as his relief, Vice Admiral Slew McCain, learned the ropes as a task group commander. Yet Halsey was in tactical command and would again be leading his carriers with the same flair and independence he had exhibited in the early days of the war.[19] The new fast battleships—in one of which, the *New Jersey*, Halsey raised his flag—were distributed among the carrier groups' screens but could be formed into a battle line as Task Force 34. Coordinating his movements only indirectly with MacArthur could entail serious risks for Halsey, given the complexity of the forthcoming invasion.

The operation began in early September 1944 with carrier strikes on Japanese airfields on Mindanao in the southern Philippines, during which Halsey was surprised at the weak enemy resistance. His task was to eliminate Japanese air defenses prior to MacArthur's landings at Mindanao on 15 November, followed by Leyte in the central islands on 20 December, and Luzon or Formosa later in the winter. Once islands were taken, they could be developed in AAF airfields to help support the next landing. The carriers shifted to targets in the Visayas group of the central Philippines on 12–13 September, again with minimal enemy response. A carrier pilot shot down over Leyte and rescued by Filipinos learned firsthand of the weakness of Japanese air defenses in the central islands, a revelation passed on to Halsey after the man was returned to the fleet by a seaplane.[20]

Halsey and his staff at once concluded that it would be possible to bypass Mindanao and assault Leyte much earlier than planned. The fast carriers and a dozen or more Seventh Fleet escort carriers would suffice to support the landing until airfields could be constructed ashore. Halsey fired off this recommendation to Nimitz at midday on 13 September. Nimitz and MacArthur concurred on the fourteenth and asked for approval from the Allied Combined Chiefs of Staff, then meeting in Canada. They, too, agreed and stepped up the Pacific timetable by two months: Leyte rather than Mindanao would be assaulted and on 20 October instead of November or December. Mindoro, just south of Luzon, was to be invaded 5 December, and Luzon itself on the twentieth, though these latter operations were later postponed. Troops earmarked for Mindanao and several lesser objectives had to be reshuffled to suit the new plan. Also, a certain risk was involved, since the seasonal rains might hamper army airfield construction on Leyte in November. But it had been a bold calculation, typical of Halsey, and showed that he had lost none of his nerve and sense of opportunity.

Halsey spent the rest of September using the fast carriers to pound Japanese air defenses in the Philippines. The final tally was nearly 900 enemy planes destroyed (mostly on the ground) and 224,000 tons of merchant and minor naval shipping sunk. The Third Fleet then retired to newly won island anchorages in the Central Pacific to prepare for the Leyte landings.[21]

Halsey's task was clear enough. The Third Fleet—or TF 38—was to isolate Leyte Island from enemy air and naval interference and seaborne troop reinforcements. This meant that his four fast carrier groups would attack Japanese airfields and shipping throughout the Philippines before, during, and after the 20 October assault. Vice Admiral Thomas C. Kinkaid's Seventh Fleet, under MacArthur's direct jurisdiction, would provide tactical support for the army troops—the older battleships, plus cruisers and destroyers, by shore bombardment, and eighteen escort carriers by close-in strafing and bombing. The key unknown factor was the Japanese fleet. Although it was not expected to sortie until landings had been made at Mindanao or Luzon on the western side of the Philippines, Nimitz hoped that the attack on Leyte would draw it out to the east of the islands, from which a retreat to its bases would be extremely hazardous.

If Japan's carriers and battleships gave battle in defense of Leyte, Nimitz left no doubt in Halsey's mind that he was to engage and destroy them. "In case opportunity for destruction of major portion of the enemy fleet is offered or can be created," read Halsey's orders, "such destruction becomes the primary task." The reason for such a direct order was Nimitz's regret that the Japanese fleet had not been decisively defeated in the Battle of the Philippine Sea in June. In that action, Spruance had kept the fast carriers close to the amphibious forces lest Japanese fleet units slip in behind them to contest the landings on Saipan. Three Japanese carriers and four hundred planes had been destroyed, but six carriers had escaped to fight again. Nimitz had not issued explicit orders to Spruance; hence his decision to give Halsey a clear mandate for Leyte. In view of Bull Halsey's aggressiveness, there seemed little chance that he would let any enemy ships slip around the Third Fleet to get at MacArthur's beachhead.[22]

So Halsey faced a potentially dual mission—shielding MacArthur from air attacks, a defensive task near Leyte; and fighting a naval battle, which would require independent, offensive tactics in the open sea. It was the classic problem that had confounded so many earlier naval commanders: Spanish and French admirals in centuries of repeated attempts to invade the Britain Isles; American admirals in the fleet problems of the 1930s; the Japanese at the Coral Sea, Midway, and Guadalcanal; and Spruance in the Marianas—if the enemy fleet appeared, which mission had priority, remaining on the defensive to guard the invasion force, or breaking away to fight an offensive naval engagement? The answer was plain enough: destroy the enemy fleet and thereby protect the landing. The difficulty, apparent ever since the Anglo-Dutch repulse of the Spanish Armada in 1588, was that very close coordination was essential between the battle fleet and the amphibious force.

No evidence exists that either Halsey or any of his staff were close students of such seemingly archaic naval history, nor indeed had they absorbed the fine "lessons" of previous such tactical choices in the Pacific war. Events were moving too quickly for relevant, in-depth war college analyses to be made. As in all wars, therefore, the tactical lessons would have to be learned anew, on the spot. How well constituted was Halsey's staff to advise the boss *and* to ensure close coordination with the amphibious forces of Kinkaid's Seventh Fleet? The latter task was not automatic; the division of theater responsibilities between Nimitz and MacArthur meant that any information between Halsey and Kinkaid had to be especially transmitted—a time-consuming chore easily overlooked in the heat of battle. The danger at Leyte was that commanders of the Third and Seventh Fleets might have to take too much tactical information for granted.[23]

Halsey had won his plaudits as Carrier Commander in 1942 by operating with a typical carrier staff—virtually all of them aviators, headed by the shrewdest tactician of them all, Miles Browning. This was the very same staff that Spruance had inherited just before Midway. It was also the one Halsey had taken to the South Pacific, where it had been reshaped from a seagoing carrier staff into a broadly based theater organization dealing with war plans, logistics, amphibious units, base development, and ship and aircraft movements. Browning had been replaced by Mick Carney; a Marine brigadier general, William R. Riley, was added for war plans; and a nonaviator, Captain Ralph E. Wilson, was made operations officer. The staff had only one career aviator, Lieutenant Commander L. J. Dow, and he was communications officer. Two others had returned to active duty—Commanders H. Douglas Moulton, air operations, and M. C. Cheek, intelligence.

During the South Pacific campaign the staff had melded into a closely knit body, adjusting to Halsey's style. Like him, it was informal, loose, even sloppy in its techniques—all traits that, however, had succeeded in winning the Solomons campaign. Halsey had brought this same theater staff with him to what was again the Carrier Command. It lacked the carrier expertise to which he had been accustomed in 1942. That now belonged to the staff of Admiral Mitscher's TF 38, but Halsey was exercising tactical command as head of the Third Fleet. Halsey and his staff were capable men, to be sure, but they had no experience as a carrier command organization. Should the Japanese fleet choose to give battle at Leyte, they would face very difficult decisions.[24]

The Third Fleet sortied early in October to eliminate land-based enemy air power north of the Philippines. The carrier planes struck Okinawa on 10 October, Aparri on northern Luzon on the eleventh, and the many airdromes on Formosa from the twelfth through the fifteenth. The Japanese reacted with fury and lost more than five hundred planes in the four-day air battle over Formosa. Two of Halsey's escorting cruisers were severely damaged, however, and had to be taken in tow to the east, toward the advanced base at Ulithi atoll in the western Carolines. Halsey and his staff decided to use this "crippled" force as bait to draw out the Japanese fleet. At first, their ploy seemed to work. Three enemy cruisers sortied from Japan, but they retired upon learning that the Third Fleet was still largely intact. Halsey and the staff had erected a game board in the *New Jersey,* on which they worked out possible Japanese fleet movements. When the enemy cruisers withdrew, they concluded that the Japanese fleet would not make a serious attempt to interfere with the Leyte operation.[25]

On 15 October the Third Fleet began striking targets on Luzon on a daily basis through the landing on the twentieth and until the twenty-third. Kinkaid's escort carriers along with AAF planes from New Guinea and Morotai joined in the attack on the central and southern Philippines. Halsey's strategic coverage of the landing was an unqualified success. The only real problem was heavy rains, which prevented the airstrips from being expeditiously completed for the AAF on Leyte. With MacArthur ashore and units of the Sixth Army moving inland, Halsey detached McCain's five-carrier task group and a sixth carrier for rest and replenishment at Ulithi, planning to rotate all four groups during what seemed to be a fairly routine covering operation. He was left with eleven fast carriers.

Suddenly, on the morning of 24 October, Halsey received word that U.S. submarines were attacking heavy enemy fleet units in the Palawan Passage west of the Philippines.[26] Indeed, they sank two cruisers and disabled a third. A search strike by carrier planes sighted the enemy force, which included several battleships. Then another, smaller gun force was spotted southwest

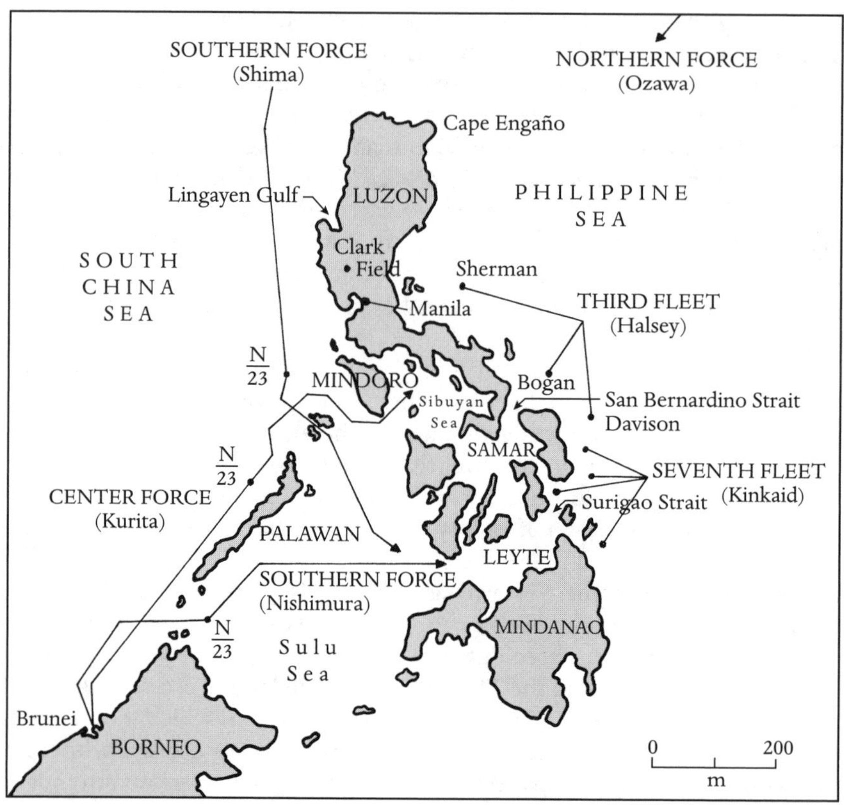

31. The Battle of Leyte Gulf, 24–25 October 1944. Positions are shown as of 1200 on 24 October. The notation N/23 indicates those at 1200 the preceding day.

of Mindanao. Both were converging on the central Philippines. Alerted that the Japanese fleet was going to contest the landings after all, Halsey ordered his three available task groups to cover the eastern exits from the Philippines—Ted Sherman's TG 38.3 off Luzon to the north; Gerald F. Bogan's TG 38.2 off San Bernardino Strait to watch for the "Center Force," as the Americans came to refer to the formidable surface-action group sighted in the Palawan Passage; and Ralph E. Davison's TG 38.4 to cover Surigao Strait and the "Southern Force." He also recalled McCain's TG 38.1, then refueling six hundred miles to the east, so far away it might arrive too late to participate in the anticipated battle. But where were the Japanese carriers?

As the Center Force entered the Sibuyan Sea, obviously aiming to pass through San Bernardino Strait, Halsey concentrated his planes against it. Sherman had to fend off repeated Japanese attacks from the airfields on

Luzon; a direct hit on the light carrier *Princeton* soon proved fatal, and she had to be scuttled. Nevertheless, Halsey's strikes mortally damaged the superbattleship *Musashi* and obliged the Center Force to turn back to the west in retreat by early afternoon. The Southern Force pressed on toward Surigao Strait, but Halsey decided to let Kinkaid's fire-support battleships deal with it in a gunnery action that night. And Sherman sent searches to the north, the direction in which Halsey suspected the Japanese carriers would appear.

By 1500 on the twenty-fourth Halsey had ably and successfully executed Nimitz's orders to turn all his attention to destroying the enemy fleet. And just in case the weakened Center Force reversed course to the east, at 1512 he issued a preparatory order for the fast battleships to form a battle line—TF 34, under Vice Admiral Willis A. Lee—for a gunnery duel at San Bernardino Strait similar to the one anticipated at Surigao Strait. It was only a contingency plan, whose execution would depend on the receipt of intelligence that the Center Force was reentering the fray. Halsey could not know that Kinkaid's communications personnel had intercepted the message and that Kinkaid concluded that the battleship task force had actually been formed! The divided chain of command now jeopardized the operation, for Kinkaid was not privy to Halsey's thinking. Nor did Kinkaid question the tactically unsound possibility that Lee's battle line—four battleships, five cruisers, and fourteen destroyers—would be detached from Halsey's formation without air cover and in range of Luzon's airfields. Yet that was not really Kinkaid's business as naval support commander.

Then, at 1640, Sherman's searches made contact with Japanese carriers 190 miles north of the Third Fleet. The discovery of this "Northern Force" of four carriers, two hybrid battleship carriers,* plus cruisers and destroyers completed the puzzle: the Japanese fleet was converging on Leyte Gulf from three directions. Excited at the prospect of annihilating Japan's carriers, Halsey considered the options with the staff. He rejected a suggestion to leave Lee's battle line (TF 34) and a carrier group off San Bernardino Strait and head north with only two groups, reasoning that he must remain tactically concentrated to repel Luzon-based air attacks and avoid losing any more ships. Divided, his fleet could be attacked piecemeal—a prospect to be avoided, according to all fleet doctrine. And if the Center Force did pass through the strait—which it could not reach before morning, at the earliest—Kinkaid's battleships could handle it after disposing of the smaller Southern Force around midnight. Halsey could even destroy the Northern

* These were the sisterships *Ise* and *Hyuga*, whose two after 14-inch turrets had been removed in 1943 to make place for a flight deck. Neither one had aircraft aboard at Leyte Gulf.

Force and turn south to cut off the Center Force should it reach Leyte Gulf. With the Northern Force now opening the distance to three hundred miles, Halsey had to act. About 1945 he put his finger on the plot of the Northern Force and told his staff, "We will run north at top speed and put those carriers out for keeps!"

In general, Halsey's tactics were sound. Although his staff was not sure whether one or two Japanese northern forces existed, they would in any case be operating in close proximity for mutual support. When at least one staff member dissented from the admiral's decision, Halsey overruled further debate. Accepting his aviators' exaggerated accounts of the damage inflicted on the Center Force, Halsey knew that the destruction of Japan's carriers would mean the end of the Japanese surface navy. In accordance with Nimitz's edict, he was going after them, and at 1950 he informed Kinkaid that he was heading north with all three carrier groups. But since he made no mention of Lee's TF 34 battle line, Kinkaid erroneously assumed that it was being left behind to cover San Bernardino Strait. Minutes later, at 2006, a night fighter reported that the Center Force was heading eastward toward the strait again after all. Halsey relayed the contact to Kinkaid and went to bed, exhausted by the day's events.[27]

Typically combative as Halsey's tactics were, they took too much for granted. Acting as tactical commander of the fast carriers, he solicited no advice from those most experienced in carrier operations—neither Mitscher, any of Mitscher's task group commanders, nor Lee. Furthermore, he continued to reject contrary views, including a message from Lee suggesting that the Northern Force was merely a decoy to lure him away from Leyte, which was in fact its mission. Then, as the carriers steamed north, Halsey slowed their speed from 25 to 16 knots, apprehensive that the Northern Force might slip around him during the night. When a night fighter sighted enemy ships eighty miles distant at 0205 on the twenty-fifth Halsey—on Mitscher's recommendation—ordered Lee to form his battle line for a night action, a delicate maneuver that required a further reduction in speed. A report that Kinkaid's battleships were engaging the Southern Force in Surigao Strait also caused Halsey to reduce his speed. Then contact was lost with the Northern Force. With the battle now enormously complicated, and without exact knowledge of the whereabouts of the Northern Force, Halsey had become uncharacteristically cautious.[28]

Inasmuch as Halsey was preoccupied with the Northern Force and Kinkaid with the Southern Force, neither man nor their staffs gave much thought to the Center Force, each assuming that the other was going to intercept it. The first message they exchanged concerning the Center Force on the twenty-fifth reached the *New Jersey* at 0648: Kinkaid asked Halsey if

TF 34 was indeed guarding San Bernardino Strait. Surprised, Halsey replied in the negative. But it was too late. At the very moment that Halsey received Kinkaid's query, the superbattleship *Yamato* and her consorts of the Center Force were sighted *visually* by Kinkaid's crews at Leyte Gulf! By that time, Halsey's planes were closing in on the decoy carriers, and as they began their attack Halsey received pleas for help from Kinkaid. Halsey simply assumed Kinkaid's old battleships and eighteen escort carriers could protect the gulf. He could not know that Kinkaid's battleships had pursued the remnants of the Southern Force sixty-five miles down Surigao Strait, nor that the planes of the escort carriers were armed to attack only shore targets, not steel ships. Confusion reigned in the navy high command. Kinkaid now knew that TF 34 was with the fast carriers, but not everyone knew it, and at 1000 Halsey received a message from Nimitz at Pearl Harbor: "Where is, repeat, where is Task Force 34. The world wonders." Though the latter phrase was probably only padding added to confuse enemy radio intercepts, the message demonstrated the sad reality that efficient communications between the Third and Seventh Fleets had broken down.[29]

After an hour of fuming at this rebuff from Nimitz and reluctantly deciding to split his force, Halsey ordered Lee's battleships and Bogan's carriers to turn south to try to cut off the Center Force. Again, he was too late. After mauling one of the Seventh Fleet's escort carrier forces, the Center Force headed back to San Bernardino Strait and escaped destruction during a night transit. Meanwhile, Halsey's carriers had sunk all four conventional carriers of the Northern Force, though not the two hybrid battleship carriers. McCain's task group reached Leyte just after noon of the twenty-fifth but inflicted little damage, while the Japanese committed their first kamikaze planes, which sank one escort carrier and damaged others. MacArthur's beachhead and most of his amphibious shipping had been saved, but ships and planes—and lives—had been lost.

The culprit in the near-debacle had been the divided command that prevented the Third and Seventh Fleets from remaining in routine communication with one another. Given such a state of affairs and the separate missions of the two admirals—a fleet action versus amphibious support—Halsey and Kinkaid had been forced to initiate special messages between one another. Neither did so effectively, though both subsequently denied any error, while analysts and historians have remained divided in their criticism ever since. Perhaps Samuel Eliot Morison came closest to the mark when he said of Halsey that "in his efforts to build public morale in America and Australia, Halsey . . . built up an image of himself as an exponent of Danton's . . . 'Audacity . . . always audacity' . . . the real reason for his fumble in the Battle for Leyte Gulf."[30]

18. The Battle of Cape Engaño, 25 October 1944. Japanese ships maneuver under attack at the battle. This photograph, taken by an aircraft from the USS *Essex* at approximately 1330, shows the light cruiser *Oyodo* in the foreground. The light carrier burning and sinking behind it is probably the *Zuiho*. (U.S. Naval Historical Center photograph, U.S. Naval Institute Photographic Collection.)

Halsey's charismatic image within the navy was undermined by having allowed his fleet to be lured away from the beachhead by a decoy force. None could fault his aggressiveness, but such a trait, wholly adequate in the dark days of 1942, was no substitute for meticulous tactics in the complicated operations of 1944. Neither Halsey nor his staff were familiar with the complexities of the Central Pacific offensive—nor did Halsey exhibit the good sense of soliciting advice from the real expert, Mitscher. He preferred direct action, without giving thorough attention to alternative courses of action or to adequate interchanges with Kinkaid.[31]

In fairness, Halsey could have been excused for having made one mistake in his otherwise sterling performance in the Pacific war. After all, Spruance had made an equally controversial decision in the Battle of the Philippine Sea, one that had resulted in the escape of the Japanese fleet. But Leyte Gulf proved to be only the first in a string of miscues and blunders during Halsey's remaining months in command of the Third Fleet—all of which occurred for similar reasons.

Following Leyte, Halsey was charged with continuing the Third Fleet's strategic support of MacArthur's operations in the Philippines. Although the Japanese fleet no longer posed a serious threat, the complications of this tedious campaign were challenging indeed: the kamikaze menace; the typhoon season; continuous operations at sea with underway replenishment; multiple missions of attacking airfields, merchant and naval shipping, coastal defenses, industrial facilities, and railroads; and enemy submarines and mines. Halsey retained the same staff, while Vice Admiral McCain relieved Mitscher at the head of TF 38. It quickly became evident that McCain lacked Mitscher's expertise and was downright slovenly in his administrative and operational habits. In a word, Halsey and McCain were too much alike, in both their personalities and style of command. Simple aggressiveness would not suffice in the final campaigns against Japan's inner defenses.

Halsey's ad hoc brand of leadership immediately became obvious to the fast carrier admirals accustomed to the precise procedures of the Spruance-Mitscher team. This had tragic consequences when, in mid-December 1944, Halsey allowed the fleet to sail directly into a typhoon; three of his unballasted destroyer escorts turned turtle and sank with heavy loss of life. Halsey defended his actions on the usual grounds—combativeness, in this case the determination to meet his support-strike schedules for MacArthur. Early the next month he took the Third Fleet into the confined waters of the South China Sea, covering MacArthur's assault at Lingayen Gulf on western Luzon, though he was more interested in finding and destroying the two hybrid carriers that had escaped his planes at Leyte Gulf. He even passed up a sizable merchant convoy in order to maintain the element of surprise against those by now nearly useless warships, which in any case he never found.

After striking Indochinese targets, the Third Fleet found its exit from the South China Sea blocked by monsoon storms, leading Halsey to request permission to withdraw through the narrow confines of Surigao Strait. Such a risky exposure to kamikaze attack led Nimitz to reject the idea and order Halsey to wait for the weather to clear to make his exit northward. And, stung by the loss of the *Princeton* off Leyte, Halsey perpetuated the reluctance he had shown in the South Pacific to take his carriers too close to enemy airfields by launching from extreme ranges—which reduced his planes' time over target and the weight of their bomb loads (because of the extra fuel needed), caused pilot fatigue and consequent losses, and thereby minimized the number and general effectiveness of his strikes.[32]

Replaced in the rotation by the Spruance-Mitscher team during the amphibious campaign for Iwo Jima and Okinawa, February to May 1945, Halsey and McCain returned to command for the opening stages of the planned invasion of Japan. Responsible only for attacking airfields in southern Japan, they promptly led the Third Fleet into another typhoon in early June. Admiral King thereupon placed the blame for getting the fleet in both typhoons squarely on Halsey. This sort of ineptitude could not be tolerated in the final decisive action of the Pacific war, and in mid-July, just as the carriers began a month of strikes on industrial targets and airfields in the Japanese homeland, King announced the command setup for the autumn invasion: Spruance would direct the assault forces, while Halsey would be assigned his by now customary mission of providing strategic cover by ranging up and down the Japanese coast. And the ineffective McCain—in ill health, anyway—would be replaced by meticulous Vice Admiral Jack Towers as commander of Task Force 38. But Japan surrendered in mid-August, making the invasion unnecessary.[33]

By V-J Day, the style of naval warfare in which Halsey had excelled—audacious, independent command—had been overtaken by the complexities of electronics, missile (kamikaze) countermeasures, and amphibious operations with enormous logistical and managerial requirements. His inspiring leadership during 1942 had been a major factor in raising American morale and turning the tide of battle in the South Pacific. For these considerable accomplishments, Halsey richly deserved his postwar promotion to the rank of fleet admiral in December 1945.

Although he had played no major role in the strategic decision-making process, which had been left to keener minds, Halsey had showed a stroke of genius in recommending bypassing Mindanao and accelerating the assault on Leyte. His miscue during the Battle of Leyte Gulf did not lead to defeat or even a major slowdown in the Philippines campaign, but it wasted lives, ships, and planes. The same can be said of his two typhoons. Aggressive leadership was Halsey's strong suit, but public pronouncements, such as the intention to ride the emperor's horse through Tokyo, served only to accentuate criticism of him within the fleet during the final twelve months of the war. Also, he was plainly tired from his long and arduous duty. Between his mistakes and his antics, he became something of an embarrassment, sadly tarnishing his otherwise outstanding war record. He retired in April 1947. Criticisms by historians and analysts plagued him through the years until his death of heart failure on 16 August 1959.[34]

In the long view of command at sea over the centuries, however, Bull Halsey's charismatic image will prevail—thanks to his dynamic personal qualities in the early carrier raids, at Guadalcanal, and in the Solomons campaign. As with Nelson before him, an idolizing public and his own men could overlook his shortcomings in their need to find comfort and security in a great war leader. Such is the stuff of legend, particularly when a hero like Halsey passes, along with his era, into the warm memory of a seemingly more innocent time.

Notes

1. U.S. Naval Academy *Lucky Bag* of 1904, p. 41; E. B. Potter, *Bull Halsey* (Annapolis: Naval Institute Press, 1985), pp. 19–21, for his forebears; oral history of Rear Admiral Malcolm F. Schoeffel, USN (Ret.), U.S. Naval Institute in 1979, p. 275, in which "Red" Schoeffel, top man in the Class of 1919, recalls Halsey's nickname.

2. *Time*, 30 November 1942 and 23 July 1945.

3. Potter, op. cit., pp. 19 ff, 100, 107, 139, and passim.

4. For Halsey's career assignments, see Clark G. Reynolds, *Famous American Admirals* (New York: Van Nostrand Reinhold, 1978), pp. 143–45; see Potter, op. cit., and Edwin P. Hoyt, *How They Won the War in the Pacific: Nimitz and His Admirals* (New York: Weybright and Talley, 1970), p. 165, for his prewar carrier duty.

5. Halsey May 1933 thesis, quoted in Gerald John Kennedy, "United States Naval War College, 1919–1941: An Institutional Response to Naval Preparedness" (Newport, R.I.: Naval War College Research Thesis, June 1975).

6. James M. Merrill, *A Sailor's Admiral: A Biography of William F. Halsey* (New York: Thomas Y. Crowell, 1976), pp. 12–14. One example of Halsey's attempts to get back to sea while assigned ashore was during his one year as commanding officer of NAS Pensacola, 1937–38. On 21 December 1937, Rear Admiral A. B. Cook, chief of the Bureau of Aeronautics, wrote him that Captain C. A. Pownall had passed on Halsey's "confidential" wish to return to sea duty. Halsey Papers, Library of Congress, Box 13.

7. Halsey to Towers, 11 July 1940; Towers to Halsey, 25 July 1940. Halsey Papers, Box 16.

8. Towers to Halsey, 6 March 1940, recommended Ernest W. Litch, H. L. Meadows, and Dixwell Ketcham. Halsey Papers, Box 16.

9. Potter, op. cit., pp. 65, 139–40, 199, 243. On Browning's rejection for flag rank and eventual relief from command of a carrier, see Nimitz to Halsey, 16 October 1942; Halsey to Nimitz, 1 January 1944; Mitscher to Nimitz, 24 May 1944 (Nimitz Papers, Library of Congress); King conversation with Walter Muir Whitehill, 31 July 1949, 11 (King Papers, Naval War College); Admiral J. J. Clark, with Clark G. Reynolds, *Carrier Admiral* (New York: David McKay, 1967), pp. 149–58.

10. Spruance to wife Margaret, 7 February, 21 March 1942. On 10 February 1942 Spruance wrote to his wife that Ernest L. Gunther had not been selected for rear admiral, which he regretted because Gunther was "the same kind of man as Bill Halsey, and I know of no higher praise." Spruance Papers, Naval War College.

11. Spruance to Margaret, 11 April 1942, Spruance Papers.

12. Potter, op. cit., pp. 157ff; Stephen D. Regan, *In Bitter Tempest: The Biography of Admiral Frank Jack Fletcher* (Ames: Iowa State University Press, 1994), pp. 206–11.

13. Quoted in Potter, op. cit., p. 175.

14. Ibid., p. 193; Merrill, op. cit., p. 53; Captain R. F. Farrington, USN, to the author, 19 March 1961, recounting Halsey's speech on board the *Saratoga* at Espiritu Santo in the summer of 1943, which Farrington regarded as "without a doubt . . . the greatest major address on record."

15. Potter, op. cit., pp. 234–47; Carney oral history, courtesy E. B. Potter, pp. 27–28, which also recounts the rumor that Carney was the third choice for chief of staff—after Admiral D. C. Ramsey, who did not want the job, and George Fort, whom Halsey regarded as unsuitable.

16. Potter, op. cit., pp. 227, 249–50, 257.

17. Ibid., pp. 216, 265–68; Carney oral history, pp. 23–25.

18. Potter, op. cit., p. 259; Clark G. Reynolds, *The Fast Carriers: The Forging of an Air Navy* (New York: McGraw-Hill, 1968; reprint, Annapolis: Naval Institute Press, 1992), pp. 117–19, 142–43.

19. See Hoyt, op. cit., pp. 428–49.

20. Potter, op. cit., pp. 277–78; Admiral W. F. Halsey, with J. Bryan III, *Admiral Halsey's Story* (New York: McGraw-Hill, 1947), pp. 199–200. The pilot was Ensign Thomas C. Tiller of the new *Hornet.*

21. Reynolds, *The Fast Carriers,* pp. 250–51.

22. Rear Admiral Samuel Eliot Morison, *History of United States Naval Operations in World War II,* 15 vols. (Boston: Little, Brown, 1947–62), vol. XII, *Leyte, June 1944–January 1945,* p. 58; see Reynolds, *The Fast Carriers,* pp. 156ff, for the Battle of the Philippine Sea.

23. Potter, op. cit., p. 290.

24. Reynolds, *The Fast Carriers,* pp. 256–58.

25. Ibid., p. 258; Morison, *Naval Operations,* XII: 91.

26. For the Battle of Leyte Gulf, see Morison, *Naval Operations,* XII; Reynolds, *The Fast Carriers,* pp. 253ff; Potter, op. cit., pp. 286ff; Thomas J. Cutler, *The Battle of Leyte Gulf* (New York: HarperCollins, 1994).

27. Vice Admiral Ralph E. Wilson, USN (Ret.), to the author, 15 August 1967; Harold E. Stassen, Halsey's flag secretary, to the author, 25 June and 12 August 1964; Rear Admiral M. C. Cheek, USN (Ret.), to the author, 16 June 1966; Halsey and

Bryan, op. cit., pp. 216–17; Halsey Action Report, Serial 0088, 13 November 1944, Naval Historical Center, Washington, D.C.; Halsey notes to Hanson W. Baldwin, cited in Reynolds, *The Fast Carriers,* p. 47, note 27; and Carney oral history, pp. 19–20. The quotation is Stassen's recollection. In his book Halsey recalled saying to Carney, "Here's where we're going. Mick, start them north."

28. Morison, *Naval Operations,* XII: 194n, 195; Theodore Taylor, *The Magnificent Mitscher* (New York: W. W. Norton, 1954; reprint, Annapolis: Naval Institute Press, 1991), pp. 262–63; Halsey and Bryan, op. cit., p. 217; conversations with Admiral Arleigh A. Burke, USN (Ret.), and Rear Admiral T. P. Jeter, USN (Ret.), Lee's chief of staff, in 1966; Vice Admiral G. F. Bogan, USN (Ret.), to the author, 11 May 1964.

29. For Kinkaid's position and actions, see Gerald E. Wheeler, *Kinkaid of the Seventh Fleet: A Biography of Admiral Thomas C. Kinkaid, U.S. Navy* (Washington: Naval Historical Center, 1995), pp. 399–406, 458–61, 482–85; for those of the escort carrier commander who bore the brunt of the attack, and his views of Halsey, see John F. Wukovits, *Devotion to Duty: A Biography of Admiral Clifton A. F. Sprague* (Annapolis: Naval Institute Press, 1995), pp. 141 ff., 189–200.

30. Rear Admiral Samuel Eliot Morison, *The Two-Ocean War* (Boston: Little, Brown, 1963), pp. 454, 475, 482; Reynolds, *The Fast Carriers,* pp. 278–81, for a summary of all commentators up to 1968. Cutler, op. cit., 287–96, assigns equal blame to Halsey and Kinkaid. Potter, op. cit., pp. 306–7, generally dodges criticism but does recount the postwar discussion between Halsey, King, and Kinkaid on pp. 370–72, 376 ff; see also Merrill, op. cit., pp. 170–76; and Wheeler and Wukovits as cited in note 29.

31. See Reynolds, *The Fast Carriers,* pp. 281–83, for some of these options.

32. Ibid., pp. 285–300.

33. Ibid., pp. 346–50, 360–75; Merrill, op. cit., pp. 216 ff for the June 1945 typhoon. See also Clark G. Reynolds, *The Fighting Lady: The New* Yorktown *in the Pacific War* (Missoula, Mont.: Pictorial Histories, 1986), pp. 297 ff.

34. I adhere to my conclusion in *The Fast Carriers,* pp. 387–88, over the roles of Halsey and McCain as fast carrier leaders: "inferior third-act heroes in the Central Pacific offensive [who] might best have served elsewhere. Their Central Pacific commands belonged to more competent officers." On page 192 of his *Fleet Tactics: Theory and Practice* (Annapolis: Naval Institute Press, 1986), Wayne P. Hughes writes: "Halsey, who fought with more heart than head, was forgiven his blunders because his command was always moving forward. . . . Nevertheless, when we rank the big-league tactical commanders of history, Halsey trails Spruance, who fought with both heart and head."

Note on Sources

Of the three biographies and one semiautobiography of Halsey, the most complete and evenhanded is that by E. B. Potter, *Bull Halsey* (Annapolis: Naval Institute Press, 1985), upon which I have leaned heavily. Well-researched and well-written though it is, however, Potter refused to criticize, pro or con, Halsey's questionable actions at Leyte Gulf, in the typhoons, or with fast carrier operations in general. Rather than making historical judgments, he prefered to let Halsey, his superiors, other critics, and "the facts" speak for themselves. James M. Merrill, *A Sailor's Admiral: A Biography of William F. Halsey* (New York: Thomas Y. Crowell, 1976) is admittedly popular and focuses almost entirely on the war years. Merrill's abridgement (not annotated) is "Fleet Admiral William F. Halsey, Jr.," in Stephen Howarth, ed., *Men of War: Great Naval Leaders of World War II* (London: Weidenfeld and Nicholson, 1992), pp. 229–43. Benis M. Frank, *Halsey* (New York: Ballatine, 1974) is a good, short wartime summary. *Admiral Halsey's Story* (New York: McGraw-Hill, 1947), written by Halsey in collaboration with J. Bryan III, is colorful and anecdotal but, not surprisingly, one-sided. Halsey's career assignments are listed in my *Famous American Admirals* (New York: Van Nostrand Reinhold, 1978).

All accounts of the wartime navy begin with Rear Admiral Samuel Eliot Morison's magisterial, semiofficial *History of United States Naval Operations in World War II*, 15 vols. (Boston: Little, Brown, 1947–62); for Halsey, see vols. III, IV, V, VI, VII, XII, XIII, and XIV, as well as the overall condensation, *The Two-Ocean War* (Boston: Little, Brown, 1963). For Leyte, see also Thomas J. Cutler, *The Battle of Leyte Gulf* (New York: HarperCollins, 1994). My *The Fast Carriers: The Forging of an Air Navy* (New York: McGraw-Hill, 1968; Annapolis: Naval Institute Press, 1992) treats Halsey as fast carrier commander during 1944–45 and is the most detailed critical account of his role as such. In his history of naval tactics, Wayne P. Hughes, Jr., *Fleet Tactics: Theory and Practice* (Annapolis: Naval Institute Press, 1986) characterizes Halsey as "rash." Edwin P. Hoyt, *How They Won the War in the Pacific: Nimitz and His Admirals* (New York: Weybright and Talley, 1970) is useful on several matters. My *The Fighting Lady: The New* Yorktown *in the Pacific War* (Missoula, Mont.: Pictorial Histories, 1986) gives the view of Halsey from one carrier in 1944–45. Admiral John S. ("Jimmy") Thach, "Halsey, McCain, and Thach," discusses Halsey's style of leadership in E. T. Wooldridge, ed., *Carrier Warfare in the Pacific: An Oral History Collection* (Washington, D.C.: Smithsonian Institute Press, 1993).

To cover particular aspects of Halsey's career, I consulted the papers of Ernest J. King and Raymond A. Spruance at the Naval War College and of Halsey, Chester W. Nimitz, and John H. Towers at the Library of Congress; action reports at the Naval Historical Center, Washington, D.C.; the U.S. Naval Academy *Lucky Bag* of 1904; the U.S. Naval Institute oral history transcript of Malcolm F. Schoeffel in 1979 and that by Benis M. Frank of Robert B. Carney in 1973 (courtesy of Potter); *Time* magazine for 30 November 1942 and 23 July 1945; and Gerald John Kennedy, "United States Naval War College, 1919–1941: An Institutional Response to Naval Preparedness" (Newport, R.I.: Naval War College Research Thesis, June 1975).

Halsey is discussed in virtually every book about the war in the Pacific and especially in several key biographies: Potter's *Nimitz* (Annapolis: Naval Institute Press, 1976); Thomas B. Buell, *The Quiet Warrior: A Biography of Admiral Raymond A. Spruance* (Boston: Little, Brown, 1974) and his *Master of Sea Power: A Biography of Fleet Admiral Ernest J. King* (Boston: Little, Brown, 1980); Theodore Taylor, *The Magnificent Mitscher* (New York: W. W. Norton, 1954; Annapolis: Naval Institute Press, 1991); my *Admiral John H. Towers: The Struggle for Naval Air Supremacy* (Annapolis: Naval Institute Press, 1991); Stephen D. Regan, *In Bitter Tempest: The Biography of Admiral*

Frank Jack Fletcher (Ames: Iowa State University Press, 1994); Admiral J. J. Clark, with me as collaborator, *Carrier Admiral* (New York: David McKay, 1967); Gerald E. Wheeler, *Kinkaid of the Seventh Fleet: A Biography of Admiral Thomas C. Kinkaid, U.S. Navy* (Washington, D.C.: Naval Historical Center, 1995); and John F. Wukovits, *Devotion to Duty: A Biography of Admiral Clifton A. F. Sprague* (Annapolis: Naval Institute Press, 1995).

Portrait Credits

Drake: Copy believed to be by Gheerharts the Younger, c. 1590, of a portrait by Segar which was destroyed in World War II. Plymouth City Museum & Art Gallery collection.

Tromp: Portrait by an unknown artist. Rijksmuseum Nederlands Scheepvaart-museum, Amsterdam.

Blake: Miniature after Samuel Cooper. The National Maritime Museum, Greenwich.

De Ruyter: Portrait by K. Dujardin. Rijksmuseum Nederlands Scheepvaartmuseum, Amsterdam; photograph by the Historical Department of the Naval Staff, The Hague.

Niels Juel: Portrait by an unknown artist. The National Historical Museum, Frederiksborg Castle, Denmark; photograph by Hans Petersen.

Hawke: Mezzotint by J. MacArdell after G. Knapton. The National Maritime Museum, Greenwich.

Suffren: Portrait by Pompeo Batoni. © Photo RMN—D. Arnaudet / G. Blot.

Nelson: Portrait by L. F. Abbott. The National Maritime Museum, Greenwich.

Miaoulis: Pencil drawing by Karl Krazeisen. The National Bank of Greece Historical Collection, Athens.

Farragut: U.S. Naval Institute Photographic Collection.

Tegetthoff: Heeresgeschichtliches Museum, Vienna.

Dewey: U.S. Naval Institute Photographic Collection.

Togo: U.S. Naval Institute Photographic Collection.

Jellicoe: U.S. Naval Institute Photographic Collection.

Scheer: Imperial War Museum, London.

Cunningham: Imperial War Museum, London.

Yamamoto: Ullstein Bilderdienst, Berlin.

Spruance: Photograph by Lieutenant Maurice Constant, USN. The National Archives, Washington, D.C.

Halsey: Official U.S. Navy Photograph, U.S. Naval Institute Photographic Collection.

Select Bibliography of the Surveys

General

Addington, Larry H. *The Patterns of War since the Eighteenth Century*. Bloomington: Indiana University Press, 1984.

Archibald, E. H. H. *The Fighting Ship in the Royal Navy, AD 897–1984*. Poole, Dorset: Blandford Press, 1984.

Beach, Captain Edward L., USN (Ret.). *The United States Navy: 200 Years*. New York: Henry Holt, 1986.

Casson, Lionel. *The Illustrated History of Ships and Boats*. Garden City, N.Y.: Doubleday, 1964.

Fioravanzo, Giuseppe, trans. Arthur W. Holst. *A History of Naval Tactical Thought*. Annapolis: Naval Institute Press, 1979.

Fuller, Major General J. F. C. *A Military History of the Western World*. Three vols. New York: Funk & Wagnalls, 1954–56.

Gibbon, Tony. *The Complete Encyclopedia of Battleships: A Technical Directory of Capital Ships from 1860 to the Present Day*. New York: Crescent Books, 1983.

Grove, Eric J. *Fleet to Fleet Encounters: Tsushima, Jutland, Philippine Sea*. London: Arms and Armour, 1991.

Hezlet, Vice Admiral Sir Arthur. *Electronics and Sea Power*. New York: Stein and Day, 1975.

Hill, J. R., ed. *The Oxford Illustrated History of the Royal Navy*. Oxford: Oxford University Press, 1995.

Hughes, Captain Wayne P., USN (Ret.). *Fleet Tactics: Theory and Practice*. Annapolis: Naval Institute Press, 1986.

Jenkins, E. H. *A History of the French Navy: From Its Beginnings to the Present Day*. Annapolis: Naval Institute Press, 1973.

Jones, Archer. *The Art of War in the Western World*. Urbana: University of Illinois Press, 1987.

Keegan, John. *The Price of Admiralty: The Evolution of Naval Warfare*. New York: Viking, 1989.

Kennedy, Paul. *The Rise and Fall of British Naval Mastery*. New York: Charles Scribner's Sons, 1976.

Lavery, Brian. *The Ship of the Line*. Two vols. London: Conway Maritime Press, 1983–84.

Lewis, Michael. *The Navy of Britain: A Historical Portrait*. London: George Allen and Unwin, 1949.

Macintyre, Donald, and Basil W. Bathe. *Man-of-War: A History of the Combat Vessel.* New York: McGraw-Hill, 1966.

Masson, Philippe, Michèle Battesti, and Jacques C. Favier. *Marine et constructions navales, 1789–1989.* Paris: Charles-Lavauzelle, 1989.

Naval Historical Center. *Dictionary of American Naval Fighting Ships.* Eight vols. Washington, D.C.: Government Printing Office, 1959–81.

Padfield, Peter. *Guns at Sea.* London: Hugh Evelyn, n.d.

Pemsel, Helmut, trans. Major i.G. D. G. Smith. *A History of War at Sea: An Atlas and Chronology of Conflict at Sea from Earliest Times to the Present.* Annapolis: Naval Institute Press, 1977.

———. *Seeherrschaft: Eine maritime Weltgeschichte von den Anfängen der Seefahrt bis zur Gegenwart.* Two vols. Koblenz: Bernard & Graefe, 1985. A major revision of the preceding work.

Potter, E. B., ed., and Fleet Admiral Chester W. Nimitz, USN, assoc. ed. *Sea Power: A Naval History.* Englewood Cliffs, N.J.: Prentice-Hall, 1960.

Reynolds, Clark G. *Command of the Sea: The History and Strategy of Maritime Empires.* New York: William Morrow, 1974.

Robison, Rear Admiral S. S., USN (Ret.), and Mary L. Robison. *A History of Naval Tactics from 1530 to 1930: The Evolution of Tactical Maxims.* Annapolis: U.S. Naval Institute, 1942.

de la Roncière, Ch., and G. Clerc-Rampal. *Histoire de la Marine Française.* Paris: Librairie Larousse, 1934.

Uden, Grant, and Richard Cooper. *A Dictionary of British Ships and Seamen.* New York: St. Martin's Press, 1980.

Willmott, H. P. *Sea Warfare: Weapons, Tactics and Strategy.* White Plains, N.Y.: Sheridan House, 1981.

Survey I: The Ship and the Gun

Addington, Larry H. *The Patterns of War through the Eighteenth Century.* Bloomington: Indiana University Press, 1990.

Black, Jeremy. *European Warfare, 1660–1815.* New Haven, Conn.: Yale University Press, 1994.

Cipolla, Carlo M. *Guns, Sails and Empires: Technological Innovation and the Early Phases of European Expansion, 1400–1700.* London: Collins, 1965.

Corbett, Julian S. *Fighting Instructions, 1530–1816.* N.P.: Navy Records Society, 1905.

Friel, Ian. *The Good Ship: Ships, Shipbuilding and Technology in England, 1200–1520.* Baltimore: Johns Hopkins University Press, 1995.

Gardiner, Robert, ed. *Conway's History of the Ship: The Line of Battle: The Sailing Warship, 1650–1840.* Annapolis: Naval Institute Press, 1992.

Lewis, Archibald R., and Timothy J. Runyan. *European Naval and Maritime History, 300–1500.* Bloomington: Indiana University Press, 1985.

Maltby, William. "Politics, Professionalism, and the Evolution of Sailing-Ship Tactics, 1650–1714," in John A. Lynn, ed., *Tools of War: Instruments, Ideas, and Institutions of Warfare, 1445–1871.* Urbana: University of Illinois Press, 1990.

Mattingly, Garrett. *The Armada*. Boston: Houghton Mifflin, 1959.

Padfield, Peter. *Armada*. Annapolis: Naval Institute Press, 1988.

———. *Tide of Empires: Decisive Naval Campaigns in the Rise of the West*. Two vols. (to 1763) to date. London: Routledge & Kegan Paul, 1979–82.

Parker, Geoffrey. *The Military Revolution and the Rise of the West, 1500–1800*. Cambridge: Cambridge University Press, 1988.

Rodgers, Vice Admiral William Ledyard, USN (Ret.). *Greek and Roman Warfare: A Study of Strategy, Tactics, and Ship Design from Salamis (480 B.C.) to Actium (31 B.C.)*. Annapolis: Naval Institute Press, 1937.

———. *Naval Warfare Under Oars, 4th to 16th Centuries: A Study of Strategy, Tactics and Ship Design*. Annapolis: Naval Institute Press, 1939.

Tunstall, Brian, ed. Dr. Nicholas Tracy. *Naval Warfare in the Age of Sail: The Evolution of Fighting Tactics, 1650–1815*. Annapolis: Naval Institute Press, 1990.

Viereck, H. D. L. *Die römische Flotte: Classis Romana*. Herford, Germany: Koehlers Verlagsgesellschaft, 1973.

Survey II: The Line of Battle

Bennett, Geoffrey. *Nelson the Commander*. New York: Charles Scribner's Sons, 1972.

Black, Jeremy, and Brian Woodfine, eds. *The British Navy and the Use of Naval Power in the Eighteenth Century*. Atlantic Highlands, N.J.: Humanities Press International, 1989.

Bromley, J. S. *Corsairs and Navies, 1660–1760*. London: Hambledon Press, 1987.

Creswell, John. *British Admirals of the Eighteenth Century: Tactics in Battle*. Hamden, Conn.: Archon Books, 1972.

Gardiner, Leslie. *The British Admiralty*. Edinburgh: William Blackwood & Sons, 1968.

Lavery, Brian. *Nelson's Navy: The Ships, Men and Organisation, 1793–1815*. Annapolis: Naval Institute Press, 1989.

Mahan, A. T. *The Influence of Sea Power upon the French Revolution and Empire, 1793–1812*. Two vols. Boston: Little, Brown, 1897.

Pope, Dudley. *At Twelve Mr. Byng Was Shot*. Philadelphia: Lippincott, 1962.

Rodger, N. A. M. *The Wooden World: An Anatomy of the Georgian Navy*. Annapolis: Naval Institute Press, 1986.

Spinney, David. *Rodney*. London: Allen & Unwin, 1969.

Symcox, Geoffrey. *The Crisis of French Sea Power, 1688–1697: From the* Guerre d'Escadre *to the* Guerre de Course. The Hague: Martinus Nijhoff, 1974.

and of the works cited under Survey I: Addington, Black, Corbett, Gardiner, Maltby, Padfield (*Tide of Empires*), Parker, and Tunstall.

Survey III: The Machine Age at Sea

Baxter, James P. *The Introduction of the Ironclad Warship*. Cambridge: Harvard University Press, 1933.

Chesneau, Roger, and Eugene M. Kolesnik, eds. *Conway's All the World's Fighting Ships, 1860–1905*. London: Conway Maritime Press, 1979.

Gardiner, Robert, ed. *Conway's History of the Ship: Steam, Steel & Shellfire: The Steam Warship, 1815–1905.* Annapolis: Naval Institute Press, 1992.

H. G., Officier de Marine. *Analyses des diverses tactiques navales publiées en europe depuis 1855.* Paris: Arthus Bertrand, [1870].

Hovgaard, William. *Modern History of Warships.* London: E. & F. N. Spon, 1920 (reprint, London: Conway Maritime Press, 1978.)

Parker, Commander Foxhall, USN. *Squadron Tactics under Steam.* New York: D. Van Nostrand, 1864.

Varfis, Commodore Konstantinos, Hellenic Navy (Ret.), President of the Organizing Committee. *Acta of the First International Colloquium on Naval History, Athens, 24–31 August 1987: The First National Fleets: The Use of Steam in Naval Warfare.* Athens: International Commission on Military History, 1988.

SURVEY IV: THE NEW STEEL NAVIES

Bainbridge-Hoff, Commander William, USN. *Elementary Naval Tactics.* New York: John Wiley & Sons, 1894.

Mahan, Captain Alfred Thayer. *The Influence of Sea Power upon History, 1660–1783.* Boston: Little, Brown, 1890.

Noel, Commander Gerard H., RN. *The Gun, Ram, and Torpedo: Manoeuvres and Tactics of a Naval Battle in the Present Day.* London: J. Griffin, 1874.

Reilly, John C., Jr., and Robert L. Scheina. *American Battleships, 1886–1923: Predreadnought Design and Construction.* Annapolis: Naval Institute Press, 1980.

Service Historique de la Marine. *Marine et technique au XIXe siècle: Actes de Colloque International . . . 10, 11, 12 juin 1987.* [Vincennes]: Service Historique de la Marine / Institut d'Histoire des Conflits contemporains, 1988.

Wilson, H. W. *Ironclads in Action.* Two vols. Boston: Little, Brown, 1896.

and of the works cited under Survey III: Chesneau and Kolesnik, and Gardiner.

SURVEY V: THE DREADNOUGHT REVOLUTION

Bacon, Admiral Sir R. H. *The Life of John Rushworth, Earl Jellicoe.* London: Cassell, 1936.

Barnett, Correlli. *The Swordbearers: Supreme Command in the First World War.* Bloomington: Indiana University Press, 1975.

Gardiner, Robert, ed. *Conway's History of the Ship: The Eclipse of the Big Gun, 1906–45.* Annapolis: Naval Institute Press, 1992.

Gray, Randal, ed. *Conway's All the World's Fighting Ships, 1906–1921.* Annapolis: Naval Institute Press, 1985.

Halpern, Paul G. *A Naval History of World War I.* Annapolis: Naval Institute Press, 1995.

Herwig, Holger. *"Luxury Fleet": The Imperial German Navy, 1888–1918.* London: George Allen & Unwin, 1980.

Hezlet, Vice Admiral Sir Arthur. *Aircraft and Sea Power.* New York: Stein and Day, 1970.

———. *The Submarine and Sea Power.* New York: Stein and Day, 1967.

O'Connell, Robert L. *Sacred Vessels: The Cult of the Battleship and the Rise of the U.S. Navy.* New York: Oxford University Press, 1991.

Scott, Admiral Sir Percy. *Fifty Years in the Royal Navy.* New York: George H. Doran, 1919.

Service Historique de la Marine. *Les marines de guerre du dreadnought au nucléar: Actes du colloque international Paris . . . 23, 24 et 25 novembre 1988.* [Vincennes]: Service Historique de la Marine, 1990.

Sumida, Jon Tetsuro. *In Defence of Naval Supremacy: Finance, Technology and British Naval Policy, 1889–1914.* Boston: Unwin Hyman, 1989.

Tarrant, V. E. *Jutland: The German Perspective.* Annapolis: Naval Institute Press, 1995.

———. *The U-Boat Offensive, 1914–1945.* Annapolis: Naval Institute Press, 1989.

Wilson, H. W. *Battleships in Action.* Two vols. London: Sampson Low, Marston, 1926 (reprint, Annapolis: Naval Institute Press, 1995).

and of the work cited under Survey IV: Reilly and Scheina.

SURVEY VI: THE ADVENT OF AIR-SEA WARFARE

Belote, James H., and William M. *Titans of the Seas: The Development and Operations of Japanese and American Carrier Task Forces During World War II.* New York: Harper & Row, 1975.

Buell, Thomas B. *The Quiet Warrior: A Biography of Admiral Raymond A. Spruance.* Boston: Little, Brown, 1974.

Chesneau, Roger, ed. *Conway's All the World's Fighting Ships, 1922–1946.* London: Conway Maritime Press, 1980.

Morison, Samuel Eliot. *History of United States Naval Operations in World War II.* 15 vols. Boston: Little, Brown, 1947–62.

Reynolds, Clark G. *The Fast Carriers: The Forging of an Air Navy.* New York: McGraw-Hill, 1968 (reprint, Annapolis: Naval Institute Press, 1992).

and of the works cited under Survey V: Gardiner, Hezlet (both titles), Service Historique de la Marine, and Tarrant (*The U-Boat Offensive*).

Index

The following abbreviations are used to specify the nationality of ships: A = Austria; C = Chile; CH = China; CS = Confederate States of America; D = Denmark; F = France; G = Germany; GB = Great Britain (or, in the case of those predating the Act of Union, England); GR = Greece; I = Italy; J = Japan; N = the Netherlands; P = Portugal; R = Russia; S = Spain; SW = Sweden; T = Turkey; US = United States of America. Merchant vessels are identified as such; all others are warships. Entries for ship types, weapons, and technologies generally relate to their development and characteristics rather than employment.

The Naval Institute Press is the book-publishing arm of the U.S. Naval Institute, a private, nonprofit, membership society for sea service professionals and others who share an interest in naval and maritime affairs. Established in 1873 at the U.S. Naval Academy in Annapolis, Maryland, where its offices remain today, the Naval Institute has members from around the world.

Members of the Naval Institute support the education programs of the society and receive the influential monthly magazine *Proceedings* and discounts on fine nautical prints and on ship and aircraft photos. They also have access to the transcripts of the Institute's Oral History Program and get discounted admission to any of the Institute-sponsored seminars offered around the country.

The Naval Institute also publishes *Naval History* magazine. This colorful bimonthly is filled with entertaining and thought-provoking articles, first-person reminiscences, and dramatic art and photography. Members receive a discount on *Naval History* subscriptions.

The Naval Institute's book-publishing program, begun in 1898 with basic guides to naval practices, has broadened its scope in recent years to include books of more general interest. Now the Naval Institute Press publishes about 100 titles each year, ranging from how-to books on boating and navigation to battle histories, biographies, ship and aircraft guides, and novels. Institute members receive discounts of 20 to 50 percent on the Press's nearly 600 books in print.

Full-time students are eligible for special half-price membership rates. Life memberships are also available.

For a free catalog describing Naval Institute Press books currently available, and for further information about subscribing to *Naval History* magazine or about joining the U.S. Naval Institute, please write to:

Membership Department
U.S. Naval Institute
118 Maryland Avenue
Annapolis, MD 21402-5035
Telephone: (800) 233-8764
Fax: (410) 269-7940
Web address: www.usni.org